The **Rough Guide** to

Guatemala

written and researched by

Iain Stewart

NEW YORK • LONDON • DELHI

www.roughguides.com

Contents

Colour section 1–24

Basics 25–70

Guide 71–418

Contexts 419–498

Language 499–510

Advertisers 511-522

Small print & Index 523-536

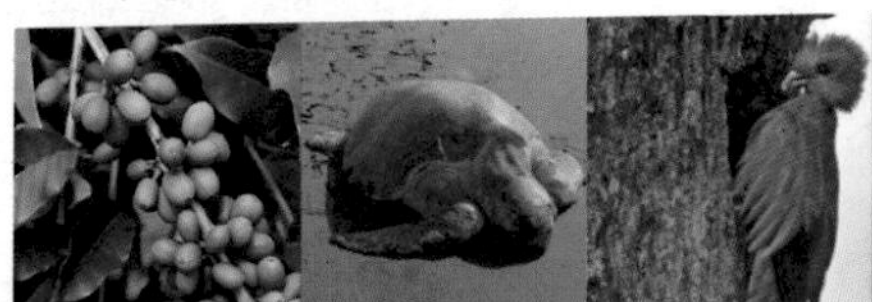

◄◄ Bus, Cuchumatanes ◄ El Baúl, Pacific coast

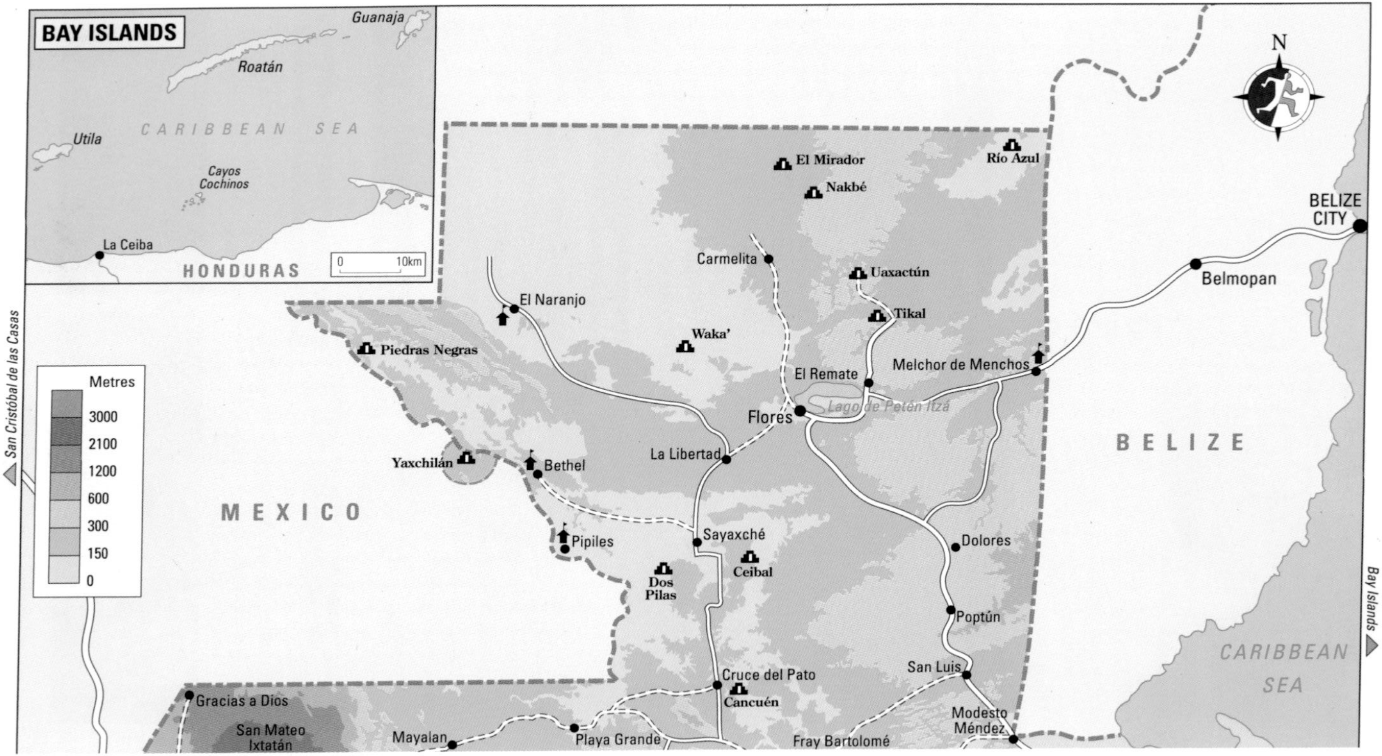

BAY ISLANDS
Guanaja
Roatán
Utila
CARIBBEAN SEA
Cayos Cochinos
La Ceiba
HONDURAS
0 10km

N
Río Azul
El Mirador
Nakbé
Carmelita
Uaxactún
Tikal
BELIZE CITY
Belmopan
El Naranjo
Waka'
Piedras Negras
Melchor de Menchos
El Remate
Lago de Petén Itzá
Flores
BELIZE
La Libertad
Yaxchilán
Bethel
MEXICO
Sayaxché
Pipiles
Ceibal
Dos Pilas
Dolores
Poptún
San Luis
Cruce del Pato
Cancuén
Gracias a Dios
San Mateo Ixtatán
Mayalan
Playa Grande
Fray Bartolomé
Modesto Méndez
CARIBBEAN SEA
Bay Islands
San Cristóbal de las Casas

Metres
3000
2100
1200
600
300
150
0

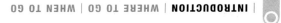

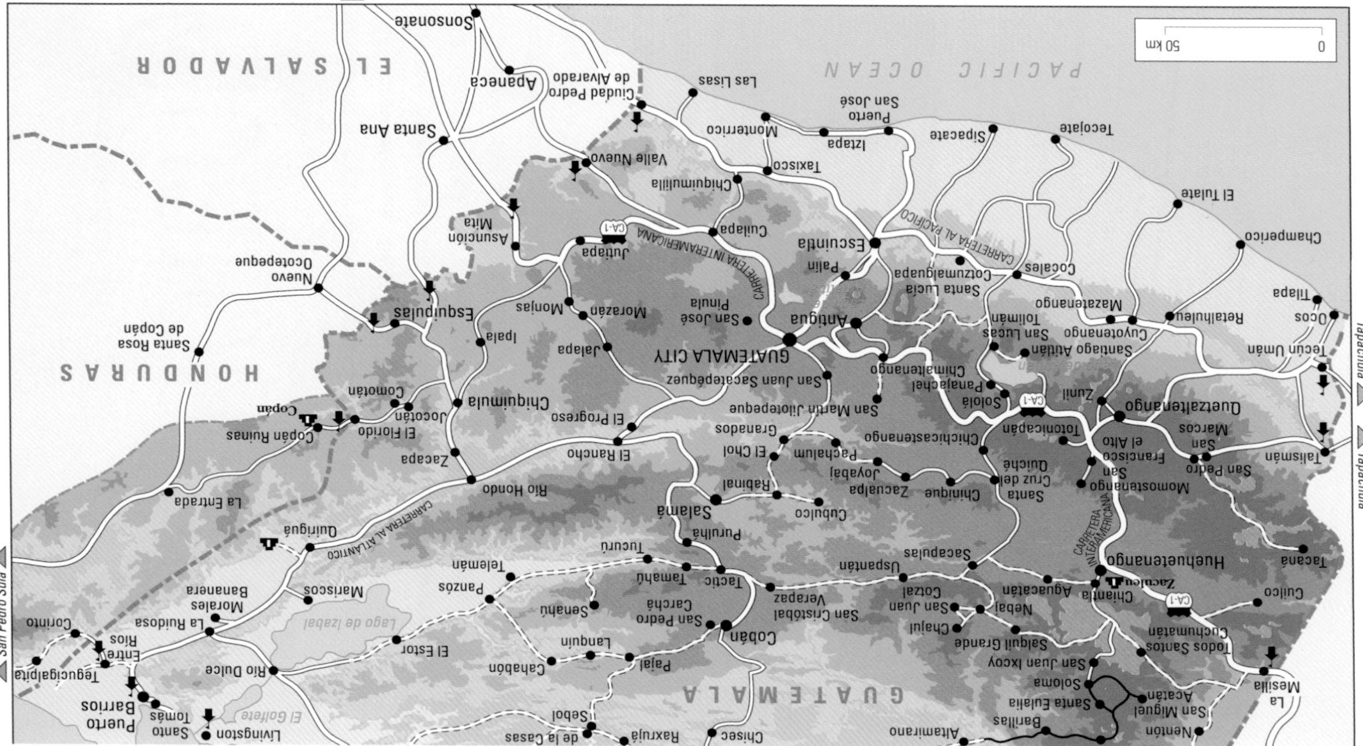
GUATEMALA
HONDURAS
EL SALVADOR
PACIFIC OCEAN
San Pedro Sula
San Salvador
Tapachula
Tapachula
GUATEMALA CITY
Antigua
Quetzaltenango
Huehuetenango
Cobán
Salamá
Escuintla
Chiquimula
Esquipulas
Santa Ana
Sonsonate
Apaneca
Ciudad Pedro de Alvarado
Las Lisas
Monterrico
Puerto San José
Iztapa
Taxisco
Chiquimulilla
Valle Nuevo
Asunción Mita
Nuevo Ocotepeque
Santa Rosa de Copán
La Entrada
Copán Ruinas
Copán
El Florido
Comotán
Jocotán
Zacapa
Río Hondo
El Rancho
El Progreso
Jalapa
Monjas
Ipala
Morazán
Jutiapa
San José Pinula
Cuilapa
Palín
Santa Lucía Cotzumalguapa
Cocales
Sipacate
Tecojate
El Tulate
Champerico
Tilapa
Ocos
Tecún Umán
Retalhuleu
Mazatenango
Cuyotenango
Santiago Atitlán
San Lucas Tolimán
Zunil
Sololá
Panajachel
Chimaltenango
San Juan Sacatepéquez
San Martín Jilotepeque
Granados
El Chol
Rabinal
Pachalum
Joyabaj
Zacualpa
Chinique
Chichicastenango
Totonicapán
Santa Cruz del Quiché
San Francisco el Alto
Momostenango
San Marcos
San Pedro
Talismán
Tacaná
Cuilco
Zaculeu
Chiantla
Aguacatán
Nebaj
Chajul
San Juan Cotzal
Sacapulas
Uspantán
San Cristóbal Verapaz
Tactic
Tamahú
Purulhá
Cubulco
Tucurú
Telemán
Panzós
Senahú
San Pedro Carchá
Lanquín
Pajal
Cahabón
El Estor
Lago de Izabal
Mariscos
Quiriguá
Morales Bananera
La Ruidosa
Río Dulce
Entre Ríos
Corinto
Tegucigalpita
Puerto Barrios
Santo Tomás
Livingston
El Golfete
Raxruhá
Sebol
de la Casas
Chisec
Altamirano
Barillas
Santa Eulalia
Soloma
San Juan Ixcoy
Salquil Grande
Todos Santos Cuchumatán
San Miguel Acatán
Nentón
La Mesilla
CARRETERA AL ATLÁNTICO
CARRETERA INTERAMERICANA
CARRETERA INTERAMERICANA
CARRETERA AL PACÍFICO
CA-1
CA-1
CA-1
CA-1
0
50 km

Introduction to Guatemala

Spanning a mountainous slice of the narrow Central American isthmus, Guatemala is a country rich with natural, historical and cultural appeal. As the birthplace and heartland of the Maya, the country is in many ways defined by the legacy of this early civilization. Although the temples and rainforest cities of the ancient Maya have been abandoned for centuries, their traditions and religious rituals, mingled with Catholic practises, endure in the western highlands to form perhaps the most distinctive indigenous identity in the hemisphere.

Countering this is a powerful **ladino** society, urban and Western in its outlook, that has been shaped by Spanish colonial and European influences. Today, however, the nation's shopping malls, cinemas, televisions and dance floors devour mainstream Latin and North American popular culture. Nevertheless, you'll come across reminders of Guatemala's **colonial past** all over the country, nowhere more so than in the graceful former capital, Antigua.

It's this outstanding cultural legacy, combined with Guatemala's natural beauty, that makes the country so compelling for the traveller. The temples of **Tikal** would be magnificent in any arena but set inside the jungles of the Reserva de la Biósfera Maya, with attendant toucans and howler monkeys, they are bewitching. Similarly, the genteel cobbled streets, Baroque church ruins and plazas of colonial **Antigua** gain an extra dimension from their proximity to the looming volcanoes that encircle

> **Tikal is the most impressive of all the Maya sites, rivalling any ruin in Latin America**

the town. This **architectural wealth** is spread to a lesser degree throughout the country – almost every large village or town boasts a giant whitewashed colonial church and a classic Spanish-style plaza. Though most of the really dramatic Maya ruins lie deep in the jungles of Petén, interesting sites are scattered throughout the land, along the Pacific coast and in the foothills of the highlands.

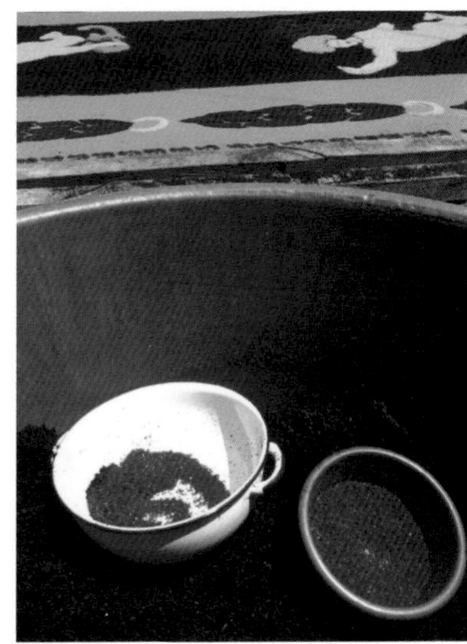

▲ Holy Week preparations, Antigua

Physically, Guatemala offers an astonishing range of **landscapes**, defined by extremes. In the south, the steamy Pacific coastal plain soars towards an awesome chain of **volcanoes** that mark the southern limit of the western highlands. North of these cones, a verdant landscape of pine-clad hills dotted with traditional villages and shimmering lakes forms the country's heartland and is home to the vast majority of Guatemala's indigenous population. Further east, towards the Caribbean coast, the terrain turns **tropical**, replete with banana plantations, coconut palms and mangrove swamps. Extensive **cloudforests** cloak the fecund Verapaz hills of central Guatemala, harbouring the elusive quetzal, Guatemala's national symbol. The vast **rainforests** of Petén occupy

▲ Temples at Tikal

Fact file

- The republic of Guatemala is situated at the northern end of the Central American isthmus, bordered by Mexico to the north and west, Belize to the northeast, and Honduras and El Salvador to the south and east. Its 108,890 square kilometres include 328km of Pacific coastline and 74km of Caribbean coast.
- Guatemala's population was estimated at 14.8 million by August 2005, with a growth rate of 2.6 percent per annum (the highest in the Western hemisphere). Eighty percent of *Guatemaltecos* live in the south of the country between the Mexican and Salvadorean borders; the northern and eastern departments are very thinly populated.
- Ethnically, the population is almost equally divided between indigenous Maya and ladinos (who are mainly of mixed race), although there are tiny numbers of black Garífuna (about 8000 in all), ethnic Chinese and non-Maya Xinca. Though Spanish is the official language, 23 other languages are spoken, including K'iche', Mam, Kaqchikel and Q'eqchi'.
- Tourism is the nation's main income earner, followed by coffee, sugar, clothing exports and bananas.
- About 63 percent of Guatemalans are nominally Roman Catholic – the lowest figure in Latin America – though many highland Maya practise a unique mix of religion that's heavily dependent on ancient religious ritual. Most others worship at US-based evangelical Protestant churches.

▲ Nebaj village costume

most of the country's north, and though these are increasingly threatened by loggers and settlers, they still are amongst the most extensive in Latin America. They're also home to **wildlife** including jaguars, tapirs, spider and howler monkeys, jabiru storks and scarlet macaws.

All of this exists against the nagging background of Guatemala's turbulent and bloody **history**. Over the years, the huge gulf between the rich and the poor, between indigenous and ladino culture, and the political left and right, has produced bitter conflict. With the signing of the 1996 peace accords between the government and the ex-guerrillas, Latin America's longest running civil war came to an end, though many of the country's deep-rooted inequalities remain. Land distribution continues to be woefully skewed in favour of agribusiness, while crime levels have soared in the absence of a functional justice system, leading to an increase in drug smuggling and gang violence. At the same time, the **economy** is still chronically weak, as income from the key coffee crop has plummeted and corruption remains endemic. Guatemala has very little industry, while poverty and malnutrition levels are some of the worst in the Americas.

Yet despite these problems, you'll find that most Guatemalans are extraordinarily courteous, and eager to help you catch the right bus or practise your Spanish. Guatemalans tend to be less extroverted than most Latin Americans and are quite formal and polite in social situations. Though decades of dictatorship and misgovernment have brought despair to many, somehow a sense of hopefulness endures that the country will one day turn the corner.

Maya fiestas

Guatemala's indigenous fiestas are some of the most compelling in Latin America: riotous, often deeply poignant and very drunken celebrations of Maya identity. Though there's often a central religious element, usually focusing on a patron saint's day, most tend to follow a familiar, tried-and-tested formula. Count on seeing a series of almost comical-looking, traditional costumed dances like the Dance of the Conquistadors, the performances charged with bitter historical sentiment and heavy symbolism. Obligatory barrages of eardrum-threatening firecrackers, wobbly fairground rides, endless marimba music and lashings of liquor complete the scene. The most spectacular events also include an additional element: the wild horse race at Todos Santos Cuchumatán (see p.218), the kite-flying extravaganzas at Santiago Sacatépequez and Sumpango (see p.104 and p.105) or the *Palo Volador* (see p.152), a Maya-style bungy jump (see p.145 and p.302).

Where to go

Whilst each region has its own particular attractions, most travellers first head to the Maya-dominated **western highlands**, and rightly so. The colour, the markets, the fiestas, the culture, and above all the people make it a wholly unique experience. And it seems almost an unfair bonus that all this is set in countryside of such mesmerizing beauty:

An archeological hotbed

The remote jungles of Petén are currently one of the most exciting archeological zones in the world, the target of more than a dozen ongoing digs that have unearthed several revelatory findings. Major progress in the reading of Maya glyphs has meant that the history of the core region, and the nature of Maya society, is becoming increasingly clear. Ruling family lineages, dates of accessions and wars and the key political alliances are all being steadily chronicled. Meanwhile, it's been established that bloodletting and human sacrifice were pivotal to Maya religious life. Recent discoveries include some stupendous Preclassic murals at San Bartolo, several magnificent stelae at Naachtún, near-pristine altarpiece panels at Cancuén and even a complete "lost city" – Wakná, located near El Mirador, found using satellite imagery.

for photographers, it's exceptional. **Antigua**, the delightful former colonial capital is another huge draw, its refined atmosphere and café society contrasting with the hectic, fume-filled bustle of Guatemala City. To the west is **Lago de Atitlán**, an astonishingly beautiful highland lake, ringed by sentinel-like volcanoes. The shores of the lake are dotted with tranquil indigenous villages such as **Santa Cruz La Laguna** and **San Marcos La Laguna**, the site of some tranquil hotels and breathtaking shoreline hikes, and **San Pedro La Laguna**, where the bohemian scene and rock-bottom prices attract travellers from all over the world. High up above the lake, the traditional Maya town of **Sololá** has one of the country's best (and least-touristy) markets, a complete contrast to the vast twice-weekly affair at **Chichicastenango**, with its incredible selection of weavings and handicrafts. Further west, the proud provincial city of **Quetzaltenango** (Xela) is a centre for language schools and also makes an excellent base for exploring the forest-fringed crater lake of **Volcán Chicabal**, the natural spa of **Fuentes Georginas** and market towns of Momostenango and San Francisco el Alto. **Huehuetenango**, the gateway to Guatemala's greatest mountain range, the **Cuchumatanes**, is a little further distant. In these granite peaks you'll find superb scenery and some of the most isolated and traditional villages in the Maya world, with **Nebaj**, in the Ixil Triangle, and **Todos Santos Cuchumatán** both making good bases for some serious hiking and adventure.

▲ Iguana

The **Pacific coast** is generally hot, dull and disappointing to visit, with scrubby, desolate beaches backed by a smattering of mangrove swamps. The sole exception is the relaxed seaside village of **Monterrico**, part of a wildlife reserve where you can watch sea turtles come ashore to lay their eggs. Inland, much of the region is devoted to commercial agriculture and dotted with bustling urban centres, though the pre-Columbian ruins of Takalik Abaj and the minor sites around the town of Santa Lucía Cotzumalguapa are worth a look if you're in the region.

None of these, however, can compete with the archeological wonders of

Men of maize

Sacred to the ancient Maya, who believed that the gods fashioned man from maize dough, corn is Guatemala's staple food. A central part of almost every meal, it's usually consumed as a *tortilla*, a flat, hand-shaped corn pancake which is toasted over a fire on a metal hot plate called a *comal*, though *tamales* (steamed corn dumplings stuffed with meat or chilli) are also eaten. Maize is deeply entwined with the national identity: the original magical realist novel, *Men of Maize*, was written by a Guatemalan, Miguel Ángel Asturias, the first Latin American to win the Nobel Prize in literature.

▲ Masks, Chichicastenango market

Petén. This unique lowland area, which makes up about a third of the country, is covered with dense tropical forest and savannah. Though loggers and ranchers have laid waste to large chunks of the terrain, much still remains to be seen, with reserves alive with wildlife and dotted with outstanding Maya ruins. From the delightful town of **Flores**, superbly situated on an islet on Lago de Petén Itzá, or the low-key village of **El Remate**, it's easy to reach **Tikal**, the most impressive of all the Maya sites, rivalling any ruin in Latin America. The region's forest also hides numerous smaller sites, including the striking **Yaxhá**, Ceibal, Uaxactún and Yaxchilán, just across the border in Mexico. Adventurous travellers may also want to seek out Petén's more remote ruins, such as the dramatic, pre-Classic sites of **El Mirador** (possibly even larger than Tikal) and Nakbé, which require days of tough travel to reach.

Finally, the **east** of the country includes another highland area, this time with little to offer the visitor, except for the compact Maya site of **Quiriguá** in the Motagua valley and the first-class ruins of **Copán**, just over the border in Honduras. Further into Honduras are the idyllic **Bay Islands**, whose pristine coral reefs offer some of the finest scuba diving and snorkelling in the

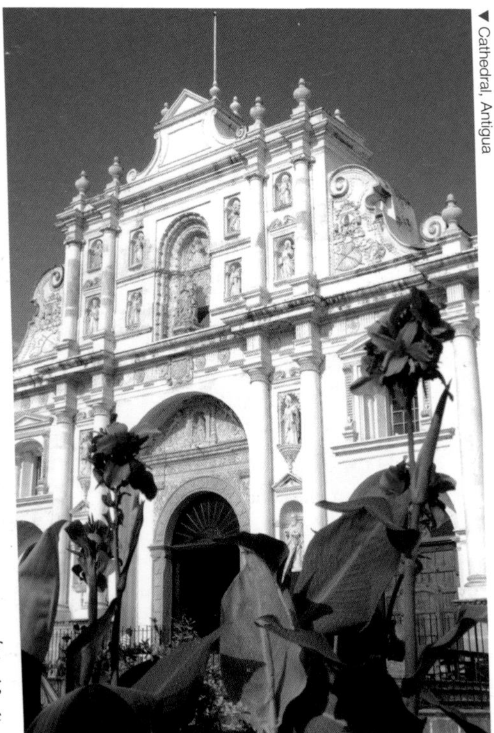
▼ Cathedral, Antigua

Caribbean. You can also travel up into the fresh green hills of the **Verapaces**, where there are stunning lakes and extensive cave systems near the settlement of **Chisec**. South of here is **Lago de Izabal**, Guatemala's largest inland lake, around whose shores there's plenty of interest, including an amazing hot spring waterfall, the Boquerón canyon and the bird-rich wetlands of the Reserva Bocas del Polochic. The lake drains into the Caribbean via the **Río Dulce**, a series of remarkable jungle-clad gorges just to the east. At the mouth of the river is the funky town of **Lívingston**, an outpost of Caribbean culture and home to Guatemala's only black community, the Garífuna.

▲ Market stall

When to go

Guatemala has one of the most pleasant climates on earth, with much of the country enjoying warm or hot days with mild evenings year-round. The immediate climate is largely determined by **altitude**. In those areas between 1300 and 1600m, which includes Guatemala City, Antigua, Lago de Atitlán and Cobán, the air is almost always fresh and the nights mild and, despite the heat of the midday sun, humidity is never a problem. Parts of the departments of Quetzaltenango, Huehuetenango and El Quiché are above this height, and so have a cooler, damper climate with distinctly chilly nights between early December and late February. Low-lying Petén suffers from sticky, steamy conditions most of the year, as do the Pacific and Caribbean coasts, though here at least you can usually

A verdant landscape of pine-clad hills dotted with traditional villages and shimmering lakes forms the country's heartland

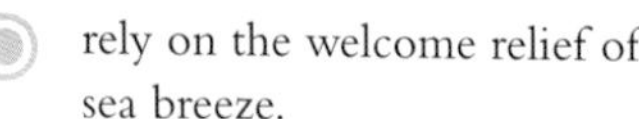

rely on the welcome relief of a sea breeze.

The **rainy season** runs roughly from May to October, with the worst of the rain falling in September and October. In Petén, however, the season can extend into December, whilst around Cobán and on the Caribbean coast it can rain at any time of the year. Even at the height of the wet season, though, the rain is usually confined to late afternoon downpours with most of the rest of the day being warm and pleasant. In many parts of the country, you can travel without disruption throughout the rainy season, although in the more out-of-the-way places, like the Cuchumatanes, flooding may slow you down. Visiting Petén's more remote ruins is best attempted between February and May, as the mud can be thigh deep during the height of the rains. The **Bay Islands' climate** is distinctly different, with clear skies between March and September, and rains starting in October and continuing until late February – Christmas and New Year are often very wet.

The **busiest times** for tourism are between December and March, and again in July and August. Language schools and hotels are fullest during these periods, and many of them hike their prices correspondingly.

Average daily temperatures (°C/°F)

	Jan	Feb	Mar	Apr	May	June	July	Aug	Sept	Oct	Nov	Dec
Guatemala City												
°C	23	25	27	28	29	27	26	26	26	24	23	22
°F	73	77	81	82	84	81	79	79	79	75	73	72
Huehuetenango												
°C	22	24	27	30	31	28	26	25	26	25	23	22
°F	72	75	81	86	88	82	79	77	79	77	73	72
Puerto Barrios												
°C	27	28	29	31	32	31	30	30	30	30	29	28
°F	81	82	84	88	90	88	86	86	86	86	84	82

32 things not to miss

It's not possible to see everything that Guatemala has to offer in one visit, and we don't suggest you try. What follows is a selective and subjective taste of the country's highlights, from active volcanoes and spectacular ruins to diverse wildlife and brash markets. They're arranged in five colour-coded categories, to help you find the best things to see, do, buy and experience. All highlights have a page reference to take you straight into the guide, where you can find out more.

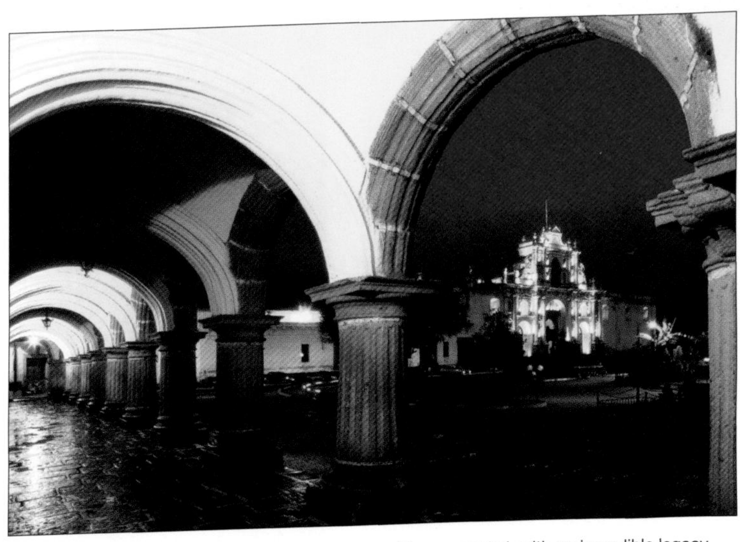

01 **Antigua** Page **105** • The serene, cultured former capital, with an incredible legacy of colonial architecture, is a UNESCO World Heritage site and one of the most elegant cities in the Americas.

02 Volcán de Pacaya Page **101** • Trek for an up-close glimpse of the smoke-belching cone of Pacaya, one of Central America's most active volcanoes.

03 Tikal Page **345** • This unmatched Maya site has it all: monumental temples and palaces set in a tropical forest reserve alive with screaming howler monkeys and chattering parakeets.

04 Quetzal Page **306** • Guatemala's national symbol inhabits the cloudforests of the Verapaces.

05 Río Dulce Page **277** • Cruise up the jungle-cloaked gorges and estuaries of Guatemala's "sweet river" by boat, and marvel at the prolific birdlife.

06 Whale shark Page **410** • Snorkel with the world's largest fish, a year-round resident in the seas just north of Utila.

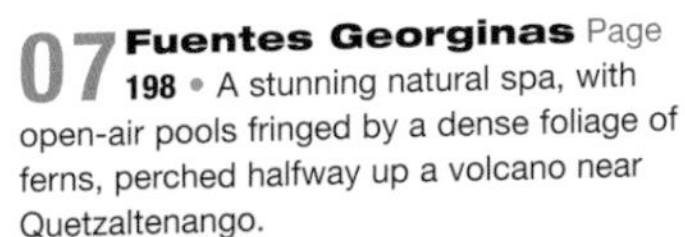

07 Fuentes Georginas Page **198** • A stunning natural spa, with open-air pools fringed by a dense foliage of ferns, perched halfway up a volcano near Quetzaltenango.

08 Chichicastenango Page **143** • Go textile and souvenir-hunting at the legendary twice-weekly market in this western highland town.

09 Chicken buses Page **45** • Garishly painted, outrageously uncomfortable, there's never a dull journey aboard Guatemala's iconic fume-belching *camionetas*.

10 Monterrico Page **250** • A rich nature reserve and village on the Pacific coast, with a sweeping beach where three species of sea turtle nest, including the giant leatherback.

11 Coffee Page **308** • Sample some of the world's finest single estate roasts in Cobán, the easy-going capital of Alta Verapaz.

12 Quiriguá Page **263** • Diminutive Maya site, where the central plaza is dotted with colossal sandstone stelae embellished with glyphs and images of the ruler, Cauac Sky.

13 Highland hiking Page **220** • Explore the beguiling high trails that crisscross the granite mountains above the traditional Mam village of Todos Santos Cuchumatán.

14 Esquipulas Page **290** • The vast basilica of Esquipulas is home to an ancient carved image of a black Christ, and the focus for Central America's largest pilgrimage.

15 San Francisco el Alto Page **203** • One of the most remarkable markets in Central America – a seething mass of highland Maya humanity.

16 Maximón Pages **174** & **198** • Visit the pagan temple of this liquor-swilling, cigar-smoking evil saint.

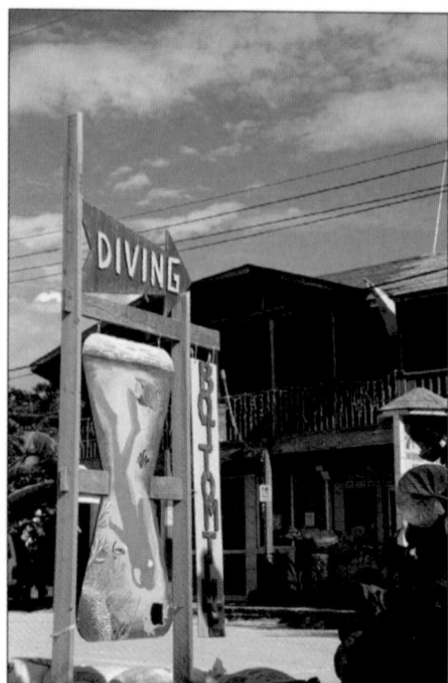

17 Scuba diving Page **413** • The Honduran Bay Islands have some of the world's cheapest scuba diving schools, as well as pristine coral reefs teeming with tropical sea life.

18 National Archeological Museum Page **92** • Guatemala City's Museo Nacional de Arqueología y Etnología contains a wonderful collection of Maya artistry and breathtakingly carved stelae, altars and lintels from many of the major Petén sites.

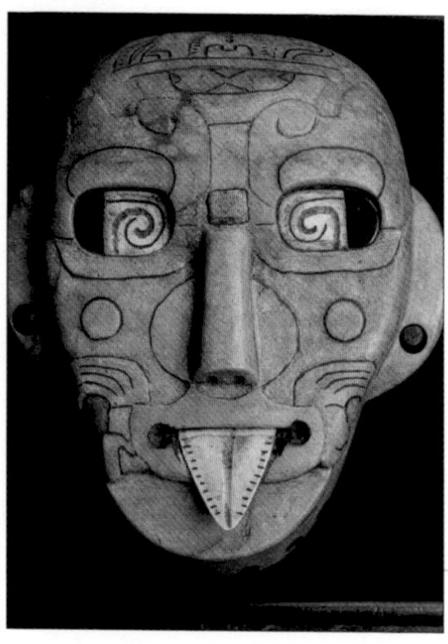

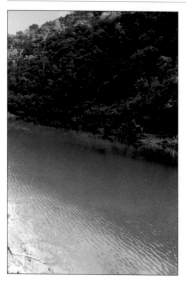

19 Lagunas de Sepalau Page **321** • Just east of the isolated town of Chisec, these beautiful jade lagoons are well off the beaten track, so you'll almost certainly be able to explore them by yourself.

20 Lívingston Page **272** • Shake your booty to the hypnotic drum-driven punta beat in the swinging Garífuna village of Lívingston.

21 Baroque churches

Page **115** • Built in a unique Iberian-American "squat-Baroque" style – to resist the ever-present threat of earthquakes – Guatemala's churches boast fabulously decorative and theatrically embellished facades.

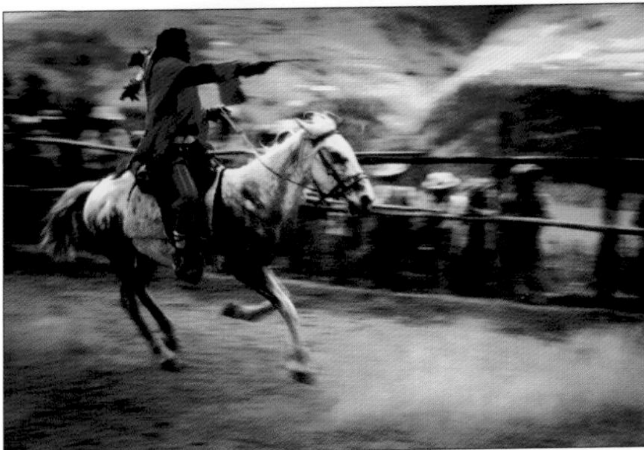

22 Todos Santos Cuchumatán

Page **218** • This normally sleepy town hosts a legendary fiesta, featuring a rip-roaring horse race, in a stunning highland valley setting.

23 Eastern highlands

Page **284** • Ancient eroded volcanoes, cacti-spiked hills, a sparkling crater lake and virtually no other tourists.

24 **Finca el Paraíso** Page **282** • Soak away the chicken bus blues at the blissful hot spring waterfall and natural pools near Finca el Paraíso.

25 **Yaxhá** Page **375** • This massive Maya site, superbly positioned on the banks of Lago de Yaxhá, mainly dates from the Classic period and is currently the subject of extensive archeological excavations.

26 **Lago de Atitlán** Page **162** • Encircled by three volcanoes, the awesome crater lake of Lago de Atitlán was famously described by Aldous Huxley as "the most beautiful lake in the world".

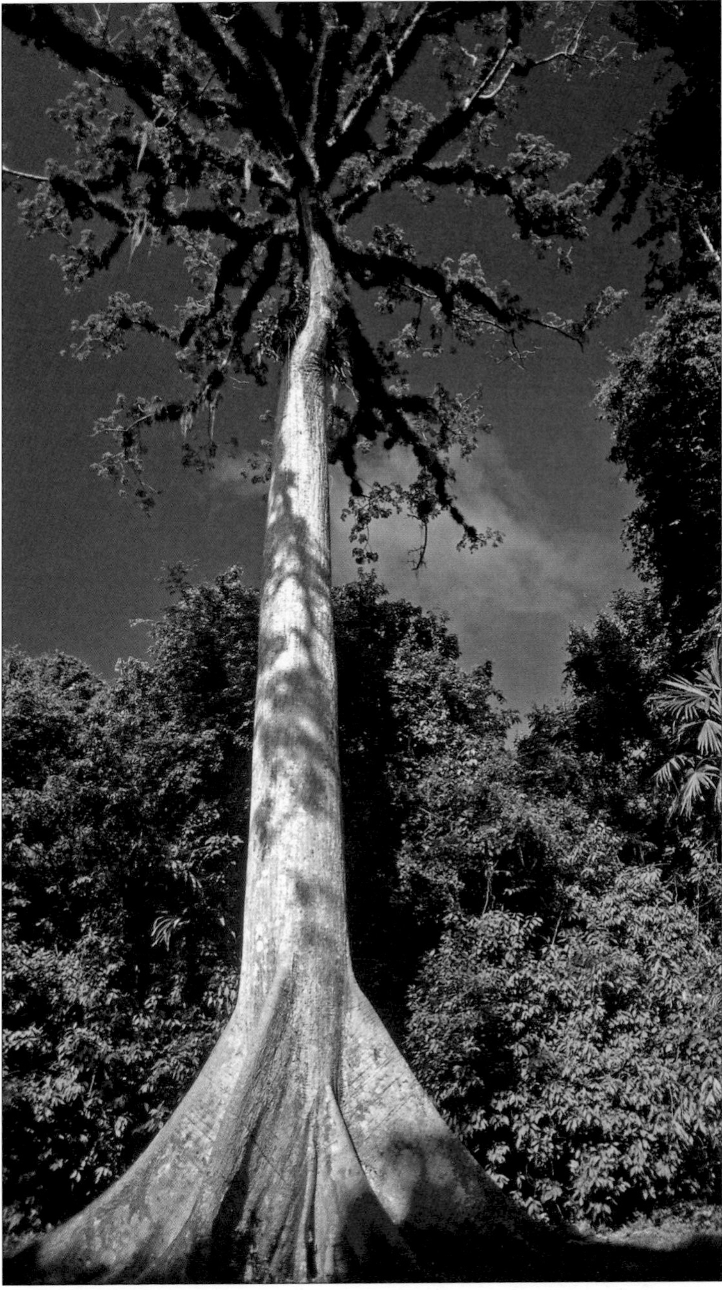

27 **Jungle trekking** Page **361** • Tramp through the Reserva de la Biósfera Maya to the jungle-choked ruins of the Preclassic cities of El Mirador and Nakbé in Petén.

28 Studying Spanish Page **64** • Latin America's leading language school centre, Guatemala has dozens of excellent institutions that offer one-on-one tuition and home-stay packages at rock-bottom rates.

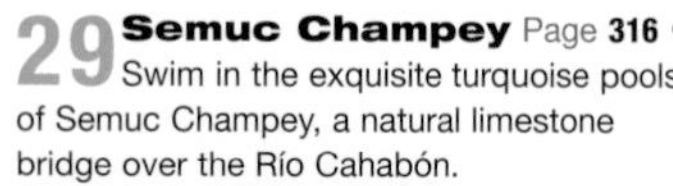

29 Semuc Champey Page **316** • Swim in the exquisite turquoise pools of Semuc Champey, a natural limestone bridge over the Río Cahabón.

30 Semana Santa Pages **112** & **174** • During Easter Week, head for either Antigua for its epic Catholic processions, or Santiago Atitlán to witness the symbolic confrontation between the evil saint Maximón and Christ.

31 Copán ruins Page **389** • There's a plethora of exquisitely carved stelae and altars, a towering hieroglyphic stairway and an outstanding site museum at the magnificent Maya ruins of Copán.

32 The Ixil Triangle Page **153** • Experience the colour, costume and bewitching scenery of three remote highland villages: Nebaj, Cotzal and Chajul.

Basics

Basics

Getting there

Most people get to Guatemala by plane, arriving in the capital, Guatemala City. There's another international airport at Flores, which is handy for the ruins of Tikal, but this is only served by a few international flights from Houston, Cancún and Belize City. Guatemalan land and sea entry points are relatively hassle-free, unless you're bringing your own transport, in which case you can expect plenty of red tape, dubious entry fees and delays.

Airfares always depend on the season, with the highest being from Christmas to February, around Easter, and in July and August. You can often cut costs by going through a specialist flight agent or by booking direct via the Internet.

If Guatemala is only one stop on a longer journey, you might want to consider buying an **airpass** that enables you to visit several other destinations in the region – though these do not offer the savings they used to as reservations changes are costly. (They also often exclude Cancún and Flores airport). You have to fly into the region on one of the participating airlines. Airlines **Taca** and **Copa** both offer similar airpass schemes linking Central American cities: flying Miami–San José–Guatemala City–LA costs from US$775. The **Mexipass**, offered by Méxicana/Aeroméxico, is another option. The best way to find out whether you might benefit from an airpass is to consult a recommended travel agent.

Guatemala City is very rarely included on standard **Round-the-World** (RTW) ticket itineraries, but a good agent can assemble one for you. That said, an RTW ticket that includes Guatemala will inevitably work out to be more expensive than many standard tickets of this type – figure on around US$2600/£1250.

Booking flights online

Booking your tickets online cuts out the costs of agents and middlemen. Good deals can often be found through discount or auction sites, though these tickets can be pretty inflexible as such sites usually offer non-refundable, non-changeable deals. Almost all airlines have their own websites, offering tickets that can sometimes be just as inexpensive – and often more flexible – as those found on discount sites.

Ⓦ **www.cheapflights.co.uk** (in UK & Ireland), Ⓦ **www.cheapflights.com** (in US), Ⓦ **www.cheapflights.ca** (in Canada), Ⓦ **www.cheapflights.com.au** (in Australia). Flight deals, plus links to other travel sites.

Ⓦ **www.cheaptickets.com** Discount flight specialists (US only). Also at Ⓣ 1-888/922-8849.

Ⓦ **www.ebookers.com** Efficient, easy to use flight finder, with competitive fares.

Ⓦ **www.etn.nl/discount** A hub of consolidator and discount agent links, maintained by the nonprofit European Travel Network.

Ⓦ **www.expedia.co.uk** (in UK), Ⓦ **www.expedia.com** (in US), Ⓦ **www.expedia.ca** (in Canada). Discount airfares, all-airline search engine and daily deals.

Ⓦ **www.flyaow.com** "Airlines of the Web" – online air travel info and reservations.

Ⓦ **www.gaytravel.com** US-based gay travel agent, offering accommodation, cruises, tours and more. Also at Ⓣ 1-800/GAY-TRAVEL.

Ⓦ **www.geocities.com/thavery2000** An extensive list of airline websites and US toll-free numbers.

Ⓦ **www.hotwire.com** Bookings from the US only. Last-minute savings of up to forty percent on regular published fares. Travellers must be at least 18 and there are no refunds, transfers or changes allowed. Log-in required.

Ⓦ **www.kelkoo.co.uk** Useful UK-only price-comparison site, checking several sources of low-cost flights (and other goods and services) according to specific criteria.

Ⓦ **www.lastminute.com** (in UK), Ⓦ **www.lastminute.com.au** (in Australia), Ⓦ **www.lastminute.co.nz** (in New Zealand), Ⓦ **www.site59.com** (in US). Good last-minute holiday package and flight-only deals.

Ⓦ **www.orbitz.com** Comprehensive Web travel source, with the usual flight, car rental and hotel deals but also great follow-up customer service.

ⓦ **www.priceline.co.uk** (in UK), ⓦ **www.priceline.com** (in US). Name-your-own-price website that has deals at around forty percent off standard fares.

ⓦ **www.qixo.com** (US). Search engine that browses dozens of airline websites, frequently coming up with bargain prices.

ⓦ **www.skyauction.com** Bookings from the US only. Auctions tickets and travel packages to destinations worldwide.

ⓦ **www.travelocity.co.uk** (in UK), ⓦ **www.travelocity.com** (in US), ⓦ **www.travelocity.ca** (in Canada), ⓦ **www.zuji.com.au** (in Australia). Destination guides, hot fares and great deals for car rental, accommodation and lodging.

ⓦ **www.travelshop.com.au** Australian site offering discounted flights, packages, insurance and online bookings. Also on ⓣ 1800/108 108.

ⓦ **travel.yahoo.com** Incorporates some Rough Guides material in its coverage of destination countries and cities across the world, with information about places to eat and sleep; also offers flight, car rental and hotel deals.

ⓦ **www.travelzoo.com** Great resource for news on the latest airline sales, cruise discounts and hotel deals. Links bring you directly to the carrier's site.

Flights from the US and Canada

Only a select number of North American airlines fly to Guatemala, with most flights routed through a few US hub cities. Flights from Atlanta, Dallas, Houston, Miami, New Orleans – and on United from LA – are non-stop. Only a handful of non-stop flights originate in New York and San Francisco. Expect to pay between US$320–540 from Miami, US$550–700 from Houston or US$390–750 from New York, depending on the time of year. Continental's new twice-weekly service also connects Houston with Flores in Petén.

From Canada, which doesn't have any non-stop flights your best bet is to fly to one of the US gateway cities and change there. Return flights from Toronto typically cost C$690–870, from Vancouver C$750–995. Consider flying via Cuba using the Havana–Guatemala City connection on Cubana, which often has competitive fares.

Airlines

Aeroméxico ⓣ 1-800/237-6639, ⓦ www.aeromexico.com. Direct flights from many US gateway cities to Mexico City, for connections on Méxicana Airlines to Guatemala City.

American Airlines ⓣ 1-800/433-7300, ⓦ www.aa.com. Daily flights from Dallas and Miami.

Continental Airlines ⓣ 1-800/231-0856, ⓦ www.continental.com. Two daily flights from Houston. Route-sharing with Air Canada means good connections from Canada.

Delta Air Lines ⓣ 1-800/241-4141, ⓦ www.delta.com. Daily flights from Atlanta.

Méxicana ⓣ 1-800/531-7921, ⓦ www.mexicana.com. Frequent flights from Chicago, Denver, LA, Newark, San Francisco, Montréal and Toronto to Mexico City, with connections to Guatemala City.

Taca ⓣ 1-888/477-8222, ⓦ www.grupotaca.com. Daily flights from Los Angeles, Miami, New York and Washington with many more options using Taca's hub airport of San Salvador.

United Airlines ⓣ 1-800/538–2929, ⓦ www.ual.com. One daily flight from Los Angeles.

US Air ⓣ 1-800/622-1015, ⓦ www.usair.com. Daily flights from Miami, with service from Fort Lauderdale planned.

Travel agents

Airtech ⓣ 212/219-7000, ⓦ www.airtech.com. Standby seat broker; also deals in consolidator fares.

Educational Travel Center ⓣ 1-800/747-5551 or 608/256-5551, ⓦ www.edtrav.com. Low-cost fares and student/youth discount offers.

eXito ⓣ 1-800/655-4053, ⓦ www.exitotravel.com. North America's top specialist for travel to Latin America. Website has a particularly useful airfare finder, with a comparison of the merits of various airpasses.

Flightcentre US ⓣ 1-866/WORLD-51, ⓦ www.flightcentre.us, Canada ⓣ 1-888/WORLD-55, ⓦ www.flightcentre.ca. Rock-bottom fares.

STA Travel US ⓣ 1-800/329-9537, Canada ⓣ 1-888/427-5639, ⓦ www.statravel.com. Worldwide specialists in independent travel; also travel insurance and car rental.

Student Flights ⓣ 1-800/255-8000 or 480/951-1177, ⓦ www.isecard.com/studentflights. Student/youth fares.

TFI Tours ⓣ 1-800/745-8000 or 212/736-1140, ⓦ www.lowestairprice.com. Well-established consolidator with a wide variety of inexpensive fares.

Travel Avenue ⓣ 1-800/333-3335, ⓦ www.travelavenue.com. Full-service travel agent that offers discounts in the form of rebates.

Travel Cuts US ⓣ1-800/592-CUTS, Canada ⓣ1-888/246-9762, ⓦwww.travelcuts.com. Popular, long-established student-travel organization, with worldwide offers.
Travelers Advantage ⓣ1-877/259-2691, ⓦwww.travelersadvantage.com. Discount travel club, with cash-back deals and discounted car rental. Membership required ($1 for a three-month trial).
Travelosophy US ⓣ1-800/332-2687, ⓦwww.itravelosophy.com. Good range of discounted and student fares worldwide.
Worldtek Travel ⓣ1-800/243-1723, ⓦwww.worldtek.com. Discount travel agency for worldwide travel.

Organized tours

There's a terrific range of organized tours to Guatemala and the Maya region. Specialist companies take escorted groups on tours to Maya ruins, colonial towns, markets and beaches, often crossing several borders, and with options including biking, diving, rafting and bird-watching. If time is short, these can be very good value.

Budget tour groups usually travel by van, staying at comfortable, family-run hotels or camping, and calling at the main tourist attractions as well as some lesser-known places. More expensive tours typically stay at luxury hotels and lodges, and can take you on expeditions with archeologists and ornithologists to remote sites and nature reserves.

Although in most cases you could organize the same or very similar itineraries yourself for a little less money, you'll need good Spanish and plenty of patience. If you're considering an upmarket package it may be impossible to negotiate a better deal on your own anyway – tour operators are able to secure reduced rates in hotels that are not normally available to independent travellers. You'll also get at least one guide for the entire trip.

Adventure trips (sea-kayaking, caving and expeditions to remote jungle ruins) are even more difficult to organize on your own, and are best done in an organized group, with expert leaders and emergency back-up.

The tour prices below do not include airfares to the region, unless stated.

US tour operators

Adventure Center ⓣ1-800/228-8747 or 510/654-1879, ⓦwww.adventure-center.com. Hiking and "soft adventure" specialists. The fifteen-day "Ancient Land of the Maya" trip costs from US$1450 and includes Nebaj and the lowland ruins of Quiriguá and Tikal.
Adventure Life ⓣ1-800/344-6118, ⓦwww.adventure-life.com. Small-group specialists using well-trained local and international guides. All the Guatemala trips (US$675–1345) offer well-structured itineraries and include options as diverse as a homestay with a local family or a night in a luxury jungle lodge.
Ceiba Adventures ⓣ1-800/217-1060, ⓦwww.ceibaadventures.com. Multi-sport adventures, including rafting, kayaking and caving, and archeological tours throughout the Maya region. The ten-day "River of Ruins" (US$2550) tour includes many of the Usumacinta sites, plus Tikal and Ceibal.
Elderhostel ⓣ1-877/426-8056 or 978/323-4141, ⓦwww.elderhostel.org. A nonprofit organization offering upmarket educational programmes for over-55s. Their "Maya and More" fifteen-day tour includes visits to Lago de Atitlán, Tikal and Copán, and costs from US$2675.
Far Horizons ⓣ1-800/552-4575, ⓦwww.farhorizon.com. Some of the very best small-group archeological trips in the region, guided by Mayanists, including a "Lost Cities of the Maya" trip that takes in the sites around the lake of Petexbatún, and Cancuén (US$4195 including airfare).
Guatemala Unlimited ⓣ1-800/733-3350, ⓦwww.guatemalaunlimited.com. Experienced company with an eight-day tour of Guatemala (US$989) plus trips to the ruins of Petén.
Latin American Escapes ⓣ1-800/510-599, ⓦwww.latinamericanescapes.com. Inexpensive Guatemalan itineraries include an intriguing market-towns trip at US$575.
Lost World Adventures ⓣ1-800/999-0558, ⓦwww.lostworldadventures.com. Very well-priced tours with accommodation in four- and five-star hotels. Four different Guatemala tours are offered, plus Maya World and Honduras trips.
Toucan Travel ⓣ805/927-5885, ⓦwww.toucantravel.com. Latin America specialists with over a dozen inexpensive, sociable tours through the Maya region and Central America, some using public buses, others mainly camping. The 14-day "Iguana" trip costs US$895.
Tropical Travel ⓣ1–800/451-8017, ⓦwww.tropicaltravel.com. Several tours in Guatemala to the highlands and beyond; sport-fishing excursions are also offered.
Wildland Adventures ⓣ1-800/345-4453, ⓦwww.wildland.com. Well-guided tours include a "Guatemalan Highlands Odyssey" (US$1395) and "Great Cities of the Maya" (US$1995).

Wilderness Travel ⓣ1-800/368-2794, ⓦwww.wildernesstravel.com. Well-organized cultural and wildlife adventure trips. There's a nine-day Ruta Maya trip through Guatemala and along the Usumacinta to Mexico from US$2695, and a nine-day "Honduras Independent Journey" (US$1895), which includes snorkeling in Roatán and two days at Copán.

Canadian tour operators

Adventures Abroad ⓣ1-800/665-3998, ⓦwww.adventures-abroad.com. Adventure specialists with a selection of comfortable small-group tours in Guatemala and the Maya region.
Gap Adventures ⓣ1-800/465-5600, ⓦwww.gap.ca. Wide range of budget group trips (some camping) with diving and kayaking; C$1750 for a 32-day "Central American Journey".

Flights from the UK and Ireland

There are no scheduled flights from the UK or Ireland to Guatemala, so flying there involves changing aircraft and sometimes airline. Most itineraries travel via the US cities of Atlanta, Dallas, Houston or Miami; however, alternatives include a new direct Madrid–Guatemala route on Iberia, plus routes via Cuba.

London airports offer the greatest variety of flights to the US and onwards to Mexico or Central America, though you can often travel from other UK airports for the same or only a slightly higher price. A scheduled return flight to Guatemala City on American (via Miami) or Continental (via Houston) will cost around £515 low season/£680 high season (excluding taxes).

From Ireland, it's often cheapest to grab a low-cost airline ticket to one of the London airports and travel on from there. Iberia has daily flights from Dublin to Madrid from where there are direct flights to Guatemala, and there are numerous possibilities via gateway cities in the US. Expect to pay around €850 low season/€1050 high season.

Many travellers opt to get to Guatemala **via Mexico** (see p.32). British Airways flies from London non-stop to Mexico City from around £415 low/£575 high. The very cheapest way to get to Guatemala from the UK is to book a charter flight to Cancún (as low as £179 return, but tickets are very rarely valid for more than one month) and then travel overland through Belize to the northern department of Petén – though this route entails around fourteen hours of bus travel just to get to the city of Flores.

If you want to travel through several countries in Central America, or even continue into South America, then it's worth considering an **open-jaw ticket** (which lets you fly into one city and out of another). The low-season price for an open-jaw flying London–Cancún and returning Guatemala City–London can be as little as £500; lots of other options are available.

On the Internet ⓦwww.cheapflights.co.uk has one of the best and fastest farefinders, allowing rapid comparisons and best-buy deals on fares to Guatemala (and Mexico and other Central American cities) from various UK airports; the site provides a link to the travel agent offering the best price. Frequently, however, no single general-travel website is consistently going to give you the best deal, so it's worth shopping around on ⓦwww.travelocity.co.uk and ⓦwww.expedia.co.uk. However, you'll often find the specialist flight agents have the best fares, backed by expert first-hand travel advice. Journey Latin America's website leads the field, closely followed by those of Trailfinders and STA Travel.

Airlines

American Airlines ⓣ0845/778 9789, ⓦwww.aa.com. Flies daily from London Heathrow to Miami, with frequent flights on to Guatemala City (some with partner Grupo Taca).
British Airways UK ⓣ0870/850 9850, Republic of Ireland ⓣ1800/626 747, ⓦwww.ba.com. Daily to Mexico City, plus codeshares with American Airlines.
Continental Airlines UK ⓣ0845/607 6760, Republic of Ireland ⓣ1890/925 252, ⓦwww.continental.com. Daily flights to Houston from London, with excellent connections on to Guatemala City.
Delta Air Lines UK ⓣ0800/414 767, Republic of Ireland ⓣ1800/768 080, ⓦwww.delta.com. Daily flights from London to Atlanta, with connections to Guatemala.
Iberia UK ⓣ0845/601 2854, Republic of Ireland ⓣ01/407 3017, ⓦwww.iberiaairlines.co.uk. Four flights a week to Guatemala direct from Madrid, though all return via San José, Costa Rica. Iberia also offer flights to Havana, from where there are daily connections to Guatemala.
Méxicana UK ⓣ020/8492 0000, ⓦwww.mexicana.com. Information, reservations and "Mexipass" airpass sales, but no flights.

Taca ⓣ0870/241 0340, ⓦwww.grupotaca.com. Agents for several Central American airlines, but no flights from Europe.

Flight and travel agents

Bridge the World UK ⓣ0870/443 2399, ⓦwww.bridgetheworld.com. Specializing in Round-the-World tickets, with good deals aimed at the backpacker market.
Journey Latin America ⓣ020/8747 3108 or 0161/832 1441, ⓦwww.journeylatinamerica.co.uk. The acknowledged leaders for airfares to Guatemala and the region, with some of the best prices on high-season flights. Also run some excellent tours (see "Tour operators in the UK").
Maxwell's Travel in Ireland ⓣ01/677-9479. Experienced in travel to Latin America, and Ireland's representatives for many of the specialist tour operators in the UK.
North South Travel ⓣ01245/608291, ⓦwww.northsouthtravel.co.uk. Small, friendly agency offering worldwide discounted fares. Profits are used to support development projects in Africa, Asia and Latin America.
South American Experience ⓣ020/7976 5511, ⓦwww.southamericanexperience.co.uk. Flights and tailor-made itinerary specialists, with competitive airfare prices on their website and high-quality tours to the Maya region.
STA Travel ⓣ0870/160 6070, ⓦwww.statravel.co.uk. Student/youth travel specialists with 250 branches worldwide, offering flights, tours, accommodation and many travel-related services, including a help desk if you have problems while abroad.
Trailfinders UK ⓣ020/7938 3939, ⓦwww.trailfinders.com, Ireland ⓣ01/677 7888, ⓦwww.trailfinders.ie. Informed travel company with a wide range of deals on flights to Central America.
USIT Northern Ireland ⓣ028/9032 7111, ⓦwww.usitnow.com, Republic of Ireland ⓣ0818/200 020, ⓦwww.usit.ie. Specialists in student, youth and independent travel – flights, trains, study tours, TEFL, visas and more.

Tour operators in the UK

Cox and Kings ⓣ020/7873 5000, ⓦwww.coxandkings.co.uk. Offers a fifteen-day "Mexico and Guatemala Grand Tour" (£2245), which visits many of the main Maya ruins, plus Lago de Atitlán and Antigua.
Dragoman ⓣ01728/861133, ⓦwww.dragoman.com. Several overland camping/hotel bus trips through Mexico and Central America, the four-week "Rum and Ruin" trip from Guatemala to Panama costs £895, plus food kitty.
Exodus ⓣ020/8675 5550, ⓦwww.exodus.co.uk. Offers seven tours that include Guatemala; the 19-day "Panamericana" trip is £1560 and uses mainly a/c minibuses.
Explore Worldwide ⓣ01252/760000, ⓦwww.exploreworldwide.com. Wide range of two- to three-week hotel-based tours; from £785 for fifteen days in Guatemala, Belize and Honduras.
Global Travel Club ⓣ01268/541732, ⓦwww.global-travel.co.uk. Small company specializing in individually arranged diving and cultural tours to Guatemala, Mexico and Belize.
Imaginative Traveller ⓣ0800 316 2717, ⓦwww.imaginative-traveller.com. Offers three low-cost tours that include Guatemala; the ten-day "Markets and Mayans" trip costs £410.
Intrepid Travel ⓣ020/8960 6333, ⓦwww.intrepidtravel.com. Small-group tours with an emphasis on cross-cultural contact and low-impact tourism.
Journey Latin America ⓣ020/8747 8315, ⓦwww.journeylatinamerica.co.uk. Wide range of high-standard group tours and tailor-made itineraries from the acknowledged experts. A thirteen-day mountain-bike trip around the Guatemalan highlands costs £995.
Kumuka ⓣ020/7397 6664 ⓦwww.kumuka.co.uk. Selection of two-week hotel-based group trips in Mexico and Central America. The "Avenue of the Volcanoes" races across four countries in 11 days and costs £530.
Reef and Rainforest Tours ⓣ01803/866965, ⓦwww.reefandrainforest.co.uk. Comfortable tailor-made and organized tours in Honduras focusing on nature reserves, Copán ruins and diving.
Scuba Safaris ⓣ01342/851196, ⓦwww.scuba-safaris.com. Knowledgeable, well-organized company, specializing in dive holidays. Around £1100–1400, depending on season, for full board in the *Fantasy Island Beach Resort* in Roatán and six days diving; live-aboard boat diving also possible. Airfare included.
Trips ⓣ0117/311 4400, ⓦwww.tripsworldwide.co.uk. Latin America and Caribbean experts who give you the chance to tailor your own trip, and build flexibility into the itinerary. Also on offer, a "Cultural Guatemala" trip (from £1895, including airfares), which covers the highlands and Tikal.
Wildlife Worldwide ⓣ020/8667 9158, ⓦwww.wildlifeworldwide.com. Superb bird-watching trips in Guatemala and Belize led by expert naturalists, visiting some remote protected areas and staying at biological stations and jungle lodges. From £1745 for a seven-day tour.

Flights from Australia and New Zealand

There are no direct flights from Australasia to Guatemala (or any other city in Central

America), so you've little choice but to fly via the US.

Flight Centres, STA and Trailfinders generally offer the lowest fares; in New Zealand also try USIT Beyond. On the Internet discounted fares can be found at Ⓦwww.travel.com.au and Ⓦwww.travelforless.co.nz.

Qantas/Méxicana offers some of the cheapest return fares to Guatemala from Australia and New Zealand, with tickets costing around A$2400–2700 (depending on the season) from Sydney via LA or NZ$2500–2800 from Auckland. If you want to visit Guatemala as part of a longer Latin American trip it often costs only a little more to book an open-jaw ticket flying into Guatemala City and returning from Panama.

Airlines

Air New Zealand Australia Ⓣ13 2476, New Zealand Ⓣ0800 737000, Ⓦwww.airnz.com. Daily to LA from Sydney and Auckland, with connections on United to Guatemala.

American Airlines Australia Ⓣ1300/130 757, New Zealand Ⓣ0800/887 997, Ⓦwww.aa.com. Daily flights from Sydney, Melbourne and Auckland to LA, with connections to Central America.

Continental Airlines Australia Ⓣ1300/361 400, New Zealand Ⓣ09/308 3350, Ⓦwww.continental.com. Teams up with Qantas and Air New Zealand to offer a through-service to Guatemala via LA and Houston.

JAL Australia Ⓣ02/9272 1111, New Zealand Ⓣ09/379 9906, Ⓦwww.jal.com. Several flights a week to Dallas/Fort Worth, LA and Mexico City from Sydney, Brisbane, Cairns and Auckland with an overnight stopover in Tokyo.

Korean Air Australia Ⓣ02/9262 6000, New Zealand Ⓣ09/914 2000, Ⓦwww.koreanair.com.au. Several flights a week from Sydney, Brisbane and Auckland to LA with an overnight stopover in Seoul.

Méxicana Australia Ⓣ03/9699 9355, New Zealand Ⓣ09/914 2573, Ⓦwww.mexicana.com. Mexipass information.

Qantas Australia Ⓣ13 1313, New Zealand Ⓣ0800/808767, Ⓦwww.qantas.com.au. Daily to LA from major Australian cities and from Auckland via Sydney.

United Airlines Australia Ⓣ13 1777, New Zealand Ⓣ09/379 3800, Ⓦwww.ual.com. Daily direct to LA from Sydney, Melbourne and Auckland with onward connections to Guatemala.

Travel agents

Flight Centre Australia Ⓣ13 31 33, Ⓦwww.flightcentre.com.au, New Zealand Ⓣ0800/243 544, Ⓦwww.flightcentre.co.nz. Rock-bottom fares worldwide.

STA Travel Australia Ⓣ1300/733 035, New Zealand Ⓣ0508/782 872, Ⓦwww.statravel.com. Worldwide specialists in low-cost flights, overlands and holiday deals. Good discounts for students and under-26s.

Student Uni Travel Australia Ⓣ02/9232 8444, Ⓦwww.sut.com.au, New Zealand Ⓣ09/379 4224, Ⓦwww.sut.co.nz. Great deals for students.

Trailfinders Australia Ⓣ02/9247 7666, Ⓦwww.trailfinders.com.au. One of the best-informed and most efficient agents for independent travellers. Agents for many adventure-travel specialists to Mexico and Central America.

travel.com.au and travel.co.nz Australia Ⓣ1300/130 482 or 02/9249 5444, Ⓦwww.travel.com.au, New Zealand Ⓣ0800/468 332, Ⓦwww.travel.co.nz. Comprehensive online travel company, with discounted fares.

Tour operators

Adventure Associates Ⓣ1800/222141, Ⓦwww.adventureassociates.com. Escorted tours and tailor-made archeological and cultural expeditions to Guatemala and the Maya region.

Adventure World Australia Ⓣ02/8913 0755, Ⓦwww.adventureworld.com.au, New Zealand Ⓣ09/524 5118, Ⓦwww.adventureworld.co.nz. Agents for many international adventure-travel companies.

Contours Ⓣ1300/135 391, Ⓦwww.contourstravel.com.au. Specialists in cultural and adventure (bike, kayak and hiking) tours to Central America.

Geckos Ⓣ02/9290 2770, Ⓦwww.geckos.com.au. Extended overland adventures from southern Mexico through Guatemala and the rest of Central America; agent for Exodus in the UK.

World Expeditions Australia Ⓣ1300/720 000, Ⓦwww.worldexpeditions.com.au, New Zealand Ⓣ0800/350 354, Ⓦwww.worldexpeditions.co.nz. Adventure company with a fine Maya World tour (A$3690) from Chiapas, Mexico, to Guatemala City via Yaxchilan and Tikal.

Overland from Mexico

It's a long haul **overland** to Guatemala from the US and Canada, with several possible routes through Mexico. In Mexico, there are Guatemalan consulates in Tapachula and

Comitán and a Belize consulate in Chetumal; for more on entry requirements, see below.

Greyhound (☎1-800/229-9424, ⓦwww.greyhound.com) runs regularly to all the major US border crossings, and some buses even take you over the border and into the Mexican bus station; in many cases you can also reserve tickets with Greyhound's Mexican counterparts. Mexican buses similarly cross the border into US bus stations.

Buses run from every Mexican border outpost to Mexico City (roughly 18–22hr), which has good bus connections to the main Guatemala border crossings. The **best route into Guatemala** takes you along the Carretera Interamericana (also known as the Panamerican Highway) through Oaxaca and San Cristóbal de las Casas (from where a direct shuttle bus runs to Antigua), over the border at La Mesilla and then on to Huehuetenango. There's another route along Mexico's Pacific coast to Tapachula, from where you can take direct buses to Guatemala City. Alternatively, there are several border crossings (see p.370) into Guatemala's northern department of Petén: the route via Frontera Corozal and La Técnica/Bethel is the most popular point of entry.

Driving south may give you a lot of freedom, but it does entail a great deal of bureaucracy. You need a separate insurance policy for Central America (sold at the Guatemalan border). Sanborn's Insurance (in US ☎1-800/222-0158, ⓦwww.sanbornsinsurance.com) arranges insurance for Mexico and Central America, and also offers legal assistance, road maps and guidebooks, and a 24-hour emergency hotline. Your car will also require an **entry permit**, for which you'll need to show the registration and license. US, Canadian, EU, Australian and New Zealand driving licenses are valid in Mexico and throughout Central America, but it's a good idea to arm yourself with an International Driving License as well. If you belong to a motoring organization at home, you may find they'll offer advice, maps and even help from reciprocal organizations in Mexico. Unleaded gasoline is widely available in the region.

Red tape and visas

Guatemalan visa entry requirements were relaxed considerably in November 2004. Citizens from nearly all Western countries need only a valid passport to enter Guatemala for up to ninety days. Passport-holders from some countries (including Russia and Jamaica) qualify for a visa, but have to get one from a Guatemalan embassy or consulate; citizens from other countries, including many in Asia and Africa, need to apply for a visa well in advance. If you're wondering whether you'll need a visa, phone an embassy for the latest entry requirements; Guatemala has embassies in all the region's capitals. You can also consult ⓦwww.migracion.gob.gt (in English and Spanish).

When you arrive at immigration you may be asked by the official how long you plan to stay, and offered thirty, sixty or ninety days. If you want ninety days, make sure you get it. Although there's no charge to enter the country, border officials at land crossings commonly ask for a fee (typically Q10, a bit more than US$1), which is destined straight for their back pockets. Travellers often avoid such payments by asking for un recibo (a receipt); if you try this, be prepared for a delay before being waved through.

If you want to **extend your visit** for up to ninety days, go to the immigration department

Useful websites

US State Department ⓦtravel.state.gov. "Consular information sheets" detailing the dangers of travelling in most countries of the world. The information can be a little alarmist.

British Foreign and Commonwealth Office ⓦwww.fco.gov.uk. Constantly updated advice for travellers on circumstances affecting safety in more than 130 countries.

Australian Department of Foreign Affairs ⓦwww.dfat.gov.au. Advice and reports on unstable countries and regions.

(*migración*) in the Inguat (tourist information) building at 7 Av 1–17, Zona 4, Guatemala City (ⓣ2361 8476; Mon–Fri 8am–2.30pm) where extensions of up to ninety days can be arranged. After 180 days all non-nationals have to leave the country for at least 72 hours.

Travelling across the border **to Honduras** is very straightforward for virtually all nationalities. Citizens of Australia, Canada, the EU, Japan, New Zealand, Norway, Switzerland and the US, with a valid passport, get a minimum thirty-day stamp at the border on arrival; this can be extended to a maximum of ninety days at immigration offices throughout the country. Officially, there are no charges to enter or leave the country by land, though border officials usually demand a dollar or more. A list of Honduran embassies can be found at ⓦwww.sre.hn (in Spanish only).

Guatemalan embassies and consulates abroad

Australia Contact Tokyo.

Belize 8 A St, King's Park ⓣ223 3150.

Canada 130 Albert St, Suite 1010, Ottawa ON K1P 5G4 ⓣ613/233-7188, ⓕ233-0135, ⓔembcanada@minex.gob.gt.

Germany Joachim-Karnatz-Allee, 45–47 Ecke Paulstrasse, 10557 Berlin ⓣ030 206 4363.

Honduras 8 C 5–38, Barrio Guamilito, San Pedro Sula ⓣ533 3560.

Italy Vía dei Colii della Farnesina, 128, 00194, Roma, ⓣ3630 3750, 3630 7392 ⓕ3291 639, ⓔembitalia@minex.gob.gt.

Japan 38 Kowa Building, 9th Floor, Room 905, 4-12-24, Nishi-Azabu, Tokyo 106-0031 ⓣ380-01830, ⓕ340-01820, ⓔembjapon@minex.gob.gt.

Mexico Embassy: Av Explanada 1025, Lomas de Chapultepec 11000, Mexico D.F. 4 ⓣ55/5540 7520. Consulates: Av Independencia 326, Chetumal, Q.R. ⓣ983 832 3045; 1 C Sur Poniente 26, Comitán, Chiapas ⓣ963 632 0491; 3 Av Norte 85, Tapachula, Chiapas ⓣ962 625 6380.

Netherlands Java Straat 44, 2585AP The Hague ⓣ302 0253, ⓕ360 2270.

New Zealand Contact Tokyo.

UK 13 Fawcett St, London SW10 9HN ⓣ020/7351 3042, ⓕ7376 5708, ⓔrobertoantoniowagner@gmail.com.

US 2220 R St NW, Washington, DC 20008 ⓣ202/745-4952, ⓦwww.guatemala-embassy.org. Consulates located in many cities, including Chicago, Houston, LA, Miami, New York, San Diego and San Francisco.

Information, websites and maps

Information about Guatemala is easy to come by inside the country, but less available in Europe or North America. There are several websites dedicated to the country, and the material produced by the country's tourist board, Inguat, is also improving, though much of it is of limited practical use. When digging out information on Guatemala, don't forget the specialist travel agents (see pp.29–32) and the embassies (see p.100).

Inguat, at 7 Av 1–17, Centro Cívico, Zona 4, Guatemala City (Ⓣ2331 1333, Ⓦwww.mayaspirit.com.gt) is usually very helpful, with a friendly team of English-speaking staff. The organization has smaller branches in Antigua, Flores, Panajachel and Quetzaltenango, and at the airports in Flores and Guatemala City. All branches should have hotel listings, transport information and dozens of brochures and leaflets. The quality of information varies, but generally the main office and the Antigua outpost are the most reliable. Inguat also maintains a telephone assistance line for tourists in Guatemala, Ⓣ2421 2810.

Current political analysis and an interesting and informative overview of the society, economy and environment of Guatemala and other Central American countries is provided by two specialist publishers: the International Relations Center in the US (Ⓦwww.irc-online.org), which produces the *Inside* series covering each country; and the London-based Latin America Bureau (Ⓦwww.lab.org.uk), an independent, nonprofit research organization whose *Guatemala In Focus* booklet is a good, if dated, general introduction to the nation.

Two highly useful **resource centres** are also located in London. The Guatemalan Maya Centre, 94A Wandsworth Bridge Rd, London SW6 2TF (Ⓣ & Ⓕ020/7371 5291, Ⓦwww.maya.org.uk; closed Jan, Easter & Aug) is one of the finest Guatemalan resource centres in the world. Membership (£5 annually) gives you access to a library (reference only) stocked with over 2500 books on Guatemala, along with several hundred videos and all the main periodicals. The centre hosts monthly cultural events, film shows and exhibitions on all things Guatemalan. It also has an outstanding textile collection, and the centre's director, Krystyna Deuss, is the acknowledged British authority on historic and contemporary Maya dress and ritual.

The other resource centre, Canning House Library, 2 Belgrave Square, SW1X 8PJ (Ⓣ020/7235 2303, Ⓦwww.canninghouse.com), has the UK's largest publicly accessible collection of books and periodicals on Latin America, with numerous shelves devoted to Guatemala and Maya issues. It's free to use, though you have to be a member to take books out and receive its twice-yearly *Bulletin*, a review of recently published books on Latin America.

Tourist information

Guatemala has several tourist offices in the US and Europe. The information lines listed below will be able to send you tourist information or direct you to your nearest office.

Canada Ⓣ613/233-2339
UK Ⓣ020/7351 3042
US Ⓣ1-800 INGUAT-1

Online resources

The Guatemala page on the Latin American Network Information Center's website, Ⓦwww.lanic.utexas.edu, is a good place to begin a search; here you'll find a comprehensive set of links to websites for everything from nonprofits and language schools to magazines and museums, as well as various academic and tourism resources. Another portal to check out is Ⓦwww.centramerica.com. An excellent site for anything about Maya culture is Ⓦwww.mostlymaya.com, while Planeta, Ⓦwww.planeta.com, is a good resource for ecotourism and independent travel in the region, run by the prolific author and journalist Ron Mader. Finally, newsgroup Ⓦrec.travel.latin-america is a huge (and generally accurate) information base.

Useful websites

Ⓦ**www.Americas.org/region_29** The latest Guatemalan news, political issues and commentary.
Ⓦ**www.aroundantigua.com** Dedicated to Guatemala's former colonial capital.
Ⓦ**www.atitlan.com** Extensive articles about the Atitlán region, rich with cultural content and some hotel and restaurant listings.
Ⓦ**www.bayislands.com** Roatán articles and listings on leisure publication *Coconut Telegraph*'s website.
Ⓦ**www.centramerica.com** Broad range of links covering countries around the region.
Ⓦ**www.copanruinas.com** Excellent, regularly updated website with news, reviews, and links to hotels and restaurants in Copán.
Ⓦ**www.famsi.org** The Web pages of the Foundation for the Advancement of Mesoamerican Studies include all the latest reports from Mayanist archeologists, epigraphers and ethnographers.
Ⓦ**www.fhrg.org** Website of the Foundation for Human Rights in Guatemala, offering an overview of the current human-rights situation plus detailed reports and news analysis.
Ⓦ**www.frmt.org** Website of Nobel Peace Prize–winner Rigoberta Menchú's foundation, which focuses on development and human-rights matters. Spanish only.
Ⓦ**www.ghrc-usa.org** Website of the Guatemala Human Rights Commission/USA, which publishes a bimonthly human-rights report plus urgent action notices.
Ⓦ**www.guatemala365.com** Good place to begin a search for a Spanish study centre, with a list of professional schools and plenty of tips.
Ⓦ**www.guatemalaweb.com** Content-rich site, with everything from ATM locations to fiesta-day dates.
Ⓦ**www.interhuehue.com** Informative, Spanish-only site with good links and listings of the Huehuetenango area.
Ⓦ**www.lanic.utexas.edu** The Latin American Network Information Center's website offers a wide range of links for Guatemala and other countries in the region.
Ⓦ**www.marrder.com/htw** The regularly updated site of *Honduras This Week*, an English-language newspaper that's the best information source about Guatemala's neighbour, publishes reliable news reports plus interesting content from regions including Copán and the Bay Islands.
Ⓦ**www.maya.org.uk** London-based Guatemalan Maya Centre's site has good articles and links, as well as news of forthcoming UK cultural events.
Ⓦ**www.mayadiscovery.com** Architecture and art of the ancient Maya, plus cultural essays about contemporary indigenous issues.
Ⓦ**www.mayaparadise.com** Useful listings and information – everything from birding to pirates – about the Río Dulce and Lago de Izabal area.
Ⓦ**www.mesoweb.com** Round-up of all the latest Mayanist developments, plus news stories about the region.
Ⓦ**www.mostlymaya.com** Good source for Maya-related content.
Ⓦ**www.planeta.com** Ecotourism and independent travel resource.
Ⓦ**www.promosaico.org** Website of Project Mosaic Guatemala, a nonprofit volunteer work organization, has dozens of opportunities and links to numerous local organizations.
Ⓦ**www.revuemag.com** Content from the popular Antigua-based tourism and travel magazine can be downloaded in PDF format.
Ⓦ**www.roatanet.com** Commerce-orientated site with decent listings and some cultural content.
Ⓦ**www.sigloxxi.com** Leading Guatemalan newspaper *Siglo XXI*'s Spanish-only website.
Ⓦ**www.stetson.edu/~rsitler/TodosSantos** Cultural content and practical coverage of the Todos Santos Cuchumatán region.
Ⓦ**www.xelapages.com** Superb, regularly updated site covering the Quetzaltenango area, with comprehensive language-school and business listings, plus a popular message board.

Maps and map outlets

Rough Guides publishes a *Guatemala and Belize* map (at a scale of 1:500,000), which also covers a sizable part of western Honduras and most of northern El Salvador. Canada's International Travel Maps and Books also publishes a good *Guatemala* map (1:470,000); both are available at retailers in North America and Europe (such as the ones listed below), in bookstores in Guatemala, as well as from online bookshops like Amazon (Ⓦwww.amazon.com). The Rough Guides map can also be purchased at Ⓦwww.roughguides.com.

Locally produced alternatives include offerings by Intelimaps and Inguat (1:1,000,000), both of which include some city maps. Virtually all car rental outlets will provide you with a map, though most are pretty ropey and don't show many of the newer roads.

The Instituto Geográfico Militar produces the only **large-scale maps** of the country. At a scale of 1:50,000, the maps cover the country in 250 sections and are accurately contoured, although many aspects are now out of date. You can consult and purchase them at the institute's offices, Av de las Américas 5–76, Zona 13, Guatemala City (Mon–Fri 9am–5pm; ⓣ2332 2611, ⓦwww.ign.gob.gt). Most can be bought for around US$6, and photocopies of these maps are usually available in hiking areas such as Todos Santos Cuchumatán and Nebaj.

In the US and Canada

110 North Latitude US ⓣ336/369-4171, ⓦwww.110nlatitude.com.
Book Passage 51 Tamal Vista Blvd, Corte Madera, CA 94925 and in the historic San Francisco Ferry Building ⓣ1-800/999-7909 or ⓣ415/927-0960, ⓦwww.bookpassage.com.
Distant Lands 56 S Raymond Ave, Pasadena, CA 91105 ⓣ1-800/310-3220, ⓦwww.distantlands.com.
Globe Corner Bookstore 28 Church St, Cambridge, MA 02138 ⓣ1-800/358-6013, ⓦwww.globecorner.com.
Longitude Books 115 W 30th St #1206, New York, NY 10001 ⓣ1-800/342-2164, ⓦwww.longitudebooks.com.
Map Town 400 5 Ave SW #100, Calgary, AB T2P 0L6 ⓣ1-877/921-6277 or ⓣ403/266-2241, ⓦwww.maptown.com.
Travel Bug Bookstore 3065 W Broadway, Vancouver, BC V6K 2G9 ⓣ604/737-1122, ⓦwww.travelbugbooks.ca.
World of Maps 1235 Wellington St, Ottawa, ON K1Y 3A3 ⓣ1-800/214-8524 or ⓣ613/724-6776, ⓦwww.worldofmaps.com.

In the UK and Ireland

Stanfords 12–14 Long Acre, London WC2E 9LP ⓣ020/7836 1321, ⓦwww.stanfords.co.uk. Also at 39 Spring Gardens, Manchester ⓣ0161/831 0250, and 29 Corn St, Bristol ⓣ0117/929 9966.
Blackwell's Map Centre 50 Broad St, Oxford OX1 3BQ ⓣ01865/793 550, ⓦmaps.blackwell.co.uk. Branches in Bristol, Cambridge, Cardiff, Leeds, Liverpool, Newcastle, Reading and Sheffield.
The Map Shop 30a Belvoir St, Leicester LE1 6QH ⓣ0116/247 1400, ⓦwww.mapshopleicester.co.uk.
National Map Centre 22–24 Caxton St, London SW1H 0QU ⓣ020/7222 2466, ⓦwww.mapsnmc.co.uk.
National Map Centre Ireland 34 Aungier St, Dublin ⓣ01/476 0471, ⓦwww.mapcentre.ie.
The Travel Bookshop 13–15 Blenheim Crescent, London W11 2EE ⓣ020/7229 5260, ⓦwww.thetravelbookshop.co.uk.
Traveller 55 Grey St, Newcastle-upon-Tyne NE1 6EF ⓣ0191/261 5622, ⓦwww.newtraveller.com.

In Australia and New Zealand

Map Centre ⓦwww.mapcentre.co.nz.
Mapland (Australia) 372 Little Bourke St, Melbourne ⓣ03/9670 4383, ⓦwww.mapland.com.au.
Map Shop (Australia) 6–10 Peel St, Adelaide ⓣ08/8231 2033, ⓦwww.mapshop.net.au.
Map World (Australia) 371 Pitt St, Sydney ⓣ02/9261 3601, ⓦwww.mapworld.net.au. Also at 900 Hay St, Perth ⓣ08/9322 5733; Jolimont Centre, Canberra ⓣ02/6230 4097; and 1981 Logan Road, Brisbane ⓣ07/3349 6633.
Map World (New Zealand) 173 Gloucester St, Christchurch ⓣ0800/627 967, ⓦwww.mapworld.co.nz.

Insurance

A comprehensive travel insurance policy is essential for visitors to Guatemala. Medical insurance (you want coverage of US$2,000,000) should include provision for repatriation by air ambulance, and your policy should also cover you for illness or injury, and against theft.

Before paying for a new policy, however, it's worth checking whether you are already covered: some all-risks home insurance policies may cover your possessions when overseas, and many private medical schemes include cover when abroad. In Canada, provincial health plans usually provide partial cover for medical mishaps overseas, while holders of official student/teacher/youth cards in Canada and the US are entitled to meagre accident coverage and hospital in-patient benefits. Students will often find that their student health coverage extends during the vacations and for one term beyond the date of last enrolment.

After exhausting the possibilities above, you might want to contact a specialist travel insurance company, or consider the travel insurance deal we offer (see box below). A typical **travel insurance policy** usually provides cover for the loss of baggage, tickets and – up to a certain limit – cash or cheques, as well as cancellation or curtailment of your journey. Most of them exclude so-called dangerous sports unless an extra premium is paid: this can mean scuba diving, whitewater rafting, windsurfing and trekking, though probably not kayaking or jeep safaris. Many policies can be chopped and changed to exclude coverage you don't need – for example, sickness and accident benefits can often be excluded or included at will. If you do take medical coverage, ascertain whether benefits will be paid as treatment proceeds or only after return home, and whether there is a 24-hour medical emergency number.

When securing **baggage cover**, make sure that the per-article limit – typically under £500 – will cover your most valuable possession. If you need to make a claim, you should keep receipts for medicines and medical treatment, and in the event you have anything stolen, you must obtain an official statement (*una afirmación*) from the police.

Rough Guides travel insurance

Health

Most visitors get home from Guatemala without experiencing any significant health problems at all. However, it's always easier to become ill in a country with a different climate, food and germs – still more so in a poor country with lower standards of sanitation than you might be used to.

It's vital to get the best health advice you can before you set off. Pay a visit to your doctor or a travel clinic (see p.42–43) as far in advance of travel as possible (at least eight weeks), and if you're pregnant or likely to become so, mention this at the outset. Many clinics also sell the latest travel health products, including mosquito nets, water filters, medical kits and so on. In addition to the websites mentioned on p.42, there are a number of books advising on health precautions and disease prevention; the best and most up to date is *The Rough Guide to Travel Health*, a pocket-sized volume packed with accurate information for all parts of the world. Finally, regardless of how well-prepared you are medically, you will still want the security of health insurance (see "Insurance").

Once you're there, what you **eat and drink** is crucial. In addition to the hazards mentioned under "Intestinal troubles" below, contaminated food and water can transmit the hepatitis A virus, which can lay a victim low for several months with exhaustion, fever and diarrhoea, and can even cause liver damage.

Vaccinations, inoculations and malaria precautions

There are no obligatory inoculations for Guatemala (unless you're arriving from a "high-risk" area of yellow fever – northern South America and equatorial Africa – in which case you need to carry your vaccination certificate). Nevertheless, there are several you should have anyway. Make sure you're up to date with polio, tetanus and typhoid vaccinations and consider having diphtheria, hepatitis A and tuberculosis (TB) jabs. Long-term travellers or anyone spending time in rural areas should think about having the combined hepatitis A and B and the rabies vaccines (though see p.41 for a caveat on that).

Malaria is a danger in some parts of the country (particularly in the rural lowlands). It's not a problem in the big cities, or anywhere over 1500m – which includes Antigua, Guatemala City, Chichicastenango, Lago de Atitlán, Quetzaltenango and virtually all of the western highlands. However, if you plan to visit any lowland areas, including Petén and the Pacific coast, you should consider taking a course of tablets.

The recommended prophylactic is **chloroquine** (inexpensive, available without prescription, and safe in pregnancy); you'll need to begin taking the pills a week before you enter an area where there's a risk of malaria and continue for four weeks after you return. An alternative (especially if you're only going for a short time) is **malarone**, which you need start only two days before you go and continue for a week after you return. Although it's a very effective, well-tolerated drug, there are some drawbacks – it's much more expensive than chloroquine, it's available on prescription only in many countries (including the UK), you can only take it for up to 28 days, and it's not suitable for pregnant women or babies.

Whichever antimalarial you choose, you should still take **precautions** to avoid getting bitten by insects: always sleep in screened rooms or under nets in lowland areas; burn mosquito coils containing permethrin (available everywhere); cover up arms and legs, especially around dawn and dusk when mosquitoes are most active; and use insect repellent containing fifty percent DEET on your skin and up to one hundred percent on clothing.

Also prevalent in some lowland areas (usually occurring in epidemic outbreaks in urban areas), **dengue fever** is a viral infection transmitted by mosquitoes which are active during the day. Fever, aches and joint pain (its old name was "lock-bone") are often followed by a rash. Though most people make a full recovery after a few days, children are particularly at risk. There is no vaccine or specific treatment, so you need to pay great attention to avoiding bites.

North Americans can get **inoculations** at any immunization centre or at most local clinics, and will have to pay a fee. Many GPs in the UK have a travel surgery where you can get advice and certain vaccines on prescription, though they may not administer some of the less common immunizations. Note too that though some jabs (diphtheria, typhoid) are free, others will incur quite a hefty charge; it can be worth checking out a travel clinic where you can receive vaccinations almost immediately, often at lower cost. In Australasia, vaccination centres are always less expensive than doctors' surgeries.

Intestinal troubles

Despite all the dire warnings given here, a bout of **diarrhoea** is the medical problem you're most likely to encounter. Even following all the usual precautions – drinking clean water (any bottled drinks, including beer and soft drinks, are already purified; see box on p.41 for more), avoiding food that has been on display for a while and steering clear of salads and raw shellfish – no one seems to avoid it altogether. Its main cause is simply the change of diet: the food in the region contains a whole new set of bacteria, and perhaps rather more of them than you're used to. If you're struck down, the best cure is the simplest one: take it easy for a day or two, drink lots of bottled water and eat only the blandest of foods – papaya is good for soothing the stomach and is also crammed with vitamins. Only if the symptoms last more than four or five days do you need to worry. Finally, if you're taking oral contraception or any other orally administered drugs, bear in mind that severe diarrhoea can reduce their efficacy.

Cholera is an acute bacterial infection, recognizable by watery diarrhoea and vomiting. However, risk of infection is considered low, particularly if you're following the health advice above, and symptoms are rapidly relieved by prompt medical attention and clean water. If you're spending any time in rural areas you also run the risk of picking up various **parasitic infections**: protozoa – amoeba and giardia – and intestinal worms. These sound (and can be) hideous, but they're easily treated once detected. If you suspect you may have an infestation, take a stool sample to a good **pathology lab** and go to a doctor or pharmacist with the test results (see "Getting medical help").

More serious is **amoebic dysentery**, which is endemic in many parts of the region. The symptoms are similar to a bad dose of diarrhoea but include bleeding too. On the whole, a course of flagyl (metronidazole or tinidozole) will cure it. If you plan to visit far-flung corners then it's worth getting hold of this before you go, and some advice from a doctor on its use.

Bites and stings

Taking steps to avoid getting bitten by **insects**, particularly mosquitoes, is always good practice. Sandflies, which are very common in the Bay Islands, are tiny, but their bites, usually on feet and ankles, itch like hell and last for days. **Ticks**, which you're likely to pick up if you're walking or riding in areas with domestic livestock (and sometimes in the forests generally), need careful removal with tweezers – those in a Swiss Army knife are ideal. Head or body **lice** can be picked up from people or bedding, and are best treated with medicated soap or shampoo; very occasionally, they may spread typhus, characterized by fever, muscle aches, headaches and eventually a measles-like rash. If you think you have it, seek treatment from a doctor.

Scorpions are common; mostly nocturnal, they hide during the heat of the day – often in thatched roofs. If you're camping, or sleeping under a thatched roof, shake your shoes out before putting them on and try not to wander round barefoot. Their sting is painful (rarely fatal) and can become infected, so you should seek medical treatment if the pain seems significantly worse than a bee sting. You're less likely to be bitten by a **spider**, but the advice is the same as for scorpions and insects: seek medical treatment if the pain persists or increases.

You're unlikely to see a **snake**, and most are harmless in any case. Wearing boots and long pants will go a long way towards preventing a bite – tread heavily and they will usually slither away. If you do get bitten, remember what the snake looked like (kill it if you can), immobilize the bitten limb and seek medical help immediately: antivenins are available in most main hospitals.

Swimming and snorkelling might bring you into contact with potentially dangerous or venomous **sea creatures**. You're extremely unlikely to be a victim of a shark attack (though the dubious practice of shark-feeding as a tourist attraction is growing, and could lead to an accidental bite), but jellyfish and most corals will sting, especially fire coral. Some jellyfish, like the Portuguese man-o'-war, with its distinctive purple, bag-like sail, have very long tentacles with stinging cells, and an encounter will result in raw, red welts. If you are stung, clean the wound with vinegar or iodine and seek medical help if the pain persists or infection develops. The spines of stingrays, stonefish and scorpion fish are all extremely poisonous, so be careful where you put your feet and hands.

Finally, **rabies** is present, but not common in Guatemala. The best advice is to give dogs a wide berth and not to play with animals at all, no matter how cuddly they may look. Treat any bite as suspect: wash any wound immediately with soap or detergent and apply alcohol or iodine if possible. Act immediately to get treatment – rabies can be fatal once symptoms appear. There is a vaccine, but it is expensive, serves only to shorten the course of treatment you need anyway and is effective for no more than three months.

Heat and altitude problems

Two other common causes of illness are **altitude** and the **sun**. The best advice in both cases is to take it easy; allow yourself time to acclimatize before you race up a volcano, and build up exposure to the sun gradually. If going to higher altitudes, you may develop symptoms of Acute Mountain Sickness (AMS), such as breathlessness, headaches, dizziness, nausea and appetite loss. More extreme cases might cause vomiting, disorientation, loss of balance and coughing up of pink frothy phlegm. The simple cure – a slow descent – almost always brings immediate recovery.

Tolerance to the sun, too, takes a while to build up: use a strong sunscreen and, if you're walking during the day, wear a hat and try to keep in the shade. Avoid dehydration by drinking plenty of water or fruit juice. The most serious result of overheating is heatstroke, which can be potentially fatal. Lowering the body temperature (by taking a tepid shower, for example) is the first step in treatment.

Getting medical help

For minor medical problems, head for a **farmacia** – look for the green cross – there's one in every town and most villages. Pharmacists are knowledgeable and helpful, and many speak some English. They can also sell

What about the water?

Contaminated water is a major cause of sickness in Guatemala and, even if it looks clean, all tap water should be regarded with caution. Stick to bottled water (*agua purificada*), which is available everywhere: in shops, restaurants and in most hotels, either in bottles or small plastic bags.

You'll only need to consider treating your own water if you plan to travel to very remote areas. Although boiling water for ten minutes kills most microorganisms, it's not the most convenient method. Water filters remove visible impurities and larger pathogenic organisms (most bacteria and cysts). Chemical sterilization with either chlorine or iodine tablets (or a tincture of iodine liquid) is effective (except in preventing amoebic dysentery or giardiasis), but the resulting liquid doesn't taste very pleasant – though it can be masked with lemon or lime juice. Iodine is unsafe for pregnant women, babies and people with thyroid complaints. Purification, involving both filtration and sterilization, gives the most complete treatment, and travel clinics and good outdoor equipment shops will stock a wide range of portable water purifiers.

drugs that are only available on prescription at home over the counter (if necessary). Every capital city has **doctors** and dentists, many trained in the US, who are experienced in treating visitors and speak good English. Your embassy will always have a list of recommended doctors, and we've included some in our "Listings" sections for the main towns.

Health insurance (see previous section) is essential and for anything serious you should to go to the best **private hospital** you can reach; again, these are located mainly in the provincial capitals. If you suspect something is amiss with your insides, it might be worth heading straight for the local **pathology lab** (all the main towns have them), before seeing a doctor, as the doctor will send you there anyway. Many rural communities have a **health centre** (*centro de salud* or *puesto de salud*), where health care is free, although there may only be a nurse or health worker available and you can't rely on finding anyone who speaks English. Should you need an injection or transfusion, make sure that the equipment is sterile (it might be worth bringing a sterile kit from home) and ensure any blood you receive is screened.

Medical resources for travellers

Websites

Ⓦ**health.yahoo.com** Information on specific diseases and conditions, drugs and herbal remedies, as well as advice from health experts.

Ⓦ**www.cdc.gov** The US government's official site for travel health.

Ⓦ**www.fitfortravel.scot.nhs.uk** Scottish NHS website carrying information about travel-related diseases and how to avoid them.

Ⓦ**www.istm.org** The website of the International Society for Travel Medicine, with a full list of clinics specializing in international travel health. Publishes outbreak warnings, suggested inoculations, precautions and other background information for travellers.

Ⓦ**www.tmvc.com.au** Contains a list of all Travel Doctor (Travellers Medical & Vaccination Centre) branches throughout Australia, New Zealand and Southeast Asia, plus general information on travel health.

Ⓦ**www.tripprep.com** Travel Health Online provides an online-only, comprehensive database of necessary vaccinations for most countries, as well as destination and medical service-provider information.

In the US and Canada

Canadian Society for International Health 1 Nicholas St, Suite 1105, Ottawa, ON K1N 7B7 Ⓣ613/241-5785, Ⓦwww.csih.org. Distributes a free pamphlet, "Health Information for Canadian Travellers", containing an extensive list of travel health centres in Canada.

Centers for Disease Control and Prevention 1600 Clifton Rd NE, Atlanta, GA 30333 Ⓣ1-800/311-3435 or 404/639-3534, Ⓦwww.cdc.gov. Publishes outbreak warnings, suggested inoculations, precautions and other background information for travellers. Useful website plus International Travelers Hotline on Ⓣ1-877/FYI-TRIP.

International Association for Medical Assistance to Travellers (IAMAT) 417 Center St, Lewiston, NY 14092 Ⓣ716/754-4883, Ⓦwww.iamat.org; and 1287 St Clair Ave W, Suite #1, Toronto, ON M6E 1B8 Ⓣ416/652-0137. A nonprofit organization supported by donations, it can provide a list of English-speaking doctors in Guatemala, climate charts, and leaflets on various diseases and inoculations.

International SOS Assistance 3600 Horizon Blvd, Suite 300, Trevose, PA, 19053 Ⓣ1-800/523-8930, Ⓦwww.intsos.com. Members receive pre-trip medical referral info, as well as overseas emergency services designed to complement travel-insurance coverage.

MEDJET Assistance Ⓣ1-800/963-3538 or 205/595-6658, Ⓦwww.medjetassistance.com. Annual membership program for travellers that, in the event of illness or injury, will fly members home or to the hospital of their choice in a medically equipped and staffed jet.

Travel Medicine Ⓣ1-800/872-8633, Ⓦwww.travmed.com. Sells first-aid kits, mosquito netting, water filters, reference books and other health-related travel products.

In the UK and Ireland

British Airways Travel Clinics 213 Piccadilly, London W1J 9HQ (Mon–Fri 9.30am–5.30pm, Sat 10am–4pm, no appointment necessary; Ⓣ0845/600 2236); 101 Cheapside, London EC2V 6DT (Mon–Fri 9am–4.30pm, appointment required; Ⓣ0845/600 2236); Ⓦwww.britishairways.com/travel/healthclinintro. Vaccinations, tailored advice from an online database and a complete range of travel health-care products.

Dun Laoghaire Medical Centre 5 Northumberland Ave, Dun Laoghaire, County Dublin Ⓣ01/280 4996, Ⓕ01/280 5603. Advice on medical matters abroad.

Hospital for Tropical Diseases Travel Clinic 2nd floor, Mortimer Market Centre, off Capper St, London WC1E 6AU (Mon–Fri 9am–4.30pm, by appointment only; ⓣ020/7388 9600, ⓦwww.thehtd.org; a consultation costs £15, which is waived if you have your injections here). A recorded Health Line (ⓣ0906/133 7733; 50p per min) gives hints on hygiene and illness prevention as well as listing appropriate immunizations.

Liverpool School of Tropical Medicine Pembroke Place, Liverpool L3 5QA ⓣ0151/708 9393, ⓦwww.liv.ac.uk/lstm/lstm. Walk-in clinic Mon–Fri 1–4pm; appointment required for yellow fever, but not for other jabs.

MASTA (Medical Advisory Service for Travellers Abroad) 40 regional clinics (call ⓣ0870/6062782 or check ⓦwww.masta.org for the nearest). Also operates a pre-recorded 24-hour Travellers' Health Line (UK ⓣ0906/822 4100, 60p per min), giving written information tailored to your journey by return of post.

Nomad Pharmacy surgeries 40 Bernard St, London, WC1N 1LE; and 3–4 Wellington Terrace, Turnpike Lane, London N8 0PX (Mon–Fri 9.30am–6pm, Sat 9am–1pm ⓣ020/7833 4114 to book vaccination appointment). They give advice free if you go in person, or their telephone helpline is ⓣ0906/863 3414 (60p per min). They can give information tailored to your travel needs.

Travel Health Centre Department of International Health and Tropical Medicine, Royal College of Surgeons in Ireland, Mercers Medical Centre, Stephen's St Lower, Dublin 2 ⓣ01/402 2337. Expert pre-trip advice and inoculations.

Travel Medicine Services PO Box 254, 16 College St, Belfast BT1 6BT ⓣ028/9031 5220. Offers medical advice before a trip and help afterwards in the event of a tropical disease.

Tropical Medical Bureau Grafton Buildings, 34 Grafton St, Dublin 2 ⓣ1850/487 674, ⓦwww.tmb.ie. Vaccinations and pre-trip consultations plus post-exposure screening at branches across Ireland.

In Australia and New Zealand

Travel Doctor (TMVC) 27–29 Gilbert Place, Adelaide, SA 5000 ⓣ08/8212 7522, ⓦwww.tmvc.com.au; 1/170 Queen St, Auckland ⓣ09/373 3531; 5/247 Adelaide St, Brisbane, Qld 4000 ⓣ07/3221 9066; 5/8–10 Hobart Place, Canberra, ACT 2600 ⓣ02/6257 7156; 270 Sandy Bay Rd, Sandy Bay Tas, Hobart 7005 ⓣ03/6223 7577; 2/393 Little Bourke St, Melbourne, Vic 3000 ⓣ03/9602 5788; Level 7, Dymocks Bldg, 428 George St, Sydney, NSW 2000 ⓣ02/9221 7133; Shop 15, Grand Arcade, 14–16 Willis St, Wellington ⓣ04/473 0991.

Costs, money and banks

By European or North American standards the cost of living in Guatemala is very low, and by Latin American standards the currency, the quetzal (Q), is relatively stable. However, fluctuations can and do take place, so we have quoted all prices in the Guide in US dollars. (In mid-2005 the rate was Q7.65 to US$1.) The US dollar is by far the most widely accepted foreign currency in Guatemala; that said, it is not a semi-official one, and you can't get by with a fistful of greenbacks and no quetzals. Euros and other foreign currencies are extremely difficult to cash.

Credit cards are very useful for withdrawing currency from bank ATMs but are rarely accepted elsewhere, so don't count on paying with them except in upmarket hotels and restaurants. Most people travel with a credit or debit card (or two), as cashpoints (ATMs) are widespread. **Travellers' cheques** and US dollar bills can also be cashed in most banks. The country's international airports have banks for currency exchange, while at the main land-border crossings there are usually banks and a swarm of moneychangers who generally give fair rates for cash. Even at the most remote border crossings, you'll usually find a wad-wielding local from whom you can get some local currency.

Costs

Guatemala is one of the cheapest countries in the Americas for travellers, though there are plenty of opportunities for a modest (or serious) splurge if you feel like it. The extremely frugal may be able to get by on around US$120 a week in most of the country, or below US$100 in a budget travellers' hub like San Pedro La Laguna. However, if you're after a little more comfort (travelling by shuttle bus and staying in rooms with a bathroom) you can expect to spend around US$160 per person per week, if you're travelling as a couple, while solo travellers should reckon on US$200 a week. For US$40–50 per day you can expect to live quite well. Things are more expensive in regions where the local economy is tourist-driven (Antigua, Guanaja and Roatán in particular), though even in these places there are some inexpensive places to stay, and it's possible to keep to a reasonable budget if you can exercise some sense of thrift.

Prices

The following prices should give you a rough idea of what you might end up paying. A basic **single room** (or a dorm bed) costs anything from US$3 to US$8, a double US$5 to US$12, while you can pay up to US$200 a night for a suite in the most luxurious establishments. **Food** prices don't vary quite as much as you might expect; eating a filling meal in a simple comedor will cost around US$2.50 anywhere in the country, while in a smarter restaurant you can expect to pay a little over double that. Anything that is imported will be expensive, so if you have a taste for fancy cheeses, wine or ice cream you'll have to pay for your indulgences. Fresh produce from the market is very good value – although to get anywhere near the price that locals pay you'll have to bargain in Spanish. Check the fixed-price goods in supermarkets first.

A bottle of Guatemalan beer costs around US$1.50 in most bars, and half that in a supermarket. Rum starts at around US$5 a bottle, while local fire-water, such as the ubiquitous Quezalteca, is even cheaper. Smokers will be pleased to find excellent Honduran cigars at bargain rates.

Transport is probably the greatest bargain, providing you stick to the "chicken buses", which charge around US$0.80 an hour. To a certain extent you get what you pay for – these buses are always crowded, slow and rudimentary in the extreme – though they can be a lot of fun. There are also better quality "pullman" buses: some are excellent, though these only serve the main highways. Travelling by car is expensive, and the cost of renting a car (from US$30 a day) is affected by accident penalty costs (sometimes over US$1000) and, of course, the cost of fuel (more than US$3 a gallon).

Generally anything produced in Central America is cheap, anything imported expensive. This applies to most tinned food, American clothing – although plenty of imitations are produced inside Guatemala – and many high-tech goods such as cameras. A student card is not very useful but may occasionally come in handy as a bargaining tool.

Credit/debit cards and travellers' cheques

Credit cards are becoming increasingly useful in Guatemala, though you shouldn't expect to be able to use them as you would in North America or Europe. They are accepted in most upmarket hotels and restaurants, but you won't be able to pay for your comedor meal or pensión bill with plastic. Beware expensive surcharges if you do want to pay by credit card.

Visa is slightly more widely accepted, though MasterCard is catching up quickly. Virtually all towns, and many gas (petrol) stations have at least one **cashpoint (ATM)**, or you can use your card to get cash over the counter at banks. For a comprehensive ATM list see Ⓦwww.guatemalatravel.com. It's important to note that most Central American ATMs do not accept five-digit PIN numbers: contact your bank at home in advance if you have one. Debit cards also work fine in Guatemala, though Cirrus brand is not as widely accepted as Plus/Electron.

Travellers' cheques are a safe way to bring money, though their usefulness is constrained by bank opening hours. It's essential to purchase US dollar cheques – other currencies including sterling- and euro-issued cheques are almost impossible to cash. American Express–branded cheques are the most widely accepted. Some banks may want to see your proof of purchase when cashing travellers' cheques; also make sure to keep the purchase agreement and a record of cheque serial numbers safe and separate from the cheques themselves.

Wiring money

Having money wired from home using one of the companies listed below is never convenient or cheap, and should be considered a last resort. It's also possible to have money wired directly from a bank in your home country to a bank in Guatemala, although this is somewhat less reliable because it involves two separate institutions.

Money-wiring companies

Travelers Express/MoneyGram
US ⓣ1-800/444-3010, Canada ⓣ1-800/933-3278, UK, Ireland and New Zealand ⓣ00800/6663 9472, Australia ⓣ0011800/6663 9472, ⓦwww.moneygram.com.

Western Union US and Canada ⓣ1-800/CALL-CASH, Australia ⓣ1800/501 500, New Zealand ⓣ0800/005 253, UK ⓣ0800/833 833, Republic of Ireland ⓣ66/947 5603, ⓦwww.westernunion.com (customers in the US and Canada can send money online).

Youth and student discounts

There are very few discounts for youth and student ID cardholders in Guatemala. Very few museums offer discounts to students, and there are no reduced prices for transportation. Some of the Antigua travel agents do offer discounted international airfares for students, though it's not so hard to get these rates if you're prepared to bargain anyway. Selected language schools issue their own student cards which qualify holders to discounts (typically ten percent) with selected internal tour operators, restaurants and cybercafés.

Getting around

With no passenger trains and few people able to afford a car, virtually everyone travels by "chicken bus" in Guatemala. These buses may be decrepit, uncomfortable, fume-filled and overcrowded, but they give you a unique opportunity to mix with ordinary Guatemalans; indeed, by sticking to sanitized tourist shuttles, you'll be missing out on one of the country's most essential experiences. More comfortable buses – some of them quite fast and luxurious – ply the main highways, but once you leave the central routes and head off on the byways, there's usually no alternative to a bumpy ride inside a chicken bus or a pick-up truck.

Successive Guatemalan governments have upgraded the country's road system, though it's still pretty inadequate, and suffers by comparison with neighbouring Mexico, or even Honduras. You'll often find yourself stuck behind smoking trucks, even on the main highways, and large swathes of the country are still only served by rutted dirt roads where the going can be painfully pedestrian. Fortunately, whatever the pace of your journey, you'll always have the spectacular Guatemalan countryside outside to wonder at.

By bus

Buses are cheap, convenient and can be wildly entertaining. For the most part the service is extremely comprehensive, reaching even the smallest of villages, and the driver will usually stop to pick up passengers anywhere, regardless of how many people are already on board. Although in very remote areas many buses leave in the dead of night and travel through the early hours to reach the morning markets, try to avoid travelling after dark, as the risk of robbery is much higher.

Guatemala has two classes of bus. **Second-class** or "**chicken buses**", known as *camionetas* in Guatemala, are the most common and easily distinguished by their trademark clouds of thick, black, noxious fumes and rasping exhausts. These are all old North American school buses, their seats designed for the under-fives, so you're liable to have bruised knees after a day or two's travel. They cram their seats, aisles and occasionally even roofs with passengers. The driver always seems to be a moustachioed ladino with an eye for the ladies and a fixation for speed and overtaking on blind corners, while his helper (*ayudante*) always seems to be overworked and under-age. It's the *ayundante*'s job to scramble up to the roof to retrieve your rucksack, collect the fares, and bellow out the destination to all and sundry. While travel by second-class bus may be uncomfortable, it is never dull, with chickens clucking, music assaulting your eardrums, and snack vendors touting for business.

Guatemala has hundreds of small bus companies, each determined to outdo the next in the garishness of their vehicles' paint jobs. Almost all chicken buses operate out of bus terminals, usually on the edge of town, and often adjacent to the market; between towns you can hail buses and they'll almost always stop for you. **Tickets** are bought on the bus, and whilst they are always very cheap, gringos do sometimes get ripped off – try to observe what the locals are paying. Fares average out at US$0.80 an hour.

The so-called **pullman** is often an old Greyhound bus, is rated as first-class, and tickets can be bought in advance. These "express" buses are about 20–30 percent more expensive than the regular buses – a little more than US$1 an hour, though there are some very swish, and more pricey, services to Petén. Pullmans are usually a little quicker than chicken buses, because they make fewer stops. Services vary tremendously: some companies' buses are very comfortable and pleasant, while other operators use decrepit buses with cracked windows and bald tyres. Officially, each passenger is allocated a seat, but on some routes it's common practice for the driver to stop en-route and fill the bus with more passengers, either standing along the aisle or squashed onto tiny camp-style seats. However, all pullmans are punctual at least.

Pullmans usually leave from the offices of the bus company – addresses are listed in the text – and on the whole they serve only the main routes, connecting the capital with Río Dulce and Flores/Santa Elena, Quetzaltenango, Huehuetenango, the Mexican border, Chiquimula and Esquipulas, Puerto Barrios, Cobán and San Salvador. This means that most long journeys can be done at least part of the way by pullman. Note that tickets are sometimes (always in Petén) collected by conductors at the end of the journey, so make sure you don't lose yours.

Providing fast, non-stop links between the main tourist centres, **shuttle buses** are now very popular in Guatemala. Conveniently, passengers are picked up from their hotels, so you won't have to lug any heavy bags around. Services are expanding rapidly and now cover virtually everywhere that tourists travel in any number. Many shuttle companies will organize an "especial" service for you even if your destination is not on a regular route. At around US$5 an hour, shuttles are expensive, but drivers are almost always more cautious than regular bus drivers, and the bus itself much cleaner.

Non-tourist **minibuses** (*microbuses*) are also becoming much more common in Guatemala. They cost the same as the larger public "chicken bus" services, and are generally a bit quicker. These buses only tend to operate where there are paved roads, such as the Santa Elena–Poptún route, and usually operate from a private terminal near the main bus station.

By air

The only scheduled internal flight currently operating in Guatemala is from the capital to Flores. It costs between US$100 and US$140 return and takes only fifty minutes (as opposed to some 8–10 hours on the bus), with four rival airlines offering daily flights. Their addresses and other details can be found in the Petén chapter; tickets can be bought from virtually any travel agent in the country. It's also possible to fly to a number of other airstrips including Copán, Poptún, Playa Grande and Sayaxché by tiny charter airlines when there's sufficient demand; details are given in the relevant chapters. Flying in Honduras is fairly inexpensive and can save a great deal of time; for details see p.398.

By car

On the whole, driving in Guatemala is pretty straightforward, and it certainly offers unrivalled freedom – though traffic is increasing and is incessantly heavy in the capital and always busy along the Interamericana and highway to Puerto Barrios. Be warned that local driving practices can be alarming at times.

Parking and security are an issue, particularly in the cities where theft and vandalism are common. Always leave your car in a guarded car park and choose a hotel with protected parking space. Even budget hotels often have this facility; appropriate recommendations can be found throughout the Guide.

Most of the main routes are paved, but beyond this the roads are often extremely rough. **Filling stations** (*gasolineras*) are reasonably common (unless you really venture off the beaten track). Fuel is extremely cheap by European standards, though above the US price. Should you break down there'll usually be an enthusiastic local mechanic, but spare parts can be a problem, especially for anything beyond the most basic of models. For obscure makes you'd be sensible to bring a basic spares kit. Tyres in particular suffer badly on the burning hot roads and rough dirt tracks. If you plan to head up into the mountains or along any of the smaller roads in Petén, you'll need high clearance and 4WD.

Local **warning signs** are also worth getting to know. The most common is placing a branch in the road, which indicates the presence of a broken-down car or something blocking the road ahead. *Derrumbes* means "landslides", *frene con motor* "brake with motor" (meaning a steep descent) and *tumulos* "bumps in the road", a favourite technique for slowing down traffic.

Renting a car costs from US$35 a day for a tiny hatchback or US$50 for a 4WD by the time you've added the extras. If you do rent, make sure you check the details of the insurance, which often does not cover damage to your vehicle at all. Always take full-cover insurance and be aware that many companies will make you sign a clause so you are responsible for the first US$1000 of damage in the event of an accident, damage or theft.

Local rental companies are in the "Listings" sections for all the main towns. There's little to be gained financially by organizing a rental in advance from home.

Car rental agencies

In North America

Avis US ⓣ1-800/230-4898, Canada ⓣ1-800/272-5871, ⓦwww.avis.com.
Budget US ⓣ1-800/527-0700, Canada ⓣ1-800/472-3325, ⓦwww.budget.com.
Hertz US ⓣ1-800/654-3131, Canada ⓣ1-800/263-0600, ⓦwww.hertz.com.
National ⓣ1-800/962-7070, ⓦwww.nationalcar.com.
Thrifty US and Canada ⓣ1-800/847-4389, ⓦwww.thrifty.com.

In Britain

Avis ⓣ0870/606 0100, ⓦwww.avis.co.uk.
Budget ⓣ01442/276 266, ⓦwww.budget.co.uk.
Hertz ⓣ0870/844 8844, ⓦwww.hertz.co.uk.
National ⓣ0870/536 5365, ⓦwww.nationalcar.co.uk.
Thrifty ⓣ01494/751 600, ⓦwww.thrifty.co.uk.

In Ireland

Avis Northern Ireland ⓣ028/9024 0404, Republic of Ireland ⓣ021/428 1111, ⓦwww.avis.ie.
Budget Republic of Ireland ⓣ09/0662 7711, ⓦwww.budget.ie.
Hertz Republic of Ireland ⓣ01/676 7476, ⓦwww.hertz.ie.
Thrifty Republic of Ireland ⓣ1800/515 800, ⓦwww.thrifty.ie.

In Australia

Avis ⓣ13 63 33 or 02/9353 9000, ⓦwww.avis.com.au.
Budget ⓣ1300/362 848, ⓦwww.budget.com.au.

Hertz ⓣ 13 30 39 or 03/9698 2555, ⓦ www.hertz.com.au.
National ⓣ 13 10 45, ⓦ www.nationalcar.com.au.
Thrifty ⓣ 1300/367 227, ⓦ www.thrifty.com.au.

In New Zealand

Avis ⓣ 09/526 2847 or 0800/655 111, ⓦ www.avis.co.nz.
Budget ⓣ 09/976 2222 or 0800/652-227, ⓦ www.budget.co.nz.
Hertz ⓣ 0800/654 321, ⓦ www.hertz.co.nz.
National ⓣ 0800/800 115 or 03/366-5574, ⓦ www.nationalcar.co.nz.
Thrifty ⓣ 09/309 0111, ⓦ www.thrifty.co.nz.

By pick-up

If you plan to visit the more remote parts of the country then it is almost inevitable that you'll be hitching a ride in a pick-up from time to time. Increasingly, pick-ups (picops) are supplementing bus services in the mountains and backroads – they are quicker, and you can't beat the open-air views (unless it's raining). In rural areas such as the Ixil triangle and northern Alta Verapaz, trucks and pick-ups are an essential form of transport for the locals. Off the main highways, many pick-ups run as a bus service, charging passengers about the same rate as chicken buses (around US$0.80 per hour).

By taxi and tuk-tuk

Taxis are available in all the main towns, and their rates are fairly low. Outside Guatemala City, metered cabs are non-existent so it's essential to fix a price before you set off. Local taxi drivers will almost always be prepared to negotiate a price for an excursion to nearby villages or sites (perhaps US$18 for a half-day or US$35 for a full day), and if time is short this can be a good way of seeing places where the bus service is awkwardly timed. If you can organize a group, this need not be an expensive option, possibly even cheaper than renting a car for the day.

Since 2004 three-wheeled Thai **tuk-tuks** have proliferated throughout Guatemala, operating as taxis, buzzing around the streets Bangkok-style. They are plentiful in Antigua and Panajachel and are likely to become much more widespread throughout the country. Always fix the fare in advance and expect to pay about 75 percent of the equivalent taxi fare.

By bike and motorbike

Bicycles are quite common in Guatemala, and cycling has to be one of the most popular sports. You'll be well received almost anywhere if you travel by bike, and if you've got the energy to make your way through the highlands it's a great way to see the country. Most towns will have a repair shop where you can get hold of spare parts, although you still need to carry the basics for emergencies on the road. Mountain bikes make the going easier, as even the main roads include plenty of formidable potholes, and it's a rare ride that doesn't involve at least one steep climb. Chicken buses will carry bikes on the roof, so if you can't face the hills then there's always an easy option. In case you didn't bring your own bike, you can **rent** them in Antigua, Panajachel and Quetzaltenango: mountain bikes can be rented by the day (about US$8) or week (US$25). In flat Utila it's easy to find a basic bike for about US$2 a day. For real two-wheel enthusiasts, Maya Mountain Bike Tours and Old Town Outfitters, both in Antigua (see p.120), offer a range of challenging bike trips.

Motorbikes are not that common in Guatemala, and locating parts and mechanical expertise can be tricky. There are rental outlets in Guatemala City, Panajachel, Antigua (see relevant "Listings") and Roatán, typically charging around US$30 a day for a 200cc machine.

By ferry and boat

Ferries operate between Puerto Barrios and Lívingston on the Caribbean coast of Guatemala; between Puerto Barrios and Punta Gorda in Belize; and in Honduras between La Ceiba and the Bay Islands of Utila and Roatán.

In Petén, there are a number of possible boat routes and trips, including the journey across the Río Usumacinta from Bethel and La Técnica to Frontera Corozal; on Lago de Petén Itzá; and irregular boats along the Río San Pedro from El Naranjo to the Mexican border and beyond. Several terrific boat trips begin near the town of Sayaxché, including the trip to Lago de Petexbatun and

Aguateca, along the Río Salinas to Benemérito, and along the Río de la Pasión to Ceibal. Precise details of schedules are given in the relevant chapters of the Guide.

Along the Pacific coast, the Chiquimulilla canal separates much of the shoreline from the mainland. If you're heading for a beach you'll find a regular shuttle of small boats to take you across the canal, including services from La Avellena to Monterrico.

Two of Guatemala's most unmissable **boat trips** are through the spectacular Río Dulce gorge starting in either Lívingston or the town of Río Dulce, and across volcano-framed Lago de Atitlán, usually starting in Panajachel.

You should be able to rent a boat somewhere on almost any of the country's other navigable waterways, though be prepared for hours of patient bargaining, as the boat owners ask serious money for any excursions.

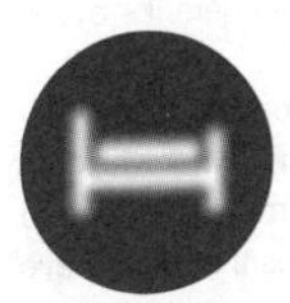

Accommodation

Guatemalan hotels come in all shapes and sizes, and unless you're really off the beaten track there's usually a good range of accommodation to choose from. Though Inguat fixes a maximum price for every hotel room in the country, there are bargains and bad deals at every level. At the top end of the scale, you can stay in some magnificent colonial hotels decorated with taste and period detail. In the mid-price bracket, you'll also find some brilliant places – you can still expect character and comfort, but perhaps without the service and facilities. But Guatemala really is a budget-travellers' dream, and you should be able to find a clean double room for US$12 (or less) in any town in the country, except the capital.

Accommodation comes under a bewildering assortment of names: *hoteles*, pensiones, *posadas*, hospedajes and *casas de huespedes*. The names don't always mean a great deal: in theory a hospedaje is less formal than a hotel, but in practice the reverse is almost as common. There are no official youth hostels in Guatemala, but independently owned backpacker-style **hostels** with dormitories are becoming more common.

Prices for rooms vary as much as anything else. On the whole you can expect the cheapest places to charge US$3–6 per person, and a reasonable but basic room with its own bathroom to cost US$12–15 (a little more in the capital). The official prices are meant to be displayed in the room, but it's well worth trying to haggle a little, or asking if there are any cheaper rooms. If travelling in a group you can often save money by sharing a larger room, which almost all the cheaper hotels offer.

Prices are at their highest in Guatemala City, where the very cheapest rooms can be very grim. Costs are also higher than average in Antigua, Río Dulce and Flores, but extremely cheap in the western highlands. At fiesta and holiday times, particularly Holy Week and Christmas, rooms tend to be more expensive and harder to find, and the summer tourist season can also be crowded.

At these times, particularly if you're going to arrive in Guatemala City at night, it's worth booking a room. Wherever you are, you'll find that most mid- and top-range hotels charge solo travellers around eighty percent of the cost of a double. Always insist on seeing your room before any money changes hands, otherwise you may find their good rooms reserved for more discerning customers. In general, the cheaper hotels (❶–❷) recommended in this book are not the very cheapest – which are often genuinely squalid, although we do list some notable bargains – but rather those one step

Accommodation price codes

All accommodation listed in this guide has been graded according to the following price scale, which refers to the price in US dollars of the cheapest double room in high season. Many places, however, will offer reductions at quieter times of the year, particularly those in the more popular tourist centres, where there is plenty of competition. It is always worth negotiating if you think the hotel is not very full.

❶ Under US$7
❷ US$7–12
❸ US$12–20
❹ US$20–30
❺ US$30–40
❻ US$40–60
❼ US$60–80
❽ US$80–100
❾ Over US$100

up. Rooms in these places will be simple, with a shared toilet and bathroom usually at the end of the corridor. In the brackets above this (❸ and ❹), you can expect a private bathroom with hot water. Rooms in the ❺ and ❻ categories should be very comfortable and attractive, while for US$60 and up (❼, ❽ and ❾), you can expect international standards of comfort and luxury, with facilities such as swimming pools, gyms and a good restaurant.

It's only in Petén, the eastern highlands, and on the Pacific and Caribbean coasts that you'll need a fan or air conditioning. In the highlands, even the luxury hotels rarely have a/c – many have lovely logwood fires to keep out the winter chill instead. Mosquito nets are not that common, even in the lowland areas, so if you plan to spend some time in Petén or by the coast it's well worth investing in one, and it's an essential purchase if you plan to so some jungle trekking.

Camping

Campsites are extremely thin on the ground in Guatemala. The main cities certainly don't have them, and there's only a handful of places in the country that offer a designated, secure place to park your tent. If you do decide to set off into the wilds, then a tent can be useful, although even here it's by no means essential.

Hiking in the highlands usually takes you from village to village, and wherever you go it's possible to find somewhere to bed down for the night. In villages that don't have hotels you should track down the mayor (*alcalde*) and ask if you can stay in the town hall (*municipalidad*) or local school. If that isn't possible, then you'll almost certainly be shown somewhere else to stay.

When it comes to hiking in the jungle you'll need to hire a guide. They usually sleep out in the open, protected only by a mosquito net, so you can either follow suit or use a tent. At most of the smaller Maya sites there are guards who will usually let you sleep in their shelters and cook on their fires. If you plan to use their facilities, bring along some food to share with them.

The other occasion for which a tent is useful is climbing volcanoes, an endeavour which often entails a night under the stars. For **renting tents**, sleeping bags, stoves and rucksacks, contact Maya Mountain Bike Tours or Old Town Outfitters in Antigua (see p.120), or Quetzaltrekkers inside the Casa Argentina hotel in Quetzaltenango (see p.195).

Communications

Guatemala's mail and telecommunication services were both relatively recently privatized and are steadily becoming more efficient. Generally, postal services are now quite reliable, though many locals use courier companies to send important packages and documents overseas. Telgua, the former state phone company, has branches throughout the country, but private communications offices and most cybercafés (which are very widespread in Guatemala) offer a much cheaper and more efficient service when you need to call abroad.

Mail

When sending mail home, the best way to ensure speedy delivery is to use the main **post office** (*correos*) in a provincial capital; this will also be the best place to send parcels. Post boxes are rare – you'll find them in the lobbies of big hotels and some tourist shops, but the best bet is to take mail to a post office. Generally, an airmail letter to the US takes about a week and to Europe from ten days to two weeks. **Receiving mail** is not generally a worry as long as you have a reliable address – many language schools and tour operators will hold mail for you. The Poste Restante (*Lista de Correos*) system is no longer operational. American Express in Guatemala City (see p.99) will also keep mail if you are a card holder or have Amex travellers' cheques.

Bear in mind it's very expensive to send anything heavy home (around US$6 per 100g to Europe and US$4 to North America) through the standard post. You may want to use a specialized shipping agency instead: see the Antigua and Panajachel "Listings" for recommended companies.

Courier companies (DHL, Federal Express etc) are establishing more and more offices throughout the region: even small towns now have them.

Phones

Telephone systems are improving in Guatemala, and though crackle-prone lines are not yet a thing of the past the system is pretty reliable, and mobile coverage now quite comprehensive. Local calls are very cheap (less than US$0.10 per minute) and long-distance domestic calls are not too expensive (around US$0.40). Call boxes (operated by a number of companies) are now widespread in urban areas; if you're going to be in Guatemala for a long stay, it's probably worth getting a local calling card (Telgua's is the most useful, followed by Telfónica) as many call boxes don't accept cash.

For **international calls**, always try to get to a private communication business (listed throughout the Guide). Cybercafés also often have inexpensive rates, and many of these places offer **webcalls**, which are extremely cheap (rates start from US$0.15 to the US and Canada, US$0.25 to the EU and a little more to the rest of the world). Connections can be a bit temperamental, however. Otherwise you're looking at around US$0.40/0.60 per minute or to the US/EU via a conventional phone line from one of these businesses. The next best way of calling home is to buy a Telgua or Telfónica phone card. As a last resort, call from a Telgua office, which can work out very expensive, or your hotel.

Taking a telephone **charge card** or calling card with you is another option. Most North

Calling home from overseas

Australia: international access code + 61 + city code

New Zealand: international access code + 64 + city code

Republic of Ireland: international access code + 353 + city code

UK and Northern Ireland: international access code + 44 + city code

US and Canada: international access code + 1 + area code

American cards work in Guatemala: AT&T, MCI, Sprint, Canada Direct and long-distance companies all enable their customers to make credit-card calls while overseas. Call your company's customer-service line to find out if they provide service from Guatemala and, if so, what the toll-free access code is. Calls made from overseas will automatically be billed to your home number. At present UK, Australian and New Zealand–issued charge cards do not function in Central America.

To make a **collect call** overseas (*llamar por cobrar*), dial ⓣ147120 from a Telgua phone, though the system does not always function well for non–North American numbers. You should be able to send (and receive) a **fax** from most telecom offices and many cybercafés.

Mobile phones

Check with your provider to see if your phone will work in Guatemala (many North American or UK phones do not function there). It's best to rent or purchase your own Guatemalan mobile; tariffs are very affordable and coverage is now extensive.

Email and the Internet

Web services are now very well-established in Guatemala. Connection speeds are generally very swift in the main urban centres but in more remote areas Guatemala's creaky power network can cause connection problems. You'll find cybercafés in virtually every town in Guatemala, and many villages. **Rates** vary considerably throughout the country: as little as US$0.80 per hour in Antigua, Quetzaltengango and Panajachel (which each have over a dozen cybercafés), and US$2–3 per hour in most other towns. In the Bay Islands, where all calls are classified as long-distance, surfing the Web works out much more pricey. Virtually all language schools are online, and many offer their students discount Internet rates upon enrolment.

It's also becoming increasingly easy to **reserve hotels**, tours and services via email, though few budget places are yet online. Additionally many towns and regions now boast superb **community websites** (see p.36), replete with accommodation, restaurant, cultural and entertainment information.

The media

Guatemala has a number of daily newspapers with extensive national coverage and a more limited international perspective. The best of the dailies are balanced, independent-minded *Siglo Veintiuno* (ⓦwww.sigloxxi.com); the most popular paper, *Prensa Libre* (ⓦwww.prensalibre.com), which features comprehensive national coverage; and forthright and outspoken *El Periódico* (ⓦwww.elperiodico.com.gt), which has some excellent investigative journalism, though can be tricky to find.

Picture-rich tabloids such as *Nuestro Diario* and *Al Día* concentrate on the shocking stories of the day. In the Quetzaltenango area, the local *Quetzalteco* is a good read; it's published three days a week. You may also come across *El Regional*, a good weekly paper which is published in both Spanish and Maya languages. As for the **periodicals**, *La Crónica* is usually a decent read, concentrating on current Guatemalan political affairs and business news with a smattering of foreign coverage.

In theory, the nation's newspapers are not subject to restrictions, though pressures and threats are still exerted by criminal gangs, the military and those in authority. Being an investigative journalist in Guatemala is a dangerous profession, and there have been several contract killings in recent years.

Slightly surprisingly for a country so dependent on tourism, the **English-language press** is pretty limited. The only publication that's widely available is *Revue* magazine, published in Antigua, which carries interesting articles about Guatemala plus some coverage of Belize, El Salvador and Honduras. It doesn't feature political issues, but there's often some cultural or historical coverage, plus plenty of accommodation, restaurant and shopping advertisements. In the Xela area, *Entremundos* (Ⓦwww.entremundos.org) is an interesting free news sheet with articles about Guatemalan society and human rights and political issues; it's distributed in the city quite widely.

For reliable, in-depth reporting, the *Central America Report* excels, with coverage of controversial news stories plus political analysis. It's published by Inforpress Centroamericana and is available by subscription only at Ⓦwww.inforpressca.com. The *Report on Guatemala*, published by Nisgua (subscription only, US$25 annually; Ⓦwww.nisgua.org) and dealing mainly with human rights, is also recommended.

As for **foreign publications**, *Newsweek* and *Time* are available in quality bookstores around the country and in some luxury hotel gift shops. Some American newspapers are also available: check in the *Camino Real Hotel* bookstore in Guatemala City and the bookshops in Antigua.

Honduran media

In Honduras, the most useful publications for travellers are *Honduras This Week* (Ⓦwww.marrder.com/htw), an excellent weekly English-language newspaper with in-depth coverage of events in Honduras, plus tourist and business information; and *Honduras Tips*, a free tourism magazine with plenty of valuable information and features, transport information, and hotel and restaurant listings. Both are widely available in Copán and the Bay Islands.

Radio and television

Guatemala has an abundance of **radio stations**, though variety is not their strong point. Most transmit a turgid stream of Latin pop and cheesy merengue, which you're sure to hear plenty of on the buses. There is a host of religious stations, too, broadcasting an onslaught of rabid evangelical lectures, services, "miracles", and so on. Try Radio Prisma on 89.7FM for jazz and *música inglés* (Western music) or La Marca on 94.1FM for rock music. If you're visiting Guatemala City, it's worth twiddling your FM dial – there can be some interesting stuff broadcast over the capital's airwaves at weekends, including European techno.

Television stations are also in plentiful supply. Viewers can choose from several local channels – Canal 3 is good for news – and a multitude of cable stations, all of them dominated by American and Mexican programmes, either subtitled or dubbed into Spanish. Many hotel rooms have cable TV, which often includes (English-language) CNN.

BBC World Service is not at all clear in many parts of Guatemala; it's usually best between 6am and 8am. For the latest frequencies consult Ⓦwww.bbc.co.uk/worldservice. For Voice of America frequencies consult Ⓦwww.voa.gov.

Eating and drinking

Guatemalan cuisine is unpretentious, filling and good value. The quality and variety of the cooking depends greatly on where you are. Eateries in places popular with tourists tend to have varied menus and plenty of choice for vegetarians, and in Antigua and Panajachel you can feast on numerous different European cuisines, several Asian ones, and even sample Middle Eastern dishes.

Elsewhere, in places orientated more to a Guatemalan clientele you're likely to be offered a lot of simply prepared grilled meat dishes and much less choice. Off the beaten path in the highlands the diet can get pretty monotonous, with things revolving around the "three-card trick" of eggs, beans and tortillas for breakfast, lunch and dinner. You'll find that the concept of healthy eating has yet to really penetrate Central America, and a lot of local food tends to be greasy and full-fat by definition.

For a list of food terminology, see the "Language" section of Contexts at the back of this book.

Where to eat

Unless you're in a tourism-orientated place, your choice is usually between a **restaurant** and a **comedor** in most Guatemalan towns. The latter is like a traditional American diner or an old-school British café; in general, these are simple local eateries serving big portions of food at inexpensive prices. In a comedor there is often no menu, and you simply ask what's on offer, or look into the bubbling pots. Restaurants, broadly speaking, are slightly more formal and expensive. On the whole you'll find restaurants in the towns, while in small villages there are usually just one or two comedores, clustered around the market area. Comedores tend to look scruffier, but the food is almost always fresh and the turnover is fast.

Many locals will very rarely venture into either a comedor or a restaurant, preferring to eat from **street food stalls**, which sell the food of the poor at rock-bottom prices; they're also usually clustered around the marketplace. If your stomach can take it, you'll often find an interesting dish to try, though hygiene standards can be questionable.

You'll find **fast-food** joints in towns and on highways, modelled on the American originals and often owned by the same companies. While on the road, you'll also come across the local version of fast food: when buses pause they're besieged by vendors offering a huge selection of drinks, sweets, local specialities and even complete meals. Treat this kind of food with a degree of caution, bearing in mind the general lack of hygiene.

Traditionally, Guatemalans eat a **breakfast** of tortillas and eggs, accompanied by the inevitable beans – and sometimes also a sauce of sour cream. **Lunch** is the main meal of the day, and this is the best time to fill up as restaurants often offer *comidas corridas*, a set two- or three-course meal that sometimes costs as little as a dollar. It's always filling and occasionally delicious. Sometimes the same deal is on offer in the evenings, but usually not, so **evening meals** are likely to be more expensive. The country's cuisine does not vary that much regionally (except on the Caribbean coast, which is quite distinct) though some areas have famous local dishes including the *kak'ik* (a turkey broth) of the Cobán area.

Vegetarians are rarely catered for specifically, except in tourist-geared restaurants and at a handful of places in Guatemala City. It is, however, fairly easy to get by eating plenty of beans and eggs (which are always on the menu) and often some guacamole. Unfortunately, beans are often fried in lard. The markets also offer plenty of superb fruit, and snacks like tostadas and *pupusas*.

Guatemalan specialities

If you're curious to try some Guatemalan dishes, markets and fiestas are particularly good grazing territory.

Nomenclature is confusing – **cornmeal** wrapped inside banana leaves or corn husks and steamed could take any number of names depending upon flavourings, and these change from region to region. Plain steamed cornmeal is a *tamal blanco*; stuff it with meat and tomato salsa, however, and it becomes either a *chuchito* or a tamale. If blended with potato, it's a *pache* – these are common in the Xela area. Near Rabinal, look out for *boxboles*, cornmeal flavoured with spices, almond and a pinch of chilli, and cooked inside a pumpkin leaf. Mixed with *frijoles*, a *tamal* is a *bollo*, *tayuyo* or *tamalito de frijol*. When sweet, it's a *camallito de cambray* (with anise) or an *elote*. Keep an eye out for a red lantern outside a house – this indicates the family has fresh tamales for sale.

The corn **tortilla** can also be prepared in a myriad of ways. Fried and topped (typically with guacamole and some salty cheese), it's a tostada, while rolled or folded around a filling – meat-and-cheese is always popular – it may be a taco, enchilada or *doblada*. Usually a salsa, based on a blend of ripe tomato and *miltomates* (green tomatoes), is served with these dishes. A *pupusa* (called a *baleada* in Honduras) is a fresh tortilla stuffed with anything, but usually including refried beans, *repollo* (pickled shredded cabbage leaves) and cheese.

Encasing food in an **egg batter** and frying it either *envueltos* ("wrapped") or *frituras* ("fritter style") is another popular cooking style. *Chiles rellenos*, chillies stuffed with vegetables and meat, are especially delicious. Simpler, often vegetarian variations, abound using green bean or cauliflower, but look out for those made with *güisquil* (squash), *flor de izote* (the slightly bitter petals of a palm) or *bledo*, a leaf similar in flavour to spinach.

Salads are often simple, though several variations are well worth trying, including *piloyada*, a hearty affair based on plump red beans with eggs, tomatoes and meat; *iguaxte*, cooked potato or vegetables flavoured with a distinct paste of pumpkin seeds, dried chillies and sometimes tomato; and *chojín,* which is radish-based and often made with cheese and either pork or pork crackling (*chicharrón*). *Fiambre*, a vast salad of pickled vegetables with cured sausage (mixed with beetroot in central Guatemala and often barley in the Quetzaltenango area) is perhaps the country's most celebrated dish; it's eaten on All Saints' Day around a family grave in the cemetery.

Many **traditional dishes** are chunky soups or subtly spiced tomato-based stews (*caldos*, *cocidos* or *sopas*). The spicy *pepián* sauce is made throughout the country and usually incorporates chicken and vegetables, but occasionally chocolate. The more lightly spiced *pulique* is flavoured with coriander and capsicum. *Suban-ik*, which hails from Chimaltenango, is a tasty dish with chicken and pork, while Cobán's *kak-ik* is a turkey broth with coriander and mint.

Sweets, snacks and desserts tend to be very sweet. *Rellenitos* – cooked mashed plantain, stuffed with sweetened beans and fried – are widely available, as is *mole de plátano*, which is plantain served in a sweet, spiced cocoa-flavoured sauce. Vegetables – for example, sweet potato, pumpkin or chayote – may be simmered in sugar syrups until they are caramelised or stuffed with a sweet mixture. Cake making is generally a specialized business, but *pastel borracho* is one that is soaked in a rum syrup before being iced, while *pastel de elote* is made with corn.

with help from Malia Dewse

Guatemalan cuisine has evolved from three distinct traditions, though they usually overlap to a great extent now to form what Guatemalans call *comida típica*.

Maya cuisine

The oldest style of cuisine is **Maya cooking**, in which the basic staples of beans and maize dominate. **Beans** (*frijoles*) are the black kidney-shaped variety and are served in two ways: either *volteados*, which are boiled up, mashed, and then refried in a great dollop; or *parados*, which are boiled up whole, with a few slices of onion and garlic, and served in their own black juice. For breakfast, beans are usually served with eggs and cream, and at other times of the day they're offered up on a separate plate from the main dish. Almost all truly Guatemalan meals include a portion of beans, and for many highland Maya, beans are the only regular source of protein.

Maize is the other essential, a food which for the Maya (and many other native Americans) is almost as nourishing spiritually as it is physically – in Maya legend, humankind was originally formed from maize. It appears most commonly as the **tortilla**, a thin pancake. The maize is traditionally ground by hand and shaped by clapping it between two hands, a method still in widespread use; the tortilla is then cooked on a *comal*, which is a flat pan of clay placed over the fire. Guatemalan tortillas should be eaten while warm, usually brought to the table wrapped in cloth.

For the Maya, the tortilla forms the hub of a meal, with beans or the odd piece of meat to spice it up. Tortillas have a lovely pliable texture, with a delicate, slightly burnt, smoky taste which will become very much a part of your trip – the smell of them is enough to revive memories years later. Where there's an option local people often serve gringos with bread, assuming they won't want tortillas.

Maize is also used to make a number of traditional **snacks**, which are sold on buses, at markets and during fiestas. The most common of these is the *tamal,* a pudding-like cornmeal package sometimes stuffed with chicken or another bit of meat. It's wrapped in a plantain leaf and then boiled. The *chuchito* is a smaller version of the *tamal*, which tends to include a bit of tomato and a pinch of hot chilli. Squash (*güisquil*) is the main Maya vegetable, often used in dishes along with meat, tomato and onion; you may also find *pacaya*, a rather stodgy local vegetable.

Chillies are the final essential ingredient of the Maya diet (especially for the Q'ek'chi). Chillies are sometimes placed raw or pickled in the middle of the table in a jar, but they're also served as a sauce – *salsa picante*. Their strength can vary tremendously, so treat them with caution until you know what you're dealing with.

A highland **breakfast** often includes a plate of *mosh*, which is made with milk and oats and tastes rather like porridge. It's the ideal antidote to the early morning chill.

Other traditional Maya dishes include a superb range of *stews* – known as *caldos* – made with duck, beef, chicken or turkey; and *fiambre*, which is the world's largest salad, a delicious mix of meat and vegetables traditionally served on the Day of the Dead (November 1), when you can usually find it in restaurants. The best chance to sample traditional food is at a market or fiesta, when makeshift comedores serve freshly cooked dishes.

Ladino cuisine

Guatemala's second culinary style is **ladino** food, which is indebted to the range of cultures that make up the ladino population. Most of the food has a mild Latin American bias, incorporating a lot of Mexican ideas, particularly tacos and enchiladas, but the influence of the United States and Europe is also strongly felt. Ladino-style food includes *bistek* (steak), *hamburguesa* and dishes like *carne adobada* (grilled pork marinated with tomato and spices), all of which are readily available in most Guatemalan towns, with rice and fries (chips) usually providing the carbohydrate (along with the ubiquitous tortillas). Guatemalan-style *ceviche* (raw fish with spicy salad) is also popular on the coasts. Ladino-style cakes and pastries are widely available, but tend to be pretty dull and dry.

Creole cuisine

The final element is **Creole** and Garífuna cooking, which incorporates the influences of the Caribbean with those of Africa, and is easy to find in Puerto Barrios and Lívingston. Here seafood dominates the scene, along with coconut and plantain. *Tapado* is probably the region's signature dish, a seafood soup that's a superb mix of fish (typically snapper), prawns, coconut milk, peppers, plantain and spices; though you'll also find plenty of grilled fish, lobster, conch fritters and *pan de coco*.

Drink

To start off the day most Guatemalans drink a cup of hot **coffee**, chocolate or tea (all of which are usually served with plenty of sugar). **Atol**, a warm, sweet drink made with either maize, rice (or even plantain) and sugar is also very popular, especially in the highlands. At other times of day, **soft drinks** and beer are usually drunk with meals. Coca-Cola, Pepsi, Sprite and Fanta (all called *aguas*) are common, as are *refrescos*, thirst-quenching water-based drinks with a little fruit flavour added. In many places, you can also get a *licuado*, a delicious, thick, fruit-based drink with either milk or water added (milk is safer).

Tap water in the main towns is purified, and you can usually taste the chlorine. However, this doesn't mean that it won't give you stomach trouble, and it's always safest to stick to bottled water (*agua pura* or *agua mineral*), which is almost always available.

Until 2002 one bland **beer** – Gallo – had an almost total monopoly in Guatemala. Then Brahva, a Brazilian brewer muscled in (they even flew the footballer Ronaldo over to promote the brand), adding some much needed variety. Gallo is a medium-strength lager-style beer that comes in 33cl or litre bottles (around US$1.50 and US$3 respectively in a bar; much less in a supermarket). Brahva comes in 33cl bottles and has a slightly spicy finish. Moza, a dark brew with a slight caramel flavour is worth trying but rarely available. Other hard-to-come-by brands (all lagers) include the premium beer Montecarlo, Dorada Draft and Cabro. Imported brands are scarce.

As for spirits, **rum** (*ron*) and **aguardiente**, a clear and lethal sugarcane spirit, are very popular and cheap. Ron Botran Añejo is a half-decent rum (around US$4 a bottle), while the fabulously smooth Ron Zacapa Centenario (around US$25 a bottle) has to be one of the world's best; indeed, it regularly wins international prizes. Hard drinkers will soon get to know Quezalteca and Venado, two readily available *aguardientes* that fire up many a fiesta. If you're after a real bargain, then try locally brewed alcohol (*chicha*), which is practically given away. Its main ingredient can be anything: apple, cherry, sugarcane, peach, apricot and quince are just some of the more common varieties.

Wine is also made in Guatemala, from local fruits or imported concentrates. It's interesting to try, but for something really drinkable stick to the more expensive imports. Chilean wines are the best value, with decent bottles available from around US$5 in supermarkets and from US$10 in restaurants.

Opening hours and public holidays

Guatemalan **opening hours** are subject to considerable local variations, but in general most offices, shops, post offices and museums are open between 8.30am and 5–6pm, though some take an hour or so break for lunch. Banking hours are extremely convenient, with many staying open until 7pm (and some as late as 8pm) from Monday to Friday, but closing at 1pm on Saturdays. You may not always be able to exchange money after 5.30pm in some places, however, even though the bank is open.

Archeological sites are open every day, usually from 8am to 5pm, though Tikal is open from 6am to 6pm. Principal public holidays, when almost all businesses close down, are listed below, but each village or town will also have its own fiestas or saints' days when most places will be shut.

Public holidays

January 1 New Year's Day
Semana Santa The four days of Holy Week leading up to Easter
May 1 Labour Day
June 30 Army Day, anniversary of the 1871 revolution
August 15 Guatemala City fiesta (Guatemala City only)
September 15 Independence Day
October 12 Discovery of America (only banks close)
October 20 Revolution Day
November 1 All Saints' Day
December 24 Christmas Eve (from noon)
December 25 Christmas
December 31 New Year's Eve (from noon)

Fiestas

Traditional fiestas are one of the great excitements of a trip to Guatemala, and every town and village, however small, devotes at least one day a year to celebration. The main day is normally prescribed by the local saint's day, though the celebrations often extend a week or two around that date. On almost every day of the year there's a fiesta in some forgotten corner of the country, and with a bit of planning you should be able to witness at least one. Most of them are well worth going out of your way for. A list of all the regional fiestas appears at the end of each chapter in the Guide.

The format of fiestas varies between two basic models (except on the Caribbean coast – see box on p.60). In towns with a largely ladino population, fairs are usually set up, and the days are filled with processions, beauty contests and perhaps the odd marching band; the nights are dominated by dancing to merengue and salsa. In the highlands, where the bulk of the population is Maya, you'll see traditional dances, costumes and musicians, and a blend of religious and secular celebration that incorporates pre-Columbian elements. What they all share is an astonishing energy and an unbounded enthusiasm for drink, dance and fireworks, all of which are virtually impossible to escape during the days of fiesta.

One thing you shouldn't expect is anything too dainty or organized: fiestas are above all chaotic, and the measured rhythms of traditional dance and music are usually obscured by the crush of the crowd and the huge volumes of alcohol consumed by participants. If you can join in the mood, there's no doubt that fiestas are wonderfully entertaining and that they offer a real insight into Guatemalan culture, ladino or indigenous.

Many of the **best fiestas** include some specifically local element, such as the giant kites at Santiago Sacatepéquez, the religious processions in Antigua, the horse race in Todos Santos Cuchumatán or the skull bearers of San José. The dates of most fiestas, along with their main features, are listed at the end of each chapter. At certain times virtually the whole country erupts simultaneously: Easter Week is perhaps the most important, particularly in Antigua, but All Saints' Day (November 1) and New Year's are each also marked by partying across the land.

Fiesta dances

In Guatemala's Maya villages **traditional dances** – heavily imbued with history and symbolism – form a pivotal part in the fiesta celebrations. The drunken dancers may look out of control, but the process is taken very seriously and involves great expense on the part of the participants, who have to rent their ornate costumes. The most common dance is the **Baile de la Conquista**, which re-enacts the victory of the Spanish over the Maya, while at the same time managing to ridicule the conquistadors. According to some studies, the dance is based in pre-Columbian traditions. Other popular dances are the Baile de los Gracejos, the dance of the jesters; the Baile del Venado, the dance of the deer; and the Baile de la Culebra, the dance of the snake; all of them again rooted in pre-Columbian traditions. One of the most impressive is the Palo Volador, in which men swing by ropes from a thirty-metre pole. Today this Maya-style bungy jump is only performed in Chichicastenango, Joyabaj and Cubulco.

Fiesta music

Guatemalan **music** combines many different influences, but yet again it can be broadly divided between ladino and Maya. For fiestas, bands are always shipped in, complete with a crackling PA system and a strutting lead singer.

Traditional Guatemalan music is dominated by the **marimba**, a type of wooden xylophone that originated in Africa. The oldest versions

Caribbean fiestas and music

Fiestas in Lívingston and the Honduran Bay Islands have different traditions from those in Guatemala and swing to other rhythms. In the Bay Islands, the Creole festivals are unabashedly hedonistic affairs, much more like a Caribbean carnival than a Latin fiesta, with floats, lashings of rum punch and plenty of heavy sexual innuendo. Reggae bass-lines boom from giant stacks of speakers and the streets and dancehalls are crammed with hip-grinding groovers. Much of the music comes from Jamaica and is sung in English, although there are popular tunes from Central America, with the most important reggae bands coming from Belize, Costa Rica and Panama. In Lívingston, on Guatemala's Caribbean coast, some of the best dancing you'll ever see is to the hypnotic drum patterns of punta, the music of the Garífuna (see pp.274–275), which betrays a distinctive West African heritage. The Garífuna really know how to party, and if you get the chance to attend a fiesta, be prepared for some explosively athletic shimmying and provocative hip movements – nineteenth-century Methodists were so outraged they called it "devil dancing". **Garífuna day** (November 26) is the ideal time to see Lívingston really celebrate, though there seems to be a punta party going on most weekends.

use gourds beneath the sounding board and can be played by a single musician, while modern models, using hollow tubes to generate the sound, can need as many as seven players. The marimba is at the heart of traditional music, and marimba orchestras play at every occasion, for both ladino and indigenous communities. In the remotest of villages you sometimes hear them practicing well into the night, particularly around market day. Other important instruments, especially in Maya bands, are the *tun*, a drum made from a hollow log; the *tambor*, another drum traditionally covered with the skin of a deer; *los chichines*, a type of maracas made from hollow gourds; the *tzijolaj*, a kind of piccolo; and the *chirimia*, a flute.

Mainstream ladino music is a blend of North American and Latin sounds, much of it originating in Miami, Colombia, the Dominican Republic and Puerto Rico, although there are plenty of local bands producing their own version of the sound. It's fast-moving, easy-going and very rhythmic, and on any bus you'll hear many of the most popular tracks. It draws on merengue, a rhythm that originally came from the Dominican Republic, and includes elements of Mexican music and the cumbia and salsa of Colombia and Cuba.

Sports and outdoor pursuits

Guatemalans have a furious appetite for spectator sports and the daily papers always devote four or five pages to the subject. Fútbol tops the bill, and if you get the chance to see a major game it's a thrilling experience, if only to watch the crowd. There's a great website, ⓦwww.guatefutbol.com, dedicated to the national sport. Otherwise North American sport predominates – baseball, American football, boxing and basketball are all popular.

Hiking is perhaps the most popular sport among visitors, particularly volcano climbing, which is certainly hard work but almost always worth the effort – unless you end up wrapped in cloud. Guatemala has 37 volcanic peaks; the tallest is Tajumulco in the west, which at 4220m is a serious undertaking, and should only be tackled when you've been acclimatized to an altitude of over 2000m for a few days. Among the active peaks, Pacaya is a fairly easy climb and a dramatic sight, although not always as active as the tour companies' photographs would have you believe. Volcano-climbing trips are organized by a number of tour groups in Antigua and Quetzaltenango (see p.120 and p.195).

Sadly, there have been some occasional **attacks** (often armed, but usually non-violent) on hikers climbing volcanoes, and around the shores of Lago de Atitlán. While these incidents have been fairly isolated, all walkers should be aware that there is an element of danger involved. It's much safer to walk in a group, and important to check local knowledge about the security situation before setting out.

As a participatory sport, fishing is also popular, with good ocean and freshwater fishing. On the Pacific side the coast offers exceptional **sport fishing**, with some of the best waters in the world for sailfish, as well as dorado, mahi mahi and some blue marlin, jack crevalle, yellow and black tuna, snappers and bonito. The Caribbean side, including Lago de Izabal, also offers excellent opportunities for snook and tarpon. In Petén the rivers and lakes are packed with sport fish, including snook, tarpon and peacock bass, and lakes Petexbatún, Izabal and Yaxjá all offer superb fishing, as do the Usumacinta and Dulce rivers. Fishing trips are organized by local agencies including Maya Expeditions (see below) and US-based Goldon Tours (ⓣ1-817/418-9779, ⓦwww.goldon.com). Sport-fishing trips are expensive however, and if you're looking for a more casual arrangement, talk to the local fishermen in Iztapa, Sayaxché or El Estor.

Guatemala's dramatic highland landscape and tumbling rivers also provide some excellent opportunities for **whitewater rafting**. Three-day trips down the Río Cahabón are organized by Maya Expeditions, 15 Calle A 14-07, Zona 10, Guatemala City (ⓣ2363 4955, ⓦwww.mayaexpeditions.com), which also run trips on the Usumacinta, Nahualate and Motagua, giving you the chance to see some very remote areas and also visit some of the country's most inaccessible Maya sites.

Scuba diving is another growing sport in this part of the world, although Guatemala has little to offer compared with the splendours of the neighbouring Belizean or Honduran coastal waters. Nevertheless, there are some diving possibilities here, including Lago de Atitlán and Lago de Izabal, as well as some reasonable Pacific and Caribbean dive sites. Highly recommended for freshwater, high-altitude dives and excellent instruction are ATI Divers, based in the *Iguana Perdida* hotel in Santa Cruz, Lago de Atitlán (see p.182).

There is also some **surfing** in Guatemala, on the Pacific coast with a small, new surf camp set up near the village of Sipacate. However, if you've come all this way for the waves, you'll probably find better breaks in El Salvador or Costa Rica.

Trouble and the police

Personal safety is a serious problem in Guatemala, partly due to a recent nationwide rise in crime, but also because some criminals actively target visitors, including tourist shuttle buses. There is little pattern to these attacks, but some areas can be considered much safer than others. Warnings have been posted in the Guide where incidents have occurred. It's wise to register with your embassy on arrival, try to keep informed of events, and avoid travelling at night.

Crime

Though Guatemala attracts around a million tourists a year and relatively few tourists have any trouble, it's essential that you try to minimize the chance of becoming a victim. **Petty theft** and pickpocketing are likely to be your biggest worry. Theft is most common in Guatemala City's Zona 1 and its bus stations, but you should also take extra care when visiting markets popular with tourists (like Chichicastenango) and during fiestas. Avoid wearing flashy jewellery and keep your money well hidden. When travelling, there is actually little danger to your pack when it's on top of a bus as it's the conductor's responsibility alone to go up on the roof and collect luggage.

Muggings and violent crime are of particular concern in Guatemala City. There's not too much danger in the daylight hours but don't amble around at night, when it's much safer to use a taxi. There have also been a few cases of armed robbery in Antigua and around Lago de Atitlán too. The Pacaya volcano is now considered safe, though there have been robberies on other volcanoes, particularly San Pedro.

If you are robbed you'll have to report it to the police, which can be a very long process and may seem like little more than a symbolic gesture; however, most insurance companies will only pay up if you can produce a police statement.

Officially, you should carry your **passport** (or a photocopy) at all times.

Drugs

Drugs are readily available in Guatemala, and the country recently became a key smuggling link in the route between Colombia and the US. Marijuana and cocaine are both readily available, and cheap heroin is also to be found on the streets. However, be aware that **drug offences** are dealt with severely. Even the possession of marijuana could land you in jail – a sobering experience in Guatemala. If you do get into a problem with drugs, it may be worth enquiring with the first policeman if there is a "fine" (*multa*) to pay, to save expensive arbitration later. At the first possible opportunity, get in touch with your embassy and negotiate through them: they will understand the situation better than you. The addresses of embassies and consulates in Guatemala City are listed on p.100.

Sexual harassment

Machismo is very much a part of Latin American culture, and many Guatemalan men consider it their duty to put on a bit of a show to impress the *gringas*. It's usually best to ignore any such hassle. Ladino towns and *cantinas* are the worst places. Indigenous society is more deferential so you're unlikely to experience any trouble in the western highlands.

The police

For Europeans and North Americans expecting to enter a police state, Guatemala may come as something of a surprise. Though there are a lot of police, soldiers and armed

Useful numbers

Police ⓣ120
Tourism Police ⓣ110
Red Cross ambulance ⓣ125

security guards on the streets, there's rarely anything intimidating about their presence.

Guatemala's civilian police force, introduced in 1997, has a poor reputation. Corruption is rampant and inefficiency the norm, so don't expect that much help if you experience any trouble. In Antigua, there's a well-established **tourist police** force, a scheme which has recently been extended to Panajachel and Tikal, and should be shortly introduced to Lívingston, among other places.

If for any reason you do find yourself in trouble with the law, be as polite as possible. Remember that bribery is a way of life here, and that corruption is widespread.

Shopping

Guatemalan craft traditions, locally known as *artesanía*, are very much a part of Maya culture, stemming from practices that in most cases predate the arrival of the Spanish. Many of these traditions are highly localized, with different regions and even different villages specializing in particular crafts. It makes sense to visit as many markets as possible, particularly in the highland villages, where the colour and spectacular settings are like nowhere else in Central America.

As for **everyday goods**, you'll find that both slide and print film are available in most towns in the country, though memory cards for digital cameras are less common, as is monochrome film. Camcorder videotapes are also widely on sale.

Artesanías

The best place to buy Guatemalan **crafts** is in their place of origin, where prices are reasonable and the craftsmen and -women get a greater share of the profit. If you haven't the time to travel to remote highland villages, the best places to head for are Chichicastenango on market days (Thurs and Sun) and the shops and street hawkers in Antigua and Panajachel.

The greatest craft in Guatemala has to be **textile weaving**. Each Maya village has its own traditional designs, woven in fantastic patterns and with superbly vivid colours. All the finest weaving is done on the backstrap loom, using complex weft float and wrapping techniques. Chemical dyes have been dominant in Guatemala for over a century now, but a few weavers are returning to use natural dyes in some areas, including Lago de Atitlán.

One of the best places to start looking at textiles is in Antigua's Nim Po't, 5 Av Nte 29 (daily 9am–9pm; Ⓣ & Ⓕ7832 2681, Ⓦwww.nimpot.com), a huge store with an excellent collection of styles and designs. Guatemala City's Museo Ixchel is another essential visit, while in Santiago Atitlán there's a good new textile museum.

You should bear in mind that while most Maya are proud that foreigners find their textiles attractive, for them clothing has a profound significance, related to their identity and history – so it's not wise for women travellers to wear men's shirts or trousers, or for men to wear *huipiles*.

Alongside Guatemalan weaving most **other crafts** suffer by comparison. However, if you hunt around, you'll find good ceramics, baskets, mats, silver and jade. Antigua has the most comprehensive collection of shops. For anything woolen, particularly blankets, head for Momostenango Sunday market.

Markets

For shopping – or simply sightseeing – the markets of Guatemala are some of the finest anywhere in the world. The large markets of

Chichicastenango, Sololá and San Francisco el Alto are all well worth a visit, but equally fascinating are the tiny weekly gatherings in remote villages like San Juan Atitán and Chajul, where the atmosphere is hushed and unhurried. In these isolated settlements market day is as much a social event as a commercial affair, providing the chance for villagers to catch up on local news, and perhaps enjoy a tipple or two, as well as sell some vegetables and buy a few provisions. Most towns and villages have at least one weekly event; for a comprehensive list, see p.129.

Work and study

Guatemala is one of the best – and most popular – places in the continent to study Spanish. The language-school industry is big business, with more than sixty well-established schools and many more less reliable set-ups. Thousands of foreigners from all over the world study each year in Guatemala – mainly travellers and college students, but also airline crew members and business people. As for work, teaching English is the best bet, though there are always opportunities for committed volunteers.

Studying Spanish

Most **language schools** offer a weekly deal that includes four or five hours one-on-one tuition a day, plus full board with a local family. This all-inclusive package works out at between US$85 and US$210 a week depending on the school and location – most are in the US$120–150 bracket. It's important to bear in mind that the success of the exercise is dependent both on your personal commitment to study and on the enthusiasm and aptitude of your teacher – if you are not happy with the teacher you've been allocated, ask for another. Insist on knowing the number of other students that will be sharing your family house; some schools (mainly in Antigua) pack as many as ten foreigners in with one family. Virtually all schools have a student liaison officer, usually an English-speaking foreigner who acts as a go-between for students and teachers, so if you're a complete beginner there will usually be someone around with whom you can communicate.

The first decision to make is to choose where you want to study. By far the most popular choices are the towns of Antigua and Quetzaltenango, though Lago de Atitlán is also starting to become an established language centre. Beautiful **Antigua** is undoubtedly an excellent place to study Spanish: though the major drawback is that there are so many other students and tourists here that you'll probably end up spending your evenings speaking English. **Quetzaltenango** (Xela) has a different atmosphere, with a stronger "Guatemalan" character and far fewer tourists, though as its popularity has grown the city's gringo scene has inevitably mushroomed. The third most popular location is now **San Pedro La Laguna** on Lago de Atitlán, which now has around a dozen schools and very cheap prices (with plenty offering a full homestay/tuition package for less than US$100 per week). As yet standards are only average in San Pedro, however. Other cities with schools include Chichicastenango, Flores, Guatemala City, Huehuetenango, Monterrico, Nebaj, Panajachel, San Andrés and San José in Petén, Todos Santas Cuchumatán and, in Honduras, Copán and Utila.

Many schools lay on **after-school activities** like salsa classes, cooking, visits to villages, films and lectures, and even trips to the coast. In Quetzaltenango most schools have a social ethos and fund development projects in the region; some offer volunteer opportunities on these projects.

Recommended language schools

Many of the schools below have academic accreditation agreements with North American and European universities; some also have US offices – consult the schools' websites for more information. The websites Ⓦwww.123teachme.com and Ⓦwww.guatemala365.com have reports and some good tips about the relative advantages of different study centres.

Antigua

APPE 6 C Poniente 40 Ⓣ7832 0720, Ⓦwww.appeschool.com.
Los Capitanes Generales 5 Av Sur 4 Ⓣ7832 8769, Ⓦwww.loscapitanes.com.
Centroamerica Spanish Academy inside La Fuente, 4 C Oriente 14 Ⓣ7832 3297, Ⓦwww.quik.guate.com/spanishacademy.
Centro Lingüístico de la Fuente 1 C Poniente 27 Ⓣ7832 2711, Ⓦwww.delafuenteschool.com.
Centro Lingüístico Maya 5 C Poniente 20 Ⓣ7832 0656, Ⓦwww.travellog.com/guatemala/antigua/clmaya/school.html.
Christian Spanish Academy 6 Av Norte 15 Ⓣ7832 3922, Ⓦwww.learncsa.com.
Probigua 6 Av Norte 41B Ⓣ7832 2998, Ⓦwww.probigua.conexion.com.
Projecto Lingüístico Francisco Marroquín 7 C Poniente 31Ⓣ7832 2886, Ⓦwww.plfm-antigua.org. The school also offers classes in Maya languages.
San José El Viejo 5 Av Sur 34 Ⓣ7832 3028, Ⓦwww.sanjoseelviejo.com.
Sevilla 1 Av Sur 8 Ⓣ7832 5101, Ⓦwww.sevillantigua.com.
Tecún Umán 6 C Poniente 34 A Ⓣ7831 2792, Ⓦwww.escuelatecun.com.
La Unión 1 Av Sur 21 Ⓣ7832 7337, Ⓦwww.launion.conexion.com.

Quetzaltenango

Casa de Español Xelajú Callejón 15, Diagonal 13–02, Zona 1 Ⓣ7761 5954, Ⓦwww.casaxelaju.com.
Celas Maya 6 C 14–55, Zona 1 Ⓣ7761 4342, Ⓦwww.celasmaya.com.
Centro Bilingüe Amerindía (CBA) 12 Av 8–21, Zona 1 Ⓣ7761 5260, Ⓦwww.xelapages.com/cba.
Centro Maya de Idiomas 21 Av 5–69, Zona 3 Ⓣ7767 0352, Ⓦwww.centromaya.org. Also offers classes in Maya languages.
Educación para Todos 12 Av 1–78, Zona 3 Ⓣ7765 0715, Ⓦwww.spanishschools.biz.
English Club International Language School Diagonal 4 9–71, Zona 9 Ⓣ7763 2198. Also offers classes in K'iche' and Mam.
Escuela Juan Sisay 15 Av 8–38, Zona 1 Ⓣ7763 1318, Ⓦwww.juansisay.com.
Guatemalensis 19 Av 2–14, Zona 1 Ⓦwww.guatemalensis.com.
Inepas 15A Av 4–59 Ⓣ7765 1308, Ⓦwww.inepas.org.
Kie–Balam Diagonal 12 4–46, Zona 1 Ⓣ7761 1636, Ⓦwww.kiebalam.com.
La Paz Diagonal 11 7–38, Zona 1 Ⓣ7761 2159, Ⓦwww.xelapages.com/lapaz.
Pop Wuj 1 C 17–72, Zona 1 Ⓣ7761 8286, Ⓦwww.pop-wuj.org.
Proyecto Lingüístico Quetzalteco de Español 5 C 2–40, Zona 1 Ⓣ7763 1061, Ⓦwww.hermandad.com. Also has sister schools on the Pacific slope and in Todos Santos Cuchumatán.
Sakribal 6 C 7–42, Zona 1 Ⓣ7763 0717, Ⓦwww.sakribal.com.

Lago de Atitlán

Casa Rosario south of Santiago Atitlán dock, San Pedro La Laguna Ⓣ5613 6401, Ⓦwww.casarosario.com.
Corazón Maya Spanish School south of Santiago dock, San Pedro La Laguna Ⓣ7721 8160, Ⓦwww.corazonmaya.com.
Escuela Jabel Tinamit off c/Santander, Panajachel Ⓣ7762 0238, Ⓦwww.jabeltinamit.com.
Jardín de América C 14 de Febrero, Panajachel Ⓣ7762 2637, Ⓦwww.jardindeamerica.com.
Mayab' Spanish School between the docks, San Pedro La Laguna Ⓣ7815 7722, Ⓦwww.mayabspanishschool.com.
San Pedro Spanish School between the piers, San Pedro La Laguna Ⓣ7715 4604, Ⓦwww.sanpedrospanishschool.com.

Huehuetenango

Xinabajul 6 Av 0–69 Ⓣ7764 1518, Ⓔacademyxinabajul@hotmail.com.

Cobán

Active Spanish School 3 C 6–12, Zona 1 Ⓣ7952 1432.
School of Arts and Language Finca Tzalampec, 16 Av 2–50, Zona 1 Ⓣ7953 9062, Ⓔalfonsotujab@yahoo.com.mx.

Monterrico

Proyecto Lingüístico ⓣ5619 8200, ⓦwww.espanol.netfirms.com.

Todos Santos Cuchumatán

Hispano Maya opposite *Hotelito Todos Santos* ⓣ7763 0717, ⓦwww.hispanomaya.org.
Nuevo Amanacer ⓔescuela_linguistica@yahoo.com.
Proyecto Lingüístico Mam contact the Proyecto Lingüístico Quetzalteco de Español in Quetzaltenango.

Nebaj

Nebaj Language School 3C, El Descanco ⓣ5801 5087, ⓦwww.nebaj.org.

Petén

Eco-Escuela San Andrés, Lago de Petén Itzá ⓣ5498 4539, ⓦwww.ecoescuelaespanol.org.
Escuela Bio-Itzá San José, Lago de Petén Itzá ⓣ7926 1363, ⓔbioitza@guate.net.
Mundo Maya ⓣ928 8321, ⓦwww.mundomayaguatemala.com.
Nueva Juventud San Andrés, Lago de Petén Itzá ⓣ711 0040, ⓦwww.volunteerpeten.com.

Copán, Honduras

Guacamaya one block north of the parque ⓣ & ⓕ651 4360, ⓦwww.guacamaya.com.
Ixbalanque two blocks west of the parque ⓣ & ⓕ651 4432, ⓦwww.ixbalananque.com.

Utila, Honduras

Central America Spanish School Main St ⓣ & ⓕ440 1707, ⓦwww.ca-spanish.com.

Volunteer and paid work

There are dozens of excellent organizations offering voluntary work placements in Guatemala. Medical and health specialists are always desperately needed, though there are always openings in other areas, from work helping to improve the lives of street children to environmental projects and wildlife conservation. The best place to start a search for organizations is on the Web or in Guatemala itself.

Project Mosaic Guatemala, 3 Av Norte, Antigua (ⓣ7832 0955, ⓦwww.promosaico.org), has links to over fifty groups, while Quetzaltenango-based Entremundos at 6 C 7–31, Zona 1 (ⓣ7761 2179, ⓦwww.entremundos.org), has excellent contacts with dozens of local development projects.

As for paid work, teaching English is your best bet, particularly if you have an ELT (English Language Teaching) or TEFL (Teaching English as a Foreign Language) qualification. Check the English schools in Guatemala City and Quetzaltenango (listed in the phone books). All language schools employ student coordinators to liaise between staff and pupils – though you'll need near-fluent Spanish. In Antigua, there are always a few vacancies for staff in the gringo bars and jade showrooms. The English-language press (the *Revue* and the *Guatemala Post*) and notice boards in the popular bars and restaurants in Antigua and Quetzaltenango also occasionally advertise vacancies. Finally, in the Bay Islands steady work is available in the dive centres for dive masters and instructors, and in the bars and restaurants, though pay is poor.

Project websites and email addresses

Ak'Tenamit ⓦwww.aktenamit.org. Health, education and agriculture volunteer positions in a large, established project, working with Q'eqchi' Maya in the Río Dulce region.
Alternatives ⓦwww.alternatives.ca. Canadian organization with numerous development projects in Central America.
Animal Aware ⓦwww.animalaware.org. Help out in an animal welfare centre near Sumpango.
Arcas ⓦwww.arcasguatemala.com. Volunteers needed in Petén to help rehabilitate animals kept illegally as pets for release back into the wild, and opportunities to help out in a sea-turtle reserve at Hawaii on the Pacific coast.
Casa Alianza ⓦwww.casa-alianza.org. Charity helping street children in Guatemala and throughout Central America. The work is extremely demanding and volunteers need to give several months' commitment.
Casa Guatemala ⓦwww.casa-guatemala.org. Teachers, doctors, nurses and helpers needed to work with street children and orphans in the Río Dulce region.
Casa Xelajú ⓦwww.casaxelaju.com/volunteer. Language school with myriad opportunities and links to social projects in the Quetzaltenango region.
Council on International Educational Exchange ⓦwww.ciee.org. Large US-based organization with many voluntary programmes.
Escuela de la Calle ⓦescueladelacalle.org. Help educate and empower street kids in Quetzaltenango.

Gap Year Ⓦ www.gap-year.com. UK-based organization with links to lots of volunteer and work placements. Also publishes the *Gap-Year Guidebook*.
Habitat for Humanity Ⓦ www.habitat.org/intl. House-building projects in Guatemala and elsewhere in Central America.
Hospital de la Familia Ⓦ www.hospitaldelafamilia.org. Doctors, nurses and medical staff needed to help out in the San Marcos region of the western highlands.
Idealist Ⓦ www.idealist.org. A massive database of links to a wide range of projects in the region – from ecotourism to human-rights work, with both voluntary and paid work opportunities.
International Voluntary Programs Association Ⓦ www.volunteerinternational.org. Dozens of voluntary opportunities throughout Central America in all fields.
NISGUA Ⓦ www.nisgua.org. Coordinates the Guatemalan Accompaniment Project, which monitors human-rights workers deemed to be at risk in Guatemala; minimum commitment of one year.
Peace Corps Ⓦ www.peacecorps.gov. US institution that recruits volunteers for two-year postings throughout Central America. Must be a US citizen.
Project Honduras Ⓦ www.projecthonduras.com. Voluntary work opportunities for medical personnel, teachers, architects and builders in Honduras.
Proyecto Eco-Quetzal Ⓦ www.ecoquetzal.org. Opportunities in the Verapaz region for people with experience in ecotourism or agriculture. A six-month commitment is required.
Remote Area Medical Corp Ⓦ www.ramusa.org. Voluntary physicians, eye specialists, surgeons, dentists, nurses and veterinarians needed to work in poor areas of Central America.
Upavim Ⓦ www.upavim.org. Community development work in Guatemala City, with opportunities for nursery workers and kids' tutors.
Volunteers for Peace Ⓦ www.vfp.org. Large US-based nonprofit group that organizes work camps in the region.

Travellers with specific needs

Whether you're trying to placate a sobbing child or steering a wheelchair around a crowded market, you'll find that most Guatemalans are extremely helpful and courteous.

Travellers with disabilities

Disabled travellers are faced with many obstacles when travelling in Guatemala. Wheelchair users will have to negotiate their way over cobbled streets, cracked (or non-existent) pavements and potholed roads in cities, towns and villages throughout the country. Getting around Guatemala by public transport can be exhausting for anyone, but trying to clamber aboard a packed chicken bus with a wheelchair or walking sticks, even with a friend to help, presents a whole set of other challenges. Nevertheless, plenty of disabled travellers do successfully get their way around the country. Most of the main sites are connected by tourist shuttle minibuses, which pick you up from your hotel, and have a driver whose job it is to assist passengers with their luggage. Many Guatemalan hotels are low rise (and larger, upmarket places often have lifts and ramps), so it shouldn't be too difficult to find an easily accessible room. You'll only find disabled toilets in the most expensive hotels, however.

Contacts in the US and Canada

Access-Able Ⓦ www.access-able.com. Online resource for travellers with disabilities.
Directions Unlimited 123 Green Lane, Bedford Hills, NY 10507 Ⓣ 1-800/533-5343 or 914/241-1700. Travel agency specializing in bookings for people with disabilities.
Mobility International USA 451 Broadway, Eugene, OR 97401 Ⓣ 541/343-1284, Ⓦ www.miusa.org. Information and referral services, access guides, tours and exchange programmes.

Society for the Advancement of Travelers with Handicaps 347 5th Ave, New York, NY 10016 ⓣ212/447-7284, ⓦwww.sath.org. Nonprofit educational organization that has actively represented travellers with disabilities since 1976. Annual membership US$45; US$30 for students and seniors.
Wheels Up! ⓣ1-888/389-4335, ⓦwww.wheelsup.com. Provides discounted airfare, tour and cruise prices for disabled travellers; also publishes a free monthly newsletter and maintains a comprehensive website.

Contacts in the UK and Ireland

Holiday Care 2nd floor, Imperial Building, Victoria Rd, Horley, Surrey RH6 7PZ ⓣ0845/124 9971 or 0208/760 0072, ⓦwww.holidaycare.org.uk. Provides free lists of accessible accommodation abroad, plus a list of accessible attractions in the UK. Information on financial help for holidays available.
Irish Wheelchair Association Blackheath Drive, Clontarf, Dublin 3 ⓣ01/818 6400, ⓦwww.iwa.ie. Useful information provided about travelling abroad with a wheelchair.
Tripscope Alexandra House, Albany Rd, Brentford, Middlesex TW8 0NE ⓣ08457/585 641, ⓦwww.tripscope.org.uk. This registered charity provides a national telephone information service offering free advice.

Contacts in Australia and New Zealand

Australian Council for Rehabilitation of the Disabled PO Box 60, Curtin ACT 2605 ⓣ02/6282 4333 (also TTY), ⓦwww.acrod.org.au. Provides lists of travel agencies and tour operators for people with disabilities.
Disabled Persons Assembly 4/173–175 Victoria St, Wellington ⓣ04/801 9100 (also TTY), ⓦwww.dpa.org.nz. Resource centre with lists of travel agencies and tour operators for people with disabilities.

Travelling with children

It can be exceptionally rewarding to travel with children in Guatemala. Most locals have children at an early age, and as families are much larger than in the West, your kids will always have some company. By bringing your children along to Guatemala, you'll take a big step toward dismantling the culture barrier, plus families can expect an extra warm welcome. Hotels, well used to putting up big Guatemalan families, are usually extremely accommodating.

Obviously, you'll have to take a few extra precautions with your children's health, paying particular care to hygiene and religiously applying sunscreen. Dealing with the sticky tropical heat of Petén is likely to be one of the biggest difficulties, but elsewhere humidity is much less of a problem. As young children are rarely enthralled by either modern highland or ancient Maya culture, you may want to plan some **excursions**: the giant Xocomil water park and Parque Xetulul theme park (see p.242 in the Guide) and Auto Safari Chapín (also see p.255) make great days out for kids. The Museo de los Niños and Aurora zoo in Guatemala City (see p.92) are a lot of fun too. Take extra care if you head for the Pacific coast beaches, as every year several children (and adults) drown in the strong undertow.

If you're planning to bring a **baby** to Guatemala, you'll find disposable nappies (diapers) are widely available in supermarkets and pharmacies in major towns; you'll need to take an extra stock if you're visiting remote areas.

Directory

Addresses Almost all addresses are based on the grid system that's used in most towns, with avenidas running in one direction (north to south) and calles in the other. All addresses specify the street first, then the block, and end with the zone. For example, the address "Av la Reforma 3–55, Zona 1" means that house is on Avenida la Reforma, between 3 and 4 calles, at no. 55, in Zona 1. Almost all towns have numbered streets, but in some places the old names are also used. In Antigua calles and avenidas are also divided according to their direction from the central plaza – north, south, east or west (*norte*, *sur*, *oriente* and *poniente*). *Diagonales* (diagonals) are what you'd expect – a street that runs in an oblique direction.

Airport departure tax For international flights it's US$30 (though it's included in the price of some tickets), while for domestic flights it's US$0.80. The tax is payable only in cash, either in quetzals or dollars.

Bags If you're planning to travel around by bus – and certainly if you're going to do some walking with your gear as well – then a backpack is by far the best option. Guatemalans have a word for backpackers, *mochileros*, and consider them to be slightly quirky because they're always running around with huge bags (*mochilas*) on their backs. Whatever you pack your stuff in, make sure it's tough enough to handle being thrown on and off the tops of buses.

Contraception Condoms (*preservativos*) are available from pharmacies in all the main towns, though they are quite pricey. Some makes of the Pill are available – mostly those manufactured in the US – but these are also expensive, so it's more sensible to bring enough to last for your entire stay. Bear in mind that diarrhoea can reduce the reliability of the Pill (or any other drug) as it may not be in your system long enough to be fully absorbed.

Electricity 110–120 volts. Plug connections (two flat prongs) are the same as those used in North America. Anything from Britain or Europe will need a transformer and a plug adapter. Cuts in the supply and wild fluctuations in the current are fairly common.

Embassies and consulates See the Guatemala City "Listings" section in Chapter 1 of the Guide. Mexico has consulates in Quetzaltenango and Retalhuleu; Honduras has consulates in Esquipulas and Puerto Barrios.

Gay travellers Homosexuality is legal for consenting adults aged 18 or over. However, though Guatemalan society is not as overtly machismo as many Latin American countries, it's wise to be discreet and avoid too much affection in public. There's a small, almost entirely male, scene in Guatemala City.

Metric weights and measures

1 ounce = 28.3 grams
1 pound = 454 grams
2.2 pounds = 1 kilogram
1 pint = 0.47 litre
1 quart = 0.94 litre
1 gallon = 3.78 litres
1 inch = 2.54 centimetres
1 foot = 0.3 metre
1 yard = 0.91 metre
1.09 yards = 1 metre
1 mile = 1.61 kilometres
0.62 miles = 1 kilometre

Guatemalan Maya also use the *legua*, a distance of about four miles, which is roughly the distance a person can walk in an hour. *Yardas* are yards, *pies* are feet.

Indigenous fabrics are often sold by the *vara*, an old Spanish measure of about 33 inches, while land is sometimes measured by the *cuerda*, a square with sides of 32 *varas*. The larger local units are the *manzana*, equivalent to three-quarters of a hectare or 1.73 acres, and the *caballeria*, which is 45.12 hectares.

Laundry Most inexpensive places will have somewhere where you can wash and dry your own clothes. Virtually every town has at least one laundry; most will wash and dry for you, costing little more than self-service laundries, which are rare.

Metric weights and measures Guatemalans use a peculiar mix of both: gasoline is sold by the gallon (*galón*) and fruit by the pound (*libra*). However, road distances are measured in kilometres (*kilometro*) and height is tracked in metres (*metros*).

Religion Guatemala is the least Catholic of all Latin American countries. It's estimated that around 35 percent of the population now belong to one of several dozen US-based Protestant churches – for more about this evangelical movement, see Contexts at the end of this book. Many of Guatemala's Catholics also continue to practice ancient Maya religious customs in the indigenous villages of the highlands. There has been a resurgence of interest in Maya spiritualism among young, educated Guatemalans since the end of the civil war, and attending "shamanic colleges" has become fashionable. Guatemala City also has tiny Jewish and Muslim communities.

Time zones Guatemala is on the equivalent of Central Standard Time in North America, six hours behind GMT. Daylight saving is not used. There is very little seasonal change – it gets light around 6am, with sunset at around 5.30pm in December and a little later in June.

Tipping In restaurants a ten percent tip is appropriate, but in most places, especially the cheaper ones, tipping is the exception rather than the rule. Taxi drivers are not normally tipped.

Toilets Nearly always Western-style (the squat toilet is very rare), with a bucket beside the bowl for your toilet paper. Standards vary greatly throughout the country, but in general the further you are from a city the worse the condition. Public toilets are few and far between; some are filthy, while others are well looked after by an attendant who usually sells toilet paper. The most common names are *baños* or *servicios*, and the signs are *damas* (women) and *caballeros* (men).

Guide

Guide

1

Guatemala City, Antigua and around

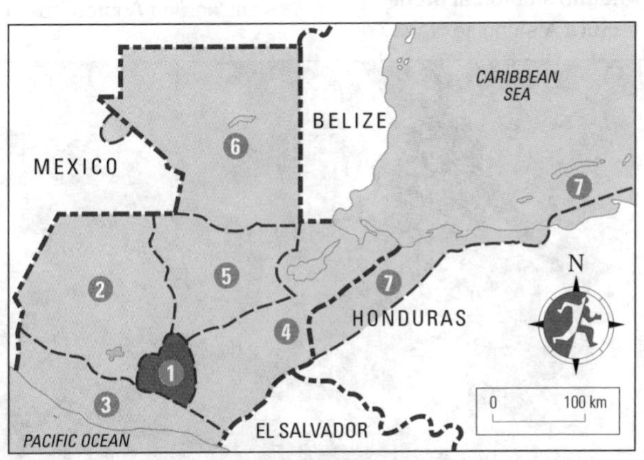

CHAPTER 1

Highlights

* **Museo Nacional de Arqueología y Etnología** Guatemala's greatest Maya sculptures and artefacts, under one roof. **See p.92**

* **Volcán de Pacaya** Hike this active volcano for a peek into its fume-belching cone. **See p.101**

* **Semana Santa** Witness the sombre ceremony and processions of the continent's most fervent Easter-week celebrations. **See p.112**

* **Antigua's colonial architecture** A stunning legacy of Baroque churches, elegant municipal buildings and graceful plazas has earned the Spainish colonial capital designation as a World Heritage site. **See pp.112–118**

* **Gourmet dining** Feast on a cornucopia of global cuisine, in sumptuous surrounds, in Antigua's remarkable array of restaurants. **See pp.118–120**

* **San Simón (Maximón)** Soak up the scene at the pagan temple of Guatemala's liquor-swilling, cigar-smoking "evil saint" in San Andrés Itzapa. **See p.128**

△ Penitents during Semana Santa, Antigua

1

Guatemala City, Antigua and around

Situated just forty kilometres apart in Guatemala's highlands, the two cities of Guatemala City and Antigua could hardly be more different. The capital, Guatemala City, is a fume-filled maelstrom of industry and commerce with few attractions to detain the traveller, though a day or two spent visiting the museums and soaking up the (limited) cultural scene won't be wasted. Antigua is everything the capital is not: tranquil, urbane and resplendent with spectacular colonial buildings and myriad cosmopolitan cafés, restaurants and hotels. Not surprisingly, most travellers choose to base themselves here.

Guatemala City sprawls across a huge upland basin, surrounded on three sides by low hills and volcanic cones. The capital was moved here in 1776 after the seismic destruction of Antigua, but the site had been of importance long before the arrival of the Spanish. These days, its shapeless and swelling mass, ringed by shanty towns, ranks as the largest city in Central America, with a metropolitan area that's home to more than three million people; and it's the undisputed centre of politics, power and wealth.

The capital has an intensity and vibrancy that are both its fascination and its horror, and for many visitors dealing with the city is an exercise in damage limitation, as they struggle through a swirling mass of bus fumes and crowds. The centre of the city is run-down and polluted, largely abandoned by the affluent middle classes and blue-chip businesses who long ago fled to the suburbs. But efforts are being made by a small group of conservationists to preserve what's left of the **centro histórico** in Zona 1, and a smattering of new cafés and bars have opened in restored buildings in the heart of the city. Some of the most exciting developments are taking place in the Cuatro Grados Norte area of Zona 4, where an expanding group of hip bars and restaurants represent the city's most interesting scene. These advances have hardly transformed "Guate" into a hotbed of culture, however, and most travellers still choose to spend as little time as possible in the place. Nevertheless the city is the crossroads of the country, and you'll almost certainly end up here at some time, if only to hurry between bus terminals or catch a plane to Petén.

Antigua, on the other hand, is the most impressive colonial city in Central America, and its tremendous wealth of architectural riches has ensured that it has become one of Guatemala's premier tourist attractions. With just 30,000 inhabitants and a small central zone, the city's graceful cobbled streets are ideal to explore on foot. Spanish architects and Maya labourers constructed a classically designed city of elegant squares, churches, monasteries and grand houses, and it's this magnificent historical legacy that ensures Antigua's continuing appeal. The city's renowned **language schools** also attract students from all over the world, with the education and tourism industries forming the city's prime source of wealth.

The countryside around Antigua and Guatemala City – a delightful landscape of volcanoes, pine forests, meadows, *milpas* and coffee farms, punctuated with villages – also begs to be explored. Looming over the capital is the **Volcán de Pacaya**, one of the most active volcanoes in Latin America. It has been spewing sulphurous gas and molten rock regularly for years now, and you can swing through the forest beneath the cone on cables in the Parque Natural Canopy Calderas. Close to Antigua the volcanoes of **Agua** and **Acatenango** are also well worth climbing, the latter offering a terrific perspective of the active neighbouring cone of Fuego.

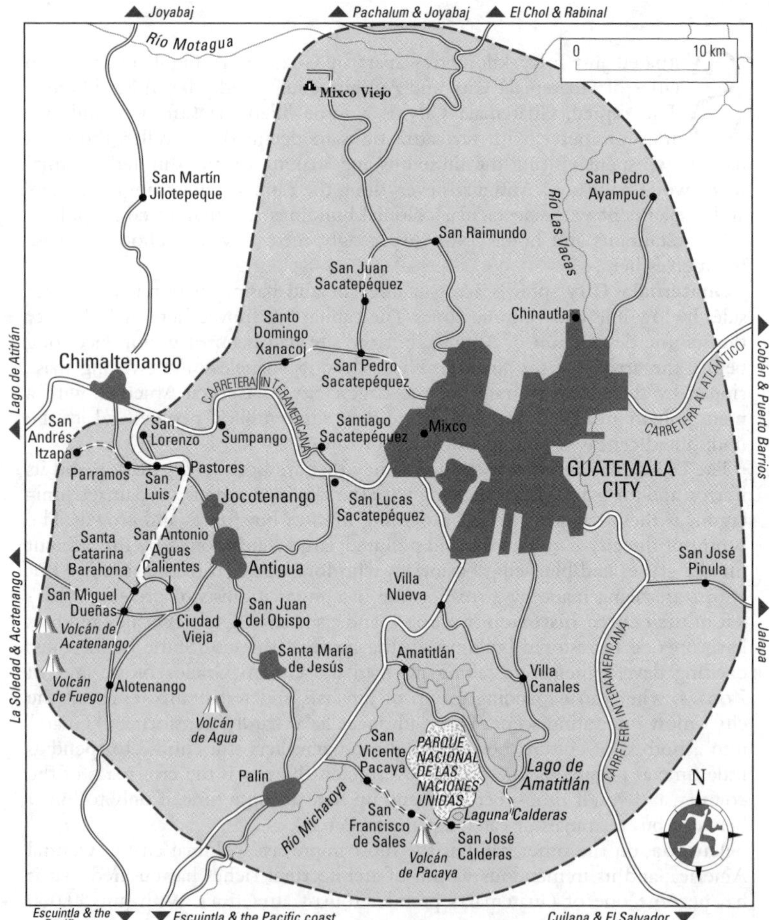

There are countless interesting villages to visit in this area, including **San Andrés Itzapa**, where there is a pagan shrine to the "evil saint" San Simón; **Jocotenango**, which boasts a pair of museums dedicated to coffee and Maya music; and Santa María de Jesús, a Maya village where the trail to the Volcán de Agua begins. The one Maya ruin in the area that can compete with the lowland sites further north is **Mixco Viejo**; it's tricky to get to unless you have your own transport, but its setting, in splendid isolation, is tremendous. Little evidence remains of the ancient capital of **Kaminaljuyú**, today almost buried in the capital's suburbs, but this was once one of the largest and most important cities of the Maya World.

Guatemala City and around

GUATEMALA CITY is not a place to visit for its beauty or architectural charm. If you arrive in the central area, your first impressions are grim, as a depressing vision of urban blight unfolds – potholed streets choked by fumes from rasping buses, thoroughfares blocked by street stalls and many of the city's fine buildings in a state of advanced decay. Understandably, few travellers take to *la capital*, and many avoid it completely.

But if you do decide to spend a day or two in the city, it does offer some metropolitan pleasures that you won't find elsewhere in the country. There are two first-rate **museums** devoted to Maya archeology and another to the country's terrific textile tradition. Culturally, a hip **artistic scene** is emerging in the small but vibrant area of Cuatro Grados Norte, where you might catch an alternative rock band or find a DJ spinning progressive electronic mixes. It's also possible to find cinemas screening independent European and Latin American movies, as well as multi-screen theatres showing Hollywood blockbusters in vast North American–style shopping malls.

Guatemala City's **climate** is also benign: the city's altitude means that the heat here never gets too oppressive, and when you escape the pollution of the central area, the lush greenery of the outer suburbs gives it a certain appeal. Its setting is also dramatic, positioned in a massive highland bowl on a site that was a centre of population and political power well before the Spanish arrived in the early sixteenth century.

That said, the disparities of life in the city are extreme, with glass skyscrapers towering over sprawling slums and shoeless widows peddling cigarettes and chewing gum to designer-clad nightclubbers. You should take a little extra care in the capital as **street crime** is a problem, mainly involving bag snatching – be particularly careful at transport terminals. Gang violence is a serious issue in the poor outer suburbs, though this rarely affects the central zones, and is highly unlikely to concern travellers.

Some history

The pre-conquest city of **Kaminaljuyú**, its ruins still scattered amongst the western suburbs, was well established here two thousand years ago. In Early Classic times (250–600AD), as a result of an alliance with the great northern power of Teotihuacán (near present-day Mexico City), Kaminaljuyú came to dominate the highlands. The city controlled key Mesoamerican trade routes and an obsidian mine at El Chayal, giving it a virtual monopoly over this essential commodity, and also had access to a supply of quetzal feathers, another highly valued item.

At the height of its prosperity, Kaminaljuyú was home to a population of some 50,000. However, following the decline of Teotihuacán and its influence, about 600 AD, it was surpassed by the great lowland centres, including Tikal, Calakmul and Yaxjá. By around 700 AD, it was abandoned.

Eight centuries later, in the early years of Spanish occupation, the only village in this area was La Ermita, founded in 1620. The tribes of the west had preoccupied the conquistadors, forcing the Spanish to establish their capital at Iximché, before eventually settling on Santiago de los Caballeros, later known as **Antigua**. But in 1773, following months of devastating earthquakes in Santiago, Capitán General Mayorga and some 4200 followers held their first planning council at Guatemala City's present site to commence construction of a **new city**. The city's layout followed the Spanish colonial model of a grid street pattern, with a main plaza plotted with a cathedral and administrative buildings. Early development was slow: the people of Antigua were reluctant to leave, despite being bullied by endless decrees and deadlines. Although waves of smallpox and cholera eventually persuaded some to move, by 1800 the population of the new capital was still only 25,000.

The splendour of the former capital was hard to recreate, and the new city's growth was steady but hardly dramatic. An 1863 census listed the main structures as 1206 residences, 7 warehouses, 130 shops, 28 churches, 1 slaughterhouse, 2 forts, 12 schools, and 25 fountains and public laundries. When Eadweard Muybridge took some of the earliest photographs of the city in 1875, it was still little more than a large village with a theatre, a government palace and a fort.

One of the factors retarding the city's growth was the existence of a major rival, Quetzaltenango (Xela), which competed with the capital in both size and importance, until 1902, when it was razed to the ground by a massive earthquake. After this, many wealthy families moved to the capital, finally establishing it as the country's primary city. By then, Guatemala City's population had already been boosted by the exodus from another major earthquake, this time in Antigua. Inevitably, the capital's turn came. On Christmas Eve 1917, Guatemala City was shaken by the first in a series of devastating tremors, and not until early February, after six long weeks of destruction, did the ground stabilize and the dust settle. This time, however, there was nowhere to run; spurred on by the celebrations of a century of independence, and the impetus of the eccentric President Ubico, reconstruction began.

Since then Guatemala City has grown at an incredible rate, tearing ahead of the rest of the country at a pace that still shows little sign of letting up. Flight from the fields, caused by a chronic shortage of land and employment in the countryside, has further boosted the city's growth; this phenomenom was exacerbated during the 36-year civil war by the army's scorched-earth tactics, employed to combat guerrilla groups. According to some estimates, six hundred new campesinos arrive in the city every day, **economic migrants** high on hope and dreams of a fresh start. In some ways the capital is becoming a city of refugees, filled with displaced people, many Maya, who struggle to settle here. The deep ravines that surround the city, thought by the original Spanish planners to offer protection from the force of earthquakes, are now filling rapidly with rubbish and shanty towns, while street crime increases daily.

Orientation, arrival and information

Although the scale of Guatemala City, with its suburbs sprawled across some 21 **zones**, can seem overwhelming at first glance, the layout is straightforward and the central area, which covers most places of interest, is not that large. Like almost all Guatemalan towns it's arranged on a strict grid pattern, with avenidas running north–south and calles east–west.

Broadly speaking, the city divides into two distinct halves. The northern section, centred on **Zona 1**, is the old part of town, containing the central plaza, or Parque Central, the main shopping streets (5 and 6 avenidas), fast-food restaurants, cinemas, the main post office, and most of the bus company terminals.

To the south, **Zona 4** serves as a buffer between the two parts of town; here you'll find the **Centro Cívico**, home of the main administrative buildings, the tourist office, the trendy Cuatro Grados Norte area, the central market, and main second-class bus terminal and the National Theatre.

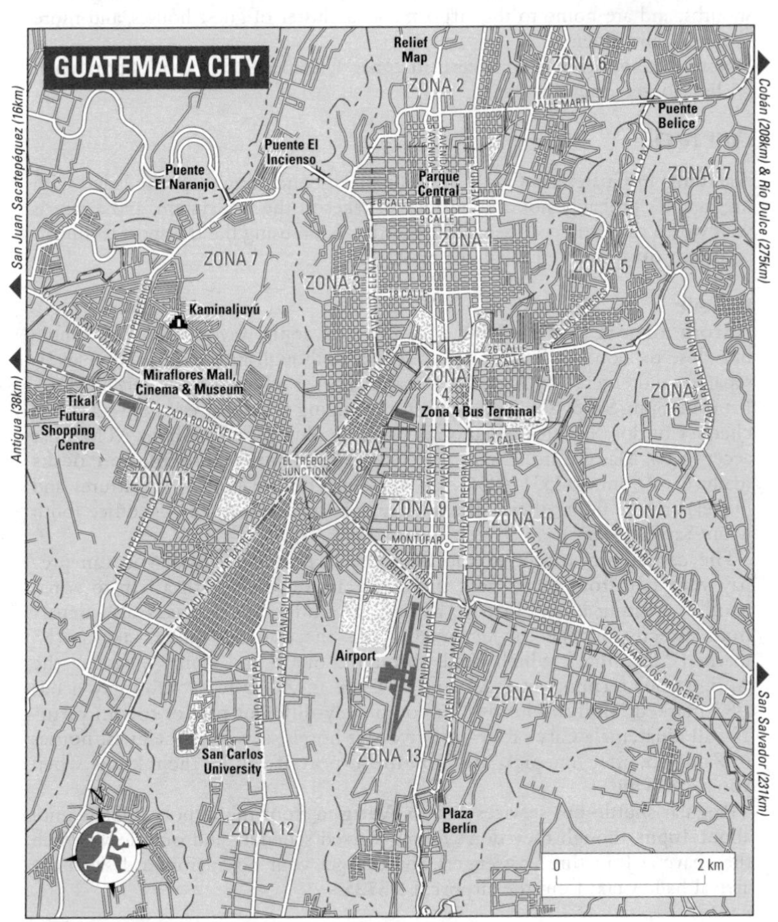

Addresses in Guatemala City

The system of **street numbering** in the capital is confusing at first, as the same numbers and street names are given to different streets in different zones. However, once learned, the system is pretty intuitive.

When it comes to finding an address, always check for the **zone** first and then the street. For example "4 Av 9–14, Zona 1" is in Zona 1, on 4 Avenida between 9 and 10 calles, house number 14. You may see street numbers written as 1a, 7a etc, rather than simply 1, 7. This is technically more correct, since the names of the streets are not One Avenue and Seven Street, but First (*primera*), Seventh (*séptima*) and so on. A capital "A" used as a suffix indicates a smaller street between two large ones: 1 Calle A is a short street between 1 and 2 calles.

Further south still, the modern half of the city comprises wealthy **zonas 9 and 10**, which are separated by the main artery of Avenida La Reforma. Continuing south, the neighbouring **zonas 13 and 14** hold wealthy, leafy suburbs, and are home to the airport, zoo, a cluster of guest houses, and more museums and cinemas.

Note that **security** is a concern in zonas 1, 2 and 4 after about 8pm, when it's best to get around by taxi.

Arrival

Arriving in Guatemala City is always a bit disconcerting. If you're laden with luggage, it's probably not a good idea to take on the bus system, and a taxi is well worth the extra cost (see p.82). For details on using the transport terminals to **move on** from the capital, see pp.98–99.

By air

Aurora airport (Ⓣ2334 7680) is in Zona 13, some way south of the centre, but close to Zona 10. The domestic terminal, though in the same complex, is separate, and entered by Avenida Hincapié. There's a Banco del Quetzal (Mon–Fri 6am–8pm, Sat & Sun 8am–6pm) for changing US dollar cash and travellers' cheques (it does *not* change euros or pounds), plus several 24-hour ATMs that accept Visa, MasterCard, Cirrus and Plus cards. **Tourist information desks** (daily 6am–9pm; Ⓣ2331 4256) can be found on the (upper) departures and (lower) arrivals floors; there's also a Telgua phone office and a post office (both Mon–Sat 7am–9pm).

The easiest way to get to and from the airport is by **taxi**: you can pre-pay your fare from a taxi desk inside the arrivals hall, with a trip to zonas 9 or 10 costing about US$10, Zona 1 around US$12. **Buses** also depart from directly outside the terminal, across the concrete plaza: take a #83 marked "Terminal", which heads through Zona 9 and Zona 4, passing the Antigua bus terminal at 5 Av and 18 Calle in Zona 1. (Confusingly, a bus #83 marked "Bolívar" heads to a completely different part of town.) Virtually all Guatemala City's four- and five-star hotels, as well as the guest houses in Zona 13, offer free pick-ups from the airport, if you let them know when you're arriving.

Regular shuttle-bus services run **to Antigua** from the airport (US$8) until about 10pm, though they don't follow a fixed schedule and only leave when they have at least three passengers. You can get your ticket from a desk in the arrival hall. A taxi from the airport is US$25.

By bus

Travelling by **first-class** (pullman) **bus**, you'll arrive at the private terminal of whichever of the dozen or so companies you're using. Most of these terminals are located in Zona 1, including those for companies which run to Petén and Mexico, Cobán and the western highlands. Note that many of these depots are located in an unsavoury part of the city; be on your guard for petty thieves and take a taxi to your hotel.

If you've come by second-class "chicken bus" **from Antigua**, you'll arrive in Zona 1 at the junction of 18 Calle, between 4 and 5 avenidas. Arriving in the city from the western highlands by second-class bus, prepare yourself for the jungle of the **Zona 4 bus terminal**, which has to rate as Guatemala City's most chaotic corner; it's also not the safest part of town after dark, so take a taxi to your hotel. The Melva terminal for San Salvador is very close by on 3 Avenida and 1 Calle.

For more information about the main bus companies and bus departure times, see "Moving on from Guatemala City" on pp.98–99.

Information and maps

The main Inguat **tourist office** (Mon–Fri 8am–4pm; ⓣ2331 1333, ⓔinformacion@inguat.gob.gt) is at 7 Av 1–17, Zona 4. The information desk on the ground floor has plenty of brochures and usually a map of the country plus someone on hand who speaks English. Another Inguat desk can be found inside the Palacio Municipal on the Parque Central (same hours as above). For detailed hiking maps, go to the Instituto Geográfico Militar (Mon–Fri 8am–4pm), Av las Américas 5–76, Zona 13. Bus #65 from the Centro Cívico gets you nearest, or take a taxi.

City transport

Even locals are often baffled by Guatemala City's anarchic web of **bus routes**. Most of Zona 1's streets are one-way, so buses return along different roads. The city authorities (who have been trying to regulate services better recently) also reroute buses from time to time. Add to this the fact that some buses with the same numbers operate along different routes, and confusion reigns – though at least fares are cheap (US$0.15).

After 10pm pick-ups known as *ruteleros* effectively operate as buses, running along the main routes all night.

Useful bus routes

83 Bolívar Airport–zoo–Blvd Liberación–Av Bolívar–5 Av–Zone 1

83 Terminal Airport–7 Av Zone 9–Zone 4 bus terminal–9 Av Zone 1

101 6 Av Zone 1–Av La Reforma–20 C Zone 10. This route passes many of the embassies, the Popol Vuh and Ixchel museums and the Los Próceres mall.

76 6 Av Zone 1–Zone 9–Obelisco–20 C Zone 10

Terminal Any bus marked "terminal" – and there are plenty of these on 4 Av in Zona 1 – will take you to the main bus terminal in Zona 4.

Bolívar/Trébol Any bus marked "Bolívar" or "Trébol" will take you along the western side of the city, down Av Bolívar and to the Trébol junction, for connections to the western highlands.

Note that Guatemala City has a ferocious **rush hour**, which leaves many roads throughout the city jammed between 6.30 and 9am and from 4 to 7.30pm.

Taxis

It's well worth taking a taxi to your hotel from the bus terminals and to get around at night. Although both metered and non-metered taxis ply the city's streets, it's best to stick to **metered cabs**: either the excellent Amarillo (Ⓣ2332 1515) cabs, which will pick you up from anywhere in the city, or Blanco y Azul (Ⓣ2360 0903), which are also reliable. The fare from Zona 1 to Zona 10 is about US$6. If you opt for a **non-metered taxi**, use your bargaining skills and fix the price beforehand.

Accommodation

Accommodation in Guatemala City comes to suit all pockets, though you'll pay more here than in the rest of the country. Most budget and mid-range hotels are in **Zona 1**, which is not a particularly safe neighbourhood at night (or a great place for wandering around in search of a room). Many travellers are now choosing to stay close to the airport, in **Zona 13**, where there are some good options – all of which offer free airport pick-ups and drop-offs, though be sure to book ahead. The disadvantage with this quiet, suburban location is that there are very few restaurants and cafés close by. Guatemala City's luxury hotels are clustered in a relatively safe part of town, in **zonas 9 and 10**, within reach of the "Zona Viva", where there's a glut of dining options, bars and nightclubs. The Zona 13 guest houses are grouped around the airport 2–3km from Zona 10.

Zona 1

Chalet Suizo 14 C 6–82 Ⓣ2251 3786, Ⓕ2232 0429. This efficient and comfortable place is opposite the police headquarters, so it should be safe enough. The Swiss-hostel-style, well-designed rooms are spotlessly clean, and there's a left-luggage facility. Private or shared bath; no double beds. ❹

Hotel Colonial 7 Av 14–19 Ⓣ2232 6722, Ⓕ2232 8671, Ⓦwww.hotelcolonial.net. Attractive hotel set in a historic building with a Spanish-style tiled lobby and a pleasingly formal dark wood and wrought iron interior. The accommodation offered is good value and comfortable, if slightly old-fashioned; the fairly large rooms come with or without private bathroom. ❹

Hotel Fénix 7 Av 15–81 Ⓣ2251 6625. This venerable place is still one of the better budget bets in the central area, and has friendly owners, clean rooms (some with private bath) and quirky café downstairs. ❷–❸

Hotel PanAmerican 9 C 5–63 Ⓣ2232 6807, Ⓕ2251 8749, Ⓦwww.hotelpanamerican.com. Historic hotel set in the heart of town, exuding a formal, civilized air. The fair-sized rooms all have cable TV and private bathrooms, and the rate includes airport transfer. The restaurant is brilliant for Sunday breakfast. ❼

Hotel Posada Belén 13 C A 10–30 Ⓣ2253 4530, Ⓕ2251 3478, Ⓦwww.guateweb.com. A peaceful refuge from the fervour of the city's streets, the *Belén* occupies a beautiful old building, with a gorgeous little garden patio. The hosts can organize excursions, including walking tours of the city centre, and offer good cooking in the hotel restaurant. No children under 5. ❻

Hotel San Martín 16 C 7–65 Ⓣ2238 0319. Nothing fancy, but very cheap, clean rooms, some with private bath. The tariffs asked represent good value at the lower end of the scale. ❷–❸

Hotel Spring 8 Av 12–65 Ⓣ2232 2858, Ⓕ232 0107. An excellent deal and a safe location, though it's perennially popular so book ahead. Spacious rooms, with or without private bath, all come with cable TV and are set around a pretty colonial courtyard. Breakfast is available, plus free mineral water. ❸–❹

Pensión Meza 10 C 10–17 Ⓣ2232 3177 or 2253 4576. Legendary travellers' hangout, with plenty of 1960s-style decadence (and guests). Che Guevara stayed here back in the day. The dorms (US$3 per person) and doubles (some with private shower) are not too clean, but remain popular. There's a nice courtyard at the rear, a useful notice board, and ping-pong, plus the helpful owner speaks English. ❷

Zonas 9 and 10

Camino Real 14 C 0–20 ⓣ2333 3000, ⓕ2337 4313, ⓦwww.caminoreal.com.gt. Guatemala's first 5-star hotel has been long favoured by visiting heads of state, though the chintzy decor now looks rather dated. Excellent location in the heart of the Zona Viva, plus in-house bars, shops, business and sports facilities – including two pools, a spacious gym and floodlit tennis courts. Rooms from US$190. ❾

La Casa Grande Av La Reforma 7–67, Zona 10 ⓣ & ⓕ2332 0914, ⓦwww.casagrande-gua.com. Elegant villa hotel, with a comfortable, homely air and a helpful, welcoming staff. The lounge has a log fire in the cooler months, plus there are several patio areas, a bar and a restaurant. It's set slightly back from the road (so front-facing rooms do get some minor traffic noise), next to the US embassy. ❼

Holiday Inn 1 Av 13–22 ⓣ2332 2555, ⓕ2332 2584, ⓦwww.holidayinn.com.gt. Located in the heart of the Zona Viva, the hotel has 204 commodious rooms and suites, with an excellent buffet breakfast included in the rate. Amenities also include a restaurant, bar, business centre and Internet café. Rooms from US$120. ❾

Hotel Carillon 5 Av 11–25, Zona 9 ⓣ2332 4267, ⓕ2332 4036, ⓔhcarillon@guate.net.gt. Slightly unusual but good-value place in a great location. All the pleasant rooms in this small hotel have wood-panelled walls and carpeted floors, en-suite bathrooms and cable TV. Breakfast is included. ❺

Hotel Casa Santa Clara 12 C 4–51 ⓣ2339 1811, ⓕ2332 0775, ⓦwww.hotelcasasantaclara.com. Attractive hotel where the 14 stylish, modern rooms all have parquet wood floors, bedside lights and cable TV; there's also a quality restaurant and (free) Internet access for guests. Call for a free shuttle from the airport. ❼

Hotel Real Inter-Continental 14 C 2–51 ⓣ2379 4444, ⓕ2379 4445, ⓦwww.interconti.com. Without doubt the city's most stylish and sumptuous five-star address. A monumental lobby featuring fine art and modern sculpture sets the tone, and a hip bar, quality French and international restaurants, and a heated outdoor pool complete the scene. The 239 wonderful rooms are supremely comfortable with great beds, and many have good city views. From US$150. ❾

Mí Casa 5 Av A 13–51, Zona 9 ⓣ2339 2247, ⓦwww.hotelmicasa.com. This suburban guest house, located on a quiet street, has seven spacious, functional rooms (with more planned), all with cable TV and most with en-suite bathroom. The friendly people who run it offer free airport pick-up and complimentary continental or Guatemalan-style breakfast; there's Internet access, too. ❺–❻

Zona 13

El Aeropuerto Guest House 15 C A 7–32 ⓣ2332 3086, ⓕ2362 1264, ⓦwww.hotelaeropuerto.centroamerica.com. A stone's throw from the international airport (call for a free pick-up), this is a convenient, comfortable place. It has nine spotless rooms, with or without private bathroom, all with attractive Maya textile bedspreads. The English-speaking management serve up a free continental breakfast, and offer email and fax facilities. ❺

Dos Lunas 21 C 10–92 ⓣ & ⓕ2334 5264, ⓦwww.xelapages.com/doslunas. An extremely well-run guest house located on a safe, quiet suburban street close to the airport, with a second location in a suburban house around the corner. Lorena Artola, the young Guatemalan owner, speaks fluent English and offers reliable travel advice, and can arrange shuttle buses and taxis and almost anything else that you'll need. Free pick-up and drop-off as well as breakfast of eggs, toast, and coffee or tea. Very popular, so it's essential to book well ahead. US$10 per bed, double with bath. ❹

Economy Dorms 8 Av 17–74, Col Aurora I ⓣ2331 8029. This friendly guest house is within a short ride of the airport, and offers four private rooms (but no dorms) in a family's house – guests are welcome to mingle in the living room with the owners. A basic breakfast and airport transfers are included. ❹

Hostal Los Volcanes 16 C 8–00 ⓣ2360 3232, ⓦwww.hostallosvolcanes.com. Decent B&B, in a modern house close to the airport, with a four-bed dorm, clean rooms (some with private bathroom) and a pleasant sitting area. The management can also arrange dinner, luggage storage and transport connections. Breakfast included. Dorm US$15 per person; doubles ❹–❺

Las Tinajas 17 C A 6-81 ⓣ2334 7809, ⓔlastinajas@turbonett.com. Good new guest house 600m from the airport, with clean, secure rooms (with or without private bathroom). There's Internet access, free pick-up from the airport, and complimentary breakfast. ❺

The City

Sights are slim on the ground in Guatemala City, but a handful of places are well worth your attention while you're here. The Ixchel, Popol Vuh and Archeological **museums** are particularly good, while a few impressive renovated buildings can be found in Zona 1. If you're interested to see how the rich let their hair down, head for the Zona Viva in Zona 10, while Zona 1 is the place to see the big-city streetlife – hawkers, market vendors, evangelical preachers and prostitutes are all here in abundance.

Zonas 1 and 2: the old city

The hub of the old city is **Zona 1**, which is also the busiest and most claustrophobic part of town. This is the run-down **centro histórico**, a squalid world of low-slung, crumbling nineteenth-century town houses and faceless concrete blocks, broken pavements, car parking lots and plenty of noise and dirt. Tentative signs of regeneration are emerging here and there, as a committed group of planners and architects attempts to preserve the capital's heritage, and clusters of new bars and cafés are opening in historic buildings. But it's a process that will take decades to achieve, with the area beset by social problems and plagued by pollution and noise from thundering fume-belching buses. That said, the streets, thick with street vendors and urban bustle, harbour a certain brutal fascination and are undeniably the most exciting part of the capital.

The Parque Central and around

Zona 1's northern boundary runs just behind the Palacio Nacional, taking in the **Parque Central**, a square that forms the country's political and religious centre and the point from which all distances in Guatemala are measured. This plaza, currently concealing a large underground car park, was originally the scene of a huge central market, which now operates from a covered site behind the cathedral (see p.86). Nowadays the square is a fairly soulless place, patronized by bored taxi-drivers, *lustradores* (shoeshiners) and plenty of pigeons; it only really comes alive on Sundays and public holidays when a tide of Guatemalans descend on the square to stroll, chat and snack or to visit the excellent *huipil* market. Next to the giant Guatemalan flag in the centre of the square is a glass case that's supposed to contain an **eternal flame** dedicated to "the anonymous heroes for peace" – sadly, its glass sides have been vandalized and there's rarely a flicker in evidence.

Most of the imposing structures that face the parque today were put up after the 1917 earthquake, with the notable exception of the blue-tile-domed **cathedral** (daily 8am–noon & 3–7pm; free), which was completed in 1868. For years its grand facade, merging the Baroque and the Neoclassical, dominated the square, dwarfing all other structures. Its solid, squat form was designed to resist the force of earthquakes and, for the most part, it has succeeded. In 1917 the bell towers were brought down and the cupola fell, destroying the altar, but the central structure, though cracked and patched over the years, remains intact. Inside there are three main aisles, all lined with arching pillars, austere colonial paintings and intricate altars supporting an array of saints. Some of this collection was brought here from the original cathedral in Antigua when the capital was moved in 1776. However, the cathedral's most poignant aspect is outside: etched into the twelve pillars that support the entrance railings are the names of thousands of the "**disappeared**" victims of the civil war – children, parents and priests – including an astounding number from the department of El Quiché.

Iglesia de San Sebastián (250m), Parque Minerva and Relief Map (1.75km)
Trébol junction (1.25km) & Kaminaljuyú (3km)
0 250 m
N
EATING & DRINKING
Altuna 13
Arguileh 17
La Bodeguita del Centro 12
Café de Centro Histórico 7
Café La Otra Puerta 5
Cafe Restaurant Pereira 16
Las Cien Puertes 4
De Imeri 1
Dos Continentes 8
El Encuentro 9
Europa Bar 11
El Gran Pavo 14
Long Wah 2
L'Ostería 18
Nuevo Mundo 15
Parrillada Doña Sara 6
Rey Sol 3
Rey Sol 2 10
SUAE 18
Sucré Salé 19
ACCOMMODATION
Chalet Suizo E
Hotel Colonial F
Hotel Fénix G
Hotel Pan American A
Hotel Posada Belén D
Hotel San Martín H
Hotel Spring C
Pensión Meza B
BUSES
Transportes Álamo ★14
Buses to Panajachel ★15
Buses to Antigua ★8
Rutas Orientales; buses to Tecún Umán and Talismán ★11
Transportes Guerra ★10
Transportes Escobar y Monja Blanca ★5
Fuente del Norte and other 1st/2nd class buses to Petén ★7
Línea Dorada ★6
ADN ★3
Los Halcones ★2
Transportes Velásquez ★13
Rápidos Zacaleu ★1
Litegua ★4
Líneas Américas ★9
Transportes Galgos ★12
Palacio Nacional
Parque del Centenario
Parque Central
Cathedral
National Library
Mercado Central
Museo Nacional de Artes y Industrias Populares
Museo Nacional de Historia
San Miguel de Capuchinas
Iglesia de San Francisco
Police Headquarters
Parque Concordia
Casa Mima
Mercado La Placita
Museo del Ferrocarril
San José Fortress
Teatro Nacional
Banco de Guatemala
Estadio Nacional Mario Flores
Gran Centro Comercial
Santa Expiatorio
IGA
CUATRO GRADOS NORTE
Cultura Hispánica
Zona 4 Bus Terminal
Iglesia Yurrita
Botanical Gardens
Politécnica
Torre del Reformador
4 CALLE
5 CALLE
6 CALLE
7 CALLE
8 CALLE
9 CALLE
10 CALLE
11 CALLE
12 CALLE
12 CALLE A
13 CALLE
14 CALLE
15 CALLE
15A CALLE
16 CALLE
17 CALLE
18 CALLE
19 CALLE
20 CALLE
21 CALLE
22 CALLE
23 CALLE
24 CALLE
25 CALLE
26 CALLE
27 CALLE
28 CALLE
29 CALLE
30 CALLE
1 CALLE
2 CALLE
4 AVENIDA
5 AVENIDA
6 AVENIDA
6 AVENIDA A
7 AVENIDA
8 AVENIDA
9 AVENIDA
10 AVENIDA
10 AVENIDA A
11 AVENIDA
12 AVENIDA
15 AVENIDA
1 AVENIDA
2 AVENIDA
AVENIDA ELENA
AVENIDA CENTRO AMÉRICA
AVENIDA BOLÍVAR
AV. LA REFORMA
RUTA 1
RUTA 2
RUTA 3
RUTA 4
RUTA 5
RUTA 6
RUTA 7
RUTA 8
VIA 1
VIA 2
VIA 3
VIA 4
VIA 5
VIA 6
VIA 7
VIA 8
VIA 9
GUATEMALA CITY: ZONAS 1 & 4

Presiding over the entire northern end of the square, the gargantuan stone-faced **Palacio Nacional** (entrance by tour only, in English or Spanish, daily 9am–4.45pm; free) faces south towards the neon maze of Zona 1. The palace was started in 1939 under the auspices of President Ubico – a characteristically grand gesture from the man who believed that he was a reincarnation of Napoleon – and completed a year before he was ousted in 1944. For decades the palace housed the executive branch of the government, and periodically its steps have been fought over by assorted coupsters. The interior of the palace is set around two attractive Moorish-style courtyards, with the most impressive rooms being the **Salas de Recepción** (State Reception Rooms), at the front of the second floor. Along one wall is a row of flags and the country's coat of arms, topped with a stuffed quetzal, while the stained-glass windows represent key aspects of Guatemalan history. Back in the main body of the building the stairwells are decorated with murals, again depicting historical scenes, mixed in with images of totally unrelated events: one wall shows a group of idealized pre-conquest Maya, and another includes a portrait of Don Quixote.

Opposite the cathedral, the western side of the Parque Central merges into the **Parque del Centenario**, former site of the Palacio de los Capitanes Generales. A long single-storey building intended to be used as the National Palace, it was completed at the end of the nineteenth century, then promptly destroyed in the 1917 earthquake. For the 1921 centenary celebration a temporary wooden structure was set up in its place, but once this had served its purpose it went up in flames. After that it was decided to create a park instead, though today's concrete expanse is unremarkable in the extreme, with an ugly, shell-shaped bandstand which is occasionally used for live concerts and evangelical get-togethers. Squatting on the western side of the Parque del Centenario is the hulking Sixties-style **Biblioteca Nacional** (National Library), housing the archives of Central America.

Around the back of the cathedral is the concrete **Mercado Central** (Mon–Sat 6am–6pm, Sun 9am–noon), with a miserable mini-plaza and car park on its roof. Taking no chances, the architect of this building, which replaced an earlier version destroyed in the 1976 earthquake, apparently modelled the structure on a nuclear bunker, sacrificing any aesthetic concerns to the need for strength. Inside, you'll find textiles, leatherware and jewellery on the top floor; fruit, vegetables, snacks, flowers and plants in the middle; and **handicrafts**, mainly basketry and *típica*, in the basement. Unexpectedly, the market is a reasonably good spot to buy traditional weaving, with a comprehensive range of cloth from all over the country on offer. It is only visited by a trickle of tourists so prices are fair and the traders very willing to bargain. This was once the city's main food market but these days it's just one of many, and by no means the largest.

A block east of the market and one block south along 10 Avenida, you reach one of the city's less well-known museums, **Museo Nacional de Historia**, 9 C 9–70, Zona 1 (Mon–Fri 9am–4.30pm; US$1.30), which features a selection of artefacts relating to Guatemalan history, including documents, clothes and paintings. Probably the most interesting displays are the photographs by Eadweard Muybridge, who, in 1875, was one of the first people to undertake a study of the country. Less impressive is the **Museo Nacional de Artes y Industrias Populares**, half a block away at 10 Av 10–72 (Tues–Sun 9am–noon & 2–4.30pm; US$1.30), with its small, sadly neglected collection of painting, weaving, ceramics, musical instruments and Maya masks.

Along 6 and 7 avenidas

The garish heart of Zona 1 is formed by **6 and 7 avenidas**, running south of the Parque Central, thick with clothes shops, restaurants, cinemas, neon signs and bus fumes. What you can't buy in the shops is sold on the pavements, while *McDonald's* and *Pizza Hut* are all very much part of the scene. It's here that most people head on a Saturday night, when the traffic has to squeeze between hordes of pedestrians. By 11pm or so, though, the streets are largely deserted, left to the cigarette sellers and street urchins.

Heading down 7 Avenida, the main **post office** (Mon–Fri 8.30am–5pm, Sat 8.30am–1pm), at the junction of 12 Calle, is a spectacular Moorish-style building with a marvellous arch that spans the road. From here it's a short walk to **Casa Mima**, at the corner of 14 Calle and 8 Avenida (Mon–Fri 9am–12.30pm & 2–6pm, Sat 9am–5pm; US$2.50), an immaculately restored late nineteenth-century town house. Inside, there's a terrific collection of original Moderne, Art Deco and French neo-Rococo furnishings, offering a fascinating glimpse of a wealthy middle-class household. There are excellent explanatory leaflets, and usually an English-speaking guide, plus a delightful little café, with good coffee and cookies, on the rear patio.

A block and a half west of here on 14 Calle are the **Police Headquarters**, which occupy an outlandish-looking mock castle complete with imitation medieval battlements. Next door, on 6 Avenida, the church of **Iglesia de San Francisco** is famous for its carving of the Sacred Heart, which, like several other of its paintings and statues, was brought here from Antigua. Building began in 1780, but was repeatedly interrupted by seismic activity – it's said that cane syrup, egg whites and cow's milk were mixed with the mortar to enhance its strength. For the most part the church fared well, but in 1917 a tremor brought down one of the arches, revealing that the clergy had used the roof cavity to store banned books.

South along 6 Avenida, things go into a slow but steady decline as the commercial chaos starts to get out of control and the pavements are swamped by temporary stalls selling clothes and pirated CDs. On the left-hand side of 6 Avenida, beneath the trees, **18 Calle** becomes distinctly sleazy, the fried-food stalls mixed in with grimy nightclubs and "streap-tease" joints. By night the streets are patrolled by prostitutes, and the local hourly-rate hotels are protected by prison-like grilles. Night or day it's best avoided. Meanwhile, over on the east side of 18 Calle, the streets around the junction with 9 Avenida house the private terminals of bus companies operating routes to the Mexican border and Petén.

Close to these bus terminals, on the east side of an open square just off 10 Avenida, lies the excellent **Museo del Ferrocarril** (Mon–Fri 9am–5pm, Sat & Sun 10am–5pm; free), a new museum dedicated to the history of Guatemalan railways. The splendidly renovated museum building was Guatemala City's main **train station** until it was mysteriously burnt down in 1996, with all its documents and records going up in smoke the night before auditors were due to start investigating the finances of the state railway company. Today only a few freight trains run (from a different terminal) in Guatemala, but you can get a great perspective of how the old network functioned here. There are several old steam engines and carriages to clamber over and examine, plus rooms stuffed with railway curiosities including staff uniforms and tickets as well as some fascinating monochrome photographs. Also on show are several lovingly polished classic cars, including a curvaceous chrome-bumpered Jaguar.

Back on 6 Avenida, just south of 18 Calle, is **La Placita**, the main food market (daily 6am–6pm), housed in a vast, multicoloured hangar. Traders who can afford it pay for a space inside, while those who can't spread themselves along the surrounding streets, which are littered with rubbish and soggy with rotten fruit. At the end of this extended block the character of the city is radically transformed as the aging and claustrophobic streets of Zona 1 give way to the broad avenues of Zona 4 and the Centro Cívico.

North to Zona 2 and the Parque Minerva

North of the old city centre is Zona 2, bounded by a deep-cut ravine that prevents the sprawl from spreading any further in this direction. Three blocks north of the Parque Central, 6 Avenida passes a small residential square, the location where **Monsignor Juan José Geradi** (see Contexts, p.444) was bludgeoned to death on April 26, 1998, two days after publishing his REMHI report into the civil war atrocities. There's a modest stone and bronze monument to Geradi in the square, and flowers and candles are often laid at the garage door of his former residence where the murder was committed. Next to the house, on the east side of the square, the modern Iglesia de San Sebastián is another place of pilgrimage, and services are held here on the anniversary of his death.

Continuing north along 6 Avenida, it's a further 1.5km to the **Parque Minerva**, also known as the Hipódromo del Norte (daily 9am–5pm; US$2), a park and sports complex on the edge of the city where fairs take place on public holidays and fiestas. Its main point of interest, however, is the decidedly quirky **relief map of the country**, which covers 2500 square metres and has a couple of viewing towers. The map was finished in 1905 and designed to have running water flowing in the rivers, although the taps are usually shut off. Its vertical scale is out of proportion to the horizontal, making the mountains look incredibly steep. It does nevertheless give you a good idea of the general layout of the country, from the complexity of the highlands to the sheer enormity of Petén. Unsurprisingly, given the perpetual border squabbles between the two countries, Belize is included as Guatemalan territory. You can get to Parque Minerva from 5 Avenida in Zona 1, from where several buses head up to Zona 2; look out for a sign on the bus displaying "Hipódromo".

The new city

South of Zona 1, the **new city** is far more spacious and the roads are much broader, though while you may have more room to breathe, the air is no less noxious. The first zone you enter is Zona 4, from where, continuing south, the new city roughly divides into two, split down the middle by Avenida La Reforma. Zonas 10 and 14, on the east side of Avenida La Reforma, form the smartest part of town, with banks, hotels, restaurants, boutiques and walled residential compounds – the natural habitat of Guatemala's wealthy elite. The western half, zonas 9 and 13, incorporating several museums, the zoo and airport and more residential suburbs, is less exclusive, but still a nice part of town.

Zona 4, the Centro Cívico and around

At the southern end of the old city, the **Centro Cívico** spans the boundaries of zones 1 and 4. At this point the avenidas from the north merge at a couple of roundabouts, from where they fan out into the more spacious southern city. Bunched around these junctions a collection of multistorey office blocks house the city's main administrative buildings, including the **Banco de Guatemala** on 7 Avenida, bedecked with bold modern murals and stylized glyphs designed by Dagoberto Vásquez – the images recount the history of Guatemala and the conflict between Spanish and Maya.

Perched on a small hilltop a few blocks northwest of here is the landmark **Teatro Nacional**, also known as the Miguel Ángel Asturias cultural centre, one of the city's most prominent and unusual structures. Completed in 1978, its design is along the lines of a huge ship, painted blue and white, with portholes as windows. Finding an entrance that isn't locked is not always easy, but it's well worth the effort for the superb **views** across the city. The complex, which also includes an open-air theatre, was actually partly built over the foundations of the **San José Fortress**, a nineteenth-century castle that was all but destroyed during the 1944 revolution. Some of the original battlements survive however, and you can enter a small section of the old castle to see the little-visited **Military Museum** (Mon–Sat 9am–4pm; US$0.75). A strange homage to the Guatemalan army, this small collection of weapons and uniforms is really only of interest to would-be *comandantes*.

Back on 7 Avenida, you'll find the main office of the country's tourist board, **Inguat** (see "Information and maps", p.81 for details) and just off it **Cuatro Grados Norte**, a hip new (largely) pedestrianized enclave centred around Vía 5 that's thick with warehouse-style restaurants and bars plus fashionable shops, as well as two **cultural centres**: the Instituto Guatemalteco Americano and the Centro Cultural de España (see p.100). Continuing south on 7 Avenida, you pass the **Iglesia Yurrita**, an outlandish building designed in an exotic neo-Gothic style that belongs more to horror movies than to the streets of Guatemala City. It was finally completed in 1944, forty years after it was originally commissioned as a private chapel by a rich philanthropist, Felipe Yurrite Casteñeda. His house, in the same style, stands alongside. The church, also known as Nuestra Señora de las Angustias, is usually open to the public (Tues–Sun 8am–noon & 3–6pm), and is well worth a look as the inside – which contains a fabulous carved wooden altar – is just as wild as the exterior.

A couple of blocks south of here is the illuminated **Torre del Reformador**, at the junction of 2 Calle. Guatemala's answer to the Eiffel Tower, this steel structure was built along the lines of the Parisian model, in honour of President Barrios, who transformed the country between 1871 and 1885; a bell in the top of the tower is rung every year on June 30 to commemorate the Liberal victory in the 1871 revolution.

The other great landmark in this part of town is the vast **Zona 4 Bus Terminal**, at 1 Calle and 4 Avenida, the country's most impenetrable and intimidating jungle, a brutal swirl of diesel fumes, petty thieves and sleeping vagrants. Adding yet more grime, and the occasional splash of colour to the scene, is the largest **market** in the city, which spreads around the terminal, across several blocks. If you can summon the energy, it's a real adventure to wander through this maze of alleys, but don't carry too much money as it's a risky part of town. To get to the bus terminal from Zona 1, take any of the buses marked "Terminal" from 6 Avenida or 10 Avenida, all of which pass within a block or two.

Across the tracks at the back of the bus terminal, just off Avenida Bolívar, is the **Santuario Expiatorio**, also known as the Iglesia Santa Cecilia de Don Bosco, a superb modern church designed (by a then-unqualified Salvadorean architect) in the shape of a fish. It's part of a church-run complex that includes clinics and schools, and is well worth a browse, above all for the fantastic mural running down the side of the interior which depicts the Crucifixion and Resurrection with vivid realism.

Zona 10: along Avenida La Reforma

Heading south of Zona 4 to Zona 10, the first place of note on Avenida La Reforma – the main artery in the south of the city – is the **Botanical**

Gardens (Mon–Fri 8am–3pm, Sat 9am–noon; US$1.20) of the San Carlos University. Inside, you'll find a beautiful, small garden with a selection of species, all neatly labelled in Spanish and Latin. In the grounds, there's also an anachronistic **natural history museum**, with a collection of mouldy stuffed birds, which includes a quetzal, and curios such as a llama skeleton, swordfish swords and some horrific pickled rodents. Continuing south along Reforma you pass the **Politécnica**, built in the style of a toy fort and still in use by the military.

Far more interesting, however, are the two privately owned **museums** on the campus of the University Francisco Marroquín, reached by following 6 Calle Final off Avenida La Reforma, heading east. **Museo Ixchel** (Mon–Fri 9am–5pm, Sat 9am–12.50pm; US$2.50) is a striking, purpose-built edifice designed loosely along the lines of a Maya temple. The capital's best-organized museum, the Ixchel is dedicated to Maya culture, with particular emphasis on traditional weaving. It contains a stunning collection of hand-woven fabrics, including some very impressive examples of ceremonial costumes, with explanations in English. There's also information about the techniques, dyes, fibres and weaving tools used, and the way in which costumes have changed over the years. Although the collection is by no means comprehensive, and the costumes lose some of their impact and meaning when taken out of the villages where they're made, this is a fascinating exhibition. The building also houses a large library, and permanent exhibitions of paintings by Guatemalan artist Andrés Curruchich, who painted scenes of rural life around San Juan Comalapa, and Carmen Peterson, who depicted traditional costumes on canvas. Don't miss the very good miniature *huipil* collection in the basement, where there's also a café.

Next door, on the third floor of the *auditorio* building, is the excellent **Popol Vuh Archeological Museum** (Mon–Fri 9am–5pm, Sat 9am–1pm; US$2.50, students US$1). Standards here are just as high as at the Ixchel, but this time the subject is archeology, with an outstanding collection of artefacts from sites all over the country. The small museum is divided into Preclassic, Classic, Postclassic and Colonial rooms and all the exhibits are of top quality. The Preclassic room contains some stunning ceramics, stone masks and *hongo zoomorfo* (sculptures shaped like mushroom heads), while highlights of the Classic room include an altar from Naranjo, some lovely incense burners, and a model of Tikal. In the Postclassic room is a replica of the Dresden Codex, one of only three extant pre-conquest Maya books, while the Colonial era is represented by assorted ecclesiastical relics and processional crosses.

A little south and east of here, centred around 10 Calle and 3 Avenida, is the swankiest commercial part of town, the **Zona Viva**, a tight bunch of expensive hotels, office blocks, restaurants, nightclubs and boutiques. This area, and the surrounding leafy streets (where the mansions' owners have numerous servants to keep the lawns clipped), has clearly escaped the Third World. If you've spent some time in the impoverished highland villages, the ostentation on show in this little enclave can come as quite a shock.

At the bottom of Avenida La Reforma is a giant roundabout known as **Parque Obelisco** – or Parque La Independencia – a regular destination for national celebrations (such as the 3000-strong all-night party when Guatemala beat Honduras in a World Cup soccer qualifier in October 2004); while close by is the up-market **Los Próceres** shopping mall. To get to Avenida La Reforma from Zona 1, take bus #82 from 10 Avenida, past the Iglesia Yurrita, and all the way along Avenida La Reforma. La Reforma is a two-way street, so you can return along the same route.

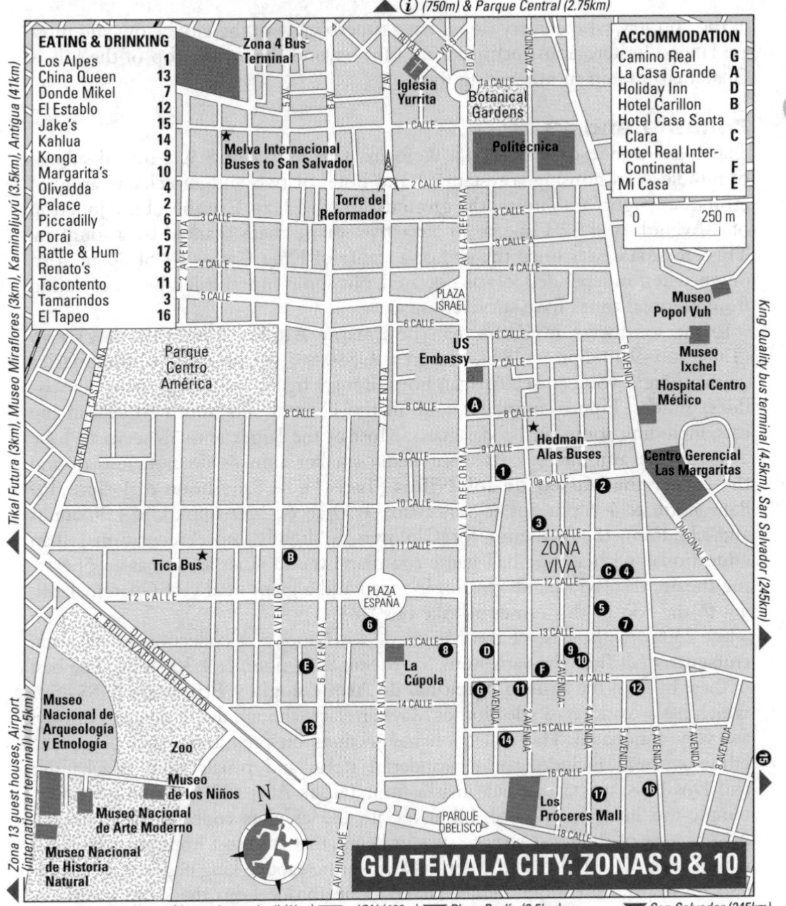

Zona 14 and around

Heading further south into Zona 14, Avenida Reforma becomes **Avenida las Américas**, where things become even more exclusive, with many of the large walled compounds belonging to embassies. Heading down Avenida las Américas, you'll pass the Instituto Geográfico Militar on the right (see "Information, websites and maps" in the Basics section of this book), and two cinema complexes, including the Cine Magic Place (see p.97). At the southern end of the avenida, behind a statue of Pope John Paul II, is the **Plaza Berlín**, from where there are stunning views of the Pacaya volcano – it's a popular spot with picnicking families at weekends, and there are also several food and drink stalls here. Running parallel to Avenida las Américas, 14 Calle – better known as **Avenida Hincapié** – gives access to the **domestic air terminal**, opposite the junction with 18 Calle.

To the east, the main highway to the border with El Salvador runs out through zonas 10 and 15. As the road leaves the city, it climbs a steep hillside and passes through one of the most exclusive and expensive residential districts in the country, where every house has a superb view of the city below, and most are ringed by ferocious fortifications. Out beyond this, at the top of the hill, is Guatemala's main motor-racing track.

Zonas 9 and 13

The western side of Avenida La Reforma falls into **Zona 9**, a mixed suburb of middle-class housing, a restaurant and hotel or two and an eclectic array of businesses. Sights are slim on the ground, though **Plaza España**, at the junction of 7 Avenida and 12 Calle, is an attractive square that's marked by a fountain. This crossroads was once the site of a statue of King Carlos III of Spain, torn down when independence was declared, but some superb tiled benches dating from colonial times have survived intact.

To the southwest, in **Zona 13**, the **Parque Aurora** houses the city's **zoo** (Tues–Sun 9am–5pm; US$2, children US$0.80; ⓦlaurorazoo.centroamerica.com), where you can see African lions, Bengal tigers, Indian elephants, crocodiles, giraffes, hippos, monkeys, and all the Central and South American big cats, including some well-fed jaguars. Most of the larger animals seem to have a reasonable amount of space, but many smaller animals do not. Just around the corner, the **Museo de los Niños** (Tues–Thurs 8am–noon & 1–5pm, Fri 8am–noon & 4–6 pm, Sat & Sun 10am–1.30pm & 2.30–6pm; US$4.30 adults and children), the Museum for Children, is slightly more recreational than educational, with a huge ball-game room and trampolines as well as an operating theatre display, a hands-on music room and a giant jigsaw of Guatemala. To get to the zoo or this museum, take bus #83.

Just 250m to the east of the Museo de los Niños is a collection of state-run **museums** (all Tues–Fri 9am–4pm, Sat & Sun 9am–noon & 1.30–4pm). The best of these by far is the **Museo Nacional de Arqueología y Etnología** (US$4.50), which has a world-class selection of Maya artefacts, though the design and displays are very antiquated. The collection has sections on prehistoric archeology and ethnology and includes some wonderful stelae and panels from Machaquilá and Dos Pilas, spectacular jade masks from Takalik Abaj and a stunning wooden temple-top lintel from Tikal. However, it's the exhibits collected from Piedras Negras, one of the most remote sites in Petén, that are most impressive. Stela 12, dating from 672 AD, brilliantly depicts a cowering captive king begging for mercy; also on display is a monumental carved stone throne from the same site richly engraved with superb glyphs and decorated with a twin-faced head.

Opposite the archeological museum, the **Museo Nacional de Arte Moderno** (US$1.50), which also suffers from poor presentation, boasts some imaginative geometric paintings by Dagoberto Vásquez, vibrant semi-abstract work by indigenous artist Rolando Ixquiac Xicará and a collection of startling exhibits by Efraín Recinos, including a colossal marimba–tank sculpture. The permanent collection also holds a selection of the bold Cubist art and massive murals of Carlos Mérida, Guatemala's most celebrated artist, which draws strongly on ancient Maya tradition. Finally, the **Museo Nacional de Historia Natural** (US$1.50) is probably the most neglected of the trio of museums, featuring a range of mouldy-looking stuffed animals from Guatemala and elsewhere as well as a few mineral samples. There's a much-mothballed plan to remodel the whole Parque Aurora area, including massive reforestation, to make the complex more appealing for visitors, but for now the only other draw is a touristy handicraft market on 11 Avenida. To get to any of these museums take bus #83 from 10 Avenida in Zona 1, or from 6 Avenida in Zona 9.

The final point of interest in the southern half of the city is the **Ciudad Universitária**, the campus of San Carlos University, in Zona 12. A huge complex, it is heavily decorated with vivid political graffiti. The San Carlos University, originally founded in Antigua by Dominican priests in 1676, is probably the best in Central America; it has an autonomous constitution and is entitled to five percent of the government's annual budget. The university also has a long history of radical dissent and anti-government protest, and hundreds of its students were victims of repression and political killings – many right-wing politicians still regard the campus as a centre of subversion. Buses marked "Universitária" travel along 4 Avenida through Zona 1 to the campus.

Zona 7: the ruins of Kaminaljuyú

Way out on the western edge of the city, beyond the stench of the rubbish dump, is the long thin arm of Zona 7, a well-established but run-down part of town that wraps around the ruins of **Kaminaljuyú** (daily 9am–4pm; park free, temple access US$4). Archeological digs on this side of the city have revealed the astonishing proportions of a Maya city that once housed around fifty thousand people and included more than three hundred mounds and thirteen ball courts. Unlike the massive temples of the lowlands, these structures were built of adobe, and most of them have been lost to centuries of erosion and a few decades of urban sprawl. Today, the archeological site, incorporating only a tiny fraction of the original city, is little more than a series of earth-covered mounds, a favourite spot for football and romance. A couple of sections have been cut into by archeologists, and by peering through the fence you can get some idea of what lies beneath the grassy exterior, but it's virtually impossible to get any impression of Kaminaljuyú's former scale and splendour – for that you'll have to visit the new Miraflores museum (see p.94).

To get to the ruins, take bus #35 from 4 Avenida in Zona 1; alternatively, any bus with a small "Kaminaljuyú" sign in the windscreen passes within a block or two.

A history of Kaminaljuyú

Despite its nondescript appearance, Kaminaljuyú, once the largest Maya city in the Guatemalan highlands, is a particularly important site. Its history falls neatly into two sections: a first phase of indigenous growth, and a later period during which migrants from the north populated the site.

First settled as far back as around 400 BC, the city had grown to huge proportions by 100 AD with some two hundred flat-topped **pyramids**. Beneath each of these structures – the largest of which reached a height of some 18m – lay entombed a member of the nobility; a few have been unearthed to reveal the wealth and sophistication of the culture. The corpses were wrapped in finery, covered in cinnabar pigment and surrounded by an array of human sacrifices, pottery, jade, masks, stingray spines, obsidian and quartz crystals. A number of carvings have also been found, proving that the elite of Kaminaljuyú were fully literate at a time when other Maya probably had no notion of writing. Many of the gods, the ceramic styles and the hieroglyphic forms from these early days at Kaminaljuyú are thought to predate those found at later centres such as Tikal and Copán. But the power of the city, pre-eminent during the Late Preclassic era, faded throughout the second and third centuries, and the site may even have been abandoned.

Kaminaljuyú's renaissance took place shortly after 400 AD, when the Guatemalan highlands suffered a massive invasion from the north and fell under the domination of Teotihuacán in central Mexico. The migrants seized the city of Kaminaljuyú and established it as their regional capital, giving them control of the obsidian mines and access to the coastal trade routes and the lowlands of Petén. With the political and economic backing of Teotihuacán, the city once again flourished, the new rulers constructing their own temples, tombs and ball courts. Numerous artefacts have been found from this period, including some pottery that's thought to have been made in Teotihuacán itself, along with endless imitations of the style. Kaminaljuyú's new-found power also played a crucial role in shaping the lowlands of Petén: it was only with the backing of the great Teotihuacán–Kaminaljuyú alliance that Tikal was able to grow so large and so fast. This role was considered of such importance that some archeologists suggest that Curl Nose, one of the early rulers at Tikal (who ascended to power in 387 AD), may actually have come from Kaminaljuyú. The fortunes of Kaminaljuyú itself, however, were so bound up with those of its northern partner that the fall of Teotihuacán around 600 AD weakened the city, resulting in its eventual demise.

Kaminaljuyú has most recently been reclaimed as an important sacred site by Maya shamen and activists, and you may well stumble across a religious ceremony going on in the grassy plazas. This was also the setting chosen by the indigenous leader Rigoberta Menchú (see pp.478–479) to celebrate her 1992 Nobel Peace Prize, when thousands thronged to the old capital.

Museo Miraflores

To gain a greater insight into the ancient city, visit the excellent, compact new **Museo Miraflores** (Tues–Sun 9am–7pm; US$5), a ten-minute walk south of the ruins, beside the very upmarket Miraflores shopping mall on Calzada Roosevelt (the main route to Antigua and the western highlands). The history of the city, and its importance as a trading centre is explained in detail, and exhibits highlight striking stone sculptures and stelae pieces, ceramics, and impressive jade jewellery and obsidian flints.

Eating, drinking and entertainment

Despite being the capital as well as the largest city in Central America, Guatemala City isn't a great place for socializing or indulging. Most of the population hurry home in the evening and, apart from a few streets in zonas 1, 4 and 10, there's little life after dark. As you would expect, **restaurants** can be found throughout the city, and they invariably reflect the type of neighbourhood they're in. Meanwhile, **nightclubs** and bars are concentrated in Zona 10. Movie-watching is hugely popular, with a good selection of cinemas.

Restaurants and cafés

In Zona 1 you'll find a great selection of inexpensive places to eat. **Lunchtime** is a particularly good time for a filling feed, when there are plenty of good Guatemalan places offering excellent set-price, three-course menus for US$2–4 a head including a *fresco* drink – try the area west of the Parque Central or around the post office. There's a cluster of **Chinese** restaurants on 6 Calle, between 4 and 3 avenidas, while vegetarian, Mexican and Italian as well as paella can also be found in Zona 1. To the south, around Cuatro Grados Norte in Zona 4, there's a lot of culinary choice, including Middle Eastern, sushi and Italian. In the smart parts of town, particularly **zonas 9** and **10** (particularly its Zona Viva), the emphasis is on upmarket cafés and glitzy dining, with a terrific selection of places (including some seriously stylish restaurants) for a splurge on Spanish, Asian or North American cuisine for upwards of US$12 a head. **Fast food** is widely available throughout the city, with both US and Central American chains aplenty.

Zona 1

Altuna 5 Av 12–31. Elegant, formal and expensive Spanish/Basque restaurant that's something of a private club for Guatemala's old-money elite in the centre of town. Majors in fish and seafood, including paella, lobster (US$15 per pound) and good *calamares* but also serves *ceviche*, pasta and Castilian treats like *bacalao* and *jamón serrano*. Definitely worth a splurge for the ambience.

Café de Centro Histórico 6 Av 9–50. Quiet, unashamedly nostalgic café on the upper floor of a beautifully restored 1930s building, replete with original tiles, wood panelling and monochrome photographs. Breakfasts, inexpensive Guatemalan dishes (like *sopa de frijoles* and *tortillas con carne*), a US$2.50 set meal, pies and salads, plus great coffee. No smoking room.

De Imeri 6 C 3–34. Old-fashioned but enjoyable café-restaurant with a rear courtyard and pleasingly formal service that's adored by its loyal clientele. Particularly good cakes, but breakfasts, salads, tacos and pasta are all on offer, as is a set lunch for US$3.50.

El Encuentro 5 Av 10–52. The civilized café-restaurant in this low-key cultural centre has some attractive original floor tiles and a short menu that includes pasta, salads and sandwiches as well as cakes and coffee.

Europa Bar 11 C 5–16. Long-running, popular expat hangout, set inauspiciously beneath a multi-storey car park. Primarily a bar, with CNN and sports on screen, but there are also cheap (though bland) eats, including sandwiches, lentil soup and spaghetti, and a few books for sale. Closed Sun.

El Gran Pavo 13 C 4–41. Fairly authentic Mexican food, at moderate prices. Things really kick off on weekends when mariachi bands prowl the tables – you'll have to put up with piped ranchero music at other times, though the long tequila list helps ease the pain. Other branches at 6 C 3–09, Zona 9; 15 Av 16–72, Zona 10; 13 C and 6 Av, Zona 10.

Long Wah 6 C 3–75, west of the Palacio Nacional. One of the better budget Chinese restaurants in this neighbourhood, consistently recommended by locals with a menu that includes *sopa mein*, *wantans*, *chop suey* and *chaw mein*. For food to go dial ⓣ2232 6611.

Nuevo Mundo 6 Av 14–79. Cheapish, centrally located Chinese restaurant, with kitsch-rich interior festooned with garish dragons, and a tooth-loosening jukebox. Try the *arroz frito a la cantonesa* washed down with *té chino verde anticancer*.

Parrillada Doña Sara corner 9 C & 9 Av. Inexpensive, informal place where the tubby chef/proprietor stands streetside stirring vast vats of paella (US$2) and *paella negra* (cooked in squid ink, US$2.75). The barbequed meats are also good. Open Mon–Sat noon–4.30pm.

Rey Sol south side of Parque Centenario. Vegetarian café-restaurant with healthy meals that include spinach lasagna and soups, wholemeal bread sandwiches, tamales, salads, "Aerobic" breakfasts, juices and *licuados*. Also sells good bread, granola, soya milk, herb teas and veggie snacks. There's a second branch at 11 C 5–51, Zona 1.

Zona 4

Arguileh Vía 5, Cuatro Grados Norte. Hip, popular Arabic-style restaurant where you sit on cushions and eat from a moderately priced Middle Eastern menu. Hubble-bubble pipes available, and some tables overlook the pedestrianized street below. Closed Mon.

Café Restaurant Pereira inside the Gran Centro Comercial mall, 6 Av and 24 C. Just a couple of blocks west of Inguat, this very popular comedor offers excellent set meals of typical Guatemalan food. Also at Av La Reforma 14–43, Zona 9.

L'Osteria Ruta 2 4–75, Cuatro Grados Norte. Informal Italian with excellent pizza and pasta (and winsome nutella flan) located in Guatemala City's boho barrio. Closed Mon.

Sucré Salé Ruta 6 8–52. Terrific, friendly little café located in the ground floor of Casa Yurrita, which adjoins the church of the same name (see p.89). All the dishes (including great soups, breakfasts, set lunches and desserts) are freshly prepared every day; there's also a shady garden. Daily 7am–3pm.

Zonas 9 and 10

Los Alpes 10 C 1–09, Zona 10. Tranquil garden café with tasty pastries, pies and crepes, and a relatively inexpensive breakfast menu considering the smart location. Closed Mon.

China Queen 6 Av 14–04, Zona 9. Excellent-value, good-quality Chinese restaurant that offers huge portions of tasty grub; the fried rice with shrimp is US$10 and enough for two.

Donde Mikel 13 C 5–19, Zona 10. Elegant, expensive Spanish restaurant whose authentic food has its regulars dreaming of the motherland, with

delicious sizzling *camarones* (shrimp) and meats served *a la plancha* (grilled). Closed Sun.
Jake's 17 C 10–40, Zona 10. European cuisine, strong on fish (try the Bayonne prawns), French classics and sweets, plus a pleasant, candle-lit atmosphere. Expensive. Closed Mon.
Margarita's 4 Av 13–20, Zona 10. Simply stunning, hip new restaurant serving excellent Italian food for around US$25–30 per person, including *bruschette*, *gnocchi* and salads. The venue's design really sets this place apart, with sumptuous seating and a separate bar area that could be straight out of New York or London.
Olivadda 12 C 4–51, Zona 10. Very smart restaurant with a stylish interior and a leafy terrace garden, majoring in authentic, moderately priced Mediterranean fare.
Palace 10 C 4–40, Zona 10. Pasta and snacks, cakes and pastries in a cafeteria atmosphere. Inexpensive.
Piccadilly Plaza España, 7 Av 12–00, Zona 9. Clean, family-orientated restaurant with decent range of pasta and pizza and some Guatemalan dishes, all at moderate prices, served along with huge jugs of beer. There's another branch in Zona 1 on 6 Av and 11 C.
Tacontento 2 Av & 14 C, Zona 10. One of the cheapest places for a serious feed in the Zona Viva, with tasty tacos, *sopa azteca* and other Mexican standards.
Tamarindos 11 C 2–19 A, Zona 10. Guatemala's most urbane restaurant, with seriously stylish furnishings, a Japanese-style garden patio, electronica on the sound system, and a fusion menu of creatively prepared Asian and Italian food. Expect to pay US$15–20 a head.
El Tapeo 6 Av 16–01 Zona 10. Enjoyable, authentic Spanish restaurant, with gingham tablecloths, posters of Almería, and excellent tapas and mains. Moderate prices.

Drinking and nightlife

Guatemala City quiets down very quickly in the evenings, though there are a few places where you can let your hair down. The three main areas – zonas 1, 4 and 10 – where people congregate each has its own distinct atmosphere. **Zona 1** has a grungy appeal and is popular with students; however, note that personal safety is a concern here, and so it's best to get around this area by taxi unless you're in a group. For a night out in Zona 1, you could do a lot worse than heading to *Las Cien Puertas* for a few drinks and then on to *La Bodeguita* to see what's on there. In **Zona 4**, the vibrant new enclave of Cuatro Grados Norte, which occupies a few pedestrianized streets around Vía 5, is a good bridge between zonas 1 and 10, with an arty, bohemian scene. It's very lively here on weekend nights, with people darting between the closely packed, cosmopolitan restaurants and hip bars – try *SUAE*. There's often an art-house film or exhibition worth catching at the Cultura Hispánica, in the heart of this area on Vía 5. More and more old warehouses are being renovated here, so the scene is sure to mushroom.

Zona Viva in **Zona 10** is where the wealthy go to have fun at the surplus of American-style bars, upmarket restaurants, and clubs playing Latino and European house music, pop hits and salsa.

There is a growing **electronica** party scene in Central America – DJ Tiesto played here in November 2004 – though few reliable venues for quality house and techno; *Porai* is one exception. The annual Rave de Castillo is certainly worth a visit, however, held at Halloween every year. For more information on DJ and live-music events consult Ⓦwww.cosmosguatemala.com.

Bars and clubs

La Bodeguita del Centro 12 C 3–55, Zona 1 Ⓣ2230 2976. Large, left-field venue with live music, comedy, poetry and all manner of arty events. Free entry in the week, around US$3.50 at weekends. Worth a visit for the Che Guevara memorabilia alone. Closed Mon.
Café La Otra Puerta Pasaje Aycinema, 9 C between 6 and 7 Av, Zona 1. Agreeable, informal place in a crumbling historic building that serves good coffee, wine and food, including pasta.
Las Cien Puertes Pasaje Aycinema, 9 C between 6 and 7 Av, Zona 1. Ever-popular bohemian bar in a beautiful run-down colonial arcade popular with artists, students and political activists. Graffiti-splattered walls, good Latin sounds and moderate prices.
Dos Continentes 10 Av 10–17, Zona 1. Scruffy but sociable bar, next door to the *Pensión Mesa*,

with draught Moza and Gallo beer, eclectic music and a good food menu, with all dishes at US$1.50.

El Establo 14 C 5–08, Zona 10. European-owned bar that attracts a middle-aged crowd. There's a large, polished wood interior, good food, and a soundtrack of decent jazz and Western pop and rock music.

Kahlua 15 C & 1 Av, Zona 10. Completely rebuilt in 2004 after a long closure, this venue looks set to be one of the most happening clubs in town, with four floors and contemporary decor.

Konga 3 Av & 13 C, Zona 10. Tropical-style-themed-club, but a good place to dance to salsa and merengue, plus a few Latin hits. Attracts a rich, young crowd.

La Ocupa Ruta 5, 8-42, Zona 4. The capital's best underground venue for house and electronica, with moderate entrance prices and Guatemala's best DJs (plus some live bands). Fri and Sat only.

Porai 4 Av & 12 C, Zona 10. One of the capital's most vibrant clubs, its dance floor semi-open to the elements, positioned under an expansive canvas canopy. Guatemalan and international DJs spin house, techno and trance, and there are occasional rock concerts, too. No dress restrictions. Thurs, Fri and Sat nights only.

Rattle & Hum 4 Av & 16 C, Zona 10. Snug and stylish Australian-owned bar, popular with expats and locals alike, with lively atmosphere and Western music on the stereo.

Renato's 13 C & Av La Reforma, Zona 9. Small, sociable and informal bar that regularly offers live music, mainly rock bands. There's a little terrace at the front.

SUAE Vía 5, Cuatro Grados Norte, Zona 4. Lounge-cum-warehouse-style bar with arresting decor (including lime green plastic sofas) and artwork, modish electronic tunes and a hip clientele. Cult movies are also shown, while the bar staff are well connected to the capital's underground rave scene.

Cinemas

The City has a good selection of cinemas, most showing films in English with Spanish subtitles. In Zona 1, four cinemas can be found on 6 Avenida between the Parque Central and the police HQ, with tickets typically running about US$2. Elsewhere, the Miraflores and neighbouring Cine Tikal Futura, Calzada Roosevelt, Zona 11, boast the best sound quality and charge around US$3.50. For **art-house movies** and the occasional classic, La Cúpula and the IGA regularly show films from Europe, North America and Latin America; most programmes are listed in the main national newspapers, including the *Prensa Libre*.

Recommended cinemas

Las Américas Av las Américas, between 8 & 9 calles, Zona 13.

Capitol 6 Av & 12 C, Zona 1.

Cine Los Próceres 16 C, Zona 10.

Cine Tikal Futura Calzada Roosevelt, Zona 11.

La Cúpula 7 Av 13–01, Zona 9.

IGA Ruta 1, Zona 4.

Lux 11 C & 6 Av, Zona 1.

Magic Place Av las Américas, Zona 13.

Miraflores Calzada Roosevelt, Zona 11.

Gay Guatemala City

Guatemala City's small **gay scene** is mostly underground and concentrated around a few (almost entirely male) venues. In **Zona 1**, *Ephebus*, 4 C 5–30, is an intimate club featuring Latin dance and house music. *El Encuentro*, 5 Av 10–52, is a popular café-bar inside a mall with frequent drinks specials; it's closed on Sundays. In **Zona 4**, *Genetic* (formerly *Pandora's Box)*, Via 3 & Ruta 3, is the city's largest gay club, and plays mainstream Latin dance and Western pop sounds to a young crowd (Saturday night only). Close by, *Mirage*, Vía 7 3–65, is a small venue open Fridays and Saturdays. *D'vino's* on Av La Reforma 7–86 is a bar-club that draws a hip crowd (Fridays only) to its Zona 9 location. Meanwhile, *Il Coliseum*, 17 Calle A 7–40, Zona 10, a gay sauna, hosts parties most nights of the week; entrance is US$10. There are no specifically **lesbian** clubs or bars in the city, but check the chat rooms at ⓦgayguatemala.com.

Listings

Airlines Airline offices are scattered throughout the city, with many along Avenida La Reforma. It's fairly straightforward to phone them, and there's nearly always someone in the office who speaks English. Note that AA and Continental passengers can check in a day early at the airlines' offices inside the *Marriott*, 7 Av 15–45, Zona 9, to pre-book seats and save queuing at the airport. Aeroméxico, Av La Reforma 7–62, Zona 9 ⓣ2361 7171; Aerocaribe (see Méxicana); Aerovías, Av Hincapié 18 C, Zona 13 ⓣ2332 5686; American Airlines, *Marriott* (see note above) and *Hotel El Dorado*, Av La Reforma 15–45, Zona 9 ⓣ2337 1177; British Airways, 1 Av 10–81, Zona 10, 6th floor of Edificio Inexa ⓣ2332 7402; Continental, *Marriott* (see note above) and 18 C 5–56, Zona 10 ⓣ2366 9985, airport ⓣ2331 2051; Copa, 1 Av 10–1, Zona 10 ⓣ2385 5500, airport ⓣ2385 0658;

Moving on from Guatemala City

To get to the **international terminal** of **Aurora airport** from Zona 1, either take bus #83 from 10 Av (30min) or take a taxi (around US$10); from Zona 10 a taxi is about US$6. There's a US$30 departure tax on all international flights – though this is included in the price of many tickets – and also a US$3 security tax; both are payable in either quetzals or dollars. The **domestic terminal** is in the same complex but only reached via Av Hincapié; you'll need to take a taxi to reach it. Note that all Taca and Tikal Jets internal flights leave from the international terminal. The domestic departure tax (US$0.80) is often not included in the ticket price.

If you're leaving by **first-class bus**, departures are from the bus company offices. Most are spread around the streets around the old train station at 18 C and 9 Av in **Zona 1**, where there are first-class departures to destinations around the country. Moving on by **second-class bus**, the main centre is the **Zona 4 terminal**. To get there, take any city bus marked "Terminal"; you'll find these heading south along 4 Av in Zona 1. Second-class **buses to Antigua** leave from a small plaza at the junction of 18 C and 5 Av.

Buses from Guatemala City

The abbreviations we've used for the bus companies are as follows:

ADN	ADN Mayan World
HA	Hedman Alas
KQ	King Quality
L	Lituega
LA	Líneas Américas
LD	Línea Dorada
LH	Los Halcones
M	Monarcas
MI	Melva Internacional
P	Pulmantur
RO	Rutas Orientales
RZ	Rápidos Zacaleu
SJ	San Juanera
TA	Transportes Álamo
TB	Ticabus
TD	Transportes Dulce María
TE	Transportes Escobar y Monja Blanca
TGG	Transportes Galgos
TGR	Transportes Guerra
TM	Transportes Marquensita
TR	Transportes Rebuli
TV	Transportes Velásquez

To	Company	Terminal	Frequency	Duration
Antigua	various (2nd)	18 C & 5 Av, Zona 1	15min	1hr
Chichicastenango	various (2nd)	Zona 4 terminal	30min	3hr 15min
Chiquimula	RO (1st)	19 C 8–18, Zona 1	20 daily	3hr 30min
	TGR (1st)	19 C 8–39, Zona 1	20 daily	3hr 30min
Cobán	TE (1st)	8 Av 15–16, Zona 1	16 daily	4hr 30min
Copán	HA (1st)	2 Av 8–73, Zona 10	1 daily	5hr

Delta Air Lines, 15 C 3–20, Zona 10, Centro Ejecutivo building ☎2337 0642; Iberia, Av La Reforma 8–60, Zona 9 ☎2332 0911, airport ☎2332 5517; Jungle Flying, Av Hincapié & 18 C, domestic terminal, Hangar L-16, Zona 13 ☎2360 4917; KLM, 6 Av 20–25, Zona 10, 5th floor of Edificio Plaza Marítima ☎2367 6179; Méxicana, 13 C 8–44, Zona 10, Edificio Edyma Plaza ☎2366 4543; Taca, Av Hincapié 12–22, Zona 13 ☎2470 8222; Racsa, airport ☎2361 5703; Tapsa, Av Hincapié 18–00, Zona 13 ☎2331 9180; Tikal Jets, Av Hincapié, Hangar J-6, Zona 13 ☎2332 5070; United Airlines, Av La Reforma 1–50, Zona 9, Edificio el Reformador ☎2336 9923.

American Express office inside Clark Tours office, 12 C 0–93, Zona 9, Centro Comercial Montúfar (Mon–Fri 8.30am–5pm; ☎2331 7422).

Baggage There's no central left-luggage facility, so you'll have to entrust any baggage to your hotel.

Banks and exchange At the airport, Banco del Quetzal (Mon–Fri 6am–8pm, Sat & Sun 8am–6pm) gives good rates; there are also several 24hr

	M (1st)	pick up from *Camino Real* hotel by request	1 daily	5hr
Cubulco	TD (2nd)	17 C & 11 Av, Zona 1	8 daily	5hr
Escuintla	various (2nd)	Zona 4 terminal	30min	1hr 15min
Esquipulas	RO (1st)	19 C & 9 Av, Zona 1	15 daily	4hr
Flores	various	17 C & 8 Av, Zona 1	19 daily	8–9hr
	LD (1st)	16 C 10–55, Zona 1	4 daily	8hr
	ADN (1st)	15C 9–18A, Zona 1	2 daily	8hr
Huehuetenango	LH (1st)	7 Av 15–27, Zona 1	3 daily	5hr 30min
	TV (1st)	20 C 1–37, Zona 1	9 daily	5hr 30min
	RZ (1st)	9C 11–42, Zona 1	3 daily	5hr 30min
La Ceiba	HA (1st)	2 Av 8–73, Zona 10	1 daily	12hr
La Mesilla	TV (1st)	20 C 1–37, Zona 1	7 daily	7hr
Monterrico	various (2nd)	Zona 4 terminal	4 daily	4hr
Panajachel	TR (2nd)	21 C 1–54, Zona 1	11 daily	3hr
Puerto Barrios	L (1st)	15 C 10–40, Zona 1	16 daily	5hr 30min
Quetzaltenango	LA (1st)	2 Av 18–74, Zona 1	6 daily	4hr
	TA (1st)	21 C 1–14, Zona 1	6 daily	4hr
	TG (1st)	7 Av 19–44, Zona 1	7 daily	4hr
	SJ (2nd)	Zona 4 terminal	10 daily	4hr 15min
Rabinal	TD (2nd)	17 C & 11 Av, Zona 1	10 daily	4hr 20min
Salamá	TD (2nd)	17 C & 11 Av, Zona 1	12 daily	3hr 30min
San Salvador	MI (1st)	3 Av 1–38, Zona 9	14 daily	5hr
	TB (1st)	11 C 2–72, Zona 9	1 daily	5hr
	KQ (1st)	Col Vista Hermosa II, Zona 15	4 daily	5hr
	P (1st)	*Holiday Inn*, Zona 10	2 daily	5hr
Santa Cruz del Quiché	various (2nd)	Zona 4 terminal	20min	4hr
San Pedro Sula	HA (1st)	2 Av 8–73, Zona 10	1 daily	8hr
Tecún Umán	various (1st)	19 Av & 8 C, Zona 1	30min	5hr
Talismán	various (1st)	19 Av & 8 C, Zona 1	30min	5hr 30min
Tapachula	LD (1st)	16 C 10–55, Zona 1	2 daily	6hr 30min
	TB (1st)	11 C 2–72, Zona 9	1 daily	6hr 30min
	TG (1st)	7 Av 19–44, Zona 1	3 daily	6hr 30min
Zacapa	RO	19 C & 9 Av, Zona 1	15 daily	3hr

MasterCard/Cirrus and Visa/Plus ATMs here. You can exchange euros (at poor rates) at Banco Uno, 18 C 5–56, Zona 10. In Zona 1, Credomatic, 5 Av & 11 C, gives Visa and MasterCard cash advances (Mon–Fri 8.30am–7pm, Sat 9am–1pm) and will cash travellers' cheques. In Zona 10, head for the Centro Gerencial Las Margaritas, at Diagonal 6 10–01, where there are several 24hr ATMs as well as banks where you can cash travellers' cheques.

Bookstores Sopho's on Av La Reforma 13–89, Zona 10, is the best bookstore for English-language fiction and literature; it also has a coffee bar. Géminis, 3 Av 17–05, Zona 14, is worth a visit if you're in the south of the city.

Car rental About a dozen companies have desks at the airport. Adaesa Renta Autos, 4 C A 16–57, Zona 1 (ⓣ2220 2180), is recommended, with a small Honda or Hyundai costing US$28 per day (with a US$440 accident deductible clause). Other companies include: Avis, 6 Av 7–64, Zona 9 ⓣ2339 3248, ⓦwww.avisenlinea.com; Hertz, 7 Av 14–76, Zona 9 ⓣ2332 2242, ⓦwww.hertz.com.gt; Tabarini, 2 C A 7–30, Zona 10 ⓣ2331 6108; and Thrifty, 6 Av 11–57, Zona 9 ⓣ2332 1456.

Dentist Central Dentist de Especialistas, 20 C 11–17, Zona 10 (ⓣ2337 1773), is the best dental clinic in the country, and superb in emergencies. Prices are reasonable.

Embassies Most of the embassies are in the southeastern quarter of the city, along Avenida La Reforma and Avenida las Américas, and they tend to be open weekday mornings only. Australia, contact the Canadian embassy; Austria, Edificio Plaza, 6 Av 20–25, Zona 10 ⓣ2364 3460; Belize, Av La Reforma 1–50, 8th floor, Suite 803, Edificio el Reformador, Zona 9 ⓣ2334 5531 or 2331 1137; Canada, 13 C 8–44, 6th floor, Edificio Edyma Plaza, Zona 10 ⓣ2333 6102; Colombia, 5 Av 5–55, Edificio Europlaza Torre I, Zona 14 ⓣ2385 3432; Costa Rica, 1 Av 15–52, Zona 10 ⓣ2363 1345; Cuba 13 C 5–72, Zona 10 ⓣ2333 7627; El Salvador, 5 Av 8–15, Zona 9 ⓣ2360 7660; Germany, Edificio Plaza Marítima, 20 C 6–20, Zona 10 ⓣ2364 6700; Honduras, 19 Av A 20–19, Zona 10 ⓣ2366 5640; Italy, 5 Av 8–59 Zona 14 ⓣ2337 4851; Mexico, 15 C 3–20, Zona 10 ⓣ2333 7254 or 2333 7255; Netherlands, 16 C 0–55, 13th floor, Torre Internacional, Zona 10 ⓣ2367 4761; Nicaragua, 10 Av 14–72, Zona 10 ⓣ2368 0785; Panama, 10 Av 18–53, Zona 14 ⓣ2368 2805; Sweden, 8 Av 15–07, Zona 10 ⓣ2333 6536; Switzerland, Torre Internacional, 16 C 0–65, Zona 10 ⓣ2367 5520; United Kingdom, Torre Internacional 16 C 0–55, 11th floor, Zona 10 ⓣ2367 5425–9; United States, Av La Reforma 7–01, Zona 10 (Mon–Fri 8am–5pm; ⓣ2331 1541).

Immigration The main immigration office (*migración*) is conveniently located on the second floor of the Inguat HQ at 7 Av 1–17, Zona 4 (Mon–Fri 8am–2.45pm; ⓣ2361 8476–9).

Internet There are plenty of cybercafés in Zona 1, including *Coffee Net* at 5 Av 11–70, and several options in Zona 10, including Web Station at 2 Av 14–63. Rates are around US$1.75 per hour.

Laundry Lavandería Obelisco, Av La Reforma 16–30, charges around US$3 for a self-service wash and dry; there's also a self-service laundry at 4 Av 13–89, Zona 1.

Libraries The Guatemalan American Institute, or IGA, at Ruta 1 and Vía 4, Zona 4, has the best library for English books. Centro Cultural de España, Vía 5, Zona 4, has a small library collection that includes a few books in English. There's also the National Library, Parque del Centenario, and specialist collections at the Ixchel and Popol Vuh museums.

Medical care Dr Manuel Cáceres Figueroa, 6 Av 8–92, Zona 9 (ⓣ2332 1506), who speaks English and German, is highly recommended for consultations; your embassy should also have a list of bilingual doctors. For emergency medical assistance, dial ⓣ125 for the Red Cross, or head for the Centro Médico, a private hospital with 24hr cover, at 6 Av 3–47, Zona 10 (ⓣ2332 3555).

Pharmacies Farmacia Osco, 16 C and 4 Av, Zona 10. There are dozens in Zona 1.

Photography To back up photos on a CD, head to cybercafé Web Station (see "Internet"). Print film is widely available, while transparency and monochrome film can be found at the camera shops on 6 Av in Zona 1.

Police The main police station is on the corner of 6 Av and 14 C, Zona 1. In an emergency dial ⓣ120.

Post office The main post office is at 7 Av and 12 C, Zona 1 (Mon–Fri 8.30am–5pm, Sat 8.30am–1pm).

Telephone Web Station (see "Internet") has very cheap international call rates (USA US$0.20; EU US$0.35). Cardphones can be found all over the city for local calls, while the main Telgua office is one block east of the post office (daily 7am–midnight).

Tours *Hotel Posada Belén* (see "Accommodation") offers excellent guided walking tours (in English and Spanish) of the historic centre of Guatemala City taking in Casa Mima, the Palacio Nacional, and cathedral and other sites for US$20pp and full-day museum tours for US$50pp. Clark Tours (see "Travel agents") also offer city tours from US$25 for a half-day tour. Chiltepe Tours (ⓣ5907 0913, ⓦwww.chiltepe.com) run an a/c tram-style bus tour between the main sites in zonas 1, 4 and 10, with pick-ups from the main luxury hotels in Zona 10 for US$15 per person.

Travel agents Flights to Petén can be booked through any of the agents along Avenida La Reforma in zonas 9 and 10, including Servisa, Av La Reforma 8–33, Zona 10 (ⓣ2332 7526). Clark Tours, Diagonal 6, 10–01, 7th floor, Torre II, Las Margaritas, Zona 10 (ⓣ2470 4700, ⓦwww.clarktours.com.gt), organizes trips to many parts of the country. Viajes Tivoli, 6 Av 8–41, Zona 9 (ⓣ2339 2260, ⓦwww.tivoli.com), is a good all-round agent with competitive rates for international flights.

Work Hard to come by. The best bet is teaching at one of the English schools; check the classified sections of the *Revue*.

Around Guatemala City

In the event you're not dashing off straight away to Antigua, a couple of destinations are suited to day-trips from the city, while the rest of the surrounding hills are easily explored using other towns as a base.

To the south the main road runs to Escuintla and the Pacific coast, passing through a narrow valley that separates the cones of the Pacaya and Agua volcanoes. Out this way is popular weekend resort **Lago de Amatitlán** and, a few kilometres further south, **Volcán de Pacaya**, one of Guatemala's three highly active cones, which often spouts smoke, gases, rocks and a plume of lava.

To the northwest of the capital, the villages of **San Juan Sacatepéquez** and **San Pedro Sacatepéquez** both have impressive markets, while further northwest lie the ruins of **Mixco Viejo**, the ancient capital of the Poqomam Maya.

South of the city

Heading out through the southern suburbs, the **Carretera al Pacífico** runs past the clover-leaf junction at El Trébol and leaves the city through its industrial outskirts. There are a swathe of new housing projects, and elaborate advertising posters on empty lots sing the merits of suburban life and mortgages. The highway runs past many of Guatemala's giant *maquila* (clothing assembly) factories and also the town of **Villa Nueva** – which has now been virtually swallowed up by the capital's sprawl. After here the valley starts to narrow, overshadowed by the volcanic cones of Agua and Pacaya.

A few kilometres east of the highway, **Lago de Amatitlán** nestles at the base of the Pacaya volcano, encircled by forested hills. It's a superb setting, but one that's been sadly undermined by the abuses the lake has suffered at the hands of property speculators (bungalows have proliferated around the shoreline) and industry (the waters of the lake are grossly polluted).

The Pacaya volcano

Heading further down the valley towards the Pacific coast, a branch road leaves the main highway to the left (east) and heads into the hills to the trailhead for the highly active **Volcán de Pacaya**. Rising to a height of 2250m, the volcano regularly spits out clouds of rock and ash in the country's most dramatic sound and light extravaganza. The current period of eruption began in 1965, and colonial records show that it was also active between 1565 and 1775. Today it certainly ranks as one of the most accessible and exciting volcanoes in Central America, and a trip to the cone is an unforgettable experience (although sulphurous fumes and very high winds can make this ascent impossible some days). The best time to watch the eruptions is at night, when the volcano often spouts plumes of brilliant orange lava.

Though it is possible to climb the cone independently, virtually everyone now chooses to join a group as part of a tour, escorted by a guide. Antigua is the best place to organize a climb; Gran Jaguar Tours, 4 C Poniente 30 (Ⓣ7832 2712), handle most tours (US$5–7 per person) or you could try Old Town Outfitters (see p.120), which run more comfortable trips that include food and drink. **Safety** on Pacaya (once the site of regular attacks by bandits) is now much less of a concern since armed park guards, who accompany groups, were posted on the volcano's slopes.

Tour minibuses drop you off in the village of **San Francisco de Sales**, where you pay a US$3.50 entrance fee to the protected Pacaya area. It's about two hours to the top from here, passing through *milpas*, thickish forest and slippery cinder, until you suddenly emerge on the lip of an exposed ridge from where you can see the cone in all its brutal beauty. In front of you is a massive bowl of cooled lava, its fossilized currents flowing away to the right; opposite is the cone itself, a jet black triangular peak that occasionally spouts molten rock and ash. From here the path passes across lava fields and between the charred stumps of trees, and then up the slippery ashen sides of the cone itself, a terrifying but thrilling ascent, eventually bringing you face to face with bubbling patches of molten magma and minor eruptions (if conditions permit). A noxious brew of sulphurous fumes (that choke the throat) swirls around the lip of the crater and you'll feel the heat of the ash and lava beneath your feet. The ascent certainly shouldn't be attempted when Pacaya is highly active – check with your tour agency about the state of the eruptions before setting out.

Parque Natural Canopy Calderas

Nestling in the northern slopes of Pacaya below the village of San Francisco de Sales is the **Parque Natural Canopy Calderas** (daily 8am–6pm; Ⓣ5538 5531, Ⓦwww.parquenaturalcalderas.com), a protected zone that encompasses a delightful highland lake and a dense patch of rainforest, close to the *aldea* of San José Calderas. The parque is a privately owned nature reserve where you can camp (US$7 per person) beside the clean lake water, go horse riding (US$8 per hour) or swing through the jungle from professionally built wooden platforms along a 700m network of cable (US$20) which slices through the forest. The reserve's owners also plan to set up a cable crossing across the lake and build cabañas and a hanging restaurant above the lake. If you go privately, stop in the village of San José and ask the mayor for the canopy tour, and well-trained guides will accompany you and show you how to use the cable canopy ropes correctly.

Onwards to the coast: Palín

Continuing towards the coast the main highway passes through **PALÍN**, whose name derives from the word *palinha*, meaning water that holds itself erect, a reference to a nearby waterfall. Home to a tiny pocket of Poqomam-speaking Maya, the town was once famous for its weaving, but these days the only *huipiles* you'll see are the purples of the village of Santa María de Jesús, connected to Palín by a back road.

The best time to visit Palín is for its Wednesday-morning **market**, which takes place under a magnificent ceiba tree in the plaza. Buses travel through every ten minutes or so, heading between the capital and the coast, so it's worth stopping off even if you just happen to be passing. Guatemala's first **motorway** (US$1 toll per car) starts just outside of town, offering a speedy route between Palín and the southern town of Escuintla, avoiding the slow lorries that clog the old road.

Northwest of the city

To the northwest of the capital lies a hilly area that, despite its proximity, is little tainted by the influence of the city. Here the hills are still covered by pine forests, and heading out this way you'll find a couple of interesting villages with markets well worth visiting. Further afield are the **Mixco Viejo** ruins, impeccably restored and enjoying the most dramatic setting of any ruins in Guatemala.

San Pedro Sacatepéquez and San Juan Sacatepéquez

Leaving the city to the northwest you travel through the suburb of **Florida**, then the road starts to climb into the hills through an area that's oddly uninhabited – save for the occasional mansion, hidden in the forest.

The first of the two villages you come to is **SAN PEDRO SACATEPÉQUEZ**, which had to be almost completely rebuilt after the 1976 earthquake. The Friday market here, though not very large, is still worth a browse. Another 6km takes you over a ridge and into the village of **SAN JUAN SACATEPÉQUEZ**. As you approach, the road passes a profusion of makeshift greenhouses where flowers are grown, an industry that has become the local speciality. Andrés Stombo brought the first carnation to Guatemala some sixty years ago. He employed the three Churup brothers, all from San Juan, and seeing how easy it was they all set up on their own. Since then the business has flourished, and there are flowers everywhere in San Juan. By far the best time to visit is for the Friday market, when the whole place springs into action and the village is packed. Keep an eye out for the *huipiles* worn in San Juan, which are unusual and impressive, with bold geometric designs of yellow, purple and green.

Buses to both villages run every fifteen minutes or so from the Zona 4 terminal in Guatemala City.

Mixco Viejo

Beyond San Juan the road divides, one branch heading north to El Chol and Rabinal along a rough dirt route (one bus a day takes this route, leaving the Zona 4 terminal in Guatemala City at 6am), the other going northwest towards **Mixco Viejo** along a smooth paved road. Taking the western route, the scenery changes dramatically, leaving behind the pine forests and entering a huge, dry valley. Small farms are scattered here and there, and the Politécnica, Guatemala's military academy, is also out this way. About thirty minutes beyond San Juan, in a massive valley, are the ruins of Mixco Viejo.

The ruins

MIXCO VIEJO was the capital of the Poqomam Maya, one of the main pre-conquest tribes. The original Poqomam language has all but died out – it's now spoken only in a few isolated areas and in the villages of Mixco and Chinautla – and the bulk of their original territory is swamped by Kaqchikel speakers. The site itself is thought to date from the thirteenth century, and its construction, designed to withstand siege, bears all the hallmarks of the troubled times before the arrival of the Spanish. Protected on all sides by deep ravines, it can be entered only along a single-file causeway. At the time the Spanish arrived, in 1525, this was one of the largest highland centres, with nine temples, two ball courts, and a population of around nine thousand.

Spanish historian Fuentes y Guzmán actually witnessed the conquest of the city, so for once there's a detailed account. At first Alvarado sent only a small force; after this group failed, the Spanish leader launched an attack himself, using his Mexican allies, two hundred Tlaxcala warriors. With a characteristic lack of subtlety he opted for a frontal assault, but his armies were attacked from behind by a force of Poqomam fighters who arrived from Chinautla. The battle was fought on an open plain in front of the city, and by sunset the Spanish cavalry had won the day, killing some two hundred Poqomam men, although the city remained impenetrable. According to Fuentes y Guzmán, the Poqomam survivors then pointed out a secret entrance to the city, allowing the Spanish to enter virtually unopposed and to unleash a massacre of its inhabitants. The survivors were resettled at a site on the edge of the city, in the suburb of Mixco, where some Poqomam is still spoken.

Today the site has been impressively restored, with its plazas and temples laid out across several flat-topped ridges. Like all the highland sites the structures are fairly low – the largest temple reaches only about 10m in height – and devoid of decoration. It is, however, an interesting site in a spectacular setting, and during the week you'll probably have the ruins to yourself, which gives the place all the more atmosphere. Buses from Zona 4 terminal pass Mixco Viejo on their way to Pachalum (4 daily); alternatively, head to San Juan Sacatepéquez from where regular shared pick-ups run to the ruins. There are cold drinks for sale at the site, and some attractive shelters where you can **camp** overlooking the ruins.

From Guatemala City to Sumpango

Heading out to the west from Guatemala City along the Carretera Interamericana to Chimaltenango, you travel through one of the central highland valleys, where a number of large villages are devoted to market gardening. The villages themselves are particularly scruffy, but their fields are meticulously neat and well taken care of, churning out a wide range of vegetables for both the domestic and export markets.

Leaving Guatemala City, the first place you pass through is **Mixco**, now absorbed into the capital's suburban sprawl. Founded in 1525 to house Poqomam refugees from Mixco Viejo, Mixco still has a large Maya population. Next along the way is **San Lucas Sacatepéquez**, just before the turning for Antigua. The village dates back to before the Conquest but these days bears the scars of the 1976 earthquake and serves the weekend needs of city dwellers, with cheap comedores and family restaurants lining the highway.

Beyond this is **SANTIAGO SACATEPÉQUEZ**, whose centre lies a kilometre or so to the north of the highway. The road to Santiago actually branches off the highway at San Lucas Sacatepéquez – and buses shuttle back and forth along the branch road. The best time to visit Santiago is on November 1, for a local fiesta to honour the **Day of the Dead**, when massive paper kites are flown in the cemetery to release the souls of the dead from their agony. The festival is immensely popular, and hundreds of Guatemalans and tourists come every year to watch the spectacle. The colourful kites, made from paper and bamboo, are massive circular structures, measuring up to 6–7m in diameter. Teams of young men struggle to get them aloft while the crowd looks on with bated breath, rushing for cover if a kite comes crashing to the ground.

At other times of the year, there are **markets** in Santiago on Tuesday and Sunday and the town has a small **museum** (Mon–Fri 9am–4pm, Sat & Sun

9am–noon & 2–4pm), just below the plaza, which is crammed with tiny Maya artefacts found locally and some traditional costumes.

The neighbouring village of **SUMPANGO**, 6km west along the Interamericana, has an identical Day of the Dead tradition – so every few years, when there's not enough wind and the kites at Santiago fail to rise to the occasion, everyone heads there in the hope of better weather.

You'll have no problem reaching either Santiago Sacatepéquez or Sumpango on fiesta day, when travel agencies and language schools send fleets of minibuses up to the villages from Antigua; to get there by public transport take any bus as far as San Lucas Sacatepéquez on the Interamericana and catch a connection there.

Antigua and around

Superbly situated in a sweeping highland valley, suspended between the cones of Agua, Acatenango and Fuego volcanoes, is one of the Americas' most enchanting colonial cities: **ANTIGUA**. In its day this was one of the great cities of the Spanish empire, ranking alongside Lima and Mexico City and serving as the administrative centre for all of Central America and Mexican Chiapas.

These days Antigua is a haven of tranquillity, and it has become the country's foremost tourist destination, a favoured hang-out among travellers looking to recharge. The beauty of the city itself is Antigua's main attraction: its neat cobbled streets and grand Baroque-style colonial buildings. You'll find the ambience here unhurried and enjoyable, with a sociable bar scene and superb choice of restaurants adding to the city's appeal. Antigua's **language schools**, some of the best in all Latin America, are another big draw, pulling in students from around the globe, and forming a vital part of the local economy. Expats, including Europeans, North Americans, South Americans and Asians, contribute to the town's cosmopolitan air, mingling with local villagers selling their wares in the streets and the middle-class Guatemalans who come here at weekends to eat, drink and enjoy themselves. The downside is that it's almost too nice: although it's a great place to wind down and eat well for a few days after you've been travelling hard, eventually this civilized, isolated world can perhaps seem a little too smug and comfortable. After a few days of sipping cappuccinos and munching cake, you could almost forget that you're in Central America at all.

Some history

Antigua was actually the third capital of Guatemala. The Spanish settled first at the site of **Iximché** in July 1524, so that they could keep a close eye on their Kaqchikel Maya allies. In November 1527, when the Kaqchikel rose up in defiance of their new rulers, the capital was moved into the Almolonga valley, to the site of **Ciudad Vieja**, a few kilometres from Antigua. In 1541, however, shortly after the death of Alvarado, this entire town was lost beneath a massive mud slide. Only then did the capital come to rest in Antigua, known in those days as *La Muy Noble y Muy Leal Ciudad de Santiago de los Caballeros de Goathemala*. Here, despite the continued threat from the instability of the bedrock – the first earthquake came after just twenty years – the capital settled and began to achieve astounding prosperity.

As the heart of colonial power in Central America, Antigua grew slowly but steadily. One by one the religious orders established themselves, competing in the construction of schools, churches, monasteries and hospitals. Bishops built grand palaces that were soon rivalled by the homes of local merchants and corrupt government officials.

The city reached its peak in the middle of the eighteenth century, after the 1717 earthquake prompted an unprecedented building boom, and the population rose to around fifty thousand. By this stage Antigua was a genuinely impressive place, with a university, a printing press, a newspaper, and streets that were seething with commercial and political rivalries. But as is so often the case in Guatemala, earthquakes brought all of this to an abrupt end. For the best part of a year the city was shaken by tremors, with the final blows delivered by two severe shocks on September 7 and December 13, 1773. The damage was so bad that the decision was made to abandon the city in favour of the modern capital: fortunately, despite endless official decrees, there were many who refused to leave and Antigua was never completely deserted.

Since then the city has been gradually repopulated, particularly in the last hundred years or so. As Guatemala City has become increasingly congested, some of its middle classes have relocated to Antigua. They've been joined by a large number of resident and visiting foreigners attracted by the city's relaxed and sophisticated atmosphere, lively cultural life, benign climate and lack of traffic congestion.

The fate of Antigua's ancient architecture has become a growing concern in recent years. Of the city's tremendous colonial legacy, many buildings still lie in atmospheric ruin, others are steadily decaying, and many others have been transformed into hotels or restaurants. Efforts are being made to preserve this unique legacy, especially after Antigua was listed as a UNESCO World Heritage site in 1979. Local **conservation** laws now in place are very strict (extensions to houses are virtually impossible) and at times verging on the absurd, with established businesses being forced to switch names to the Castilian Spanish equivalent and owners having to paint their premises in officially sanctioned Antigüeño colour schemes. More commendably, the ongoing construction of a new ring road around the west of Antigua, and the exclusion of trucks from the city streets have helped reduce noise and environmental pollution considerably.

Arrival

Antigua is laid out on the traditional grid system, with avenidas running north–south, and calles east–west. Each street is numbered and has two halves, either a north and south (*norte/sur*) or an east and west (*oriente/poniente*), with the plaza, the **Parque Central**, regarded as the centre. Despite this apparent simplicity, poor street lighting, the recent revival of using old street names, and a local law banning overhanging signs – a bid to preserve the colonial character – ensure that most people get lost here at some stage. However, the town is small and if you get confused, remember that the Agua volcano, the one that hangs most immediately over the town, is to the south.

Arriving by bus, whether from Guatemala City or Chimaltenango, you'll end up in the main bus terminal, a large open space beside the market, three

Tourist crime in Antigua

Visitors to Antigua should be aware that crimes against tourists – mainly street robberies – do occur infrequently. In recent years, a much more visible tourist police presence has helped security, but it's still wise to follow the usual precautions: try to avoid walking alone late at night or to isolated spots during the day. If you want to visit viewing spots, such as the *cruce* overlooking Antigua, inform the tourist police and they will accompany you.

long blocks to the west of the plaza. The noise, fumes and bustle of this part of town are similar to any other in Guatemala, and you may well be greeted by a hustler or two trying to push a hotel or language school. To get to the centre of town, cross the broad tree-lined street outside the terminal and walk straight up the street opposite (4 Calle Poniente), which leads directly to the plaza. If **arriving by taxi** or shuttle, you'll be dropped off wherever you like.

Information

The **tourist office** (Mon–Fri 8am–1pm & 2–5pm, Sat & Sun 9am–1pm & 2–5pm; Ⓣ7832 0763, Ⓔinfo-antigua@inguat.gob.gt), on the south side of the plaza, dispenses excellent, if occasionally overly cautious, information. English is spoken and you can pick up a free map and get advice about monuments and city walks. You'll find the **tourist police** just off the Parque Central on 4 Avenida Norte (Ⓣ7832 7290), who will try to help you with any difficulties, though few officers speak English. Twice daily, they will escort visitors up to the Cerro de la Cruz, which offers a panoramic view of Antigua and the surrounding volcanoes, and also to the city cemetery on request.

The most comprehensive **guidebooks** devoted to Antigua are *Antigua Guatemala: The City and Its Heritage* by Elizabeth Bell and *Antigua for You*, by Barbara Balchin De Koose. Both are available from bookshops in town (see p.121). Although **guides** of the human variety are often to be found in the plaza, hustling for business, it's better to take a city tour (see p.121).

Notice boards in various popular tourist venues advertise everything from salsa classes to apartments and private language tuition. Probably the most useful are those at *Doña Luisa's* restaurant, 4 C Oriente 12, and the Rainbow Reading Room, 7 Av Sur 8.

Accommodation

Antigua has an excellent selection of hotels and hostels, and whether you're after a room in a colonial mansion or a bed in a dorm, you shouldn't have a problem (except around Holy Week, see p.112, when the place is packed and prices soar). Rates are often slashed in mid-range and luxury hotels at quiet times of year.

Would-be guides often greet arriving bus passengers with offers of a hotel; be aware, though, that they get paid a commission if you take a room, so if you arrive at the hotel with one in tow your bargaining powers have already been affected – only at very busy times is it worth taking one of these guides up.

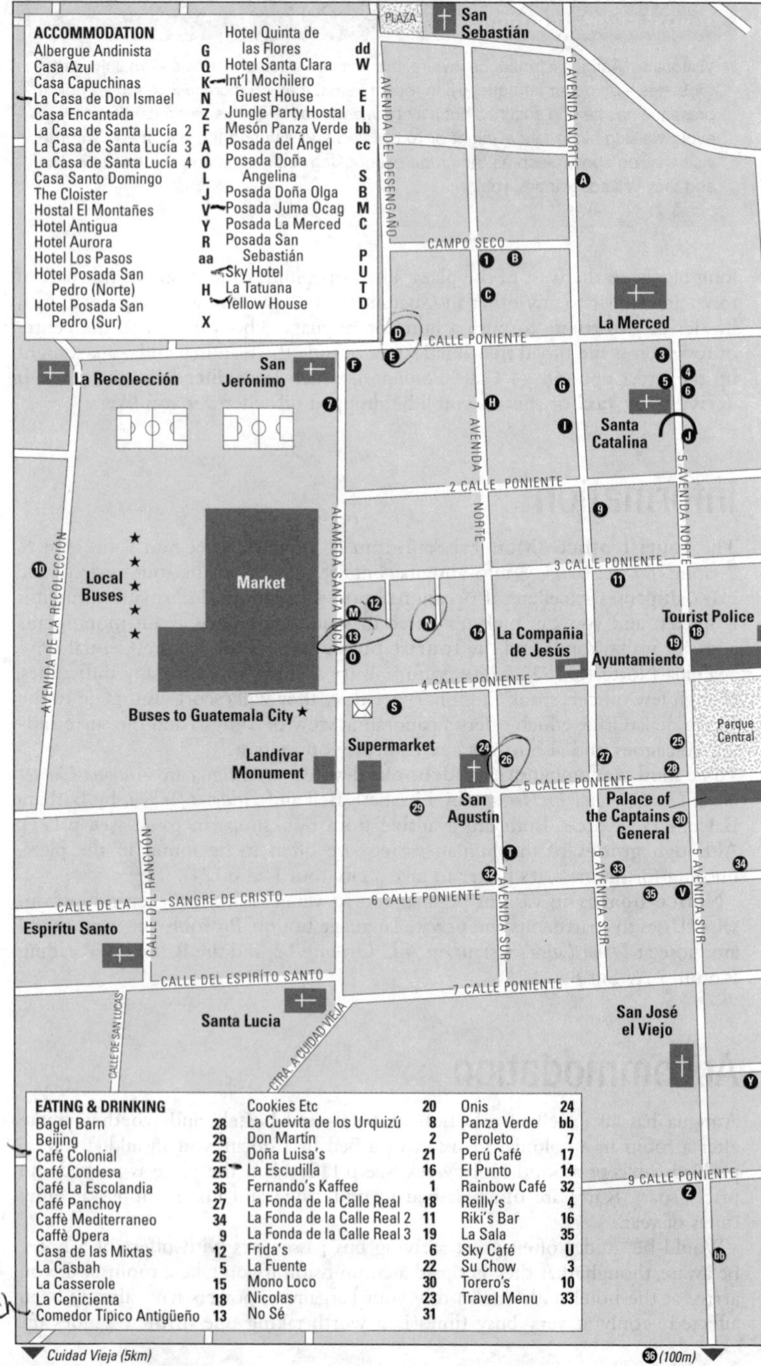

San Felipe (750m) & Jocotenango (2km)
ACCOMMODATION
Albergue Andinista G
Casa Azul Q
Casa Capuchinas K
La Casa de Don Ismael N
Casa Encantada Z
La Casa de Santa Lucía 2 F
La Casa de Santa Lucía 3 A
La Casa de Santa Lucía 4 O
Casa Santo Domingo L
The Cloister J
Hostal El Montañes V
Hotel Antigua Y
Hotel Aurora R
Hotel Los Pasos aa
Hotel Posada San Pedro (Norte) H
Hotel Posada San Pedro (Sur) X
Hotel Quinta de las Flores dd
Hotel Santa Clara W
Int'l Mochilero Guest House E
Jungle Party Hostal I
Mesón Panza Verde bb
Posada del Ángel cc
Posada Doña Angelina S
Posada Doña Olga B
Posada Juma Ocag M
Posada La Merced C
Posada San Sebastián P
Sky Hotel U
La Tatuana T
Yellow House D
PLAZA
San Sebastián
6 AVENIDA NORTE
AVENIDA DEL DESENGAÑO
CAMPO SECO
La Merced
1 CALLE PONIENTE
La Recolección
San Jerónimo
7 AVENIDA NORTE
Santa Catalina
5 AVENIDA NORTE
2 CALLE PONIENTE
3 CALLE PONIENTE
AVENIDA DE LA RECOLECCIÓN
Local Buses
Market
ALAMEDA SANTA LUCIA
Tourist Police
La Compañia de Jesús
Ayuntamiento
4 CALLE PONIENTE
Buses to Guatemala City
Parque Central
Supermarket
Landívar Monument
San Agustín
5 CALLE PONIENTE
Palace of the Captains General
CALLE DEL RANCHÓN
6 AVENIDA SUR
5 AVENIDA SUR
7 AVENIDA SUR
CALLE DE LA SANGRE DE CRISTO
6 CALLE PONIENTE
Espiritu Santo
CALLE DEL ESPIRITO SANTO
7 CALLE PONIENTE
Santa Lucia
CALLE DE SAN LUCAS
CTRA. A CUIDAD VIEJA
San José el Viejo
9 CALLE PONIENTE
EATING & DRINKING
Bagel Barn 28
Beijing 29
Café Colonial 26
Café Condesa 25
Café La Escolandia 36
Café Panchoy 27
Caffè Mediterraneo 34
Caffè Opera 9
Casa de las Mixtas 12
La Casbah 5
La Casserole 15
La Cenicienta 18
Comedor Típico Antigüeño 13
Cookies Etc 20
La Cuevita de los Urquizú 8
Don Martín 2
Doña Luisa's 21
La Escudilla 16
Fernando's Kaffee 1
La Fonda de la Calle Real 18
La Fonda de la Calle Real 2 11
La Fonda de la Calle Real 3 19
Frida's 6
La Fuente 22
Mono Loco 30
Nicolas 23
No Sé 31
Onis 24
Panza Verde bb
Peroleto 7
Perú Café 17
El Punto 14
Rainbow Café 32
Reilly's 4
Riki's Bar 16
La Sala 35
Sky Café U
Su Chow 3
Torero's 10
Travel Menu 33
Cuidad Vieja (5km)
36 (100m)

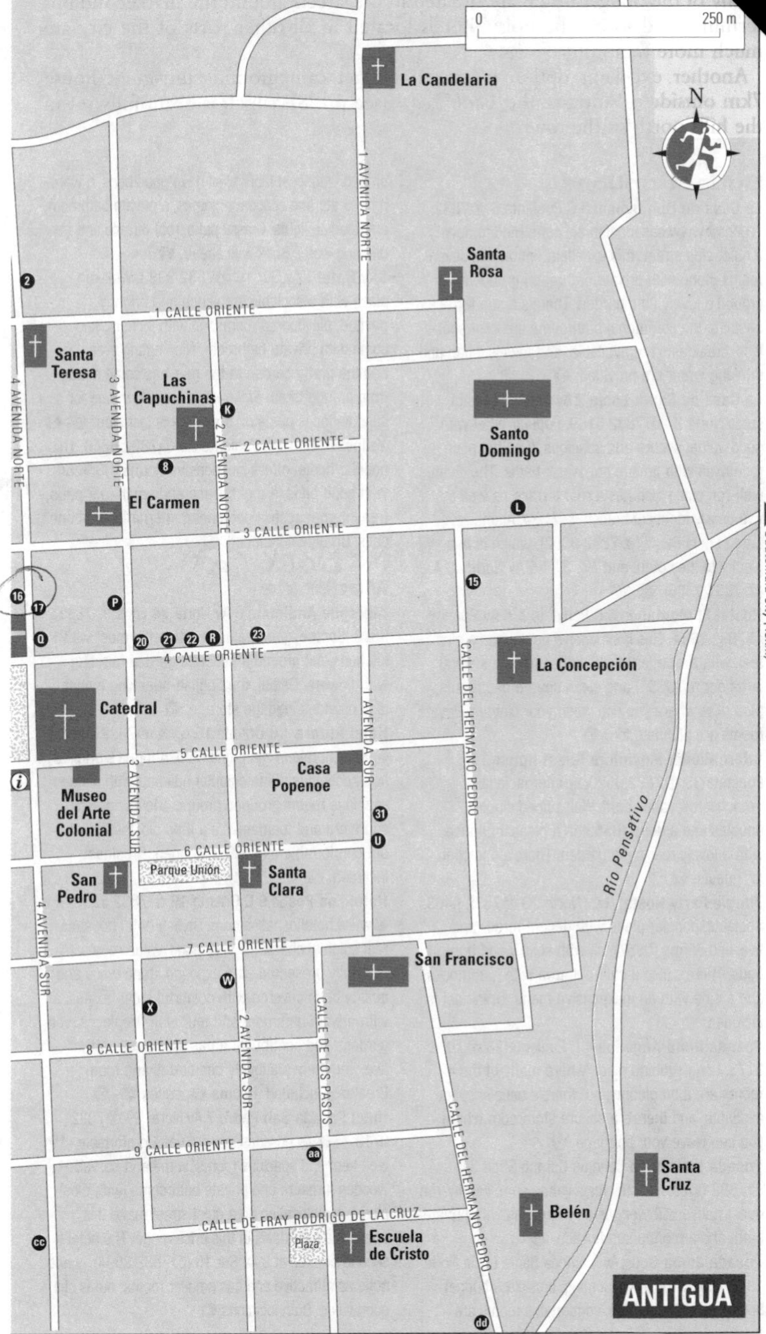

0
250 m
N
La Candelaria
Santa Rosa
Santo Domingo
Santa Teresa
Las Capuchinas
El Carmen
Catedral
Museo del Arte Colonial
Casa Popenoe
La Concepción
San Pedro
Parque Unión
Santa Clara
San Francisco
Santa Cruz
Belén
Escuela de Cristo
Plaza
1 AVENIDA NORTE
2 AVENIDA NORTE
3 AVENIDA NORTE
4 AVENIDA NORTE
1 AVENIDA SUR
2 AVENIDA SUR
3 AVENIDA SUR
4 AVENIDA SUR
1 CALLE ORIENTE
2 CALLE ORIENTE
3 CALLE ORIENTE
4 CALLE ORIENTE
5 CALLE ORIENTE
6 CALLE ORIENTE
7 CALLE ORIENTE
8 CALLE ORIENTE
9 CALLE ORIENTE
CALLE DE FRAY RODRIGO DE LA CRUZ
CALLE DEL HERMANO PEDRO
CALLE DE LOS PASOS
Río Pensativo
Guatemala City (43km)
San Juan del Obispo (5km) & Santa María de Jesús (11km)
ANTIGUA

: budget hotels are situated in the streets around the market and bus d so can be noisy; hotels located in all other parts of the city are tranquil.

:xcellent option is a great budget campground-cum-guest house : of Antigua, the *Earth Lodge* (see p.128), which is beautifully set in :th of the town.

Budget options

La Casa de Don Ismael 3 C Poniente 6 ⓣ7832 1932, ⓦwww.casadonismael.com. Hidden down a quiet side street, this excellent option has seven rooms (none with private bathroom) grouped around a lovely little garden. There's a sun terrace upstairs, the communal bathrooms are kept spotless, breakfasts are available, and towels, soap and drinking water are provided. ❸

La Casa de Santa Lucía 2 Av Alameda Santa Lucía Norte 21 ⓣ7832 6189. Popular hotel with good-value, secure and spacious, if a little plain, rooms, all with private hot-water baths. The clean, well-run place also has a roof terrace as well as two nearly identical branches: *No. 4*, Alameda Santa Lucía Sur 5 (ⓣ7832 3302), which is two blocks to the south, and *No. 3*, at 6 Av Norte 43 A (ⓣ7831 1386). ❸

Hostal El Montañes 6 C Poniente & 5 Av Sur ⓣ7832 8804. This inexpensive hostel has a nice feel, with a wonderful colonial courtyard, several large dorms (US$5) and clean shared bathrooms, plus *pilas* where you can wash your clothes. Private rooms are planned, too. ❷

International Mochilero Guest House 1 C Poniente 33 ⓣ7832 0520, ⓔinternacional_mochilero@yahoo.com. Well-priced singles, doubles and a dorm (US$5) in a pleasant house with a lovely rear patio garden. There's a kitchen for guests. ❷

Jungle Party Hostal 6 Av Norte 20 ⓣ7832 0463. Sociable, popular place with decent three- and five-bed dorms (US$7), all with solid wood bunk beds. There's also a chill-out area with hammocks, and a café with an inexpensive menu. Breakfast is included. ❸

Posada Doña Angelina 4 C Poniente 33 ⓣ7832 5173. Long-running place where many of the 42 rooms are a bit gloomy, but there's usually space available, and there's a secure storeroom where you can leave your baggage. ❷

Posada Doña Olga Callejón Campo Seco 3A ⓣ7832 0623, ⓔhotelolga@yahoo.com. Family-run guest house with very clean rooms, all with private bath, and a rooftop sun terrace. ❸

Posada Juma Ocag Av Alameda Santa Lucía Norte 13 ⓣ7832 3109. A welcoming, first-class budget hotel. The eight spotless, comfortable rooms are draped with local fabrics; all have good beds, a wardrobe or storage space for clothes, a private bathroom, and reading lights. Grassy patio, roof terrace and free drinking water. Book well ahead. ❸

Sky Hotel 1 Av Sur 15 ⓣ7832 3383. Well-run place with a sociable ambience and brightly painted, tile-floored rooms, all with lockers, and some with private bathroom. Nice sitting area, and the pretty garden at the rear has some shade from orange trees. *Sky Café*, a popular venue for a sundowner, is upstairs; breakfast is included. ❷–❸

Yellow House 1 C Poniente 24 ⓣ7832 6646. This popular hostel offers inexpensive dorms (US$6.50) with good beds, a roof terrace and small rear patio, free Internet access and cheap international phone calls. Breakfast included. ❸

Moderate

Albergue Andinista 6 Av Norte 34 ⓣ & ⓕ7832 3343. Secure, good-value apartments, most with kitchens, set around a peaceful garden bursting with flowers. Daniel, the English-speaking owner, also provides luggage storage. ❹

Hotel Aurora 4 C Oriente 16 ⓣ & ⓕ7832 0217, ⓦwww.hotelauroraantigua.com. Antigua's original hotel occupies a fine colonial building with sixteen spacious rooms grouped around a lovely grassy courtyard and fountain. It's a little old-fashioned, but comfortable and well-managed. Breakfast included. ❻

Hotel Los Pasos 9 C Oriente 19 ⓣ7832 5252, ⓦwww.hotellospasos.com. Stylish hotel boasting real colonial character. Very good-value rooms, tastefully presented with exposed stone walls and quality beds covered with colourful local textiles, all with private bathroom and four with fireplaces. The gardens and communal areas are equally attractive, and there's a lovely beamed dining room. Breakfast included. Rooms ❹, suites ❻–❼

Hotel Posada San Pedro 7 Av Norte 29 ⓣ7832 0718, ⓦwww.posadasanpedro.net. Comfortable, well-kept and spacious rooms, with hand-carved wooden furniture and private bathrooms (with tubs), plus a good location on a quiet street make this one of the best deals in this price range. The hotel's second branch, at 3 Av Sur 15 (ⓣ7832 3594), is not quite as attractive and has smaller rooms, but is still good value. Both locations ❹

Hotel Santa Clara 2 Av Sur 20 ⓣ7832 0342. Tranquil location and spacious, clean rooms – most with two double beds and all with private bath (some have tubs) – set around a pleasant little courtyard. Parking available. ❹

Posada La Merced 7 Av Norte 43a ⓣ7832 3197, ⓦwww.merced-landivar.com. Excellent Kiwi-owned hotel with a good choice of cheerful rooms (some set around a garden patio), all with reading lights, safes, spotless private bathrooms and nice decorative touches. Children are made very welcome; there's also a well-equipped kitchen for guests' use. Discounts outside peak season. Rooms ❹–❺, suite ❻, apartment ❽

Posada San Sebastián 3 Av Norte 4 ⓣ & ⓕ7832 2621, ⓔsnsebast@hotmail.com. Charming, conveniently located establishment with nine rooms, each decorated with antiques. There's also a gorgeous little bar, a roof terrace and complimentary breakfast. ❻

La Tatuana 7 Av Sur 3 ⓣ7832 1223. Small hotel with five bright rooms, all with private bath and decent-quality beds, a quiet location and a roof terrace. Book well ahead as it's good value and always popular. ❺

Expensive

Casa Azul 4 Av Norte 5 ⓣ7832 0961, ⓦwww.casazu.guate.com. Small, elegant hotel, just off the plaza, with huge, extremely stylish rooms – those on the upper level enjoy great city views – set in a converted colonial mansion. Extras include sauna, hot tub and a delightful pool. ❽

Casa Capuchinas 2 Av Norte 7 ⓣ & ⓕ7832 0121, ⓦwww.casacapuchinas.com. Lovely little guest house whose trump card is a wonderfully peaceful location and private garden. There are just five rooms, all with huge beds, fireplaces and decoration that shows a personal touch. Breakfast included. ❽

Casa Encantada 9 C Poniente 1 ⓣ7832 7903, ⓦwww.casaencantada-antigua.com. Sumptuous new place with ten immaculate, stylish rooms, most with a four-poster bed, and all with delightful bathrooms. There's also a small pool, a rooftop bar and a breakfast area. Rooms ❽, suites ❾ US$110–140

Casa Santo Domingo 3 C Oriente 28 ⓣ7832 0140, ⓦwww.casasantodomingo.com.gt. One of Central America's most impressive hotels – a converted colonial-era convent where the rooms and corridors are bedecked in ecclesiastical art and paraphernalia. There's no lack of luxury here; most of the 125 rooms and suites have a fireplace, all have king-size or two double beds. High-season rates start at US$190, but discounts available at off-peak times. ❾

The Cloister 5 Av Norte 23 ⓣ7832 0712, ⓦwww.thecloister.com. Set almost under Antigua's famous arch, this tasteful, upmarket B&B has seven beautifully furnished rooms around a flowering courtyard. There's a real air of tranquillity here, plus a well-stocked private library and reading room. ❽–❾

Hotel Antigua 8 C Poniente 1 ⓣ7832 0288, ⓕ7832 0807, ⓦwww.portahotels.com/hotelantigua.htm. Large establishment set in spacious grounds, offering rooms appointed with tasteful colonial-style furniture and log-burning fireplaces to ward off the winter chill. US$110, including breakfast. ❾

Hotel Quinta de las Flores C del Hermano Pedro 6 ⓣ 832 3721, ⓕ7832 3726, ⓦwww.quintadelasflores.com. A little out of town, but this hotel's spectacular garden, with a swimming pool and many rare plants, shrubs and trees, make it a wonderful place to relax. The rooms and *casitas* (each sleeping five, with two bedrooms and kitchen) are attractively decorated; there's also a restaurant. ❼

Mesón Panza Verde 5 Av Sur 19 ⓣ7832 2925, ⓦwww.panzaverde.com. Stylish, immaculately furnished hotel with wonderful doubles and suites spread throughout two colonial-style buildings. The hotel is also home to one of Antigua's premier restaurants and an art gallery, while other perks include a lap pool and a healthy complimentary breakfast. ❼–❾

Posada del Ángel 4 Av Sur ⓣ7832 5303, ⓕ7832 0260, ⓦwww.posadadelangel.com. Luxurious B&B with five suites, all outfitted with huge beds and sumptuous furnishings, including rugs and textiles. There's also a small heated lap pool, a library and a roof terrace with great views. President Clinton stayed here during his 1999 visit (in the Rose suite). Prices rise on weekends. US$150–200. ❾

The City

In accordance with its position as the seat of colonial authority in Central America, Antigua was once a centre of secular and religious power, trade and,

Semana Santa in Antigua

Antigua's **Semana Santa (Holy Week) celebrations** are perhaps the most extravagant and impressive in all Latin America, a week of vigils, processions and pageants commemorating the most solemn week of the Christian year. The celebrations start with a procession on Palm Sunday, representing Christ's entry into Jerusalem, and continue through the week, climaxing on Good Friday. On Thursday night the streets are carpeted with meticulously drawn patterns of coloured sawdust, and on Friday morning a series of processions re-enacts the progress of Christ to the Cross. Setting out from the churches of La Merced and Escuela de Cristo and the village of San Felipe at around 8am, groups of penitents, clad in purple or white and wearing peaked hoods, carry images of Christ and the Cross on massive platforms, accompanied by solemn dirges played by local brass bands and clouds of incense. After 3pm, the hour of the Crucifixion, the penitents change into black.

It is a great honour to be involved in the procession but no easy task – the great cedar block carried from La Merced weighs some 3.5 tonnes and needs eighty men to lift it. Some of the images displayed date from the seventeenth century, and the procession itself is thought to have been introduced by Alvarado in the early years of the Conquest.

Check the exact details of events with the tourist office, which should be able to provide you with a map detailing the routes of the processions. During Holy Week hotels in Antigua are often full, and the entire town is packed on Good Friday. But even if you have to make the trip from Guatemala City or Lago de Atitlán, it's well worth it, especially on Friday.

above all, wealth. Here the great institutions competed with the government to build the country's most impressive buildings. Churches, monasteries, schools, hospitals and grand family homes were constructed throughout the city, all with tremendously thick walls to resist earthquakes. Today, Antigua has an incredible number of ruined and restored **colonial buildings**, and although these constitute only part of the city's original architectural splendour, they do give an idea of its former extravagance. Mentioned below are only some of the remaining examples; armed with a map from the tourist office you could spend days exploring the ruins. However, the prospect of visiting the lot can seem overwhelming; if you'd rather just see the gems, make La Merced, Las Capuchinas, the Casa Popenoe and San Francisco your targets.

The Parque Central

Antigua's focal point has always been its commanding central plaza, the **Parque Central**. In colonial times the plaza held a bustling market, which was cleared periodically for bullfights, military parades, floggings and public hangings. The calm of today's shady plaza, largely isolated from the city's traffic and replete with well-tended flowering scrubs, is relatively recent. Don't miss the risqué central fountain, its water jets gushing from the nipples of breast-squeezing mermaids.

The Cathedral of San José

The most imposing of the surrounding structures is the **Cathedral of San José**, on the eastern side, its intricate facade evocatively illuminated at night. The first cathedral on this site was begun in 1545, using some of the vast fortune left by Alvarado's death. However, the execution was so poor that the structure was in a constant state of disrepair, and an earthquake in 1583 brought down much of the roof. In 1670 it was decided to start on a new cathedral worthy of the town's role as a capital city. For eleven years the town watched as conscripted Maya laboured and the most spectacular colonial building in Central America took shape. The scale of the new cathedral was astounding: a vast dome, five naves, eighteen chapels, and a central chamber measuring 90m by 20m. Its altar was inlaid with mother-of-pearl, ivory and silver, and carvings of saints and paintings by the most revered of European and colonial artists covered the walls.

The new cathedral was strong enough to withstand the earthquakes of 1689 and 1717, but its walls were weakened and the 1773 earthquake brought them crashing to the ground. Today, two of the chapels have been restored as the **Church of San José**, which opens off the Parque Central; inside it is a figure of Christ by the colonial sculptor Quirio Cataño, who also carved the famous Black Christ of Esquipulas (see p.291). Behind the church, entered from 5 Calle Oriente (entrance fee US$0.40), are the remains of the rest of the structure, a mass of fallen masonry, rotting beams, broken arches and hefty pillars, cracked and moss-covered. Buried beneath the floor are said to be some of the great names of the Conquest, including Alvarado; his wife, Beatriz de la Cueva; Bishop Marroquín; and the historian Bernal Díaz del Castillo. At the very rear of the original nave, steps lead down to a burial vault that's regularly used for Maya religious ceremonies, an example of the coexistence of pagan and Catholic beliefs that's so characteristic of Guatemala.

The Palace of the Captains General

Along the entire south side of the Parque Central runs the squat two-storey facade of the **Palace of the Captains General**, with a row of 27 arches along each floor. It was originally built in 1558, but as usual this first version was destroyed by earthquakes. It was rebuilt in 1761, only to be damaged again in 1773 and finally restored along the lines of the present structure. The palace was home to the colonial rulers and also housed the barracks of the dragoons, the stables, the royal mint, law courts, tax offices, great ballrooms, a large bureaucracy, and a lot more besides. Today it contains the headquarters of the Sacatepéquez police department and the tourist office, and a few market stalls.

The Ayuntamiento

Directly opposite, on the north side of the plaza, is the **Ayuntamiento**, the city hall, also known as the *Casa del Cabildo*, or town house. Dating from 1740, its metre-thick walls balance the solid style of the Palace of the Captains General. Unlike most others, this building survived earlier rumblings and wasn't damaged until the 1976 earthquake, although it has since been repaired. The city hall was abandoned in 1779 when the capital moved to today's site in Guatemala City, but it was later reclaimed for use by the city's administration. If you climb to the upper level of the building, there's a wonderful vista of the three volcanoes that ring the city, especially fine at sunset.

The Ayuntamiento also holds a couple of minor museums. The first of these, the **Museo de Santiago** (Tues–Sun 9am–4pm; US$1.20, Sun by donation), houses a collection of colonial artefacts, including bits of pottery, a sword said to have been used by Alvarado, some traditional Maya weapons, portraits of stern-faced colonial figures, and some paintings of warfare between the Spanish and the Maya. At the back of the museum is the old city jail, beside which there used to be a small chapel where condemned prisoners passed their last moments before being hauled off to the gallows in the plaza. Also under the arches of the city hall, the **Museo del Libro Antiguo** (same hours and fees as above) is located in the rooms that held the first printing press in Central America. The press arrived here in 1660, from Puebla de los Ángeles in Mexico, and churned out its first book three years later. A replica of the press is on display alongside some copies of the works produced on it.

South and east of the Parque Central

Across the street from the ruined cathedral, in 5 Calle Oriente (Calle de La Universidad), is the old **Seminario Tridentino**, one of the great colonial schools. It was founded at the start of the seventeenth century for some fifteen students, and later expanded to include the Escuela de Guadalupe, a special school for indigenous Maya of high birth, so that local people could share in the joys of theology. The structure is still in almost perfect condition, but it's now divided up into several separate homes, so the elaborate stucco doorway – one of the city's finest – is all you'll get to see.

A little further up the same street is the **Museo de Arte Colonial** (Tues–Fri 9am–4pm, Sat & Sun 9am–noon & 2–4pm; US$3), housed in the former premises of the University of San Carlos Borromeo. The founding of a university was first proposed by Bishop Marroquín in 1559, but it wasn't until 1676 that the plan was authorized, using money left by the bishop. Classes began in 1681 with seventy students applying themselves to everything from law to the Kaqchikel language. At first only pure-blooded Castilians could study here, but later a broader spectrum of the population was admitted. The Moorish-style courtyard, deep-set windows and beautifully ornate cloisters make it one of the finest architectural survivors in Antigua. The museum contains a good collection of brooding religious art, sculpture, furniture, murals depicting life on the colonial campus, and a seventeenth-century map of Antigua by the historian Antonio de Fuentes y Guzmán.

Further west up 5 Calle Oriente, on the corner of 1 Avenida Sur, the superbly restored colonial mansion **Casa Popenoe** (Mon–Sat 2–4pm; US$1.20) offers a welcome break from church ruins as well as a window into domestic life in colonial times. The house, originally built in 1634 was in ruins when, in 1932, Dr Wilson Popenoe, a United Fruit–company scientist, began its comprehensive restoration. Sifting through the rubble piece by piece, the doctor and his wife restored the building to its former glory, filling it with an incredible collection of colonial furniture and art. Among the paintings are portraits of Bishop Marroquín and the menacing-looking Alvarado himself. Every last detail has been authentically restored, down to the original leather lampshades painted with religious musical scores and the great wooden beds, decorated with a mass of accomplished carving. The kitchen and servants' quarters have also been carefully renovated, and you can see the bread ovens, herb garden and pigeon loft, which would have provided the original occupants with their mail service. A narrow staircase leads up from the pigeon loft to the roof, from where there are spectacular views over the city and volcanoes. Dr Popenoe died in 1972, but two of his daughters still live in the house.

Around Parque Unión

A block south and a block west of the parque, on 6 Calle Oriente, two churches face each other at opposite ends of the slim, palm-tree-lined plaza of **Parque Unión**. At the western end is the **San Pedro Church** and hospital. Originally built in 1680, and periodically crammed full of earthquake victims, the church was finally evacuated in 1976 when one of the aftershocks threatened to bring down the roof. Reconstruction was completed in 1991 and the facade now has a polished perfection that's strangely incongruous in Antigua. At the other end of the plaza is the convent and church of **Santa Clara**, founded in 1699 by nuns from Puebla in Mexico. In colonial times this became a popular place for well-to-do young ladies to take the veil, as the hardships were none too hard, and the nuns earned a reputation for their cooking, by selling bread to the aristocracy. The huge original convent was totally destroyed in 1717, as was the second in 1773, but the current building was spared in 1976 and its ornate facade (floodlit at night) remains intact. In front of Santa Clara are the huge arches of an open-air *pila*, a washhouse where local women gather to scrub, rinse and gossip.

Just southwest on 1 Avenida Sur, the imposing **church of San Francisco** (daily 8am–6pm) is one of the oldest churches in Antigua. Dating from 1579, it grew into a vast religious and cultural centre that included a school, a hospital, music rooms, a printing press and a monastery. The church originally boasted highly decorative mouldings and sculpture along its nave, but these were ruined by earthquakes and were left off during restoration in 1960. Inside the church is the tomb of **Hermano Pedro de Betancourt**, a Franciscan from the Canary Islands who founded the Hospital of Belén in Antigua and is credited with powers of miraculous intervention by the faithful – hundreds of little plaques give thanks for his services, while Pope John Paul II made him Central America's first saint in 2002. The **ruins** (same hours; US$0.40) of the monastery are among the most impressive in Antigua, and you're welcome to picnic next to the colossal fallen arches and pillars on the pleasant grassy verges.

North of the Parque Central

Setting out northwards from the Parque Central, you'll find the remains of the hermitage of **El Carmen** on 3 Avenida Norte. This was originally one of the city's great churches, first built in 1638 and rebuilt many times since: the top half of the facade finally collapsed in 1976 but the remains hint at its former glory.

Just northeast of here, at the junction of 2 Calle Oriente and 2 Avenida Norte, is the site of **Las Capuchinas** (Tues–Sun 9am–5pm; US$3.75), the largest of the city's convents, whose ruins are some of the best preserved but least understood in Antigua. The Capuchin nuns, who came from Madrid, were rather late on the scene, founding the city's fourth convent in 1726. They were only granted permission by the colonial authorities on the condition that the convent would exact no payment from its novices. The Capuchin order was the most rigorous in Antigua. Numbers were restricted to 25, with nuns sleeping on wooden beds with straw pillows. Once they had entered the convent it's thought the women were not allowed any visual contact with the outside world; food was passed to them by means of a turntable and they could only speak to visitors through a grille.

The ruins are the most beautiful in Antigua, with fountains, courtyards and massive earthquake-proof pillars. The tower or "retreat" is the most unusual feature, with eighteen tiny cells set into the walls of its top floor, each having its own independent sewage system. Two of the cells have been returned to their original condition to demonstrate the extreme austerity of the nuns' lives. The lower floor is dominated by a massive pillar that supports the structure above and incorporates seventeen small recesses, some with rings set in the walls. Theories about the purpose of this still abound – as a warehouse, a laundry room, a communal bath or even a torture chamber – though most scholars now agree that it probably functioned as a storage room, and the rings were meat

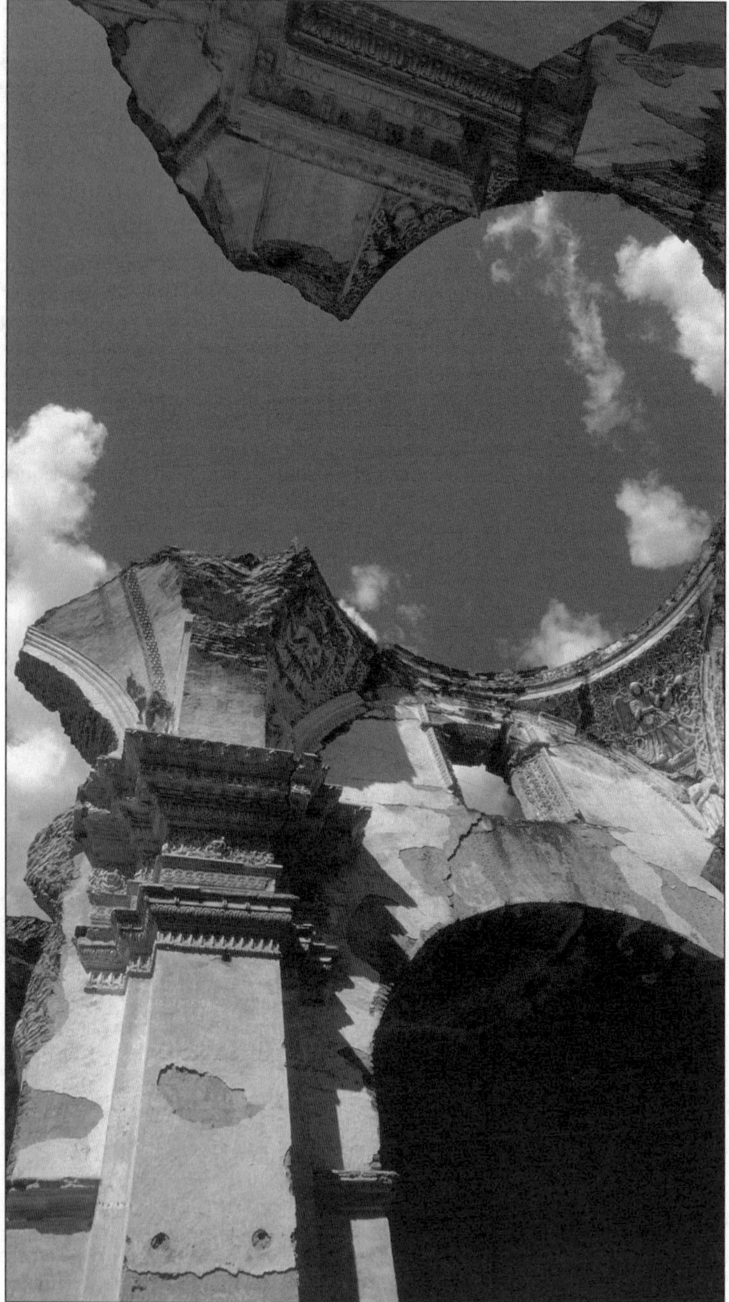

△ Ruins, Antigua

hooks. The exterior of this architectural curiosity is also interesting, ringed with small stone recesses that represent the Stations of the Cross.

Heading northwest, the church and convent of **Santa Teresa**, located where 4 Avenida Norte meets 1 Calle, was originally founded by a Peruvian philanthropist for a group of Carmelite nuns from Lima; these days, however, it serves as the city jail.

A block further west along 1 Calle is the church of **La Merced**, which boasts one of the most intricate and impressive facades in the entire city. It has been beautifully restored, painted mustard yellow and white, and crammed with plaster moulding of interlaced patterns. Look closely and you'll see the outline of a corn cob, a design not normally seen on Catholic churches and probably added by the original Maya labourers. The church is still in use, but the cloisters and gardens lie ruined, exposed to the sky. In the centre of one of the courtyards is a monumental tiered fountain with four pools that's known as the *Fuente de Pescados*; the pools were used by the Mercedarian brothers for breeding fish. The colonial fountain in front of the church is also worth a look for its superbly preserved carved decoration.

From La Merced it's a few steps to 5 Avenida Norte, spanned by the **arch of Santa Catalina**, one of Antigua's most emblematic structures and all that remains of the original convent founded here in 1609. By 1697 it had reached maximum capacity with 110 nuns and six novices, and the arch was built in order that they could walk between the two halves of the establishment without being exposed to the pollution of the outside world. Somehow it managed to defy the constant onslaught of earthquakes and was restored in the middle of the nineteenth century; it is now a favoured, if clichéd, spot for photographers as the view to the Volcán de Agua is unobstructed from here.

Further out to the northeast along 1 Avenida Norte, the badly damaged ruins of the churches of **Santa Rosa**, **Candelaria** and **Nuestra Señora de los Dolores del Cerro** are of interest to ruined-church buffs only.

West of the Parque Central

The last of the major ruins lie west of the plaza, near the bus station. At the junction of 4 Calle Poniente and 6 Avenida Norte stands **La Compañia de Jesús**, an educational establishment and church that was operated by the Jesuits until King Carlos III of Spain, feeling threatened by their tremendous and growing power, expelled them from the colonies in 1767. Renovated recently by Spanish experts, the building now hosts cultural exhibitions and events.

Turning to the right in front of the bus station, walk to the end of tree-lined Avenida Alameda Santa Lucía, and you reach the spectacular remains of **San Jerónimo** (daily 9am–5pm; US$3.75), a school built in 1739. The site, with its well-kept gardens woven between the huge blocks of fallen masonry and crumbling walls, is regularly used as a spectacular site for classical music concerts. Behind San Jerónimo, a cobbled road leads to the even larger, and more chaotic, ruin of **La Recolección** (daily 9am–5pm; US$2.25), where the middle of the church is piled high with the remains of the roof and walls. Recolectos friars first arrived here and asked for permission to build in 1685, but it wasn't until 1701 that they started the church, and a further fourteen years before it was finished. Only months after its completion, the church was brought to the ground by a huge earthquake. This second version was destroyed in 1773 and has been steadily decaying ever since.

On the southern side of the bus station, along Avenida Alameda Santa Lucía, is an imposing monument to **Rafael Landívar** (1731–93), a Jesuit

Volcano tours from Antigua

Volcán de Pacaya (see p.101) near Guatemala City is a spectacular and very active volcano, which regularly spews towering plumes of smoke and brilliant orange sludge – though such fire 'n' brimstone shows only happen sporadically. Gran Jaguar Tours, 4 C Poniente 30 (ⓣ7832 2712, ⓦwww.granjaguar.com), offer basic trips for US$5–7 per person, while Old Town Outfitters (see p.120) charge US$25–30 per person, using comfortable minibuses and including a packed lunch. Entrance to the Pacaya National Park is an additional US$3.

Other cones to climb include **volcanoes Agua** (see p.127) and **Acatenango** (see pp.124–126), the toughest climb in this region, which gives a great view of the highly active neighbouring cone of **Fuego**.

composer who is generally considered the finest poet of the colonial era. Along with the other members of his order, he was banished from the Americas in 1767. Walking back to the plaza along 5 Calle Poniente, you'll pass the **Iglesia de San Agustín**, the remains of a vast convent complex that once occupied about half the block but has stood derelict since the earthquake of 1773, after which the Augustinians followed the government in the exodus to Guatemala City.

Eating

Antigua boasts a terrific array of **cafés** and **restaurants**, with most types of global cuisine represented. It's possible to snack well for a few bucks or dine in style for around US$12–15 a head, and round it off with a great espresso or latte. The only thing hard to come by is authentic Guatemalan comedor food – which will be a relief if you've been subsisting on nothing but eggs and beans in the mountains.

The best **deli** is *Epicure*, 6 Av Norte 35A, where you'll find lots of gourmet treats produced in Guatemala, including salami and sausages, and some fine cheeses, as well as wine and culinary treats from Europe, North America and Asia. They'll also make you up a sandwich here.

Cafés

Bagel Barn 5 C Poniente 2, just off the plaza. Inexpensive breakfasts, tasty (if a little pricey) bagels and good coffee. They also show movies here.

Café Condesa west side of Parque Central – go through the Casa del Conde bookshop. Refined, bourgeois, but enjoyable place to enjoy an excellent (if expensive) breakfast, coffee and cake, or lunch. The cobbled patio and period charm create a nice tone for the long, lazy Sunday brunches (US$7.50) favoured by Antiguan society.

Café La Escolandia 5 Av Sur. A wonderfully peaceful café attached to a plant nursery, about 800m south of the parque, which offers breakfasts and *pan de hierbas* sandwiches, pies and salads.

Caffè Opera 6 Av Norte 17. Swanky, expensive café with lavish wall-to-wall operatic paraphernalia, comfortable seating and a tiled floor. Good for coffee and a *panini* (though the *licuado* prices are stratospheric); they also offer daily specials that might include *gnocchi* or *lomito*. Closed Wed.

La Cenicienta 5 Av Norte 7. Bizarre Guatemalan attempt to re-create a Victorian tearoom – with reasonable enough quiche, cakes and sweet snacks that granny would approve of – though the coffee is very weak. No smoking.

Cookies Etc 3 Av Norte 7. Small place with a near endless list of yummy cookies, as well as sandwiches, muffins and free coffee refills. Takeouts available.

Doña Luisa's 4 C Oriente 12. Long-running café-restaurant set in a historic colonial mansion that's highly popular with foreigners and locals. The menu is pretty basic – sandwiches, burgers and salads (try the *ensalada taco guatelmalteco*) – but the in-house bakery really is the best in town. Bread and pastries can be purchased from an adjoining shop.

Fernando's Kaffee 7 Av Norte 43. Unquestionably some of the finest coffee – ground and roasted on the premises – in Antigua. The house blend is selected by a friendly, English-speaking Guatemalan perfectionist, while the home-made pastries, ice cream and cakes are equally splendid.

La Fuente 4 C Oriente 14. Attractive, moderately priced courtyard restaurant/café where you can eat a decent plate of pasta, a sandwich or soup and sip good coffee. On Saturdays indigenous women set up a *huipil* market around the central fountain.

Peroleto Alameda Santa Lucía Norte 36. Hole-in-the-wall cabin with cheap, healthy breakfasts, fruit juices and delectable cakes.

Rainbow Café 7 Av Sur 8. Long-standing café-restaurant with a bohemian atmosphere and a great menu of imaginative salads and vegetarian choices, shakes and juices. There's live music most nights (around a campfire when weather permits) and occasional cultural events, too. Also home of one of Antigua's best secondhand bookshops and travel agents.

Restaurants

Beijing 5 C Poniente 15C. Competent, if not compelling, fairly pricey Chinese and East Asian food, with good noodle and rice dishes, and Vietnamese spring rolls prepared with a few imaginative twists. Inexpensive set-lunch menu.

Café Colonial 7 Av Norte 3. Superb, very clean and well-run little place with plenty of tasty Guatemalan dishes at rock bottom rates: US$2.50 for a plate including rice and a drink.

Café Panchoy 6 Av Norte 1B. Good-value cooking with a real Guatemalan flavour, served around an open kitchen. Dishes include top steaks and *chiles rellenos*. Excellent margaritas, too. Closed Tues.

Caffè Mediterraneo 6 C Poniente 6A. Real Italian cooking, with fresh pasta, *bruschette* and decent wine. Very civilized and popular with Antigua's resident foodies. Closed Tues.

Casa de las Mixtas 1 Callejón, off 3 C Poniente. Clean, friendly, better-than-average comedor, with bright, attractive decor and very extensive breakfast options.

La Casserole Callejón de la Concepción 7. Elegant restaurant, in a pretty garden patio shaded by a lime tree, which consistently delivers first-rate French cuisine – leave some room for the epic desserts. Also features wines of the month. Closed Mon.

Comedor Típico Antigüeño Alameda Santa Lucía Sur 5. Canteen-like comedor opposite the bus terminal and market, with cheap breakfasts and US$2 set lunches (such as *pollo a la carbón*, *pepián* and *adobado*), which all include a soup starter.

La Cuevita de los Urquizú 2 C Oriente 9. This popular, canteen-like place offers a good opportunity to gorge on an array of typical Guatemalan dishes for US$4.30 per head, including a drink and sweet. Open daily 9am–7pm.

Don Martín 5 C Poniente 15C. Smallish, slightly out-of-the-way place which nevertheless has some of the most creative and appetizing Guatemalan food-with-a-twist in Antigua, plus an Italian dish or two. The classically trained chef's moderately priced menu includes a *plato típico*, *pepián* (spicy meat stew) and pasta. Closed Mon.

La Escudilla 4 Av Norte 4. Agreeable, excellent-value courtyard restaurant offering a choice of European dishes (including salads and plenty of vegetarian options) and a US$2.75 set meal that's a steal. Always busy, but you can have a drink, if you have to wait, in *Riki's Bar*, which is in the same premises.

La Fonda de la Calle Real three branches: upstairs at 5 Av Norte 5; 5 Av Norte 12; and a third (the nicest location) at 3 C Poniente 7. Excellent for authentic Guatemalan specialities including *caldo real* (chicken soup), *pepián* or charcoal-grilled meats. Closed Wed.

Frida's 5 Av Norte 29. Lively atmosphere, especially at weekends, with great Mexican food served up in surrounds festooned with 1950s Americana.

Nicolas 4 C Oriente 20. The most opulent restaurant in town, benefiting from a stunning setting in a historic house awash with chandeliers and modish contemporary seating. Gourmet-geared menu includes Asian fusion dishes, New Zealand lamb and fresh lobster, while the wine list is extensive and well chosen. Around US$30–35 a head. Closed Wed, and Sun evenings.

Panza Verde 5 Av Sur 19. Highly rated, stylish and consistently good European restaurant, whose Swiss chef has created a well-chosen menu of fish and meat mains and desserts to die for. The setting is elegant, too, with tables grouped around a delightful courtyard garden.

Perú Café 4 Av Norte 7. Enjoyable, casual place with a dining room off a small patio. There's interesting fare including *sausa seco de res* (beef in coriander sauce) and Peruvian-style *ceviche*.

El Punto 7 Av Norte 8A. The most authentic Italian place in town, with meat, pasta and *gnocchi* at moderate prices as well as some interesting wines. Rated highly by Antigua's foodie expats. Closed Mon.

Su Chow 5 Av Norte 38. Good, inexpensive Chinese food, cooked and served by a charming Belizean family.

Travel Menu 6 C Poniente 14. Enjoyable, inexpensive Dutch-owned place serving up large portions of very tasty Latin and Western food, with an atmospheric candlelit setting.

Drinking, nightlife and entertainment

Evening activity tends to wax and wane depending on the attitude of town hall: periodically, a mayor will clamp down on licensing laws and close down **bars** and restrict **nightlife**, which is curtailed officially anyway by a "dry law" that forbids the sale of alcohol after 1am. Antigua's main *zona viva* (lively zone) is centred around the arch on 5 Av Norte, though there are also some good bars on 1 Av Norte. The club scene here is small but lively, drawing a crowd from Guatemala City. Illegal **"after hours" parties** are held most weekends in private houses, publicized by flyers and word-of-mouth, and featuring local and visiting DJs.

A number of small video **cinemas** show a range of Western films on a daily basis; weekly listings are posted on notice boards all over town. The main cinemas are Cinema Bistro, 5 Av Sur 14, and Maya Moon, 6 Av Norte 1A; the *Bagel Barn*, 5 C Poniente 2, and *Café 2000*, 6 Av Norte, also show films. The Proyecto Cultural El Sitio, at 5 C Poniente 15, has a fairly good choice of Latin American and art-house movies.

Bars and clubs

La Casbah 5 Av Norte 30. Nightclub with a spectacular venue overlooking the floodlit ruins of a Baroque church, attracting a well-heeled crowd. Commercial Latin house is the main musical flavour, and drinks are expensive. Mon–Wed free, Thurs, Fri & Sat around US$3.50.

Mono Loco 2 Av Norte 6B. Huge, clichéd gringo sports-bar-style place, with mediocre mainstream music and dreary food. For some reason, however, it's one of the most popular places in town.

No Sé 1 Av Norte 11C. Highly enjoyable American-owned bar, slightly disheveled in appearance and featuring eclectic background sounds and an open mike and live music some nights. A short menu offers filling food at fair rates, plus there's a rear tequila/mescal bar, secondhand bookstore and video room.

Onis 7 Av Norte & 6 C Poniente. Hip, boho two-storey bar which serves some snacks and has stunning views over the ruined church of San Agustín. Rarely gets that busy.

Reilly's 5 Av Norte 31. The city's first Irish bar is a highly popular meeting point and has a daily special menu (with fish 'n' chips some nights), and a great quiz on Sunday evenings.

Riki's Bar 4 Av Norte 4. Still one of the most happening bars in town due to its excellent location inside *La Escudilla*, eclectic funk, jazz and lounge music policy, and double-dose happy hour (7–9pm).

La Sala 6 C Poniente 9. Spacious, sociable bar, with a good drinks list and a mix of locals and foreigners. It's heaving every weekend.

Sky Café 1 Av Norte. Terrific views from the upper deck, great tunes and an infectious vibe make this one of Antigua's main drinking dens, from around sunset onwards.

Torero's Av de la Recolección. *Discoteca* for salsa and merengue aficionados, popular with gringas and their Spanish teachers, though the location behind the bus station is inconvenient – take a taxi.

Listings

Adventure sports Maya Mountain Bike Tours, 1 Av Sur 15 (☎7832 3383), have an excellent range of trips, plus bike rental; Old Town Outfitters, 6 C Poniente 7 (☎7832 4243, ⓦwww.bikeguatemala.com), run volcano hikes, mountain-bike excursions and rock-climbing trips for all levels, and offer tent, sleeping bag, pack and bike rental.

Banks and exchange Banco Industrial, 5 Av Sur 4, just south of the plaza, has a 24hr ATM for Visa/Plus cardholders; Banco del Quetzal, on north side of the plaza, has a MasterCard/Cirrus ATM.

Bike rental Maya Mountain Bike Tours and Old Town Outfitters (see "Adventure sports", above) rent mountain bikes from around US$8 a day, US$28 weekly.

Bookstores Casa del Conde and Un Poco de Todo are both on the west side of the plaza. For second-hand books, *Rainbow Café*, 7 Av Sur 8, has the largest selection, or try *No Sé* at 1 Av Norte 11C.

Car and motorbike rental Avis, 5 Av Norte 22 (ⓣ & ⓕ832 2692), and Tabarini, 6 Av Sur 22 (ⓣ7832 8107, ⓦwww.tabarini.com), both have cars from around US$35 a day and Jeeps from US$50. La Ceiba, 6 C Poniente 6 (ⓣ7832 4168), rent 250cc motorbikes for US$8 per hour or US$30 a day.

City tours Excellent walking tours (US$18) are led by historian Elizabeth Bell, *Hotel Casa Santo Domingo* (ⓣ & ⓕ7832 5821, ⓦwww.antiguatours.net), both have cars from around US$35

Gym La Fábrica, C Del Hermano Pedro 16 (ⓣ7832 0486), has excellent facilities, including running machines, weights, and dance, aerobics, step and martial arts classes.

Horse-riding Ravenscroft Stables, 2 Av Sur 3, in the village of San Juan del Obispo (ⓣ7832 6229). It's on the road up to Santa María de Jesús.

Internet There are dozens of cybercafés; rates are set at around US$1.25 an hour. Conexión, in the *La Fuente* courtyard at 4 C Oriente 14 (daily 8.30am–7pm), is probably the best set-up, with flat screens and fast connections. Funky Monkey, 5 Av Sur 6 (next to *Mono Loco*), is another good place.

Laundry Rainbow Laundry, 6 Av Sur 15 (Mon–Sat 7am–7pm).

Libraries and cultural institutes El Sitio, 5 C Poniente 15 (ⓣ7832 3037), has an active theatre, library and art gallery, and regularly hosts exhibitions and concerts; see the *Revue* or *Guatemala Post* for listings.

Studying Spanish in Antigua

Antigua's **language schools** are a key local employer, with a couple of dozen or so established schools, and many more less reliable set-ups, some operating in the front room of someone's house. Whether you're just stopping for a week or two to learn the basics, or settling in for several months in pursuit of total fluency, there can be no doubt that this is one of the best places in Latin America to learn Spanish: it's a beautiful, relaxed town, lessons are inexpensive (though tend to cost more than in other areas of Guatemala) and there are several superb schools.

Choosing a school

The following schools are well established, recommended and towards the top end of the price scale, charging between US$130 and US$190 per week for four hours daily one-on-one tuition and full family-based lodging and meals.

APPE 6 C Poniente 40 ⓣ7832 0720, ⓦwww.appeschool.com

Los Capitanes Generales 5 Av Sur 4 ⓣ7832 8769, ⓦwww.loscapitanes.com

Centroamerica Spanish Academy inside *La Fuente*, 4 C Oriente 14 ⓣ7832 3297, ⓦwww.quik.guate.com/spanishacademy

Centro Lingüístico de la Fuente 1 C Poniente 27 ⓣ7832 2711, ⓦwww.delafuenteschool.com

Centro Lingüístico Maya 5 C Poniente 20 ⓣ7832 0656, ⓦwww.travellog.com/guatemala/antigua/clmaya/school.html

Christian Spanish Academy 6 Av Norte 15 ⓣ7832 3922, ⓦwww.learncsa.com

Probigua 6 Av Norte 41B ⓣ7832 2998, ⓦwww.probigua.conexion.com

Proyecto Lingüístico Francisco Marroquín 7 C Poniente 31 ⓣ7832 2886, ⓦwww.plfm-antigua.org. Also offers classes in Maya languages.

San José El Viejo 5 Av Sur 34 ⓣ7832 3028, ⓦwww.sanjoseelviejo.com

Sevilla 1 Av Sur 8 ⓣ7832 5101, ⓦwww.sevillantigua.com

Tecún Umán 6 C Poniente 34 A ⓣ7831 2792, ⓦwww.escuelatecun.com

La Unión 1 Av Sur 21 ⓣ7832 7337, ⓦwww.launion.conexion.com

Moving on from Antigua

Because of its small size, and its position off the Interamericana, few **bus routes** originate in Antigua. If you're heading to anywhere in the east of the country, take the first bus to Guatemala City and change there or, for convenience, consider a shuttle minibus service. If you're heading into the western highlands, with the exception of Panajachel, it's usually best to catch the first bus to Chimaltenango and transfer there. The following buses leave from the main terminal by the market unless stated otherwise.

Guatemala City 1hr. A constant flow of buses leaves for the capital (Mon–Sat 4am–7.30pm, Sun 6am–8pm).

Ciudad Vieja every 30min; 20min

Chimaltenango, via Parramos every 20min; 40min

Escuintla, via El Rodeo hourly; 1hr

Panajachel 1 daily at 7am from 4 C Poniente 34; 2hr 30min

San Antonio Aguas Calientes every 30min; 20min

Santa María de Jesús every 30min; 30min

Yepocapa and **Acatenango** 8 daily; both 40min.

Shuttles

Minibus **shuttle services** run from Antigua to many parts of the country and can be booked through most travel agents, including Atitrans (see "Listings"). Shuttles are a lot more expensive than public buses, but they are much more comfortable and a bit quicker. There are very frequent airport and Guatemala City shuttles (US$7–10) depending on the time of day; several daily buses to Panajachel (US$12); at least one daily shuttle to Monterrico (US$7–10). Chichicastanango (US$12) is very well served on market days (Thurs & Sun). For Copán, Honduras, travel agency Monarcas (see "Listings") has a daily bus at 4am.

When there's enough demand, shuttles also run to Río Dulce (around US$35), Quetzaltenango (US$25), Huehuetenango (US$35) and San Cristóbal de las Casas, Mexico, for US$50 (contact Monarcas).

Medical care There's a 24hr emergency service at the Santa Lucía Hospital, Calzada Santa Lucía Sur 7 (Ⓣ7832 3122). Dr Aceituno, who speaks good English, has a surgery at 2 C Poniente 7 (Ⓣ7832 0512).

Pharmacies Farmacia Santa María, west side of the plaza (daily 8am–10pm).

Police The police HQ is on the south side of the plaza, next to the tourist office (Ⓣ & Ⓕ7832 0251). The tourist police are just off the plaza on 4 Av Norte (Ⓣ7832 7290).

Pool hall 3 C Poniente 4–5 A. Very much a male-dominated institution, although tourists of either sex are welcome, providing they can handle the smell.

Post office Av Alameda Santa Lucía, opposite the bus terminal (Mon–Fri 8am–4.30pm). Federal Express, 2 C Poniente 3.

Shopping Nim Po't, 5 Av Norte 29, sells some of the finest textiles in the country at fair prices. The warehouse-like store is something of a museum of contemporary Maya weaving, with a stunning array of complete costumes, as well as books on Maya culture and some souvenirs. La Fuente centre, at 4 C Oriente 14, has a number of upmarket clothing and handicraft stores, while Al Pie del Volcán, on 4 Av Norte 7, also sells quality handicrafts.

Supermarket La Bodegona, at 4 C Poniente and Alameda Santa Lucía.

Swimming pool The *Radisson Villa Antigua*, 9 C, just south of town on the road to Cuidad Vieja, has two (non-heated) pools that non-guests can use for US$5 per day, which also gives you access to a small gym and sauna.

Taxis On the east side of the plaza, by the market or call Ⓣ7832 0479. For a female cab driver, call Chiqui on Ⓣ5715 5720.

Telephones The Telgua office is just south of the plaza on 5 Av Sur (7am–10pm), but rates are higher here than anywhere else and you'll have to queue. You can netcall on good lines at Conexión and Funky Monkey (see "Internet") for around US$0.30 to North America, US$0.40 per hour to

Europe, and US$0.50 per hour to Australia, New Zealand and the rest of the world.

Travel agents Of the dozens of travel agents in Antigua, some of the most professional are: Adventure Travel Center Viareal, 5 Av Norte 25B (Ⓣ7832 0162, Ⓔviareal@guate.net), which is good for adventure and sailing trips; Atitrans, 6 Av Sur 8 (Ⓣ7832 3371, Ⓦwww.atitransguate.com), the best in town for shuttle buses; Monarcas, Av Alameda Santa Lucía 7 (Ⓣ7832 1939, Ⓔmorarcas@conexion.com.gt), which organize direct daily shuttle buses to Copán as well as Maya culture and ecology tours; the very efficient Rainbow/Arco Iris, 7 Av Sur 8 (Ⓣ & Ⓕ7832 4202, Ⓦwww.guatemalareservations.com; Viajes Tivoli, at 4 C Oriente 10, east of the plaza (Ⓣ7832 4274, Ⓔantigua@tivoli.com.gt), a recommended all-rounder.

Around Antigua: villages and volcanoes

The countryside surrounding Antigua is superbly fertile and breathtakingly beautiful. The valley is dotted with small villages, ranging from the ladino coffee centre of Alotenango to the traditional indigenous village of Santa María de Jesús, while there are two museums in Jocotenango just north of Antigua. None is more than an hour away and all make interesting day-trips. For the more adventurous, the **volcanic peaks** of Agua and Acatenango offer strenuous but superb hiking. A third, Fuego, has been far too active to climb in recent years.

San Antonio Aguas Calientes

South of Antigua, the Panchoy valley is a broad sweep of farmland, overshadowed by three volcanic cones and peppered with olive-green coffee bushes. The highway passes a string of villages as it heads to Escuintla and the Pacific coast.

The first of these, a couple of kilometres from Antigua, is the indigenous village of **SAN ANTONIO AGUAS CALIENTES**, set to one side of a steep-sided bowl beneath the peak of Acatenango. San Antonio is famous for weaving, characterized by its complex floral and geometric patterns, and there's an indoor textile market next to the plaza where you can find a complete range of the local output. This is also a good place to learn the traditional craft of back-strap weaving; if you're interested, the best way to find out about possible tuition is simply by asking the women in the market.

Adjoining San Antonio is the village of **SANTA CATARINA BARAHONA**, which has a modest ruined colonial church. Out on the edge of the village, a five-minute walk up from the plaza, there's also a small outdoor municipal swimming pool (Tues–Sun 9am–6pm). You'll find a decent comedor, the *Restaurante y Cafeteria Gaby*, two blocks east of the plaza. **Buses** from the terminal in Antigua run a regular service to San Antonio and Santa Catarina every hour.

Ciudad Vieja and Alotenango

Three kilometres beyond San Antonio is **CIUDAD VIEJA**, a scruffy and unhurried village with a distinguished past: it was near here that the Spanish established their second capital of Guatemala, Santiago de los Caballeros, in 1527. Today, however, there's no trace of the original city, and all that remains from that time is a solitary tree, in a corner of the plaza, which bears a plaque commemorating the site of the first mass ever held in the country. The plaza also boasts an eighteenth-century colonial church that has recently been restored.

A further 10km down the valley, the ragged-looking village of **ALOTENANGO** is dwarfed by the often smoking, scarred cone of the Fuego volcano, which has

The unlucky one

After abandoning their short-lived first settlement near the Kaqchikel capital of Iximché, the Spanish founded **Santiago de los Caballeros** on St Celia's Day in 1527. Set amid perfect pastures in the shadow of the Acatenango and Agua volcanoes, the new city quickly flourished, and within twenty years things had really started to take shape, with a school, a cathedral, monasteries, and farms stocked with imported cattle. But while the bulk of the Spaniards were still settling in, their leader, the rapacious **Alvarado**, was off in search of action, wealth and conquest. In 1541 he set out for the Spice Islands, travelling via Jalisco, where he met his end, crushed to death beneath a rolling horse.

When news of Alvarado's death reached his wife, **Doña Beatriz**, she plunged the capital into an extended period of mourning, staining the entire palace with black clay, inside and out. She appointed herself as her husband's replacement, and on September 9, 1541, she became the first woman to govern in the Americas, signing the declaration as *La sin ventura* (the unlucky one) – a fateful premonition.

On the night of Beatriz's inauguration, an earthquake shook Volcán de Agua's crater, releasing a great wave of mud that swept away the capital, killing the new ruler and most of her courtiers. Today the exact site of the original city is still the subject of some debate, but the general consensus puts it about 2km to the east of Ciudad Vieja.

been in a state of constant eruption since the arrival of the Spanish. Given its recent record, it's best to forget about climbing the cone and view it instead from the neighbouring volcano of Acatenango. Beyond Alotenango, a smooth paved highway continues down the valley to **Escuintla**, passing the village of El Rodeo.

To get to Ciudad Vieja or Alotenango, there's a steady stream of **buses** leaving from outside the terminal in Antigua: the last one returns from Alotenango at around 7pm.

Acatenango and Fuego volcanoes

A short way beyond Ciudad Vieja, a road branches off to **SAN MIGUEL DUEÑAS**, a dried-out, scrappy-looking sort of place where the roads are lined with bamboo fences and surrounded by coffee fincas. There's little to delay you in San Miguel itself, but a kilometre before the village the **Valhalla Organic Farm** (daily 8am–5pm) is well worth investigating. Owned by an eccentric American, Lorenzo Gottschamer, the farm has nearly 60,000 macadamia nut trees, using non-grafted stock (which bear bigger crops and are more disease resistant). Visitors are very welcome, and a short tour will reveal all the secrets of nut harvesting and roasting, while later there's a chance to sample delicious macadamia pancakes or buy cosmetics and chocolates.

San Miguel Dueñas is also the best starting point for climbing the Acatenango and Fuego volcanoes. **Buses** head out to San Miguel every half-hour or so from the terminal in Antigua, but most terminate in the village. If you're making for the volcanoes, it's best to take a taxi from Antigua to La Soledad (around US$12), where you'll find the trailhead, to get an early start. Alternatively, sporadic pick-ups run from San Miguel Dueñas, or it's a two-hour walk.

Climbing Acatenango

Several travel agencies in Antigua run hiking trips (see p.120) up **Acatenango** but it's also possible to do it yourself. The trail starts in **LA SOLEDAD**,

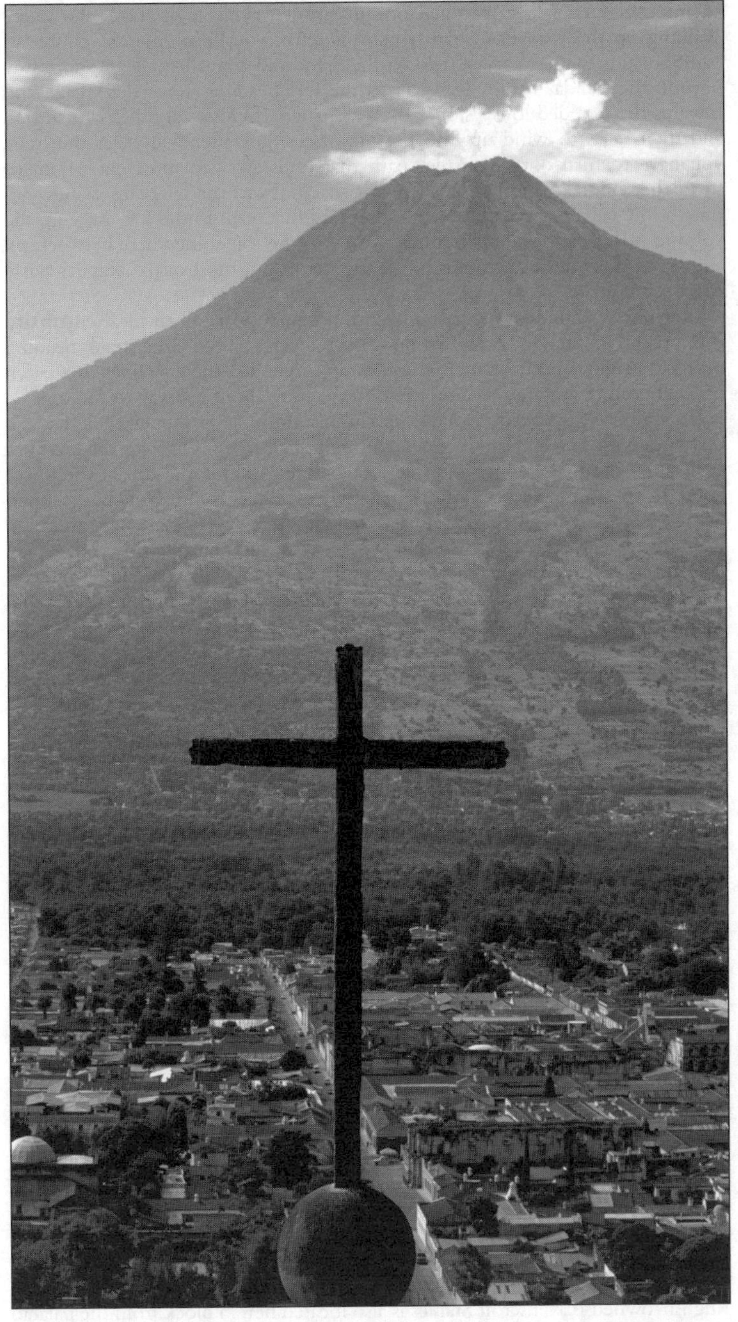

△ Volcán de Agua

an impoverished village perched on an exposed ridge high above the valley. Walking up the road from San Miguel Dueñas, you come upon a cluster of bamboo huts, with a soccer field to the right and a small *tienda*. A short way beyond the tienda, a track leads up to the left, heading above the village and towards the wooded lower slopes of Acatenango. It crosses another largish trail and then starts to wind up into the pine trees. Just after you enter the trees, you have to turn onto a smaller path that leads away to the right; 100m or so further on, take another small path that climbs to the left. This brings you onto a low ridge, where you meet a thin trail that leads to the left, away up the volcano – this path eventually finds its way to the top, somewhere between six and seven hours away. At times it's a little vague, but most of the way it's fairly easy to follow.

After ninety minutes you pass a beautiful grassy clearing, an ideal **campsite** – the path cuts straight across, so don't be tempted by the larger track heading off to the right. Another ninety minutes up, a wooden shelter clings to a patch of level ground among the pine trees: You're now about halfway to the top.

The trail itself is a pretty exhausting climb, a thin line of slippery volcanic ash that rises with unrelenting steepness through thick forest. Only for the last 50m or so does it emerge above the tree line, before reaching the top of the lower cone. To the south, another hour's gruelling ascent, is the main cone, accessed via a great grey bowl that rises to a height of 3975m. From here there's a magnificent view out across the valley below. On the opposite side is the Agua volcano and, to the right, the fire-scarred cone of Fuego. Looking west you can see the three cones that surround Lake Atitlán and beyond them the Santa María volcano, high above Quetzaltenango.

When it comes to getting down again, the direct route towards Alotenango may look invitingly simple but is in fact very hard to follow. It's easiest to go back the same way that you came up.

San Juan del Obispo, Santa María de Jesús and Volcán de Agua

Southeast of Antigua the smooth paved road to Santa María de Jesús runs out along a narrow valley, sharing the shade with acres of coffee bushes. Before it starts to climb, the road passes the village of **SAN JUAN DEL OBISPO**, invisible from the road but marked by what must rank as the country's finest bus shelter, beautifully carved in local stone. The village itself is unremarkable, although it does offer a good view of the valley below. What makes it worth a visit is the **Palacio de Francisco Marroquín**, who was the first bishop of Guatemala. The place is currently home to a dozen or so nuns, and if you knock on the great wooden double doors one of them will give you a tour in Spanish (daily 8am–5pm; free). Marroquín arrived in Guatemala with Alvarado and is credited with having introduced Christianity to the Maya, as well as reminding the Spaniards about it from time to time. On the death of Alvarado's wife he assumed temporary responsibility for the government, and was instrumental in the construction of Antigua. He died in 1563, having spent his last days in the vast palace that he'd built for himself here in San Juan. The palace interior, arranged around two small courtyards, is spectacularly beautiful and several rooms still contain their original furniture, as well as a portrait of Marroquín himself. Attached to the palace is a fantastic church and chapel with ornate wood carvings, plaster mouldings and austere religious paintings. The excellent, English-owned Ravenscroft Stables is also located here, a block from the palacio (see Antigua "Listings" for more information).

Hourly **buses** to San Juan leave from the market in Antigua (7.30am–6.30pm; 20min) terminating in the churchyard. Alternatively, you could catch one heading for Santa María de Jesús and ask the driver to drop you here.

Santa María de Jesús

Up above San Juan the road arrives in **SANTA MARÍA DE JESÚS**, starting point for the ascent of the Agua volcano. Perched high on the shoulder of the volcano, the village is some 500m above Antigua, with magnificent views over the Panchoy valley and east towards the smoking cone of Pacaya. It was founded at the end of the sixteenth century for the Maya transported from Quetzaltenango: they were given the task of providing firewood for Antigua and the village earned the name "Aserradero", lumber yard. Since then it has developed into a farming community where the women wear beautiful purple *huipiles* (although the men have recently abandoned traditional costume). The village has a certain scruffy charm, with the only place **to stay** being the hospedaje *El Oasis* (Ⓣ7832 0130; ❶), just off the plaza on the road into town; it's a friendly, clean institution which serves meals that are as simple as the rooms. The owner, Aurelio, can organize guides for the hike up Agua as well as horse-riding trips.

Buses run from Antigua to Santa María every thirty minutes or so from 6am to 7pm; the trip takes thirty minutes. Beyond Santa María, the road continues down the east side of the volcano to the village of Palín, on the Guatemala City–Escuintla highway. Few buses cover this route, but you shouldn't have to wait long to hitch a lift on a pick-up.

Volcán de Agua

Agua is the easiest and by far the most popular of Guatemala's big cones to climb, and on Saturday nights dozens of people spend the night at the summit. It's an exciting ascent with a fantastic view to reward you at the top. The trail starts in Santa María de Jesús – to reach it, head straight across the plaza, between the two aging pillars, and up the street opposite the church doors. Take a right turn just before the end, and then continue past the cemetery and out of the village. From here on it's a fairly simple climb on a clear, garbage-strewn path, cutting across the road that goes some of the way up. The climb takes five to six hours, and the peak, at 3766m, is always cold at night. There is shelter (though not always room) in a small chapel at the summit, however, and the views certainly make it worth the struggle.

Sadly, there have been (very occasional) robberies of hikers reported on the outskirts of Santa María in recent years, so before starting an ascent it's safest to check out the situation first at Inguat in Antigua or consider going with a group tour (see p.118).

Antigua to Chimaltenango

Heading to the western highlands, a single-lane highway heads north of Antigua through a succession of villages – though a new multi-lane highway will add a speedy bypass to the north in the next few years. The nearest of these villages, **SAN FELIPE DE JESÚS**, is so close that you can walk there: just a kilometre or so north of Antigua following 6 Avenida Norte. San Felipe has a small, Gothic-style church housing a famous image of Christ, Jesús Sepultado, said to have miraculous powers. Severely damaged in the 1976 earthquake, the church has been well restored since, and there's a fiesta here on August 30 to celebrate the anniversary of the arrival of the image in 1670. The village's other attraction is a **silver workshop**, where silver mined in the highlands of Alta Verapaz is worked and sold. To find the workshop, follow the sign to the Platería Típica La Antigüeña.

Merging into San Felipe to the west, the grimy suburb of **JOCOTENANGO**, "place of bitter fruit", is set around a huge, dusty plaza where there's a magnificent, but weathered, dusty pink Baroque church. In colonial times, Jocotenango was the gateway to Antigua, where official visitors would be met to be escorted into the city. Long notorious for its seedy bars, the town's main industries are coffee production and wood carving. There's an excellent selection of bowls and fruits in the family-owned Artesanías Cardenas Barrios workshop on Calle San Felipe, where they have been working at the trade for five generations.

Joco's newest attractions are 500m west of the plaza in the **Centro La Azotea** cultural centre (Mon–Fri 9am–4.30pm, Sat 9am–2pm; US$3.50, including tour in English or Spanish). **Casa K'ojom**, which forms one half of the centre, is a purpose-built museum dedicated to Maya culture, especially music. The history of indigenous musical traditions is clearly presented from its pre-Columbian origins, through sixteenth-century Spanish and African influences – which brought the marimba, bugles and drums – to the present day, with audiovisual documentaries of fiestas and ceremonies. Other rooms are dedicated to the village weavings of the Sacatepéquez department and the cult of Maximón (see p.174). Next door, the **Museo de Café** is an extensive plantation dating from 1883, offers the chance to look around a working organic coffee farm. All the technicalities of husking, sieving and roasting are clearly explained, and you're served a cup of the aromatic homegrown brew after your tour. Special minibuses leave from Antigua's 4 C Oriente (just east of the plaza) hourly to the Centro La Azotea; alternatively, catch one of the buses from the Antigua terminal that pass Jocotenango every twenty minutes on their way to Chimaltenango.

If you're keen on a rural base near Antigua, consider staying at the **Earth Lodge** (Ⓣ5664 0713 or 5613 6934, Ⓦwww.welcometoearthlodge.com; ❷–❹, including all meals), a wonderful new guest house and campground (US$7 per person) occupying a forty-acre plot high in the hills above Jocotenango and about 7km northeast of Antigua, with stunning views of the Panchoy valley and its volcanoes. There's a warm welcome from the Canadian-American owners, and the accommodation includes solid, comfortable A-frame cabañas and dorms (US$9.50 per bed) in a wood cabin. You'll also find a *chuj* (Maya

The wicked saint of San Andrés Itzapa

San Andrés shares with many other western highland villages (including Zunil and Santiago Atitlán) the honour of revering **San Simón**, or Maximón, the wicked saint, whose image is housed in a pagan chapel in the village. His abode is home to drunken men, cigar-smoking women and hundreds of burning candles, each symbolizing a request. Curiously this San Simón attracts a largely ladino congregation and is particularly popular with prostitutes. Inside the dimly lit shrine, the walls are adorned with hundreds of plaques from all over Guatemala and Central America, thanking San Simón for his help. For a small fee, you may be offered a *limpia*, or soul cleansing, which involves one of the resident women workers beating you with a bushel of herbs, while you share a bottle of local firewater, *aguardiente*, with San Simón (it dribbles down his front) and the attendant, who will periodically spray you with alcohol from her mouth. If you are in the region, try to get to San Andrés on October 28th when San Simón is removed from his sanctuary and paraded through the town in a pagan celebration featuring much alcohol consumption and dancing.

Fiestas

Although the region around Guatemala City and Antigua is not prime fiesta territory, a few villages, listed below, have some firmly established traditions and dramatic celebrations. Also listed here are some events in villages not covered in the text that may be worth visiting around fiesta time, if you're in the area.

January

1–4 Fraijanes

1–5 Santa María de Jesús, main day 1st

Varies San Pedro Ayampuc

February

First Friday in Lent Antigua; San Felipe de Jesús has a huge pilgrimage

March

6–14 Villa Canales, main day 14th

6–20 San Pedro Pinula, main day 19th

18–20 San José del Golfo, main day 19th

Holy Week

Celebrated with fervour in Antigua (see box, p.112)

April

26–30 Palencia, main day 30th

May

1 Guatemala City; Labour Day is marked by marches and protests

1–7 Amatitlán, main day 3rd

June

24 Comalapa

22–27 San Juan Sacatepéquez, main day 24th

27–30 Yepocapa, main day 29th

July

25 Antigua, in honour of Santiago

24–30 Palín, climaxes on final day

August

4 Mixco

15 Jocotenango

15 Guatemala City

September

29 San Miguel Dueñas; dances include Los Toritos

October

18 San Lucas Sacatepéquez; dances include Moors and Christians

28 San Andrés Itzapa; all-nighter with San Simón paraded through the town

November

1 Sumpango and Santiago Sacatepéquez, massive paper kites flown in village cemeteries

20–28 San Catarina Pinula, main day 25th

27–Dec 1 San Andrés Itzapa, main day 30th

December

4–9 Chinautla, main day 6th

6–11 Villa Nueva, main day 11th

sauna); good walking trails; and plenty of space for frisbee throwing, football or swinging in a hammock. If you're willing to work for four hours a day on the ranch, rates are reduced by forty percent. A free pick-up from Antigua is also offered.

Another 4km brings you to **SAN LORENZO EL TEJAR**, which has some superb hot springs. To reach the springs turn right in the village of **San Luis Las Carretas**, from where the springs are signposted; they're at the end of a narrow valley, a couple of kilometres from the main road. If you want to bathe in the sulphurous waters, you can either use the cheaper communal pool or, for a couple of dollars, rent one of your own – a little private room with a huge tiled tub set in the floor. The baths are open daily from 7am to 5.30pm, except Tuesday and Friday afternoons, when they are closed for cleaning; Sundays can get very busy with local families.

From San Luis the road passes a turn-off for the new Antigua bypass highway that will eventually connect Chimaltenango with Santa Catarina Barahona, and then climbs out of the Panchoy valley through **Parramos**, a dusty, overgrown farming village. A couple of kilometres beyond Parramos, a side road branches to **SAN ANDRÉS ITZAPA**, one of the many villages badly hit by the 1976 earthquake. Tragically, San Andrés also hit the headlines at the end of 1988, when it was the scene of the largest massacre since the return of civilian rule, when 22 corpses were found in a shallow grave. Today, however, San Andrés' main claim to fame is as home to the cult of San Simón, or Maximón (see box, p.128). To pay the so-called wicked saint a visit, head for the central plaza from the branch road into the village, turn right when you reach the church, walk two blocks, then up a little hill and you should spot street vendors selling charms, incense and candles. If you get lost, ask for the Casa de San Simón. The other point of interest in the village is the particularly intricate weaving of the women's *huipiles*. The patterns are both delicate and bold, similar in many ways to those around Chimaltenango. San Andrés' Tuesday market is also worth a visit.

From Antigua a few direct buses run to San Andrés Itzapa; you can also take a **bus** heading to Chimaltenango, via Parramos (not using the new highway), from the terminal in Antigua (hourly 5.30am–7pm; 40min). Get the driver to drop you off at the turn-off, from where frequent pick-ups and minibuses head into San Andrés.

After the turning for San Andrés, the road drops through pine trees to the **Laguna de los Cisnes**, a small boating lake surrounded by cheap comedores and swimming pools, and then on to Chimaltenango.

Travel details

Guatemala City is at the transport heart of the country, with literally thousands of buses travelling in and out of the city each day connecting it with provincial capitals and tiny villages alike. Most of these routes are covered in the "Travel details" sections of other chapters; for the main **bus services** from Guatemala City, however, see the "Moving on" box on pp.98–99; for buses from Antigua, see p.122.

International **flights** depart from Guatemala City's Aurora airport, and at least ten domestic flights connect the capital with Flores in Petén, the site of the only other international airport in the country. Most Flores-bound departures are in the early morning, at around 7am; tickets for the 50min trip can be bought from virtually any travel agent in the capital (see p.101) or Antigua (see p.123) and cost from US$120 return.

2

The western highlands

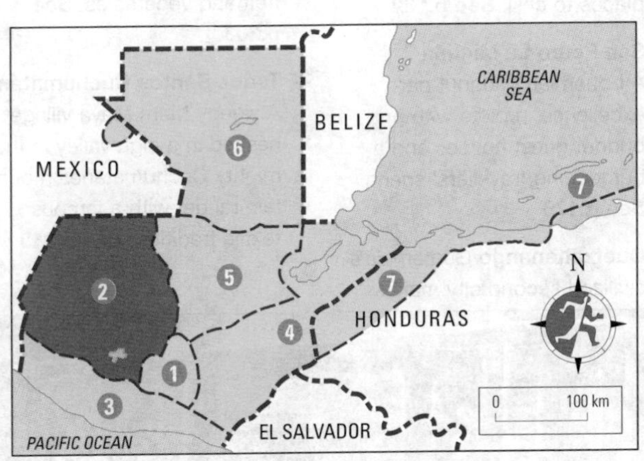

CHAPTER 2

Highlights

* **Chichicastenango** Hunt for textiles and souvenirs at this scenic town's legendary market. **See p.143**

* **The Ixil Triangle** Hike the hillside trails of this remote, intensely traditional, indigenous region. **See p.153**

* **Lago de Atitlán** An awesome steep-sided crater lake, ringed by volcanoes and diminutive indigenous villages, with a plethora of idyllic places to chill. **See p.162**

* **San Pedro La Laguna** A bohemian hangout par excellence, replete with budget guest houses and a burgeoning travellers' scene. **See p.176**

* **Quetzaltenango** Guatemala's civilized second city makes an excellent base for studying Spanish, and for any number of fascinating day-trips. **See p.186**

* **Fuentes Georginas** A blissfully relaxing natural spa, with warm pools framed by lush ferns and forest, situated halfway up a volcano near Quetzaltenango. **See p.198**

* **San Francisco el Alto** Its weekly market is a maelstrom of highland humanity, animals, fruit and vegetables. **See p.203**

* **Todos Santos Cuchumatán** A sleepy Mam Maya village nestled in a high valley in the mighty Cuchumatanes mountain range, with a famous textile tradition. **See p.218**

△ Village church, San Mateo Ixtatán

2

The western highlands

Guatemala's western highlands, stretching from the outskirts of Antigua to the Mexican border, are perhaps the most beautiful and captivating part of the entire country. The area is defined by two main features: a chain of awesome volcanoes that lines its southern side, and the high Cuchumatanes mountain range that dominates the north of the region. Strung between these two natural barriers is a series of spectacular forested ridges, lakes, gushing streams and plunging, verdant valleys.

It's an astounding landscape, blessed with tremendous fertility but cursed by instability. More than a dozen cones loom over the western highlands, including the three highly active volcanoes of **Pacaya**, **Fuego** and **Santiaguito**, all emitting plumes of sulphurous smoke and occasionally spewing out showers of molten rock. Two major fault lines also cut through the area, making earthquakes a regular occurrence. The most recent major quake occurred around **Chimaltenango** in 1976 – it left 25,000 dead and around a million homeless. But despite its sporadic ferocity the countryside is outstandingly beautiful, with irrigated valleys and terraced hillsides carefully crafted to yield the maximum potential farmland.

The highland landscape is controlled by many factors, but above all **altitude**. At lower levels the vegetation is almost tropical, supporting dense forests and crops of **coffee**, **cotton**, **bananas** and **cacao**. Higher up in the hills, **pine**, **cedar** and **oak** forests are interspersed with patchwork fields of **maize** and potatoes. In the highest terrain, known as the *altiplano*, the land is largely treeless and often wrapped in cloud, suited only to hardy herds of sheep and goats. The seasons also play their part: in the rainy season, from May to October, the land is superbly green with life from emerging young crops, while during the dry winter months the hillsides gradually turn a dusty yellow.

The Maya highlands

The western highlands are home to one of the American continent's largest groups of surviving indigenous people, the **Maya**, who have lived here continuously for the past two thousand years. The Maya still form the vast majority of the population in this region, and despite the Spanish conquest, their society, languages and traditions remain largely unchanged.

In the days of Classic Maya civilization (300–900 AD), the western highlands were a peripheral area, with the great developments taking place in the

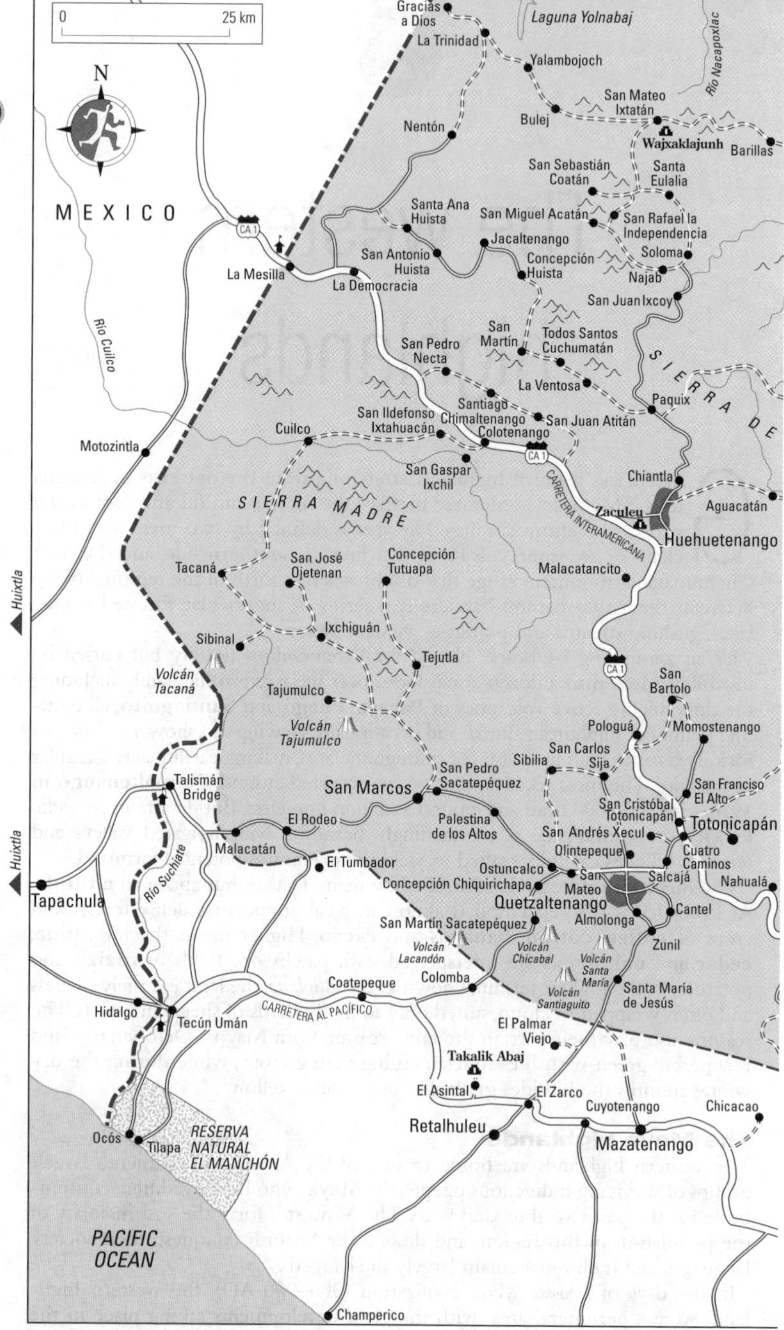
San Cristóbal de las Casas
0 25 km
N
MEXICO
Río Cuilco
Motozintla
Huixtla
Huixtla
Tapachula
Gracias a Dios
Laguna Yolnabaj
La Trinidad
Yalambojoch
Río Nacapoxlac
San Mateo Ixtatán
Bulej
Nentón
Wajxaklajunh
Barillas
San Sebastián Coatán
Santa Eulalia
Santa Ana Huista
San Miguel Acatán
San Rafael la Independencia
CA 1
Jacaltenango
San Antonio Huista
Concepción Huista
Soloma
La Mesilla
La Democracia
Najab
San Juan Ixcoy
San Martín
Todos Santos Cuchumatán
San Pedro Necta
SIERRA DE
La Ventosa
Paquix
Santiago Chimaltenango
San Ildefonso Ixtahuacán
San Juan Atitán
Cuilco
Colotenango
San Gaspar Ixchil
CARRETERA INTERAMERICANA
Chiantla
SIERRA MADRE
Zaculeu
Aguacatán
Huehuetenango
Tacaná
San José Ojetenan
Concepción Tutuapa
Malacatancito
Ixchiguán
Sibinal
Tejutla
Volcán Tacaná
San Bartolo
Tajumulco
Volcán Tajumulco
Pologuá
Momostenango
San Carlos Sija
Sibilia
San Pedro Sacatepéquez
Talismán Bridge
San Marcos
San Francisco El Alto
San Cristóbal Totonicapán
Totonicapán
Palestina de los Altos
El Rodeo
San Andrés Xecul
Malacatán
Río Suchiate
Olintepeque
Cuatro Caminos
El Tumbador
Ostuncalco
San Mateo
Salcajá
Nahualá
Concepción Chiquirichapa
Quetzaltenango
Cantel
Almolonga
San Martín Sacatepéquez
Zunil
Volcán Lacandón
Volcán Chicabal
Volcán Santa María
Coatepeque
Colomba
Santa María de Jesús
Volcán Santiaguito
Hidalgo
Tecún Umán
CARRETERA AL PACÍFICO
El Palmar Viejo
Takalik Abaj
El Asintal
El Zarco
Cuyotenango
Chicacao
Retalhuleu
Mazatenango
Ocós
Tilapa
RESERVA NATURAL EL MANCHÓN
PACIFIC OCEAN
Champerico

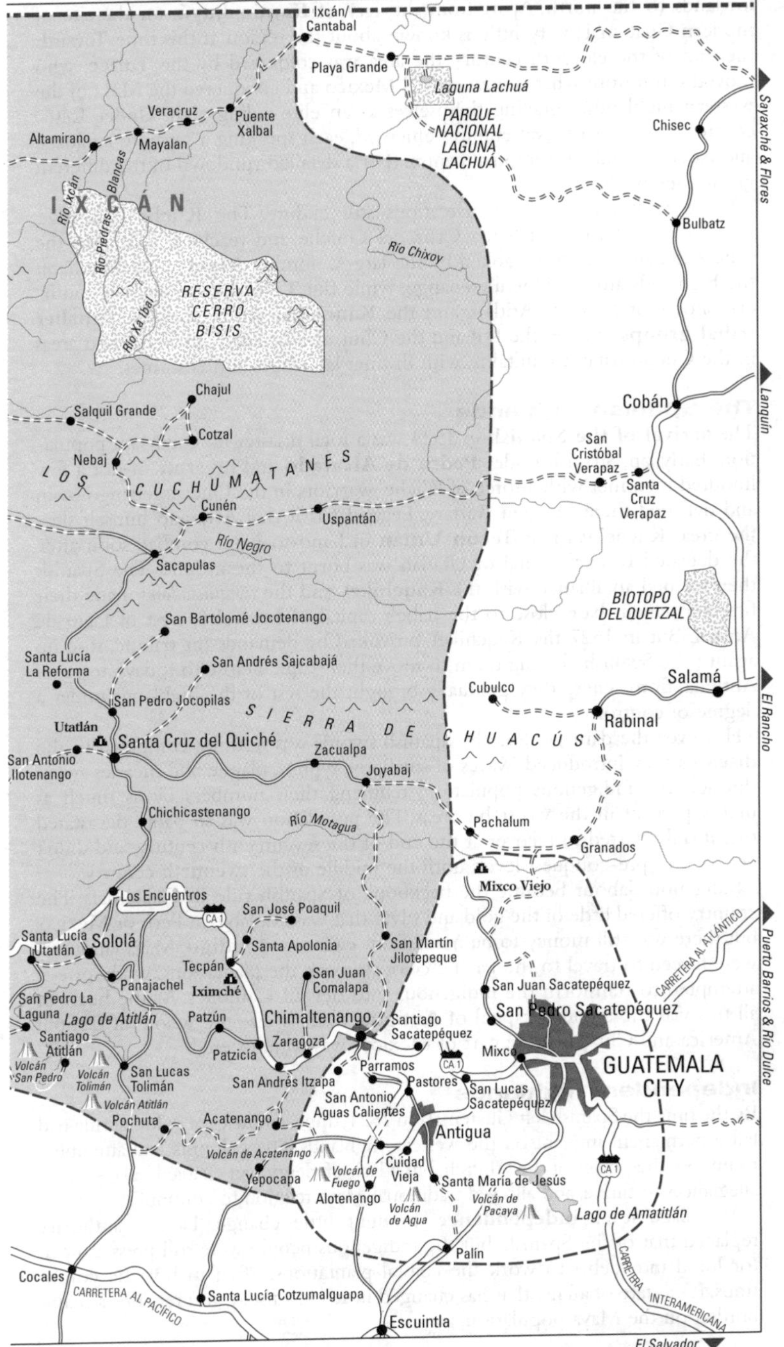

Ixcán/
Cantabal
Playa Grande
Laguna Lachuá
PARQUE
NACIONAL
LAGUNA
LACHUÁ
Sayaxché & Flores
Chisec
Veracruz
Puente
Xalbal
Altamirano
Mayalan
Río Ixcán
Río Piedras Blancas
IXCÁN
Bulbatz
Río Chixoy
RESERVA
CERRO
BISIS
Río Xa Ibal
Chajul
Lanquín
Cobán
Salquil Grande
Cotzal
San
Cristóbal
Verapaz
Nebaj
LOS
CUCHUMATANES
Santa
Cruz
Verapaz
Cunén
Uspantán
Río Negro
Sacapulas
BIOTOPO
DEL QUETZAL
San Bartolomé Jocotenango
Santa Lucía
La Reforma
San Andrés Sajcabajá
Salamá
Cubulco
El Rancho
San Pedro Jocopilas
SIERRA DE CHUACÚS
Rabinal
Utatlán
Santa Cruz del Quiché
San Antonio
Ilotenango
Zacualpa
Joyabaj
Chichicastenango
Río Motagua
Pachalum
Granados
Mixco Viejo
Los Encuentros
CA 1
San José Poaquil
CARRETERA AL ATLÁNTICO
Puerto Barrios & Río Dulce
Santa Lucía
Utatlán
Sololá
Santa Apolonia
San Martín
Jilotepeque
Tecpán
Iximché
San Juan
Comalapa
Panajachel
San Juan Sacatepéquez
San Pedro La
Laguna
Lago de Atitlán
Patzún
Chimaltenango
San Pedro Sacatepéquez
Santiago
Atitlán
Zaragoza
Santiago
Sacatepéquez
Volcán
San Pedro
Volcán
Tolimán
Patzicía
Mixco
CA 1
GUATEMALA
CITY
San Lucas
Tolimán
San Andrés Itzapa
Parramos
Pastores
Volcán Atitlán
San Antonio
Aguas Calientes
San Lucas
Sacatepéquez
Pochuta
Acatenango
Antigua
Volcán de Acatenango
Cuidad
Vieja
Volcán de
Fuego
Yepocapa
Santa María de Jesús
CA 1
Alotenango
Volcán
de Agua
Volcán de
Pacaya
Lago de Amatitlán
Palín
CARRETERA INTERAMERICANA
Cocales
CARRETERA AL PACÍFICO
Santa Lucía Cotzumalguapa
Escuintla
El Salvador

lowlands to the north. Apart from the city of **Kaminaljuyú**, on the site of modern Guatemala City, little is known about the region at this time. Towards the end of the eleventh century the area was colonized by the **Toltec**, who moved south from what is now central Mexico and conquered the Maya of the western highlands, installing themselves as an elite ruling class. Under Toltec control a number of rival empires emerged, each speaking a separate language and based around a ceremonial centre. (For a detailed rundown of the different groups, see p.426.)

These traditional tribal demarcations still endure. The **K'iche'** language, centred on the town of Santa Cruz del Quiché and reaching west into the Quetzaltenango valley, is spoken by the largest number. **Mam**-speakers inhabit the highlands around Huehuetenango, while the **Tz'utujil** occupy the southern shores of Lago de Atitlán, and the **Kaqchikel** are to the east. **Smaller tribal groups**, such as the Ixil and the Chuj, also occupy clearly defined areas in the Cuchumatán mountains, with distinct languages and costumes.

The Spanish highlands

The **arrival of the Spanish** in 1523 was a total disaster for the Maya population. Early on, Spanish leader **Pedro de Alvarado** and his army of just a few hundred men met with a force of K'iche' warriors in the Quetzaltenango basin and defeated them in open warfare. Legend has it that Alvarado himself slew the great K'iche' warrior **Tecún Umán** in hand-to-hand combat; soon after, the defeated K'iche' capital of Utatlán was burnt to the ground. The Spanish then formed an alliance with the **Kaqchikel**, and the *conquistadores* made their first permanent base close to the tribe's capital of **Iximché**, west of Lago de Atitlán. But in 1527 the Kaqchikel, provoked by demands for tribute, rose up against the Spanish, forcing them to move their capital close to today's town of Antigua, from where they gradually brought the rest of the highlands under a degree of control.

However, the damage done by Spanish swords was nothing compared to the **diseases** they introduced. Waves of smallpox, typhus, plague and measles swept through the indigenous population, reducing their numbers by as much as ninety percent in the worst-hit areas. The population was so badly devastated that it only started to recover at the end of the seventeenth century, and didn't get back to pre-conquest levels until the middle of the twentieth century.

Indigenous labour became the backbone of Spanish rule in Guatemala. The country offered little of the gold and silver that was available in Peru or Mexico, but there was still money to be made from **cacao** and **indigo**. Maya labourers were forced to travel to the Pacific coast to work the plantations, while priests attempted to transform the indigenous into devout Catholics. At the heart of all this was the colonial capital of **Antigua**, from where the whole of Central America and Chiapas (now part of Mexico) was administered.

Independent highlands

By the time the Spanish left Guatemala in 1821, three centuries of colonial rule had left a permanent imprint on the western highlands. The colonists had attempted to impose the power of the Church, but a lack of clergy had enabled village-based allegiances to thrive, and allowed traditional Maya religion to continue.

At village level, **independence** brought little change. Ladino authority replaced that of the Spanish, but the indigenous people were still press-ganged (or lured into debt) to work the coastal plantations, often in horrific conditions. It's a state of affairs that has changed little even today, and remains a major burden on the Maya population.

Fresh pressures emerged in the 1970s as the Maya were caught up in waves of political violence. **Guerrilla movements** sought support from the indigenous population and established themselves in the western highlands, particularly the departments of El Quiché, Huehuetenango, Sololá and Totonicapán. The Maya became the victims in this process, as they were caught between the guerrillas and the army. A total of 440 villages were destroyed during the conflict; around 180,000 died and thousands more fled the country, seeking refuge in Mexico.

Indigenous society has also been besieged in recent years by a holy tidal wave of American **evangelical churches** (see p.465), whose influence undermines local hierarchies, dividing communities and threatening Maya culture.

Market days

Throughout the western highlands **weekly markets** are the main focus of economic and social activity, drawing people from the area around the town or village where they're held. Make an effort to catch as many market days as possible – they're second only to local fiestas in offering a glimpse of a way of life unchanged for centuries.

Monday
Chimaltenango; San Juan Atitán; Santa Bárbara; Zunil.

Tuesday
Chajul; Comalapa; Olintepeque; Patzún; Salcajá; San Andrés Semetabaj; San Antonio Ilotenango; San Marcos; San Pedro Jocopilas; Sololá; Totonicapán; Yepocapa.

Wednesday
Almolonga; Chimaltenango; Colotenango; Cotzal; Huehuetenango; Momostenango; Palestina de Los Altos; Patzicía; Sacapulas; San Sebastián.

Thursday
Aguacatán; Chichicastenango; Chimaltenango; Jacaltenango; La Libertad; Nebaj; Panajachel; Patulul; Patzite; Patzún; Sacapulas; San Juan Atitán; San Lucas Tolimán; San Luis Jilotepeque; San Mateo Ixtatán; San Miguel Ixtahuacán; San Pedro Necta; San Pedro Pinula; San Rafael La Independencia; Santa Bárbara; Santa Cruz del Quiché; San Pedro Sacatepéquez; Soloma; Tajumulco; Tecpán; Totonicapán; Uspantán; Zacualpa.

Friday
Chajul; Chimaltenango; San Andrés Itzapa; San Francisco el Alto; San Martín; Santiago Atitlán; Sololá; Tacaná.

Saturday
Almolonga; Colotenango; Cotzal; Ixchiguan; Malacatán; Nentón; Palestina de los Altos; Patzicía; Santa Clara La Laguna; Santa Cruz del Quiché; Todos Santos Cuchumatán; Totonicapán; Yepocapa.

Sunday
Aguacatán; Cantel; Chichicastenango; Chimaltenango; Cuilco; Huehuetenango; Jacaltenango; Joyabaj; La Libertad; Malacatancito; Momostenango; Nahualá; Nebaj; Nentón; Ostuncalco; Panajachel; Patzite; Patzún; Sacapulas; San Bartolo; San Carlos Sija; San Cristóbal Totonicapán; San Juan Comalapa; San Lucas Tolimán; San Luis Jilotepeque; San Martín Jilotepeque; San Mateo Ixtatán; San Miguel Acatán; San Miguel Ixtahuacán; San Pedro Necta; San Pedro Sacatepéquez; Santa Bárbara; Santa Cruz del Quiché; Santa Eulalia; Sibilia; Soloma; Tacaná; Tecpán; Tejar; Uspantán; Yepocapa; Zacualpa.

With the signing of the 1996 **peace accords** however, political tensions have lifted and there is evidence of a new self-confidence within the highland Maya people. With the guerrilla groups now disbanded and the army back in their barracks, the threats, intimidation and deaths that the native population suffered during the war years are over, even if a new series of challenges remain.

Poverty levels are still some of the worst in the hemisphere, exacerbated by high birth rates, underemployment and institutionalized racism. Nevertheless, a reawakened sense of pride in Maya identity is coming to the fore, with indigenous leaders such as Nobel Peace Prize–winner Rigoberta Menchú (see pp.478–479) serving in the Berger government and educated young Maya rising to positions of prominence.

Maya society is becoming increasingly vulnerable, as the allure of "El Norte" (the US) entices more and more jobless young men away from the highlands. It's often the most remote traditional villages that have been most affected by this emigration, and though many return with money to invest in their communities, social structures are inevitably disrupted and centuries-old customs threatened.

Despite these pressures, you'll find that more than a dozen Maya languages are still spoken in the highlands, native costume continues to be worn in most areas and the 260-day Tzolkin Maya calendar remains in use in some villages. Trade is still as much a social function as an economic one, with life centring on the village and its own civil and religious hierarchy, and subsistence farming of maize and beans remaining at the heart of Maya existence. It is this unique culture, above all else, that is Guatemala's most fascinating feature.

Visiting Maya **villages** during the week, you may find them almost deserted – their permanent populations are generally small, though they may support five or ten times as many scattered rural homesteads. It's on **market** and **fiesta** days, when the villages fill to bursting, that you can most clearly sense the values of the Maya world – in the subdued bustle and gossip of the market, or the intense joy of celebration.

Where to go

You're spoilt for choice in the western highlands, with beautiful highland scenery yielding atmospheric **villages** of cobbled lanes and whitewashed colonial churches at every turn. Along with the colourful market towns and spectacular mountainscapes for which the region is famed, a few fascinating **historical sites**, such as the pre-conquest cities of Iximché, Utatlán and Zaculeu, are also worthy of your attention – although they don't bear comparison to Tikal and the lowland sites.

Travelling west from Guatemala City, the Carretera Interamericana sweeps through a densely populated region around the scruffy town of Chimaltenango before climbing steadily into the highlands. Just north of the highway in the department **El Quiché** is the renowned market town of **Chichicastenango** and the ruins of **Utatlán**, near the departmental capital of **Santa Cruz del Quiché**. To the south of Quiché, **Lago de Atitlán** is the jewel of the western highlands, ringed by volcanoes and some of the country's most fascinating villages – it's reached via the colourful town of **Sololá**, and **Panajachel**, an attractive lakeside resort. To the north are the wildly beautiful peaks of the **Cuchumatanes**, beneath which nestle the towns of the **Ixil Triangle**, remote and intensely traditional communities at the end of a tortuous bus journey. Heading on to the west is Guatemala's second city, **Quetzaltenango** (Xela), an ideal base for visiting local villages or climbing the near-perfect volcanic cone of **Santa María**. Beyond this, the border with Mexico is marked by the departments of **San Marcos** and **Huehuetenango**, both of which offer superb mountain scenery, dotted with isolated villages, the pick of which is the beautifully situated **Todos Santos Cuchumatán**.

Buses flow continuously along the Carretera Interamericana, and tourist shuttle buses serve all the main centres. Some buses branch off the highway onto minor roads to more remote areas: travelling on these roads can sometimes be a gruelling experience, particularly in northern Huehuetenango and El Quiché, but the scenery makes it well worth the discomfort. The most practical plan of action is to base yourself in one of the larger places and then make a series of day-trips to markets and fiestas, although even the smallest villages will usually offer some kind of accommodation.

Into the highlands: the Carretera Interamericana

The serpentine **Carretera Interamericana** forms the main artery of transport in the highlands, and this highway and its junctions will inevitably become very familiar. The first of three major junctions that you'll quickly get to know is **Chimaltenango**, an important town (and capital of its own department) from where you can make connections to or from Antigua. Continuing west, **Los Encuentros** is the next main junction, where one road heads off to the north for Chichicastenango and another branches south to Panajachel and Lago de Atitlán. Beyond this, the highway climbs high over a mountainous ridge before dropping to **Cuatro Caminos**, from where side roads lead to Quetzaltenango, Totonicapán and San Francisco el Alto. The Carretera Interamericana continues on to Huehuetenango before it reaches the Mexican border at La Mesilla. Virtually every bus travelling along the highway will stop at all of these junctions, and you'll be able to buy fruit, drink and fast food from an army of vendors, some of whom will storm the bus looking for business, with others content to dangle their wares at your window from the street.

Chimaltenango and around

Grimy **CHIMALTENANGO**'s main focal point is the Carretera Interamericana, which cuts through the southern side of the town, bringing with it an endless flow of trucks and buses. The town extracts what little business it can from this stream of traffic, and the roadside is crowded with cheap comedores, mechanics' workshops and sleazy bars. There's absolutely no reason to hang around here – especially with Antigua so near – and you should take care with your bags if you are changing buses as pickpockets have been known to target disorientated travellers.

Chimal has the misfortune of being positioned right on the continental divide and suffered terribly from the 1976 earthquake, which flattened much of the surrounding area. Today's town testifies to rapid and unfinished reconstruction, with dirt streets, breeze-block walls and an air of weary desperation.

The town's **plaza**, two blocks north of the highway, is more attractive and sedate, with a church that combines the Gothic and the Neoclassical, an impressive colonial fountain positioned exactly on the continental divide – half the water drains to the Caribbean, the other half to the Pacific – and a striking peace monument that depicts a Maya woman bearing a broken rifle over her head. The best place to eat is *Km 56* on the highway itself, where you can choose from an excellent selection of grilled meats and Guatemalan specialities.

Buses passing through Chimaltenango run to all points along the Carretera Interamericana, and those headed for Antigua leave every twenty minutes between 5am and 7pm from the market in town – though you can also wait at the turn-off on the highway.

San Martín Jilotepeque

To the north of Chimaltenango, it's 19km past plunging ravines and pine forests to the village of **SAN MARTÍN JILOTEPEQUE**. San Martín had to be rebuilt following the 1976 disaster, but the sprawling Sunday market is well worth a visit and the weaving here, the women's *huipiles* especially, is some of the finest you'll see – with intricate and ornate patterning, predominantly in reds and purples.

Buses to San Martín leave the market in Chimaltenango every thirty minutes from 5am to 6pm for the forty-minute trip. To the north of San Martín the road continues to **Joyabaj**. Only five daily buses cover this isolated route, though it's usually possible to catch a ride in a pick-up at other times.

San Juan Comalapa, Patzicía and Patzún

Heading west from Chimaltenango, a series of turnings lead off the Carretera Interamericana to interesting but seldom-visited villages. The first of these, 16km to the north of the road on the far side of a deep-cut ravine, is **SAN JUAN COMALAPA**. The village was founded by the Spanish, who brought together the populations of several Kaqchikel centres. A collection of eroded pre-Columbian sculptures is displayed in the plaza, where there's a monument to Rafael Alvarez Ovalle, a local man who composed the Guatemalan national anthem. Looking out over the plaza is a fine, recently restored Baroque church that dates from colonial times.

In the past few decades, the villagers of Comalapa have developed something of a reputation as **folk artists**. The tradition began with **Andrés Curuchich** (1891–1969), who painted simple scenes documenting village life, such as fiestas, funerals and marriages, with a clarity that soon attracted the attention of outsiders. Throughout the 1950s he became increasingly popular, exhibiting in Guatemala City, and later as far afield as Los Angeles and New York, and was awarded Guatemala's highest civilian honour, the Order of the Quetzal. There is a permanent exhibition devoted to his paintings at the Museo Ixchel in Guatemala City.

Inspired by his example and the chance of boosting their income, forty to fifty painters are now working here, including two or three women – although success is considerably more difficult for them as painting is generally perceived as a man's task. Several **galleries** in the streets around the plaza show the work of these artists, and a new museum, the Museo de Arte Maya, is also planned. Local artists have also contributed to a huge new mural – taking in the Maya creation myth, the Conquest and the guerrilla war – which adorns the village's cemetery wall.

Comalapan **weaving** is of the highest standards, using styles and colours characteristic of the Chimaltenango area. Traditionally, the weavers work in silk and an untreated natural brown cotton called *cuyuxcate*, although these days they mainly use ordinary cotton and synthetic fibres.

If you want to **stay** here, the clean and attractive *Hotel Pixcayá*, 0 Av 1–82 (☎7849 8260; ❷–❸), is good value with rooms with or without private bathroom. Several comedores are located around the plaza. As ever, the best time to visit is for the **market**, on Sunday, which brings people out in force. **Buses** to Comalapa run hourly from Chimaltenango (45min), though microbuses and pick-ups also wait at the highway turn-off. The service is always better on a market day.

Patzicía and Patzún: a route to the lake

Further to the west another branch road runs down towards Lago de Atitlán, connecting the Carretera Interamericana with several small villages. First is **PATZICÍA**, its bedraggled-looking appearance belying its history of independent defiance, as in 1944 it was the scene of a Maya uprising that left some three hundred dead. Believing that a nationwide rebellion against ladino rule had begun, villagers charged through the town killing any non-indigenous inhabitants they could set hands on. Armed ladinos, arriving from the capital, managed to put down the uprising, killing the majority of the rebels. Ironically enough, the Declaration of Patzicía was signed here in 1871, setting out the objectives of the liberal revolution.

PATZÚN, 11km from the main highway heading towards Lago de Atitlán, suffered terrible losses in the 1976 earthquake. A monument in the plaza remembers the 172 who died, and a new church stands beside the shell of the old one, an even more poignant memorial. Traditional costume is still worn here and the colourful Sunday market is well worth a visit. Outside the twin churches the plaza fills with traders, with the majority of the women dressed in the brilliant reds of the local costume.

Beyond Patzún it's possible to continue all the way to the small village of **Godínez**, high above the northern shore of Lago de Atitlán, and further on to Panajachel and San Lucas Tolimán. Pick-ups, tourist shuttles and five daily buses make this trip, but the road is fairly rough, plunging down the side of a thickly forested ravine. If you're driving, you should bear in mind that this has been the scene of occasional armed robberies and attacks, though incidents have decreased in recent years. **Buses** to Patzún leave the Zona 4 terminal in Guatemala City every hour; you can also pick them up in Chimaltenango or at the turning for Patzicía.

Tecpán and Iximché

The small town of **TECPÁN** lies just a few hundred metres south of the Carretera Interamericana, ninety minutes or so from Guatemala City. This may well have been the site chosen by Alvarado as the first Spanish capital, to which the Spanish forces retreated in August 1524, after they'd been driven out of Iximché. Today it's a modest place of little interest, apart from its fine sixteenth-century Baroque **church**, complete with a magnificent original beamed ceiling and silver altars.

Iximché, the pre-conquest capital of the Kaqchikel, is about 5km to the south, on a beautiful exposed hillside site, isolated on three sides by plunging ravines and surrounded by pine forests. From the early days of the Conquest, the Kaqchikel allied themselves with the Spanish, so the structures here suffered less than most. Since then, however, time and weather have taken their toll, and the majority of the buildings, originally built of adobe, have disappeared, leaving only a few stone-built pyramids, clearly defined plazas and a couple of ball courts. Nevertheless the site, which housed a population of about ten thousand, is very atmospheric, and its grassy plazas are marvellously peaceful, especially during the week, when you may well have the place to yourself.

The Kaqchikel Maya established their capital here in about 1470 after a long conflict with the neighbouring K'iche', and from that time on were almost continuously at war with other tribes. Despite this, they devoted a lot of energy to the building and rebuilding of their new capital, and trenches dug into some of the structures have revealed as many as three superimposed layers. When the Spanish arrived, the Kaqchikel were quick to join forces with Alvarado in order to defeat the K'iche'. Grateful for the assistance, the Spanish established their first headquarters near here on May 7, 1524 – probably where Tecpán stands today. The Kaqchikel referred to Alvarado as *Tonatiuh*, the son of the sun, and as a mark of respect he was given the daughter of a Kaqchikel king as a gift.

On July 25, 1524, the Spanish renamed the new settlement **Villa de Santiago**, declaring it their new capital. But within months the Kaqchikel had risen in rebellion, outraged by Alvarado's demands for tribute. The conquistador retaliated by burning Iximché and forcing the Kaqchikel to flee into the mountains from where they waged a guerrilla war against the invaders until 1530. The Spanish capital was moved from Tecpán to the greater safety of Ciudad Vieja, a short distance from Antigua.

More than four hundred years later, the Campesino Unity Committee, a predominantly Maya group, met here in February 1980 and issued the **Declaration of Iximché**. Provoked by the massacre of their leaders during a peaceful occupation of the Spanish embassy in Guatemala City, the declaration identified this atrocity as the latest episode in more than four centuries of state-sponsored genocide against the Maya race. The storming of the embassy led to the Spanish government breaking off diplomatic relations with Guatemala for five years.

The site

The **ruins of Iximché** (daily 8am–5pm; US$3.20) are made up of four main plazas, a couple of ball courts and several small pyramids. In most cases only the foundations and lower parts of the original structures were built of stone, while the upper walls were of adobe, with thatched roofs supported by wooden beams. You can make out the ground plan of many of the buildings, but it's only the most important all-stone structures that still stand. The most significant buildings were those clustered around courts A and C, which were probably the scene of the most revered rituals. On the sides of **Temple 2** you can make out some badly eroded murals, the style of which is very similar to that used in the codices.

It's thought that the site itself, like most of the highland centres, was a ceremonial centre used for religious rituals, and Maya worship still takes place here down a small trail through the pine trees behind the final plaza. The settlement was thought to have been inhabited only by the elite, with the rest of the population living in the surrounding hills and coming to Iximché only to attend festivals and to defend the fortified site in times of attack. Archeological digs here have unearthed a number of interesting finds, including the decapitated heads of sacrifice victims, burial sites, grinding stones, obsidian knives, a flute made from a child's femur, and large numbers of incense burners. There was surprisingly little sculpture, but most of that which was found resembled that of the ruins of Zaculeu and Mixco Viejo, both of which were occupied at around the same time.

Iximché's shady location is perfect for a picnic or barbeque, and you can buy *aguas* at the site. **To get there**, hop off any bus travelling along the Carretera Interamericana at the turn-off for Tecpán. The centre of town is about 500m from the road, from where buses and microbuses leave for the ruins (every 45min; 10min). Be back on the Carretera Interamericana by 5.30pm to be sure of a bus onwards.

El Quiché

At the heart of the western highlands, sandwiched between the Verapaces and Huehuetenango, is the department of **El Quiché**. Like its neighbours, El Quiché encompasses the full range of Guatemalan scenery: in the south a fertile and heavily populated area includes the upper reaches of the Motagua valley, while to the north the landscape becomes increasingly dramatic, rising to the massive, rain-soaked peaks of the **Cuchumatanes**, beyond which the land drops away into the inaccessible rainforests of the **Ixcán**.

The department takes its name from the greatest of the pre-conquest tribal groups, the **K'iche'**, who overran much of the highlands by 1450 from their capital at Utatlán. Although their empire was in decline by the time the Spanish arrived, they were still the dominant force in the region and confronted the conquistadors at a site near Quetzaltenango. The K'iche' were easily defeated though, and the Spanish were able to negotiate alliances with former K'iche' subjects, playing one tribe off against another, and eventually overcoming them all. Today these highlands remain a stronghold of Maya culture, and El Quiché, scattered with small villages and mountain towns, is the scene of some superb fiestas and markets.

With little in the way of plunder, this remote, mountainous terrain remained an unimportant backwater for the Spanish, although in later years it did become a source of cheap labour. The region became a centre of guerrilla activity in the late 1970s – hardly surprising, after two hundred years of abuse at the hands of the state – and quickly became the scene of unrivalled repression in Guatemala, as tens of thousands of villagers were wiped out by the armed forces. Catholic priests, who were often connected with the cooperative movement, were also singled out and murdered; indeed, the Church withdrew all its priests from the department in 1981.

For the traveller, El Quiché has a lot to offer, in both the accessible south and the wilder north. **Chichicastenango**, one of the country's most popular destinations, is the scene of a vast, twice-weekly market and still a pivotal centre of Maya religion. Beyond this, at the heart of the central valley, is the departmental capital of **Santa Cruz del Quiché**, stopping-off point for the ruins of **Utatlán**. Further to the north the paved road ends and the mountains really begin. Travelling here can be hard work, but the extraordinary scale of the scenery makes it all well worthwhile. Isolated villages, set in superb highland bowls, sustain a wealth of indigenous culture and occupy a misty, mysterious world of their own. Passing over the Sierra de Chuacús, and down to the Río Negro, you reach **Sacapulas** at the base of the **Cuchumatanes**. From here you can travel across the foothills to Cobán in the east or Huehuetenango to the west, or, for real adventure, up into the mountains to the three towns of the **Ixil Triangle** – Nebaj, Chajul and Cotzal.

The road for Chichicastenango and the department of El Quiché leaves the Carretera Interamericana at Km127.3, the **Los Encuentros** junction.

Chichicastenango

Heading north from Los Encuentros, you soon drop down through dense, aromatic pine forests into a deep ravine housing a tributary of the Río Motagua.

The road then begins a tortuous ascent from the valley floor around a seemingly endless series of switchbacks until it reaches **CHICHICASTENANGO**, 17km from the junction. Dubbed Guatemala's "Mecca del Turismo" by Inguat, this is a compact and traditional town of cobbled streets, where old abode houses topped with red-tiled roofs sit alongside modern concrete structures. Twice a week the town's highland calm is shattered as the Sunday and Thursday **markets** attract a myriad of day-tripping tourists and commercial traders, as well as Maya weavers from throughout the central highlands. On these days you'll probably find yourself embroiled in one of provincial Guatemala's rare traffic jams, as traders, tourists and locals all struggle to reach the town centre.

The market is by no means all that sets Chichicastenango apart, however, and for the local Maya population it's an important centre of culture and religion. Long before the arrival of the Spanish this area was inhabited by the Kaqchikel,

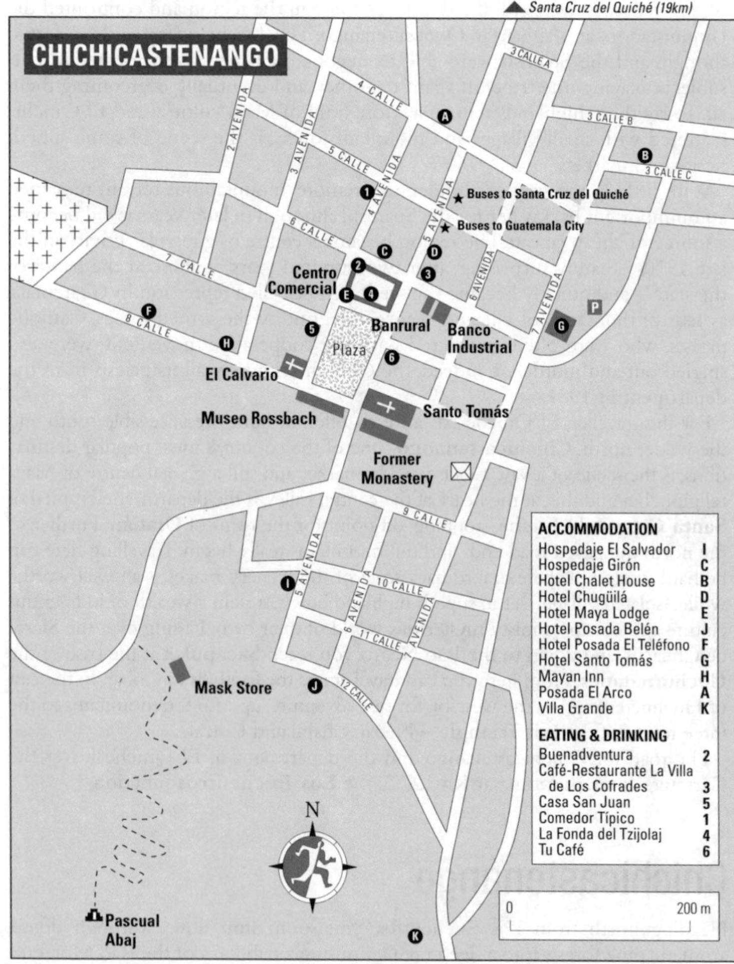

whose settlements of Patzak and Chavier were under threat from the all-powerful K'iche'. In a bid to assert their independence, the Kaqchikel abandoned the villages in 1470 and moved south to Iximché, from where they mounted repeated campaigns against their former masters. Chichicastenango itself was founded by the Spanish in order to house K'iche' refugees from Utatlán to the north, which they conquered and destroyed in 1524. The town's name is a Nahuatl word meaning "the place of the nettles", accorded it by Alvarado's Mexican allies.

Over the years, Maya culture and folk Catholicism have been treated with a rare degree of respect in Chichicastenango, although inevitably this blessing has been mixed with waves of arbitrary persecution and exploitation. Today the town has an incredible collection of Maya artefacts, parallel indigenous and ladino governments, and two churches that make no effort to disguise their acceptance of unconventional pagan worship. Locals adhere to the ways of traditional weaving, the women wearing superb *huipiles* with flower motifs. The men's costume of short trousers and jackets of black wool embroidered with silk is highly distinguished, although it's very expensive to make and these days almost all men opt for Western dress. For Sundays and fiestas, however, a handful of *cofradres* (elders of the religious hierarchy) still wear the traditional clothing and parade through the streets bearing spectacular silver processional crosses and antique incense burners.

Chichicastenango's appetite for religious fervour is especially evident during the **fiesta** of Santo Tomás, from December 14 to 21. It's a spectacular occasion, with attractions including the *Palo Volador* (in which men dangle by ropes from a twenty-metre pole; see p.468), a live band or two, a massive procession, traditional dances, clouds of incense, gallons of *chicha* and deafening fireworks. On the final day, all babies born in the previous year are brought to the church for christening. Easter, too, is celebrated here with tremendous energy and seriousness.

Arrival and information

There's no bus station in Chichi, although the corner of 5 Calle and 5 Avenida operates loosely as a terminal. **Buses** heading between Guatemala City and Santa Cruz del Quiché pass through here every twenty minutes or so, pausing to load up passengers. In Guatemala City buses leave from the terminal in Zona 4, from 4am to about 5pm; coming from Antigua, you can easily connect with these buses in Chimaltenango. On market days several **shuttle services** run the route from Antigua to Panajachel via Chichi, allowing you to spend a few hours at the market before continuing on to Lago de Atitlán; and the reverse journey is possible from Panajachel too. Four direct chicken buses also run from Pana (and more on market days), or you can take any bus up to Los Encuentros and change there.

There's currently no tourist information available in Chichi. If you're bitten by market fever and need to **change money**, you'll find a glut of banks, with plenty open on Sundays: Banrural on 6 Calle (Tues–Sun 9am–5pm) also has a MasterCard/Cirrus ATM, or, almost next door, Banco Industrial (Mon 10am–2pm, Wed–Sun 10am–5pm) has an ATM for Visa/Plus cardholders. For **Internet** access head to Acses at 6 C 4–52 (US$1.80 per hour).

Accommodation

Hotels can be in short supply on Saturday nights before the Sunday market, but you shouldn't have a problem on other days. Prices can also rise on market days, though at other times you can usually negotiate a good deal.

Hospedaje El Salvador 5 Av 10–09 ⓣ7756 1329. Venerable budget hotel with a bizarre external colour scheme and a warren of bare but fairly tidy rooms at cheap prices. Should be space here, even before market days, but beware that hot water can be erratic. ❷

Hospedaje Girón 6 C 4–52 ⓣ7756 1156, ⓕ7756 1226. Well-priced, comfortable rooms with pine furnishings – most with private bath – plus parking. Good value for single travellers. ❸

Hotel Chalet House 3 C 7–44 ⓣ7756 1360, ⓕ7756 1793. Welcoming hotel set on a quiet street with thirteen double rooms, all with private bathrooms (some have a tub) and comfortable beds. Highland wool blankets and textiles add a pleasing decorative touch. Breakfast is available. ❹

Hotel Chugüilá 5 Av 5–24 ⓣ7756 1134, ⓕ7756 1279. Rambling hotel, with a selection of spacious rooms, all on different levels and some with fireplaces. Rooms vary in quality a little (if not in price), so ensure you take a look at your digs first. Secure parking. ❺

Hotel Maya Lodge 6 C A 4–08 ⓣ7756 1167. This hotel has real colonial character, with nine large tiled rooms, all with solid wooden furniture, set off a courtyard. It's fractionally overpriced, so try asking for a discount. ❺

Hotel Posada Belen 12 C 5–55 ⓣ & ⓕ7756 1244. Large place with plenty of space, but not overly attractive rooms; some have private bath, however, and many have stunning views. ❷

Hotel Posada El Teléfono 8 C 1–64 ⓣ7756 1197. Friendly, fairly new guest house with 14 small, clean, bare rooms scattered up and down steep staircases. The beds all have woolen blankets and the communal bathroom is kept tidy. ❷

Hotel Santo Tomás 7 Av 5–32 ⓣ7756 1061, ⓕ7756 1306. Spacious, modern rooms, all well appointed, with pleasant bathrooms boasting tubs, and set around two colonial-style courtyards and a (heated) swimming pool. The hotel, which has ample restaurant facilities and lounge areas, is block booked by huge tour groups on market days, however. ❼

Mayan Inn 8 C and 3 Av ⓣ7756 1176, ⓕ7756 1212, ⓦwww.mayaninn.com.gt. Chichi's longest-established hotel offers very comfortable rooms with colonial-style furniture and fireplaces. Pity the staff decked out in mock-traditional dress, though. ❽

Posada El Arco 4 C 4–36 ⓣ7756 1255. Excellent guest house, run by friendly English-speaking brothers, with seven large, attractive rooms with good wooden beds and reading lights. Room nos. 6 and 7 have access to a pleasant terrace; there's also a beautiful garden and stunning countryside views. ❹

Villa Grande 1km south of centre ⓣ7756 1053, ⓦwww.villasdeguatemala.com. This large hotel occupies a fine hillside position with good views, but its rather perfunctory, modern-ish rooms let the place down a little. It does have a restaurant and pool, however. ❻–❼

The Town

Though most visitors come here to see the market, Chichicastenango also offers an unusual insight into traditional religious practices in the highlands. At the main **Santo Tomás Church** in the southeast corner of the plaza, the local K'iche' Maya (called *Maxeños*) have been left to adopt their own style of worship, blending pre-Columbian and Catholic rituals. The church was built in 1540 on the site of a Maya altar, and rebuilt in the eighteenth century. It's said that indigenous locals became interested in worshipping here after Francisco Ximénez, the priest from 1701 to 1703, started reading their holy book, the **Popol Vuh** (see p.148). Seeing that he held considerable respect for their religion, they moved their altars from the hills and set them up inside the church. Today, this ancient, unique hybrid of Maya and Catholic worship still takes place in the church.

Before entering the building it's customary to make offerings in a fire in front of the church or burn *copal* and *estoraque* incense in perforated cans, a practice that leaves a cloud of thin, sweet smoke hanging over the steps. Inside is an astonishing scene of avid worship. A soft hum of constant murmuring fills the air, as the faithful kneel to place candles on low-level stone platforms for their ancestors and the saints. For these people the entire building is alive with the souls of the dead, each located in a specific part of the church. The place of the "first-people", the ancient ancestors, is beneath the altar railing; former

Chichicastenango's market

There's been a **market** at Chichicastenango for hundreds, if not thousands, of years, and despite the twice-weekly invasions local people continue to trade their wares alongside the tourist-geared stalls of bric-a-brac. On Sundays and Thursdays, Chichicastenango's streets are lined with stalls and packed with buyers, and the choice is overwhelming, ranging from superb-quality Ixil *huipiles* to wooden dance-masks, and everything in between, including pottery, gourds, machetes, belts and a gaudy selection of fabrics. You can still pick up some authentic weaving, but you need to be prepared to wade through a lot of very average material – and haggle hard. Your chances of getting a good deal are better before 10am, when the tourist buses arrive from the capital, or in the late afternoon once things have started to quiet down. The best of the stuff from the local villages is generally found in the centre of the plaza. Prices are pretty competitive, but for a real bargain you need to head further into the highlands – though Panajachel is a better bet for *típica* clothes.

For a brilliant **vantage point** over the vegetable market, head for the indoor balcony on the upper floor of the Centro Comercial building on the north side of the plaza. You'll be able to gawp down on the villagers below (as well as take photographs without fear of being intrusive) as they haggle and chat over bunches of spring onions. It's possible to pick out costumes from all over the highlands, including *huipiles* from the Atitlán villages of San Antonio and Santa Catarina Palopó, and even from as far away as Chajul; the funky "space cowboy" shirts and pants are worn by men from the neighbouring Sololá area.

officials are around the middle of the aisle; ordinary folk to the west in the nave; and deceased native priests beside the door. Equally important are the Catholic saints, who receive the same respect and are continuously appealed to with offerings of candles and alcohol. Last, but by no means least, certain areas within the church, and particular patterns of candles, rose petals and *chicha*, are used to invoke specific types of blessings, such as those for children, travel, marriage, harvest or illness. Don't enter the building by the front door, which is reserved for *cofrades* and senior church officials, but through the **side door**. It's deeply offensive to take **photographs** inside the building – don't even contemplate it.

Beside the church is a former **monastery**, now used by church administrators. This is where Spanish priest Francisco Ximénez first discovered the Popol Vuh (see box, p.148), a masterpiece of indigenous literature, buried amongst the parish archives in the early eighteenth century.

On the south side of the plaza, often hidden by stalls on market day, **Museo Rossbach** (Tues, Wed, Fri & Sat 8am–noon & 2–4pm, Thurs 8am–4pm & Sun 8am–2pm; US$0.75) houses a wide-ranging collection of pre-Columbian artefacts, mostly small pieces of ceramics (including some demonic-looking incense burners), jade necklaces and earrings, and stone carvings (some 2000 years old). Some interesting old photographs of Chichi as well as local weavings and masks are also on display.

On the west side of the plaza, the whitewashed **El Calvario** chapel is like a miniature version of Chichi's main church. Inside, the atmosphere is equally reverential as prayers are recited around the smoke-blackened wooden altar, and women offer flowers and stoop to kiss a supine image of Christ, entombed inside a glass cabinet, which is paraded through the street during Holy Week. The steps are also the scene of incense-burning rituals, and the chapel is considered good for general confessions and pardons.

The Popol Vuh

Written in Utatlán shortly after the arrival of the Spanish, the more than nine thousand lines of the **Popol Vuh** detail the cosmology, mythology and traditional history of the K'iche'. The first of the two parts of this sacred poem is an account of the K'iche's **creation** by their god, who is known as Heart of Sky. According to the Popol Vuh, at first there was only water and sky; the creator then formed earth and mountains, plants and trees. Heart of Sky turned his attention to animals, and created creatures of the forest including deer, birds and jaguars. Unsatisfied with these animals – which could only howl, roar or squawk – the creator fashioned humans from corn paste after twice failing to make man from mud and wood. The Popol Vuh then recounts the adventures of the ancestors of mankind, the hero (or wizard) twins Hunahpú and Xbalanqué, which culminate in an epic struggle with the death lords of Xibalbá, the Maya underworld. The twins ultimately triumph, and the cycle of creation is born.

The Popol Vuh's second half describes the wanderings of the K'iche' ancestors as they migrate south from the Toltec area of Mexico and settle in the highlands of Guatemala. Evidence gathered by archeologists and epigraphers strongly supports the accuracy of this part of the epic. The book concludes with a history of K'iche' royalty, and suggests a shared lineage with these kings and their gods. Dennis Tedlock's translation of the Popol Vuh (see "Books", p.495) is regarded as the definitive text.

The shrine of Pascual Abaj

The churches are certainly not the only scenes of Maya religious activity, however; the hills that surround the town, like so many throughout the highlands, are topped with shrines. The closest of these, less than a kilometre from the plaza, is known as **Pascual Abaj**. Although the site is regularly visited by tourists, it's important to remember that the Maya ceremonies held here are deeply serious and you should keep your distance and be sensitive about taking any **photographs**. The shrine is laid out in a typical pattern with several small altars facing a stern-looking pre-Columbian sculpture. Ceremonies, usually overseen by a shaman, always incorporate clouds of incense, liquor-swilling and incantations, along with offerings of flowers and maybe a sacrificed chicken. In 1957, during a bout of religious rivalry, Pascual Abaj's altars were smashed by reforming Catholics, but the traditionalists gathered the scattered remains and patched them together with cement and a steel-reinforcing rod.

To get to Pascual Abaj, walk south downhill along 5 Avenida from the Santo Tomás church, take the first right, 9 Calle, and follow this as it winds its way out of town. You'll soon cross a stream, after which a well-signposted route takes you through the courtyard of a workshop making wooden masks. If a ceremony is in progress, you may be able to pick out Pascual Abaj by a thin plume of smoke. Continue to follow the path uphill for ten minutes through a dense pine forest to the shrine.

Eating

Chichi offers little in the way of fancy cuisine, but plenty of good-value Guatemalan comedor food. For smarter surrounds head to either the *Hotel Santo Tomás* or the *Mayan Inn*. The plaza on **market days** is the place to come for authentic highland eating: try one of the makeshift food stalls, where you'll find cauldrons of stews and broths.

Buenadventura upper floor, inside the Centro Comercial. Offers a terrific view of the vegetable market and simple, no-nonsense food – the breakfasts are some of the cheapest in town.

Café-Restaurant La Villa de Los Cofrades 6 C and 5 Av, first floor. Good set meals – soup, a main dish and salad, fries and bread – for under US$4, plus great *churrascos* and breakfasts. Real coffee and wine available, too.

Casa San Juan beside El Calvario church. Modish bar-restaurant with a stylish interior and plenty of artwork on display. Imaginatively prepared sandwiches and Guatemalan cooking, including *pepián de pollo* and tasty chorizo.

Comedor Típico 4 Av, between 5 and 6 calles. Good, clean and cheap place for local food, with some great lunchtime set meals.

La Fonda del Tzijolaj upper floor of the Centro Comercial. The name may be unpronounceable, but the food is moderately priced, tasty and reliable – and the balcony views of the church of Santo Tomás are unrivalled. Try the delicious *chiles rellenos*.

Tu Café east side of plaza. Unpretentious place run by a friendly Guatemalan who worked as a cab driver in New York for many years. There's plenty of breakfast choice, *antojitos*, sandwiches and *carne adobada*, plus all lunchtime mains come with rice, salad and soup.

Santa Cruz del Quiché and around

The capital of the department of El Quiché, **SANTA CRUZ DEL QUICHÉ**, lies half an hour north of Chichicastenango. A good paved road connects the two towns, running through pine forests and ravines, and past the **Laguna Lemoa**, a lake which, according to local legend, was originally filled with tears wept by the wives of K'iche' kings after their husbands had been slaughtered by the Spanish. Quiché, as it is usually called, is an easy-going but uneventful town with no attractions. It is, however, the transport hub for the department and the most direct route to the Ixil Triangle, as well as being the only practical place to base yourself for a visit to the nearby ruins of **Utatlán**.

The Town

Dominating the central **plaza** of Santa Cruz del Quiché is a large colonial church, built by the Dominicans with stone from the ruins of Utatlán. The clock tower beside it is also said to have been built from Utatlán stone, stripped from the temple of Tohil. In the middle of the plaza, a defiant statue of the K'iche' hero Tecún Umán stands prepared for battle. His position is undermined somewhat by an ugly urban tangle of hardware stores and shabby *panaderías* that surround the square. The large, infamous military garrison that used to occupy the northeast corner of the square was closed by President Berger in 2004. **Market** days here are the same as in Chichicastenango – Thursday and Sunday – with stalls sprawling over most of the area south and east of the plaza, spreading down to the bus station. Palm weaving is a local speciality, and Maya people can sometimes be seen threading a band or two as they walk through town. Many of the palm hats on sale throughout the country were put together here, but if you want to buy you'll have to look hard and long to find one that fits a gringo head.

Moving on from Chichicastenango

Direct buses head to Guatemala City every twenty minutes or so (3hr), the last one leaving at around 6pm, and seven buses daily head westwards to Quetzaltenango between 6am and 3pm (2hr 30min). For Antigua, catch a Guatemala City–bound bus and change at Chimaltenango, except on market days when you can get a direct shuttle, if funds permit. If you're heading north, it's often quickest to take the first bus to Santa Cruz del Quiché (every 20min; 30min), from where buses go to Nebaj or Uspantán. If you need a **shuttle bus** from Chichicastenango, head to Chichi Turkaj Tours, 5 Av 5–24 (ⓣ5698 7825).

Practicalities

The **bus terminal**, a large, grubby open-aired affair, is about four blocks south and a couple east of the central plaza. Connections are generally good from Quiché. Second-class buses to Guatemala City leave every twenty minutes until 5pm (3hr 30min), all via Chichicastenango (30min) and Los Encuentros (1hr). If you're heading up to the northern mountains, regular services run to Nebaj (7 daily; 2hr 45min), Joyabaj (hourly; 2hr 15min), Uspantán (7 daily; 3hr 30min) and Quetzaltenango (10 daily; 3hr). Several **banks** will change your travellers' cheques, including Banrural (Mon–Fri 8.30am–6.30pm, Sat 9am–1pm), which has a MasterCard ATM, and Bancafé (Mon–Fri 8.30am–6pm, Sat 8.30am–1pm), with a Visa ATM; both are located at the northwest corner of the plaza.

There's a limited range of **hotels** in Quiché and nothing luxurious. The best two are the *Hotel Maya Quiché*, a block west of the plaza at 3 Av 4–19, Zona 1 (Ⓣ7755 1464; ❸), which is a friendly place with big clean rooms, some with bathroom; and the modern *Hotel Rey K'iche*, two blocks north of the bus station at 8 C 0–39, Zona 5 (Ⓣ7755 0824; ❸), which has spotless rooms, most with cable TV and private bath, plus a good comedor. The best budget choice, *Posada Calle Real*, at 2 Av 7–36 (Ⓣ7755 1438), lies two blocks south of the plaza and has bare but clean rooms. If that's full, head to the *Hotel San Pascual*, at 7 C 0–43, Zona 1 (Ⓣ7755 1107; ❷); it's also south of the plaza and has tidy rooms on two floors around a patio.

Most **places to eat** in Quiché are close to the plaza. The large *El Torito Steakhouse*, 7 C 1–73, just southwest of the plaza, is one of the smartest places, with kitsch cowboy decor and a menu that's a real carnivore's delight – try the sausages or *chuletas*. On the west side of the plaza, *La Pizza de Ciro* dispenses fairly uninspiring pizzas, while close by are several so-so bakeries with dry pastries and cakes. For a no-nonsense comedor meal, try *Restaurante Las Rosas*, 1 Av 1–28.

The ruins of Utatlán (K'umarkaaj)

Early in the fifteenth century, riding on a wave of successful conquest, the K'iche' king Gucumatz (Feathered Serpent) founded a new capital, K'umarkaaj. A hundred years later the Spanish arrived, renamed the city **Utatlán**, and then destroyed it. Today the **ruins** (daily 8am–5pm; US$1.80) can be visited, about 4km to the west of Santa Cruz del Quiché.

According to the Popol Vuh, Gucumatz was a lord of great genius, assisted by powerful spirits. And there's no doubt that this was once a great city, with several separate citadels spread across neighbouring hilltops. It housed the nine dynasties of the tribal elite, including the four main K'iche' lords, and contained a total of 23 palaces. The splendour of the city embodied the strength of the K'iche' empire, which at its height boasted a population of around a million.

By the time of the Conquest, however, the K'iche' had been severely weakened and their empire fractured. They first made contact with the Spanish on the Pacific coast, suffering a heavy defeat at the hands of Alvarado's forces near Quetzaltenango, including the loss of their leader Tecún Umán. The K'iche' then invited the Spanish to their capital, a move that made Alvarado distinctly suspicious. On seeing the fortified city, the conquistador feared a trap and captured K'iche' leaders Oxib-Queh and Beleheb-Tzy. His next step was characteristically straightforward: "As I knew them to have such a bad disposition to service of his Majesty, and to ensure the good and peace of this land, I burnt them, and sent to burn the town and destroy it."

The site

Utatlán is nowhere near as grand as the large ruins of Petén, but its dramatic setting, surrounded by deep ravines and pine forests, is impressive, and its historical significance intriguing. Little restoration has taken place since the Spanish destroyed the city, and only a few of the main structures are still recognizable, most buried beneath grassy mounds and shaded by pine trees. The small **museum** has a scale model of what the original city may once have looked like.

The central plaza is almost certainly where Alvarado burned the two K'iche' leaders alive in 1524. Nowadays it's where you'll find the three remaining **temple buildings**, the great monuments of Tohil, Auilix and Hacauaitz, which were simple pyramids topped by thatched shelters. The Temple of the Sovereign Plumed Serpent once stood in the middle of the plaza, but these days just the foundations of this circular tower can be made out. The only other feature that's still vaguely recognizable is the **ball court**, which lies beneath grassy banks to the south of the plaza.

Perhaps the most interesting thing about the site today is that *costumbristas* (Maya religious practitioners) still come here to perform sacred rituals that predate the arrival of the Spanish by thousands of years. The entire area is covered in small burnt circles – the ashes of incense – and chickens are regularly sacrificed in and around the plaza.

Beneath the plaza, a long constructed **tunnel** runs underground for about 100m. Follow the sign for *la cueva*; the entrance is usually littered with empty incense wrappings and *aguardiente* liquor bottles. Inside are nine shrines, the same number as there are levels of the Maya underworld, Xibalbá. Devotees pray at each shrine, but it is the ninth one, housed inside a chamber, which is most actively used for sacrifice, incense and alcohol offerings. Why the tunnel was constructed remains uncertain, but local legends suggest that it was dug by the K'iche' to hide their women and children from the advancing Spanish, whom they planned to ambush at Utatlán. Others believe it represents the caves of Tula mentioned in the Popol Vuh (see p.148). Whatever the truth, today the tunnel is the focus for Maya rituals and a favourite spot for sacrifice, the floor carpeted with chicken feathers, and candles burning in the alcoves at the end. Tread carefully inside the tunnel, as some of the side passages end abruptly with precipitous drops. If a ceremony is taking place, you'll hear the mumbling of prayers and smell incense smoke as you enter, in which case it's wise not to disturb the proceedings by approaching too closely.

To **get to** Utatlán from Santa Cruz del Quiché, you can walk or take a taxi (expect to pay about US$8 for a return trip, with an hour at the ruins). It's a pleasant forty-minute stroll, heading south from the plaza along 2 Avenida, then turning right down 10 Calle, which will take you all the way out to the site.

A rough road continues west from the ruins to San Antonio Ilotenango and on to Totonicapán. A fair amount of traffic passes along this back route, which takes in some superb high ground.

East to Joyabaj

A good, smooth paved road runs east from Santa Cruz del Quiché, beneath the impressive peaks of the **Sierra de Chuacús**, through a series of villages set in beautiful rolling farmland. The first of these, **Chiché**, is a sister village to Chichicastenango, with which it shares costumes and traditions, though the market here is on Wednesday. Next is **Chinique**, followed by larger **Zacualpa**, which has Thursday and Sunday markets in its beautiful broad plaza. The latter village's name means "where they make fine walls", and in the hills to the north are the remains of a pre-conquest settlement.

The small town of **JOYABAJ**, the last place out this way, also has a small archeological site to its north. During the colonial period, Joyabaj was an important staging post on the royal route to Mexico, but all evidence of its former splendour was lost when the 1976 earthquake almost totally flattened the town, killing hundreds of people. The crumbling facade of the colonial church that stands in front of the new prefabricated version is one of the few physical remains. In recent years the town has bounced back, however, and it is now once again a prosperous traditional centre. The Sunday **market**, which in fact starts up on Saturday afternoon, is a huge affair well worth visiting, as is the **fiesta** in the second week of August – five days of unrelenting celebration that includes some fantastic traditional dancing and the spectacular *Palo Volador*, in which "flying" men or *ángeles* spin to the ground from a huge wooden pole: a pre-conquest ritual now performed in only two other places in the country. Though the fiesta is in many ways a hybrid of Maya and Christian traditions, the *ángeles* symbolize none other than the wizard twins of the Popol Vuh, who descend into the underworld to do battle with the Lords of Death.

It's possible to **hike** from Joyabaj, over the Sierra de Chuacús, to Cubulco in Baja Verapaz. It's a superb but exhausting hike, taking at least a day, though it's perhaps better done in reverse (as described on p.304).

Practicalities

Buses run between Guatemala City and Joyabaj, passing through Santa Cruz del Quiché about every forty minutes (8am–3.30pm from the capital and 3am–3pm from Joyabaj). Joyabaj has a few basic **pensiones**, (among which the *Hospedaje Mejia* (❶), on the plaza, is one of the best), plenty of **comedores** and a **bank**, the G&T Continental, with a branch on the Parque Central.

It's also possible to do a loop back towards Guatemala City via a rough, seldom-travelled route that passes through **Pachalum**, where there's the excellent, clean *Hotel Nancy* (❷), northwest of the plaza, and the ruins of **Mixco Viejo**. One daily bus (leaving at 2.30am) operates this route, though pick-ups run at other times.

To the Cuchumatanes: San Andrés Sajcabaja, Sacapulas and Uspantán

The land to the north of Santa Cruz del Quiché is sparsely inhabited and dauntingly hilly. About 17km northeast of town, only accessed by a rough dirt track, the *Posada San Rafael* (Ⓣ5570 3336, Ⓦwww.posada-sr.com; ❹–❺) is a wonderful rural hotel, set in the grounds of an old finca near the village of **SAN ANDRÉS SAJCABAJA**, deep in the glorious Quiché hills. The French–Guatemalan owners offer horse-riding to the minor Maya ruins of Chijoj (with an impressive ball court) and Xepatzac, indigenous villages, hot springs and waterfalls, and serve up delicious organic food. If you call first, there's a good chance that someone will pick you up from Santa Cruz del Quiché, as very few buses run up this way; alternatively, ask around at the bus station to see if there's a pick-up leaving for San Andrés. The journey takes an hour.

Heading out of Santa Cruz, the road passes through **San Pedro Jocopilas** before skirting the western end of the Sierra de Chuacús and eventually dropping to the isolated town of **SACAPULAS**, an hour and a half from Quiché. Set in a spectacular position on the Río Negro beneath the dusty foothills of the Cuchumatanes, Sacapulas has a small colonial church, with some finely carved wooden images of saints, and a good market every Thursday and Sunday, held beneath the two huge ceiba trees in the plaza. Some of the women still wear impressive *huipiles* and tie their hair with elaborate pom-poms, similar to those of Aguacatán.

Since long before the arrival of the Spanish, **salt** has been produced here in beds beside the Río Negro, a valuable commodity that earned the town a degree of importance. Legend has it that the people of Sacapulas originally migrated from the far north, fleeing other savage tribes. The town's original name was Tajul, meaning "hot springs", but the Spanish changed it to Sacapulas, "the grassy place", as they valued the straw baskets made locally. Along the riverbank, downstream from the bridge, there are several little pools where warm water bubbles to the surface, used by local people for washing. On the opposite bank trucks and buses break for lunch at some ramshackle comedores and fruit stalls.

Getting to Sacapulas is straightforward – catch any bus from Santa Cruz del Quiché heading to Uspantán or Nebaj. Leaving can be a bit tricky in the late afternoon when buses south to Quiché are fewer, with the last departing around 4pm. There are seven daily buses to Nebaj (1hr 45min), two daily buses to Huehuetenango, at 4.30am and 5.30am (2hr), and seven buses to Uspantán (2hr), plus regular pick-ups on all routes. If you do get stuck here, you'll find two good, but basic, hospedajes: *Hospedaje y Restaurant Río Negro* (Ⓣ5410 8168; ❶) and *Comedor y Hospedaje Tujaal* (❷); neither place has private bathrooms, but both serve good food. The owners of the latter spot own a separate restaurant, also called the *Tujaal*, right on the riverbank, where you can enjoy excellent *comida típica* with a view of the Cucumatanes mountain chain. There's a **bank** on the north side of the plaza, Banrural, where you can cash travellers' cheques and dollars.

East to Uspantán, and on to Cobán

East of Sacapulas, a dirt road rises steeply, clinging to the mountainside and quickly leaving the Río Negro far below. As it climbs, the views are superb, with tiny Sacapulas dwarfed by the sheer enormity of the landscape. The road eventually reaches a high valley and arrives in **USPANTÁN**, a small town lodged in a chilly gap in the mountains and often soaked in steady drizzle. Rigoberta Menchú, the K'iche' Maya woman who won the 1992 Nobel Peace Prize, is from Chimel, a tiny village in this region. But probably the only reason you'll end up here is in order to get somewhere else. With the **buses for Cobán** and San Pedro Carchá leaving at around 3am and 5am, the best thing to do is go to bed (unless you can get a ride in a pick-up). Uspantán has several friendly pensiones, all basic but clean and very cheap: *Galindo* (❶), on 5 Calle, and *La Uspanteka* (❶), on 4 Calle, are two of the best. There are seven daily buses between Uspantán and Quiché via Sacapulas, and regular pick-ups too.

The Ixil Triangle: Nebaj, Chajul and Cotzal

High up on the spine of the Cuchumatanes, in a landscape of steep hills, bowl-shaped valleys and gushing rivers, is the **Ixil Triangle**. Here Nebaj, Chajul and Cotzal, three remote and extremely traditional towns, share a language spoken nowhere else in the country. This triangle of towns forms the hub of the **Ixil-speaking region**, a massive highland area which drops away towards the Mexican border and contains at least 120,000 inhabitants. These lush and rain-drenched hills are hard to reach and have proved notoriously difficult to control, and today's relaxed atmosphere of highland Maya colour and customs conceals a bitter history of protracted conflict.

The beauty of the landscape and the strength of indigenous culture in the Ixil are both overwhelming. When church leaders moved into the area in the 1970s, they found very strong communities in which the people were reluctant to accept new authority for fear that it would disrupt traditional structures, and where women were included in the process of communal decision-making. Counterbalancing these strengths are the horrors of the human rights abuses that took place here during the civil war, which must rate as some of the worst anywhere in Central America.

Before the arrival of the Spanish, Nebaj was a sizable centre, producing large quantities of jade and possibly allied with the Mam capital, Zaculeu. The Conquest was particularly brutal in these parts, however. After several setbacks, the Spaniards finally managed to take Nebaj in 1530, by which time they were so enraged that the town was burnt to the ground and the survivors enslaved as punishment for their resistance. In the years that followed, the land was repeatedly invaded by the Lacandón Maya from the north and swept by devastating epidemics. Things didn't improve with the coming of independence: the Ixil were regarded as a source of cheap labour and forced to work on the coastal plantations. It is estimated that between 1894 and 1930 six thousand labourers migrated annually to work on the harvest, suffering not only the hardship of the work, but also exposure to a number of new diseases. Many never returned, and even today large numbers of local people still migrate to the coast, Guatemala City and even the US in search of work.

In the late 1970s and 1980s, the area was hit by waves of horrific violence as it became the main theatre of operation for the Guerrilla Army of the Poor (the EGP). Caught up in the conflict, the people suffered enormous losses, with the majority of the smaller villages destroyed by the army and their inhabitants herded into "protected" settlements. Since the 1996 peace accords, normality steadily returned to the area, as villagers have returned to the old sites and rebuilt their homes.

Despite this terrible legacy, the fresh green hills are some of the most beautiful in the country, and the three towns are friendly and accommodating, with a relaxed and distinctive atmosphere in a misty world of their own.

Nebaj and around

NEBAJ is the centre of Ixil country and the largest of the three settlements. Until a few years ago, virtually all structures in the town were single-storey dwellings of adobe walls, but concrete buildings are becoming more common, particularly in the centre of town. Nevertheless, the town remains highly atmospheric and attractive, if a little scruffy around its edges, and is beginning to pull in a trickle of adventure-minded travellers, drawn by the superb highland hiking, a new language school, and the opportunity to get off Guatemala's main gringo trail.

The **textiles** woven here are unusual and intricate, especially the women's *huipiles*, which are a mass of complex geometrical designs. Until very recently, greens, yellows, reds and oranges were omnipresent, worn with brilliant red *cortes* (skirts), though fashion-conscious young Maya women are now choosing to wear clothes of other hues and these days it's not that unusual to see blue *cortes* instead of red. The most spectacular part of Ixil Maya *traje* is the dramatic women's headcloth, a length of hand-loomed fabric that's decorated with

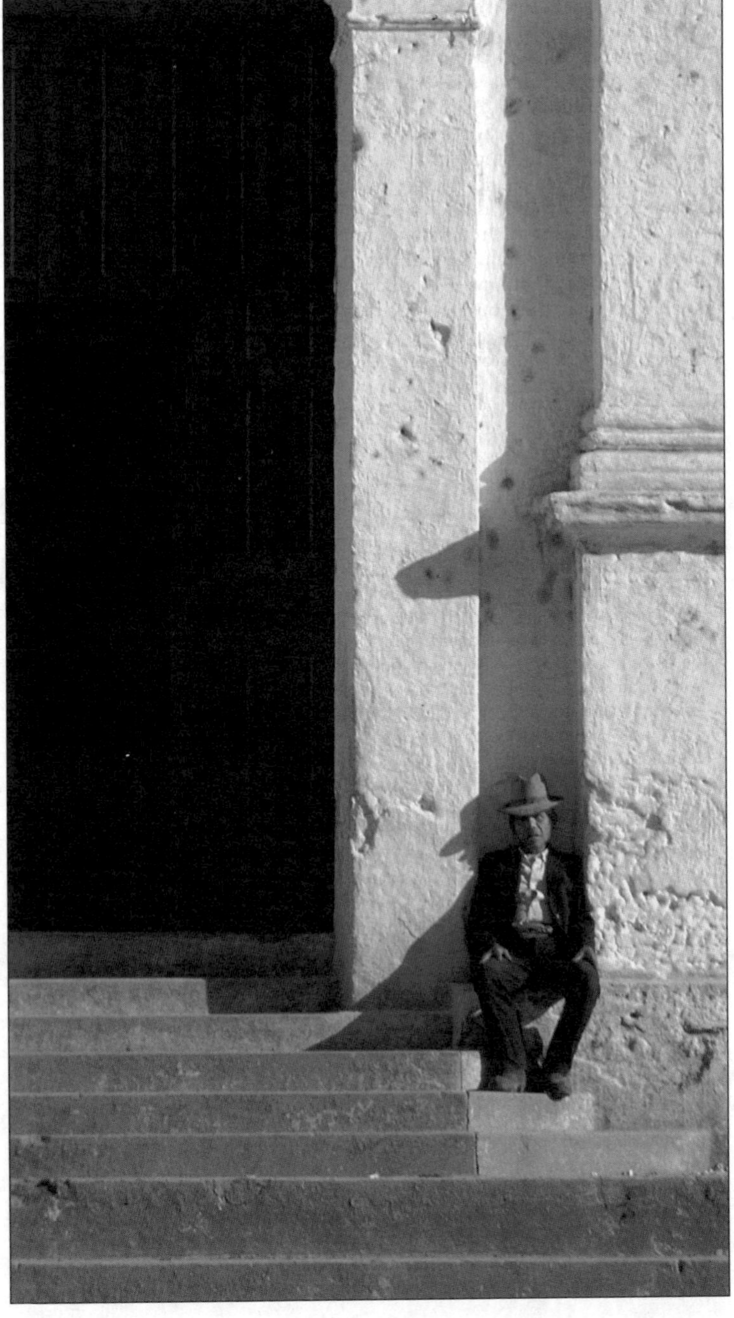

△ A Nebajeño relaxing outside the town church

"pom-pom" tassles that they pile up above their heads. Almost no men now wear traditional dress, preferring to buy secondhand North American clothes from the market. The scarlet male ceremonial jackets are dusted down for fiestas, however; formal looking and ornately decorated, they're modelled on those worn by Spanish officers. As soon as you arrive in town, you'll likely be hassled by an army of young girls, desperate to sell their clothing.

Nebaj's **plaza** is the focal point for the community and houses the main municipal buildings and the large whitewashed Catholic church – inside its door on the left are dozens of crosses, forming a memorial to those killed in the civil war. There's not that much to do in Nebaj itself, though the small **market**, a block east of the church, is worth investigation. It's fairly quiet most days, but presents the best photographic opportunities, as you can capture Nebajeños going about their daily business without too much disturbance. On Thursday and Sunday the numbers swell and traders visit from out of town selling North American secondhand clothing, stereos from Taiwan and Korea, and chickens, eggs, fruit and vegetables from the highlands. If you're in town for the second week in August, you'll witness the **Nebaj fiesta**, which includes processions, dances, drinking, fireworks and a marimba-playing marathon.

Guerrilla warfare in the Ixil Triangle

The bitter **civil war** of the late 1970s and early 1980s ravaged the western highlands, and left the Ixil Triangle among the areas most devastated by the conflict between the Guatemalan army and the insurgent Ejército Guerrillero de los Pobres (the EGP, or Guerrilla Army of the Poor). By 1996, when the guerrilla war officially ended, nearly all of the region's smaller villages had been destroyed and fifteen to twenty thousand people had been killed, with tens of thousands more displaced. Most of the victims were villagers, dying not because of their political beliefs but because they had been caught between the army, who viewed the war as a battle for the survival of the state, and the EGP, who saw the creation of a liberated zone in the Ixil as the springboard to national revolution.

The severity of the violence is a measure of the success of the EGP, who fought the army in northern Quiché for more than two decades. The EGP first entered the area in 1972, when a small group of guerrilla fighters (some of whom had been involved in the 1960s guerrilla campaign) crossed the Mexican border and began building links with locals. With little military presence in the area at the time, they were able to work swiftly, impressing the Ixil Maya with their bold plans for political and social revolution. The guerillas opened their military campaign in 1975 with the assassination of Luis Arenas, the owner of Finca La Perla, to the north of Chajul, where hundreds of labourers were kept in a system of debt bondage. The EGP shot Arenas in front of hundreds of his employees as he was counting the payroll. According to the group, "shouts of joy burst from throats accustomed for centuries only to silence and lament, and with something like an ancestral cry, with one voice they chanted with us our slogan, 'Long live the poor, death to the rich.'" But other accounts describe how people walked for days to pay their last respects to Arenas.

Such early actions prompted a huge response from the armed forces, which began killing, kidnapping and torturing suspected guerrillas and sympathizers. The organization was already well entrenched, however, and the army's brutality only served to persuade more and more people to seek protection from the guerrillas. By late 1978, the EGP were regularly occupying villages, holding open meetings and tearing down debtors' jails. In January 1979 they killed another local landowner, Enrique Brol, of Finca San Francisco near Cotzal. On the same day, the EGP also briefly took control of Nebaj itself, summoning the whole of the town's population,

Arrival and information

The *El Descanso* centre on 3 Calle, two blocks north and one west of the plaza, is a one-stop shop for Nebaj visitors and easily the best place to go for **information** on local activities and an Internet connection. Here, you'll find Trekking Ixil, which offers a range of inexpensive guided walks (from around US$7 per person) – from day hikes to Acul and Cocop to four-day trips across the mountains staying in *posadas comunitarias* (guest houses) and eating local meals in remote villages. Next door, Pablo's Tours, 3 C 3–20 (Ⓣ7755 8287, Ⓔpablostours@hotmail.com), can also arrange hiking trips, horse-riding excursions or a shuttle bus. The *Descanso* team also operate the Ⓦwww.nebaj.org website (Spanish only) and are affiliated with the **Nebaj Language School** (see p.66), which is in the same building.

For your **banking** needs, Banrural, on the north side of the plaza, has a 5B ATM for MasterCard/Cirrus cards, and Bancafé, near the market on 2 Av, has a Visa/Plus ATM and exchanges both cash and travellers' cheques.

The **bus terminal** is two blocks southeast of the plaza. Getting to Nebaj is straightforward enough, with seven daily buses from Santa Cruz del Quiché (2hr 45min), while **getting around** the Ixil Triangle involves using a pick-up or two

including Western travellers staying at *Las Tres Hermanas*, to the central plaza, where they denounced the barbaric inequalities of life in the Ixil.

The army responded with a wave of horrific attacks on the civilian population. Army units swept through the area, committing atrocities, burning villages and massacring thousands, including women and children. Nevertheless, the strength of the guerrillas continued to grow, and in 1981 they again launched an attack on Nebaj, by then a garrison town. Shortly afterwards the army chief of staff, Benedicto Lucas García (the president's brother), flew into Nebaj and, in a simple speech before the townspeople, he warned them that if they didn't "clean up their act" he'd bring five thousand men "and finish off the entire population".

After the ouster of President Lucas García in the military coup of early 1982, the army changed its tactics. The new president, **General Ríos Montt**, used anti-Communist propaganda and conscripted civilian patrols (PACs), which were placed on the conflict's front lines, to ensure the loyalty of the people. Villagers were given ancient M1 rifles and told to protect their communities from the guerrillas. Meanwhile, the army began aggressive sweeps through the highlands, bringing displaced people back into Nebaj to be fed and eventually settled in new "model" villages. With the EGP retreating to more remote terrain, Ixil communities began to adapt to the army's newfound dominance, and many opted to reject contact with the guerrillas.

Hit hard, the EGP responded with desperate acts. On June 6, 1982, guerrillas stopped a bus near Cotzal and executed thirteen civil patrol leaders and their wives; eleven days later a guerrilla column entered the village of Chacalté, where the civil patrol had been particularly active, and killed a hundred people, wounding thirty-five.

The army's offer of amnesty, twinned with a continuous crackdown on the guerrillas, soon drew refugees out of the mountains: between 1982 and 1984 some 42,000 people turned themselves in, fleeing a harsh existence under guerrilla protection. By 1985 the guerrillas had been driven back into a handful of mountain strongholds in Xeputul, Sumal and Amachel, all to the north and west of Chajul and Cotzal. Skirmishes continued until the mid-1990s, but ceased with the signing of peace accords. Since then, ex-guerrillas and former civil patrol members have resettled the old village sites and begun the task of rebuilding communities.

from time to time. Bus schedules are not set in stone, but buses usually depart for Chajul at 10am and 3pm (1hr); Cotzal at 12.30pm and around 3.30pm (50 min); and Salquil Grande at 11.30am (1hr). Additional buses depart Nebaj early in the morning on market days in Chajul (Tues and Fri) and Cotzal (Wed and Sat).

Moving on from Nebaj, buses head for Quiché at 1am, 2am, 3am, 4am, 5.30am, 8am and 11am, and a direct bus to Guatemala City departs at 11pm. A new daily service to Cobán was slated to begin in 2005. (For Huehuetenango you'll have to change in Sacapulas.) Arrive early to grab a seat on all routes. Pick-ups and trucks supplement the buses: the best place to hitch south is on the road out of town, past the *Hotel Ixil*; heading north, wait by the gas station just beyond the *Hospedaje Ilebal Tenam*. For shuttle buses to destinations around the country, such as Antigua, Quetzaltenango and Cobán, contact Pablo's Tours – though these can be pricey unless you have a group.

Accommodation

You'll find little in the way of luxury in Nebaj, though standards have improved considerably recently and what there is does have an inimitable charm. There are few street signs, so you'll probably have to rely on the children who act as guides – none of the hotels is more than a few minutes' walk from the terminal.

Anexo Hotel Ixil 250m southeast of the plaza ☎7756 0036. Agreeable place with twelve clean and decent-sized rooms, with tiled floors, TVs and private bathrooms, all set around a garden courtyard. Safe parking. ❸

Hospedaje Ilebal Tenam 400m north of the plaza on the road to Chajul/Cotzal ☎7755 8039. Well-run hospedaje with selection of smallish but very clean rooms, situated around a triangular courtyard. Some rooms have TVs and private bathrooms, and reliably hot showers. Safe parking. ❶–❷

Hospedaje Nebajeñese a block northwest of the plaza ☎7755 8071. Simple place with bare but serviceable rooms (with two, three or four beds) that's run by a very friendly family. They also own the store below and can provide meals. Hot water all day. ❶

Hotel Ixil 200m south of the plaza on the road to Sacapulas ☎7756 0036. Some of the large, bare rooms are a little damp, though the setting, around a courtyard, is pleasant. Warmish shower. ❶

Hotel Shalom one block north of the plaza ☎7756 0000 or 7755 8031. Large rooms all with desk, chest-of-drawers and TV, plus a sitting area upstairs. ❸

Hotel Turansa one block west of the plaza ☎7755 8219 or 5715 7803. Two-storey green-and-white block with smallish but neat rooms featuring pine furnishings, comfortable beds, cable TV and private bathrooms. Safe parking. ❷

Hotel Villa Nebaj two minutes' walk north of the plaza ☎7755 8115 or 5715 1651. Garishly painted, new four-storey construction that's something of a blot on the landscape, though the accommodation is extremely comfortable – all the very clean, attractive rooms have quality beds, bedside lights, TVs and phones, and most have a bathroom. Safe parking. ❸–❹

Eating

The best places to eat are the *Maya-Inca*, on 5 C, which is owned by a friendly Peruvian–Guatemalan couple and serves tasty local and Peruvian dishes (and huge breakfasts), and *El Descanso*, which has well-prepared, inexpensive Guatemalan food, as well as sandwiches and cakes. For a meat feast, *Asados el Pasabien* on the road south to Sacapulas excels for *churrascos*, *chuletas* and chicken, while *Cesar's*, on 2 Av opposite Bancafé, serves up reasonable pizzas. For entertainment, most of the raving in town is courtesy of Nebaj's burgeoning evangelical church scene, with four-hour services involving much wailing and gnashing of teeth; alternatively, head to *El Descanso* for a beer, where many development-project workers gather.

Walks around Nebaj

In the hills that surround Nebaj there are several beautiful **walks**, with one of the most interesting taking you to the village of **Acul**, two hours away.

Starting from the church in Nebaj, head east downhill along 5 Calle past the *Hotel Turansa*. At the bottom of the dip, the road divides close to the *Tienda y Cantina*, and here you take the right-hand fork and head out of town.

Just after you pass the last houses, you'll see some pre-Columbian burial mounds to your right. These are still used for religious ceremonies, and if you take a close look you'll find burnt patches marking the site of offerings. Since the mounds are usually planted with maize they can be a bit difficult to spot, but once you get up higher above the town they're easier to make out.

Beyond this the track carries on, switchbacking up a steep hillside, and heads over a narrow pass into the next valley, where it drops down into the village. **ACUL** was one of the original so-called "model villages" into which people were herded after their homes had been destroyed by the army. It's steadily developing its identity with the efforts of the United Nations and other organizations; the municipality now has a population of around four hundred Ixil and K'iche' Maya families. You can **stay** here at the very basic but friendly *Hostal Doña Magdelena* (❶), where they also serve meals. If you walk through the village and out the other side and then bear right, you soon arrive at the *Finca San Antonio* (☎5599 3352; ❹), a wonderful Swiss-style chalet set in a neat little meadow where they rent out delightful rooms with pine beds and a verandah. An Italian–Guatemalan family have lived here for more than fifty years, making several varieties of some of the country's best **cheese**. Non-guests are welcome to have a look around – especially if they buy some produce. José Azzari, who founded the finca, died in 1990, at the ripe old age of 99, though his sons continue to farm here.

Sadly, a second, shorter walk to a beautiful little **waterfall**, La Cascada de Plata, is so strewn with trash that it's not worth the effort unless a clean-up has been undertaken (check in *El Descanso*). Take the road to Chajul and turn left just before it crosses the bridge, a kilometre or two outside Nebaj. Don't be fooled by the smaller version you'll come to shortly before the main set of falls.

A third half-day circular walk climbs up the steep eastern edge of the natural bowl that surrounds Nebaj to the village of **COCOP** and back to the main Nebaj–Cotzal road. Starting from Bancafé in the centre of town, walk along 2 Avenida through the market area, then past *Anexo Hotel Ixil* until the end of the road, bear right, and then take the first left downhill to the bridge. Cross the bridge, and continue walking until you reach the pueblo of **Xemamatzé** on the edge of Nebaj. This village used to be home to a huge internment camp where Ixil villagers who had surrendered to the army were subject to lengthy "repatriation" treatment before being allowed to return to their native villages. In Xemamatzé take the well-trodden trail uphill just after the *Pepsi tienda* sign, and after five minutes there's a green signpost to **COCOP** – this trail climbs steadily for about an hour to 2300m. Back across the valley there are spectacular views towards Nebaj. When the trail eventually begins to level out, directly facing a maize field, the path then turns a sharp left and continues round the mountain. The path grips the side of the slope and twists and turns, then gradually starts to descend as the small village of Cocop comes into view below. The village has recently been rebuilt on old foundations, after it was razed to the ground during the civil war, and 98 villagers were massacred by the army. Today it's a pretty little settlement in a delightful setting beside a gurgling river, with a few stores where you can buy a warm fizzy drink. If you want to **stay**, ask for Gaspar Brito (the village's tourism coordinator), who will organize a bed and may show you Cocop's *cusha* liquor distillery. To head back, walk straight ahead from the crossroads in the centre of the village, past the Emmanuel church for a lovely hour's stroll along the V-shaped valley through sheep-filled meadows. At the end of the trail is the village of **Río Azul** on the main Cotzal–Nebaj road from where you can wait for a pick-up, truck or bus, or hike back to Nebaj in an hour and a half.

West to Salquil Grande

Another possible excursion from Nebaj takes you to the village of **SALQUIL GRANDE**, 23km to the west. A road runs out this way, through the village of Tzalbal, and across two huge and breathtaking valleys. New villages, built to replace those burnt to the ground by the army, pepper the hillsides, their tin roofs still clean and largely rust-free. They are inhabited by people who spent the war years either starving in the mountains or shut away in the refugee camps of Nebaj. A daily **bus** leaves for Salquil Grande from the market in Nebaj at around 11.30am; alternatively, catch one of the trucks or pick-ups heading this way – there's always more traffic for the Tuesday market. The village doesn't have anywhere to stay, but pick-ups return to Nebaj throughout the afternoon. Continuing west from Salquil Grande, a very rough track runs some 44km to join up with the main Huehuetenango–Barillas road, a spectacular way of reaching the Paquix junction for the turn-off for Todos Santos Cuchumatán.

The landscape around Salquil Grande is supremely beautiful and best enjoyed on foot. A good hike takes you to the little village of **Parramos Grande** in around two hours. Starting from the statue of a soldier on the edge of Salquil Grande, you want to take the path to the right, and when this divides take a left through the *milpa*, heading downhill. Along the way you pass a couple of beautiful waterfalls, so if the sun's shining you can always pause for a chilly dip.

San Juan Cotzal and Chajul

Buses run from Nebaj to the Ixil Triangle's two other towns, San Juan Cotzal and Chajul, though it's best to coincide your visit with market days when there's more going on, as well as more traffic on the move. (Cotzal holds its market on Wednesday and Saturday, while Chajul does so on Tuesday and Friday.) Plenty of pick-ups supplement these buses; the last usually leave both towns at around 4.30pm, as do aid agency four-wheel drives. Sunday is also a good day to travel because villagers from the other two Ixil towns visit Nebaj for its weekly market, heading back after 11am.

Walking from Cotzal to Chajul

Though a newish unpaved road connects Cotzal and Chajul, it's also possible to hike (roughly 2hr 15min) an indirect route through some beautiful Ixil scenery before joining the road for the last two or three kilometres. From Cotzal's church take the road downhill that heads toward the Finca San Francisco, passing a school and a football pitch on your right. Just before the bridge, leave the road and take the path that follows the Río Tichum for about five minutes, until you reach another bridge. Cross the second bridge and take the left-hand path uphill through maize fields (the right-hand path leads to the village of Xepalma). After thirty minutes you'll reach a ridge, marking the border between two municipalities, from where you can see the white bulk of Chajul's church. Continue down a muddy path through woodland and you'll come to a large fenced-off field. Turn to the left and follow the fence until you reach a large path; turn right here and you'll shortly reach the Cotzal–Chajul road. From here, it's about an hour to Chajul: turn right and follow the road down a small valley before climbing very steeply to the village.

SAN JUAN COTZAL is the closer town to Nebaj, forty minutes to over an hour away depending on the state of the road. The town is beautifully set in a gentle dip in the valley, sheltered beneath the Cuchumatanes and often wrapped in a damp blanket of mist. In the 1920s and 1930s, this was the largest and busiest of the three Ixil towns, as it was from here that the fertile lands to the north were colonized. Once a road reached Nebaj in the 1940s, however, Cotzal was somewhat eclipsed, although there is still a higher concentration of ladinos here. Cotzal attracts very few Western travellers, so you may find that many people assume you're an aid worker or attached to a fundamentalist church.

Although there's little to do in town, there is some great **hill walking** close by. If you want to stay, a small, very basic unmarked **pensión** (❶) lies two blocks from the church; otherwise you may find the farmacia in the corner of the plaza will rent you a room (1). *La Maguey* **restaurant**, in a front room a block behind the church, serves up reasonable, if bland, food.

Last but by no means least of the Ixil settlements is **CHAJUL**, replete with a good stock of old adobe houses, their wooden beams and red-tiled roofs blackened by the smoke of cooking fires. It is also the most traditional and least bilingual of the Ixil towns. The streets are usually bustling with activity: you'll be met by an army of small children, and the local women gather to wash clothes at the stream that cuts through the middle of the village. Here boys still use blowpipes to hunt small birds, a skill that dates from the earliest of times but is now little used elsewhere. The women of Chajul are terrific weavers, their *huipiles* richly embroidered with animals and symbols, filling the streets with colour. Until the past few years, all the textiles created here used to be woven in red, though nowadays blue is almost as common. Look out, too, for the women's earrings which are made of old coins strung up on lengths of wool. The traditional red jackets of the men are an extremely rare sight these days. Make sure you visit the shop run by the local weaving cooperative, Va'l Vaq Quyol, between the church and the market, where you'll find some of the best-quality handmade textiles in the country at very decent prices.

The colonial church on the plaza, a huge old structure full of gold leaf and boasting a fine wooden ceiling of massive beams, is home to the **Christ of Golgotha** and the target of a large pilgrimage on the second Friday of Lent – a particularly good time to be here. The two angels that flank the image were originally dressed as policemen, after a tailor who'd been cured through prayer donated the uniforms so that his benefactor would be well protected. Later they were changed into army uniforms, and recently they've been toned down to look more like boy scouts.

Chajul's plaza was the place where Rigoberta Menchú, in her autobiography, describes the public execution of her brother at the hands of the army. According to Menchú, her brother and several other suspected communists and labour organizers were brought before the town's population by the army, all showing signs of hideous torture. She describes the commander delivering an anti-communist lecture, then ordering the prisoners to be burnt alive. Although there is no doubt that atrocities took place, painstaking investigation by author David Stoll, and evidence by EGP member Mario Payeras, contradicts Menchú's version of events – eyewitnesses testify that the prisoners were machine-gunned, and the date of the killings is in dispute, as is the fact that Menchú was there at all. Though the show-trial execution was horrific enough under any circumstances, the reliability of Menchú's account has undoubtedly come into question.

If you want to **stay**, the very basic – and pretty filthy – *Hospedaje Cristina* (❶) is two blocks south of the church. The best place to eat is the clean *Comedor*

Las Gemelitas, two blocks downhill from the church. Local families also rent out beds in their houses to the steady trickle of travellers now coming to Chajul; you won't have to look for them, they will find you. The Banrural on the plaza will change dollars and travellers' cheques.

Beyond the triangle: the Ixcán

The thinly populated area north of the Ixil Triangle known as the **Ixcán**, which drops down towards the Mexican border to merge with the Lacandón rainforests, has long been one of Guatemala's great untamed frontiers. Like the Ixil Triangle, this region, a former EGP stronghold, was heavily fought over until the mid-1990s. In the 1960s and 1970s, land-hungry migrants from Quiché and Huehuetenango began moving here, carving out new farms from the forest. After a few years of extreme hardship, and assisted by Maryknoll missionaries, they established thriving communities. The land yielded two crops a year and produced an abundance of fruit, coffee and cardamom. The settlers built health clinics and churches, established a system of radio communication and a transport network, and began applying for collective land titles. However, the EGP moved into the Ixcán in the early 1970s, and a decade later bitter fighting between the insurgents and the army devastated the area, with virtually every village burned to the ground and thousands fleeing to Mexico.

Now many refugees and ex-guerrillas have returned to northern Ixcán, and a number of new villages and resettlement camps have been established. The backroads route across the very northern part of Ixcán from Playa Grande to Barillas is covered on p.323, though currently only very rough tracks (and no public transport) link this area with the Ixil.

Lago de Atitlán

Lake Como, it seems to me, touches the limit of the permissibly picturesque; but Atitlán is Como with the additional embellishments of several immense volcanoes. It is really too much of a good thing. After a few days of this impossible landscape one finds oneself thinking nostalgically of the English Home Counties.

Aldous Huxley, *Beyond the Mexique Bay* (1934)

Whether or not you share Huxley's refined sensibilities, there's no doubt that **LAGO DE ATITLÁN** is astonishingly beautiful, and most people find themselves captivated by the lake's scenic excesses. Indeed, the effect is so intoxicating that a handful of gringo devotees have been rooted to its shores since the 1960s, and today Atitlán rates as the country's number one tourist attraction.

Hemmed in on all sides by volcanoes and steep hills, it's at least 320m deep and has no visible outlet, draining as it does through an underground passage to the Pacific coast. The lake water itself is an irregular shape, with three main inlets. It measures 18km by 12km at its widest point, and shifts through an astonishing range of blues, steely greys and greens as the sun moves across the sky. In the morning the surface of the lake is normally calm and clear, but by early afternoon the *xocomil*, "the wind that carries away sin", blows from the coast, churning the surface and making travel by boat quite a rock 'n' roll experience. A north wind, say the Maya, indicates that the spirit of the lake is discarding a drowned body, having claimed its soul.

Another remarkable aspect of the Atitlán area is the strength of Maya culture evident in its lakeside villages. Despite the holiday homes and the thousands of tourists that venture here each year, many of the pueblos remain intensely traditional – **San Antonio Palopó**, **Santiago Atitlán** and **Sololá**, in the hills above the lake, are some of the very few places in the entire country where Maya men still wear *traje*. Around the southwestern shores, from Santiago to San Pedro La Laguna, the indigenous people are **Tz'utujil** speakers, the remnants of one of the smaller pre-conquest tribes, whose capital was on the slopes of the San Pedro volcano. On the other side of the water, from San Marcos La Laguna to Cerro de Oro, **Kaqchikel** is spoken, marking the western barrier of this tribe.

Thirteen villages grace the shores of the lake – from cosmopolitan **Panajachel** to tiny, isolated **Tzununá** – with many more in the hills behind. The villages are mostly subsistence farming communities, and it's easy to hike and boat around the lake staying in a different one each night. The lakeside area has been heavily populated since the earliest of times, but it's only relatively recently that it has attracted large numbers of tourists. For years few people stayed outside Panajachel, but hotels, guest houses and tourism facilities have recently spread to most villages.

Tourist crime around Lake Atitlán

The robbery of hikers is rare but not unknown in the Atitlán area, and a couple of rapes have been reported in the past five years. Statistically, the chance of you becoming a victim is extremely small, and hundreds of hikers enjoy trouble-free walks around the lakeshore every month. Nevertheless, if you plan to hike any of the volcanoes, or the trails between San Pedro and Santa Cruz, check out the security situation first. Guest-house staff in Santa Cruz are usually well informed, and some language-school teachers in San Pedro can advise you about the situation; as can the tourist office in Panajachel.

Atitlán's beauty remains overwhelming, although recent pressures are decidedly threatening. Despite its status as a national park, large swathes of the coastline are now owned by foreigners and wealthy investors from Guatemala City. A population boom in the Maya villages has also had a damaging impact as the desperate need to cultivate more land leads to deforestation and soil erosion. According to a 2004 report published in *Prensa Libre*, a third of the indigenous children that live in the lake environs suffer from malnutrition, and the villages of San Pedro, San Juan La Laguna and San Pablo La Laguna were all given food aid that year. Meanwhile, the fishing industry, once thriving on the abundance of small fish and crabs, has been crippled by the introduction of **black bass**, which eat the smaller fish and water birds, and are, moreover, much harder to catch.

Where to go

Most people reach the lake via Panajachel, a small town on the northern shore which is now dominated by tourism. It makes a good base for exploring the surrounding area, either heading across the lake or making day-trips to **Chichicastenango**, **Nahualá**, **Sololá** and **Iximché**. Panajachel has an abundance of cheap hotels and restaurants and is well served by buses. To get a sense of a more typical Atitlán village, however, travel by boat to Santiago Atitlán or San Antonio Palopó, while for an established travellers' scene and a surplus of cheap hotels, try **San Pedro**. Meanwhile, **Jaibalito**, **Santa Cruz La Laguna** and **San Marcos** are the places to head for if you're looking for real peace and quiet and some good hikes.

The **website** Ⓦ www.atitlan.com has some good historical and cultural information and up-market accommodation options.

Sololá and around

A couple of kilometres to the west of Los Encuentros, at the El Cuchillo junction, the road for Panajachel branches off the Carretera Interamericana. Dropping towards the lake it arrives first at **SOLOLÁ**, the departmental capital and the gateway to the lake, which is perched on a natural balcony some 600m above the water. Overlooked by the majority of travellers, the town itself isn't much to look at, with a huge central plaza (that's good for people watching) with a clock tower on one side and a modern church on the other. However, its **Friday market** (there's also a smaller one on Tuesdays) is one of Central America's finest, a mesmeric display of colour and commerce that Aldous Huxley described as "a walking museum of fancy dress". From as early as 5am the lanes around the plaza are packed, drawing traders from all over the highlands, as well as thousands of Sololá Maya, the women covered in striped red cloth and the men in their outlandish "space cowboy" shirts, woollen aprons and wildly embroidered trousers. Weaving is a powerful creative tradition in the lives of Sololá Maya and each generation develops a distinctive style based upon previous designs.

In common with only a few other places in the country, Sololá has parallel indigenous and ladino governments, and is one of Guatemala's largest Maya towns. Tradition dominates daily life here and the town is said to be divided into sections, each administered by a Maya clan, just as it was before the Conquest. The town's symbol, still seen on the back of the men's jackets, is an abstraction of a bat, referring to the royal house of Xahil, who were the rulers of the Kaqchikel at the time of the Spanish invasion.

Another interesting time to visit Sololá is on Sunday, when the **cofradías**, the elders of the indigenous religious hierarchy, parade through the streets in ceremonial costume to attend the late-morning Mass. They're easily recognizable, carrying silver-tipped canes and wearing broad-brimmed hats and particularly elaborate jackets. Inside the church the sexes are segregated, and the women wear shawls to cover their heads.

Virtually no one stays in Sololá, but the *Hotel y Restaurante Posada del Viajero*, on the east side of the plaza, offers basic **rooms** (❷) and good *comida típica*. The clean *Comedor Las Rosas,* on the north side of the plaza, is another good dining option. For **bus** times, refer to the Panajachel schedules, as all buses travelling between Panajachel and Los Encuentros pass through Sololá. Minibuses also run regularly between Sololá and Los Encuentros. The last bus to Panajachel passes through Sololá at around 7pm.

Nearby villages

Several other villages can be reached from Sololá, most of them within walking distance. About 8km to the east is tiny **Santa María Concepción**, an exceptionally quiet farming village with a spectacularly restored whitewashed colonial church whose altar has some wonderful gilded cherubs. The walk out here, along a dirt track skirting the hills above Panajachel, offers superb views across the lake. No buses, but the odd pick-up plies this route.

Four kilometres to the west of Sololá, along another dirt road and across a deep-cut river valley, **San José Chacayá** has a tiny colonial church with thick crumbling walls but little else. Another 8km further along the track is **Santa Lucía Utatlán**, which can also be reached along a paved road that branches off the Carretera Interamericana. From Santa Lucía, set back from the ridge of hills overlooking the water, you can then get a bus or pick-up, or continue hiking around the lake using the paved road that passes through Santa María Visitación and Santa Clara and then plummets down to San Pablo La Laguna on the lakeshore.

On the hillside below Sololá, **San Jorge La Laguna** is a tiny hamlet perched above the lake with sweeping views whose villagers have been chased around the country by natural disasters. The settlement was founded by refugees from the 1773 earthquake in Antigua, and its original lakeside incarnation was swept into the water by a landslide, persuading the people to move up the hill.

Panajachel

Ten kilometres beyond Sololá, separated by a precipitous descent, is **PANAJACHEL**. Over the years what was once a small Maya village has become

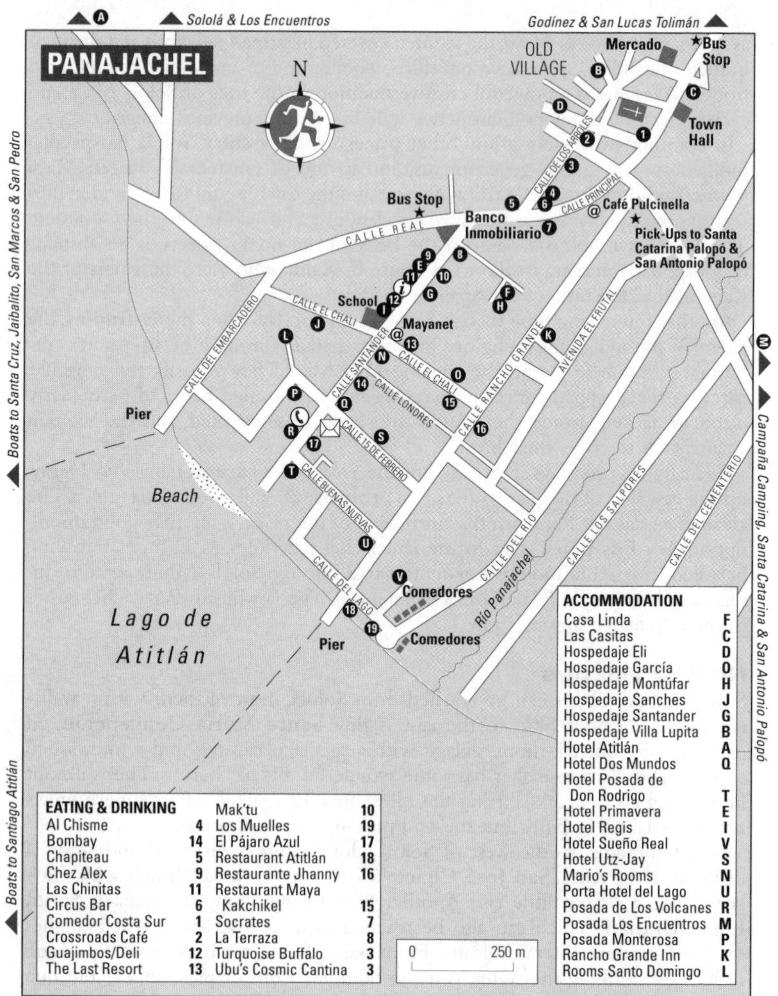

something resembling a resort, with a sizable population of long-term foreign residents, whose numbers are swollen in the winter by an influx of North American seasonal migrants and a flood of tourists. Back in the 1960s and 1970s, Panajachel was the premier Central American hippie hangout, though it's now fully integrated into the tourism mainstream and is as popular with Guatemalans (and Mexicans and Salvadoreans) as Westerners. The lotus-eaters and crystal-gazers have not all deserted the town, though – many have simply reinvented themselves as capitalists, owning restaurants and exporting handicrafts. There is much talk about Atitlán being one of the world's few vortex energy fields, along with the Egyptian pyramids and Machu Picchu. Though you are unlikely to see fish swimming backwards or buses rolling uphill to Sololá, the lake does have an undeniable draw and attracts a polyglot population of healers, therapists and masseurs to Panajachel. In many ways it's this **gringo** crowd that gives the town its modern character and identity – vortex energy centre or not.

Not so long ago (although it seems an entirely different age) Panajachel was a quiet little village of **Kaqchikel** Maya, whose ancestors were settled here after the Spanish crushed a force of Tz'utujil warriors on the site. In the early days of the Conquest, the Franciscans established a church and monastery in the village, using it as the base for their regional conversion campaign. Today the old village has been enveloped by a construction boom, and though most of the new buildings are pretty nondescript, its lakeside setting is superb. Most of the Maya continue to farm in the river delta behind the town, and the Sunday market, bustling with people from all around the lake, remains oblivious to the tourist invasion.

Arrival and information

Most buses from Sololá stop beside Calle del Embarcadero and then again at the end of the main drag, Calle Santander, which runs down to the lakeshore. Pana has two piers, where you'll find boats to towns around the lake (see box below). The Inguat **tourist office** is on Calle Santander (daily 9am–5pm; ⓣ7762 1392), with English-speaking staff, basic hotel information, and boat and bus schedules. **Tuk-tuks** are everywhere in Pana, while taxis usually wait outside the post office – you can call one on ⓣ7762 1571. You'll find at least a dozen or so inexpensive **Internet** cafés around town, with rates around US$1.25 an hour. Among the best are *Mayanet*, midway along Calle Santander, and *Café Pulcinella*, at C Principal 0–72, which also bakes a mean pizza and sells Chianti by the glass.

Pana also has two language schools where you can **study Spanish** (see p.65).

Accommodation

The streets of Panajachel are overflowing with inexpensive **hotels**, and there are plenty of "**rooms**". Campers are well served at shady *Campaña* (ⓣ7762 2479; US$3 per person), on the corner of the road to Santa Catarina and Calle

Boats

Most lakeside villages are served by **lanchas**, small, fast boats which depart when the owner has enough passengers to cover fuel costs. You usually won't have to wait long, but at quiet times of year you may have to hang around for 30min or a little more. Panajachel has two piers. The **main pier**, at the end of Calle del Embarcadero, serves the villages on the northern side of the lake: Santa Cruz (about 15min), Jaibalito (25min), Tzununá (30min) and San Marcos (40min). This pier is also home to direct (15min) and non-direct (50min) boats to San Pedro, from where you can easily get to San Juan and San Pablo. The **second pier**, at the end of Calle Rancho Grande, is for Santiago Atitlán (1hr by ferry or 20min by *lancha*) and lake tours. The last boats on all routes leave around 6.30pm.

A semi-official **fare system** is in place: tourists pay US$1.30 for a short trip, US$2–2.50 for a longer journey. Locals pay less. Some *lancheros* try to charge more for the last boat of the day. **Tours of the lake** (US$8), visiting San Pedro, Santiago Atitlán and San Antonio Palopó, can be booked in virtually any travel agent (see p.171); all leave around 9am and return by 4pm.

del Cementerio, over the river bridge. There's a kitchen and storage facilities, hook-up facilities, sleeping bags and tents for rent, and a few little clean cabañas (❷), too.

Budget

Casa Linda down an alley off the top of C Santander ⓣ7762 0386. Not the cheapest hospedaje, but the central garden is undeniably beautiful, and the management friendly. Some rooms have private bath. ❷

Las Casitas C Principal, near the market ⓣ7762 1224, ⓦwww.hotellascasitas.net. Clean, friendly and safe, with tastefully decorated rooms sporting quality beds and reading lamps; most also have private bath. It is quite a walk from the lakeshore, however. ❸

Hospedaje Eli Callejón del Pozo, off C de los Arboles ⓣ7762 0148. Ten clean, cheap rooms overlooking a pretty little garden in a quiet location. ❶

Hospedaje García C El Chali ⓣ7762 2187. An abundance of featureless but perfectly reasonable budget rooms, with good prices for single travellers. ❷

Hospedaje Montúfar down an alley off the top of C Santander ⓣ7762 0406. Very clean, secure accommodation on three separate floors and a quiet location make this a good choice. Triples also available. ❷

Hospedaje Sanches C El Chali. Quiet location, friendly management and clean rooms, on two levels, which are a little larger than average for this price category. ❶

Hospedaje Santander C Santander ⓣ7762 1304. Agreeable place with a leafy courtyard and clean, inexpensive rooms, some with private bath. ❷

Hospedaje Villa Lupita Callejón El Tino ⓣ7762 1201. Excellent-value family-run place on a quiet lane in the old village. Sixteen rooms, all with bedside lights, rugs and mirrors, some with private bath. There's also a sun terrace and free purified water and coffee. ❷

Mario's Rooms C Santander ⓣ7762 1313. Appealing, clean rooms, some airy and light with private bath, others more basic. ❷

Posada Monterosa C Monterrey ⓣ7762 0055. Neat little hotel with attractive, recently renovated en-suite rooms. Secure car parking. ❸

Rooms Santo Domingo down a path off C Monterrey ⓣ7762 0236. Very inexpensive, age-old place, set well away from the bustle of C Santander. Super-basic rooms all face a charming little garden, with more expensive en-suite options upstairs. ❶–❸

Moderate

Hotel Dos Mundos C Santander ⓣ7762 2078, ⓕ7762 0127. Just off the main drag, this hotel has comfortable rooms set to one side of a large private garden, where there's also a small swimming pool. Breakfast is included; and there's an authentic in-house Italian restaurant and espresso bar. ❻

Hotel Primavera C Santander ⓣ7762 2052, ⓦwww.primaveraatitlan.com. A classy minimalist-style place where the rooms boast magnolia walls, pale wood and a notable absence of *típica* textiles. The smart restaurant downstairs, *Chez Alex*, is highly acclaimed. ❺

Hotel Regis C Santander ⓣ7762 1149, ⓕ7762 1152, ⓦwww.atitlan.com/regis.htm. Age-old colonial-style establishment with pleasant individual bungalows and rooms, all with cable TV, though the real attraction is the natural hot spring in the grounds. ❻

Hotel Sueño Real C Ramós ⓣ7762 0608, ⓕ7762 1097. Welcoming little hotel, close to the lakeshore in a quiet location and run by a friendly family. The ten attractive rooms all have private bath and TV. ❹

Hotel Utz-Jay C 15 de Febrero ⓣ7762 0217, ⓦwww.hotelutzjay.com. A lovely place, occupying a large plot of land featuring a tranquil garden and an in-house *tuj* herbal sauna. The stylish rooms and adobe-and-stone *casitas* all have hand-carved furniture, rugs and private bath; the nicest (nos. 1, 7, 8 and 12) face the garden. There's also a selection of excellent tours and ample parking. ❹

Posada de los Volcanes C Santander ⓣ7762 0244, ⓦwww.posadadelosvolcanes.com. Bright, clean rooms, all with good beds, private bath and cable TV. Slightly overpriced, however, so try asking the helpful management for a discount at quiet times of year. ❺

Posada Los Encuentros Callejón Chotzar 0-41, ⓣ7762 2093, ⓦwww.atitlan.com/losencuentros. Comfortable, welcoming American-owned B&B with large rooms and an apartment, a lovely leafy garden, sauna and gym, located about a fifteen-minute walk from C Principal. ❺–❻

Rancho Grande Inn C Rancho Grande ⓣ7762 2255, ⓦwww.ranchograndeinn.com. Attractive, nicely appointed bungalows bedecked with local textiles and set in spacious gardens with a swimming pool. A filling breakfast is included. ❺–❻

Luxury

Hotel Atitlán 1km west of the centre ⓣ7762 1441 or 7762 1416, ⓦwww.hotelatitlan.com. A wonderful lakeside location, and the luxurious rooms (from US$130) have all the mod-cons and volcano views. Highlights include extensive, beautifully maintained gardens and a swimming pool. ❾

Hotel Posada de Don Rodrigo C Santander ⓣ & ⓕ7762 2322 or 7762 2329, ⓦwww.hotelposadadedonrodrigo.com. Colonial-style hotel with large outdoor pool, sauna and squash court. Most of the accommodation, if comfortable enough, lacks a lake view, so go for a room in the new wing (nos. 301–311), which offers better value, vistas and much more space for a few dollars more. ❽

Porta Hotel del Lago Right on the lakeshore ⓣ7762 1555, ⓦwww.portahotels.com. All-inclusive hotel with pool, Jacuzzi, sauna, gym and a very corporate, "international" flavour – only the great volcano views remind you that you're in Guatemala. Doubles US$140 low season, US$160 high season. ❾

The Town

Panajachel is one of those inevitable destinations for travellers, and although no one ever owns up to actually liking it, most people seem to stay for a while. The **old village** – a handful of narrow lanes grouped around a stone-faced Catholic church that dates from 1567 – is not particularly picturesque, though it is worth a little exploration. Curiously, the main municipal buildings are not positioned around the dusty plaza in front of the church (the usual layout in Guatemala) but scattered around the streets nearby. You'll find a small **marketplace**, very much geared to local needs rather than tourist tastes, a block to the north of the church.

There's far more hustle and bustle in evidence along Pana's main drag, **Calle Santander**, which cuts a colourful path through the modern heart of the town. This kilometre-long street boasts dozens of stores and stalls, loaded up with a kaleidoscopic collection of weaving and handicrafts from all over Guatemala, as well as an amazing selection of places to eat, drink and surf the Net. Street hawkers, weighed down with armfuls of *típica* textile shirts and gaudy trinkets, ply their goods with daunting persistence here, and buzzing tuk-tuk three-wheelers weave their way along the lane touting for business.

At the southern end of Calle Santander, Pana's **beach** is a modest stretch of sand that offers reasonable swimming and sunbathing. Water quality has improved recently with the construction of a fairly high-tech sewage-treatment plant – though there are nicer spots for a swim. You can also rent out kayaks from Pana beach (note that the lake is usually calmer in the morning), or even scuba dive with ATI Divers (see "Listings").

Cultural sights are hardly abundant in Pana, though there is the stylish **Museo Lacustre** (daily 8am–6pm; US$4.50, students US$2.75) dedicated to the Atitlán region. Located in the grounds of the *Hotel Posada de Don Rodrigo* on Calle Santander, it has well-presented displays in Spanish and English, outlining the turbulent geological history that led to the creation of the lake. There's also an interesting collection of Maya artefacts, including Preclassic and Classic-era ceramics and some wonderfully grotesque ceremonial incense burners.

Eating, drinking and entertainment

Panajachel has an abundance of **restaurants**, most catering to the cosmopolitan tastes of its visitors. You'll have no trouble finding tasty Italian, Mexican and Mediterranean dishes. For really cheap and authentically Guatemalan food, plenty of comedores can be found on and just off the beach promenade and close to the market.

Al Chisme C de los Árboles. Stylish café-restaurant with a menu including snacks (bagels and crepes) and pasta, fish and meat mains as well as veggie options. There's a set menu at around US$3.50 and live jazz some nights. Closed Wed.

Bombay halfway along C Santander. Interesting vegetarian menu which, despite the name, has little Indian about it, instead featuring offerings such as Indonesian *gado-gado,* Mexican dishes, pita bread sandwiches and organic coffee.

Chez Alex halfway along C Santander. Probably the flashest place in town, majoring in European classics, with trout and lobster on the menu. It's expensive, however, and the wine list is pretty basic.

Las Chinitas northern end of C Santander. Pan-Asian cuisine, particularly Nonyan (Malay-Chinese) dishes – try the *gulai curry malay.* Also has tasty stir-fries, Singapore salad and *sate.* Cooking standards have slipped a little recently, but still worth a try. Closed Mon.

Comedor Costa Sur just off C Principal, in the old village. Pana's best comedor: clean and inexpensive and great for breakfast or lunch, with a bargain US$2 fried-fish set menu on offer some days.

Crossroads Café C del Campanario, in the old village. Easily Pana's finest coffee – selected, blended and roasted by a South African barista – plus herbal teas, real hot chocolate and fresh pastries. Closed Sun and Mon and for siesta 1–4pm.

Deli halfway down C Santander. Healthy meals, snacks, salads, sandwiches, pastries, bagels, cakes, wine and tea. Service is friendly, but can be more than a little lethargic.

Guajimbos halfway down C Santander. Ideal for a South American–style feast, all the meat – including kebabs, *chorizo* and giant steaks – is barbecued on a giant *parrilla.* They also serve Chilean wine by the glass and offer well-priced breakfasts. Closed Thurs.

The Last Resort C El Chali. Looks vaguely like an English pub, but does the best American buffet breakfasts in town. Also pasta, steaks and vegetarian dishes, served in huge portions.

Los Muelles lakeside, by the Santiago Pier. Right above the water, with stunning views, this simple place is quite inexpensive for the lakeside location. Menu includes fish (including *mojarra*), *caldos* and sandwiches.

El Pájaro Azul C Santander. Elegant French-style brasserie with good sweet and savoury crepes, salads and sandwiches.

Restaurante Atitlán lakeside, by the Santiago Pier. Fine position, with great views, and a reliable menu offering big portions of Guatemalan favourites.

Restaurante Jhanny halfway down C Rancho Grande. Reliable, flavoursome and filling Guatemalan food; the tables are nicely arranged around a little garden.

Restaurant Maya Kakchikel C El Chali 2–25. There's no sign outside, but this is a good, inexpensive place run by a friendly indigenous family that serves huge *caldos* and has a decent set menu.

La Terraza northern end of C Santander. Formal, expensive European restaurant, with a few Asian-style dishes, mains that include *pollo a la pimento verde*, and a tapas menu, too.

Nightlife

Panajachel buzzes at weekends and during holidays, when many young Guatemalans head to the lake to drink and flirt. Things are quieter at other times, however. One of the most popular places in town at the time of research was the new *Mak'tu* bar on C/Santander which has a big garden and **live bands** most nights. Many other bars and clubs are located around the southern end of Calle de los Árboles, where you'll find the *Circus Bar* for live music plus *El Aleph*, and the *Chapiteau* **nightclub**. Close by on C Principal, *Socrates* is a mainstream disco-club where a young local crowd gather to dance to Latin pop and merengue. Alternatively, *Ubu's Cosmic Cantina*, on Calle de los Árboles, is a more relaxed US-style bar with a big screen for sports fans and movie buffs. **Movies** are also shown at the Carrot Chic and Turquoise Buffalo cinemas on Calle de los Árboles, and there's a **pool hall** in the old village, near the post office.

Listings

Banks and exchange Banco Inmobiliario, at C Santander and C Principal (Mon–Fri 9.30am–5pm, Sat 9am–12.30pm); there's a 5B ATM opposite for MasterCard/Cirrus cards; Banco Industrial, C Santander, has a Visa/Plus ATM.

Bicycle and motorbike rental Moto Servicio Queche, C de los Árboles and C Principal (☎7762 2089), rents mountain bikes for US$1 an hour, or US$6 a day, and 200cc bikes for US$8 an hour, or US$28 a day.

Bookstores The Gallery, Calle de los Árboles, stocks a reasonable choice of secondhand titles and a few interesting new books in English. Libería Libros del Lago, C Santander 9, has a good selection of books on Maya culture, maps and guidebooks.

Laundry Lavandería Automatico, C de los Árboles 0–15 (Mon–Sat 7.30am–6.30pm). US$3.50 for a full load washed, dried and folded.

Medical care Dr Edgar Barreno speaks good English; his surgery is down the first street that branches to the right off C de los Árboles (☎7762 1008).

Pharmacy Farmacia La Unión, C Santander.

Police On the plaza in the old village (☎7762 1120).

Post office C Santader and C 15 de Febrero, or try Get Guated Out on C de los Árboles (☎7762 0595) for bigger shipments.

Telephone Many of the businesses and cybercafés on C Santander offer the best rates to call long-distance; *Café Internet*, on C Principal, charges US$0.30 per minute to North America and US$0.50 to Europe. Otherwise Telgua (daily 7am–midnight) is near the junction of C Santander and C 15 de Febrero.

Travel agents Unión Travel, C Santander & C El Chali (☎7762 2426, www.igoguate.com); Servicios Turísticos Atitlán, C Santander, near C 15 de Febrero (☎7762 2075, www.atitlan.com).

Water sports Canoes, kayaks and windsurfers can be rented on the main beach. Scuba divers can dive the lake with ATI Divers based in Santa Cruz, but they have an office in Pana at Plaza Los Patios, C Santander (☎7762 2621), next to *Las Chinitas* restaurant; one fun-dive is US$25, while a PADI Open Water course is US$175.

Around Panajachel

About 2km west of Panajachel, the **Reserva Natural Atitlán** (8am–5pm, US$5) is a privately run forest reserve on the steep slopes of the lake. Also known as the Finca San Buenaventura, the reserve's land used to form one of the largest coffee farms in the Atitlán region. There are several walking trails (20–75 minutes) through dense foliage, and viewing platforms from where spider monkeys and small mammals like possums and kinkajous are often spotted. Inside the reserve there's a **butterfly park** with dozens of species, including golden orange monarchs and blue morphos, plus a breeding laboratory, and there are also orchid gardens and aviaries. To **get to** the reserve head for the *Hotel Atitlán* (see p.169), from where signposted trails lead to the adjacent reserve.

Elsewhere around the lake

The villages that surround the lake are all easily accessible. For an afternoon's outing, head along the shore southeast of Panajachel to **San Antonio** and **Santa Catarina Palopó**. If you want to spend a day or two exploring the area, then it's well worth crossing the lake to **Santiago Atitlán** and **San Pedro La Laguna**. It's perfectly feasible to walk round the whole lake in four to five days; alternatively, you could cut out a section or two by catching a boat between villages. Perhaps the finest **walking** is on the western side, between San Pedro and Santa Cruz, which is around a six-hour hike.

The eastern shore

There are two roads around the lake's eastern shore from Panajachel: one clings to the shoreline, and the other runs parallel up along the ridge of hills towards Godínez. Next to the lake, backed up against the slopes, are a couple of villages, the first of which, **SANTA CATARINA PALOPÓ**, is just 4km from Panajachel. The people of Santa Catarina used to live almost entirely by fishing and trapping crabs, but these days the black bass have put an end to all that and they've turned to farming and migratory work, with many of the women travelling to Panajachel and Antigua to peddle their weaving. The women's *huipiles* here are unusual in that they have dazzling zigzags in vibrant shades of turquoise or purple, though the traditional design was predominantly red with tiny geometric designs of people and animals. The changes are partly due to a North American who visited the village in the 1970s and commissioned a *huipil* to be made in purple, blue and green as opposed to the traditional colours. These new shades became very popular in the village and are now worn almost universally.

Leaving Santa Catarina, much of the shoreline has been bought and developed, and great villas, ringed by impenetrable walls and razor wire, have come to dominate the environment. Here you'll find the landmark *Hotel Villa Santa Catarina* (ⓣ7762 1291, ⓦwww.villasdeguatemala.com; ❼), which enjoys a prime lakeside plot, with 36 very comfortable **rooms**, a pool and a well-regarded restaurant. A kilometre beyond Santa Catarina, high above the lakeshore, the luxurious *Casa Palopó Hotel* (ⓣ7762 2270, ⓦwww.casapalopo.com; doubles from US$140, suites US$165; ❾) offers stunning rooms with wood-beam ceilings and wrought-iron beds – and each suite has a private sun terrace – in a converted villa. Beyond here, the road winds around the shore for another 2km until you reach another upmarket place, the *Bella Vista Ecolodge* (ⓣ7762 1566, ⓦwww.santomasatitlanlodge.guate.com; ❼), with fourteen attractive bungalows set in extensive shady grounds, all boasting great views, plus a pool and restaurant. Continuing along the lakeside road, just as the steep profile of San Antonio comes into view, the road dips and passes a beautiful secluded little beach, almost hidden among the reeds. San Antonio is a further 2km from here.

Two kilometres on from the beach, **SAN ANTONIO PALOPÓ** is a larger and more traditional village, squeezed in beneath a steep hillside. The village is also on the tour group itinerary, which has encouraged some persistent sales techniques on the part of the inhabitants. The hillsides above San Antonio are well irrigated and terraced, reminiscent of rice paddies, and most men wear the village *traje* of red shirts with vertical stripes and short woollen kilts. Women wear almost identical shirts, made of the same fabric but with subtle variations to the collar design. The whitewashed central church is worth a look; just to the left of the entrance are two ancient bells, while inside is a model of the birth of Jesus, San Antonio–style, with Joseph wearing the village costume.

One of the best ways to visit the two villages is on foot from above the lake. Catch a bus from Panajachel towards Godínez, and get off at the *mirador* about a kilometre before Godínez. From here you can enjoy some of the best lake views of all, and there are various paths that lead to San Antonio (about a thirty-minute walk) through vegetable terraces of spring onions and tomatoes. Alternatively, you can catch a pick-up from Panajachel, via Santa Catarina, to San Antonio; they leave when full (you shouldn't have to wait more than 30min) between 6am and 6pm from Calle Principal. The last pick-up returns to Panajachel from San Antonio at around 5.30pm.

If you decide **to stay** in San Antonio, there are two options: the mid-range *Hotel Terrazas del Lago* (ⓣ7762 1288, ⓕ7762 0157; ❺), by the water, which has comfortable rooms and beautiful views; or the very simple but clean pensión (❶) owned by Juan López Sánchez, near the entrance to the village. Try the comedor below the church for a cheap **meal**.

The higher road to San Lucas Tolimán

The higher of the two roads around the lake's eastern shore heads back into the rich river delta behind Panajachel, before climbing up above the lake to **San Andrés Semetabaj**, where there's a fantastic ruined colonial church. A path opposite the church's main entrance leads back to Panajachel, winding down through fields and coffee bushes – a nice walk of an hour or so. Beyond San Andrés the road curves around the edge of the ridge, offering a sweeping view of the lake below and the irregular cone of the Tolimán volcano opposite, and arriving eventually in Godínez. A short way before is the *mirador* mentioned above, from where paths lead down to the lakeside village of San Antonio Palopó.

At **Godínez**, a ramshackle and wind-blown village, the road divides, one way running out to the Carretera Interamericana (through Patzicía and Patzún – though if you're driving, you should bear in mind there have been occasional attacks and robberies on this road), and the other on around the lake to the village of **SAN LUCAS TOLIMÁN** in the southeast corner. Set apart from the other villages in many ways, this is probably the least attractive of the lot. The surrounding land is almost all planted with coffee, which dominates the flavour of the place. The indigenous people take a poor second place to the sizable ladino population, and the easy-going atmosphere of the lake is tempered by the influence of the Pacific coast. The setting, however, is as spectacular as always. The village is at the back of a small inlet of reed beds, with the Tolimán volcano rising above. Both the Tolimán and Atitlán **volcanoes** can be climbed from here, though taking a guide is recommended as the trails are difficult to find – ask at your hotel or the town hall. The main **market** days are Thursday and Sunday.

If you need somewhere to **stay**, head for the *Hotel Villa Real Internacional*, 7 Av 1–84 (Ⓣ7722 0102; ❸), with reliable hot showers, safe parking and a restaurant; or consider the tranquil *Hotel Tolimán* (Ⓣ7722 0033, Ⓦwww.atitlan/toliman.htm; ❻), which has lovely grassy lakefront grounds with a pool, comfortable rooms and complimentary breakfast. For good, inexpensive food, head to *La Fonda* close to the plaza.

San Lucas sits at the junction of the roads to the coast and Santiago Atitlán, and **buses** regularly thunder through in both directions. Eight daily buses run to Cocales and on to Guatemala City, mainly in the early morning, with the last bus at about 3pm. Hourly buses depart for Santiago (20 min) between 5am and 6pm, while five daily buses connect the town with Panajachel (1hr), running mostly in the morning though the last one leaves at 4pm. *Lanchas*, which don't run to a fixed schedule, also connect San Lucas with Panajachel (20 min; US$2.75), some calling in at San Antonio and Santa Catarina on the way.

Santiago Atitlán

In the southwest corner of the lake, set to one side of a sheltered horseshoe inlet, **SANTIAGO ATITLÁN** is overshadowed by the cones of the San Pedro, Atitlán and Tolimán volcanoes. It's the largest and most important of the lakeside villages, and also one of the most traditional, being the main centre of the Tz'utujil-speaking Maya. At the time of the Conquest, the Tz'utujil had their fortified capital, **Chuitinamit-Atitlán**, on the slopes of San Pedro, while the bulk of the population lived spread out around the site of today's village. Alvarado and his crew, needless to say, destroyed the capital and massacred its inhabitants, assisted this time by a force of Kaqchikel Maya, who arrived at the scene in some three hundred canoes.

Today Santiago is an industrious sort of place, in a superb setting. During the day the town becomes fairly commercial, its **main street** (which runs up from the dock) lined with weaving shops and art galleries, so expect to be hustled by persistent hawkers, particularly if you visit during the huge Friday-morning **market**.

Holy smoke

Easter celebrations are particularly special in Santiago, and as Holy Week draws closer the town comes alive with expectation and excitement. **Maximón** maintains an important role in the proceedings. On the Monday of Holy Week his effigy is taken to the lakeshore where it is washed, on the Tuesday he's dressed, and on the Wednesday the idol is housed in a small chapel close to the plaza. Here he waits until Good Friday, when the town is the scene of a huge and austere religious procession, the plaza packed with everyone dressed in their finest traditional costume. Christ's image is paraded solemnly through the streets, arriving at the church around noon, where it's tied to a cross and raised above the altar. At around 3pm it's cut down from the cross and placed in a coffin born by penitents, who emerge from the church for a symbolic confrontation in the plaza between Christ and Maximón, who is carried out of an adjoining chapel by his bearer.

The presence of Maximón, decked out in a felt hat and Western clothes, with a cigar in his mouth, is scorned by reforming Catholics and revered by the traditionalists. The precise origin of the saint is unknown, but he's also referred to as San Simón, Judas Iscariot and Pedro de Alvarado, and always seen as an enemy of the Church. Some say that he represents a Franciscan friar who chased after young indigenous girls, and that his legs are removed to prevent any further indulgence. "Max" in the Mam dialect means tobacco, and Maximón is always associated with ladino vices such as smoking and drinking; more locally he's known as *Rij Laj or Rilej Mam*, the powerful man with a white beard. Throughout the year he's looked after by a *cofradía*; if you feel like dropping in to pay your respects to him, ask for "*La Casa de Maximón*" and someone will show you the way. Take along a packet of cigarettes and a bottle of Quezalteca for the ever-thirsty saint and his minders, who will ask you to make a contribution to fiesta funds. For details on visiting San Simón in Zunil and for a warning about the gravity of the process, see p.198. For more on indigenous religion, see the Contexts section of this book.

There's not that much to see in Santiago, but you could drop into the new weaving museum, **Museo Cojolya** (Mon–Fri 9am–4pm, Sat 9am–1pm; free), about 100m up the main drag from the dock, on the left. Here you'll find excellent displays (in English and Spanish) about the tradition of backstrap weaving in Santiago, and you can see some of the weavers in action at 11am and 1pm daily. They sell a range of very good quality shirts, bags and souvenirs here too.

Otherwise the fabulous old colonial Catholic **church** is well worth a look for its fascinating Maya religious detail. Its huge central altarpiece, carved when the church was under *cofradía* control, culminates in the shape of a mountain peak and a cross, symbolizing the Maya world tree. Dozens of statues of saints (all bedecked in indigenous attire) line the walls. On the right as you enter, a stone memorial commemorates **Father Stanley Rother**, an American priest who served in the parish from 1968 to 1981. Father Rother was a committed defender of his parishioners in an era when, in his own words, "shaking hands with an Indian has become a political act". Branded a communist by President García, he was assassinated by a paramilitary death squad like hundreds of his parishioners before and after him. His body was returned to his native Oklahoma for burial, but not before his heart was removed and buried in the church. There's an informative article about the church on Ⓦwww.mesoweb.com.

As is the case in many other parts of the Guatemalan highlands, the Catholic Church in Santiago is locked in bitter rivalry with several evangelical sects, who are building churches here at an astonishing rate. Their latest construction, right beside the lake, is the largest structure in town. Folk Catholicism plays an important role in the life of Santiago, and the town is one of the main places where Maya pay homage to **Maximón**, the "evil" saint. It costs US$0.25 to enter his abode and US$1.30 to take his picture.

The traditional costume of Santiago, still worn a fair amount by the older men, is both striking and unusual. The men wear long shorts, which, like the women's *huipiles*, are white- and purple-striped, intricately embroidered with birds and flowers. Some women also wear a *xk'ap*, a band of red cloth approximately 10m long, wrapped around their heads, which has the honour of being depicted on the 25 centavo coin. Sadly, this headcloth has almost gone out of use, though you may still see it at fiestas and on market days, when it's worn by canny girls eager to attract the eye of tourists (and charge for a photo).

Around Santiago: volcanoes and the nature reserve

The land around Santiago is mostly volcanic, with only the odd patch of fertile soil mixed in with the acidic ash. Farming, fishing and the traditional industry, the manufacture of *cayucos* (canoes), are no longer enough to provide for the population, and a lot of people travel to the coast and beyond, or work on the coffee plantations that surround the volcano. The Tolimán and Atitlán **volcanoes** can both be climbed from here, but it's always best to take a guide to smooth the way as there have been robberies – ask at *Hotel Chi-Nim-Ya* (see below), or at one of the restaurants.

If you're here for the day, then you can walk out of town along the track to San Lucas Tolimán, or rent a **canoe** and paddle out into the lake – just ask around at the dock. To the north of Santiago is a small island which has been designated a **nature reserve**, originally for the protection of the *poc*, or Atitlán grebe, a flightless water bird. The *poc* used to thrive in the waters of the lake but two factors have now driven it into extinction: the overcutting of reeds where it nested and the introduction of the predatory black bass, which ate all the young birds. Despite the disappearance of the *poc*, the island is still a beautiful place to spend an hour or two and is a fine destination if you're paddling around in a canoe.

Santiago Atitlán practicalities

Boats to Santiago leave from the beach in Panajachel at 8.35am, 10.30am, 1pm and 4.30pm – the trip takes about an hour. Unscheduled, and much faster (20min), *lanchas* connect the two towns at other times. Four daily boats make the return trip at 6am, 11.45am, 1.30pm and 3pm (plus supplementary *lanchas*), while nine daily boats head to San Pedro La Laguna, leaving between 6am and 5pm (40min).

The village is well connected by **bus** to almost everywhere except Panajachel. From the Parque Central, buses depart for Cocales and Guatemala City (7 daily between 3am and 3pm) and regular pick-ups leave for San Lucas Tolimán. Meanwhile, pick-ups leave for San Pedro from a stop by the *Hotel Chi-Nim-Ya*.

As for **accommodation**, two backpacker favourites are the basic, clean and friendly *Hotel Chi-Nim-Ya* (ⓣ7721 7131; ❷), on the left uphill from the dock, where some rooms have private bath; and the good-value *Hotel Tzutuhil*, in the centre of town (ⓣ7721 7174; ❷). For something special, there are a couple of good options which can be reached by road or water-taxi from the dock. The *Posada de Santiago*, 1km south of town (ⓣ & ⓕ7721 7167, ⓦwww.posadadesantiago.com; ❻), is a luxury lakeside B&B, with rooms in stone cabins (each with its own log fire), a few budget options, a fine restaurant and a

The expulsion of the army from Santiago Atitlán

Santiago Atitlán's recent history, like that of so many Guatemalan villages, is marked by trouble and violence. The village assumed a unique role, however, when it became the first in the country to successfully expel the armed forces. Relations between the army and the village had been strained since the early 1980s, when the army, wary of the presence of ORPA guerrillas in the area, established a permanent base in Santiago. The army accused the villagers of supporting the insurgents and attempted to terrorize the population into subservience. Throughout the 1980s villagers were abducted, tortured and murdered – around three hundred were killed over an eleven-year period.

Under civilian rule after 1986, the guerrilla threat dropped off considerably, and the people of Santiago grew increasingly confident and resentful of the unnecessary army presence. Matters came to a head on the night of December 1, 1990, when two drunken soldiers shot a villager. The men fled to the army base on the outskirts of the village, but they were soon followed by an unarmed crowd, which eventually numbered around two thousand. Believing that they were about to be overwhelmed, the six hundred soldiers inside the garrison opened fire on the crowd, killing thirteen people, including three children, and wounding a further twenty. Following the incident some twenty thousand villagers signed a petition calling for the army's expulsion from Santiago. After intense international pressure, the army finally withdrew, shutting down the base.

Difficulties then arose with the police, when, on December 6, the local civil patrol discovered a group of policemen on a suspicious night-time mission. A mob soon surrounded the police station, and the police were also forced to leave. When replacements arrived from Guatemala City, Santiago's residents refused to sell the new recruits any food for two weeks – and it was a month before they agreed to allow them use of the public toilet.

In June 1991, Santiago's example was followed by neighbouring San Lucas Tolimán, where the killing of a community leader by a soldier led to the army's expulsion there, too. Other villages in sensitive areas, including Joyabaj and Chajul, subsequently took steps to shut down army bases. The 1996 peace accords went some way toward curtailing military interference in civilian affairs, and in 2004 President Berger slashed military numbers considerably. Increasing societal instability, however, has seen troops once again return to the streets in some areas and resume highway patrols as well.

pool. About a ten-minute walk north of the dock, *Hotel Bambú* (Ⓣ7721 7332; ❻) has beautiful thatch-roofed stone bungalows and rooms, all with lake views, plus an excellent restaurant with Spanish specialities and fine wines.

Of the **restaurants** in town, the inexpensive *Wach'alal*, about 400m up from the dock, is a good option for grilled meats, fish or soup; while *Restaurant El Pescador*, a bit further on, is a formal place with good views of Santiago's street life and a menu that includes black bass and *churrascos* for around US$5–7.

San Pedro La Laguna

Around the other side of the San Pedro volcano is the village of **SAN PEDRO LA LAGUNA**, which has now usurped Panajachel to become the centre of Guatemala's travelling scene. Generally, this status involves little more than playing host to colourful foreigners who have set up home here, and the young, mainly European travellers who flock here in droves. More than anywhere else in Guatemala, San Pedro has a distinctive bohemian feel, and there's plenty of bongo-bashing and bong-smoking counterculture in evidence. Yet despite the obvious culture clash between locals (most of whom are evangelical Christians) and travellers, everyone seems to get on reasonably well.

In recent years, San Pedro has also established itself as a **language school** centre, the beautiful location drawing increasing numbers of students. The tuition is pretty variable, though standards are steadily improving and prices are extremely cheap, ranging from US$85 to US$110 per week for four hours' one-on-one tuition and full board with a local family (see p.65 for a list of recommended institutions).

The setting is spectacular, with the San Pedro volcano rising to the east and a ridge of steep hills running behind the village. To the east of the Panajachel dock a line of boulders juts out into the water – an ideal spot for an afternoon of swimming and sunbathing.

Tradition isn't as powerful here and only a few elderly people, mostly men, wear the old costume, although there is a sense of permanence in the narrow cobbled streets and old stone houses. Pedreños are famed for their *cayucos* (canoes), made from the great cedar trees that grow on the slopes of the San Pedro volcano. They also have a reputation for driving a hard bargain when

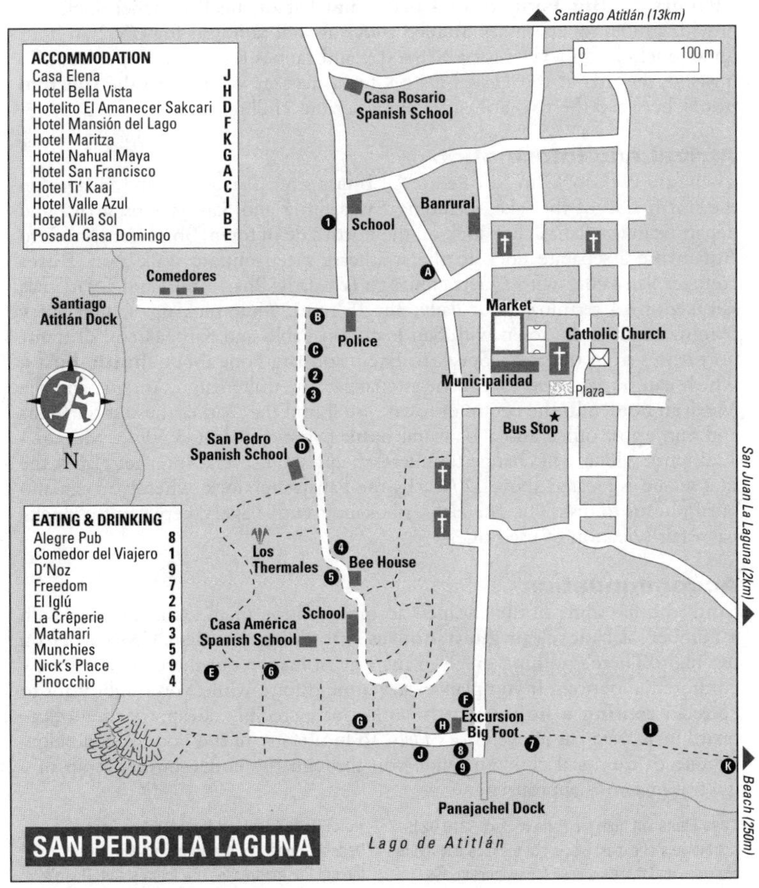

trading their coffee and avocados, and have managed to buy up a lot of land from neighbouring San Juan, with whom there's endless rivalry.

The **San Pedro volcano**, which towers above the village to a height of some 3020m, is largely covered with tropical forest; get an early start to maximise your chances of a clear view and to avoid the worst of the heat. It can be climbed in four to five hours, and takes between two and three hours to descend. The peak itself is ringed by forest, which blocks the view over San Pedro, although an opening on the south side gives excellent views of Santiago. You should definitely use the service of an official **guide** to lead you up the volcano's slopes as there have been attacks on tourists in the past and the paths are very tricky to follow. The introduction of a new village-based **guide office** in June 2005 should improve security considerations considerably, however; it costs around US$5 per person to climb the volcano, depending on the numbers in your group. Excursion Big Foot (see below) also offer guided tours (about US$4–5 per person for a group of five) up a neighbouring peak, nicknamed "Indian Nose", which provides stunning vistas of the lake and its three volcanoes. The summit is regularly used for Maya religious ceremonies – if you do happen to come across a ritual during your hike, it's best not to take photographs.

Excursion Big Foot (☎5204 6267), just left of the Panajachel dock, can provide guides for the hikes detailed above as well as horses for US$2 an hour (guide included), bicycles for US$8 a day and canoes for US$1.30 per hour. To unwind, see Ada at the *Hotel Villa Sol* for a massage or head to the **thermal pools**, between the two docks, for some serious chilling time.

Arrival and information

There are two docks in San Pedro. All **boats** from Panajachel and villages on the north side of the lake, including Santa Cruz and San Marcos, arrive and depart from the Panajachel dock on the north side of town. Boats from Santiago Atitlán use a separate dock to the southeast, a ten-minute walk away. **Buses** connect San Pedro with Quetzaltenango (six daily; 2hr 15min) and Guatemala City's Zona 4 terminal (four daily; 3hr 15 min), while pick-ups (about every 30min) connect the town with San Juan, San Pablo and San Marcos; all transport leaves from the plaza. Speak to Excursion Big Foot about **shuttle buses**, which can be arranged to Chichicastenango, Quetzaltenango, Antigua and the Mexican border. In the centre of town, you'll find the market (busiest on Thurs and Sun), post office and a Banrural **bank** (Mon–Fri 9am–5.30pm, Sat 9am–12.30pm), which will change travellers' cheques. Of several Internet places, the best set-up is located above *D'Noz* by the Panajachel dock, where you can also burn photos to disk. The *Bee House* bookshop-cum-bakery, between the docks, has a fair selection of used titles.

Accommodation

San Pedro has some of the cheapest accommodation in all Latin America, with a number of basic, clean **guest houses** that charge less than US$3 a person per night. There's nothing much in the way of luxury, but there are a few new comfortable options. If you plan to stay around for a while, you might want to consider **renting a house**, which works out incredibly cheap; try the noticeboard in *D'Noz* bar above *Nick's Place*. To locate any of the hotels listed below, let one of the local children guide you through the coffee bushes; a tip of a quetzal or two is appropriate.

Casa Elena left from the Pana dock ☎5310 9243. Not the very cheapest place, but the nine tidy rooms are clean and there's a dock for swimming. ❷

Hotel Bella Vista left from the Pana dock. Decent budget hotel with clean, bare rooms, though the mattresses are foam slabs. There's a kitchen and a garden with hammocks at the back. ❶

Hotel Mansión del Lago right above the Pana dock ⓣ5811 8172 or 7721 8195, ⓦwww.hotelmansiondellago.com. The most comfortable place in San Pedro, where the spotless, superb-value rooms all have nice pine beds, private bath and balcony areas with lake views. Also has a rooftop Jacuzzi and Internet café. Book ahead at weekends. ❷

Hotel Martiza right from the Pana dock. Friendly, cheap, family-run place with a kitchen and a garden. ❶

Hotel Nahual Maya left from the Pana dock, ⓣ7721 8158. Well-run, friendly new place with tidy en-suite rooms (and most with two beds) facing a lawn. ❷

Hotel San Francisco uphill from the Santiago dock ⓣ7721 8016. Neat little rooms, some with bathrooms, most with lake-view balconies and all have access to kitchen facilities. Highly popular, so book ahead. ❶

Hotel Ti'Kaaj near the Santiago dock. Very basic rooms, but there's also a lovely shady garden with hammocks. ❶

Hotel Valle Azul turn right from the Pana dock, ⓣ5207 7292. Vaguely Soviet-style concrete monster of a hotel, but the clean, bare rooms (some with private bath) are reasonable enough. ❶

Hotel Villa Sol near the Santiago dock ⓣ2334 0327. Plenty of space here, but the multitude of clean, sparse rooms are set in somewhat souless blocks. Bizarrely – despite the location – none enjoy lake views. ❶–❷

Hotelito El Amanecer Sakcari between the docks ⓣ5812 1113. Friendly, family-run place with ten attractive rooms, all with private bath and most with wonderful lake views. ❷

Posada Casa Domingo between the docks. Six attractive, clean rooms, all with tiled floors, private bath and good mattresses, facing Volcán San Pedro. Ultra-basic cell-like accommodation in a separate block also available. ❶–❷

Eating and drinking

San Pedro's **cafés** and **restaurants** have a decidedly international flavour, and most are also excellent value for money. Vegetarians are well catered for, and there are also a few typical Guatemalan comedores in the centre of the village and by the Santiago dock. For a **drink**, there's a cluster of places close to the Pana dock: *D'Noz* is a great place to hear some electronica and house music; they also show a **film** nightly at 7.30pm. Nearby, the *Alegre Pub* has Premiership football and nightly drinks and food specials like fish 'n' chips or pie 'n' mash. *D'Noz* also organize DJ-driven **parties** on full moons and other occasions.

Comedor del Viajero south side of town. One of the best-run comedores in town, with tasty and inexpensive Guatemalan grub and a daily set lunch.

D'Noz above *Nick's Place*. Very popular bar-restaurant with a menu that includes baguettes, croissants, and soup with garlic bread. Open until 1am.

Freedom turn right from the Pana dock. An inexpensive menu and great views of the lake from its terrace make this spot popular at all times of day. Great margaritas and live music some nights.

El Iglú between the docks. Good ice cream and shakes, though the coffee is very pricey.

La Crêperie turn left from the Pana dock. Pretty authentic, flavoursome crêpes and snacks.

Matahari turn right from the Santiago dock. The best comedor in San Pedro, this clean place has good Guatemalan grub and amazingly good fries.

Munchies between the docks. Veggie stronghold where you can tuck into a healthy soup or salad in a pleasant patio setting.

Nick's Place by the Pana dock. Popular, locally owned restaurant with a superb-value menu of international and Guatemalan food (most meals cost around US$2) and a fine lakefront location.

Pinocchio between the docks. Decent Italian, where you can feast on lake fish, pizza or pasta in a pretty garden setting.

The northern shore

The **northern side** of the lake harbours a string of isolated villages, including some of the most traditional settlements of the central highlands. From San Pedro, a rough road runs as far as Tzununá and from there a spectacular path continues all the way to Sololá. Non-direct *lanchas* to Panajachel will call in at any village en route, but the best way to see this string of isolated settlements is **on foot**: it makes a fantastic day's walk (though see warning, p.164). A narrow strip of level land is wedged between the water and the steep hills most of the way, and where this disappears the path is cut into the slope, yielding dizzying views of the lake below. It takes between five and six hours to walk from San Pedro to Santa Cruz, but if you want some very rewarding hiking, this is the section of the lake to hit. You can get drinks, snacks and meals at several of the villages along the way, while San Juan, San Marcos, Jaibalito and Santa Cruz all have accommodation.

From San Pedro it's just 2km to **SAN JUAN LA LAGUNA**, at the back of a sweeping bay surrounded by shallow beaches. The village specializes in the weaving of *petates*, mats made from lake reeds, and there are two large weaving co-ops, Las Artesanías de San Juan, signposted on the left from the dock and the Asociación de Mujeres de Color, on the right – both have plenty of goods for sale. Next to the latter, the simple *Hospedaje Estrella del Lago* (Ⓣ7759 9126; ❶) has eleven secure rooms (and eleven more on the way), none with private bath, and a guests' kitchen. Uphill, in the centre of the village, you'll find a quiet comedor, *Restaurant Chi'nimaya*, and almost next door, a shrine to **Maximón** (see p.174). Inside you'll find the evil saint dressed in local garb – as this shrine attracts fewer visitors than those elsewhere, you may want to bring him some liquor or a cigar. Pick-ups run between San Pedro and San Juan about every thirty minutes.

Leaving San Juan, you'll pass below the Tz'utujil settlement of **SAN PABLO LA LAGUNA**, perched high above the lake a fifteen-minute walk away, and connected by a precipitous but paved road to the Carretera Interamericana. The village's traditional speciality is the manufacture of rope from the fibres of the maguey plant; you can sometimes see great lengths being stretched and twisted in the streets. Continuing along the lakeside road, however, the route cuts through extensive coffee plantations and past terraced fields planted with spring onions.

San Marcos La Laguna

Guatemala's premier New Age centre, the tiny village of **SAN MARCOS LA LAGUNA**, is about a two-hour walk from San Pedro, or a twenty-minute ride in one of the regular pick-ups that bump along the road between the villages. The land close to the lakeshore – densely wooded with banana, mango, jocote and avocado trees – is where San Marcos' bohemian hotels and guest houses have been sensitively established, while the Maya village is centred on higher ground away from the shore. Relationships between the two communities remain a little distant. Apart from a huge new stone **church**, built to replace a colonial original destroyed in the 1976 earthquake, there are no sights in the Maya village – though you can surf the **Internet** at HML next to the *municipalidad*.

San Marcos has a decidedly tranquil appeal – there's little in the way of partying and no bar scene at all. One of the main draws is the *Las Pirámides* yoga and meditation retreat, and there's a surplus of auxiliary practitioners and masseurs, plus the requisite organic bakery and a healing centre – San Marcos Holistic Center – offering acupuncture, reflexology and natural remedies; it's located next to the *Unicórnio*. There's excellent swimming from a number of wooden jetties by the lakeshore, and a mesmerizing view of Atitlán's three volcanoes, including a perspective of the double-coned summit of Tolimán, plus glimpses of the grey 3975m peak of Acatenango, more than 50km to the east.

Accommodation

San Marcos' hotels and guest houses are best reached from the westernmost of San Marcos' two docks, where *Posada Schumann* and *Las Pirámides* have jetties (look out for the mini-pyramid): all accommodation is signposted from there. Avoid the unfriendly *Hotel Jivana*.

Aculaax ⓔniecolass@hotmail.com. An astonishing labour of love, this fantasy ecohotel was built by an (eccentric) German visionary craftsman from thousands of recycled bottles and wood, with stained-glass detailing and giant glass butterflies doubling as lampshades. Most rooms have hand-painted murals and bathrooms, while the 'Mirador' also has a kitchen. It *has* to be seen. ❸–❹

Hotel La Paz ⓣ5702 9168. Comfortable, rustic rooms, a bungalow (with three beds) and an excellent dorm (US$4.50) set in spacious grounds which also feature a sauna/massage room. Home cooking is often available; Benjamin, the Guatemalan owner, once ran a restaurant in Liverpool. ❷–❸

Hotel San Marcos Cheap, bare but clean rooms in a concrete block, none with private bath. ❶

El Paco Real ⓣ5918 7215. Attractive, well-constructed stone bungalows, some sleeping up to four, set in a shady garden. No private bathrooms, but the communal facilities are kept spotless; there's also a good, in-house Mexican restaurant (closed Mon). ❷

Las Pirámides ⓣ5205 7151, ⓦwww.laspiramides.com.gt. Meditation retreat centre set in leafy grounds. Monthly courses, which begin the day after the full moon (though you can also enroll on a daily or weekly basis), include hatha yoga, healing and meditation techniques, plus days of fasting and silence and plenty of esoteric pursuits. All accommodation is in comfortable, pyramid cabañas; there's also delicious vegetarian food. US$10–12 per person per day includes courses but not food. ❸–❹

Posada Schumann ⓣ5202 2216. Wonderful, solar-powered lakeside hotel with rooms and stone bungalows, which sleep between two and six (nos. 8 and 10 have stupendous volcano views). There's also a great restaurant (the US$10 dinner includes a drink, while breakfast is US$3.50), a private wooden jetty for sunbathing and swimming, and a Maya-style sauna. ❹–❻

Unicórnio ⓦwww.hotelunicornio.com. Inexpensive, idiosyncratic English-Guatemalan-owned place with small A-frame huts and rooms (none with bath) in a nice garden, with a kitchen and sauna. ❷

Eating

The choice of places to eat in San Marcos is fairly limited, though there's a pretty good range of cuisines. Inexpensive Guatemalan food is available at the *Comedor Marquensita* and *Sonoma* (both close to the church in the village) and great meat dishes are on offer at *Jeff's Burger Shack* on the road to San Pablo. Closer to the lakeshore, *Il Giardino* serves wonderful Italian and Latin American food, while some of the hotels have restaurants attached – *El Paco Real* has superb Mexican food; *Posada Schumann* has a good menu for healthy Guatemalan food (dinner is US$10 including a drink); and *Las Pirámides* offers excellent veggie food (including delicious sandwiches and salads). For the best views, head for the fairly expensive, French-owned *Tul y Sol*, right by the lake, which has good cooking, including *bistek al vino* and *pescado a la plancha*, and fine sandwiches. Meanwhile, *Moonfish*, close to the western end of the lakeshore, is the best café.

Tzununá to Paxanax

Beyond San Marcos, the villages en route have a greater feeling of isolation, and you'll find the people surprised to see you and often eager for a glimpse of passing gringos. Nowhere is this more true than in **TZUNUNÁ**, the next place along the way, where women occasionally run from oncoming strangers, sheltering behind the nearest tree in giggling groups. They wear beautiful red *huipiles* striped with blue and yellow on the back. The village originally sat at the lakeside, but after it was badly damaged by a flood in 1950 the people rebuilt their homes on higher ground. Here the road indisputably ends, giving way to a narrow path cut out of the steep hillside, which can be a little hard to follow as it descends to cross small streams and then climbs again around the rocky outcrops.

The next, slightly ragged-looking place is **JAIBALITO**, an isolated lakeside settlement nestling between soaring *milpa*-clad slopes. The village remains resolutely Kaqchikel – very little Spanish is spoken, and few women have ever journeyed much beyond Lago de Atitlán – though the opening of two new hotels means that outside influence is growing. Almost lost amongst the coffee bushes, 70m north of the main pathway, the Norwegian-owned *Vulcano Lodge* (ⓣ5410 2237, ⓔvulcanolodge@hotmail.com) occupies a tranquil spot. Although it lacks lake views, it does have a well-tended garden bursting with flowering shrubs and scattered with sun loungers and hammocks. There's good European and Guatemalan food in the restaurant and a choice of spotless, comfortable rooms (❸–❹) or a very stylish two-bedroomed suite (❻).

Heading west, it's a steep five-minute walk up along the cliff path to the spectacularly sited *La Casa del Mundo* (ⓣ5218 5332, ⓦwww.lacasadelmundo.com; ❸–❺). It's an astounding place, the culmination of twelve years' work by the warm American host family, with a range of atmospheric accommodation, including a budget room, doubles (room nos. 1 and 3 have the best views), detached stone cabins and a suite. There's also a great restaurant (dinner is US$9 per person), and guests can rent kayaks and use the lakeside hot tub (US$35 for up to 10 people). From Jaibalito it's less than an hour to Santa Cruz along a glorious, easy-to-follow path that parallels the steep hillside.

The Maya village of **SANTA CRUZ LA LAGUNA**, set well back from the lake on a shelf 150m or so above the water, is the largest in this line of villages, with a population approaching 5000. Santa Cruz's hotels are all at the lakeshore below. There isn't much to see in the village, apart from a fine sixteenth-century church, and most people spend their time chilling out with a book or **swimming** in the lake. Note that the water is cleaner away from the hotels, towards Paxanax, and keep an eye out for speeding local boatmen while you're in the water, as collisions have occurred. Alternatively, there's some excellent **hiking**, including a walk to a waterfall above the village football pitch, and another to Sololá along a spectacular path that takes around three hours. Staff at the *Iguana Perdida* or the *Hotel Arca de Noé* should be able to get you on the right track for these walks.

Of all the shore hotels around Lago de Atitlán, the *Iguana Perdida* (ⓣ5706 4117, ⓦwww.laiguanaperdida.com; ❷), owned by an English–American couple, has the most sociable atmosphere. The rooms are fairly basic – with dorms (US$3), singles and twin-bedded doubles (the "Jerry Garcia" room has its own balcony with views) – but it's the gorgeous, peaceful site overlooking the lake that really makes this place. Dinner (US$5.50) is a wholesome three-course communal affair, after which the story-telling often runs long into the night. The *Iguana* is also home to a professional PADI dive school, ATI Divers (ⓣ7762 2621), where all levels of scuba training are offered and a single fun-dive costs US$25. Ask about hiring the four-metre "ocean kayak", if you want to explore the lake; alternatively, get steamed up inside the Maya-style *chuj* sauna.

Next door, the slightly more expensive *Hotel Arca de Noé* (ⓣ5306 4352, ⓔthearca@yahoo.com; ❸–❺) is also a good place, with attractive rooms, most with private bath, and comfortable bungalows. You'll marvel at the uninterrupted views of the lake from the spacious terraced gardens, plus there's good home cooking, with large breakfasts for US$4 and dinner for US$8. A friendly English–French couple manages the place for half the year, while the Austrian owners take over for the rest. On the other side of the main dock, the *Casa Rosa* (ⓣ5390 4702; ❸–❹) offers beautiful, peaceful gardens, decent though unexceptional rooms and a restaurant. Service standards are not always the highest here, however, and perhaps consequently the hotel is less popular than the others.

Beyond Santa Cruz a lakeside path wriggles past luxury villas for a kilometre to the small bay of **PAXANAX**, which is ringed by about twenty holiday homes and is the site of the superb-value *Villa Sumaya* (Ⓣ5617 1209, Ⓦwww.villasumaya.com; ❺–❻). This American-owned, luxury guest house has seven rooms, each of which enjoys stupendous lake views and has plush beds, stylish decor and access to a shared verandah with hammocks. Also on hand is a great restaurant, a library, and a hot tub and sauna. Kayaks can be rented and massages and yoga sessions arranged.

Beyond Paxanax the path that runs directly to Panajachel is very hard to follow, and distraught walkers have been known to spend as long as seven hours scrambling through the undergrowth. **Lanchas** will call in at Paxanax, if they see you waving from the pier beside *Villa Sumaya*, but as there's very little traffic from here it's often best to retreat back to Santa Cruz to move on.

Along the Carretera Interamericana: Los Encuentros to Cuatro Caminos

Heading west from the Los Encuentros junction to Cuatro Caminos and the Quetzaltenango valley, the Carretera Interamericana runs through some fantastic high mountain scenery. The views alone are superb, and if you have a Sunday morning to spare then it's well worth dropping into Nahualá for the market. The **Los Encuentros** junction (at Km 127.3 on the Carretera Interamericana) is for Chichicastenango, while about 2km beyond here the **El Cuchillo** junction serves Sololá and Panajachel. The last buses to Chichicastenango, Panajachel, Quetzaltenango and Guatemala City pass through these junctions at around 6.30pm.

Nahualá

West of Los Encuentros the Carretera Interamericana runs through some spectacular and sparsely inhabited countryside. The only place of any size before Cuatro Caminos is **NAHUALÁ**, "place of sorcerers", a small and intensely traditional town a kilometre or so to the north of the highway, at the base of a huge, steep-sided and intensely farmed bowl. The unique atmosphere of isolation from and indifference to the outside world makes Nahualá one of the most impressive and unusual K'iche' towns.

The town itself is not much to look at, a sprawl of old cobbled streets and adobe houses mixed with newer concrete structures, but the inhabitants of Nahualá have a reputation for fiercely preserving their independence and have held out against ladino incursions with exceptional tenacity. At the end of the nineteenth century the government confiscated much of their land, as they did throughout the country, and sold it to coffee planters. In protest, the entire male population of Nahualá walked the 150km to Guatemala City and demanded to see President Barrios in person, refusing his offers to admit a spokesman and insisting that they all stood as one. Eventually, they were allowed into the huge reception room where they knelt with their foreheads pressed to the floor, refusing to leave until they were either given assurances of their land rights or allowed to buy the land back, which they had done twice before. The action managed to save their land that time, but since then much of it has gradually been consumed by coffee bushes all the same.

On another occasion, during the 1930s under President Ubico, ladinos were sent to the town as nurses, telegraph operators and soldiers. Once again the Nahualáns appealed directly to the president, insisting that their own people should be trained to do these jobs, and once again their request was granted. Ubico also wanted to set up a government-run drink store, but the villagers chose instead to ban alcohol, and Nahualeños who got drunk elsewhere were expected to confess their guilt and face twenty lashes in the town's plaza.

These days the ban's been lifted, and if you're here for the fiesta on November 25 you'll see that the people are keen to make up for all those dry years. However, only a handful of ladinos live in the town, and the indigenous Maya still have a reputation for hostility, with rumours circulating about the black deeds done by the local shamen. You don't have much to worry about if you drop in for the **Sunday market**, though, as this is one time that the town is full to bursting and the people seem genuinely pleased to welcome visitors. There is also a smaller market on Thursdays.

The town is also a major centre of artisan craft. The **weaving** is outstanding: the *huipiles*, designed in intricate geometrical patterns of orange on white, particularly impressed the Spanish because they featured a double-headed eagle, the emblem of the Habsburgs who ruled Spain at the time of the Conquest. The men wear bright yellow and pink shirts with beautifully embroidered collars; short woollen "skirts" called *rodilleras*, which are worn with white trousers underneath; and huge hats and leather sandals very similar to those of the ancient Maya. Woollen garments, including *capixay* cloaks and jackets, are also woven locally. The town is also famous for its woodwork, and Nahualá carpenters churn out a good proportion of the country's hand-carved pine and cedar wood bedsteads and wardrobes.

To get to Nahualá take any bus along the Carretera Interamericana between Los Encuentros and Cuatro Caminos, and get off at the Puente Nahualá, from where it's a kilometre or so uphill from the bus shelter. Although a few very basic pensiones (all ❶) can be found in the centre of town, it's best to visit on a day-trip from Chichicastenango, Panajachel or Quetzaltenango.

Santa Catarina and the Alaskan heights

Beyond Nahualá the highway climbs westwards, up a mountainous ridge and passes the entrance road to **SANTA CATARINA IXTAHUACÁN**, a sister and bitter rival of Nahualá, just north of the highway. Santa Catarina used to be located on notoriously unstable land on the south side of the Carretera Interamericana, only moving to its present position in December 2000 after huge sink holes destroyed several houses. The costumes and traditions of Santa Catarina and Nahualá, which are together known as the **Pueblos Chancatales**, are fairly similar, and they're both famous as producers of *metates*, the stones used for grinding corn. These days much corn-grinding is done by machine, and they've turned to making smaller toy versions and rustic wooden furniture – both of which you'll see peddled by the roadside.

Just west of Santa Catarina, the highway bottoms out on a flat plateau high up in the hills – one of the most impressive sections of the Carretera Interamericana. Known as **Alaska**, this exposed tract of land, where the men of both Nahualá and Santa Catarina graze sheep, shines white with frost in the early mornings. At more than 3000m, almost on a level with the great cones, the view is fantastic – this is one of the highest points anywhere on the highway (indeed, it's second only to the Cerro de la Muerte in Costa Rica, which reaches 3300m). Away to the east a string of volcanoes runs into the distance, and to the west the Totonicapán valley stretches out below you.

Further on, as the road drops over the other side of the ridge, the Quetzaltenango valley opens out to the left, a broad plain reaching across to the foot of the Santa María volcano. At the base of the ridge, the highway arrives at the **Cuatro Caminos** crossroads, the key junction for the Quetzaltenango area. Turning right here leads to Totonicapán, left to the city of Quetzaltenango, and straight on for Huehuetenango and the Mexican border.

Quetzaltenango and around

To the west of Lake Atitlán, the highlands rise to form a steep-sided ridge topped by a string of forested peaks. On the far side of this is the **Quetzaltenango basin**, a sweeping expanse of level ground that forms the natural hub of the western highlands. The Quetzaltenango basin is perhaps the most hospitable part of this region, encompassing a huge area of fertile farmland that has been densely populated since the earliest of times. Originally part of the Mam kingdom, the K'iche' Maya overran this area sometime between 1400 and 1475, retaining control until the arrival of the Spanish. Today, the western side of the valley is Mam-speaking and the east K'iche'. It was here that conquistador Pedro de Alvarado first struggled up into the highlands, having already confronted one K'iche' army on the coast and another in the pass at the entrance to the valley. Alvarado and his troops came upon the abandoned city of Xelajú (near Quetzaltenango) and were able to enter it without encountering any resistance. Six days later they fought the K'iche' in a decisive battle, massacring the Maya warriors – legend has it that Alvarado himself killed the king, Tecún Umán, in hand-to-hand combat. The victorious Spanish subsequently founded a new town, Quetzaltenango, "the place of the quetzals", the name probably chosen because of the brilliant green quetzal feathers worn by the K'iche' nobles and warriors, including, no doubt, Tecún Umán himself.

Where to Go

The city of **Quetzaltenango** can't claim to be a tourist attraction in its own right, but its ordinariness is in many ways its strength – a resolutely Guatemalan highland centre, off the main gringo trail but with a hospitality and friendliness that belies its size. It certainly makes an excellent base for exploring this part of the country, making day-trips to markets and fiestas, basking in hot springs, or hiking in the mountains. Bus connections are superb to all parts of the western highlands; alternatively, the city's well-regarded tour agencies can whisk you around the main sights in shuttles if time is tight, or if you appreciate a little more comfort.

The Xela plain and surrounding hills feature numerous smaller towns and villages, mostly indigenous agricultural communities and weaving centres. On **market and fiesta days** these villages explode into life; you should certainly try to get to San Francisco el Alto or Almolonga, both of which offer a terrific assault on the senses, their streets packed with colour. The pick of the region's **hiking** is the wonderful excursion up to Volcán Chicabal's crater lake, while if you really yearn to get off the beaten path, the remote high-country landscapes in the neighbouring department of San Marcos are wildly impressive.

Quetzaltenango (Xela)

Totally unlike the capital, and only a fraction of its size, Guatemala's second city, **QUETZALTENANGO (XELA)**, has the slightly subdued provincial atmosphere that you might expect in the capital of the highlands. Bizarre

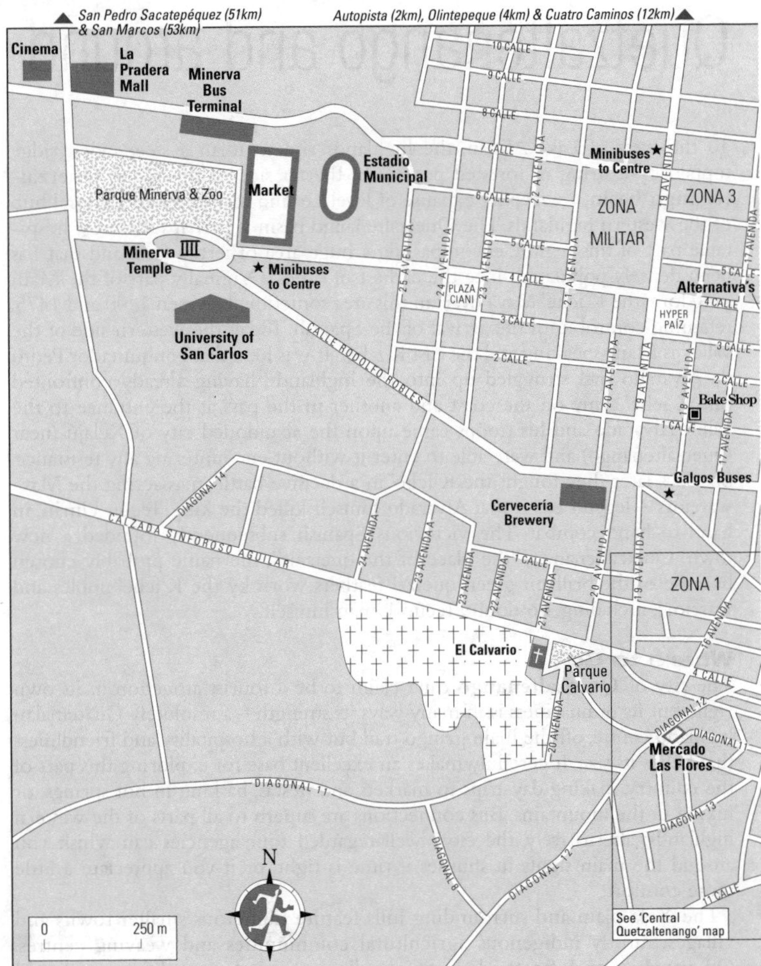

though it may seem, Quetzaltenango's character and appearance is vaguely reminiscent of an industrial town in northern England – grey and cool with friendly, down-to-earth inhabitants. Ringed by high mountains, and bitterly cold in the early mornings, the city wakes up slowly, only getting going once the warmth of the sun has made its mark. The main plaza, heavily indebted to Neoclassicism, is a monument to stability, with great slabs of grey stone belying a history of turbulence and struggle. The heart of town has the calm order of a regional administrative centre, though things deteriorate as you head away from the plaza, with thick traffic and fumes blighting the highland air, particularly around the main bus terminal. Locally, the city is usually referred to as Xela (pronounced "shey-la"), a shortening of the K'iche' name of a nearby pre-conquest city, Xelajú. Meaning "under the ten", the name is probably a reference to the surrounding peaks.

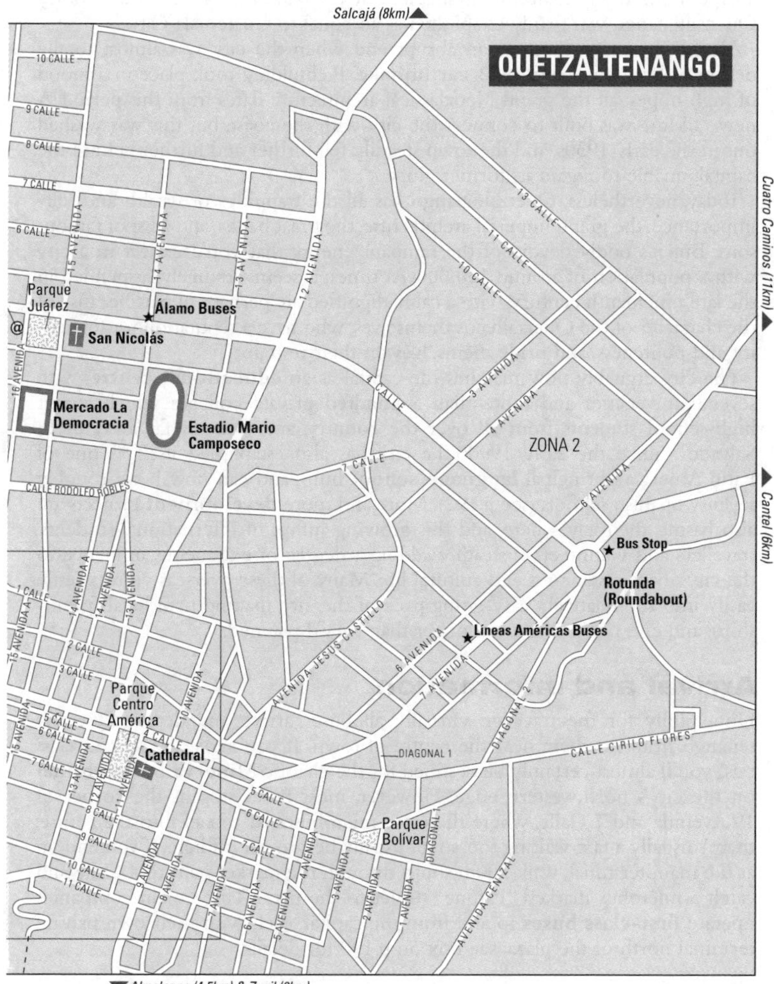

A brief history

Under colonial rule Quetzaltenango flourished as a commercial centre, benefiting from the fertility of the surrounding farmland and good connections to the port at Champerico. When the prospect of independence eventually arose, the city was set on deciding its own destiny. After the Central American Federation broke with Mexico in 1820, Quetzaltenango declared itself the capital of the independent state of **Los Altos**, which incorporated the modern departments of Huehuetenango, Sololá, San Marcos and Totonicapán. But the separatist movement was soon brought to heel by President Carrera in 1840, and a later attempt at secession, in 1848, was put down by force. Despite having to accept provincial status, the town remained an important centre of commerce and culture, consistently rivalling Guatemala City. The coffee boom at the end of the last century was particularly significant, as Quetzaltenango controlled some of the richest coffee land in the country. Its wealth and population grew rapidly, incorporating a large influx of German immigrants, and by the end of the nineteenth century Quetzaltenango was firmly established as an equal to Guatemala City.

All this, however, came to an abrupt end when the city was almost totally destroyed by the massive **1902 earthquake**. Rebuilding took place in a mood of high hopes; all the grand Neoclassical architecture dates from this period. A new rail line was built to connect the city with the coast, but this was washed out in the early 1930s, and the town steadily fell further and further behind the capital, unable to regain its former glory.

Today, nevertheless, Quetzaltenango has all the trappings of wealth and self-importance: the grand imperial architecture, the great banks, and a list of famous sons. But it's oddly devoid of the rampant energy that you'd expect in a city with a population of around 130,000. At times, it seems strangely suspended in the late nineteenth century, with a calm, dignified air, perhaps in part because of the character of the Quetzaltecos themselves, who have a reputation for formality and politeness, and pride themselves on their restraint.

The city arguably now matches the capital as an **educational centre**, with several universities and more than a hundred private colleges which attract high-school students from all over the country, and from as far away as El Salvador. Since the early 1990s the city has also established itself as one of Latin America's principal **language school** hubs, and can now boast roughly seventy Spanish schools (see p.192). More and more **development** projects are also basing themselves here, and this growing influx of international students, travellers and volunteers is steadily adding a degree of extraneous influence to the city's bars, restaurants and cultural life. Many of these overseas visitors settle easily into the relatively easy-going pace of the city, making firm local friendships, and end up staying a lot longer than they'd planned.

Arrival and information

Unhelpfully for the traveller, virtually all buses arrive and depart Quetzaltenango from nowhere near the centre of town. If you arrive by second-class bus, you'll almost certainly be destined for the chaotic **Minerva bus terminal** on the city's northwestern edge. However, most buses stop at the corner of 19 Avenida and 7 Calle, where there are microbuses that head into the centre; there's usually a taxi waiting too, so it's usually best to get off here. If you end up at the main terminal, walk 300m south through the market stalls to 4 Calle and catch a microbus marked "Parque" to get to the plaza. Three main companies operate **first-class buses** to and from the capital, each with their own private terminal north of the plaza; see box on p.190 for details.

The tourist office, on the main plaza (Mon–Fri 8am–1pm & 2–5pm, Sat 8am–1pm; ⓣ7761 4931), has maps and local information. But you'll almost certainly find Adrenalina Tours and the Casa Iximulew travel agencies (see p.195) more helpful and better informed. The excellent **website** ⓦwww.xelapages.com, devoted to all things Quetzaltenango, is a great resource too, with comprehensive hotel and accommodation listings, lots of good cultural information and useful forums.

Orientation and city transport

Quetzaltenango is laid out on a standard grid pattern, somewhat complicated by a number of steep hills. Basically, **avenidas** run north–south, and **calles** east–west. The oldest part of the city, focused around the plaza, is made up of tightly grouped narrow streets while in the newer part, reaching out towards the Minerva terminal, the blocks are larger. The city is divided up into **zones**, although for the most part you'll only be interested in zonas 1 and 3, which contain the central plaza area and the Minerva bus terminal respectively.

When it comes to **getting around**, most places are within easy walking distance – except the Minerva terminal. To get there, catch one of the regular microbuses that run from the junction of 4 Calle and 13 Avenida, at the back of the Pasaje Enríquez.

Accommodation

Once you've made it to the plaza you can set about looking for somewhere to stay. Most of the **hotels** in town tend to be a bit dark and old-fashioned, even in the mid-range of the market, and not especially good value for money compared with Antigua or Panajachel. However, all but one of the places listed below are within ten minutes' walk of the centre. If you want to stay for while, *Casa Mañen* has **apartments** for rent. Alternatively, for a superb rural location near Quetzaltenango, head to *Hotel Las Cumbres* (see p.198).

Casa Argentina 12 Diagonal 8–37 ⓣ7761 2470. Xela's definitive budget choice, run by a very hospitable family, with a myriad (43 at the last count, including 4 with bathroom) of comfortable rooms, a large dorm (US$2.50 a bed), a kitchen, sun terrace, and a neighbouring café. It's a ten-minute walk from the plaza, and also the home of Quetzaltrekkers (see p.195). ❶–❷

Casa Kaehler 13 Av 3–33 ⓣ7761 2091. Attractive guest house set in a lovely old building with seven spotless rooms (one with bathroom) set around a patio. Good value, secure and always popular. ❸

Casa Mañen 9 Av 4–11 ⓣ7765 0786, ⓦwww.comeseeit.com. Immaculate, very well run boutique-style hotel, that's good value for money and certainly the best bet in this category. Spacious rooms are decorated with local textiles and have fireplaces and cable TV, while the two huge suites offer sofas and fridges. There's also a wonderful rooftop terrace and a large complimentary breakfast, plus the Texan owners are a mine of information about the area. Rooms ❻–❼, suites ❾

Hostal Don Diego 7 C 15–20 ⓣ7761 6497, ⓔdondiegoxela@hotmail.com. Good new option with a pleasant courtyard, guests' kitchen, laundry facilities, and twelve basic rooms. Very inexpensive weekly and monthly rates. ❷

Hotel del Campo Carretera al Pacífico Km 224, Zona 5, 4km east of the town centre ⓣ7761 1663, ⓕ7761 0074. Huge, modern, three-star hotel with a swimming pool and a decent restaurant. Rooms are spacious, and all have private bathrooms and cable TV. Though it's good value, it's only really an option if you have your own transport. ❻

Hotel Casa Florencia 12 Av 3–61 ⓣ7761 2811, ⓦwww.xelapages.com/florencia/index.htm. Just north of the main plaza, with nine fairly comfortable, large en-suite rooms, all of which have wood-panelled walls, flowery bedspreads and fitted carpets – but no outside windows. ❹

Hotel Modelo 14 Av A 2–31 ⓣ7761 2529, ⓕ7763 1376. A good mid-range choice, this historic hotel has a classy air, a wonderful dining room and spacious rooms. Most rooms face a small garden courtyard and tend to lack natural light, however. Try to avoid the streetside rooms on weekend nights, when the area can be noisy, and if you stay in the annex, where the rooms are cheaper, be sure to ask the caretaker to heat up the hot-water boiler adequately. ❹–❺

Hotel Villa Real Plaza 4 C 12–22 ⓣ7761 4045, ⓔvillareal@xelaenlinea.com. Comfortable enough hotel with 54 rooms, located across the plaza from the *Bonifaz*, to which it is a modern(ish) rival – the decor and ambience are a little soulless, however. ❻

Hotel Virginia 11 Av 8–11 ⓣ7761 7355. This good-value new hotel has twenty carpeted rooms with nice wooden beds and decent mattresses, desks and cable TV. The design of the building – it's above a basement car park – is a bit bizarre though. ❺

Pensión Altense 9 C 8–48 ⓣ7761 2811. Old-fashioned place with fairly spacious, clean (if not "Swiss clean") rooms, most of which have a TV and private shower. Safe parking. ❷–❸

Quetzaltenango transport connections

As the focus of the western highlands, Quetzaltenango is served by literally hundreds of buses. **Getting to Quetzaltenango** is fairly straightforward: there are direct pullmans from Guatemala City, and at any point along the Carretera Interamericana you can flag down a bus for Xela (they pass about every 30 minutes) or take the first bus as far as the Cuatro Caminos junction and change there. Coming from the coast you can catch a bus from the El Zarco junction, Mazatenango or Retalhuleu. **Leaving the city**, there are plenty of direct buses, but unless you're heading east along the Carretera Interamericana most are second class and leave from the Minerva terminal.

Shuttle buses are offered by travel agents such as Adrenalina Tours, which operate a comprehensive service to destinations including Panajachel, Huehuetenango, Antigua and Guatemala City.

Pullman buses

All first-class buses run to Guatemala City only. On Sundays, it's essential to book ahead for services to the capital. If you're heading for Antigua and want to travel by pullman as far as possible, get the driver to let you off in Chimaltenango, and catch a connecting bus from there.

Líneas Américas 7 Av 3–33, Zona 2 (ⓣ7761 2063). 6 daily.

Transportes Alamo 14 Av 5–15, Zona 3 (ⓣ7761 7117). 6 daily.

Transportes Galgos 21 C 0–14, Zona 1 (ⓣ7761 2248). 7 daily.

Second-class ("chicken") buses

The main routes from Xela are listed below; all of these buses leave from the **Minerva terminal**. Transport details to villages in the Quetzaltenango area are given in the relevant accounts.

To	Frequency	Journey time
Chichicastenango	10 daily	2hr 30min
Coatepeque	every 30min	1hr 45min
Guatemala City	19 daily	4hr
Huehuetenango	22 daily	2hr
La Mesilla	6 daily	3hr 30min
San Francisco el Alto	every 20min	45min
Malacatán	every 30min	3hr
Momostenango	every 45min	1hr 15min
Panajachel	6 daily	2hr 30min
Retalhuleu	every 30min	1hr 15min
San Marcos	hourly	1hr 30min
San Pedro La Laguna	6 daily	2hr 15min
Tecún Umán	hourly	3hr
Totonicapán	every 30min	1hr
Zunil	every 30min	30min

Pensión Andina 8 Av 6–07 ☎7761 4012. Cheap, bare and fairly tidy rooms, some with private bath (hot water 6–9am only). ❶

Pensión Bonifaz northeast corner of the plaza ☎7761 2182, ©bonifaz@intel.net.gt. Landmark hotel, founded in 1935, with character, comfort and a well-regarded (though overpriced) restaurant. Although it retains an air of faded upper-class pomposity, it's still one of the better places in town, and it has a pool. ❼

The City

Quetzaltenango does not have an excess of sights, but if you have a day to spare then it's well worth wandering through the streets, soaking up the atmosphere and taking in the museums. The hub of the place is the **central plaza**, officially known as the Parque Centro América. Here you'll find the requisite stone benches and well-tended flowers and scrubs as well as a monument to former President Barrios – all overshadowed by a mass of Greek columns. With an atmosphere of dignified calm, the plaza is the best place to appreciate the sense of self-importance that accompanied the city's rebuilding after the 1902 earthquake. The buildings have a look of defiant authority, although there's none of the buzz of business that you'd expect – except on the first Sunday of the month when it plays host to a good artesanías market, with blankets, basketry and piles of *típica* weavings for sale.

Studying Spanish in Quetzaltenango

With dozens of language schools, many of a very high standard, Quetzaltenango is now one of the most popular places in the world to **study Spanish**. Although the days are long gone when schools could boast about the absence of foreigners in the town, Quetzaltenango is still less visited than Antigua and its relatively large population means that you shouldn't have to share a family home with other gringos. Moreover, because tourism is not that important here, fewer local people speak English, so many students find that the city is an excellent place to progress quickly in their language studies. An added benefit of choosing to study in Quetzaltenango is that most schools fund community and environmental projects, like supporting the education of students from poor backgrounds or reforestation initiatives.

All of the schools listed here are well established, employ professional teachers and offer intensive Spanish classes plus the chance to live with a local family (usually with full board). In addition, they often run trips to places of interest around Quetzaltenango, such as Fuentes Georginas or the beach, and hold lectures on political and social issues – some even offer salsa classes, too. Nearly all schools have a student liaison officer who speaks English to act as a go-between for students and teachers. You can expect to pay from US$130 to US$150 a week (often a little more in July and August) for four or five hours of individual tuition from Monday to Friday and seven nights' full-board accommodation with a family. For background information about studying Spanish in Guatemala, see the Basics section of this book.

Casa de Español Xelajú Callejón 15, Diagonal 13–02, Zona 1 ⓣ7761 5954, ⓦwww.casaxelaju.com.

Celas Maya 6 C 14–55, Zona 1 ⓣ7761 4342, ⓦwww.celasmaya.com.

Centro Bilingüe Amerindía (CBA) 12 Av 8–21, Zona 1 ⓣ7761 5260, ⓦwww.xelapages.com/cba.

Centro Maya de Idiomas 21 Av 5–69, Zona 3 ⓣ7767 0352, ⓦwww.centromaya.org. Also offers classes in Maya languages.

Educación para Todos 12 Av 1–78, Zona 3 ⓣ7765 0715, ⓦwww.spanishschools.biz.

English Club International Language School Diagonal 4 9–71, Zona 9 ⓣ7763 2198. Also offers classes in K'iche' and Mam.

Escuela Juan Sisay 15 Av 8–38, Zona 1 ⓣ7763 1318, ⓦwww.juansisay.com.

Guatemalensis 19 Av 2–14, Zona 1 ⓦwww.guatemalensis.com.

Inepas 15 A Av 4–59 ⓣ7765 1308, ⓦwww.inepas.org.

La Paz Diagonal 11 7–38, Zona 1 ⓣ7761 2159, ⓦwww.xelapages.com/lapaz.

Kie–Balam, Diagonal 12 4–46, Zona 1 ⓣ7761 1636, ⓦwww.kiebalam.com.

Pop Wuj 1 C 17–72, Zona 1 ⓣ7761 8286, ⓦwww.pop-wuj.org.

Proyecto Lingüístico Quetzalteco de Español 5 C 2–40, Zona 1 ⓣ7763 1061, ⓦwww.hermandad.com. Also has a sister school on the Pacific slope.

Sakribal 6 C 7–42, Zona 1 ⓣ7763 0717, ⓦwww.sakribal.com.

The Greek columns were probably intended to symbolize the city's cultural importance and its role at the heart of the liberal revolution, but today many of them do nothing more than support street lights. The northern end of the plaza is dominated by the grand Banco de Occidente, complete with sculptured flaming torches. On the west side is Bancafé, and the impressive and slowly gentrifying **Pasaje Enríquez**, which was planned as a sparkling arcade of upmarket shops, spent many years derelict, and has now been partially renovated. Inside you'll find Xela's hippest spot, the *Salón Tecún* bar, a friendly place for meeting other travellers; a frenetically busy cybercafé; a swish new Tex-Mex restaurant; and a travel agency. Below the Pasaje Enríquez, towards the bottom of the square, is a curious little museum, the **Museo del Ferrocarril de Los Altos** (Mon–Fri 8am–noon & 2–6pm, Sat 9am–1pm; US$0.75), which focuses on the ill-fated railway line that connected Xela with Reu in the 1930s.

At the bottom end of the plaza, next to the tourist office, the **Casa de la Cultura** (Mon–Fri 8am–noon & 2–6pm, Sat 9am–1pm; US$0.75) is the city's most blatant impersonation of a Greek temple, with a bold grey frontage. The main part of the building is given over to an odd mixture of local exhibits. On the ground floor, to the left-hand side, you'll find a display of assorted documents, photographs and pistols from the liberal revolution and the State of Los Altos (see p.432), sports trophies, and a room dedicated to the marimba. Upstairs there are some modest Maya artefacts, historic photographs and a bizarre natural history room where, amongst the dusty displays of stuffed bats and pickled snakes, you can see the macabre remains of assorted freaks of nature, including a four-horned goat.

Along the eastern side of the plaza is the **cathedral**, with a new cement version set behind the spectacular crumbling front of the original. There's another unashamed piece of Greek grandeur, the **municipalidad**, or town hall, a little further up. Take a look inside at the courtyard, which has a neat little garden set out around a single palm tree. Between the cathedral and the Casa de la Cultura, the old **mercadito** still functions, although nowadays it's eclipsed by the larger market near the bus terminal in Zona 3. Beside it, there's a grim three-storey shopping centre, the **Centro Comercial Municipal**.

Beyond the plaza

Away from the plaza the city spreads out, a mixture of the old and new. The commercial heart is 14 Avenida, complete with pizza restaurants and neon signs. At the top of 14 Avenida, at its junction with 1 Calle, stands the restored **Teatro Municipal**, another spectacular Neoclassical edifice. The plaza in front of the theatre is dotted with busts of local artists, including Osmundo Arriola (1886–1958), Guatemala's first poet laureate, and Jesús Castillo, "the re-creator of Maya music" – another bid to assert Quetzaltenango's cultural superiority. On clear days, there's a spectacular perspective of the Volcán Santa María from the steps of the plaza.

Further afield, the city's role as a regional centre of trade is more in evidence. Out in Zona 3 is the **Mercado La Democracia**, a vast, covered market complex with stalls spilling out onto the streets. A couple of blocks north of the market, next to the Parque Juárez, stands the modern **Iglesia de San Nicolás**, a bizarre and ill-proportioned neo-Gothic building, sprouting sharp arches.

On the western edge of town, there's another Greek-style monument: the **Minerva Temple**. Built to honour President Barrios' enthusiasm for education, it makes no pretence at serving any practical purpose. Just behind the temple is a little **zoo** (Tues–Sun 9am–5pm; free), doubling as a playground. Crammed into the tiny cages are a collection of birds, monkeys, pizotes, wild boar and some wild cats, including a miserable-looking lion. Below the temple are the sprawling **market** and **bus terminal**. It's here that you can really sense the city's role as the centre of the western highlands, with indigenous traders from all over the area doing business, and buses heading to or from every imaginable village and town. Just behind the market, the spanking new shopping mall **La Pradera** boasts over a hundred stores, and there's a neighbouring multiplex cinema. To get to this side of the city, take a microbus from the corner of 13 Avenida and 4 Calle in Zona 1, at the rear of the Pasaje Enríquez.

Eating

Quetzaltenango has a fairly moderate choice of restaurants, suiting its character as a modest, unpretentious city. Almost nowhere opens before 8am, so forget early breakfasts.

Asados Puente 7 C and 14 Av. This clean, Guatemalan-American-owned restaurant has a nice rear patio and is great for moderately priced meat dishes, including tasty *longaniza* sausages.

Bake Shop 18 Av and 1 C, Zona 3. Fine, Mennonite-run bakery whose tasty pastries and breads are served at Xela's best restaurants. 9am–6pm Tues & Fri only.

Blue Angel Video Café 7 C 15–19. Popular, sociable travellers' hangout with a daily video programme, plus great salads and sandwiches.

Café Baviera 5 C 12–50, a block from the plaza. Anachronistic, pine-panelled coffeehouse, with plenty of period photos of Xela's local notables on the walls. Although known for its coffee, the atmosphere is pretty subdued. There's also a selection of teas, as well as cakes, sandwiches and soups, plus a no-smoking area.

Cardinali's 14 Av 3–41. Reliably good, atmospheric Italian place with gingham tablecloths and Chianti flasks on the walls. It's best for pizza or pasta and offers huge portions at reasonable prices. For delivery call ⓣ7761 0924.

Casa Babilón 13 Av and 5 C. Friendly French-Guatemalan-owned place dispensing wonderful, filling sandwiches, tacos, crêpes, plus fondues (US$8 a pot). The menu also features a good selection of salads (including "winsome spinach and five cheese") and wine by the glass. Recommended. Closed Sun.

Dos Tejanos 4 C 12–33. Located inside the Pasaje Enríquez, this Texan-owned restaurant is a stylish place to feast on terrific barbecued ribs, brisket and chicken, as well as tasty Tex–Mex dishes. Mains run between US$3 and US$10.

La Luna 8 Av 4–11. Crammed with curios and antiques, *La Luna* has seven different varieties of drinking chocolate, though the food is mediocre. Weekends 4–9pm only.

Pensión Bonifaz in the hotel of the same name, corner of the plaza. Worth a visit, as it's a pleasingly civilized spot for a cup of tea, a cake, and the chance to rub shoulders with the town's elite, though the restaurant is expensive and the cooking only average.

El Rincón de los Antojitos 15 Av and 5 C. This friendly little French-Guatemalan restaurant has specialities like *hilachas* (beef in tomato sauce) as well as some French dishes.

Royal Paris 14 Av A 3–06. Authentic, enjoyable French-owned restaurant with a winsome menu of really flavoursome dishes, plus snacks like *croque monsieur*. Prices are moderate, given the quality of the cuisine.

Sagrado Corazón 1 14 Av 3–08. Run by a formidable *señora*, this small, informal place is a great spot to try Guatemalan specialities like *pepián* or *jocón* (meat cooked with peppers and tomatillos).

Sagrado Corazón 2 9 C 9–00. Agreeable comedor, not connected to the establishment above, with good-value breakfasts, a huge US$2.50 set lunch and friendly service.

La Taquería 8 Av & 5 C. Enjoyable Mexican food, moderately priced and fairly authentic.

Ut'z Hua 12 Av & 3 C. Diners sit under a *palapa* roof at this intimate, busy place specializing in Guatemalan cuisine. There's an excellent choice of mains, costing about US$3–4, including *jocón*, *quichóm*, local sausages, *mojarra* fish and seven kinds of soup.

Drinking, nightlife and entertainment

After dark, things are generally quiet in the week, but a number of lively **bars** fill up at the weekend. There's also a small **club** scene. For a night out, start at the most popular drinking den in town, the *Salón Tecún*, where they serve a mean *Cuba libre* and draught beer, and then head on to 14 Avenida A, which has become something of a **Zona Viva** in recent years. Here you'll find several bars, some with dancing. *El Duende* is a bar-club with Latin house, salsa and merengue; underneath it, *La Bodega Duende* has good DJs at weekends. *Fratta's*, a little further up the same street, has a big salsa night on Wednesdays, while *Hektisch*, over on 15 Avenida is the hippest club in town, with a cutting-edge selection of music, including hard techno, hip-hop and drum 'n' bass. For a quieter drink, try the intimate *Bajo La Luna*, on the corner of 4 Calle and

8 Avenida, where you can choose from a great selection of bottled wines and tuck into platters of cheese and ham.

Quetzaltenango is a good place to catch a **movie**. In the centre of town, Cine Paraíso, 1 C 12–20, shows a variety of interesting Latin and Western films, while a multi-screen theatre is located by La Pradera mall, near the Minerva terminal. To find **what's on** in Xela, pick up a copy of the free listings magazine, *Fin de Semana*, available in many of the popular bars and cafés or the *Quetzalteco* newspaper.

Listings

Banks and exchange Several banks on the main plaza will change travellers' cheques, including Banrural (Mon–Fri 9am–7pm, Sat 9am–1pm), which has a MasterCard/Cirrus ATM, and Banco Industrial (Mon–Fri 9.30am–6.30pm, Sat 9.30am–1.30pm), with a Visa/Plus ATM.

Bike rental Vrisa bookstore (see below) has bikes for US$3.50 per day, US$9 per week and US$19 per month.

Bookstores Vrisa, 15 Av 3–64, has over 5000 used titles. El Libro Abierto, 15 Av A 1–56, Zona 1, has political, social and anthropological books on Guatemala, guidebooks and some used titles.

Car rental Tabarini, 9 C 9–21 (Ⓣ7763 0418), has cars from US$28 per day.

Consulates Mexican Consulate, 9 Av 6–19, Zona 1 (Mon–Fri 9am–noon & 2–3pm). Most nationalities do not need a visa or tourist card; if you do, hand in your paperwork in the morning and collect it in the afternoon.

Internet There are at least two dozen places in Xela where you can surf the Net, including Maya Communications, above *Salón Tecún* in the Plaza Central, and Alternativa's at 16 Av 3–35, Zona 3. Xela's cybercafés are generally open until 9pm or later and charge around US$1.25/hr.

Laundry MiniMax, 4 Av and 1 C, Zona 1 (Mon–Sat 7am–7pm); US$2.50 for a full-load wash and dry.

Medical care Hospital San Rafael, 9 C 10–41, Zona 1 Ⓣ7761 4414.

Post office 15 Av and 4 C.

Telephone Alternativa's (see "Internet" above) has the best rates: webcalls on clear lines are US$0.10 per minute to the US and Canada, US$0.25 to Europe. You'll pay much more at the main Telgua office, 15 Av and 4 C.

Tours and travel agencies Adrenalina Tours, inside Pasaje Enríquez, Plaza Central (Ⓣ7761 4509, Ⓦwww.adrenalinatours.com), offers volcano climbs (Volcán Santa María costs from US$15 per person), shuttle buses, airline tickets and various tours of the Xela region, including trips to Zunil, Fuentes Georginas and San Andrés Xecul. Maya Explorer, 1 Av A 6-59 (Ⓣ7761 5057, Ⓦwww.mayaexplor.com), is an experienced agency that organizes trips to most of the volcanoes and sights around Xela. Quetzaltrekkers, inside *Casa Argentina* (see "Accommodation", p.189; Ⓣ7761 4520, Ⓦwww.quetzalventures.com), offers cultural tours and hiking trips to volcanoes, with all profits going to a charity for street children.

Around Quetzaltenango

The Xela area offers some of the country's most evocative highland scenery, with volcanic cones soaring above forested ridges, and a number of fascinating indigenous villages to explore. Straddling the coast road south of the city are **Almolonga** and **Zunil**, where you'll find superb hot springs, including **Fuentes Georginas**, a wonderful natural spa. Just west of here, the **Santa María volcano**, towering above Quetzaltenango is a terrific, if exhausting, excursion. The most accessible climb in the area lies southwest of the city, up **Volcán Chicabal** to an exquisite crater lake set in the extinct volcano's cone.

Heading northwards, the traditional Maya town of **Olintepeque** is renowned for its shrine devoted to the pagan saint of San Pascual. A little further distant are **Totonicapán**, a departmental capital, and the famous market town of **San Francisco el Alto**, perched on a rocky outcrop. Beyond here, in

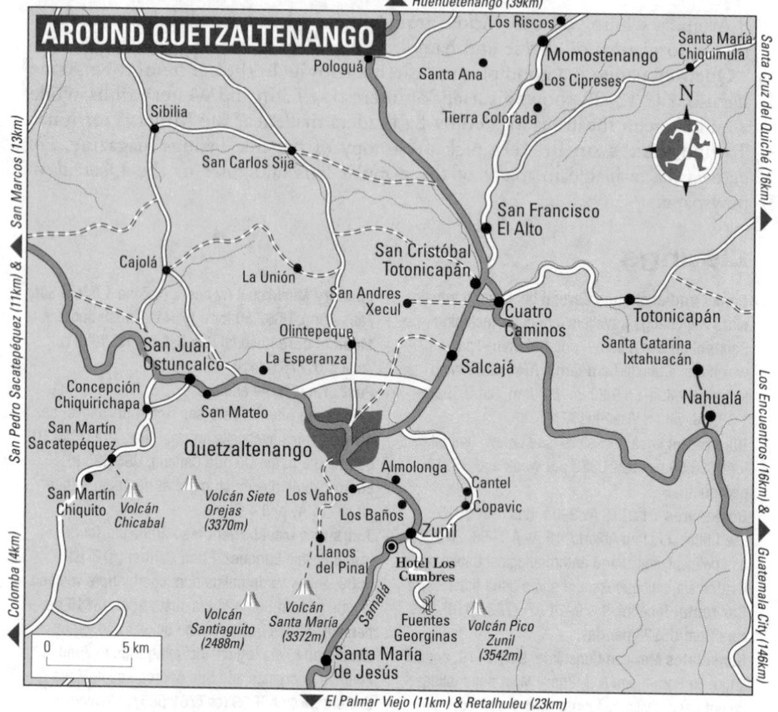

the midst of a pine forest, lies **Momostenango**, the country's principal wool-producing centre. Maya culture remains strong throughout this network of simple rural towns and villages, whose lifeblood is a series of weekly markets.

South to Almolonga and Zunil

The most direct route from Quetzaltenango to the coast takes you through a narrow gash in the mountains to the village of **ALMOLONGA**, sprawled around the sides of a steep-sided, flat-bottomed valley just 5km from Quetzaltenango. Almolonga is K'iche' for "the place where water springs", and streams gush from the hillside, channelled to the waiting crops. This is the market garden of the western highlands, where the flat land is far too valuable to live on and is parcelled up instead into neat, irrigated sections.

In markets throughout the western highlands, the women of Almolonga corner the vegetable trade; it's easy to recognize them, dressed in their bold, orange zigzag *huipiles* and wearing beautifully woven headbands. The village itself has **markets** on Wednesday and Saturday mornings – the latter being the larger one – when the elongated plaza is ringed by trucks and crammed with people, while piles of scrubbed radishes and gleaming carrots are swiftly traded between the two. The Almolonga market may not be Guatemala's largest, but it has to be one of the most frenetic, and is well worth a visit. While you're here, it's also worth dropping by the village **church**, an arresting banana-yellow and white affair that backs onto the plaza. Inside, beneath the cupola, there's a wonderfully gaudy gilded altar complete with a silver statue of a crusading

San Pedro, complete with bible, set behind protective bars. Pay the caretaker a quetzal and the whole altar lights up in a riot of technicolour fluorescent tubes, including a halo for the saint.

A couple of kilometres beyond the village lie **Los Baños**, where about ten different operations offer a soak in waters heated naturally by the volcano; Fuentes Saludable and El Recreo (daily 5am–10pm) are good options. For a couple of dollars you get a private room, a sunken concrete tub, and enough hot water to drown an elephant. In a country of lukewarm showers, it's paradise, and the baths echo to the sound of indigenous families, some of whom queue barefoot for the pleasure of a good scrub. Below the road, between the baths and the village, there's a warm swimming pool known as Los Chorros – follow the sign to Agua Tibia – which you can use for a small fee.

If, on the other hand, you'd prefer to immerse yourself in steam, you're in luck as this also emerges naturally from the hillside. To hike to the **vapores**, as they're known, get off the bus halfway between Quetzaltenango and Almolonga at the sign for Los Vahos, and head off up the track. Take the right turn after about forty minutes, and follow this track for another thirty minutes, and you'll come to the steam baths. Here you can sweat it out for a while in one of the rooms and then step out into the cool mountain air, or have a bracing shower to get the full sauna effect.

Buses run to Almolonga from Quetzaltenango every fifteen minutes from the Minerva terminal, stopping to pick up passengers at the junction of 9 Avenida and 10 Calle in Zona 1. They pause in Almolonga itself before going on to the baths, and, although the baths stay open until 10pm, the last bus back is at around 7.30pm.

Beyond Los Baños the road heads through another narrow gully to join the main coast road in Zunil. If you're bound for Zunil, buses pass this way every thirty minutes or so.

Cantel, Zunil and the Fuentes Georginas

Many buses to the coast avoid Almolonga, leaving Quetzaltenango via the **Las Rosas** junction and passing through **CANTEL FÁBRICA**, an industrial village built up around an enormous textile factory. The factory's looms produce a range of cloths, using indigenous labourers, German dyes, English machinery, and a mixture of American and Guatemalan cotton. The village was originally known as Chuijullub, a K'iche' word meaning "on the hill", and this original settlement (now called Cantel – Cantel Fábrica simply means "Cantel Factory") can still be seen on a height overlooking the works.

A kilometre beyond Cantel on the road to Zunil is the **Copavic glass factory**, one of Guatemala's most successful cooperatives. Copavic uses one hundred percent recycled glass and exports the finished product all over the world. Visitors are welcome to see the glass-blowers in action (Mon–Fri 8am–1pm), or visit the factory shop (Mon–Fri 8am–5pm & Sat 8am–noon), which sells a fine selection of glasses, vases, jugs and other assorted goods.

Further down the valley is **ZUNIL**, another centre for vegetable growing. As at Almolonga, the village is split in two by the need to preserve the best land.

The plaza is dominated by a beautiful white colonial church with twin belfries and a magnificent Baroque facade – complete with a Buddha-like figure, a quetzal and vines. Inside an intricate silver altar is protected behind bars. The women of Zunil wear vivid purple *huipiles* and carry incredibly bright shawls, and during the Monday market the plaza is awash with colour. Just below the plaza is a **textile cooperative** (Mon–Sat 8.30am–5pm, Sun 2–5pm), where hundreds of women market their beautiful weavings; lessons are also offered

Visiting San Simón in Zunil

Zunil's reputation for the worship of San Simón is well founded, and as in Santiago Atitlán you can pay a visit to the man himself with a minimum of effort. Every year on November 1, at the end of the annual fiesta, San Simón (also known as Maximón) is moved to a new house; discreet enquiries will locate his current home. Here his effigy sits in a darkened room, dressed in Western clothes, and guarded by several attendants, including one whose job it is to remove the ash from his lighted cigarettes – this is later sold off and used to cure insomnia, while the butts are thought to provide protection from thieves. San Simón is visited by a steady stream of villagers, who come to ask his assistance, using candles to indicate their requests: white for the health of a child, yellow for a good harvest, red for love and black to wish ill on an enemy. The petitioners touch and embrace the saint, and just to make sure that he has heard their pleas they also offer cigarettes, money and rum. The latter is administered with the help of one of the attendants, who tips back San Simón's head and pours the liquid down his throat, presumably saving a little for himself. Meanwhile, outside the house a small fire burns continuously and more offerings are given over to the flames, including whole eggs – if they crack it signifies that San Simón will grant a wish.

If you visit San Simón, you will be expected to contribute to his upkeep (US$0.50 or so). While the entire process may seem chaotic and entertaining, it is in fact deeply serious and outsiders have been beaten up for making fun of San Simón – so proceed with respect.

David Dickinson

here. Zunil is also renowned for its adherence to the cult of **San Simón** (or Maximón), the evil saint. In the face of disapproval from the Catholic Church, the Maya are reluctant to display their Judas, who also goes by the name Alvarado, but his image is usually paraded through the streets during Holy Week, dressed in Western clothes and smoking a cigar. At other times of year, you can meet the man himself (see box above).

In the hills above Zunil are the **Fuentes Georginas**, a spectacular natural spring spa. Unfortunately, the heated water that feeds the pools has been more tepid than steaming hot for the past few years – perhaps due to a nearby hydroelectric power scheme, which has disturbed the supply. Nevertheless, the location on the evergreen slopes of Volcán Pico Zunil, and the exhilarating journey to the pools – up a road which switchbacks through magnificent volcanic scenery – make a visit well worthwhile anyway. The baths (US$2) themselves are surrounded by fresh green ferns, thick moss and lush forest, and to top it all there's a restaurant with a well-stocked bar beside the main pool. You can also rent one of the pleasant rustic stone **bungalows** for the night (Ⓣ7765 4442; ❹), complete with bathtub, two double beds, fireplace (wood is provided) and barbecue. Pick-ups leave the plaza in Zunil and cost US$5 per trip, no matter how many passengers there are; it's another US$5 for the return ride.

Buses to Cantel and Zunil run from Quetzaltenango's Minerva bus terminal every thirty minutes or so, though you can also catch a bus from the centre of town beside the Shell gas station at 10 Calle and 9 Avenida in Zona 1. The last bus back from Zunil leaves at around 7pm. All buses to the coastal town of Retalhuleu also pass through this way.

Just a kilometre beyond Zunil is one of Guatemala's most enjoyable **places to stay**, the spa hotel *Las Cumbres* (Ⓣ7767 1746; ❺–❻), perched on the side of a steep slope with tremendous views across the valley to the forested foothills of the Volcán Pico Zunil. It's a tremendously well-run hotel, with a dozen or so

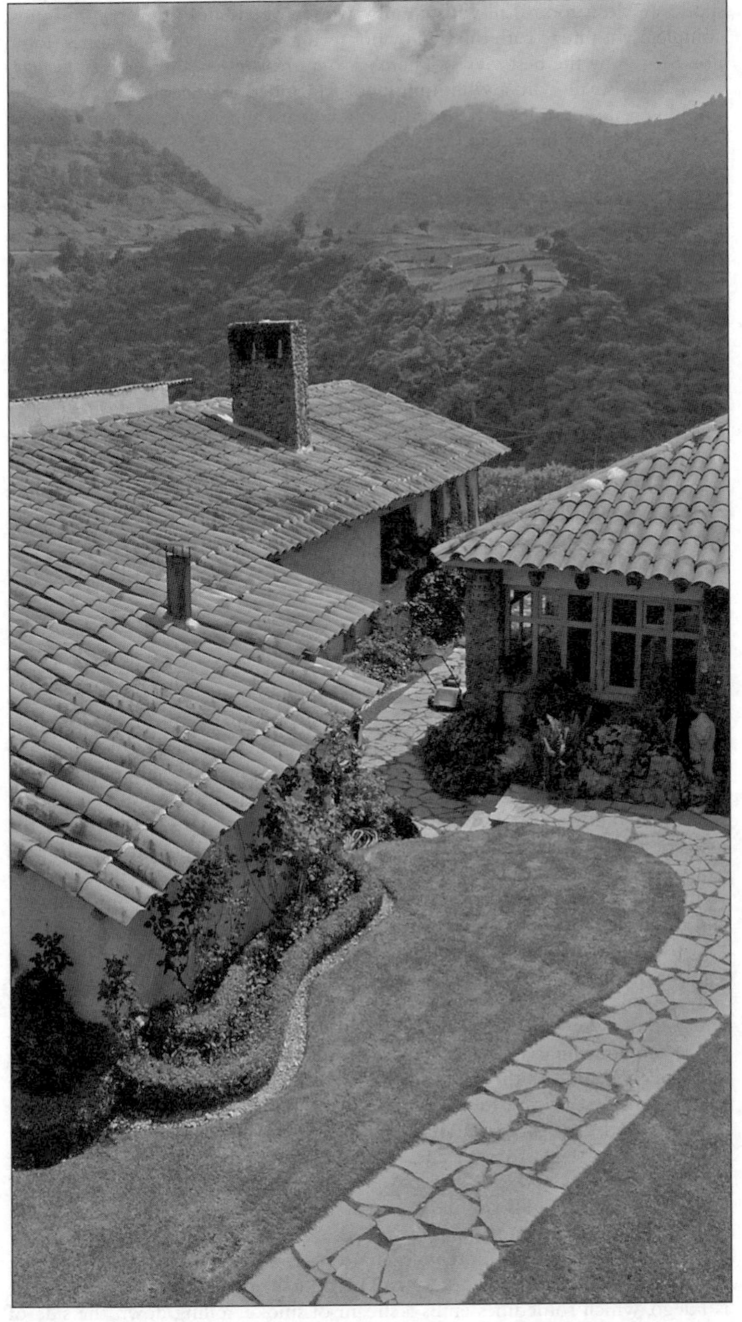

△ View from *Las Cumbres* hotel

spotlessly clean rooms, all with chunky wooden beds and fireplaces, and most complete with huge bath tubs fed by hot spring water and private saunas (room nos. 6–9 enjoy the best views). There's also a great restaurant with tasty *comida típica* and a small gym; a swimming pool is planned. No alcohol is served and smoking is not permitted. If you just want a steam and a soak, seven great sauna rooms (US$3 per hour) can be used by visitors.

Volcán Santa María

Due south of Quetzaltenango, the perfect cone of the **Volcán Santa María** rises to a height of 3772m. From the town only the peak is visible, but seen from the rest of the valley the entire cone seems to tower over everything around. The view from the top is, as you might expect, spectacular, and if you're prepared to sweat out the climb, you certainly won't regret it. It's possible to climb the volcano as a day-trip, but to really see it at its best you need to be on top at dawn, either sleeping on the freezing peak, or camping at a site part-way up and climbing the final section in the dark by torchlight. Either way you need to bring enough food, water and stamina for the entire trip, and you should be acclimatized to the altitude before attempting it.

For more **information** on climbing Santa María, or any of the volcanoes in the region, contact Adrenalina Tours or Casa Iximulew (see p.189). Sadly, you should also check the current security situation with either of these tour operators or on the forum of Ⓦwww.xelapages.com, as robberies have been reported.

Climbing the cone

To get to the start of the climb, you need to take a pick-up (approximately hourly between 7am and 5pm) to the village of **Llanos del Pinal**; pick-ups leave from the El Calvario church, beside Quetzaltenango's main cemetery on the south side of the Calzada Sinforoso Aguilar road. The village is set on a high plateau beneath the cone, and drivers will drop you off at the right spot, close to where the paved road ends. From here, the road heads uphill, soon becoming a trail. Painted arrows mark the way along this first section. As you push on, the path soon arrives at a flat football-pitch-sized grassy area, about ninety minutes to two hours from the start – an ideal place to **camp**. The path cuts off to the right from here, heading more or less straight up the side of the cone, a muddy and backbreaking climb of two or three hours.

At the top the cone is a mixture of grass and volcanic cinder, usually frozen solid in the early morning. The highest point is marked by an altar where the Maya burn copal and sacrifice animals, and on a clear day the **view** will take your breath away – as will the cold if you get here in time to watch the sun rise. In the early mornings the Quetzaltenango valley is blanketed in a layer of cloud, and while it's still dark the lights of the city create a patch of orange glow; as the sun rises, its first rays eat into the cloud, revealing the land beneath.

Below, to the south, is the angry, lava-scarred cone of **Santiaguito**, which has been in constant eruption since 1902. Every now and then it spouts a great grey cloud of rock and dust hundreds of metres into the air. To the west, across a chaos of twisting hills, are the cones of Tajumulco and Tacaná, marking the Mexican border. But most impressive is the view to the east. Wrapped in the early morning haze, four more volcanic cones can be seen, two above Lago de Atitlán and two more above Antigua. The right-hand cone in this second pair is Fuego, which sometimes emits a stream of smoke, rolling down the side of the cone in the early morning.

West to San Juan Ostuncalco and Laguna Chicabal

Heading west from Quetzaltenango, a good paved road runs 15km along the valley floor to the prosperous village of **SAN JUAN OSTUNCALCO**, the commercial centre for the west side of the Xela plain. The large Sunday market draws people from all the surrounding villages; here you can see the furniture made locally from wood and rope, painted in garish primary colours. The village's other famous feature is the Catholic church's *Virgen de Rosario*, who is reputed to have miraculous powers. Almost merging into Ostuncalco, its centre just 2km or so to the south, is the quiet, traditional village of **CONCEPCIÓN CHIQUIRICHAPA**, which hosts a very local market on Thursday, attended by only a few outsiders and conducted in hushed tones. **Buses** and microbuses run every thirty minutes between Quetzaltenango and Ostuncalco.

Beyond Chiquirichapa the road to the coast climbs into the hills and through a gusty pass before winding down to **SAN MARTÍN SACATEPÉQUEZ**, also known as San Martín Chile Verde, an isolated Mam-speaking village set in the base of a natural bowl and hemmed in by steep, wooded hills. The village was abandoned in 1902 when the eruption of the Santa María volcano buried the land beneath a metre-thick layer of pumice stone, killing thousands. These days both the people and fertility have returned to the land, and the village is once again devoted to farming. The men of San Martín wear a particularly unusual costume, a long white tunic with thin red stripes, ornately embroidered around the cuffs and tied around the middle with a red sash; the women wear beautiful red *huipiles* and blue *cortes*.

A two-hour hike from San Martín brings you to **Laguna Chicabal**, a spectacular lake set in the cone of the Chicabal volcano that is the site of Maya religious rituals. To get there, get the bus to drop you off the stop for "la laguna", head down to a small bridge, then uphill to the Arca de Noe yellow-and-red church, where you bear left. The dirt track climbs steeply uphill for forty minutes before levelling out near the entrance to the Chicabal reserve (US$1.80 entrance) where there's a football field and some *palapa*s, each with four bunk beds (US$3 per person), a comedor and a shop.

A signposted route then ascends again through a forest, winding around the cone to the rim, from where there are two routes to the lake: either to the left via a *mirador* (from where there are stunning views of the emerald lagoon, and the volcanoes of Santa María and Santiaguito, Tajamulco and Tacaná), or alternatively via precipitous steps straight down to the shore. At the water's edge, you come into a different world, eerily still, disturbed only by the soft buzz of a hummingbird's wings or the screech of parakeets. Small sandy bays bear charred crosses and bunches of fresh-cut flowers mark the site of ritual sacrifice. On May 3 every year *costumbristas* gather here for ceremonies to mark the fiesta of the Holy Cross: at any time, but on this date especially, you should take care not to disturb any rituals that might be taking place. You are welcome to camp at the shore, though you'll have to bring all your own supplies.

Buses run between the Minerva terminal in Quetzaltenango and Coatepeque (for the coast) passing San Martín every 30 minutes or so. The journey time is 40 minutes; the last returns from San Martín about 6pm.

Olintepeque and around

To the north of Quetzaltenango, perched on the edge of the flat plain, is the small textile-weaving town of **OLINTEPEQUE**. According to some accounts this was the site of the huge and decisive battle between the Spanish and K'iche' warriors, but these days it's better known as a peaceful little place with a fascinating pagan shrine and a great Tuesday **animal market**. This gets going soon after daylight, winding down by midday, by which time hundreds of pigs-on-leads, chickens, goats and cattle have been prodded and poked over, bought and sold.

Olintepeque's other curious attraction, the **Capilla de Rey San Pascual**, lies right in the centre of town, behind the huge mustard-coloured Catholic church. This pagan temple is dedicated to an idol, believed by devotees to have supernatural powers: numerous plaques on the walls of his shrine commissioned by believers give thanks to San Pascual for his ability to heal the sick (and bring misfortune to enemies). San Pascual is certainly a curious sight: a foot-high effigy with an exposed skull bedecked in gaudy-coloured robes, surrounded by hundreds of candles and offerings of flowers. A flight of steps leads up to an exposed platform known as the *quemadero* ("bonfire") where the faithful whisper incantations through clouds of pungent *copal* (pine incense) smoke. **Buses** for Olintepeque (20min) leave from the Minerva terminal in Quetzaltenango every thirty minutes.

Olintepeque was a staging post on the old road to Huehuetenango, and although only local traffic heads this way nowadays you can still follow the route. Leaving Olintepeque the road climbs the steep hillside onto a plateau, arriving at the village of **SAN CARLOS SIJA**, 22km from Quetzaltenango and the hub of a fertile yet isolated area. The only real reason to come out here is for the wonderful views, or to visit the small Sunday market. If you don't want to return the same way, pick-ups run from San Carlos to the Carretera Interamericana, just 10km away, where there's plenty of traffic to Quetzaltenango via Cuatro Caminos or on to Huehuetenango.

Northeast to Cuatro Caminos

Between the Cuatro Caminos junction and Quetzaltenango, heavy traffic cuts right through the unappealing ladino town of **SALCAJÁ**, one of Guatemala's main commercial weaving centres. Lengths of fabric, much of it woven for the *cortes* worn by Maya women, are often stretched out by the roadside, either to be prepared for dyeing or laid out to dry.

Salcajá's other claim to fame is that (according to some historians at least) it was the site of the first Spanish settlement in the country. Its modest-looking Iglesia de San Jacinto, with a simple facade embellished with plasterwork pineapples and bananas, is therefore regarded as the first Catholic foundation in Guatemala. The ideal time to visit Salcajá is for its Tuesday market, after which you might want to sample a drop of the local *caldo de fruitas* (fruit-based) or *rompopo* (egg and aguardiente) liquor. Many places can sell you a dram, including the pink house numbered 5–23, next to the basketball court on the west side of the church.

A couple of kilometres beyond Salcajá, a left turn runs to the edge of the valley and the village of **SAN ANDRÉS XECUL**. Bypassed by almost everything, and enclosed by steep, dry hills to the rear, the breezeblock grey suburban outskirts present an unfavourable first impression that doesn't do the village justice. Facing the central plaza, San Andrés' canary yellow Catholic **church** is quite astonishing, with a facade that's a riot of vines dripping plump, purple fruit, and podgy little angels scrambling across the surface. The twin jaguars at the top are said to represent the hero twins of the Maya holy book, the Popul Vuh. Inside there are some fabulously chintzy chandeliers made of glass stones, coins and rosary beads.

The village's other religious activities are less orthodox. In the 1970s the artist Carmen Petterson even claimed to have discovered that a "university" for *brujos* was operating in the village, attracting young students of shamanism from K'iche' villages throughout the country. Her observations remain unsubstantiated, but there's no doubt that San Andrés is an important Maya religious centre. Uphill on 1 Calle at **La Casa de Maximón**, Guatemala's pagan saint (see p.198) holds court and a wooden case contains some rare Maya ceramics. Continuing up 1 Calle, you'll reach the yellow-and-green Calvario church, next to which is a Maya altar that's actively used for ceremonies and often shrouded in thick *copal* smoke. There are said to be dozens more in the hills around the town.

Hourly **buses** leave the Minerva terminal in Quetzaltenango for San Andrés, the last returns at around 5pm; or you can easily get a bus or pick-up from the filling station 2km beyond Salcajá on the road to Cuatro Caminos.

At **Cuatro Caminos**, the most important junction in the western highlands, the main roads from Quetzaltenango and Totonicapán intersect with the Carretera Interamericana. Here you'll find all the usual highlights of Guatemalan road junctions: cheap motels, pricey fruit stalls and shanty-like comedores. More importantly, up until about 7pm, there's a stream of buses heading for Quetzaltenango, Huehuetenango, Guatemala City and smaller villages along the way.

One kilometre to the west, the ladino town of **SAN CRISTÓBAL TOTONICAPÁN** is built at the junction of the Sija and Salamá rivers. It's generally a quiet place that holds a position of importance as a source of **fiesta costumes**, which can be rented from various outfitters. If you'd like to see one of these, drop in at 5 Calle 3–20, where they rent costumes for around US$50 a fortnight, depending on age and quality. The colossal Baroque **colonial church**, on the other side of the river, is the main landmark in town, with a magnificent wood-beamed roof and some fantastic frescoes. Look out, too, for the extravagant side altars with images of saints made from ornate silverwork – St Michael is particularly striking. Easter week is an impressive time to visit San Cristóbal, when there are huge processions to the church, or you could drop by for the Sunday market. **Buses** going to San Francisco el Alto pass by the village – they leave from the Minerva terminal.

San Francisco el Alto and Momostenango

From a magnificent hillside setting, the small market town of **SAN FRANCISCO EL ALTO** overlooks the Quetzaltenango valley. It's worth a visit for the view alone, with the great plateau stretching out below and the cone of the Santa María volcano marking the opposite side of the valley. At times a layer of early morning cloud fills the valley, and the volcanic cone, rising out of it, is the only visible feature.

The **Friday market** – the largest weekly market in the country – is an equally good reason for visiting the village. Traders from every corner of Guatemala make the trip, many arriving the night before, and some starting to sell as early as 4am by candlelight. Throughout the morning a steady stream of buses and trucks fills the town to bursting; by noon the market is at its height, buzzing with activity.

The town is set into the hillside, with steep cobbled streets connecting the different levels. Two areas in particular are monopolized by specific trades. At the very top is an open field used as an **animal market**, where everything from pigs to parrots changes hands. The teeth and tongues of animals are inspected by the buyers, and at times the scene degenerates into a chaotic wrestling match, with pigs and men rolling in the dirt. Below this is the town's plaza, dominated by **textiles** and clothing. Most of the stalls deal in imported *ropa americana* and denim, but under the arches and in the covered area opposite the church you'll find a decent selection of traditional cloth. (For a really good view of the market and the surrounding countryside, pay the church caretaker a quetzal and climb up to the church roof.) Below, the streets are filled with vegetables, fruit, pottery, furniture, cheap comedores and plenty more. By early afternoon the numbers start to thin out, and by sunset it's all over – until the following Friday.

Plenty of **buses** connect Quetzaltenango with San Francisco, leaving every twenty minutes from 6am or so from the Minerva terminal; some also stop at the rotunda on the east side of town. San Francisco's best place to stay is the *Hotel Galaxia*, 2 C 1–81 (☎7738 4007; ❷), which is nothing special but does have tidy bare rooms with private bathrooms. For a bite there are some simple comedores but little else; *La Fuente* on 3 Avenida is not bad. Bancafé on 2 Calle has a Visa ATM, and changes travellers' cheques.

Momostenango

Above San Francisco a smooth paved road continues over the ridge, then drops down through pine forests to **MOMOSTENANGO**, less than an hour away. This small, isolated town is the centre of **wool** production in the highlands, and Momostecos travel throughout the country peddling their blankets, scarves and rugs. Years of experience have made them experts in the hard sell and given them a sharp eye for tourists. The wool is also used in a range of traditional costumes, including the short skirts worn by the men of Nahualá and San Antonio Palopó as well as the jackets of Sololá. The ideal place to buy Momostenango blankets is in the **Sunday market**, which fills the town's two plazas, or the smaller Wednesday occasion.

A visit at this time will also give you a glimpse of Momostenango's other feature: its rigid adherence to Maya tradition. Opposite the entrance to the church, you may see people making offerings of incense and alcohol on a small fire, muttering their appeals to the gods. Momostenango's religious **calendar**, like that of only one or two other villages, is still based on the 260-day *Tzolkin* year – made up of thirteen twenty-day months – which has been in use since ancient times. The most celebrated ceremony is *Guaxaquib Batz*, "Eight Monkey", which marks the beginning of a new year. Originally, this was a purely pagan ceremony, starting at dawn on the first day of the year, but the Church has muscled in on the action and it now begins with a Catholic service the night before. The next morning the people make for Chuitmesabal (Little Broom), a small hill about 2km to the west of the town. Here offerings of broken pottery are made before age-old altars. (Momostenango means "the place of the altars".) The entire process is overseen by shamans responsible for communicating with the gods. At dusk the ceremony moves to Nim Mesabal (Big Broom), another hilltop, where the *costumbristas* pray and burn incense throughout the night.

As a visitor, however, even if you could plan to be in town at the right time, you'd be unlikely to see any of this, and it's best to visit Momostenango for the market, or for the fiesta on August 1. If you decide to stay for a day or two, you can take a walk to *los riscos*, a set of bizarre sandstone pillars on the northern edge of town, or beyond to the **hot springs** of Pala Chiquito about 2km further on. Throughout the day weavers work at the springs washing and shrinking their blankets – it's always best to go early, before most people arrive and the water is discoloured by soap.

Practicalities

Hospedaje Paglóm (❶) on 1 Calle has cleanish, plain rooms, but serves good grub; you'll find comedores on the main plaza. There's also a Bancafé **bank**, 1 Calle and 1 Avenida (Mon–Fri 9am–4pm, Sun), which has a Visa ATM and changes cash and travellers' cheques.

Buses run here from the Minerva terminal in Quetzaltenango, passing through Cuatro Caminos and San Francisco el Alto on the way, every 45 minutes from 7am (1hr 15min). The last bus returns at 4pm. On Sunday, special early-morning buses leave Quetzaltenango every thirty minutes from 6am, some stopping at the rotunda.

Totonicapán

TOTONICAPÁN, capital of one of the smaller departments, is a pleasant, if unremarkable, provincial centre reached down a direct road leading east from Cuatro Caminos. Entering the village you pass one of the country's finest *pilas* (communal washing places), ringed with Gothic columns. Surrounded by rolling hills and pine forests, the town stands at the heart of a heavily populated and intensely farmed region. The Toto valley has always held out against outside influence, isolated in a world of its own, and in 1820 was the scene of one of the most famous **Maya rebellions**, sparked by demands for tax. The indigenous people expelled all of the town's ladinos and crowned their leader, Antanasio Tzul, the "king and fiscal king". His reign lasted only 29 days, ending when crack state troops from the capital violently quashed the rebellion – a stone memorial commemorates the event in the town's southern plaza.

Tensions in the town boiled over again in August 2001, after the Portillo government announced a VAT increase. Angry demonstrations ignited into widespread rioting during which FRG (Portillo's party) offices, a bank, the local tax office, the mayor's house and a radio station were burned down. The riots were only quelled when a state of emergency was declared and army tanks were sent in to restore order.

Periodic rebellions aside, Totonicapán is normally a quiet place whose faded glory is ruffled only by the Tuesday and Saturday markets, which fill the two plazas to bursting. Until fairly recently a highly ornate traditional costume was worn here. The women's *huipiles* were some of the most elaborate and colourful in the country, and the men wore trousers embroidered with flowers, edged in lace, and decorated with silver buttons. Today, however, all this has disappeared and the town has instead become one of the chief centres of **commercial weaving**. Along with Salcajá it produces much of the *jasped* cloth worn as skirts by the majority of indigenous women: the machine-made *huipiles* of modern Totonicapán are used throughout the highlands as costume. To take a closer look at the work of local artisans, head for the town's **visitor centre**, the Casa de la Cultura, 8 Av 2–17 (Mon–Sat 9.30am–5pm; Ⓦlarutamayaonline.com/aventura.html). It organizes guided walks around the fringes of town (US$6–15, price depends on numbers) that take in sacred Maya sites, mask and fiesta costume-making workshops and weavers' houses (lunch included); the funds raised help benefit the community. The only other sight here is located just north of the two plazas: a grand, recently restored municipal **theatre** – a Neoclassical structure echoing the one in Quetzaltenango.

Totonicapán is very quiet after dark; if you do want to stay, however, the best **hotel** is the modern *Hotel y Centro de Convenciones Totonicapán*, at the junction of 8 Calle and 8 Avenida (Ⓣ7766 4458, Ⓦwww.larutamaya.net/hct; ❺). It features large, comfortable rooms, all with cable TV and private bathroom;

a restaurant; and a car park. Otherwise *Hospedaje San Miguel*, a block from the plaza at 8 Avenida and 3 Calle (☎7766 1452; ❷–❸), is quite acceptable; only some of the rooms here have private bathrooms and TVs, though, and note that prices rise before market days. The *Pensión Blanquita* (❶) is a friendly and basic alternative opposite the gas station at 13 Avenida and 4 Calle. For somewhere **to eat**, try one of the comedores scattered around the town's two plazas, or the restaurant in the *Hotel y Centro de Convenciones Totonicapán*. **Buses** for Totonicapán leave Quetzaltenango's Minerva terminal between 6am and 5pm every 30min, passing through Cuatros Caminos.

The Department of San Marcos

Leaving Quetzaltenango you can head west to the rather neglected, little-visited department of **San Marcos** – a potential **route to Mexico** by the coastal crossing, and the home of the country's highest volcano, **Tajumulco**. Set in some of the finest highland scenery in Guatemala, the area offers excellent **hiking**.

West of Quetzaltenango the main road heads out of the valley through San Mateo and Ostuncalco and climbs a massive range of hills, dropping down on the other side to the village of Palestina de Los Altos. Beyond this it weaves through a U-shaped valley to the twin towns of **San Marcos** and **San Pedro Sacatepéquez**. These towns form the core of the country's westernmost department that once served as a major trade route. There's little to detain you in either place, but they make useful bases for a trip into the mountainous countryside to the north.

San Pedro Sacatepéquez and San Marcos

SAN PEDRO SACATEPÉQUEZ is the larger and busier of the two towns, a bustling and unattractive commercial centre with a huge plaza that's the scene of a market on Thursday and Sunday. In days gone by this was a Maya settlement, famed for its brilliant yellow weaving, in which silk was used. Over the years the town has been singled out for some highly questionable praise: in 1543 the king of Spain, Carlos V, granted the headmen special privileges as thanks for their assistance during the Conquest, and in 1876 the town was honoured by President Rufino Barrios, who with a stroke of his pen raised the status of the people from Indians to ladinos.

A dual carriageway road connects San Pedro with its sister town of **SAN MARCOS**, 2km west. Along the way, a long-running dispute about the precise boundary between the two towns has been solved by the construction of the departmental headquarters at **La Unión**, halfway between the two. The building, known as the **Palacio Maya**, is an outlandish and bizarre piece of architecture that goes some way to compensate for the otherwise unrelenting blandness of the two towns. The structure itself is relatively sober, but its facade is covered in imitation Maya carvings. Elaborate decorative friezes run around the sides, two great roaring jaguars guard the entrance, and above the main doors is a fantastic clock with Maya numerals and snake hands. A few kilometres away there's a spring-fed **swimming pool**, where you can while away an hour or two: to get there walk from the plaza in San Pedro down 5 Calle in the direction of San Marcos, and turn left in front of the Templo de Candelero along 2 Avenida. Follow this road through one valley and down into a second, where you take the left turn to the bottom.

The pool – marked simply *Agua Tibia* – is open from 6am to 6pm; a small entrance fee is charged.

San Marcos, officially the capital of the department, once stood proud and important on the main route to Mexico, but these days the focus of trade has shifted south and articulated lorries roar along the coastal highway instead.

Practicalities

The best **places to stay** are in San Marcos. *Hotel Fairmont*, 10 C 8–74 (Ⓣ7760 4893; ❷), has clean, plain rooms; while *Hotel Pérez*, 9 C 2–25 (Ⓣ7760 1007; ❸), is a dignified and longstanding establishment with en-suite rooms and a restaurant.

Both towns have their fair share of cheap **comedores**, but San Pedro boasts real Italian food, too, thanks to *La Cueva de los Faraones*, at 5 C 1–11. Banrural, at 8 Av 7-43 in San Marcos, has a 5B ATM which accepts Visa and MasterCard; you can cash travellers' cheques here, too.

Second-class **buses** run every 30 minutes from Quetzaltenango to San Marcos via San Pedro (1hr 30min) from 5am until 5pm. Marquensita pullmans go direct from San Marcos to Guatemala City, passing through the plaza in San Pedro eight times daily from 2.30am until 4pm.

To Tacaná and the high country

Some magnificent high country lies northwest of San Pedro, strung up between the Tajumulco and Tacaná volcanoes and forming an extension of the Mexican Sierra Madre. A rough dirt road runs through these mountains, connecting a series of isolated villages which lie exposed in the frosty heights.

Leaving San Pedro to the north, the road climbs steeply, winding up through thick pine forests and emerging onto a high, grassy plateau. Here it crosses a great boggy expanse to skirt around the edge of **Volcán Tajumulco**, whose 4220-metre peak is the highest in Central America. It's best climbed from the roadside hamlet of **Tuichán** (the exact drop-off point is called Llana de la Guardia) from where it's about five hours to the summit. It's not a particularly hard climb as long as you're **acclimatized** to the altitude – the risk of sickness is a serious concern at this height. Quetzaltrekkers and Adrenalina Tours, both in Quetzaltenango, conduct guided trips up Tajumulco. Skies are clearest between September and February.

Up here the land is sparsely inhabited, dotted with adobe houses and flocks of sheep and goats. The rocky ridges are barren and the trees twisted by the cold. The air is thin and what little breath you have left is regularly taken away by the astonishing views which – except when consumed in the frequent mist and cloud – open up at every turn. After Tuichán the village of **Ixchiguán**, on an exposed hillside at 3050m, is the first place of any size, surrounded by bleak rounded hills and in the shadow of the two towering volcanic cones. Buses generally stop in Ixchiguán for lunch, giving you a chance to stretch your legs and thaw out with a steaming bowl of *caldo*.

Moving on, the road climbs to the **Cumbre De Cotzil**, a spectacular pass which reaches some 3400m and marks one of the highest points on any road in Central America. From here on it's downhill all the way to the scruffy village of **TACANÁ**, a flourishing trading centre that signals the end of the road – 73km from San Marcos and less than 10km from the Mexican border. Up above the village, spanning the border, is **Volcán Tacaná** (4064m), which can be climbed from the village of Sibinal. It's technically active, but last erupted in 1855, so it should be safe enough. Unless you're setting out to climb one of the volcanoes, there's not much to do out this way; however, the bus ride alone, bruising though it is, offers some great scenery. Four **buses** a day leave the terminal in San Pedro for Tacaná, mainly in the late morning; some pick-ups also make the four-hour trip. There's also a bus service to Sibinal and Concepción Tutuapa – at similar times. In Tacaná, the *Hotel Pérez* (❶) is clean and very cheap, and the town has a couple of comedores.

Heading on from Tacaná, pick-ups provide links with Cuilco (from where there are regular buses to Huehuetenango) and to a remote crossing point on the Mexican border called Niquimiul (foreigners are not permitted to leave Guatemala here, though).

Towards the Mexican border

The main road through San Pedro continues west, through San Marcos and out of the valley. Here it starts the descent towards the Pacific plain, dropping steeply around endless hairpin bends and past acre after acre of coffee bushes. Along the way, the views towards the ocean are superb. Eventually, you reach the sweltering lowlands, passing through San Rafael and El Rodeo with their squalid shacks for plantation workers. About an hour and a half out of San Pedro, you arrive in **MALACATÁN**, a relatively sedate place by coastal standards. If you get stuck here on your way to or from the border, try the *Pensión Lucía*, on the plaza (Ⓣ7776 9415; ❷), or *Hotel Don Arturo*, 5 C & 7 Av (Ⓣ7776 9169; ❹), for somewhere more comfortable. Contrary to popular belief, there is no Mexican consulate in Malacatán, but if you need a bank, Bancafé has a Visa ATM and changes travellers' cheques.

Buses between Malacatán and San Marcos run about every 45min from 5am to 5pm. Trucks and minibuses leave Malacatán for the border at Talismán every 30min, while plenty of pullmans pass through the town on their way between the border and the capital. (See Chapter 3 for more details on this border crossing.)

Huehuetenango and the Cuchumatanes

The **department of Huehuetenango**, slotted into the northwest corner of the highlands, is a wildly beautiful part of the country that's bypassed by the majority of visitors. The area is dominated by the mountains of the **Cuchumatanes** but also includes a limestone plateau in the west and a strip of dense jungle to the north. With adequate time and a sense of adventure, this can be one of the most rewarding and spectacular parts of the country to explore.

Travelling along the Carretera Interamericana, which runs to the Mexican border, you can only get a peripheral sense of the isolated nature of this massive landscape. With more time and energy to spare, a trip into the mountains to **Todos Santos Cuchumatán**, or even all the way out to **San Mateo Ixtatán**, reveals an exceptional wealth of Maya culture. It's a world of jagged peaks and deep-cut valleys, where Spanish is definitely the second language, and where women rigidly adhere to traditional costume. Heavily populated before the Conquest, the area has pre-Columbian ruins scattered throughout the hills, with the largest at **Zaculeu**, immediately outside **Huehuetenango**, a surprisingly lively town with good budget hotels and some decent restaurants, cafés and bars.

Despite the initial devastation, the arrival of the Spanish had surprisingly little impact in these highlands, with some of the communities remaining amongst the most traditional in Guatemala. A visit to these mountain villages, either for a market or fiesta (and there are plenty of both), offers an ideal opportunity to see Maya life at close quarters.

Heading on from Huehuetenango you can be at the **Mexican border** in an hour and a half, reach Guatemala City in five or six hours, or use the back roads to travel across the highlands through **Aguacatán** towards Sacapulas, Nebaj or Cobán.

From Cuatro Caminos to Huehuetenango

Heading northwest from Cuatro Caminos, the Carretera Interamericana climbs steadily, stepping up out of the Xela valley onto a broad plateau thick with fields of wheat and dotted with houses. The only village along the way is **POLOGUÁ**, where there are a couple of comedores and a small weekly market; the fiesta here is from August 21 to 27.

Beyond Pologuá the road turns towards the north and leaves the corn-covered plateau, crossing the crest of the hills and skirting around the rim of a huge sweeping valley. To the east a superb view opens out across a sea of pine forests, the last stretch of more or less level land before the mountains to the north. Way out there in the middle is Santa Cruz del Quiché and closer to hand, buried in the trees, lies Momostenango. Once over the ridge the road winds its way down towards Huehuetenango. The first place inside the department is the ladino village of **Malacatancito**, where Mam warriors first challenged the advancing Spanish army in 1525.

Huehuetenango

Five kilometres from the highway, at the foot of the mighty Cuchumatanes, the town of **HUEHUETENANGO** is a departmental capital and the focus of trade and transport for a vast area of northwest Guatemala. Its atmosphere is provincial and pretty relaxed, though heavy traffic, much of which thunders through the town centre, reduces this appeal somewhat. The name is a Nahuatl word meaning "the place of the old people", and before the arrival of the Spanish it was the site of one of the residential suburbs that surrounded the Mam capital of Zaculeu. Under colonial rule it was a small regional centre with little to offer beyond a steady trickle of silver and a stretch or two of grazing land. The supply of silver dried up long ago, but other minerals are still mined, and coffee has been added to the area's produce.

Arrival and information

Like most Guatemalan towns, Huehuetenango, known simply as Huehue, is laid out on a grid pattern, with avenidas running one way and calles the other. It's fairly small so you shouldn't have any real problems finding your way around, particularly once you've located the Parque Central. A helpful **information**

office sits at 2 Calle, just off the plaza (Mon–Fri 8am–1pm & 2–5pm; ⓣ5539 1984, Ⓔglendy@asocuch.com), though you'll probably get better practical information from the staff at Adrenalina Tours (see "Listings").

All buses stop at the chaotic **bus terminal**, halfway between the Carretera Interamericana and town (Los Halcones pullmans continue on to their offices in town). Microbuses make continuous trips between the town centre and the bus terminal.

Chicken buses to Huehuetenango leave Guatemala City every thirty minutes or so and travel along the Carretera Interamericana. Fifteen daily pullman buses also run this route (see p.99 for details); all will stop and pick you up at the main junctions along the highway if they have room. Direct second-class services from Quetzaltenango are also available. Buses depart from the Mexican border at La Mesilla every thirty minutes until 7pm.

Accommodation

Huehuetenango has a pretty good range of **hotels**, but no luxury options. If you don't care to venture into town, you'll find a few mid-priced options located near the bus terminal.

Casa Blanca 7 Av 3–41 ⓣ & Ⓕ7769 0777. Modern mid-range hotel, with a good restaurant (open 6am–10pm) and spacious garden, built in colonial style. The rooms all have private bath and cable TV – try to book one upstairs as most of those below have little natural light. ❹

Hotel Central 5 Av 1–33 ⓣ7764 1202. Slightly scruffy budget hotel, with largish rooms in a creaking old wooden building, plus a fantastic comedor. No singles or private baths. ❶

Hotel Los Cumbres 4 C 6–83 ⓣ7764 1189. Clean, plain, smallish rooms, some with bathroom, grouped around a covered courtyard which doubles as a parking area. ❶–❷

Hotel Gobernador 4 Av 1–45 ⓣ & ⓕ7764 1197. One of the best budget hotels in town, run by a very friendly family, with decent-sized rooms, some with bath, and reliable hot showers. ❷

Hotel Guatemex south side of bus terminal ⓣ7769 0398. The best inexpensive hotel close to the terminal, this place has good rooms in three price categories – the higher up you go, the nicer they become. All have decent-quality beds and TV, and towels are provided. ❷–❸

Hotel Mary 2 C 3–52 ⓣ7764 1618, ⓕ7764 7412. This well-run hotel is centrally located and has small, bright and pleasant rooms – all have cable TV and most have a private shower. ❷–❸

Hotel Maya 3 Av 3–55 ⓣ7764 0369, ⓕ7764 1622. Good-value place, with very spacious if slightly plain rooms, all with TV and bathroom, plus parking. ❹

Hotel San Luis de la Sierra 2 C 7–00 ⓣ & ⓕ7764 1103. Attractive, modern hotel with en-suite rooms, all with cable TV and nice pine beds and tables; some have wonderful views of the mountains. There's ample parking and a fair restaurant. ❹

Hotel Zaculeu 5 Av 1–14 ⓣ7764 1086, ⓕ7764 1575. Something of an institution in Huehue, this long-running hotel has an in-house restaurant and rooms ranging from a bit musty in the old block to more spacious (and pricey) in the new one. All come with cable TV and private bath, however. ❹–❺

Todos Santos Inn 2 C 6–74 ⓣ7764 1241. A decent, friendly budget hotel, though the rooms (some with private bath) do vary in quality – those upstairs are bright and cheery, others less well presented. The shared bathrooms are clean, and there are cheap rates for single travellers. ❶–❷

The Town

Huehuetenango is a likeable if unremarkable provincial town, its character best expressed in the unhurried atmosphere of the attractive **plaza**, where shaded walkways are surrounded by grand administrative offices. Overlooking this square, perched above the pavements, are a shell-shaped bandstand, a clock tower and a grandiose Neoclassical church, a solid whitewashed structure with a facade that's crammed with Doric pillars and Grecian urns. In the middle of the plaza, there's a **relief map** of the department with flags marking the villages. The details are vague and the scale a bit warped, but it gives you an idea of the mass of rock that dominates the region, and the deep river valleys that slice into it.

If that all seems a bit sedate, wander over a few blocks to the **market** area, where the streets are crowded with traders from Mexico and campesinos from every corner of the department. Centred on 1 Avenida, this part of town is always alive with activity, its streets packed with people and littered with rotten vegetables.

Eating and drinking

Most of the better **restaurants** are either in the central area around the plaza, or a short walk to the southwest around 6 Calle (which also acts as a focal point for nightlife in Huehue). *Mi Tierra*, on 4 Calle, is always a safe, if hardly lively, choice for a drink; while *Bob's Bar* on 2 Calle attracts a young crowd and has pool tables and a sports-bar feel. *Disco Cactus* on 6 Calle is the most happening **club** in town, with Latin chart tunes, a little house and some salsa, too.

El Boquerón 6 Av 6–37. Simple little place that's great for roasted chicken, grilled *lomito*, and Mexican-style dishes such as fajitas and *rellenitos*.

La Cabaña del Café 2 C 6–50. Logwood café with an excellent range of coffees, including cappuccino, and sandwiches (there's even roast beef), plus great cakes.

Café Gallery Cake 3 C & 6 Av. Pleasant, civilized café with flavoured coffee, a good breakfast, cakes and pancakes as well as a set lunch. Closes at 8pm and all day Sun.

Café Jardín 3 C and 6 Av. Cheap, friendly place with good Guatemalan-style *comida típica*, a US$2.50 set lunch, snacks and breakfast.

El Comal 6 C 6–35. Agreeable restaurant in a covered courtyard setting with *carne asada*, *caldos* and Mexican food – the tasty tacos are US$0.40 each.

La Fonda de Don Juan 2 C 5–35. Large, vaguely Mediterranean-looking restaurant with gingham tablecloths, though the pizza, pasta and burgers are a bit overpriced and portions could be bigger. There's a daily set lunch here, too, for US$2.75.

Grill Parrilladas 6 C. A young local crowd hits this large, fairly pricey, bustling restaurant for its good grilled meat dishes, pasta (try the *fettuccini tres quesos*), salads, *ceviche* and *mariscos*.

Mi Tierra 4 C 6–46. Great little café-restaurant, set in a covered patio with a welcoming atmosphere and a menu offering plenty of choice, including *papas fritas*, fajitas, plus grilled chicken and pork mains. It also serves proper coffee and has a no-smoking section, Internet facilities and a good notice board.

Listings

Banks Banco G&T Continental on the plaza has an ATM which accepts Visa and MasterCard. Banco Industrial on 6 Av has a Visa/Plus network ATM.

Immigration Inside the Farmacia el Cid on the plaza's south side.

Internet Génesis on 2 Calle and Interhuehue on 3 Calle both charge around US$1.25 an hour.

Language schools Huehuetenango is a good place to learn Spanish as you don't rub shoulders with many other gringos. Academia de Español Xinabajul, 6 Av 0–69 (Ⓣ & Ⓕ7764 1518, Ⓔacademiaxinabajul@hotmail.com), receives positive reports from students. Abesaida Guevara de López gives good private lessons: call Ⓣ7764 2917.

Moving on from Huehuetenango

Virtually all transport leaves from the main **bus terminal** on the edge of town. Microbuses connect the town centre with the terminal, leaving from 6 Av, between 2 and 3 C. The terminal is an outdoor affair, dusty and scruffy but pretty well laid out. Each bus company has its own office, at which you should ask for the latest schedule as the timetables painted on the walls are often wrong. Also note that it is standard practice, even for second-class buses, to buy your ticket in advance from the relevant office. Generally, buses for all destinations leave more frequently in the mornings.

Buses to the **Mexican border** (1hr 45min) leave every half-hour from 5am onwards, with the last departure at 6pm. Buses also depart every thirty minutes from 4am to 6pm to **Quetzaltenango** (2hr). Three companies operate pullman buses to **Guatemala City** (6hr): Los Halcones, 7 Av 3–62 (Ⓣ7764 2251), have buses at 4.30am, 7am and 2pm, which depart from their own terminal; Transportes Velásquez and Rápidos Zacaleu together have twelve departures from the main terminal. Second-class buses to Guatemala City also leave from the main bus terminal every thirty minutes. If you want to go to **Antigua**, take a capital-bound bus and change at Chimaltenango; for **Lake Atitlán** or Chichicastenango change at Los Encuentros.

Heading north into the Cuchumatanes mountains, some buses to Todos Santos (7 daily; 2hr 30min) continue on to San Martín and Jacaltenango. Several companies offer buses for Barillas (8 daily; 6hr), all via Soloma and San Mateo Ixtatán; four daily buses also run to San Miguel Acatán and San Rafael La Independencia. Buses to all the above destinations stop beside El Calvario church on the western outskirts of Huehue, though you may not get a seat if you alight here. Meanwhile, Nentón (4hr) and Gracias a Dios (5hr 30min) are served by three daily buses, and Yalambojoch by two daily buses (5hr 30min).

To the west, five daily buses head for isolated Cuilco (3–4hr), while hourly buses travel **east** to Aguacatán (1hr). Recently, only one daily bus has been making the trip to Sacapulas (at 2.30pm) – check schedules as the road has been under construction – although pick-ups regularly run from Aguacatán to Sacapulas.

Finally, pick-ups to **San Juan Atitán** leave from outside the *Cafetería Tucaná*, 2 C 2–15, the last at about 4pm; and buses to **Zaculeu ruins** from the corner of 2 Calle and 7 Avenida.

Laundry Turismundo Commercial Centre, 3 Av 0–15.
Mexican consulate Inside the Farmacia el Cid on the plaza's south side (ⓣ7764 1366).
Post office 2 C 3–54 (Mon–Fri 8am–4.30pm).
Shopping Superb weaving is produced throughout the department and can be bought in the market or at Artesanías Ixquil – located at 1 C 1–115, a fifteen-minute walk north of the plaza up 6 Av to the top of a hill, then on the right – where both the prices and quality are high. If you have the time and interest, travel to the villages and buy direct from the producers.
Supermarket Paiz, southwest of the town centre at 6 C and 10 Av.
Telephone Telgua, next to the post office at 2 C 3–54 (daily 7am–10pm), though it's much cheaper to call abroad (and nationally) from the phone stalls on the plaza's west side.
Tour operator Adrenalina Tours, next to *Mi Tierra* at 4 C 6–38 (ⓣ7736 2615, ⓦwww.adrenalinatours.com), has an excellent selection of tours in the Huehue department, including trips to remote Laguna Yolnabaj on the border with Mexico. Speak to them about shuttle buses to Quetzaltenango and Todos Santos as well.

Zaculeu

A few kilometres to the west of Huehuetenango are the ruins of **ZACULEU**, capital of the **Mam**, who were one of the principal pre-conquest highland tribes. The site (daily 8am–6pm; US$3.20) includes several large temples, plazas and a ball court, but unfortunately it was restored pretty unsubtly by a latter-day colonial power, the United Fruit Company, in 1946 and 1947. The walls and surfaces were levelled off with a layer of thick white plaster, leaving them stark and undecorated. There are no roof-combs, carvings or stucco mouldings, and only in a few places does the original stonework show through. Even so, the site does have a peculiar atmosphere of its own and is worth a look; surrounded by trees and neatly mown grass, with fantastic views of the mountains, it's an excellent spot for a picnic.

Not all that much is known about the early history of Zaculeu as no Mam records survived the Conquest. The site is thought to have been a religious and administrative centre housing the elite, with the bulk of the population living in small surrounding settlements or scattered in the hills. Zaculeu was the hub of a large area of Mam-speakers, its boundaries reaching into the mountains as far as Todos Santos and along the Selegua and Cuilco valleys, an area throughout which Mam remains the dominant language.

To put together a history of the site means relying on the records of the K'iche', a more powerful neighbouring tribe. According to their mythology, the K'iche' conquered most of the other highland tribes, including the Mam, some time between 1400 and 1475: the Popol Vuh tells that "our grandfathers and fathers cast them out when they inserted themselves among the Mam of Zakiulew". The K'iche' maintained their authority under the rule of the leader Quicab, but following his death in 1475 the subjugated tribes began to break away from the fold. As a part of this trend, the Mam managed to reassert their independence, but no sooner had they escaped the clutches of one expansionist empire, than the **Spanish** arrived with a yet more brutal alternative.

At first the Spaniards devoted themselves to conquering the K'iche', still the dominant force in the highlands. They then turned their attention to the Mam, especially after being told by Sequechul, leader of the K'iche', that a plan to burn the Spanish army in Utatlán had been suggested to his father by **Caibal Balam**, king of the Mam. In response, Spanish leader Pedro de Alvarado dispatched an army under the command of his brother Gonzalo to mete out punishment. The Spanish were met by about five thousand Mam warriors near the present-day-village of Malacatancito, and promptly set about a massacre.

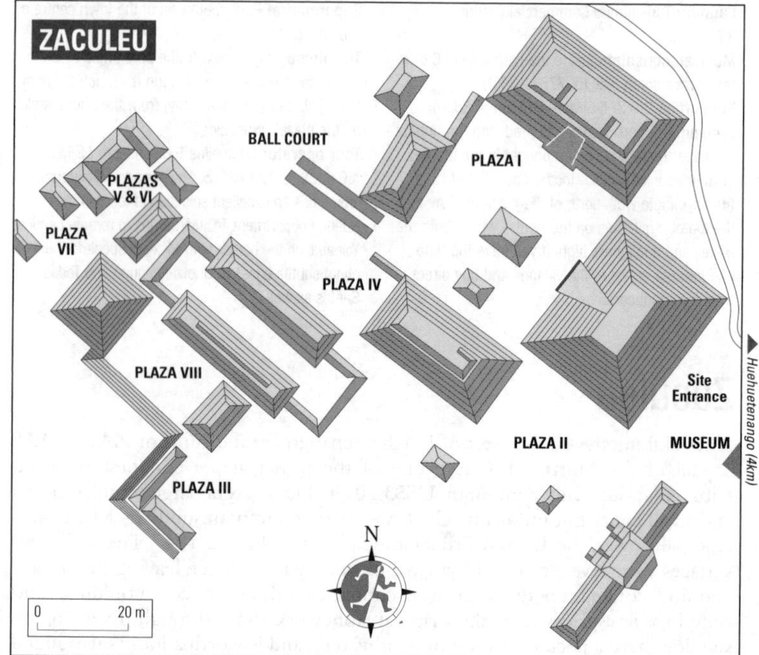

Seeing that his troops were no match for the Spanish, Caibal Balam withdrew them to the safety of Zaculeu, where they were protected on three sides by deep ravines and on the other by a series of walls and ditches. The Spanish army settled outside the city, preparing themselves for a lengthy siege, while Gonzalo offered the Maya a simple choice – become Christians "peacefully" or face "death and destruction".

Attracted by neither option they struggled to hold out against the invading force. At one stage a relief army of eight thousand arrived from the mountains, but again they were unable to ruffle Gonzalo's well-disciplined ranks. Finally, after about six weeks under siege, his army starving to death, Caibal Balam surrendered to the Spanish. With the bitterest of ironies a bastardized version of his name has been adopted by one of Guatemala's crack army regiments – the "Kaibiles", who have been held responsible for numerous massacres during the 1970s and early 1980s.

Excavations at the site have unearthed hundreds of burials carried out in an unusual variety of ways; bodies were crammed into great urns, interred in vaults and even cremated. These burials, along with artefacts found at the site, including pyrite plaques and carved jade, have suggested links with Nebaj. There's a small **museum** on site (daily 8am–noon & 2–6pm) with examples of some of the burial techniques used and some interesting ceramics found during excavation.

To get to Zaculeu from Huehuetenango, take one of the buses to the "ruinas" that leave every thirty minutes from 7 Avenida between 2 and 3 calles.

Chiantla

The village of **CHIANTLA** is backed right up against the mountains, 5km to the north of Huehuetenango. The main point of interest here is the colonial church. Built by Dominican friars, the church is now the object of one of the country's largest pilgrimages, held annually on February 2 in honour of its image of the **Virgen del Rosario**. Legend has it that the image of the Virgin was given to the church by a Spaniard named Almengor, who owned a silver mine in the hills. Not only did it proceed to yield a fortune, but on his last visit to the mine, the entire thing caved in just after Almengor had surfaced – thus proving the power of the Virgin. She is also thought to be capable of healing the sick, and at any time of the year you'll see people who've travelled from all over Guatemala asking for her assistance. A mural inside the church depicts a rather ill-proportioned Spaniard watching over the Maya toiling in his mines, while on the wall opposite the Maya are shown discovering God. The precise connection between the two is left somewhat vague, but presumably the gap is bridged by the Virgin. This is also the town where Rigoberta Menchú attended convent school, according to her biographer David Stoll, though the Nobel Prize laureate has denied receiving a formal education.

Buses from Huehuetenango to Chiantla travel between the main bus terminal and Chiantla every fifteen minutes until 7.30pm. You can catch one as it passes the plaza in the town centre, or wait at the Calvario (by the junction of 1 Av and 1 C), instead of heading out to the terminal.

East to Aguacatán

To the east of Huehuetenango, a dirt road turns off at Chiantla to weave along the base of the Cuchumatanes, through dusty foothills, to **AGUACATÁN**. This small agricultural town is strung out along one main street, shaped entirely by the dip in which it's built. The village was created by Dominican friars, who in the early years of the Conquest merged several smaller settlements inhabited by two distinct peoples. The remains of one of the pre-conquest settlements can still be seen a couple of kilometres to the north, and minute differences of dress and dialect linger – indeed, the village remains loosely divided along pre-Columbian lines, with the Chalchitek to the east of the market and the Awakatek to the west. It used to be said that both people spoke Awakateko, but in the past few years it's been decided locally that the 18,000 or so people in this valley speak separate languages.

During the colonial period gold and silver were mined in the nearby hills, and the Maya are said to have made bricks of solid gold for the king of Spain, to persuade him to let them keep their lands. Today the town is steeped in tradition and the people survive by growing vegetables, including huge quantities of garlic, much of it for export.

Aguacatán's vast Sunday **market** gets under way on Saturday afternoon, when traders arrive early to claim the best sites. On Sunday morning a steady stream of people pours down the main street, cramming into the market and plaza, and soon spilling out into the surrounding area. Around noon the tide turns as the crowds start to drift back to their villages, with donkeys leading their drunken drivers. Despite the scale of the market, its atmosphere is subdued and the pace unhurried: for many it's as much a social event as a commercial one.

The traditional costume worn by the women of Aguacatán is unusually simple: their skirts are made of dark blue cotton and the *huipiles*, which hang loose, are decorated with bands of coloured ribbon on a plain white background. This plainness, though, is set off by the local speciality – the *cinta*, or headdress, an intricately embroidered piece of cloth combining blues, reds, yellows and greens, in which the women wrap their hair.

Aguacatán's other attraction is the source of the **Río San Juan**, which emerges from beneath a nearby hill, fresh and cool. The source itself, bubbling up beneath a small bush and then channelled by concrete walls, looks a bit disappointing to the uninitiated (though as far as cavers and geologists are concerned, it's a big one), but if you have an hour or two to kill it's a good place for a chilly swim – for which you have to pay a small fee. To get there walk east along the main street out of the village for about a kilometre, until you see a sign directing you down a track to the left. From the village it takes about twenty minutes.

Ten daily **buses** run from Huehuetenango to Aguacatán between 6am and 4pm (1hr). The best **place to stay** (and eat) is *Hotel y Restaurant San Juan* (Ⓣ7766 0110; ❶–❸), two blocks north of the plaza, where there are clean, tidy rooms with or without bath; they serve a mean *pollo dorado* here, too. The simple *Hospedaje Aguacateco* (Ⓣ7766 0180, ❶), in an ancient wooden building, is more basic and no rooms have private bath here. There's a branch of Banrural that will change travellers' cheques on the main street.

Beyond Aguacatán the road runs out along a ridge, with fantastic views stretching out below, eventually dropping down to the Chixoy valley and the riverside town of **Sacapulas** an hour and a half to the east. There's a lot of work being done on this road, which is steadily being improved and will eventually be paved, so expect delays. Only one bus a day heads this way, passing through Aguacatán at 3.30pm, though regular pick-ups make the trip, too.

The Cuchumatanes

The **Cuchumatanes**, rising to a frosty 3837m just to the north of Huehuetenango, are the largest non-volcanic peaks in Central America. The mountain chain rises from a limestone plateau close to the Mexican border, reaches its full height above Huehuetenango, and falls away gradually to the east, continuing through northern Quiché to form part of the highlands of Alta Verapaz. Appropriately enough, the name translates as "that which was brought together by great force", from the Mam words *cucuj*, to unite, and *matan*, superior force.

The mountain scenery is magnificent, ranging from wild, exposed craggy outcrops to lush, tranquil river valleys. The upper parts of the slopes are barren, scattered with boulders and shrivelled cypress trees, while the lower levels, by contrast, are richly fertile, cultivated with corn, coffee and some sugar. Between the peaks, in the deep-cut valleys, are hundreds of tiny villages, isolated by the enormity of the landscape. This area had little to entice the Spanish, and even at the best of times they only managed to exercise vague control, occasionally disrupting things with bouts of religious persecution or disease, but rarely maintaining a sustained presence. Following the initial impact of the Conquest, the people were, for the most part, left to revert to their old ways, and their traditions are still very much in evidence today, showing through in the fiestas, costumes and folk Catholicism.

More recently, the mountains were the scene of bitter fighting between the army and guerrilla forces. In the late 1970s and early 1980s, a wave of violence and terror swept across the area, sending thousands fleeing across the border to Mexico. These days things have calmed down, and most families have returned from exile and settled back to life in their old communities.

Travel here is slow and not easy – hotels and restaurants are basic at best and buses are packed – but if you can summon the energy it's an immensely rewarding area, offering a rare glimpse of Maya life and some of the country's finest fiestas and markets. The mountains are also ideal for hiking, particularly if you've had enough of struggling up volcanoes.

Where to go

The region offers a good chunk of Guatemala's most spectacular scenery and most absorbing villages. The most accessible of these, and the only one yet to receive a steady trickle of tourists, is **Todos Santos Cuchumatán**, which is also one of the most interesting. At any time of year, the town's Saturday market is well worth visiting, and its horse-race fiesta on November 1 has to be the most outrageous in Guatemala. From Todos Santos, you can walk over the hills to **San Juan Atitán**, or head on down the valley to **Jacaltenango**. Further into the mountains is the traditional village of **San Rafael La Independencia** from where you can explore more terrific mountain scenery and isolated Maya shrines. North of here, the village of **San Mateo Ixtatán**, which has markets on Thursday and Sunday, is another fascinating place with strong Maya cultural traditions. Beyond San Mateo is **Barillas**, a ladino town from where the jungle lowlands beyond are being colonized. One of the roughest roads in the country swings east from here to Playa Grande in Alta Verapaz.

From Huehuetenango to Paquix

Heading north out of Huehuetenango, the road to the Cuchumatanes – smoothly paved until Soloma – passes through Chiantla before beginning the long climb up the vertiginous south face of the mountain chain. Buses sway around endless switchbacks as they struggle up the arid hillside, but the views back across the valley are superb. If you're driving, you can stop at a *mirador* almost at the top of the 1000-metre ascent for a spectacular vista of the chain of volcanoes away to the south, including the near-flawless coned peak of the Volcán Santa María.

At the top of the slope, 1km after the *mirador*, a signposted dirt track heads off to the right to the *Unicórnio Azul* (Ⓣ5205 9328, Ⓦwww.unicornioazul.com; ❼), 6km from the paved road, a wonderful French-Guatemalan-owned ranch that organizes superb **horse-riding** excursions (a one-hour ride is included in the room rate). Accommodation is in attractive adobe-walled rooms and the food (breakfast is complimentary, dinner is US$7) is farm fresh and very filling. The same turn-off from the highway also heads east across the hills, via San Nicolás to Salquil Grande – this rough road can be impassable during heavy rains, but if you're in search of an unpredictable adventure it makes a spectacular trip.

Back on the paved road north, you enter into the *región andina* or *altiplano*, a desolate, grassy 3000-metre-high plateau suspended between the peaks that's strewn with boulders and usually wrapped in cloud in the late afternoon. At this altitude the air is cool, thin and fresh, the ground sometimes hard with frost and occasionally dusted with snow. About 10km beyond the *mirador* is the **Paquix junction**, where you'll find a couple of comedores, a gas station and the turn-off for Todos Santos.

Todos Santos Cuchumatán

Taking the western turn at the Paquix junction, a beautifully scenic road heads across the *altiplano* towards the tiny village of **La Ventosa**, perched between peaks at an altitude of around 3400m. From here a trail leads north to **La Torre** (at 3837m the highest non-volcanic mountain in Guatemala). It's around an hour and a half to the top, a stunning hike that passes one-room adobe farmsteads and then weaves through a pine and cedar tree forest before arriving at the summit, which is topped with antennae. On clear days (mornings are best) a jagged profile of distant volcanoes, from Tacaná to Tolimán, pierces the horizon to the south.

Continuing along the road west of La Ventosa, you'll soon start to see villagers wearing the traditional costume of Todos Santos, the men in their red-and-white-striped trousers, black woollen breeches and brilliantly embroidered shirt collars; the women in dark blue *cortes* and superbly intricate purple *huipiles*. Further down, at the bottom of the steep-sided, deep-cut river valley, is **TODOS SANTOS CUCHUMATÁN** itself – strung out along an elongated main street that's plotted with tiendas and some venerable old wooden houses. There's an excellent community **website** – Ⓦwww.stetson.edu/~rsitler/TodosSantos – dedicated to the Todos Santos region.

Todos Santos was originally put on the map by the writer Maud Oakes (whose *The Two Crosses of Todos Santos* was published in 1951) and photographer Hans Namuth, who has been recording the faces of the villagers for more than forty years. It's the endurance of tradition and the isolation that have made the village so attractive to visitors, and photographers in particular, though you should be wary of taking pictures of people – particularly of children. Rumours persist locally that some foreigners steal babies, and a tragic misunderstanding led to the death of a Japanese tourist here in 2000.

As usual, most of the people the village serves don't actually live here. The immediate population is around 2000, but there are perhaps ten times that many in the surrounding hills who are dependent on Todos Santos for trade, supplies and social life. This population is more than the land can support, and many travel to the coast, the capital and the US in search of work. One annual

Learning Spanish or Mam in Todos Santos

Todos Santos is home to two **language schools**. The well-regarded Hispano Maya (Ⓦwww.hispanomaya.org), opposite the *Hotelito Todos Santos*, offers Spanish instruction, while Nuevo Amanacer (Ⓔescuela_linguistica@yahoo.com), another good institution that's located about 150m along the main street west of the parque, teaches Spanish and Mam (it also offers weaving classes).

As Spanish is the second language here (after Mam), students only get a limited chance to practise it with their Mam-speaking host families. However, if you're looking for **cultural exchange**, you'll find the courses highly rewarding – especially if you don't mind pretty basic living conditions. Some students can be placed with ladino, Spanish-speaking families, though these houses are in short supply. Courses – which consist of four to five hours' instruction a day – plus accommodation and meals with a local family cost between US$100 and US$120 a week. A percentage of the profits from both schools goes to local development projects, and after-school activities such as hikes are also arranged.

A third school, the Proyecto Lingüístico de Español, has recently closed, and had developed a poor reputation for not supporting projects its directors, the Calmo brothers, had committed to.

event brings them all home, however – the famous November 1 **fiesta** for All Saints (*todos santos*). For three days the village is taken over by unrestrained drinking, dance and marimba music. The event opens with an all-day **horse race**, which starts out as a massive stampede. The riders tear up the course, thrashing their horses with live chickens, pink capes flowing out behind them. At either end of the run they take a drink before burning back again. As the day wears on some riders retire, collapse, or tie themselves on, leaving only the toughest to ride it out. On the second day, "The Day of the Dead", the action moves to the cemetery, with marimba bands and drink stalls setting up amongst the graves for a day of intense ritual that combines grief and celebration. By the end of the fiesta, the streets are littered with bodies and the jail packed with brawlers.

If you can't make it for the fiesta, the Saturday **market** also fills the village – although it's nothing like as riotous – and is well worth checking out. You may even catch some marimba the night before. During the week the village is fairly quiet, although it's a pleasant and peaceful place to spend some time and the surrounding scenery is unbelievably beautiful. Moreover, since the **language schools** opened in Todos Santos (see box, p.218), an embryonic "gringo scene" has developed, revolving around the schools' evening events. This is either a bonus or spoils the whole place – depending on your point of view.

Todos Santos is one of the few places where people are still said to use the 260-day *Tzolkin* calendar, which dates back to Maya times. Above the village – follow the track that goes up behind the *Comedor Katy* – is the small Maya site of **Tojcunanchén**, where you'll find a couple of grass-covered mounds sprouting pine trees. The site is occasionally used by *costumbristas* for the burning of incense and the ritual sacrifice of animals.

Practicalities

Seven daily **buses** leave Huehuetenango for Todos Santos (2hr 30min), the last at 3pm – get there early to mark your seat and buy a ticket. A couple of buses carry on through the village, heading further down the valley to Jacaltenango. Check the latest schedule at the Hispano Maya.

Of the places **to stay**, *Hospedaje Casa Familiar* (ⓣ7783 0656 or 7758 3283; ❷), just uphill from the plaza, has basic but clean wooden rooms, and the views from its terrace café are breathtaking. The good *Hotelito Todos Santos* (ⓣ7783 0603; ❷) – turn left just before you reach the *Casa Familiar* – has small clean rooms, a few with bathroom, friendly staff and a comedor. (Next door, a new hotel was being built that should be the most comfortable place in town.) Just uphill from the end of this street, *El Viajero* (❷) is a two-storey concrete structure with simple, fairly clean rooms, none with showers, and safe parking. Two other very cheap "hotels" in Todos Santos, *Hospedaje La Paz* and *Las Olguitas* (both ❶), are both extremely rough.

For a **meal**, very inexpensive and tasty *comida típica* is served at the *Comedor Kary*, just behind the church; a veggie meal goes for US$1. The hospitable *Comedor Katy* does tasty food too, though the gringo prices are too high here for such a basic joint. The food at the *Casa Familiar* is also a bit steep, though at least you have the best views in town from the terrace as compensation. Some 250m east of the plaza, the *Restaurant Chuchumajlaán* styles itself as the fanciest place in town, with steaks and pizza on the menu, though the food is only average. Last but certainly not least is *Rebecca's* bookstore, just east of the plaza, where the friendly American owner offers spaghetti, omelettes, stir-fries and sandwiches as well as tea and coffee, and the opportunity to browse lots of titles, particularly fiction.

You'll find a Banrural **bank** on the plaza which will change travellers' cheques. If you want to take a shirt, pair of trousers or *huipil* home with you, you'll find two excellent co-ops selling quality **weavings**: one is located next to the *Casa Familiar* and the other (named Cooperativa Estrella de Occidente) is just east of the plaza on the main street – there's a slow, pricey **Internet** place above the latter too. Most of the fun of Todos Santos is simply hanging out, but it would be a shame not to indulge in a traditional **smoke sauna** (*chuc*) while you're here. Most of the guest houses will prepare one for you.

Hikes from Todos Santos

The scenery around Todos Santos is some of the most spectacular in all Guatemala: there's no better place to leave the roads and set off on foot. In a day you can walk across to **San Juan Atitán**, and from there continue to the Carretera Interamericana or head on to **Santiago Chimaltenango**. From the highway you'll be able to catch a bus back to Huehuetenango for the night, and if you make it to Santiago you shouldn't have any problem finding somewhere to stay. Thursday is the best day to do this hike – if you set out early in the morning (around 6.30am) you can arrive in San Juan before the market there has finished.

Alternatively, you can walk down the valley from Todos Santos to **San Martín** and on to **Jacaltenango**, a route which offers superb views. There's a hotel in Jacaltenango, so you can stay the night and then catch a bus back to Huehuetenango in the morning.

Walking to San Juan Atitán

The village of **SAN JUAN ATITÁN** is around five hours from Todos Santos, across a beautiful, isolated valley. The walk follows the path that heads up behind the *Comedor Katy*, passes the ruins and climbs steeply above the village through endless muddy switchbacks, bearing gradually across to the right. You reach the top of the ridge after about an hour and, if the skies are clear, you'll be rewarded by an awesome view of the Tajumulco and Tacaná volcanoes. Here the path divides: to the right are the scattered remains of an ancient cloudforest and a lovely grassy valley, while straight ahead is the path to San Juan, dropping down past some huts, through beautiful forest. The route takes you up and down endless exhausting ridges, through lush forests, and over a total of five gushing streams, only the first and third of which are bridged.

Beside the first stream is an idyllic spot where a family have set up home – they may allow you to **camp** here, especially if you share your rations. Between the fourth and fifth streams – about three hours on from Todos Santos – you'll find an ideal place for a **picnic** overlooking the valley. Having crossed the thinly inhabited valley, the path swings up to the left and on to the top of another pass, about three and a half hours from Todos Santos. From here you can see the village of San Juan, strung out along the steep hillside in a long thin line, though it is still more than an hour's walk away. To head down into the village follow one of the left-hand trails that goes out along the hillside and then drops down amongst the houses. There are several paths to choose from – all cross a series of deep ravines before emerging onto the main track that runs through the village.

Built on treacherously unstable land, San Juan is regularly hit by landslides that sweep whole houses into the valley below. The government has proposed that the entire village be moved, but the people have so far resisted this idea. It's an intensely traditional place: all the men wear dark-brown woolen *capixayes* (a kind of knee-length poncho) over a scarlet shirt, held in place by a sash, and plain white trousers. The high-backed sandals worn here are a style depicted in ancient Maya carving – they are also worn in some of the villages around San Cristóbal de las Casas in Chiapas, Mexico.

Like most of these mountain villages, San Juan is a pretty quiet place, active only on market days, Monday and Thursday. The central square has a giant palm tree and a pretty garden, and from the marketplace, below the health centre, there are spectacular views across the valley.

If you want to **stay**, the *Hospedaje San Diego* (❶), on the hill above the plaza, makes a very basic but friendly place to rest, and the family may cook you supper on request. Alternatively, there's the *Hospedaje Jímenez* (❶), beside the church. For **food**, the small comedor beneath the *San Diego* serves reasonable meals, but watch out for the fearsome *picante* sauce. Pick-ups to Huehuetenango leave every couple of hours or so from 6am (1hr). From Huehuetenango, the pick-ups for San Juan leave from outside the *Cafetería Tucaná*, 2 C 2–15, the last at about 4pm. Get there early for a space. In this direction the journey can take a little longer.

On to Santiago Chimaltenango

SANTIAGO CHIMALTENANGO, which everyone in the region simply calls "Chimbal", makes a good alternative destination. If you want to go straight here from Todos Santos, turn right when you reach the top of the pass overlooking San Juan, head along the side of the hill and over another pass into a huge bowl-like valley. The village lies on the far side. If you're coming from San Juan, follow the track straight through the village and you'll come to the same pass in just over an hour. From the top of the pass, follow the main track down into the valley as it bears around to the right, towards the village – about one and a half hours from the top. Although it's not as attractive as some of the other villages of the region, Chimbal does retain some character, with narrow cobbled streets and adobe houses juxtaposed with modern concrete structures. The women here wear terrific red *huipiles*, criss-crossed with white thread, and pile up their hair up into buns with slender lengths of scarlet cloth.

Pick-ups run down the valley through coffee plantations to the village of San Pedro Necta, and beyond to the Carretera Interamericana, or you can walk to the highway in two or three hours. *Mini Tienda La Benedición* (❶), below the market, is a very basic **place to stay** here.

From Todos Santos to San Martín and Jacaltenango

Heading down the valley from Todos Santos, the road arrives at the one-street village of **SAN MARTÍN**, a three-hour walk away. It is inhabited almost entirely by ladinos, but has a Friday market that attracts indigenous people from the land all around, including many from Todos Santos. A little beyond the village the road down the valley divides, with a right fork that leads 11km around the steep western edge of the Cuchumatanes. On a clear day there are spectacular views, reaching well into Mexico. At the end of the old road, on a rocky outcrop, is the poor and ragged village of **Concepción Huista** from where a road plunges to Jacaltenango, the final destination of two of the Todos Santos buses, which return from there to Huehuetenango at about 3am and 4am. You should be able to hitch a ride in a pick-up at other times however.

Perched on a plateau overlooking the limestone plain that stretches out across the Mexican border, **JACALTENANGO** is the heart of an area that was once very traditional, inhabited by a small tribe of Akateko speakers. Several notable books about Maya customs were researched here in the early twentieth century, including the classic *The Year Bearer's People* by Douglas Byers (for more on Maya religion and prayersayers, see box below). More recently, the village's most famous resident, Víctor Montejo, documented his experiences during the dark days of the civil war, when he worked here as a teacher, in his book *Testimony: Death of a Guatemalan Village* (for more about this and other tomes about Guatemala, see the Contexts section of this book).

Things have calmed down considerably since then, however, and in recent years the surrounding land has been planted with coffee, and waves of ladinos have swelled the population of the town. Today the place has a calm and fairly prosperous feel to it. The pick of several simple pensiones is the *Hospedaje Buen Samaritario* (❶); you'll find plenty of comedores along the side of the market, which is at its busiest on Sunday.

The town can also be reached by a branch route that leaves the Carretera Interamericana close to the Mexican border. Four daily **buses** run from Huehuetenango to Jacaltenango, the last departing at 5pm; the last bus leaves Jacal for Huehue at 2pm – though it's always good to check the timetable at the terminal.

The high road to Barillas

North of the Paquix junction (see p.217), a single road, paved until Soloma, runs across the mass of the Cuchumatanes, crossing the exposed central plateau and snaking across vast valleys before finally dropping into the more temperate coffee

The Maya priests of the Cuchumatanes

The high peaks and rugged terrain of the Cuchumatanes guard one of the country's most traditional Maya cultures. Ethnographer Krystyna Deuss, author of a forthcoming book on the region and its unique Maya customs, has been studying rituals in these remote communities for more than twenty years, focusing her attention on the prayersayers, who occupy a position parallel to that of local priests. Here she explains their role and some of the key rituals surrounding their office.

Some of the purest **Maya rituals** today can be found among the Q'anjob'al of the northwestern Cuchumatanes. The office of **alcalde resador** (chief prayersayer) still exists here and the 365-day *Haab* calendar is used in conjunction with the 260-day *Tzolkin*. The former ends with the five days of *Oyeb' ku'*, when adult souls leave the body; the return of the souls on the fifth day brings in the new year. As this always falls on a day of *Watan*, *Lambat*, *Ben* or *Chinax*, these four day lords are referred to as the "Year Bearers" or "Chiefs". Depending on the community, the *Haab* year begins either at the end of February or the beginning of March, coinciding with the corn planting season.

The duty of the *alcalde resador* is to protect his village from evil and ensure a good harvest by praying for rain at planting time and for protection against wind, pests and disease while the corn is maturing. His year of office – during which he and his wife must remain celibate – begins on January 1, the day all the voluntary municipal officials change; in the towns of Santa Eulalia, Soloma and San Miguel Acatán where traditions are particularly strong, he lives in a house which has been specially built for him. Traditionalists regularly visit to ask for prayers and leave gifts of corn, beans, candles and money. On the altar of the house stands the **ordenanza,** a chest that not only contains religious icons but also ancient village documents, a throwback to the time when religious and civil authorities worked as one. The chest now serves both as a symbol of authority and as a sacred object, and can only be opened by the *alcalde* country around Barillas. This magnificent highland area, one of the most isolated parts of Guatemala, encompasses a network of deeply traditional indigenous villages and three separate **linguistic zones**: between San Juan Ixcoy and Santa Eulalia, Q'anjob'al is spoken; around San Miguel Acatán, it's Acateko; and in the San Mateo Ixtatán region the language is Chuj.

The road to Barillas was something of a one-way street until the past few years, but new bridges across the mighty rivers of the Ixcán and road improvements have opened up an enticing, if challenging, route east into Alta Verapaz, and regular buses and pick-ups now connect Barillas with Playa Grande.

To San Juan Ixcoy

Beyond Paquix the road runs through a couple of magical valleys, where great grey boulders lie scattered among ancient-looking oak and cypress trees, their trunks gnarled by the bitter winds. A few families manage to survive the rigours of the altitude, collecting firewood and tending flocks of sheep. Sheep have been grazed here since they were introduced by the Spanish, who prized this wilderness as the best pasture in Central America, though lamb is very rare on the menus up here, or anywhere in Guatemala.

Continuing north the road gradually winds down off the plateau, emerging on the other side at the top of an incredibly steep valley. This northern side of the Cuchumatanes contains some of the most dramatic scenery in the entire country, and the road is certainly the most spine-chilling. Here the road clings to the hillside, cut out of the sheer rock face that drops hundreds of metres

resador, in private, once a year. The *resador*'s whole day is spent in prayer: at his home altar before the *ordenanza*, in church and at sacred village sites marked by crosses. Prayers for rain are often accompanied by the ritual sacrifice of turkeys whose blood is poured over the candles and incense destined to be burned at the sacred places the following day. These ceremonies are not open to the general public.

Festivals more in the public domain happen on January 1 when the incumbent *alcalde resador* hands over to his successor. In **Soloma** after an all-night vigil the *ordenanza* is carried in procession to the middle of the market square and put on a makeshift altar under a pine arch. When the incoming group arrives there are prayers and ritual drinking, and they receive their wooden staffs of office; after this, the outgoing *alcalde resador* (usually a man in his sixties or seventies) is free to leave for his own home. The new prayersayer's group stays in the marketplace, collecting alms and drinking until 3pm, when they carry the *ordenanza* back to the official residence in a somewhat erratic procession. Notwithstanding a further night of vigil and ceremonial drinking, at 7am the following morning the *alcalde resador* sets out on his first prayer-round to the sacred mountains overlooking the town.

In **San Juan Ixcoy** the year-end ceremonies differ in that the new *resador* is not appointed in advance. Here the outgoing group carries the *ordenanza* to a small chapel outside the church on the night of the 31st and leaves it in the care of a committee of traditionalists. The usual all-night vigil with prayers, ritual drinking and collecting alms continues throughout the following day while everyone waits anxiously for a candidate to turn up. As the office of *resador* is not only arduous, and with dwindling support from the community, also expensive, the post is not always filled on January 1. The *ordenanza* sometimes stays locked in the chapel for several days before a volunteer (usually an ex-prayersayer) takes on the office again rather than let the *ordenanza* and the tradition be abandoned.

–Krystyna Deuss, the Guatemalan Maya Centre, London

to the valley floor. On your right, as the road plunges in altitude, are the two huge incisor-shaped rocky outcrops, known locally as the **Piedras de Captzín**, which are sacred to the Q'anjob'al Maya of these parts.

The first village reached by the road is **SAN JUAN IXCOY**, an apple-growing centre drawn out along the valley floor. There's no particular reason for breaking the journey here, but if you do the basic *Hotel Captzín de Tomas* (☎7780 6152; ❶) has invigoratingly hot showers, and the *Comedor El Viajero* two doors down serves up cheap meals. In season, around the end of August, passing buses are besieged by an army of fruit sellers. This innocent-looking village has a past marked by violence. On the night of July 17, 1898, following a dispute about pay, the Maya of San Juan murdered the local labour contractor, and in a desperate bid to keep the crime secret they slaughtered all but one of the village's ladino population. The authorities responded mercilessly, killing about ten Maya for the life of every ladino. In local mythology the revolt is known as *la degollación*, the beheading.

There are twelve daily **buses** between Huehuetenango and San Juan Ixcoy (2hr 45min).

Soloma

Over another range of hills, and down in the next valley, is the town of **SOLOMA**, the largest, busiest and richest of the settlements in the northern Cuchumatanes. Its flat valley floor was once the bed of a lake, and the steep hillsides still come sliding down at every earthquake or cloudburst. Soloma translates (from Q'anjob'al, the dominant language on this side of the mountains) as "without security", and its history is blackened by disaster; it was destroyed by earthquakes in 1773 and 1902, half burnt down in 1884, and decimated by smallpox in 1885. The long white *huipiles* worn by the women of Soloma are similar to those of San Mateo Ixtatán and the Lacandones, and are probably as close as any in the country to the style worn before the Conquest. These days they are usually donned only for the **market** on Thursday and Sunday, by far the best time to visit, though there are always a few stalls to browse here anyway.

About three hours from Huehuetenango, Soloma makes a good spot to break the trip and has several **places to stay**. The best just-above-budget place is the clean, friendly *Hotel Estrella del Norte*, Diagonal 1 6–10 (☎5715 7636; ❷–❸), where all rooms have TV and most a bathroom. *Hotel Cáucaso*, a block north-east of the plaza (☎7810 6113; ❶), will just about do for a night, with grim, very basic rooms, all with showers. Moving up in quality, the towering *Hotel Don Chico* (☎7780 6087; ❸), north of the plaza, is the smartest place in town, and has underground parking. The comfortable, modern rooms, well priced for solo travellers, have tiled floors, private bathrooms and TV. The best **comedor** in town is here too, on the lower level of the same hotel, or try *Restaurante California* on the south side of the plaza. You can check your emails (slowly) at Impresiones Casteñada, one block west of the plaza, while Bancafé, one block north of the plaza, has a Visa ATM and will change travellers' cheques. **Buses** from Huehuetenango pass through Soloma about every hour on their way to Barillas and other villages to the north; the last bus leaves Huehue at 5pm.

Santa Eulalia

Leaving Soloma the paved road soon ends, and you continue over another range of hills to the large village of **SANTA EULALIA**, where highland religious ritual is adhered to very strongly. The church here is fascinating, a large, dusty pink-coloured building where the faithful assemble on their knees to recite prayers, and the air is thick with the smoke from hundreds of candles. Many then stop to burn incense at a separate Maya altar, wrapped in smoke, in front of the church. The clean and very cheap *Hotel y Restaurante Eulalense* (☎7765 9634; ❶), just below the church, has hot water and neat little rooms, while next door the *Cafetería Margol* serves up tasty *comida típica*.

Beyond Santa Eulalia is the Cruce Pett junction after which the Barillas road pushes on north through pastureland, skirting patches of pine forest, with exhilarating views west into Mexico. The sense of isolation is immense up on this beautiful 3000-metre-high plateau, and you'll barely see a soul except for shepherd boys and their goats.

San Rafael La Independencia, San Miguel Acatán and around

At the **Cruce Pett** junction, 5km north of Santa Eulalia, there are three comedores and a branch road that cuts off to the west, curving around the peaks of the Cuchumatanes to the village of **SAN RAFAEL LA INDEPENDENCIA**, 11km to the southwest. Perched on a west-facing outcrop with magnificent views down towards the Mexican border, this peaceful Akateko-speaking settlement amounts to not much more than a scattering of old timber houses and utilitarian concrete structures. Nevertheless, it makes an enjoyable place to spend a day or two, at the heart of a very traditional region where Maya customs remain very strongly observed. The Centro Cultural Maya Akateko (☎7779 7239), above the *municipalidad*, has a fascinating collection of old artefacts, including polychrome ceramics, obsidian flints, a two-metre blowpipe and some interesting photographs. The staff here can put you in touch with guides (Pedro Juan Méndez Martinez is recommended) who can lead you to the Maya ruins of **Tenam**, the Chimbam chapel, Xeyatak ceremonial centre, and the numerous sacred caves and altars that dot the hills around. A new yellow **hotel** is being built on the way in from Cruce Pett, or you can stay in basic rooms above the *Tienda San Andrés* (❶), a block downhill from the plaza, though there's no hot water here.

From San Rafael it's just 4km to the larger, much less attractive village of **SAN MIGUEL ACATÁN**, where you'll find a couple of hospedajes (❶), plenty of comedores, a Sunday market and a branch of Banrural that will change travellers' cheques. **Buses** leave Huehuetenango for San Miguel, via San Rafael, four times daily (4hr 30min). If you want to return via a different route, a narrow but reasonable dirt road heads southeast from San Miguel through a series of remote, steep-sided valleys and the tiny village of **Najab**, to join up with the Huehue–Barillas road just north of Soloma. You'll have to hitch a ride in a pick-up if you want to take this route, as there are no buses.

From San Miguel Acatán, a spectacular day-long **hike** takes you along the edge of the mountains to Jacaltenango. Setting out from San Miguel, cross the river and follow the trail that bears to the right as it climbs the hill opposite. At the fork, halfway up, take the higher path that crosses the ridge beside a small shelter. On the other side it drops down into the head of the next valley. Here you want to follow the path down the valley on the near side of the river, and through the narrow gorge to an ancient wooden bridge. Cross the river and climb up the other side of the valley, heading down towards the end of it as you go. The path that heads straight out of the valley runs to Nentón, and the other path, up and over the ridge to the left, heads towards **Jacaltenango**. Along the way there are stunning views of the rugged peaks of the southern Cuchumatanes and the great flat expanse that stretches into Mexico – on a clear day you can see the Lagunas de Montebello, a good 50km away, over the border. On the far side of the ridge, the path eventually drops down to Jacaltenango through the neighbouring village of San Marcos Huista: some eight or nine tough but worthwhile hours in all from San Miguel.

San Mateo Ixtatán

Back on the high road to Barillas, it's a further 24km from Cruce Pett to **SAN MATEO IXTATÁN**, the most traditional, and quite possibly the most interesting, of this string of villages. Its name derives from the Nahuatl for "abundance of salt", which is still a major industry in the communally owned mines around the village. Little more than a thin sprawl of wooden-tiled houses, the village tumbles down a steep east-facing hillside, occupying the ground between two plunging river valleys. The people here speak **Chuj** and form part of a Maya group who occupy the extreme northwest corner of the highlands and some of the jungle beyond; their territory borders that of the Lacandón, a jungle tribe never subjugated by the Spanish, who constantly harassed these villages in colonial times. The best time to visit, other than for the fiesta (September 17–21), is on a market day, Thursday or Sunday – during the rest of the week the village is virtually deserted.

Traditional dress is becoming less common, but the older women here still wear unusual and striking *huipiles*, long white gowns embroidered in brilliant reds, yellows and blues, radiating out from a star-like centre. You may also see men wearing short woollen poncho-like tunics called *capixayes*, often embroidered with flowers around the collar and quetzals on the back.

San Mateo's cream-coloured **church**, its wonky facade embellished with niches and the images of saints, is one of the most interesting in Guatemala, with a pagan character that barely offers a passing reference to conventional Catholicism. Smoke from a Maya altar attended by *costumbristas* drifts across the courtyard in front of the church, while inside devotees kneel on the bare earth of the nave clutching candles, the stone walls reverberating with the constant murmur of solemn incantations.

The best of the three very simple places to **stay** in San Mateo is *Hotel Ixtateco* (Ⓣ7756 6586; ❶), which has hot water. *Restaurante Wajxaklajunh*, above the police station, is clean and cheap. The **cybercafé** Wajxaklajunh.com, which charges US$0.90 per hour, is run by the development project Ixtatán Foundation (Ⓦwww.ixtatan.org), whose staff are a good source of information about the village and its traditions, as is their website. Eight daily **buses** leave Huehuetenango for San Mateo (5hr 15min). It's also possible to travel by pick-up from San Mateo northwest to the village of **Yalambojoch** in around two and a half hours (see p.231).

Below the village are the quite substantial unrestored Maya ruins of **Wajxaklajunh**, which enjoy a magical position overlooking the San Mateo valley and down to ridge after ridge of hills on the horizon to the east. Here you'll find several temples, including the pyramid-shaped structure known as Yolk'u, meaning "inside the warm place", a ball court and a couple of weathered stelae shaded by cypress trees.

Barillas and around

Beyond San Mateo the road drops steadily east to **BARILLAS**, an unlovely ladino frontier town 28km away in the relative warmth of the lowlands and devoted to coffee production. A lot of development projects are based here, but any cosmopolitan extraneous influence is negligible. At least *Hotel el Quetzal* (❷), bordering the plaza, is clean and friendly, and *Hotel Sol* (Ⓣ7870 2618; ❷) next to the bus station is also good; and there are several comedores in town.

There are eight daily buses to Barillas from Huehuetenango, passing through all the villages en route, and the journey takes six hours. There's also an airstrip here, so you may be able to hitch a ride on one of the missionary flights (three weekly; US$35) in a five-seater plane to Guatemala City.

About 18km to the north of the village (take the dirt road towards the village of Yolhuitz) is the beautiful hourglass-shaped **Laguna Maxbal**, which is ringed by forest – locals say it's possible to see a quetzal bird here some mornings. Heading west from Barillas, a very rough road penetrates a landscape of pastureland and patches of thick, uninhabited jungle known as the **Ixcán** – this terrain slopes down into the Usumacinta river basin. Regular picks-ups and one daily bus push through this near-forgotten corner of the country, covering the route from Barrillas to Playa Grande in five hours or more, depending on the state of the road.

West to the Mexican border

From Huehuetenango the Carretera Interamericana runs for 79km through the narrow Selegua valley to the Mexican border at **La Mesilla**. Travelling direct this takes less than two hours on one of the buses that thunder out of Huehuetenango every thirty minutes or so between 5am and 6pm. Along the way, just off the main road, are some interesting traditional villages, largely oblivious to the international highway that carves through their land. Most are best reached as day-trips out of Huehuetenango.

The first of these, 22km from Huehue, is **San Sebastián Huehuetenango**, a quiet little place barely 200m north of the highway. The village was the site of a pre-conquest centre, and of a settlement known as Toj'jol, which was swept away by the Río Selegua in 1891. Further on the road runs through a particularly narrow part of the valley known as **El Tapón**, "the cork", and past a turning for San Juan Atitán (12km) and another for San Rafael Petzal, 2km from the main road. Beyond this it passes roads that lead to Colotenango, Nentón and Jacaltenango.

You pass one last roadside village, La Democracia, before reaching the border at **LA MESILLA** where there's a bank and plenty of money changers. If you get stuck here, there's **accommodation** at the *Hotel Maricruz* (❷), which is clean, with private bathrooms and a restaurant, or at the slightly cheaper *Hospedaje Marisol* (❷). The two sets of customs and immigration are 3km apart; collective taxis (US$0.50) run between the immigration points, and on the Mexican side you can pick up buses from the border settlement of **Ciudad Cuauhtemoc** to **Comitán**, or even direct to **San Cristóbal de las Casas**. Heading into Guatemala, buses to Huehuetenango leave the border every thirty minutes (1hr 45min) until roughly 7pm; wherever you're aiming for in Guatemala, it's best to take the first bus to Huehue and change there.

Colotenango, San Ildefonso Ixtahuacán and Cuilco

The most important of the villages reached from the highway is **COLOTENANGO**, perched on a hillside 1km or so south from the main road. The municipality of Colotenango used to include San Rafael Petzal and San Ildefonso, until 1890 when they became villages in their own right. Ties are still strong, however, and the red *cortes* worn by the women of all three villages are almost identical. Colotenango remains the focal point for the smaller settlements,

Fiestas

The western highlands are the home of the traditional Guatemalan fiesta. Every village and town, however small, has its own saint's day, around which a fiesta is based that can last anything from a day to two weeks. All of these fiestas involve traditional dances that mix pre-Columbian moves with more modern Spanish styles, and each has its own signature event, whether it's a horse race or a firework spectacular.

January

3–8 El Tumbador, department of San Marcos
3–6 San Gaspar Ixchil, a tiny village on the road to Cuilco
9–15 Sibilia, main day 13th
10–16 Santa María Chiquimula, in honour of the Black Christ of Esquipulas
12–16 La Libertad
12–15 Chinique, a very traditional fiesta
12–16 Colomba
13–16 Nentón
15–17 San Antonio Ilotenango
18–20 San Sebastián Coatan
19–21 Santa Lucía La Reforma
19–24 Ixtahuacán
22–26 San Pablo La Laguna, main day 25th
23–27 San Pablo, department of San Marcos

February

Jan 28–Feb 2 Chiantla, main day 2nd
Jan 28–Feb 2 Jacaltenango
1–4 Cunén, main day 2nd
6–10 Patzité, El Quiché, main day 8th
8 San Juan Ostuncalco
8–13 Santa Eulalia, main day 8th
Varies Palestina de Los Altos, department of San Marcos, celebrating the first Friday in Lent

March

14–20 San José El Rodeo, main day 19th
19 San José Poaquil, near Chimaltenango
Varies Chajul and La Democracia, the second Friday in Lent marked by huge pilgrimages

Holy Week

Santiago Atitlán, Maximón paraded through the streets, usually on the Wednesday; San Cristóbal Tonicapán, the biggest processions in the Xela area

April

22–28 San Marcos, main day 25th
24 San Jorge La Laguna
25 San Marcos La Laguna
29–May 4 Barillas
30–May 4 La Esperanza
Varies Zacualpa and Aguacatán, fiestas to mark forty days from Holy Week

May

1–3 Cajola
6–10 Uspantán, main day 8th
8–10 Santa Cruz La Laguna

8–10 Santa Cruz Balanya, department of Chimaltenango
20 Patzún

June

12–14 San Antonio Palopó, Lago de Atitlán, main day 13th
12–14 San Antonio Huista
21–25 San Juan Ixcoy, north of Huehuetenango
21–25 Olintepeque, just north of Quetzaltenango
22–25 San Juan Cotzal, main day 24th
22–26 San Juan Atitán, main day 24th
23–26 San Juan La Laguna, main day 24th
24 Comalapa
24–30 San Pedro Sacatepéquez
26–30 Soloma, main day 29th
27–30 San Pedro Jocopilas
27–30 San Pedro La Laguna, main day 29th
28–30 Almolonga, main day 29th
Varies Corpus Christi celebrations, held throughout Guatemala in June, are particularly spectacular in Patzún

July

1–4 Santa María Visitación, near Sololá, main day 2nd
12–17 Huehuetenango
21–August 4 Momostenango, the 25th is a very important day in the Maya religious calendar, and the 1st is the main fiesta day
22–27 Tejutla, main day 25th
22–27 San Cristóbal Totonicapán, main day 25th
22–27 Chimaltenango, main day 26th
22–27 Patzicía, main day 27th
23–26 Malacatancito
23–27 Santiago Atitlán, main day 25th
25–27 Santa Ana Huista, main day 26th
29–31 Ixchiguan, main day 31st

August

1–4 Sacapulas, main day 4th
9–15 Joyabaj, main day 15th. Superb fiesta, traditional dances here include the *Palo Volador*
10–13 Santa Clara La Laguna, main day 12th
11–17 Sololá, main day 15th
12–15 Nebaj, main day 15th
12–15 Colotenango, main day 15th
12–18 Cantel, near Quetzaltenango, main day 15th
12–15 Tacaná, main day 15th
14–19 Santa Cruz del Quiché, main day 18th
18–25 San Bartolo, main day 24th
21–27 Pologuá
22–28 Salcajá, main day 25th
22–25 Sipacapa
27–30 Sibinal, main day 29th

September

12–18 Quetzaltenango, main day 15th
17–21 San Mateo Ixtatán, main day 21st

Fiestas *(contd...)*

21 San Mateo, west of Quetzaltenango
24–30 Totonicapán, main day 29th
25–30 San Miguel Acatán, main day 29th
26–Oct 5 Tecpán

October
1–6 San Francisco el Alto, main day 4th
2–6 Panajachel, main day 4th
15–20 San Lucas Tolimán, Lago de Atitlán, main day 18th
21–Nov 2 Todos Santos Cuchumatán, a long warm-up to the big day

November
1–2 Todos Santos Cuchumatán, a wild, alcohol-infused horse race on the 1st, with everyone heading to the cemetery on the 2nd for All Souls' Day
7–12 San Martín Jilotepeque, main day 11th
14–18 Malacatancito, main day 18th
23–26 Nahualá, main day 25th
22–26 Zunil, main day 25th
24–26 Santa Catarina Ixtahuacán, main day 25th
25 Santa Catarina Palopó, Lago de Atitlán
27–Dec 1 Cuilco, main day 28th
27–Dec 1 San Andrés Semetabaj, main day 30th
27–Dec 1 San Andrés Xecul, main day 30th

December
1–4 Santa Bárbara
5–8 Huehuetenango, main day 8th
5–8 Concepción Huista, main day 8th
7 The Burning of the Devil is celebrated in most highland towns with bonfires and men running around dressed as devils
7–9 Concepción
9–14 Malacatán
11–15 Santa Lucía Utatlán, main day 13th
14–21 Chichicastenango, very impressive fiesta, main day 21st
25–28 Chiché, main day 28th

and its Saturday market is the largest in the Selegua valley. From early Saturday morning the plaza is packed, and the paths that lead into the village are filled with a steady stream of traders, indigenous families, cattle, chickens, reluctant pigs and the inevitable drunks. Here you'll see people from all of the surrounding villages, most of them wearing traditional costume. The village is also worth visiting during Holy Week, when elaborate and violent re-enactments of Christ's Passion take place (the bravest of villagers takes the role of Judas, and is shown no mercy by the rest), and for its fiesta from August 12 to 15.

To get to Colotenango from Huehuetenango, take any **bus** heading towards the Mexican border and ask the driver to drop you at the village. They'll usually leave you on the main road just below, from where you have to cross the bridge and walk up the hill. The journey from Huehuetenango takes around 45 minutes.

On to San Ildefonso and Cuilco

Behind Colotenango a dirt road goes up over the hills and through a pass into the valley of the Río Cuilco. Here it runs high above the river along the top of a ridge, with beautiful views up the valley: below you can make out the tiny village of San Gaspar Ixchil, which consists of little more than a church and a graveyard.

Another few kilometres brings you to the larger village and mining centre of **SAN ILDEFONSO IXTAHUACÁN**. Similar in many ways to Colotenango, it has a large and traditional Maya population. In 1977 the place achieved a certain notoriety after its miners were locked out of the mine because they'd tried to form a union. In response to this they decided to walk the 260km to Guatemala City in order to put their case to the authorities. At the time this was a bold gesture of defiance and it captured the imagination of the entire nation. When they eventually arrived in the capital 100,000 people turned out to welcome them.

Beyond San Ildefonso the road slopes down towards the bottom of the valley and crosses the river before arriving at **CUILCO**, a sizable ladino town 36km from the Carretera Interamericana that marks the end of the road. The Mexican border is just 15km away, and the town maintains cross-border trade links both inside and outside the law. Beyond today's village are the ruins of an earlier settlement known as **Cuilco Viejo**. Cuilco has also earned itself something of a reputation for producing heroin, but anti-drug campaigns have stamped out a lot of poppy cultivation in recent years.

Buses run between Huehuetenango and Cuilco at 5am and 2pm, returning at 7am and 8.30am, so if you come out this way you'll probably end up having to **stay**: the *Hospedaje Osorio* (❶) is on the main street. Bizarre though it sounds, a vast new five-storey "tourist complex" is also under construction and should be open by the time you read this. If the roads are in reasonable condition, trucks and pick-ups run south from Cuilco to the mountain village of Tacaná, from where there is a regular bus service to San Pedro.

North to Nentón and Yalambojoch

A short distance before the border, from the roadside village of **Camoja Grande**, a road, paved in parts, leads off to the north, running parallel to the border. It heads across a dusty white limestone plateau to the village of **Nentón**, then continues up into the extreme northwest corner of the country, where there are a couple of wonderful natural attractions. The first of these is the startling **El Cimarrón** *cenote* (a sink hole in the limestone crust), a near-perfect cylindrical depression measuring about 500m wide and around 300m deep. Locals attest all sorts of legends to the *cenote*, and say that the bottom (which harbours a lake and dense forest) is unexplored. El Cimarrón is about 4km from the tiny village of **La Trinidad**, which is 35km north of Nentón.

East of La Trinidad, it's 9km along a dirt track to the larger village of **YALAMBOJOCH**, something of a transport hub for these parts, with two daily **buses** (both leaving in the early morning) for Huehue and pick-ups for San Mateo Ixtatán. It's also the jumping-off point for the spectacular cobalt blue waters of **Laguna Yolnabaj**, a large lake 5km to the north, that's also known as Laguna Brava. Locals, many of whom are *repatriados* (returned refugees from Mexico), have launched a reforestation programme around the lake, and successfully fought off American real-estate speculators (so far). Adrenalina Tours (see p.213), based in Huehuetenango, run trips to Laguna Yolnabaj.

The recent history of Yalambojoch is bound up with that of **Finca San Francisco**, a smaller village a further 3km to the east. In 1982 the army massacred around three hundred people here and the entire population of the surrounding area fled for their lives, crossing the border into Mexico. After more than a decade, people started to return, and today life in the region seems to have returned to normal. Finca San Francisco has a small Maya temple, and also a plaque commemorating those who died in the massacre.

Finally, there is a remote **border crossing** into Mexico at Gracias a Dios (5km northwest of La Trinidad), but according to officials only Guatemalans and Mexicans are permitted to cross. It's a ten-minute walk from Gracias a Dios to Carmixán in Mexico and bus services do connect. If you have an exit stamp, and you do make it over the border, head straight for Comitán and get your Mexican entry stamp there.

Travel details

Buses

An almost constant stream of buses plies the Carretera Interamericana – between roughly 8am and 6pm you should never have to wait more than twenty minutes for one – and the major towns of the western highlands are generally just off the highway. The main routes from these hubs are covered below, while other, more local schedules are provided in the relevant accounts throughout the chapter.

Chichicastenango to: Guatemala City (every 20min; 3hr); Quetzaltenango (10 daily; 2hr 30min); Santa Cruz del Quiché (every 20min; 30min).

Chimaltenango (the junction for Antigua) to: Antigua (every 20min; 40min); Guatemala City (every 20min; 1hr); Quetzaltenango (every 30min; 3hr).

Huehuetenango to: Aguacatán (10 daily; 1hr); Guatemala City (15 daily pullmans, plus half-hourly chicken buses, 6hr); La Mesilla (26 daily; 1hr 45min); Quetzaltenango (22 daily; 2hr); Todos Santos Cuchumatán (7 daily; 2hr 30min).

Panajachel to: Antigua (1 daily at 10.45am; 3hr); Chichicastenango (5 daily Thurs & Sun, 1–2 daily other days; 1hr 30min); Cocales (8 daily; 2hr); Guatemala City (10 daily; 3hr 30min); Quetzaltenango (6 daily, 2hr 30min).

Quetzaltenango to: Chichicastenango (10 daily; 2hr 30min); Guatemala City (19 pullmans, plus half-hourly chicken buses; 4hr); Huehuetenango (22 daily; 2hr); Momostenango (every 45min; 1hr 15min); Panajachel (6 daily; 2hr 30min); San Francisco el Alto (every 30min; 45min); San Pedro La Laguna (6 daily; 2hr 15min); Totonicapán (every 30min; 1hr); Santa Cruz del Quiché (10 daily; 3hr); Zunil (every 30min; 25min).

San Marcos to: Guatemala City (8 daily; 5hr 30min); Malacatán (hourly; 1hr 30min); Quetzaltenango (hourly; 1hr 30min).

Santa Cruz del Quiché to: Guatemala City, via Chichicastenango (every 20min; 3hr 30min); Joyabaj (hourly; 2hr 15min); Nebaj (7 daily; 2hr 45min); Quetzaltenango (10 daily; 3hr); Uspantán (7 daily; 3hr 30min).

3

The Pacific coast

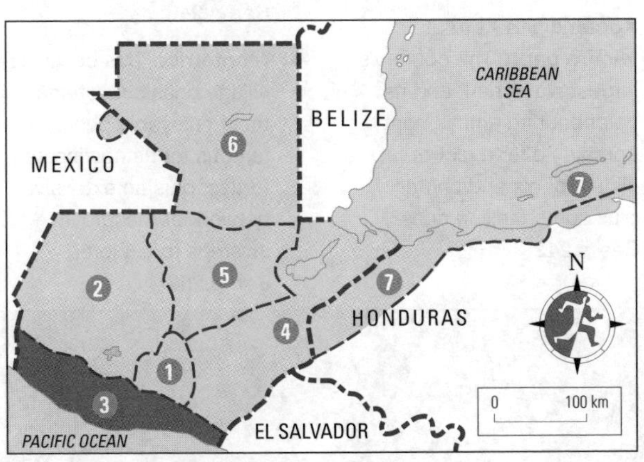

CHAPTER 3

Highlights

* **Tilapa** and **Tilapita** Palm trees line these fine, black-sand beaches, whose gently shelving profile makes this stretch one of the coast's best spots for a swim. See p.239

* **Takalik Abaj** This small but rewarding archeological site features well-executed Olmec and Maya carvings. See p.241

* **Xocomil** and **Xetulul leisure parks** The country's largest water park and its neighbouring amusement complex offer a glut of slides, pools and chutes, plus some thrilling rides. See p.242

* **Santa Lucía Cotzumalguapa** A rich assortment of Pipil-carved stone monuments lies scattered about the sugarcane fields near this Pacific-coast town. See p.245

* **La Democracia** A startling collection of pot-bellied carved stone sculptures, or "fat boys", inhabit this village's main plaza. See p.246

* **Monterrico** This oceanside village boasts Guatemala's most enjoyable beach, famous for its nesting sea turtles, plus an extensive network of mangrove swamps to explore. See p.250

△ Leatherback hatchling

3

The Pacific coast

A chain of volcanoes divides the cool air of the mountains from a sweltering strip of low-lying, tropical, ladino-populated land, some 300km long and 50km wide. Usually known simply as **La Costa**, this fairly featureless yet supremely fertile coastal plain – once swamp, forest and savannah – is today a land of vast fincas, dull commerce-driven towns and ramshackle seaside resorts scattered along an unrelentingly straight, black-sand shoreline.

Prior to the arrival of the Spanish, the Pacific coast was as rich in wildlife as the Petén, while several Mesoamerican cultures once flourished in the region, leaving some important archeological sites. Today it's large-scale agriculture – sugarcane, palm oil, cotton and rubber plantations – that dominates and accounts for a substantial proportion of the country's exports. Only in some isolated sections, particularly in the extensive mangrove swamps, can you still get a sense of the maze of tropical vegetation that once covered this area. One place is the **Monterrico Reserve**, where the unique coastal environment is protected, offering a refuge to sea turtles, iguanas, crocodiles and an abundance of bird life.

Many of the region's archeological sites have been either reclaimed by the jungle or swallowed up by agribusiness, though you can glimpse the extraordinary art of the Pipil – the main tribal group indigenous to the area at the time of the Conquest – around the town of Santa Lucía Cotzumalguapa. Nowhere near as spectacular as the sites of the Petén, these carvings are almost lost in fields of sugarcane, though some are still regularly used for religious rituals. The one site in the area that comes close to ranking with those elsewhere in the country is **Takalik Abaj**, outside Retalhuleu. For a fascinating insight into the Preclassic era of the Pacific littoral, the ruins are well worth a visit as a detour on your way to or from Mexico, or as a day-trip from Xela or Retalhuleu. Much excavation is yet to be done, but the structures bear significant Maya and Olmec influence.

The main attraction of the region should be the **coastline**, though sadly much of it is mosquito-ridden and dotted with scruffy palm huts, pig pens and garbage, with a dangerous undertow. The hotels are some of the country's worst, so if you're desperate for a quick dip and a fresh shrimp feast, you're usually better off taking a day-trip from the capital or from Quetzaltenango.

Generally, wave conditions are much better in El Salvador and Mexico, but a few hardy souls are attempting to create a **surf scene** around the village of **Sipacate**, though accommodation and facilities are very basic at the moment. The one place on the Pacific coast that is definitely worth investigating is the nature reserve of **Monterrico**, which harbours one of the country's finest beaches, with a superb stretch of clear, clean sand.

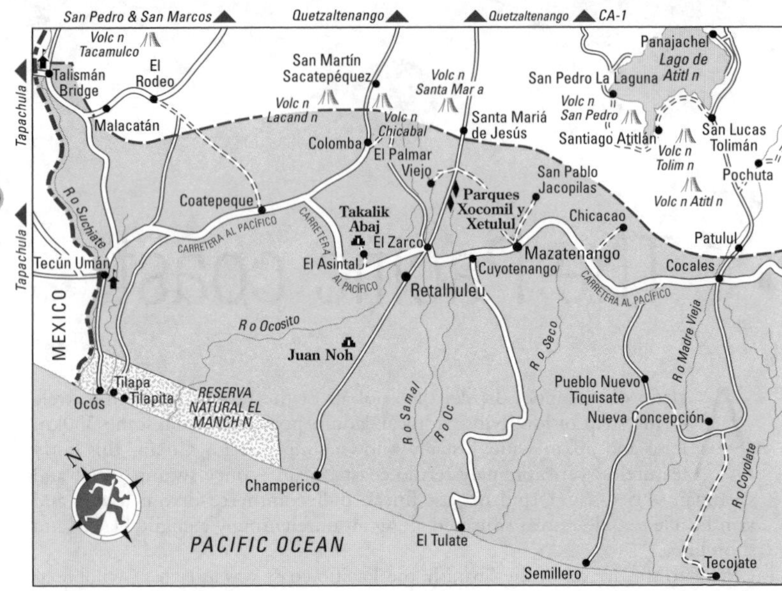

The main transport link in this region is the coastal highway, the **Carretera al Pacífico** (CA-2), the country's fastest road. This is the usual route for pullman buses speeding between Guatemala City and the Mexican border, so travel is normally swift and comfortable.

Some history

The earliest history of the Pacific coast remains something of a mystery, with the only hints being offered by the remnants of two distinct languages: **Zoquean**, now only spoken by a tiny population over the Mexico–Guatemala border, and **Xincan**, which is thought to have been spoken throughout the eastern area of Guatemala but can now only be heard in an isolated part of the Zacapa department. However, the extent to which these languages are evidence of independent tribes, and how these tribes might have lived, remains mere speculation. It's generally held that the sophisticated **Olmec** influence – in what is now Mexico – spread along the Pacific coast, influencing both the emerging **Ocós** and **Iztapa** cultures, which thrived here after 1500 BC. These were small, village-based societies that developed considerable skills in the working of stone and pottery. It's also generally believed that the great cultural developments of the Maya, including writing and the Maya calendar, reached the southern area of the Maya region via the Pacific coast.

What is certain is that some time between 400 and 900 AD the entire coastal plain was overrun by the **Pipil**, who migrated south from the Central Highlands and Veracruz area of Mexico, possibly driven out by the chaos that followed the fall of the ancient Mesoamerican metropolis of Teotihuacán. (The Pipil language is actually an antiquated form of Nahuatl, the official language of the Aztec empire.) These migrants brought with them their architectural styles and artistic skills, and the remains of their civilization show that they used a foreign calendar and worshipped the gods familiar in Mexico. The Pipil built

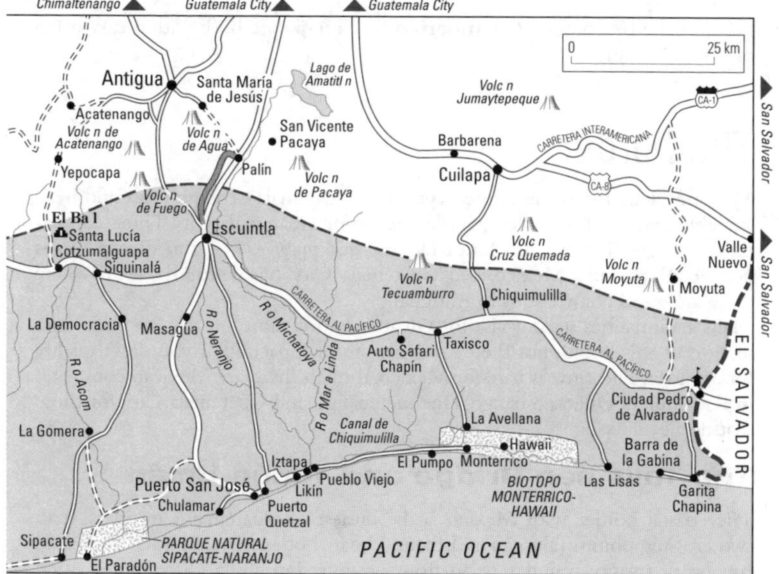

half a dozen sites, all compact ceremonial centres with rubble-filled pyramids. Their main produce was cacao, from which they extracted the beans to make a chocolate drink and to use as a form of currency. But by the time of the Conquest the ever-expanding tribes of the highlands had started to encroach upon the coastal plain and claim a slice of the action.

The first **Spaniards** to set foot in Guatemala did so on the Pacific coast, arriving overland from the north. Pedro de Alvarado's first confrontation with K'iche' warriors came here in the heat of the lowlands, before he headed up towards Quetzaltenango. Once they'd established themselves, the Spanish dispatched a handful of Franciscans to convert the coastal population, and were faced with a long, hard fight from the Pipil. In **colonial times** the land was mostly used for the production of indigo and cacao, and for cattle ranching, but the inhospitable climate and accompanying disease soon took their toll, and for much of that era the coast remained a miserable backwater. It was only after **independence** that commercial agriculture began to dominate this part of the country. The lower slopes of the mountains, known as the Boca Costa, were the first to be covered in huge coffee plantations; later, rubber, banana and sugarcane plantations spread across the land below. By the early twentieth century, the area was important enough to justify the construction of two railways to the coast (connecting Guatemala City with Puerto San José and Quetzaltenango with Retalhuleu), as well as a line to the Mexican border.

Today the coastal strip is the country's most intensely farmed region, with entire villages being effectively owned by vast fincas. Much of the nation's income is generated here and the main towns are alive with commercial activity, ringed by the ostentatious homes of the wealthy and dominated by the assertive machismo of ladino culture. Typically, most towns here are breathless and ugly, though **Retalhuleu** is a little more attractive and sedate. If you plan to spend any time on the coast, **Monterrico** is your best bet, but if you just want to head for the beach, then **Champerico** and **Tilapa** are both within easy reach of Quetzaltenango.

The border

Most travellers forgo the limited appeal of Guatemala's Pacific coast and head straight from the border to Quetzaltenango or Guatemala City. Three companies – Galgos, Ticabus and Línea Dorada (see pp.98–99) – run **direct buses** between Tapachula, Mexico, and Guatemala City (via Escuintla, from where there are good connections to Antigua).

Few nationalities need a visa for Guatemala (for more on this, see the Basics section of this book), but there's a consulate in Tapachula if you don't qualify for a waiver. The same is true for Mexico, though there are Mexican consulates in Retalhuleu, Quetzaltenango, Huehuetenango and Guatemala City for those that do need a visa.

The Talismán Bridge and Tecún Umán

The coastal border with Mexico is the busiest of Guatemala's frontiers, with two crossing points, Talismán and Tecún Umán, both open 24 hours. Minibuses run every twenty minutes or so from posts to Tapachula (30 minutes away) until 9pm.

The northernmost of the two crossings is the **Talismán Bridge**, also referred to as El Carmen, where the countries' customs and immigration posts are split by the Río Suchiate. This is the more relaxed of the two as there's nothing here but a few huts and a couple of basic pensiones. On the Guatemalan side, there is a regular flow of trucks, minibuses and buses leaving for **Malacatán**, where you'll find hotels and buses for San Marcos, Quetzaltenango and the western highlands. If you're heading for Guatemala City, there's usually a bus waiting at the border – if not, go to Malacatán and catch one from there.

The **Tecún Umán** crossing, on the edge of the dusty, bustling border town of Ciudad Tecún Umán, is favoured by most Guatemalans and all commercial traffic. The town has an authentic frontier flavour with all-night bars, lost souls, contraband and moneychangers, and its streets are almost permanently choked by a chaos of articulated lorries and buses, with cycle rickshaws (charging US$1.30 to Immigration) snaking through the traffic. Everything and everyone is on the move, and after one look at the place you'll want to join them. If for some reason you get stuck here, head for the *Hotel Pirámide* at 3 Av 4–46 (☎7776 8472; ❸) or the *Hotel Don José*, 2 C 3–42 (☎7776 8164; ❸). Again, there's a steady stream of buses connecting the border with Guatemala City, Coatepeque and Retalhuleu.

South to Ocós, Tilapa and Tilapita

South of Tecún Umán, a paved road running parallel to the border passes endless palm-oil plantations to **OCÓS**, a forlorn beachfront village of sand streets running past rows of squalid palm huts and breeze-block shacks. Between 1250 and 1100 BC this area was a centre of the Ocós people, a network of small fishing and farming villages that comprised one of the earliest civilizations on the Pacific coast. No evidence of this society remains today, however, so it's best to head straight for the ferry (US$0.40pp) that crosses the Río Naranjo.

Undertow

Most of Guatemala's Pacific coastline is affected by a strong undertow, which occurs when big waves break on a shore with a steep profile. Because there's nowhere for the water to escape, it retreats backwards under the next breaking wave, creating a downwards force close to the shore. Unless you're very confident in the ocean, it's best not to mess around if the surf is big. By not getting out of your depth, you can use your feet to jump up into the oncoming waves and let their force push you toward the shore. If you do get caught in an undertow, don't panic, as the downward force only lasts a second or two and you'll soon surface. Catch a breath, duck under the next breaker, and then work your way steadily back to shore.

On the river's other bank, the simple resort town of **TILAPA** is a much better bet for spending some time by the sea. The dark-sand beach here has a relatively gently shelving profile compared with many places on this coast, so the undertow is less fierce and it's easier for children to paddle in safety. Tilapa's sandy lanes are also largely devoid of rubbish, and there's a row of comedores dispensing good, fresh prawns and fish, plus cold Gallo beer. You'll also find a couple of very inexpensive, basic **hospedajes** (❶) with foam mattresses – bring your own mosquito net. The coastline here forms part of the **Reserva Natural El Manchón**, which covers some 30km of prime turtle-nesting beach and extends around 10km inland to embrace a belt of swamp and mangrove, which is home to crocodiles, iguanas, kingfishers, storks, white herons, egrets and an abundance of fish. There's usually a lonely Peace Corps worker stationed here to look after the reserve who's sure to appreciate some company and bound to be a good source of local information (just ask for the "gringo").

If you're interested in exploring the area's **wetlands** you shouldn't have any trouble finding a boatman willing to take you on a tour of the canals and lagoons. Or you could catch one of the sporadic boats from the dock (US$0.40 per person, or you can hire your own for US$3) that head over to tiny **Tilapita**, where there's an even more agreeable beach. Here there's a real opportunity to get away from it all and enjoy a superb stretch of clean, dark sand and the ocean (with not too much undertow). You'll find an excellent new **hotel** here, *El Pacífico* (❸), owned by local landowner Alex Mata. It has eighteen screened rooms, all with two double beds and a fan, and most with bathroom; there's good food available too.

Buses run between Tilapa and Coatepeque hourly from 5am to 6pm (1hr 30min), and about every ninety minutes between Coatepeque and Ocós (1hr 30min).

The coastal highway: Coatepeque and Retalhuleu

East from the Mexican border, **COATEPEQUE** is the first place of any importance on the main road, a furiously busy, purely commercial town where most of the locally produced coffee is processed. The action is centred on the **bus terminal**, an intimidating maelstrom of sweat, mud and energetic chaos: buses run every thirty minutes from here to the two Mexican border crossings and Quetzaltenango (via both Colomba and Zunil) until about 7pm, and hourly to Guatemala City until 6pm.

Coatepeque practicalities

Coatepeque's shabby streets and relentless tropical heat offer very little to deter the visitor. If for some reason you do get stuck here, one of the best places to **stay** is the *Hotel Villa Real*, 6 C 6–57 (Ⓣ7775 1308, Ⓕ7775 1939; ❹), a modern hotel with clean rooms, a restaurant with tasty local food, and secure parking. The *Europa*, 6 C 4–01 (Ⓣ7775 5334), just off the plaza, is of a similar standard, though the food is not as good here. The best budget hotel is the family-run *Hotel Baechli*, 6 C 5–35 (Ⓣ7775 1483; ❷), which has plain rooms with fans and TV, plus secure parking.

For **changing money**, there's a branch of the Banco del Occidente (Mon–Fri 9am–7pm, Sat 9am–1pm) on the central plaza, with several more banks nearby.

Retalhuleu and around

Beyond Coatepeque lies the most densely populated section of the Pacific coast, centred on **RETALHULEU**, the region's largest town. The town is usually referred to as **Reu** (pronounced "Ray-oo"), which is what you should look for on the front of buses. Set a few kilometres south of the Carretera al Pacífico and surrounded by the walled homes of the wealthy, Retalhuleu has managed to avoid the worst excesses of the coast, protected to some extent by a combination of wealth and tradition. The town was founded by the Spanish when they merged two neighbouring Maya villages, and until the past few decades the women maintained the tradition of wearing no blouse.

Today, Retalhuleu is a relatively civilized place compared with the chaos evident elsewhere on the coast. Grand-looking palm trees line the entrance road to the town, while the **plaza** retains a modest degree of faded authority – here you'll find the towering Greek columns that define the *municipalidad*, and a large, attractive colonial church. The mood is relaxed and easy-going, and in the warmth of the evening young couples canoodle on the park benches and munch ice cream. If you have time to kill, pop into the small **Museo de Arqueología y Etnología** in the *municipalidad* (Tues–Sat 8am–5.30pm; US$0.20). Rooms are divided into Preclassic, Classic and Postclassic Maya periods and display a collection of anthropomorphic figurines, mostly heads. Many show a strong Mexican influence in their design, with large earplugs a common feature. Upstairs, a fascinating collection of photographs, dating back to the 1880s, provides an excellent historic record of the town's changing streetscapes and industries, demonstrating the extent to which its leading citizens tried to create a bourgeois haven among the festering plantations.

Retalhuleu practicalities

Budget **accommodation** is in short supply in Retalhuleu. The best moderately priced places are the new *Hotel Génesis*, 6 C 6–29 (Ⓣ7771 2855; ❸), where all the rooms have a/c, TV and private bathroom; and *Hotel América*, 8 Av 9–32 (Ⓣ7771 1154; ❸), which has clean but non-a/c rooms with private bath. If you want a bit more luxury, try the modern *Hotel Posada de Don José*, 5 C 3–67 (Ⓣ771 0180, Ⓦwww.don-jose.com; ❻), which has good a/c rooms, a decent restaurant and a large pool.

The **plaza** is the hub of the town's activity, and around its fringes are three **banks**, including the Banco Industrial, with a Visa ATM. The best **restaurants** are also close by: try the dark wood surrounds of the *Cafetería la Luna* for inexpensive Guatemalan meals and snacks, *El Volován* for cakes and pastries, or *Punto Frio* for breakfasts, meals and good ice cream. The most stylish place for a drink is *Lo de Chaz*, 5 C 4–83, just west of the plaza, where they also serve food.

Buses running along the coastal highway almost always pull in at the Retalhuleu terminal on 7 Avenida and 10 Calle, a ten-minute walk from the plaza. There's a half-hourly service to and from Guatemala City, the Mexican border and Quetzaltenango; regular buses also depart for Champerico and El Tulate. Retalhuleu has a **Mexican consulate** at 5 Calle and 3 Avenida (Mon–Fri 4–6pm).

Takalik Abaj

The archeological site of **Takalik Abaj** (daily 7am–5pm; US$3.20, guide US$6.50), some 15km west of Retalhuleu, has cast fresh light on the development of early Maya civilization, particularly the influence of **Olmec** culture. The city presided over trade routes between Mexico and El Salvador, controlling the movement of jade, cacao and obsidian. Formerly known as Abaj Takalik, it's still being excavated, with an unlooted Maya royal grave being uncovered here in 2002. Today only its former urban centre is part of the archeological site, while the city's outskirts are spread over five coffee plantations. First settled around 1000 BC, its early ceremonial buildings and monuments were executed in Olmec style between 800 and 400 BC, including the characteristic pot-bellied humans with swollen eyelids. But by the late Preclassic period, Maya-style carvings of standing rulers were beginning to replace Olmec art. Later in the Classic era some of the Maya world's most exquisite jade masks were created here – they now reside in Guatemala City's Museo Nacional de Arqueología y Etnología (see p.92).

The first substantial structure you encounter is **Terraza 3**, a low, rectangular stepped temple with three stone Olmec-head statues facing a ceremonial Maya altar. Some of the finest carved stelae have been placed in front of **Temple 12**, the largest at the site with a 56-metre-wide base: Monument 67, which depicts a jaguar head; toad-like Monument 68; Monument 9, a rare representation of an owl; and, most impressive of all, the grouping of **Altar 8** and **Monument 5** (which has a date of 126 AD and shows twin kings presiding over bound captives). Facing Temple 12 is **Temple 11**, resembling a grassy mound, which is mid- to late Classic Maya and has seven more stelae in front of it. More good carvings lie round the back of Temple 12 including Olmec-style Monument 99, which shows a baboon-like creature with a protruding jaw.

Behind Temple 12 is a small building which acts as the site **musuem**, containing a model of Takalik Abaj along with assorted carvings and ceramics. There are also several fairly miserable animal enclosures which contain pizotes, spider monkeys and porcupines, among other creatures. You should be able to get a warm fizzy *agua* near the entrance, but there's no food available.

To **get to Takalik Abaj**, take a local bus from Reu to **El Asintal**, a small village 15km to the west, from where you can either hire a pick-up or walk the four kilometres to the site through coffee and cacao plantations. If you're driving, take the highway to Mexico from Reu and take the Astinal turn-off.

There are two places to stay, both in rural locations, nearby. If you continue along the same minor road from El Astinal past the ruins, it's a further two kilometres to a working coffee and sugar finca, the *San Isidro Piedra Parada*, that also offers bed and breakfast (❻) in an elegant main house. A tour of the finca, which employs 80 workers, is included; packages can be arranged by Adrenalina Tours in Quetzaltenango (see p.195). Continuing further along the main highway to Mexico, there's a turn-off at Km 190.5 to a wonderful new eco-resort, *Takalik Maya Lodge* (Ⓣ2337 0037, Ⓦwww.takalik.com; ❾). One of the finest places along the Pacific coast, it offers stylish and attractive accommodation in two separate buildings, horse-riding, guides for the ruins, excursions, and a pool.

Retalhuleu towards Quetzaltenango

North of Retalhuleu on the Carretera al Pacífico, the **El Zarco** junction marks the start of one of the country's most scenic roads, which heads up into the highlands towards Quetzaltenango, passing two impressive leisure parks and the deserted remains of the village of El Palmar Viejo. It then skirts the plunging lower slopes of the Santa María and Zunil volcanoes before emerging in the valley of Quetzaltenango, some 47km from Reu.

Xocomil and Xetulul theme parks

Some 6km north of the Zarco junction is a theme-park complex – two have been built, another two are planned – landscaped into the foothills of the highlands. The **Parque Acuático Xocomil** (Thurs–Sun 9am–4pm; US$10, children US$6.75) is a vast complex containing 1.2km of water slides, wave pools and artificial rivers amidst grounds replete with Maya temples and copious greenery. The neighbouring **Parque Xetulul** (Thurs–Sun 10am–6pm; US$25.50, children US$12.75, ride package US$6.50 extra) is divided into different zones, with the Plaza Chapina having recreations of famous Guatemalan buildings, the Plaza Italia showcasing an imitation Trevi fountain, and Plaza Francia boasting replicas of Parisian structures such as the Gare de France. The park has some terrific rides, including the thrilling La Avalancha rollercoaster, and, like its sister complex, it is clean, well-run and extremely popular with Guatemalan families. **Buses** between Retalhuleu and Quetzaltenango pass the water park every thirty minutes in daylight hours.

El Palmar Viejo

Beyond these parks it's about 14km to the left-hand turn-off that leads to the absorbing remains of the village of **El Palmar Viejo**. After torrential rains in 1998, the Río Nimá burst its banks and mud flows swept through the centre of this farming community, powerful enough to cut the village church in two and leave its western facade hanging over a ravine. Villagers were evacuated to the other side of the highway – and while the remains of El Palmar Viejo hardly amount to a Guatemalan Pompeii, the overgrown ghost town makes an intriguing sight and represents a haunting reminder of the destructive powers of Hurricane Mitch, which killed hundreds in Guatemala and thousands in Honduras and Nicaragua.

Fizzy-drink vendors and pick-ups congregate near the ravine, where there's a rickety bridge. If you cross this bridge and follow a path that winds past boulders left by the mud flows, then across a much smaller second wooden bridge over a river, and around a patch of jungle, there's a pretty hourglass-shaped **laguna** (though its colour turns to muddy brown in the rainy season), bordered by *milpas* and rainforest, that's an ideal spot for a swim or picnic. The lake is about a fifteen-minute walk from the ravine.

To get to El Palmar Viejo you can either take any bus heading between Retalhuleu and Quetzaltenango and get off at the El Palmar Viejo turn-off, from where you can walk or wait for a pick-up to cover the 3.5km route. There are also tours from Quetzaltenango (see p.195).

Champerico

South from Retalhuleu a paved road heads to the beach at **CHAMPERICO**, which, though it certainly doesn't feel like it, is the country's third port. Founded in 1872, it was originally connected to Quetzaltenango by rail and enjoyed a brief period of prosperity based on the export of coffee. In 1934, Aldous Huxley passed through, but was distinctly unimpressed: "Then suddenly, vast and blank, under a glaring white sky, the Pacific. One after another, with a succession of dreary bumps, the rollers broke on a flat beach." Huxley was fortunate enough to board a steamer and escape what he called "the unspeakable boredom of life at Champerico". If anything, things have gotten worse, as barely any trade passes through the port these days, and the rusting pier, the only feature to disturb the coastline, will doubtless soon sink beneath the waves. Champerico still supports a handful of fishermen, but spends most of its time waiting for the weekend, when hordes of weary city-dwellers descend on the coast. The **beach** is much the same as anywhere else, although its sheer scale is impressive. As elsewhere along this stretch of coast, it's essential to watch out for the dangerous **undertow**, even though lifeguards are present. On a more positive note, decent meals are widely available: try the *Restaurant Monte Limar* or the *Alcatraz* for fried shrimp and fish or, for a treat, feast on paella at the *Hotel Miramar*, 2 Calle and Av Coatepeque (Ⓣ7773 7231; ❷), which also has a fantastic wooden bar – the best place in town to tackle your thirst – and dark, windowless rooms. Just over the street, the *Martita* (❷) is a less-attractive alternative.

Buses run between Champerico and Retalhuleu every ten minutes or so from 7am to noon; the last bus leaves Champerico at 7.30pm. If you're heading anywhere else, catch a bus from Champerico to Retalhuleu (from where there are buses to Quetzaltenango every thirty minutes).

Cuyotenango to Cocales

Beyond Retalhuleu the highway runs east to **CUYOTENANGO**, one of the older settlements along the road, having started life as a pre-conquest Kaqchikel village before becoming an important colonial town. The narrow streets and some of the older buildings bear witness to this distinguished past, but the thunder of the highway, which cuts right through the town, overwhelms all else, and its larger neighbours, Mazatenango and Retalhuleu, have long since consumed any importance that Cuyotenango once held.

Another branch road turns off for the beach here, heading 45km south to **EL TULATE**, where the village and the ocean are separated from the mainland by a narrow expanse of mangrove swamp. The beach itself, lined with palm trees, is another featureless strip of black sand, though the waves are a little less brutal here than at other beaches along this stretch of coast. The village's isolation is a definite bonus, though the only places to stay are on the reed mattresses in the shacks adjoining the open-air fried fish 'n' shrimp restaurants. **Buses** struggle down to El Tulate every hour or so from Mazatenango and Retalhuleu, with the last bus back to Mazatenango at 5pm and the last to Retalhuleu at 6pm: small boats meet the buses to ferry passengers from the end of the road to the village.

Back on the highway, the next stop is **MAZATENANGO**, another seething commercial town. There are two sides to "Mazate", as it's generally known. The main street, which runs down the side of the market, past the filling stations and bus terminal, is characteristic of life along the coastal highway, redolent of diesel fumes and cheap commercialization. The other half of town, centred on the plaza, is quieter, calmer and more sophisticated, with long shaded streets. There's no particular reason to linger in Mazatenango, but if you do find yourself here for the night, budget **accommodation** options include *Hotel La Cabaña*, 2 C 2–10, Zona 2 (Ⓣ7872 1635; ❷), which offers good-value rooms with private bath and parking. If you want somewhere more comfortable, head for *Hotel Alba*, on the main highway heading for Mexico (Ⓣ7872 0264; ❹), which also has secure parking and a restaurant. For **food**, try *Cardinali's*, 10 C 4–36, for the best pizza on the south coast, or *Croissants Pastelería* on the plaza, for coffee and cakes. There are a couple of cinemas in Mazatenango and plenty of **banks**.

Buses can be caught at the small terminal above the market on the main street, or outside the filling stations on the highway, which is where most of the pullmans stop. Services run very regularly in both directions along the coastal highway – and also to Quetzaltenango (every 30 minutes until 6pm) and to El Tulate, Chicacao and Pueblo Nuevo Tiquisate (every hour or so from 8am to 4pm).

East to Cocales

Continuing east from Mazatenango the main road passes the turn-off for Chicacao, a coffee centre from where pick-ups run to Santiago Atitlán and **Pueblo Nuevo Tiquisate**, once the local headquarters of the all-powerful United Fruit Company, whose banana plantations stretched almost as far as its political influence. From the latter town you can take a local bus to El Semillero or El Tecojate. The better beach is at **El Semillero**, where there's a terrific expanse of dark sand that's the occasional location for full-moon parties organized by the Rainbow Gathering tribe, a big hippie party collective – check in *D'noz* bar in San Pedro La Laguna for details of the latest events.

About 30km beyond Mazatenango is **COCALES**, a crossroads town from where a road and **buses** run north to Santiago Atitlán, Panajachel and San Lucas Tolimán. The best option is to take the first pick-up or bus to Santiago Atitlán and catch a boat from there to other points around the lake. The last bus to Santiago leaves Cocales at around 5pm, but plenty of pick-ups also run this route.

From Cocales, a road also heads south to the agricultural centre of **NUEVA CONCEPCIÓN**, an inconspicuous little place that catapulted into the headlines in the 1980s as the home parish of Guatemala's most radical priest, **Padre Andrés Girón**, who founded the country's first significant land-reform movement since the Arbenz government of 1949–54. During the civil war, Girón spoke out eloquently on behalf of campesinos and led fifteen thousand peasants in a four-day march to Guatemala City. Although he received numerous death threats and was later expelled from the Catholic Church, Girón continues to campaign.

Santa Lucía Cotzumalguapa and around

Another 23km along the Carretera al Pacífico brings you to **SANTA LUCÍA COTZUMALGUAPA**, a pretty uninspiring Pacific town a short distance north of the highway. The only reason to visit the area is to take in the Pipil and Maya **archeological** sites and carvings around Santa Lucía, the colossal Olmec carved figures at nearby La Democracia, or the **surf** at Sipacate to the south.

Santa Lucía Cotzumalguapa

This largely featureless place is rightly bypassed by most travellers, but if you have an hour or two to kill in the area, a group of unusual carvings and archeological remains, scattered in the surrounding cane fields around the town, are worth a visit. Bear in mind, though, that getting to them is not easy unless you rent a taxi. As usual, the **plaza** is the main centre of interest, a shady square that's disgraced by one of the ugliest buildings in the country, a horrific green and white concrete municipal structure. Several cheap, scruffy **hotels** can be found close to the plaza, but the nearest half-decent place is *Hotel Internacional* (☎7882 5504; ❸), just south of the main highway, which has clean rooms with fans. About 400m west of here, the *Hotel Santiaguito* (☎7882 5435; ❻) is a slick motel with a swimming pool and a restaurant. Other **food** options include the *Comedor Lau*, on 3 Avenida, which does reasonable Chinese meals, and the *Cevichería La Española*, on 4 Avenida a block south of the plaza, which is fine for fresh seafood and a drink. Several **banks** will change your travellers' cheques; Banco Industrial on 3 Avenida has a Visa/Plus ATM.

Pullman **buses** passing along the highway will drop you at the entrance road to town, ten minutes' walk from the centre, while second-class "direct" buses from the capital go straight into the terminal, a few blocks from the plaza. Buses to Guatemala City leave the terminal hourly from 3am to 4pm, or you can catch a pullman from the highway.

Sites around Santa Lucía Cotzumalguapa

A tour of the **sites** around Santa Lucía Cotzumalguapa can be an exhausting and frustrating process, taking you through a sweltering maze of cane fields. Doing the whole thing on foot is certainly the cheapest way, but also by far the hardest. Note that wandering about the cane fields alone is never a good idea, though if you are determined to, do so in the mornings when, as locals would say, "the thieves are still sleeping". You're far better off taking a round trip by taxi instead – you'll find plenty in the plaza in varying degrees of decrepitude – and, if you bargain, US$10 should cover all the sites. If you only want to see one of the sites, Bilbao is just a kilometre or so from the centre of town and features some of the best carving. If you do get lost just ask for *las piedras*, as they tend to be known locally.

Bilbao

In 1880, more than thirty Late Classic stone monuments were removed from the Pipil site of **Bilbao**, and nine of the very best were shipped to Germany. Four sets of stones are still visible in situ, however, and two of them perfectly illustrate the magnificent precision of the carving, beautifully preserved in slabs of black volcanic rock. To **get to** the site, walk uphill from the plaza, along 4 Avenida, until you reach the Convento Las Hermanas where you bear left, following a dirt track along the side of a cane field. About 200m further on is a fairly wide path leading left into the cane for about 20m. This brings you to two large stones carved with bird-like patterns, with strange circular glyphs arranged in groups of three: the majority of the glyphs are recognizable as the names for days once used by the people of southern Mexico. In the same cane field, further along the same path, is another badly eroded stone, and a final set with a superbly preserved set of figures and interwoven motifs.

Finca El Baúl

The second site is about 5km further afield in the grounds of the **Finca El Baúl**, reached by following 3 Avenida north out of town. The hilltop site has two stones, one a standing figure wearing a skirt and a spectacular headdress, the other a massive half-buried stone head, with wrinkled brow and patterned headdress, possibly that of Huhuetéotl, the fire god of the Mexicans. In front of the stones is a set of small altars on which local people make animal sacrifices, burn incense and leave offerings of flowers. Recent excavations here have revealed a network of buried causeways – one stretches to the north to a site called **Gloria**, where some giant carved stones have been unearthed – you can view these in the Popul Vuh museum in Guatemala City. El Baúl also makes an ideal shaded spot for a **picnic** lunch, with fine vistas towards the twin peaks of volcanos Agua and Fuego to the north.

The next stones of interest are at the **finca** itself, a few kilometres further away from town, where the carvings include some superb heads, a stone skull, a massive jaguar and an extremely well-preserved stela of a ball-court player (monument 27) dating from the Late Classic period. Alongside all this antiquity is the finca's old steam engine, a miniature machine that used to haul the cane along a system of private tracks. As the finca has its own **bus service** you may be able to get a ride: buses leave from the Tienda El Baúl, a few blocks uphill from the plaza, four or five times a day, the first at around 7am and the last either way at about 6pm.

Finca Las Ilusiones

On the other side of town, the third site is at **Finca Las Ilusiones**, where another collection of artefacts and some stone carvings has been assembled in the **Museo Cultura Cotzumalguapa** (Mon–Fri 8am–4pm, Sat 8am–noon; US$1.25). Two of the most striking figures here are an Olmec-style pot-bellied statue (monument 58), probably from the middle Preclassic era, and a copy of monument 21 which bears three figures, the central one depicting a ball player. There are several other carved pieces, including a fantastic stela, plus some more replicas, and thousands of small stone carvings and pottery fragments. To **get there**, walk east along the highway for about 1km and follow the signs on the left. If you want to learn more about the latest archeological investigations around Santa Lucía Cotzumalguapa, check out Ⓦwww.famsi.org.

La Democracia and Sipacate

Heading east from Santa Lucía Cotzumalguapa the coastal highway arrives next at **Siquinalá**, a run-down sort of place from where another branch road heads to the coast. Along the way, 9km to the south, **LA DEMOCRACIA** is an orderly little town that's of particular interest as the home of another collection of archeological relics. To the east of town lies the archeological site of **Monte Alto**; many of the best pieces that have been found there are now spread around the town plaza under a vast ceiba tree. These "fat boys" are massive stone heads with simple, almost childlike faces, grinning with bizarre, Buddha-like contentment. Some are attached to smaller rounded bodies and rolled over on their backs, clutching their swollen stomachs like stricken Teletubbies. The figures are strikingly similar to ancient Olmec sculptures found near Villahermosa in the Gulf of Mexico, and they probably date from the mid-Preclassic period around 500 BC. Also on the plaza, the town **museum** (Tues–Sun 8am–noon & 2–5pm; US$1.30) houses carvings, ceremonial yokes worn by ball-game players, pottery, grinding stones, a wonderful jade mask and a few more carved heads.

The road continues 21km further south to **La Gomera**, a mid-sized agricultural centre where buses usually wait for a while, and beyond to the coast at the low-key village of **SIPACATE**, located inside the Parque Natural Sipacate-Naranjo, a mangrove coastal reserve that's also home to Guatemala's best **surf**. The beach here is separated from the village by the black waters of the **Canal de Chiquimulilla** (which parallels Guatemala's southern coast from here to Las Lisas, 100km to the east) across which boats ferry a steady stream of passengers. Beachside there's an embryonic but developing surf scene. Waves average six feet, and are most consistent between December and April (for more details see

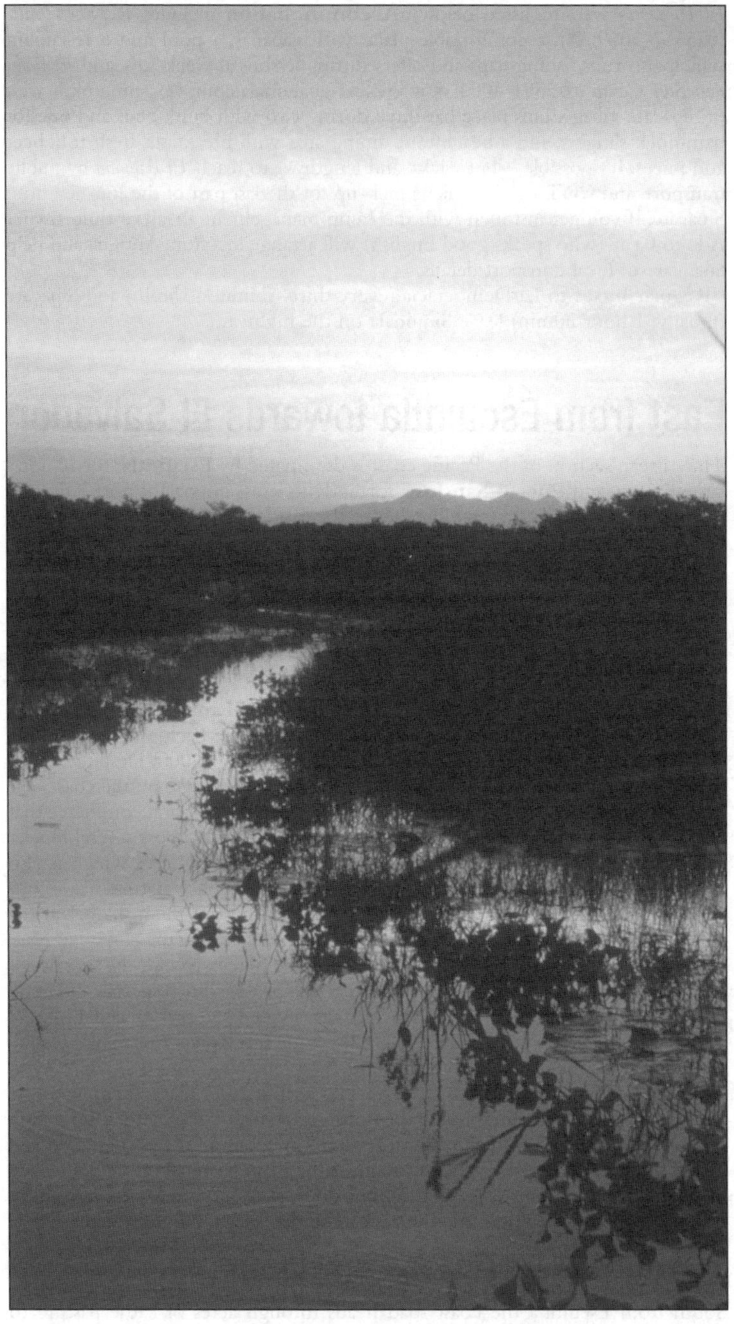

△ Mangrove swamp, Monterrico

El Paradon's website, listed below). **Accommodation** includes *Rancho Carillo* (ⓣ5517 1069; ❹), a comfortable place with cabañas, a pool and a restaurant which also runs fishing trips and offers surfing lessons at weekends, and *El Paradon Surf Camp* (ⓣ5591 4004, ⓦwww.surf-guatemala.com; ❷), some 6km west of Sipacate village. This place has three dorms, two with bunk beds and one for hammock slingers, and a beachfront dining area with breakfasts, fresh fish, beer and juices. It's possible – but tricky and lengthy – to reach *El Paradon* by public transport, and you'll need to take a pick-up for the last part of the journey from Sipacate. If you get in touch with the camp management ahead of time, owner Adolfo Cruz (who speaks good English) will arrange lifts from Antigua and help take care of local transport details.

Regular **buses** to La Democracia (every thirty minutes; 15min) and Sipacate (6 daily; 1 hour 30min) leave Siquinalá on the highway.

East from Escuintla towards El Salvador

The eastern section of the Pacific coast is dominated by **Escuintla**, the region's largest town, and **Puerto San José**, formerly its most important port – though neither town is at all attractive. Further to the east is **Monterrico**, an impressive beach where you'll find the coast's most important wildlife reserve, a protected area of mangrove swamps that's home to some superb birdlife. Beyond that the coastal highway runs to the border with El Salvador, with branch roads heading off to a couple of small seashore villages.

Escuintla

Located at the junction of the two principal coastal roads from the capital, **ESCUINTLA** is the largest and most important of the Pacific towns, ranking as Guatemala's third largest city with a population of 92,000. Despite its size there's nothing to see here, but you do get a good sense of life on the coast – its heat, pace and energy, and the frenetic industrial and agricultural commerce that drives it. Below the plaza a huge, chaotic **market** sprawls across several blocks, spilling out into 4 Avenida, the main commercial thoroughfare, which is also notable for a mock castle that functions as the town's police station.

There are plenty of cheap **hotels** near 4 Avenida, most of them sharing in the general air of dilapidation; for a/c and secure parking head for the fair-value *Hotel Costa Sur*, 12 C 4–13 (ⓣ7888 1819; ❸). Among the **places to eat**, the best deal is at *Pizzería al Macarone*, 4 Av 6–103, which has inexpensive lunch specials and good ice cream. As for **banks**, there's a Bancafé with a Visa ATM at 4 Av and 12 C.

Buses to Escuintla leave Guatemala City from the Zona 4 terminal, passing the Treból junction every 30 minutes until 7pm, returning from 8 C and 2 Av in Escuintla. For other destinations, there are two terminals: for places en route to the Mexican border, buses run through the north of town and stop by the Esso station opposite the Banco Uno (take a local bus up 3 Av); buses for the coast road and inland route to El Salvador are best caught at the main terminal on the south side of town, at the bottom of 4 Av (local bus down 4 Av). Buses leave every thirty minutes for Puerto San José and the eastern border, and hourly to Antigua.

To the coast: Puerto San José

South from Escuintla the coast road heads through acres of cattle pasture to **PUERTO SAN JOSÉ**, the capital's nearest and most popular, if ramshackle, resort. Opening as a port in 1853, San José was once Guatemala's main shipping terminal, funnelling goods to and from the capital. Now, however, the port has been made virtually redundant by the container port of Puerto Quetzal, a few kilometres to the east, and both town and port are somewhat run-down and sleazy. Everything here is geared to extracting as many quetzales as possible from the rowdy day-trippers who fill the beaches at weekends.

The shoreline is separated from the mainland by the Canal de Chiquimulilla, which divides the black-sand beach from the main resort area. This is where you'll find all the **bars** and **restaurants**, most of them crowded at weekends with big ladino groups feasting on seafood and playing the jukebox until the small hours. The **hotels**, most of them in the same area, are not at all enjoyable, catering as they do to a largely drunken clientele, with high prices and low standards. If you do need to stay, one of the better deals is at the *Casa San José Hotel*, on Av del Comercio (Ⓣ7776 5587; ❹), where you'll find a pool and restaurant; for something cheaper, try the basic *Viñas del Mar*, which is right on the beach (❸). If you want to spend a few days on the coast, head along to Iztapa or Monterrico.

Buses between the plaza in San José and the Zona 4 bus terminal in Guatemala City run every thirty minutes or so all day, with many services continuing on to Iztapa.

Chulamar and Likín

Leaving San José and following the coast in either direction brings you to the beach resorts of Guatemala's wealthy elite, who abandoned Puerto San José to the capital's working class and established their own enclaves, with holiday homes built in a pale imitation of California. The first of these, **CHULAMAR**, lies about 5km west of Puerto San José and can only be reached by private car or taxi. Here you'll find another strip of sand separated from the land by the muddy waters of the canal and also the swanky *Radisson Villas del Pacífico* (Ⓣ7881 1028; ❾), with three pools, manicured grounds and luxurious accommodations – a room plus all meals and drinks costs US$170 per day during the week, US$210 at weekends.

East of San José, past the container terminal at Puerto Quetzal, is the other main upmarket resort in the area, **BALNEARIO LIKÍN**. Here a complete residential complex has been established, based around a neat grid of canals and streets. The ranks of second homes have speedboats and swimming pools, and the entire compound comes complete with an armed guard. It's deserted here during the week, when there are no boats to shuttle you to the beach, but at weekends you can drop by to watch the rich at play.

Iztapa and along the coast to Monterrico

Further east the road comes to an end at **IZTAPA**, another venerable port that now serves the domestic tourist industry. Of all the country's redundant ports, Iztapa is the oldest, as it was here that the Spanish chose to harbour their fleets. In the early days, Spanish leader Pedro de Alvarado used the port to build the boats that took him first to Peru and then on the trip to the Spice Islands from which he never returned.

There's little sense of this historical past in Iztapa today, but the town is a bit less forlorn than most of the resorts along the Pacific strip, if hardly an architectural beauty. The beach itself, a bank of black sand, is on the other side of the Canal de Chiquimulilla at a separate village called **Pueblo Viejo**. A small **ferry** crosses the canal for a couple of quetzales per passenger or US$2.25 per vehicle to Pueblo Viejo. There are few **hotels** in Iztapa and Puerto Viejo, though the welcoming, family-run *Sol y Playa Tropical* (Ⓣ7881 4365; ❹) is recommended, with rooms (all with private bath, and with or without a/c) set around a decent-sized pool that's surrounded by palms and banana trees. For a **meal**, *Rancho San Rafael*, right by the ferry stop in Iztapa, offers good seafood: *ceviche*, fish and *caldo de mariscos*. **Buses** run from the Zona 4 bus terminal in Guatemala City to Iztapa every hour (5am–5pm).

Beyond Iztapa a smooth paved road traces the 25km coastline from Pueblo Viejo to Monterrico, through a littoral landscape punctuated with loofa farms. Thanks to the improved road, large swathes of this unspoiled coastline are now being snapped up by property speculators. About 6km before Monterrico in the pueblo of El Pumpo, the *Utz Tzaba* (Ⓣ5318 9452, Ⓦwww.utz-tzaba.com; ❼–❾) is a smart new Dutch-owned place with ten immaculate rooms and four bungalows (each with living room and two bedrooms) on a spacious seafront plot where the lawns are kept well clipped; there's a large pool and a bar area, and best of all an empty stretch of clean, dark sand to enjoy and explore.

From Pueblo Viejo, five **buses** a day go to **Monterrico** – at 8am, 10am, noon, 1.30pm and 4pm – plus irregular pick-ups.

Monterrico and around

The setting of **MONTERRICO** is one of the finest on the Pacific coast, with the scenery reduced to its basic elements: a strip of dead-straight sand, a line of powerful surf, a huge empty ocean and an enormous curving horizon. The village is scruffy, but friendly and relaxed, and is separated from the mainland by the waters of the Canal de Chiquimulilla, which weaves through a fantastic network of **mangrove swamps**. Mosquitoes can be a problem during the wet season.

Monterrico sits at the heart of the **Biotopo Monterrico–Hawaii**, a nature reserve that embraces a twenty-kilometre-long beach-blessed slice of the Pacific littoral and includes a vital turtle-nesting ground, abundant wetlands, and the small villages of Monterrico and Hawaii. Sadly, however, the reserve's officially protected status does not prevent mounds of domestic rubbish being dumped in it, nor the widespread theft of turtle eggs. That said, it's well worth making your way to Monterrico, if only for the fantastically beautiful ocean setting, though if you intend to swim it's worth remembering that there's a vicious **undertow** along the entire southern coast of Guatemala. Lifeguards are posted here at weekends, but swimmers regularly get into trouble and drownings are not uncommon.

Arrival and information

Because of the hassles involved in travelling by pubic transport to Monterrico, most people now use the fast direct **shuttle bus** services (US$7–10; see box, p.122) that leave Antigua daily.

If you do opt for **public transport**, you have two options: arriving via Iztapa, or from Taxisco on the coastal highway. Buses from Guatemala City's Zona 4 terminal pass through Taxisco every thirty minutes en route to Chiquimulilla and the border with El Salvador at Ciudad Pedro de Alvarado. From Taxisco, buses trundle down the 17km south to La Avellana, from where boats shuttle passengers (US$0.40) and cars (US$7) back and forth to Monterrico on the opposite side of the mangrove swamp. The last buses leave Taxisco for Guatemala City around 6pm.

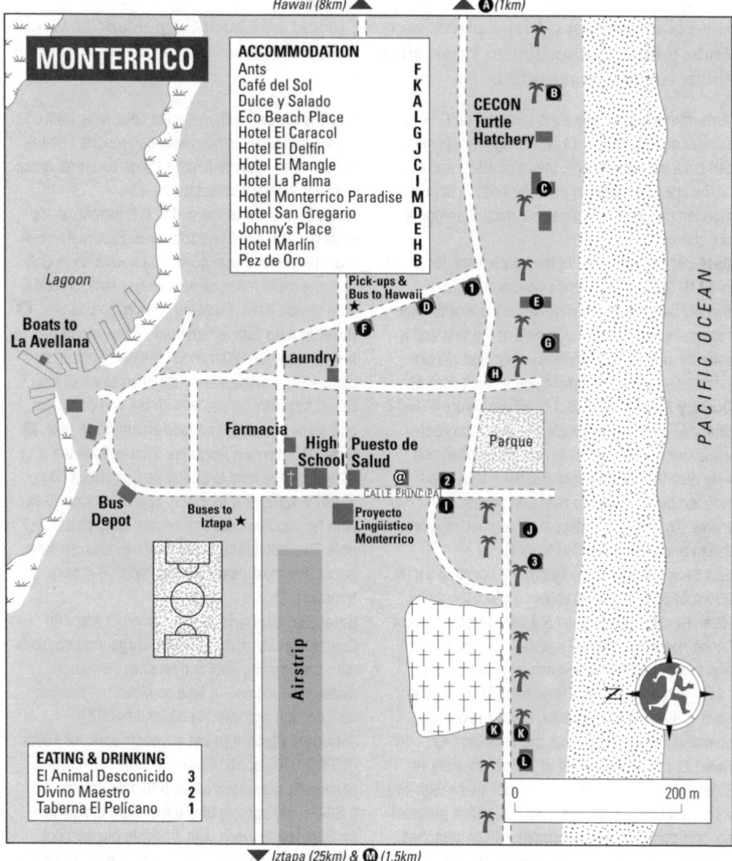

From the dock in Monterrico, Calle Principal (actually a meandering dirt track) passes through the coconut palms past tiendas, a football pitch and plenty of pigs, chickens and dogs. Continue past a group of open-air restaurants and you'll soon hear the pounding of the Pacific and see what all the fuss is about: Baule beach.

It's possible to **study Spanish** in Monterrico at the good Proyecto Lingüístico Monterrico (Ⓣ5619 8200, Ⓦwww.espanol.netfirms.com) where a study package costs US$85 for twenty hours of teaching, and includes accommodation in a bedroom in the school building (where there's a kitchen). Check out the community **website**, Ⓦwww.playademonterrico.com, for up-to-date hotel information and some community news.

Internet access at US$1.75 per hour is available on the main drag from a nameless cybercafé. There are no **banks** in Monterrico, but you can cash travellers' cheques in Taxisco; the nearest ATMs are in Chiquimulilla.

Accommodation

All Monterrico's **accommodation** is centred right on or just off the beach. Note that many places have reservation numbers in Guatemala City and others use cellular phones. Many places increase prices by about 20 percent at weekends, when it's also best to book ahead. Avoid the *Hotel Baule Beach* as regular thefts have been reported.

Ants turn left just before the farmacia on C Principal, second right, and it's on the right (no phone). Set back from the beach, this spot offers some of the cheapest rates in town for beds in decent wooden cabañas with mosquito nets. Bathrooms are shared. ❷

Café del Sol turn right at the beach, walk for 250m ⓣ5810 0821, ⓦwww.cafe-del-sol.com. Good, friendly Swiss-Guatemalan-owned place with large rooms – some beachside, others at the rear and a *mirador* room with sea views – with and without private bathroom. Tasty food and a small pool. ❹

Dulce y Salado 2km east of village centre ⓣ5817 9046, ⓦwww.ducleysalado.dk. New, excellent-value place with a great beachside location and very nice thatched bungalows, each with good wooden beds, mosquito nets and private bathrooms. There's also a decent-sized pool, plus fine Italian and Latin American food. ❸

Eco Beach Place turn right at the beach, walk for 250m ⓣ5611 6637, ⓔecobeachplace@hotmail.com. Next to the *Café del Sol*, this attractive guest house has a hospitable English-speaking owner and large comfortable rooms (some sleep up to four); all but one have private bath. There's good grub, a nice lounge/bar area, a small pool and stunning Pacific vistas from the verandah. ❹

Hotel El Caracol turn left at the beach, walk for 120m ⓣ5693 0430. Small, sociable place with two rooms that have bathroom and fan, plus a pleasant six-bed dorm (US$5 per person) with an attached bathroom. The young Israeli-Canadian owners also offer body-board rental (US$3 per hour). ❷–❸

Hotel El Delfín at the end of C Principal, on the right ⓣ5702 6701 Long-running backpackers' place with plenty of dark, pokey rooms, all with ancient mattresses, fan and nets. Friendly enough, and has a small pool, but head elsewhere unless it's a very busy time of year. ❷

Hotel El Mangle turn left at beach, walk for 300m ⓣ5514 6517 or 5490 1336. Popular, ever-expanding, agreeable place with selection of pleasant, small rooms, all with mosquito nets, fans, bathrooms and little terraces with hammocks. Friendly Guatemalan management, leafy garden area, small pool and beachside restaurant. ❸

Hotel La Palma at the end of C Principal, on the right ⓣ5705 4707 or 2363 4905. Extremely clean French-American-run guest house with six doubles and one triple room, all with ceiling fans, around a little grassy patio. Excellent French food as well. ❸

Hotel Marlín turn left just before the end of the beach, walk for 120m ⓣ5715 4104. Good new place with a single-storey thatched block of nine tidy, if smallish rooms, all with fan and bathroom and some with a/c, that face an attractive pool. ❹

Hotel Monterrico Paradise 2km outside the village, on the road to Iztapa (in Guatemala City ⓣ2478 4202, ⓕ478 4595). Spacious bungalows with two double beds and private bath, plus a pool. The restaurant, though decent, charges silly prices. It's most easily reached with your own transport. ❼

Hotel San Gregario behind *Johnny's Place* (in Guatemala City ⓣ2238 4690). Large modern block with a swimming pool and recently renovated motel-style rooms – a little soulless, but comfortable enough and offering a/c and bath. ❺

Johnny's Place turn left at beach, walk for 150m ⓣ5812 0409 or 5611 0444. Popular travellers' place with separate male and female dorms (US$4–5 per person) plus good-sized bungalows for four people, each with a private plunge pool. There are also hammocks, a communal room and a good café-restaurant with ocean views and fairly-priced tacos and pasta. Prices 20 percent higher at weekends. ❷–❺

Pez de Oro turn left at beach and walk for 350m ⓣ5204 5249 or 2368 3684. Eleven very attractive cottages, all with good beds, nice wooden furniture, verandahs and hammocks. The smallish swimming pool is shaded by coconut palms; there's also an Italian restaurant with excellent pasta, fish, and wine by the glass. ❺

Eating and drinking

When it comes to **eating** in Monterrico, you can either dine at one of the hotels on the beach – which can be pricey – or at one of the comedores in the village. The best of the basic eateries is *Divino Maestro*, where they do good *camarones al ajo*, while the finest cuisine in town can be found at the *Hotel La Palma* – where the French chef/owner might be rustling up *moules* or other delicious Gallic fare – and at Swiss-owned *Taberna El Pelícano* (closed Tues), just inland from *Johnny's Place*. Here, pasta dishes are only US$3 and *ragout de pescado* costs US$8.

Elsewhere, there's good, inexpensive vegetarian food at *Johnny's* and filling grub at *Café del Sol*, while the best Italian food is at *Dulce y Salado*, with *Pez de Oro* ranking second best. By far the liveliest bar is the beachfront *El Animal Desconicido*, which hammers out an eclectic selection of rock and dance music and serves up a mean cocktail.

Monterrico's beach, mangrove swamp and turtle hatchery

Monterrico's impressive **beach**, a prime turtle-nesting ground (see box, pp.254–255), is a fifty-metre-wide strip of dark grey sand that's continuously pummelled by the Pacific. Its steep profile means there's usually a strong **undertow** – take particular care when the waves are big. You'll find the beach is near-deserted away from the village centre, with just the odd holiday home or fisherman's *palapa* between the shoreside palms. Squadrons of pelicans – flying in formation and nicknamed the "Monterrico air force" by locals – skim over the ocean, angling their wings to clip the crest of the wave as they glide along the coastline.

Behind the beach and village, the extensive **mangrove swamp** is an unusually rich environment, formed as rivers draining from the highlands find their path blocked by the black sands of the beach and spill out into this enormous watery expanse before finally finding their way to the sea through two estuaries, 30km to the east and west of the village. These dark, nutrient-rich waters are superbly fertile, and four distinct types of mangrove form a dense mat of branches, interspersed with narrow canals, open lagoons, bullrushes and water lilies. The tangle of roots acts as a kind of marine nursery, offering small fish protection from their natural predators, while above the surface the dense vegetation and ready food supply provide an ideal home for hundreds of species of bird and a handful of mammals, including racoons, iguanas, alligators and opossums.

A trip into the swamp is an adventure, taking you through a complex network of channels, beneath a dense canopy of vegetation. The best way to explore the area is with a **guide**. Conservation group CECON, which administers the Monterrico reserve and is part of the University of San Carlos, has trained local guides – look for them on the beachfront outside the group's visitor centre (they should be sporting an ID badge). Otherwise most of the hotels can recommend a local boatman, or you could even rent a small *cayuco* (US$1.25 per hour) and paddle around yourself from the ferry dock. Note that if you rent a larger boat with an engine you won't see as much because the noise of the engine will frighten off the wildlife. You shouldn't expect to encounter the anteaters and racoons that hang around the swamp whichever way you travel, but you probably will see a good range of bird life, including kingfishers, white herons and several species of duck. The Palmilla lagoon is a particularly good spot. Failing all else, the trip is worthwhile just to watch the local fishermen casting their nets.

Be sure to drop by the headquarters of CECON, which also runs the renowned local **turtle hatchery**. The visitor centre (daily 8am–noon & 2–5pm; US$1) occupies a large beachside area where the hatchery has a shaded section of sand where **turtle eggs** are reburied after they have been laid. A short trail runs from the headquarters along the edge of the reserve, past enclosures of freshwater turtles, alligators and green iguanas, which are also bred for release into the wild. The organization seeks Spanish-speaking volunteers, as well as contacts with overseas universities. If you're interested in helping out, write to CECON USAC, Reserva Natural Monterrico, 06024 Taxisco, Santa Rosa.

The turtles of Monterrico

The huge, sparsely populated expanses of beach around Monterrico are prime nesting sites for three types of **sea turtle**, including the largest of them all, the giant leatherback. The reserve was originally established to protect the turtles from the soup pot and curb the collection of their eggs, which are considered an aphrodisiac in Guatemala. Further dangers to the turtles include being hunted for their shells, drowned inside fishing nets and poisoned by pollution, especially plastic bags that resemble jellyfish, a favourite food. Turtles almost always nest in the dark, and on a moonless night in egg-laying season you have a good chance of seeing one in Monterrico.

Leatherback (*Dermochelys coriace*). The gargantuan leatherback is by far the largest of the world's turtles, growing to more than 2m in length and weighing up to 900 kilos. Called *baule* in Spanish, the leatherback gives the beach at Monterrico its name. It feeds almost exclusively on jellyfish, diving as deep as a kilometre beneath the sea in search of its prey. As its name suggests, it's the only turtle not to have a hard exterior shell; instead it has a layer of black, soft, rubbery skin. The leatherback frequents tropical and Arctic waters from Malaysia to Scotland and makes one of the longest migrations of any creature on earth. The species, which has been around for 200 million years, is in severe danger of extinction as a result of long-line fishing and gill-netting. It nests at Monterrico between mid-October and late December.

Olive Ridley (*Lepidochelys olivacea*). Spread throughout the tropical waters of the Pacific, Atlantic and Indian oceans, the Olive Ridley is the most numerous of the world's eight species of marine turtle and also one of the smallest, typically around 80cm long and weighing around 35kg. Olive Ridleys gather in huge numbers off favoured beaches to mate, after which the females return en masse to nest. They are common visitors at Monterrico (where they are known as *parlamas*) during their nesting season between July and December.

East Pacific Black Turtle (*Chelonia agassizi*). The East Pacific Black Turtle nests only on the Pacific coast between California and Ecuador, and is not found anywhere else in the world. It reaches more than a metre in length and has a characteristic dark heart-shaped shell. Some scientists believe it to be a subspecies of the more common green turtle, which shares a similar shell outline and can be found throughout the tropics. Its nesting season at Monterrico is the same as that of the Olive Ridleys, from July to December.

East to Hawaii

About 7km east along the beach from Monterrico, isolated **HAWAII** is another relaxed fishing village that has attracted a handful of regular visitors, including some wealthy Argentineans from Guatemala City who have built second homes on the beach. Locals live by fishing and farming and there's a large **turtle project**, run by the Association to Rescue and Conserve Wildlife (ARCAS), which releases ten thousand turtles each year into the wild. Volunteers are always needed (at any time of year, though June to November is the main nesting season), and though they prefer you to get in touch first, you can always just show up. The work is primarily nocturnal, with volunteers walking the beach collecting sea-turtle eggs and assisting in the management of the hatcheries. You can also assist in environmental education, mangrove reforestation, construction, and caiman and iguana captive-breeding. Accommodation costs US$50 a week (meals not included). Contact ARCAS, 4 Av 2-47, Zona 8, Mixco, San Cristóbal, Guatemala City (Ⓣ2478 4096, Ⓦwww.arcasguatemala.com). You can visit Hawaii on a day-trip from Monterrico, by catching a pick-up, the occasional public bus, or by renting a boat from the dock (about US$35 round trip).

Eggs and hueveros

All the species of turtle use similar **nesting** techniques, hauling themselves up the beach, laboriously digging a hole about 50cm deep with their flippers, and then with great effort depositing a clutch of a hundred or so soft, golf-ball-sized eggs. The turtles then bury the eggs and race back into the ocean. The eggs of the two smaller turtles take around fifty days to hatch, those of the leatherback require 72. When their time comes, the tiny turtles, no larger than the palm of your hand, use their flippers to dig their way out and make a mad dash for the water, desperately trying to avoid the waiting seabirds. Once they are in the water, their existence is still very hazardous for the first few years of their lives; only one in a hundred makes it to maturity.

Watching a turtle lay her eggs at Monterrico should be a memorable experience, but the presence of the local *hueveros* (egg collectors) will probably ensure that it's not. In season, Baule beach is lined with sentries, torches in hand, scanning the waves for turtles. After a turtle comes ashore and lays its eggs, these poachers dive in and harvest them – sometimes going so far as to pick up and dump the turtles elsewhere (unless it's a leatherback) before delving straight into the nest. Most foreign witnesses are content to take a photo and touch one of the bewildered creatures before it claws its way back to the ocean (note that you shouldn't use flash photography as it can upset and disorient the turtles), although some braver souls have challenged the *hueveros* and been threatened with machetes.

Officially, the taking of eggs is outlawed, but an informal deal has been struck so that out of every clutch of eggs collected, a dozen are donated to the reserve's turtle hatchery, from where around five thousand baby turtles are released each year. It's hoped that this agreement will ease relations between the local community, who sell the eggs for US$2 a dozen, and the conservationists.

During nesting season, visitors can donate to the project by backing a turtle hatchling in the Saturday "**turtle race**" on the beach. The sponsor of the winning baby turtle gets a dinner for two at a shoreside restaurant. However, most experts are now uneasy about encouraging such races (as well as close contact or "petting" of turtles), as the races involve grouping baby hatchlings together in buckets for days, a practice which disorients the turtles and interferes with the natal homing instinct by which they return to their beach of birth.

From Escuintla to El Salvador

Heading east from Escuintla the coastal highway brings you to **TAXISCO**, a quiet farming centre, famous for its cheese, which is set to the north of the main road. From here a branch road runs to La Avellana, from where you can catch a boat to Monterrico. Buses to Taxisco leave from the Zona 4 terminal in Guatemala City, calling at Escuintla and usually going on to the El Salvador border. If you get stuck in Taxisco, make for the fairly comfortable *Hotel Jeresol* (ⓣ7874 9114; ❸), on the main street.

Shortly before it reaches Taxisco the highway passes one of Guatemala's most unusual tourist sights, the **Auto Safari Chapín** (Tues–Sun 9am–5.30pm; US$4.75), Central America's only safari park. The park lies about a kilometre south of the highway (at Km 87.5) on land owned by one of the country's great *fincero* families, whose older generation were enthusiastic big-game hunters who covered the walls of the main hacienda with the heads and skins of animals from every corner of the globe. Their children, however, developed a strong dislike for these exploits and insisted on bringing their animals home alive. The end result is a safari park that includes giraffes, hippos, a pair of black rhinos, African lions, pumas, deer, tapir, antelope, coyotes and a superbly comprehensive collection of Central American animals, snakes and birds. Sadly, their elephant died after he was fed a piece of plastic, but aside from this mishap the animals are well cared for. Indeed, every species, except for the black rhino, has been successfully bred here in captivity.

The park is set up and managed in a very Guatemalan style, catering almost exclusively to domestic tourists, who like to make a day of it, picnicking, feasting in the restaurant and swimming in the pools. The entrance fee entitles you to a swim and a trip through the park in a minibus, although you can drive yourself if you have a car. There is also a small walk-through zoo, laid out around a lake, which is largely devoted to Central American wildlife.

Chiquimulilla and Las Lisas

Beyond Taxisco is **CHIQUIMULILLA**, from where another branch road heads up into the eastern highlands, through acres of lush coffee plantations, to the town of Cuilapa. Chiquimulilla is another fairly nondescript town that serves as a market centre for the surrounding area, but you might easily come here to change money, in which case Banrural, at 1 Calle and 1 Avenida, Zona 3, has a 5B ATM which takes Visa and MasterCard. If you need a bed, try the *Hotel*

Fiestas

Ladino culture dominates on the Pacific coast – despite the presence of a massive migrant labour force – so fiestas here tend to be more along the lines of fairs, with parades, amusement rides, fireworks, sporting events and heavy drinking. You'll see very little in the way of traditional costume or pre-Columbian dances, although marimba bands are popular and many of the fiestas are still based on local saints' days. Nevertheless, there's no doubt that the people of the coast like to have a good time and know how to enjoy themselves. Allegiances tend to be less local than those of the Maya population, and national holidays are celebrated as much as local ones.

January

11–18 Cuyotenango, main day 15th, events include some traditional dancing

12–15 Taxisco, events include bullfighting

12–16 Colomba, events include bullfighting

February

Varies Tecún Umán

March

11–19 Coatepeque, main day 15th

16–22 Puerto San José, main day 19th

Varies Ocós

April

30–May 4 Chiquimulilla, main day 3rd

July

25 Coatepeque, in honour of Santiago Apóstol

August

4–8 Champerico, main day 6th

October

20–26 Iztapa, main day 24th

November

23–26 Siquinalá

December

6–12 Retalhuleu, main day 8th

6–15 Escuintla, main day 8th

18–21 Chicacao, includes traditional dancing

31 La Democracia

San Carlos, Barrio Santiago (☎7885 0187; ❷), or the excellent-value *Turicentro Baru* (☎7885 0374; ❹), on the main highway at Km 114.5, which has motel-style rooms, most with a/c and TV, and a pool.

The town is in the heart of ladino cowboy country and superb **leather goods**, including machete cases and saddles, are handcrafted in the market, so you may want to do a little shopping. From the small bus terminal, a block or so from the plaza, there's a steady flow of traffic, about every thirty minutes to both the border and Guatemala City via Taxisco, and hourly to Cuilapa, departing from the other side of the market.

Heading on towards the border, the highway is raised slightly above the rest of the coastal plain, giving great views to the sea. A few kilometres south of the road, archeological digs at a long-forgotten Maya site called **La Nueva** have recently yielded some fascinating stelae and evidence that more than five thousand people lived here between the years 250 and 900 AD.

A short distance before the border a side road runs off to the seashore village of **LAS LISAS**, another good spot for spending time by the sea – especially if you plan to stay at the wonderful new hotel *Isleta de Gaia* (☎7885 0044, Ⓦwww.isleta-de-gaia.com; ❼–❾). This idyllic place, located on a little sandy islet, has twelve gorgeous bamboo-and-thatch bungalows with either ocean or lagoon views, a big pool, fine-quality European restaurant and a lovely clean beach – though again watch out for the undertow. Deep-sea fishing trips can be arranged here.

Pick-ups and hourly **buses** run between Las Lisas and Chiquimulilla 8am to 5pm (1hr 30min).

The border with El Salvador

The coastal highway finally reaches the border with El Salvador at the small settlement of **CIUDAD PEDRO DE ALVARADO**. Most of the commercial traffic and all of the pullman buses use the highland route to El Salvador, and consequently things are fairly quiet and easy-going here; though the border is open 24 hours. Should you get stuck for the night, try *Hotel Los Cuernos* (❸), which has clean rooms with private bath; more basic hotels and comedores can be found on the El Salvador side of the border. Second-class buses run to and from the Zona 4 terminal in Guatemala City every thirty minutes or so between 1am and 5pm, all of them travelling via Escuintla.

Travel details

Buses

Buses are the best way to get around on the Pacific coast, and the main highway, from Guatemala City to the Mexican border, is served by a constant flow of pullmans. Fewer pullmans head in the other direction, to the border with El Salvador, though there is a regular stream of second-class buses. On either of these main routes you can hop between buses and expect one to come along every thirty minutes or so, but if you plan to leave the highways, then it's best to travel to the nearest large town and find a local bus from there.

The coastal highway

Buses travelling from Guatemala City to the **Mexican border** (5hr) call every thirty minutes or so at all the main towns along the coastal highway. The bulk of these leave from the terminal at 19 Calle and 9 Avenida in Zona 1. The main companies plying the route to the Talismán and Tecún Umán border crossings are Fortaleza del Sur (22 daily, midnight–7pm; ⓣ2230 3390) and Chinita (14 daily, 1am–6pm; ⓣ2251 9144); both outfits have offices on 19 Calle between 8 and 9 avenidas in Zona 1. In addition, Galgos (2 daily), Línea Dorada (1 daily) and Tica Bus (1 daily) all run direct buses to **Tapachula** in Mexico (see p.99 for their addresses).

Heading in the other direction, buses leave every 30 minutes for **Taxisco** (3hr) and **Chiquimulilla** (3hr 30min) from the Zona 4 terminal in Guatemala City. Many buses continue on to the border with El Salvador at **Cuidad Pedro de Alvarado** (1hr from Chiquimulilla). Buses from the border to Guatemala City leave hourly from 6am to 5pm.

Coatepeque to: Retalhuleu (50min); Tecún Umán (40min).
Cocales to: Escuintla (30min).
Escuintla to: Antigua (1hr 15min); Guatemala City (1hr).
Retalhuleu to: Cocales (50min); Mazatenango (30min).

Branching off the coastal highway

To Champerico: From Retalhuleu (every 30min; 1hr 20min).
To Iztapa (via Puerto San José): From Guatemala City, Zona 4 terminal (hourly; 2hr 30min).
To Las Lisas: From Chiquimulilla (hourly; 1hr).
To Monterrico: From Pueblo Viejo (4 daily; 1hr). From Taxisco, via La Avellana (3hr 20min). From La Avellana, you must continue by boat (30min).
To Ocós: From Coatepeque (5–8 daily; 1hr 30min).
To Puerto San José: From Guatemala City, Zona 4 terminal (every 30 min; 2hr); hourly buses continue on to Iztapa (30min from San José).
To Tilapa: From Coatepeque (hourly; 1hr 30min).

East to the Caribbean

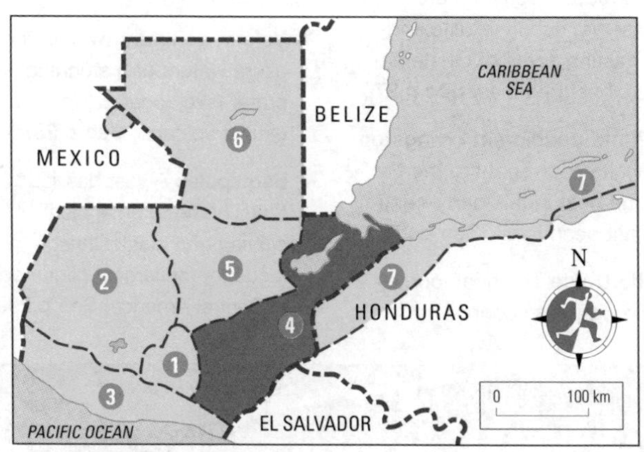

CHAPTER 4 Highlights

* **Quiriguá's carvings** Gawk at the monumental stelae stones, the largest in the Maya world, and the bizarre altars in the great plaza of this fascinating site. **See p.263**

* **Hotel del Norte** Enjoy the faded Caribbean class of Puerto Barrios' oldest hotel. **See p.268**

* **Punta de Manabique** A Caribbean-coast nature reserve, rich in wildlife and boasting some of Guatemala's best beaches. **See p.270**

* **Punta dancing in Lívingston** Shake your booty to the Garífuna beat in this party-central Caribbean town. **See p.272**

* **Río Dulce** The boat journey through this soaring, jungle-clad gorge is an exhilarating trip. **See p.277**

* **Hot spring waterfall** Soak away an afternoon or two at the exquisite hot spring–fed waterfall at the Finca el Paraíso. **See p.282**

* **Eastern highlands** An evocative landscape of ancient, eroded volcanoes, and parched, cacti-studded hills dotted with hard-drinking cowboy towns. **See p.284**

* **Volcán de Ipala** Swim in the azure waters of a stunning crater lake, located atop an extinct volcano. **See p.287**

* **Esquipulas** A vast basilica that's home to an ancient carving of a black Christ – the focus for the largest pilgrimage in Central America. **See p.290**

△ Hotel del Norte, Puerto Barrios

4

East to the Caribbean

The main highway northeast from the capital, the Carretera al Atlántico, at first descends through a particularly arid, virtually unpopulated region before meeting up with the Río Motagua at the El Rancho junction, where the road is surrounded by desert. From here on the highway runs through the **Motagua valley**, a broad corridor of low-lying land that separates the Sierra del Espíritu Santo, marking the border with Honduras, from the Sierra de las Minas. This valley soon opens out into a massive flood plain with the parallel ridges rising on either side. The land here is fantastically fertile and lush with vegetation at all times of the year, and the air is thick with humidity.

Dampened by tropical heat and repeated cloudbursts, the eastern section of the valley was densely populated in Maya times, when it served as an important trade route connecting the highlands with the Caribbean coast, and also was one of the main sources of jade. Following the decline of the Maya civilization, the area lay virtually abandoned until the end of the nineteenth century when the **United Fruit Company** cleared and colonized the land, planting thousands of acres with bananas and reaping massive profits. At the height of its fortunes, the company was powerful enough to bring down the government and effectively monopolized the country's trade and transport. Today bananas are still the main crop, though cattle are becoming increasingly important; the Carretera al Atlántico, which thunders through the valley, is also vital to the region's prosperity, and carries the bulk of Guatemala's foreign trade.

For the traveller, the Motagua valley is the main route to and from Petén, and most people get no more than a fleeting glimpse of it through a bus window. But two fascinating Maya sites are in this area: **Quiriguá**, just 4km from the main road, and the great ruins of **Copán**, across the border in Honduras (a side trip of a day or two) and covered in depth in Chapter Seven.

The region to the north of the Motagua valley is dominated by the subtropical **Río Dulce** and **Lago de Izabal**, a vast expanse of freshwater ringed by isolated villages, swamps, hot springs and caves. From Lago de Izabal, you can sail to the Caribbean past a manatee nature reserve and through the spectacular gorges of the **Río Dulce** to the coast at **Lívingston**, a laid-back town that's home to Guatemala's black Garífuna people. Boats connect Lívingston with the largely forgettable port of **Puerto Barrios**, jumping-off point for the coastal route into Honduras or boats to Belize.

Also covered in this chapter is the **eastern highlands**, a seldom-visited part of the country that spreads to the south and east of the capital. Its dry ladino lands are dominated by parched hills and ancient, eroded volcanoes, while the towns here are hot and dusty. The scenery is magnificent in places, but the region offers

little for the traveller, save the beautiful isolation of the **Ipala volcano**, with its stunning crater lake, and the curious holy town of **Esquipulas**, home of the famous Black Christ, the scene of Central America's largest annual pilgrimage.

The Motagua valley

Leaving Guatemala City, the Carretera al Atlántico also forms the main route to Cobán, until the road divides at the **El Rancho junction**, besides the decaying carcass of a huge abandoned paper mill. Here a branch road climbs into the highlands of the Verapaces, while the main highway continues down the Motagua valley through a dry and distinctly inhospitable landscape. The first place of any note is the **Río Hondo junction** where the road divides, with one arm heading south to Esquipulas and the three-way **border** with Honduras and El Salvador and the main branch continuing on to the coast. At the junction, you'll find an army of food sellers swarming around every bus that stops and a line of comedores, as well as a number of motels scattered around. Río Hondo is home to the impressive, well-organized Valle Dorado water park (daily 8.30am–5.30pm; US$6 per day), where a plethora of slides and pools set in shady grounds makes for a popular weekend retreat for Guatemalans. If you stay at the *Valle Dorado* motel, at Km 149 (Ⓣ7933 1111, Ⓦwww.hotelvalledorado.com; ❻), you get free entry to the park. For a cheaper bed, try *Hotel Nuevo Pasabién* (Ⓣ7934 7201, Ⓔpasabien@infovia.com.gt; ❺), with spacious air-conditioned bungalows and a pool, or the simpler *Hotel Santa Cruz* (Ⓣ & Ⓕ7934 7112; ❹), both at Km 126.

On down the valley the landscape starts to undergo a radical transformation; the flood plain opens out and the cacti are gradually overwhelmed by a profusion of tropical growth. It is this supremely rich flood plain that was chosen by both the Maya and the United Fruit Company, to the great benefit of both. Here the broad expanse of the valley is overshadowed by two parallel mountain ranges: to the northwest, the **Sierra de las Minas**, and on the other side, the **Sierra del Espíritu Santo**, along the border with Honduras.

The ruins of Quiriguá

Of one thing there is no doubt; a large city once stood there; its name is lost, its history unknown; and no account of its existence has ever before been published. For centuries it has lain as completely buried as if covered with the lava of Vesuvius. Every traveller from Yzabal to Guatimala [sic] has passed within three hours of it; we ourselves had done the same; and yet there it lay, like the rock-built city of Edom, unvisited, unsought, and utterly unknown.

John Lloyd Stephens (1841)

In 1841, John Stephens was so impressed with the ruins at **Quiriguá** that he planned to take them home, using the Río Motagua to float the stones to the Caribbean so that "the city might be transported bodily and set up in New York". Fortunately, the asking price was beyond his means and the ruins remained buried in the rainforest until 1909, when the land was bought by the United Fruit Company.

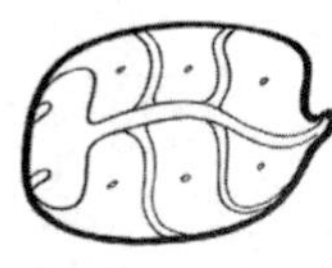
▲ Quiriguá emblem glyph

Today things are somewhat different: the ruins themselves are partially restored and reconstructed, and banana plantations stretch to the horizon in all directions. Few travellers visit Quiriguá, which is a shame because it does have some of the finest of all Maya carving. Only nearby Copán can match the magnificent stelae, altars and zoomorphs that are covered in well-preserved and superbly intricate glyphs and portraits.

A dense patch of lush rainforest surrounds the ruins, and weather conditions are decidedly **tropical**. Indeed, cloudbursts are the rule and the buzz of mosquitoes is almost uninterrupted – take repellent.

A brief history of Quiriguá

Quiriguá's history starts a short distance from the existing site, near the hospital in the village, where two stelae and a temple have been unearthed, marking the site of an earlier ceremonial centre. From there it moved to a second location nearby, where another stela has been found, before finally settling at the main site you see today.

The **early history** of Quiriguá is still fairly vague, and all that is certain is that towards the end of the Late Preclassic period (400 BC–250 AD) migrants

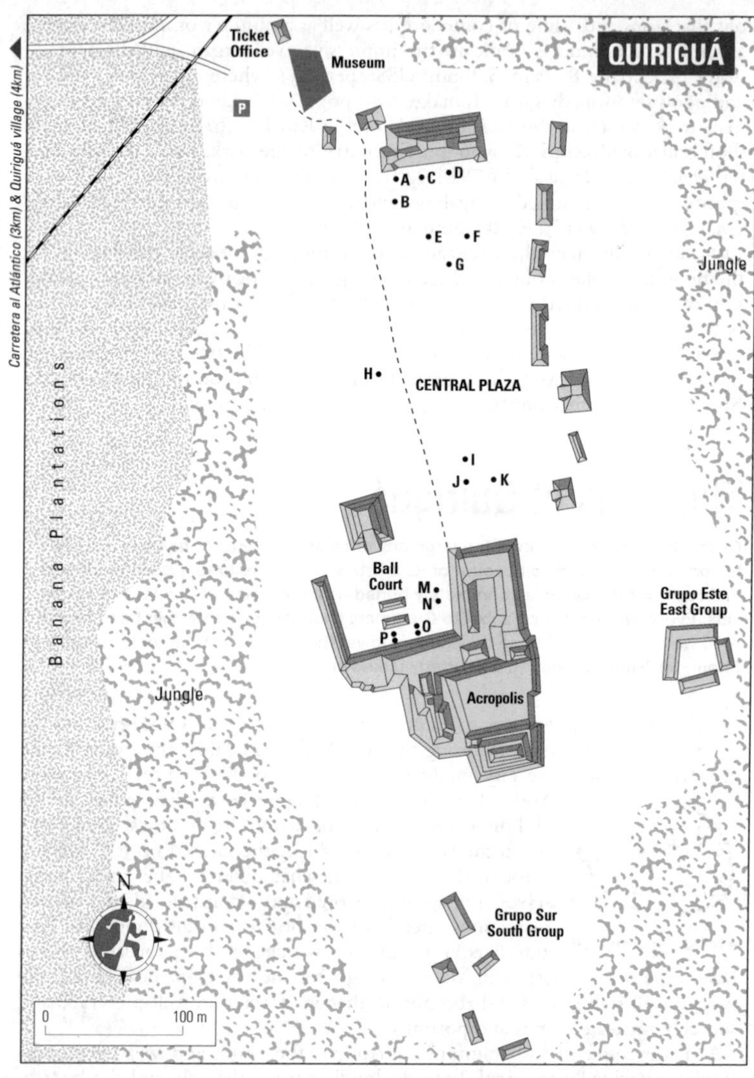

from the north, possibly Putun Maya from the Yucatán peninsula, established themselves as the rulers here. Thereafter, in the Early Classic period (250–600 AD), the centre was dominated by Copán and doubtless valued for its position on the banks of the Río Motagua, an important trade route, and as a source of jade, which is found throughout the valley. At this stage the rulers themselves may well have come from Copán, just 50km away. There certainly seem to have been close ties between the two sites: the architecture, and in particular the carving that adorns it, makes this very clear.

In the Late Classic period (600–800 AD) Quiriguá really started to come into its own. The site's own name glyph is first used in 731, just six years after its greatest leader, **Cauac Sky**, ascended to the throne. As a member of the long-standing Sky dynasty, Cauac Sky took control of a city that had already embarked upon a campaign of aggressive expansion, and was in the process of asserting its independence from Copán. In 737 matters came to a head when he captured Eighteen Rabbit, Copán's ruler, thus making the final break (see p.392). For the rest of his 56-year reign the city experienced an unprecedented building boom: the bulk of the great stelae date from this period and are decorated with Cauac Sky's portrait. For a century Quiriguá dominated the lower Motagua valley and its highly prized resources. Cauac Sky died in 771 and was succeeded 78 days later by his son, Sky Xul, who ruled for nineteen years until being usurped by Jade Sky, who took the throne in 790. Under Jade Sky, Quiriguá reached its peak, with fifty years of extensive building, including a radical reconstruction of the acropolis. But from the end of Jade Sky's rule, in the middle of the ninth century, the historical record fades out, as does the period of prosperity and power.

The ruins

Entering the site beneath the ever-dripping trees, you emerge at the northern end of the **Great Plaza**. To the left-hand side of the path from the ticket office and new museum is a badly ruined pyramid; directly in front of this are the **stelae** for which Quiriguá is justly famous. The nine stelae in the plaza are the tallest in the Maya world and their carving is some of the best. The style, similar in many ways to that of Copán, always follows a basic pattern, with portraits on the main faces and glyphs covering the sides. As for the figures, they represent the city's rulers, with Cauac Sky depicted on no fewer than seven (A, C, D, E, F, H and J). Two unusual features are particularly clear: the vast headdresses, which dwarf the faces, and the beards, a fashion that caught on in Quiriguá thirty years after it became popular in Copán. Many of the figures are shown clutching a ceremonial bar, the symbol of office, which has at one end a long-nosed god – possibly Chaac, the rain god – and at the other the head of a snake. The glyphs, crammed into the remaining space, record dates and events during the reign of the relevant ruler.

Largest of the stelae is E, which rises to a height of 8m and weighs 65 tonnes – it was originally sunk about 3m into the ground and set in a foundation of rough stones and red clay, but was reset in 1934 using concrete. The stelae are carved out of an ideal fine-grained sandstone, from a quarry about 5km from the site. The stones were probably rolled to the site on skids, set up, and then worked by sculptors standing on scaffolding. Fortunately for them the stone was soft once it had been cut, and fortunately for us it hardened with age.

Another feature that has helped Quiriguá earn its fame are the bizarre **zoomorphs**: six blocks of stone carved with interlacing animal and human figures. Some, like the turtle, frog and jaguar, can be recognized with relative ease, while others are either too faded or too elaborate to be accurately made out. The best of the lot is P, which shows a figure seated in Buddha-like pose, interwoven with a maze of others. The zoomorphs are usually referred to as altars and thought to be connected with the stela-altar complexes at Tikal, but their size and shape make this seem unlikely.

Around the plaza are several other interesting features. Along the eastern side are some unrestored structures that may have had something to do with Quiriguá's role as a river **port** – since the city's heyday the river has moved at least 1km from its original course. At the southern end of the plaza, near the main zoomorphs, you can just make out the shape of a **ball court** hemmed in on three sides by viewing stands, although the actual playing area is still buried beneath tons of accumulated soil. The **acropolis** itself, the only structure of any real size that still stands, is bare of decoration. Trenches dug beneath it have shown that it was built on top of several previous versions, the earliest ones constructed out of rough river stones. Apart from these central structures, there are a few smaller unrestored complexes scattered in the surrounding forest, but nothing of particular interest.

Quiriguá practicalities

The **ruins** (daily 7.30am–5pm; US$4) are situated some 70km beyond the junction at Río Hondo, and 4km from the main road, reached down a side road that serves the banana industry. All buses running between Puerto Barrios and Guatemala City pass by – just ask the driver to drop you at the ruins and you'll end up at the entrance road, which is about four hours from Guatemala City. From here there's a fairly regular bus service to the site itself, as well as a number of motorbikes and pick-ups that shuttle passengers back and forth. The entrance to the ruins is marked by a ticket office, a couple of mini-tiendas, a coconut vendor or two and a car park. A small site **museum** has informative displays about the site's historical significance and its geopolitical role in Maya times as well as a diorama showing the extent of the ruins that remain unexcavated.

To get back to the highway, wait until a bus or taxi motorbike turns up. Buses, often packed with plantation workers, are the most likely to stop at the barrier. If you want to walk back to Quiriguá village, you can take a short cut by heading towards the highway for 2km along the access road to the highway, then turning left (west) and following the (disused) train track – it's a further kilometre to the village.

There's nowhere to stay at the ruins themselves, but two **hotels** can be found in the **village** – also known as Quiriguá – which is just off the highway, about 2km back towards Guatemala City. Nowadays it's a run-down sort of place, strung out along the railway track, but in the past it was famous for its hospital of tropical diseases, run by the United Fruit Company. This imposing building, which still stands on the hill above the track, is now a state-run workers' hospital. Next to the hospital is the plaza, where you'll find the decent *Hotel y Restaurante Royal* (☎7947 3639; ❷–❸), with old rooms downstairs (though some are some windowless) and more modern rooms on the upper floor, and a dependable comedor-style menu. The gloomy *Hotel el Eden* (☎7947 3281; ❷), next to the old station, also serves **meals**.

To the coast: Puerto Barrios

Heading on towards the Caribbean, an additional 15km brings you to **La Trinchera**, junction for the branch road to Mariscos on the shores of Lago de Izabal. Further down the Motagua valley the road pushes on through an evergreen landscape of cattle ranches and fruit trees, splitting again at the junction for the twin towns of **MORALES** and **BANANERA**, a ramshackle collection of wooden huts and railway tracks that was the headquarters of the United Fruit Company (see p.433) for much of the twentieth century. Today these squalid towns are of no interest at all except as the transport hub of the lower Motagua, served by all the second-class buses for Petén and a regular shuttle of minibuses to and from Río Dulce. Non-direct Litegua buses between Puerto Barrios and Guatemala City also pull in here.

A short distance beyond the turn for Morales/Bananera, you pass the **Ruidosa junction**, from where the highway to Petén heads northwest, out over the Río

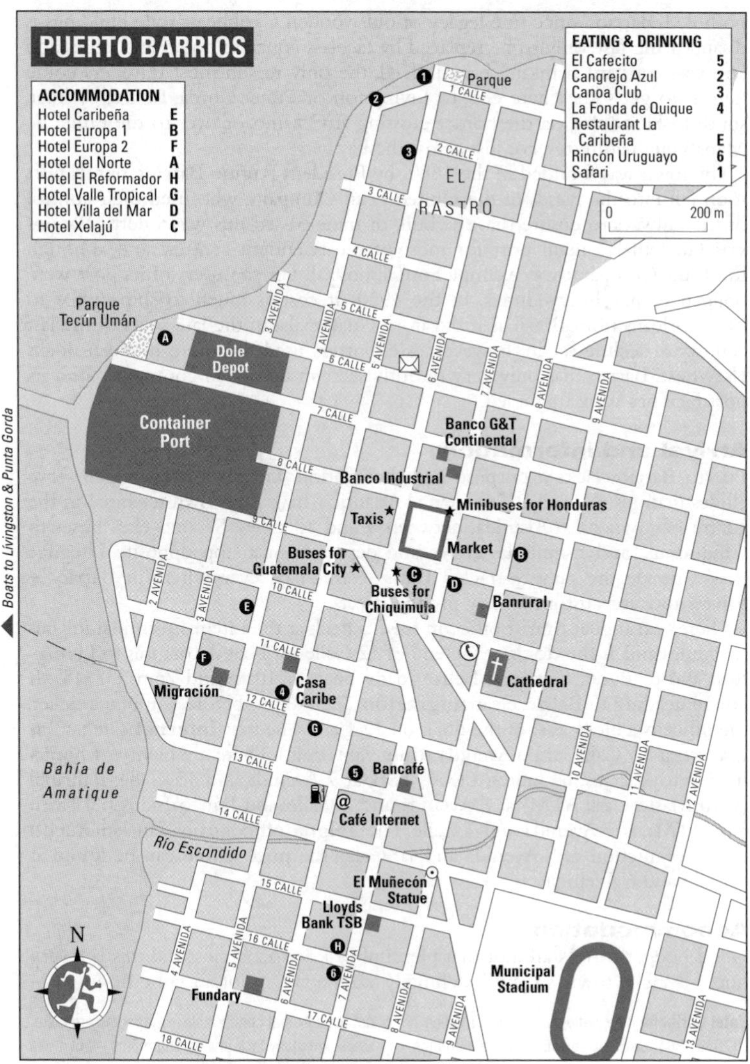

Dulce. A further 50km to the northeast and you reach the Caribbean, with the road dividing for the last time, right to the old port of Puerto Barrios and left to Puerto Santo Tomás de Castillo, the modern town and dock.

Puerto Barrios and around

At the final junction on the highway, unless you happen to be driving a banana truck, the turn for **PUERTO BARRIOS** is the one to take. Hot and sprawling, the town is a pretty forlorn place, its wide, poorly lit streets badly potholed. Barrios' once fine legacy of old wooden Caribbean-style buildings is disappearing fast, only to be replaced by faceless concrete hotels and stores and an excess of hard-drinking bars. Indeed, the only reason most travellers come here is to get somewhere else: to Lívingston or Punta Gorda, Belize, by boat, south to Honduras via the border crossing at Corinto, or over to the Punta de Manabique nature reserve just across the bay.

The town was founded in the 1880s by President Rufino Barrios, but its port soon fell into the hands of the United Fruit Company, who used their control of the railways to ensure that the bulk of trade passed this way. Puerto Barrios was Guatemala's main port for most of the twentieth century, and although the Fruit Company was exempt from almost all tax, the users of its port were obliged to pay heavy duties. In the 1930s it cost as much to ship coffee to New Orleans from Brazil as it did from Guatemala. In the late years of the last century a decline set in, however, as exporters used the more modern docks elsewhere. Barrios has only very recently seen an upturn in commerce after its port facilities were upgraded.

Arrival and information

Puerto Barrios lacks a purpose-built bus station. Litegua **buses**, which serve all destinations along the Carretera al Atlántico, have their own terminal in the centre of town on 6 Avenida, between 9 and 10 calles. Second-class buses to Chiquimula and Esquipulas arrive and depart from a stop opposite Litegua's depot, beside the railway tracks. **Taxis** seem to be everywhere in Barrios – drivers toot for custom as they ply the streets.

There's no Inguat tourist office in town: check at the Litegua terminal for bus schedules and at the **dock** at the end of 12 Calle for boat departures to Lívingston and to Punta Gorda in Belize (daily boats at 10am and 2pm; US$15). If you're heading to Belize, clear **migración** (7am–8pm) before you buy a ticket; the office is a block east of the dock on 12 Calle. The best **Internet** café is *Café Internet*, at 13 Calle and 6 Avenida (daily 9am–9pm). There are plenty of **banks** in Puerto Barrios, including Lloyds TSB, at 7 Avenida and 15 Calle; Banrural (with MasterCard ATM) at 8 Avenida and 9 Calle; and Banco Industrial (with Visa ATM), at 7 Avenida and 7 Calle. The **Telgua** office (daily 7am–midnight) is at the junction of 8 Avenida and 10 Calle; the **post office** can be found at 6 Calle and 6 Avenida.

Accommodation

Good budget **hotels** are not that plentiful in Puerto Barrios, and this is a very hot and sticky town, so you'll definitely want a fan, if not air conditioning.

Hotel Caribeña 4 Av, between 10 and 11 calles ⓣ7948 0384. Large place with good-value rooms (some with a/c) including doubles, triples and quadruples; friendly management and a quality seafood restaurant attached. ❷–❹

Hotel Europa 2 3 Av and 12 C ⓣ948 1292. Clean, safe and friendly place, ideally located for the dock. All the good-value rooms have fan and private shower and there are fair rates for single travellers. The almost identical *Hotel Europa 1* is at 8 Av and 8 C (ⓣ948 0127). Both ❸

Hotel del Norte 7 C and 1 Av ⓣ7948 0087. This classic Caribbean-style wooden hotel is one of the most atmospheric places to stay in the country. It's not actually that comfortable – the rooms are quite small and many lack private bathrooms – but it has a nice swimming pool, and a location, overlooking the Bahía de Amatique, that's magnificent. There's a separate block with modern a/c rooms, too. Best of all is the mahogany-panelled restaurant and bar – though the food doesn't match the decor. ❸–❹

Hotel El Reformador 7 Av & 16 C ⓣ7948 0384. Efficiently run place with a restaurant and well-kept, modern rooms, all with cable TV and either fan or a/c. ❸–❹

Hotel Valle Tropical 12 C, between 5 and 6 aves ⓣ948 7084. Large motel-style block with well-equipped, if bland, rooms; all have a/c, TV, bathroom and double bed. There's safe parking, a swimming pool and a restaurant. ❻

Hotel Villa del Mar 9 C & 7 Av ☎948 1011. Safe and friendly family-run hospedaje positioned above a *cafetería* close to the market. The fifteen small rooms are bare but serviceable, but only one has a private bath. ❷

Hotel Xelajú 9 C, between 6 and 7 aves ☎948 0482. It looks grim from the outside, but this cheap place has acceptable, if not spotless, rooms. ❷

The Town and around

The main **market**, sprawling around disused railway lines at the corner of 9 Calle and 6 Avenida, is the town's main focus and the best place to start to get a grip of Barrios' modern identity. Here lines of ladino vendors furiously whisk up lush fruit *licuado* drinks from a battery of blenders, while Garífuna women swat flies from piles of *pan de coco*. West along 7 Calle from here, it's about 800m to the last surviving landmark to Barrios' Caribbean architectural heritage, the elegant *Hotel del Norte* (see "Accommodation"), its timber corridors warped by a century of storms and salty air – be sure to take a look inside at the colonial-style bar and dining room. Next to the hotel, there are a tiny park and pier, where you gaze out over the glistening waters of the Bahía de Amatique.

Across the bay, 7km west of Puerto Barrios, is **Santo Tomás de Castillo**, the newest port facility in the country. To look at the concrete plaza, the planned housing and the fenced-off docks, you'd never guess that the place had a moment's history, but oddly enough it's been around for a while. It was founded in 1604 by the Spanish, who inhabited it with some Black Caribs, the survivors of an expedition against pirates on Roatán Island. The pirates in turn sacked Santo Tomás, but it was revived in 1843, when a Belgian colony was established here. Today it's connected by a regular shuttle of local buses to Puerto Barrios, though other than the docks themselves there's nothing much to see.

Eating

For a cheap feed, there's an abundance of **comedores** and snack bars around the market – look out for *pan de coco* (coconut bread) and local speciality *tortillas de harina* (wheat tortillas stuffed with meat and beans). Otherwise, most of the restaurants in town are quite expensive by Guatemalan standards. Puerto Barrios really excels at **fish and seafood**, and you should certainly try some *tapado* (seafood soup with coconut, plantain and spices) while you're here, though it's not a cheap dish to prepare.

El Cafecito 13 C, between 6 & 7 aves. The only proper café in town, with espresso and cappuccino, bagels, cakes and some Portuguese dishes.

Cangrejo Azul end of 4 Av. Close to the *Safari*, this rival seafood restaurant has marginally cheaper prices, and a dining table or two on stilts out in the bay. Try the *camarones al ajo* or *sopa pescado*.

La Caribeña 4 Av, between 10 and 11 calles. Big barn of a restaurant inside the *Hotel Caribeña* that does a superb *caldo de mariscos* (seafood soup).

La Fonda de Quique 12 C & 5 Av. Formal little a/c restaurant, with proper tablecloths and a menu that specializes in seafood.

Rincón Uruguayo 7 Av and 16 C. Meat-eaters won't do better than this (relatively) moderately priced place, which excels at *parrilladas* (South American–style meat barbecues). They also offer the odd vegetarian dish like barbecued spring onions and *papas asados*. Closed Mon.

Safari northern end of 5 Av. Ten minutes from the centre, this locally renowned restaurant is a very large place with huge (if a little pricey at around US$7–9 a main) portions of seafood. It's rarely that busy, however, and a bit overrated.

Drinking, clubs and cultural activities

As befits a port, Puerto Barrios has its share of striptease **bars** – a lot of the action is centred around 6 and 7 avenidas and 6 and 7 calles. Reggae and punta

Puerto Barrios: travel connections

Litegua **pullmans** – which are some of the country's best – ply the Carretera al Atlántico to Guatemala City fifteen times daily from 1am to 4pm (5hr–5hr 30min) from their private terminal just southeast of the market on 6 Av. Eight of these travel via a detour to Morales, which adds up to 30 minutes to the journey; the other seven *especiales* travel direct to the capital. Tickets can be bought in advance, although it's not necessary except perhaps on a Sunday afternoon. **Second-class buses** go from Puerto Barrios to Chiquimula every hour from 6am to 5pm (4hr). If you're heading for Río Dulce, take any bus heading west and change at La Ruidosa junction.

Lanchas leave for Lívingston from the Muelle Municipal **dock** at the end of 12 Calle when full (about every 40min; 6.30am–6pm; US$3.50; 30min); a much slower daily ferry departs at 10am and 5pm (US$1.50; 1hr 30min). To Punta Gorda in Belize, a *lancha* leaves at 10am and 2pm (US$16; 1hr 15min). If you're heading to Belize, remember to clear **migración** (7am–8pm) first; the office is on 12 Calle, a block inland from the dock. Departure times are subject to change, so check them at the dock first.

rock are the sounds on the street in Barrios, and you'll catch a fair selection at weekends in the *Canoa Club*, on 5 Av and 2 C. For more cerebral pursuits, Casa Caribe, on the corner of 11 C and 5 Av, is a small **culture centre** which features art and photographic exhibitions and occasional classical concerts.

Overland to Honduras

Puerto Barrios is an excellent jumping-off point to the north coast of Honduras and the Bay Islands, a fairly straightforward journey via San Pedro Sula, Honduras's second city. To **get to Honduras** from Barrios, minibuses depart from the marketplace (every 30min; 6.30am–4.30pm) and pass through the town of Entre Ríos (for *migración*) before continuing on to the border (1hr). You may be asked for an unofficial "exit tax" (US$1–2) on the Guatemalan side and an entry fee of a similar sum from the Hondurans. On the other side, pick-ups and microbuses leave the border to the village of **Corinto**, 4km away, from where buses depart for Puerto Cortés (every 90min; 2hr 30min) via the pretty village of Omoa. If you set out early from Puerto Barrios, you should get to San Pedro Sula by lunchtime, and it's certainly possible to catch an afternoon flight to one of the Bay Islands (see Chapter Seven) and catch a sunset cocktail at one of the beach bars. San Pedro Sula is well connected with Puerto Cortés by Citul and other buses (every 30min 5am–7.30pm; 1hr 15min); the Citul terminal is located just across the plaza from the *migración*.

Punta de Manabique

North of Puerto Barrios, the hooked peninsula that juts into the Bahía de Amatique, the **Punta de Manabique**, contains virtually all Guatemala's finest Caribbean beaches and offers superb ecotourism opportunities. Most of the area has been designated a nature reserve, the Biotopo Punta de Manabique, which is managed by the conservation group **Fundary**. It's one of the richest wetland habitats in Central America, and the swamps, mangroves and patches of flooded rainforest are home to caimen, iguana, spider and howler monkeys, peccary, plus a few manatee, some jaguar, tapir and bountiful birdlife, including the extremely rare yellow-headed parrot (*Amazona oratrix*). The reserve also includes the adjacent coastal water and the only coral-reef outcrops in Guatemalan waters.

About 1000 people, mainly immigrants from western Guatemala, eke out a living in Manabique, surviving by subsistence fishing (mainly for sardines, which are then salted) and hunting (particularly iguana) and cultivating small rice paddies. Their livelihood is increasingly under threat from cattle ranchers who are starting to encroach into the drier lands in the south of the reserve. Most locals are very poor, and Fundary have been busy establishing basic healthcare measures, setting up schools and providing teachers, and raising environmental awareness. They've also been working to develop **ecotourism** in the area, an initiative that's included the establishment of a hotel lodge, *El Saraguate* (reservations through Fundary; US$8 per bed), which offers four clean rooms, each with three or four beds, and a restaurant which serves simple but excellent meals: lobster, grilled fish and chicken dishes. From the lodge there's a purpose-built wooden walkway over nearby swampland, jungle paths and coastal walks along stunning palm-fringed white-sand beaches, as well as excellent swimming. Boat trips also can be arranged along the **Canal Inglés** ("English Channel") – named after British loggers who dug a ten-kilometre trench between Laguna Santa Isabel and the Río Piteros – which offers superb bird-watching. Local guides can be hired at the hotel, while sport fishing in the Bahía la Graciosa or open sea can be organized, too. It's also possible to **camp** (US$3 per person) at the reserve's scientific research station, which is a kilometre east of the Punta de Manabique in Cabo Tres Puntos.

To **get to** Manabique, you have two choices. To explore the area properly, head to Puerto Barrios and get in touch with Fundary, 17 Calle between 5 and 6 avenidas (Ⓣ7948 0435, Ⓣ & Ⓕ7948 0944, Ⓔmanabique@intelnet.net.gt; or in Guatemala City, Diagonal 6 17–19, Zona 10; Ⓣ7333 4957, Ⓦwww.guate.net/fundarymanabique). The group can arrange for you to arrive via boat (around US$70 return for up to eight people), a necessity as there are no roads to Manabique. Packages are also available from US$95 per person for two nights of accommodation, meals and transportation. Boats leave from the pier in Puerto Barrios. The other alternative is to travel to Manabique on a day-trip (around US$25 per person) from Lívingston, though a minimum of six people is usually necessary. These outings usually focus on spending a day at the beach, though there's nothing to stop you from hiring a guide locally on arrival to explore the wetlands. Tours can be arranged by several travel agents, including Exotic Travel (see p.272), based in the *Bahía Azul* restaurant.

Lívingston, Río Dulce and Lago de Izabal

Guatemala is at its most sultry and tropical in the fascinating region fringing the nation's slither of Caribbean coastline. The area's distinctive identity – more reminiscent of neighbouring Belize than the bulk of the country – is most apparent in **Lívingston**, which draws travellers eager to experience the intoxicating music and culture of the Garífuna people. Inland from Lívingston it's easy to spend several days exploring the plunging gorges of the **Río Dulce** and the shoreline of the huge, freshwater **Lago de Izabal**, with its hot springs and lakeside hotels. The western fringes of the lake, best explored from the sleepy town of **El Estor**, are protected as part of the **Reserva Bocas del Polochic**, which harbours a tremendous variety of wildlife (including alligators, iguanas and turtles, as well as large numbers of migratory birds and resident parrots and toucans).

Leaving El Estor it's possible to travel up through the isolated Polochic valley towards Cobán and the Verapaces, or even take an adventurous route that spirals up the shoulder of the Sierra de la Cruz mountains to Cahabón, just down the road from Lanquín and Semuc Champey. If you're heading to the Petén, you'll find a steady stream of buses (night and day) from **Río Dulce Town**, an unlovely transport hub with several banks and a cybercafé or two.

Lívingston

Looking out over the Bahía de Amatique and only accessible by boat, **LÍVINGSTON** not only enjoys a superb setting but also offers a unique fusion of Guatemalan and Caribbean culture in which marimba mixes with Marley. Many locals call the town La Buga ("the mouth"), referring to its location at the mouth of the Río Dulce. Along with several other villages in Central America, Lívingston provides a hub for the displaced **Garífuna**, or black Carib people, who are now strung out along the Caribbean coast between southern Belize and northern Nicaragua. To a lesser extent, the town also acts as a focal point for the Q'eqchi' Maya of the Río Dulce region.

Lívingston is undoubtedly one of the most fascinating places in Guatemala, and many visitors find the languid rhythm of life here hypnotic. The town is as popular with weekending Guatemalans as it is with international travellers, and offers a welcome break from mainstream Latino culture. Carib **food** is generally excellent and more varied than the usual comedor dishes, and Garífuna punta rock and reggae make a pleasant change from the standard merengue beat. Although certainly not unaffected by the pressures of daily life in Central America, the general atmosphere is pretty chilled.

Arrival and information

The only way you can get to Lívingston is **by boat**, either from Puerto Barrios, the Río Dulce, Belize or, occasionally, from Omoa in Honduras. Wherever you come from, you'll arrive at the main dock on the south side of town, where a dreadlocked hotel or ganja hustler may greet you – most are not that pushy.

Lívingston is a small place with only a handful of streets, and you can see most of what there is to see in an hour or so. Straight ahead up the hill is Calle Principal, the main drag with most of the restaurants, bars and shops, and the **immigration office** (daily 6am–7pm), where you can get an exit stamp, if you're heading for Belize, or an entrance stamp, if you've just arrived.

For **changing money**, try either Bancafé (with Visa ATM) or Banrural, both on the main drag. The **Telgua** office (daily 7am–midnight) is on the right, up the main street from the docks, next door to the **post office**. Several places offer **Internet** access: try Buganet (where you can transfer photos to CD) or Happy Fish on the main drag – rates are around US$2.50 an hour.

Exotic Travel (Ⓣ7947 0049, Ⓔkjchew@hotmail.com), in the same building as the *Bahía Azul* restaurant, and *Happy Fish* (Ⓣ7902 7143), just down the road, are the best **travel agents** in town. The helpful owners can arrange **trips**

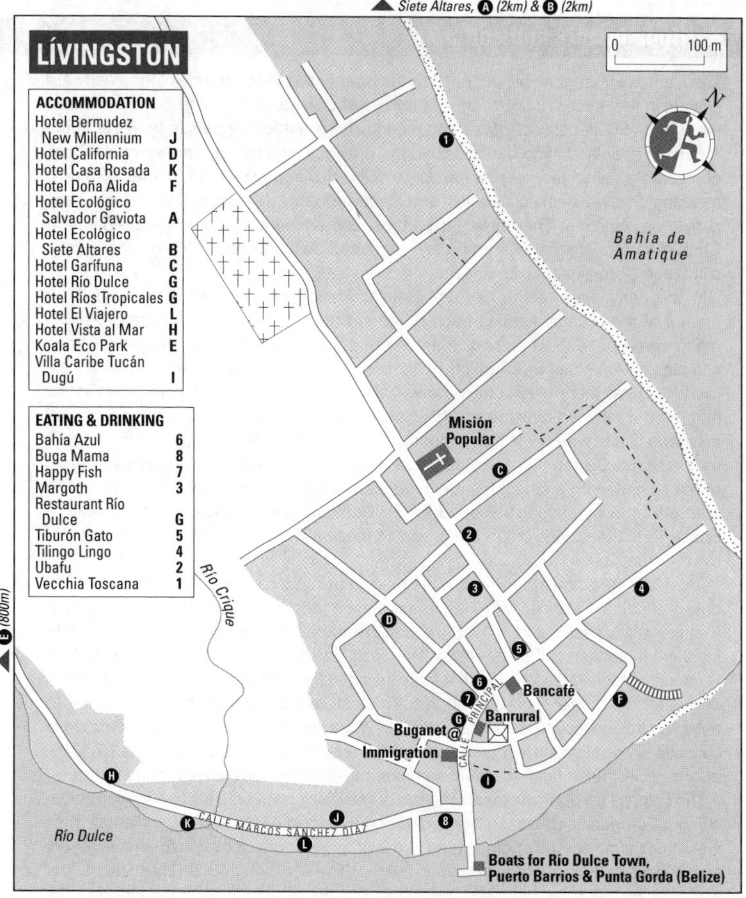

(minimum six people) around the area, including visits to the fine white-sand beach of Playa Blanca (US$10) and the Sapodilla Cayes off Belize for **snorkelling** (US$30). Several companies, including Exotic Travel, run morning boat trips up the Río Dulce (US$9 per person).

Scheduled **ferry boats** leave for Puerto Barrios daily at 5am and 2pm (1hr 30min), supplemented by **lanchas**, which leave when full (roughly every 40min 6.30am–5.30pm; 30min). Boats also run to Punta Gorda in **Belize** on Tuesdays and Fridays at 7am (1hr) and to Omoa in **Honduras** when there are sufficient numbers (US$35 per person, minimum 6 people; 2hr 30min). Combined boat/shuttle bus tickets are sold by Exotic Travel to Antigua, Copán (both US$30), San Pedro Sula (US$35) and La Ceiba (US$45).

Tickets (US$10 per person) for the **river trip up the Río Dulce** can be booked by any travel agent in Lívingston. Most *lanchas* leave at around 9am. The trip takes around 2hr 30min, depending on how many stops the skipper makes – most stop at the Castillo de San Felipe but are otherwise eager to get to Río Dulce Town as quickly as possible. If you want a more leisurely cruise so

Garífuna history and culture

The Garífuna trace their history back to the island of **St Vincent**, one of the Windward Islands in the eastern Caribbean. At the time of Columbus's landing in the Americas, the islands of the Lesser Antilles had recently been settled by people from the South American mainland, who had subdued the previous inhabitants, the Arawaks. These new people called themselves *Kalipuna*, or *Kwaib*, from which the names *Garífuna*, meaning "cassava-eating people", and *Carib* probably derived; St Vincent was then known as Yurimein. The natives the Europeans encountered were descendants of Carib men and Arawak women. A few thousand descendants of the original Caribs still live in Dominica and St Vincent.

In the early seventeenth century, Britain, France and the Netherlands vied for control of the islands, fighting each other and the Caribs. The admixture of African blood came in 1635 when two Spanish ships, carrying slaves from Nigeria to their colonies in America, wrecked off St Vincent and the survivors took refuge on the island. At first there was conflict between the Caribs and the Africans. The Caribs had been weakened by wars and disease, however, and eventually the predominant race was black, with some Carib blood. These people became known by the English as the **Black Caribs** – in their language they were *Garinagu*, or *Garífuna*. For most of the seventeenth and eighteenth centuries, St Vincent was nominally under British control but in practice it belonged to the Garífuna, and in 1660 with the Treaty of Basse Terre the islands of Dominica and St Vincent were granted "perpetual possession" to the Caribs.

A century later, however, Britain attempted to gain full control of St Vincent, but was driven off by the Caribs, with French assistance. Another attempt twenty years later was more successful, and in 1783 the British imposed a treaty on the Garífuna, allowing them more than half of the island. The treaty was never accepted, however, and the Garífuna continued to defy British rule, resulting in frequent battles in which the French consistently lent the Garífuna support. The last serious attempt by the Garífuna to establish their independence took place in 1795, when both sides suffered horrendous casualties. The Garífuna lost their leader, Chief Joseph Chatoyer, and on June 10, 1796, after a year of bitter fighting, the French and the Garífuna surrendered to the British.

The colonial authorities could not allow a free Black society to survive among slave-owning European settlers, so it was decided to deport the Garífuna population. They were hunted down, their homes (and in the process some of their culture) destroyed, and hundreds died of starvation and disease. The survivors, 4300 Black Caribs and 100 Yellow Caribs, as they were designated by the British, were transported to the nearby island of Balliceaux; within six months more than half of them had died, many of yellow fever. In March 1797, the remaining survivors were loaded aboard ships and sent to **Roatán**, one of the Bay Islands, off the coast of Honduras (see Chapter Seven). One of the ships was captured by the Spanish and taken to Trujillo, on the mainland, while barely 2000 Garífuna lived to make the landing on Roatán, where the British abandoned them.

that you can take in the attractions along the way, and perhaps stop for a swim, you're looking at chartering a boat: speak to agents Exotic Travel or Happy Fish, or try bargaining hard with the *lancheros* based at the dock.

Accommodation

There are plenty of cheap **hotels** in town, though not much choice in the mid-range and luxury brackets. You'll find a couple of places right on the beach, but these are quite a hike from town. Book ahead on holidays, but at other times you should easily be able to find a bed.

Perhaps in response to pleas for help from the Garífuna, who continued to die on Roatán, the Spanish Commandante of Trujillo arrived and took possession of the island, shipping survivors to Trujillo where they were in demand as labourers. The Spanish had never made a success of agriculture here and the arrival of the Garífuna, who were proficient at growing crops, benefited the colony considerably. The boys were conscripted and the Garífuna men gained a reputation as soldiers and mercenaries. Soon they began to move to other areas along the coast, and in 1802, 150 of them were brought as wood-cutting labourers to southern Belize, from where they moved along the Caribbean coast and settled in Lívingston in 1806.

By the start of the twentieth century, the Garífuna were well established in the Lívingston area, with the women employed in bagging and stacking *cohune* nuts and the men working as fishermen. As in the previous century, the Garífuna continued to travel widely in search of work, and in World War II Garífuna men supplied crews for both British and US merchant ships. Since the 1970s, many have left Central America for the US, where there's now a 50,000-strong population in New York, plus smaller Garífuna communities in New Orleans and Los Angeles. There's even a community in London. Today most Garífuna live in villages along the Caribbean coast of Honduras (where they number more than 100,000) with smaller populations in Belize (around 16,000) and Nicaragua.

Most Garífuna speak Spanish (and some English) plus the unique Garífuna **language** that blends Arawak, French, Yuroba, Banti and Swahili words. Though virtually all worship at either Catholic or evangelical churches, their Afro-Carib **dugu** (religion) – centred on ancestor worship and comparable in some respects to Haitian voodoo – continues to be actively practised. *Dugu* is immersed in ritual, and death is seen as the freeing of a spirit, a celebration which involves dancing, drinking and music. Garífuna music, or **punta**, is furiously rhythmic, characterized by mesmeric drum patterns and ritual chanting, and it's very easy to hear its West African origins.

For many Guatemalans, the Garífuna remain something of a national curiosity, a mysterious and somewhat mistrusted phenomenon. They are not only subjected to the same discrimination that plagues the Maya population, but also viewed with a strange awe that gives rise to a range of fanciful myths. Uninformed commentators have argued that their society is matriarchal, polygamous, and directed by a secret royal family. Accusations of voodoo and cannibalism are commonplace too, while it's claimed that the women speak a language incomprehensible to the men, passing it on only to their daughters. The prejudices, and the isolated nature of the community – numbering only around 6000 in Guatemala – mean many young Garífuna are more drawn to African-American (hip-hop) and also Jamaican (rastafari) influence than Latin culture.

For more on the Garífuna, consult ⓦwww.garifuna.com or the September 2001 feature in the *National Geographic* magazine.

Hotel Bermudez New Millennium C Marcos Sánchez Díaz ⓣ7947 0476. A big, ugly three-storey concrete block of a hotel, but the management is hospitable and there are good views of La Buga from the communal corridors. The large, bare rooms all have screened windows and private bath; those on the upper floors are better. ❷

Hotel California turn left just before the *Bahía Azul* restaurant. Clean hotel, offering reasonable if sparse rooms, all with fan and most with private bath. ❷

Hotel Casa Rosada C Marcos Sánchez Díaz, about 400m left of the dock ⓣ7947 0303, ⓦwww.hotelcasarosada.com. The ownership has recently changed but standards remain as high at this delightful hotel, with a harbourfront plot and lush, spacious grounds. The small, cheery wooden cabins are a little overpriced (and lack private bath) but do have real charm. Excellent, wholesome meals served as well. ❹

Hotel Doña Alida turn right immediately after the *Tucán Dugú*, then walk north 250m ⓣ7947 0027. Welcoming owners and a selection of spacious modern rooms in a quiet cliffside location, with a little beach below. Room nos. 10 and 11 both have excellent sea (and sunset) views. ❸–❹

Hotel Ecológico Salvador Gaviota Playa Quehueche ⓣ5514 3275, ⓔhotelsgaviota@hotmail.com. This isolated place on the way to the Siete Altares is right on a slim, clean beach, with rooms and thatched cabañas with bath in grassy grounds. Tasty, inexpensive local food including fresh fish is available. You can walk to the centre of town in about half an hour, or a *lancha* ride is around US$3 per person from the main dock. ❷

Hotel Ecológico Siete Altares Playa Quehueche ⓣ5205 7864, ⓦwww.geocities.com/sietealtares. Attractive beachfront hotel featuring comfortable en-suite cabañas that sleep two to six, and a restaurant serving good breakfasts, pasta and seafood. *Lanchas* charge US$3 to take you here from the centre of town, which is about 2.5km away. ❹

Hotel Garífuna turn left off C Principal towards the *Ubafu* bar and walk 250m ⓣ7948 1091. Well-managed and secure locally owned guest house with good-value if fairly featureless rooms, all with fan and private shower. ❷

Hotel Río Dulce C Prinicpal ⓣ7947 0764. This place only has a handful of plain rooms, both above and behind the restaurant, but they're kept clean, and soap and towels are provided. ❷

Hotel Ríos Tropicales C Principal ⓣ7947 0158. Attractive hotel with pleasant, well-presented wood-panelled rooms, some very spacious, with good beds and fans. The small sunny patio at the rear is a nice retreat, with hammocks for chilling. ❸

Hotel El Viajero C Marcos Sánchez Díaz ⓣ5718 9544. Friendly family-run place with cheap rooms, all with fan and some with private bath, though the beds are ancient. There's a snack bar, too. ❶–❷

Hotel Vista al Mar C Marcos Sánchez Díaz, about 450m left of the dock ⓣ7947 0131. Simple but attractive rooms in a wooden building, all with good fans and some with private bath; one has a little deck balcony overlooking a creek. Run by amiable Latino locals who also manage a comedor. ❸

Koala Eco Park C Marcos Sánchez Díaz, 1.5km west of the dock ⓔgezza1510@yahoo.com.au. New Aussie-Garífuna-owned place on a large shady plot with three cabañas (one has private bath), camping and hammock space, a huge pool and full-sized pool tables. Good cooking, too. It's about a 25-minute walk from the dock, however. Rates increase in high season. ❸

Villa Caribe Tucán Dugú first on the right, uphill from the jetty ⓣ7947 0072, ⓦwww.villasdeguatemala.com. Lívingston's only luxury hotel, with spacious, attractive modern rooms boasting balconies with views to the bay. Pleasant bar, swimming pool and lush gardens. Rooms start at just over US$100 per night. ❾

The Town and around

There's not much to do in town itself, other than relax in local style. The local palm-fringed **beaches** are quite narrow and, though not of the Caribbean-dream variety, do offer plenty of pleasant places to take a swim. Everywhere you'll find that the sand slopes into the sea very gradually. Sadly, it's best to explore the more isolated beaches away from town in a group, as attacks on tourists have been occasionally reported.

The most popular side-trip is to the **Siete Altares**, an imposing series of waterfalls – much more impressive in the rainy season – 5km northwest of town. Though incidents have diminished in recent years as police patrols have increased, you should still not take anything of value; the safest option is to hire a local guide or visit as part of a **tour**. To **get there** follow the street past the *Ubafu* bar and turn right by the *African Place* hotel to the beach, then follow the sand away from town to the west. After a couple of kilometres, wade (or get one of the waiting boatmen to punt you) across a small river and, just before the beach eventually peters out, take a path to the left. Follow this inland and you'll soon reach the first of the falls; to reach the others, scramble up, and follow the water. All of the falls are idyllic places to swim, but the highest one is the best of all.

Eating and drinking

Lívingston is a great place to eat out. For local food, you must try the *tapado* (coconut-based fish soup): *Tiburón Gato*, *Tilingo Lingo* or *Margoth* are good places to hit. Elsewhere, the restaurant in the historic Caribbean-style *Hotel Río Dulce* (on the left up from the jetty) has a superb menu, with plenty of fish and seafood, salads, and imaginative European cuisine; while *Buga Mama*, just left of the jetty, has good shrimp, fish and pasta. *Hotel Casa Rosada* also has great (mainly) vegetarian food, including curries and grilled conch – dinner here is US$9. For Italian food head to the authentic *Vecchia Toscana*, right on the beach, where they have a wood-fired oven for pizza, and great pasta. The *Bahía Azul*, on the main street, is another popular place with an inexpensive menu (including *coco burguesa)* and an excellent terrace for watching streetlife. For evening **entertainment**, Lívingston has lots of groovy hangouts, including *Ubafu*, usually the most lively bar, and the *Coco Bongo* club, on the beach, where you'll hear Jamaican reggae and pure Garífuna punta rock. You can catch video movies at the *Black Sheep*, on Calle Principal, next to the *Bahía Azul*.

The Río Dulce

In a few moments we entered the Río Dulce. On each side, rising perpendicularly from three to four hundred feet, was a wall of living green. Trees grew from the water's edge, with dense unbroken foliage, to the top; not a spot of barrenness was to be seen; and on both sides, from the tops of the highest trees, long tendrils descended to the water, as if to drink and carry life to the trunks that bore them. It was, as its name imports, a Río Dulce, a fairy scene of Titan land, combining exquisite beauty with colossal grandeur. As we advanced the passage turned, and in a few minutes we lost sight of the sea, and were enclosed on all sides by a forest wall; but the river, although showing us no passage, still invited us onward.

John Lloyd Stephens (1841)

Another excellent reason to come to Lívingston is the spectacular trip up the **Río Dulce**, a roughly 30-kilometre journey that eventually brings you to Río Dulce Town and the highway to Petén. From Lívingston, the river passes through a system of gorges with sheer, 100-metre-high rock faces draped in tropical vegetation and cascading vines. Here and there you might see some white herons or flocks of squawking parakeets as you cruise upriver taking in the stunning tropical scenery. A few kilometers from Lívingston there's a delightful river tributary, **Río Tatín**, which most boatmen venture up into briefly. On the banks of this tributary, *Finca Tatín* (Ⓣ5902 0831, Ⓦwww.fincatatin.centroamerica.com; ❷–❸) offers rustic dorms (US$6 per bed) and private rooms with bathroom (all accommodation has mosquito nets) set in dense jungle and accessible only by boat. The guest house's rainforest habitat does mean that you will encounter plenty of bugs and wildlife, so it's probably not the place for arachnophobes. However, the hospitable Argentinean owners offer a warm welcome, and there's excellent, healthy food (lunch is US$3.50, dinner US$4.50), kayaks for hire, table tennis, walking trails and Spanish classes available. Q'eqchi' Maya guides also can be arranged to accompany you to local villages and caves, as well as Ak'Tenamit.

A further kilometre west along the Río Dulce is **Ak'Tenamit** (Ⓦwww.aktenamit.org), a health and development centre which caters to the needs of around fifty recently established Q'eqchi' Maya villages. Until the American Guatemala Tomorrow Fund came to work here, the people had neither schools,

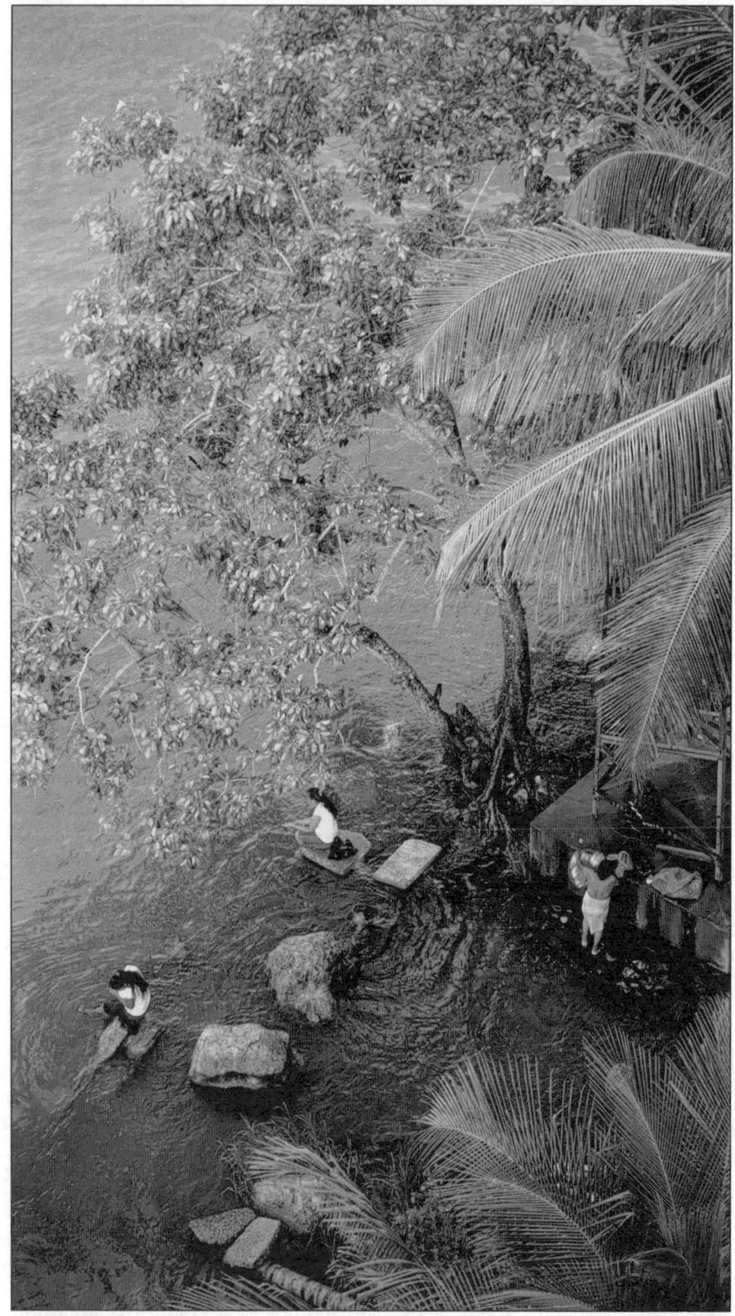

△ Río Dulce

medical care, nor much else. Now there is a 24-hour clinic, a primary school for several hundred children, a secondary college, and a new senior high-school is planned. Self-help programmes, a women's craft-making cooperative, an ecotourism centre and Maya cultural initiatives have also been launched – and a new ceremonial temple will be consecrated in the area soon. Volunteer doctors, nurses and dentists who can commit themselves for at least one month are very welcome, and visitors are invited to take a look around.

Travel another kilometre or so upriver and you'll find a spot where warm sulphurous waters emerge from the base of a cliff – a good place for a dip. Just beyond, the gorge opens into a small lake, **El Golfete**, on whose northern shore is the **Biotopo Chocón Machacas** (daily 7am–4pm; US$5), a government-sponsored nature reserve designed to protect the habitat of the **manatee**, or sea cow, a threatened species that's seen around here from time to time. The manatee is a massive seal-shaped mammal which lives in both sea- and freshwater and, according to some, gave rise to the myth of the mermaid. Female manatees breastfeed their young, clutching them in their flippers, though – tipping the scales at as much as a ton – they're hardly as dainty as your fairytale mermaids. The reserve also protects the forest that still covers much of the lake's shore, and has some specially cut trails where you might catch sight of a bird or two, or if you've plenty of time and patience, even a tapir or jaguar.

At the western end of the Golfete is another **charity operation**, this one an orphanage for 250 children from the capital, who are often referred here by the judicial system. Casa Guatemala is an astonishing success story, and has grown (despite a huge earthquake in 1999 that demolished most of the buildings) to include a hostel, *Hotel Backpackers* (see p.281), where some of the older children work, a farm, fish pond, greenhouses and a meat store in Río Dulce Town. The charity runs on donations and income generated with the help of volunteers, who do anything from teaching to construction work. Volunteers with the right background, who can stay a few months (preferably six), are always desperately needed. The work is hard and conditions are pretty basic, but for those who can take it, it's time very well spent. For contact information, see "Work and Study" in the Basics section of this book.

Lago de Izabal and around

Heading on upstream, across the Golfete, the river closes in again and passes the marina and bridge at the squalid settlement of **RÍO DULCE TOWN** (sometimes also known as Fronteras), on the northern side of the river. The waterfront away from Río Dulce Town is a favourite playground for wealthy Guatemalans, with boats and hotels that would put parts of California to shame; the shores of **Lago de Izabal** beyond hide increasing numbers of elite properties behind high walls and dense foliage. The road for Petén crosses the river, and the boat trip from Lívingston comes to an end.

The beautiful tropical area along the lush banks of the Río Dulce and Lago de Izabal is a tourist destination in its own right, with plenty to keep you occupied for a few days and a genuinely relaxed atmosphere. A road around the northern shore of the lake provides a route up to the Verapaces (see p.317), passing the idyllic **hot spring waterfall** close to the *Finca El Paraíso* and the towering **Boquerón canyon**. On the western side of the lake, the small town of **El Estor** is an excellent alternative base to explore these sights and the biodiverse wetlands of the **Reserva Bocas del Polochic**. The restaurant *Río Bravo* and the *Hacienda Tijax* hotel are good places for gleaning **information**; alternatively, consult Ⓦ www.mayaparadise.com, a comprehensive **website** which covers the Río Dulce region.

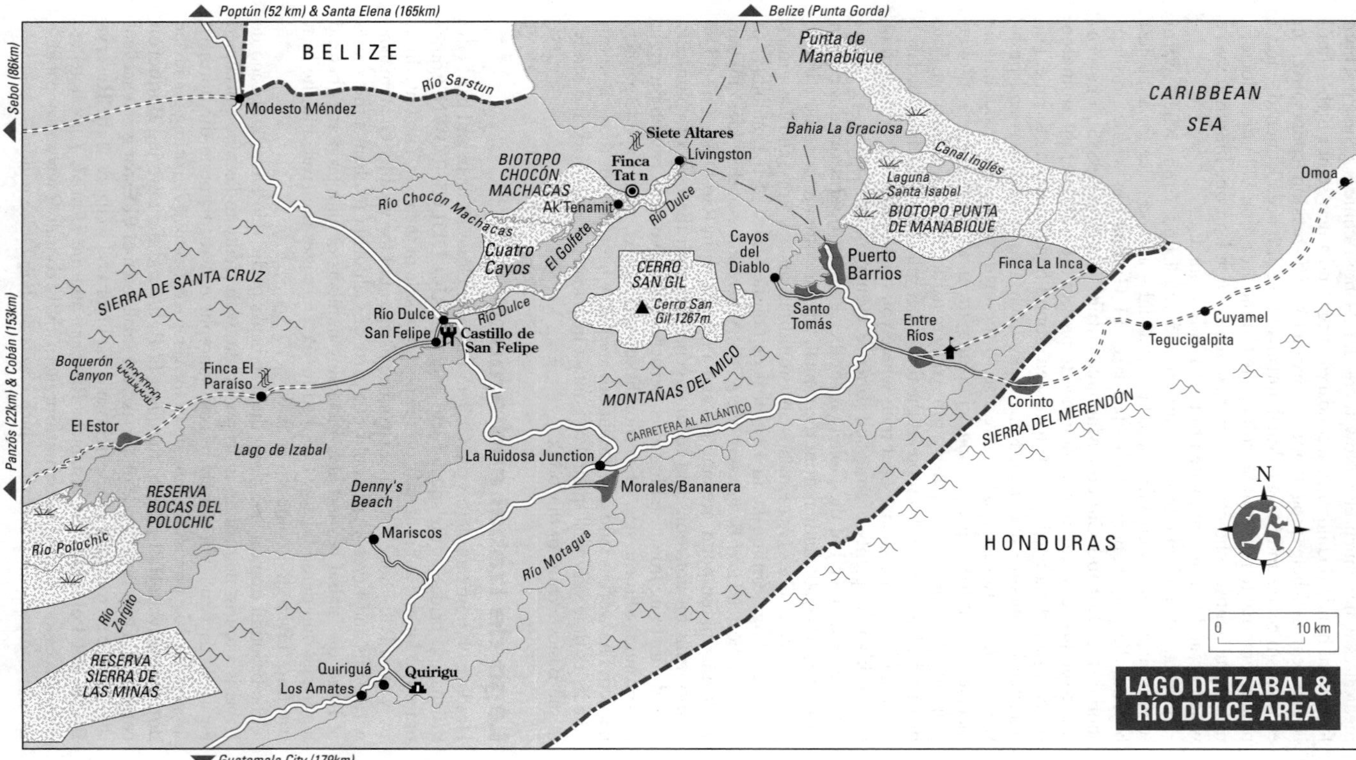
LAGO DE IZABAL & RÍO DULCE AREA
0
10 km
N
Poptún (52 km) & Santa Elena (165km)
Belize (Punta Gorda)
Sebol (86km)
Panzós (22km) & Cobán (153km)
Puerto Cortés (14km) & San Pedro Sula (71km)
Guatemala City (179km)
BELIZE
CARIBBEAN SEA
HONDURAS
Río Sarstun
Modesto Méndez
Punta de Manabique
Bahía La Graciosa
Canal Inglés
Laguna Santa Isabel
BIOTOPO PUNTA DE MANABIQUE
Omoa
Siete Altares
Livingston
Finca Tat n
BIOTOPO CHOCÓN MACHACAS
Ak'Tenamit
Río Dulce
Río Chocón Machacas
Cuatro Cayos
El Golfete
CERRO SAN GIL
Cerro San Gil 1267m
Cayos del Diablo
Puerto Barrios
Santo Tomás
Finca La Inca
Cuyamel
Tegucigalpita
Entre Ríos
Corinto
SIERRA DEL MERENDÓN
SIERRA DE SANTA CRUZ
Río Dulce
San Felipe
Castillo de San Felipe
MONTAÑAS DEL MICO
CARRETERA AL ATLÁNTICO
Boquerón Canyon
Finca El Paraíso
El Estor
Lago de Izabal
La Ruidosa Junction
Morales/Bananera
RESERVA BOCAS DEL POLOCHIC
Denny's Beach
Mariscos
Río Polochic
Río Motagua
Río Zarquito
RESERVA SIERRA DE LAS MINAS
Quiriguá
Quirigu
Los Amates

Practicalities in and around Río Dulce Town

The town is little more than a truck stop, where traffic for Petén pauses before the long stretch to Flores. Río Dulce is actually a new name given to a couple of older settlements, Fronteras to the north and El Relleno to the south, which have been connected by a monstrous concrete road bridge, obliterating almost any sense of tranquillity in the area immediately around. However, get a little bit away from the town and there's plenty to see.

As for **places to stay**, the Swiss-owned *Casa Perico* (ⓣ5909 0721, ❷–❸), 1km northeast of the bridge up a small lakeside inlet, is a good spot for budget travellers. Built on small stilts above the water and swampland with cabins at the end of wooden walkways, the guest house offers dorm beds (US$5.50) and basic rooms (US$6.75 per person) along with a profusion of hammocks, a lively atmosphere and great food. Call them for a free *lancha* pick-up. *Hotel Backpackers* (ⓣ7930 5169, ⓔcasaguatemala@guate.net), underneath the south side of the bridge, has dorm beds (US$4), hammock space (US$2.50) and private doubles (❸). Owned by the nearby Casa Guatemala children's home, many of the young staff are former residents; it's a good place to pick up information about the Río Dulce region.

On the north side of the bridge, *Hotel Río Dulce* (ⓣ7930 3179; ❸) has clean, neat doubles with fans. *Hacienda Tijax* (ⓣ7930 5505, ⓦwww.tijax.com), two minutes by water-taxi from the north side of the bridge, is a bit more comfortable. Nicely located on the lakefront, you'll also find a remarkable canopy jungle walk (US$12), hiking trails and horse-riding (US$20 for 2hr 30min), plus a swimming pool; *Tijax* also operates as a working teak and rubber farm. Accommodation is either in basic rooms (❸), A-frame cabins with or without bathrooms (❸–❹) or bungalows (❻), and the food is tasty, if a little overpriced. The only upmarket place in the area, *Hotel Catamaran* (ⓣ7930 5494; ❼) occupies a great position on a tiny private island, a five-minute *lancha* ride from Río Dulce Town. The grounds are lovely, and there's a restaurant, bar and tennis courts. The cabañas are comfortable enough, but not exceptional, however.

As for **restaurants**, *Río Bravo*, on the north side of the bridge, is a good place to meet other travellers, eat pizza or pasta and drink the night away – you can also surf the **Internet** and make radio contact with most places around the river and lake here. Next door, *Bruno's* serves international food and offers North American news and sports coverage – it's very popular with the sailing fraternity. They have Internet facilities here, too. For cheap grub, there's a strip of pretty undistinguished comedores on the main road close to the bus stop. Meanwhile, *Casa Perico* has a popular Saturday barbeque. Several **banks** have set up shop in Río Dulce, including Banrural, with a MasterCard ATM, and Banco Industrial, with a Visa ATM.

Moving on from Río Dulce, buses leave every thirty minutes or so to both Guatemala City and Flores via Poptún until around 6pm. If you're heading towards Puerto Barrios, take the first bus or minibus to La Ruidosa junction (every 30min) and pick up a connection there. Between 6am and 4pm, buses around the lakeshore depart for El Estor every ninety minutes (1hr 45min); they leave outside *Pollolandia* in Río Dulce Town. If you're heading for Lívingston via the Río Dulce gorge, *lancha* captains will ambush you as soon as you step off a bus; *colectivo* boats (US$10 per person) leave Río Dulce Town from a designated dock on the north side of the bridge, west bank of the river. Downstream, the trip takes around one and a half hours. The boatmen usually stop at a couple of islets to look at nesting cormorants and pelicans, and another place where water lilies are profuse, but do *not* generally stop to let you off at the Castillo de San Felipe.

For a more leisurely **cruise** along the Río Dulce or to *Finca Paraíso* (both US$25 round trip), the *Shin-Tzu* catamaran, docked at *Tijax* (see p.281; ⓣ5493 0865) fits the bill nicely. For the more ambitious, wonderful sailing trips to the Belizean cayes on *That*, a nineteen-metre (62ft) trimaran leave from *Bruno's* (ⓣ5529 0829, ⓦwww.that-boat.com). A five-day trip costs US$375, including two dives and all meals. Scuba courses are also offered. Avoid trips on John Clarke's catamaran, as we have received a number of complaints.

Castillo de San Felipe

Looking like a miniature medieval castle and marking the entrance to Lago de Izabal, the *castillo* (8am–5pm; US$1.30) is a tribute to the audacity of British pirates, who used to sail up the Río Dulce to raid supplies and harass mule trains. The Spanish were so infuriated by this that they built the fortress to seal off the entrance to the lake, and a chain was strung across the river. Inside there are a maze of tiny rooms and staircases, plus plenty of canons and panoramic views of the lake.

The hot spring waterfall and Boquerón canyon

Beyond the *castillo*, the broad sweep of Lago de Izabal opens before you, with great views of the fertile highlands beyond the distant shores. Some 25km from Río Dulce, a **hot spring waterfall** (daily 8am–6pm; US$1.30) in land owned by the *Finca el Paraíso*, 300m north of the road, is one of Guatemala's most remarkable natural phenomena. Bathtub-temperature spring water cascades into pools cooled by a separate chilly flow of fresh river water, creating a sublime, steamy spa-like environment where it's easy to soak away an afternoon. Above the waterfall is a series of caves whose interiors are crowded with extraordinary shapes and colours – made even more memorable by the fact that you have to swim by torchlight to see them (bring your own flashlight). Two kilometres south of the waterfall, the *Finca el Paraíso* **hotel** (ⓣ7949 7122; ⑤) sits on the waterfront, with two rows of large, comfortable, but rarely occupied cabañas and a reasonably good, if pricey, restaurant. The hotel enjoys a delightfully peaceful location and there's good swimming from the black-sand beach. Buses and pick-ups between Río Dulce and El Estor pass the hot springs and hotel hourly in both directions.

Continuing west along the lakeshore, it's a further 7km to the **Boquerón canyon**, completely hidden yet just 500m from the road. Near-vertical cliffs soar to more than 250m above the Río Sauce, which flows through the bottom of the startling jungle-clad gorge, the river bed plotted with colossal boulders. To see the canyon, you'll have to employ one of the local boatmen who wait at the end of the signposted track from the main road. They'll paddle you upstream in logwood canoes for a small fee. The return trip takes thirty minutes or so, though it's possible to get your boatman to drop you off and return to pick you up later in the day. If you want to explore Boquerón further, the canyon extends for an additional 5km; make sure you have sturdy footwear and enjoy a scramble.

El Estor

Heading west beyond Boquerón, it's just 6km to the sleepy lakeside town of **EL ESTOR**, allegedly named by English pirates who came up the Río Dulce to buy supplies at "The Store". It's an easy-going, friendly place which was briefly energized in the mid-1960s by the discovery of high-grade nickel deposits. A mine opened in 1977, functioned for a couple of years at reduced capacity, and was then shut down. In 2004 plans were announced to offer new concessions to a Canadian mining company, raising the possibility of a resumption of strip mining. Of course the environmental impact that this would bring to the area – the nickel is just below the top soil – would seriously impact the vast eco-tourism potential of the region, just when El Estor is starting to attract a trickle of travellers.

There are no sights in El Estor itself, though you'll find a pool in the plaza which harbours fish, turtles and alligators. Keep an eye out, too, for huge green iguanas in the trees around town; locals shoot at them with slingshots. However, the town does have a friendly, relaxed atmosphere, particularly in the warmth of the evening when the streets are full of activity, and you could easily spend a few days exploring the surrounding area – including the hot spring waterfall, the Boquerón canyon and Bocas del Polochic – much of which remains undisturbed. For local **information** the best contacts are Hugo at *Hugo's Restaurant*, or Oscar Paz, who runs the *Hotel Vista del Lago* and is an enthusiastic promoter of the area. He will arrange a boat and guide to explore any of the region's attractions. Banrural, on 3 C and 6 Av, changes travellers' cheques.

Accommodation

The town has an excellent choice of good-quality budget **places to stay**, though nothing much in other price categories.

Hotel Central 5 Av & 2 C ⓣ7949 7244. Just north of the plaza, this is an excellent deal with spotless modern rooms, each with private bath and fan. ❷

Hotel Ecológico Cabañas del Lago ⓣ & ⓕ7949 7245. Set in a tranquil lakeside plot a kilometre east of the centre, the bungalows here are comfortable, spacious and attractive. There's a private sandy beach here too. Hugo, the owner, will take you there if you drop in at his restaurant in the plaza. ❹

Hotel Villela 6 Av 2–06 ⓣ7949 7214. A long-standing reasonable enough place with simple, if slightly tired-looking rooms, some with private shower, surrounding a pretty garden. ❷

Hotel Vista del Lago lakeside ⓣ7949 7205. El Estor's most atmospheric hotel is a beautiful old wooden building by the dock; the owners claim that it's the original "store" that gave the town its name. It offers small clean rooms with private bath, with those on the second floor boasting superb views of the lake. ❸

Restaurant Chaabil lakeshore on 3 C ⓣ7949 7272. This place is a good choice where the cabaña-style rooms have chunky wooden beds and private bathrooms. ❸

Eating and entertainment

There's not too much to get excited about when it comes to **food**, but *Restaurant Chaabil* at the western end of 3 Calle is the fanciest place in town and has good seafood, while *Hugo's Restaurant* and *Café El Portal* score for *comida típica* – both are on the main plaza. For good inexpensive **breakfasts** or snacks head to the clean, friendly *Cafetería Santa Clave*, three blocks west of the plaza at 3 C 7–75. There's a great **pool hall** just south of the plaza at 2 Calle and 5 Avenida where you can play for less than a dollar an hour. Its enthusiastic DJ-minded owner lets rip a frighteningly eclectic mix of rock, pop and dance from colossal speakers most nights.

Reserva Bocas del Polochic

Encompassing a substantial slice of lowland jungle on the west side of the lake, the **Bocas del Polochic** nature reserve is one of the richest wetland habitats in Guatemala. The green maze of swamp, marsh and forest harbours at least 224 different species of birds, including golden-fronted woodpeckers, Aztec parakeets and keel-billed toucans. It's also rich in mammals, including howler monkeys, which you're virtually guaranteed to see (and hear), plus rarely encountered manatees and tapirs. There's good accommodation next to the tiny Q'eqchi' village of **SELEMPÍM** in the heart of the reserve – the large mosquito-screened wooden house with bunk beds (US$12 per person per day, including three substantial meals) provides villagers with employment. Locals also lead guided walks up into the foothills of the Sierra de las Minas and conduct kayak tours of the river delta.

The major drawback for visitors wanting to get to the reserve is that it's only accessible by infrequent public *lanchas* or expensive chartered boats. If you do want to go, drop by Defensores de la Naturaleza, at 5 Avenida and 2 Calle in El Estor (Mon–Fri 9am–5pm; ⓣ7949 7427 or 5815 1736, ⓦwww.defensores.org.gt); the group, who manage Bocas del Polochic (and the neighbouring Reserva Sierra de las Minas), can help with information and boat schedules. Three weekly public *lanchas* run to and from Selempím on Monday, Wednesday and Saturday, leaving Selempím at 7am and returning from El Estor at 11am (US$7; 1hr 15min) – check times at Defensores' office. Day-trips to the fringes of the reserve cost around US$35; ask Hugo or Oscar to recommend a local boatman. A special charter to Selempím costs around US$80 (return).

Mariscos and Denny's Beach

MARISCOS, the main town on the south side of Lago de Izabal, sees very few visitors now that the road around the northern shore of the lake is complete. In its day, however, it was an important stopping-off point, where travellers heading for the capital would disembark and continue overland. Nowadays, there's no longer a ferry service to El Estor, though the odd *lancha* (US$4.50; 1hr) does cover the route when enough passengers can be amassed. It's pretty much a one-street town, with a couple of cheap hotels – *Hotel Karinlinda* (❷) is the best bet – a police station, a supermarket and *Restaurante Margarita's* at the pier. Regular microbuses connect the town with the La Trinchera junction at Km 217 on the Carretera al Atlántico.

If you're craving a good swim, you can't do better than head for **Denny's Beach** (ⓣ5398 0908 or 5709 4990), a resort that's a ten-minute water-taxi (US$2) ride from the pier at Mariscos (or 40 minutes from Río Dulce Town). It's an ideal place to get away from it all, with nice private cabañas (❸) and a dorm (US$5 per bed) above the sandy beach; you can also camp or sling a hammock (both US$3 per person). There's an open-air bar and restaurant, where the menu includes omelettes, sandwiches and fish, and a warm welcome from owner Dennis Gulck, who has lived here for years. Horse-riding in the Sierra de las Minas, wake boarding and boat trips around the lake can be organized.

The eastern highlands

The eastern highlands, often just called El Oriente, connect Guatemala City with El Salvador and Honduras and must rank as the least-visited part of the entire country. The population here is almost entirely latinized, speaking Spanish and wearing Western clothes, although many are by blood pure Maya. Only a very few elderly people, in a couple of isolated areas, still speak Poqomam Maya, the region's indigenous language. The ladinos of the east have a reputation for behaving like cowboys, and demonstrations of macho pride are common.

The landscape lacks the immediate appeal of the western highlands. Not only are its peaks lower, but its features are generally less clearly defined. The volcanoes, unlike the neatly symmetrical cones of the west, are heavily eroded, merging with the lower-lying hills. Close to the border with El Salvador the hills are incredibly fertile and the broad valleys lush with vegetation, but in the north of the area, around the key town of **Chiquimula**, the landscape is very different, with dry rounded peaks and dusty fields.

On the whole you're unlikely to head this way unless you're on your way somewhere else. Buses for **San Salvador** pass through the southern side of the eastern highlands, while in the north of the region a good road branches off the Carretera al Atlántico and skirts the towns of **Zacapa** and Chiquimula. From Chiquimula it's a short hop to the ruins of Copán over in Honduras, while **Esquipulas**, with its famous basilica, and the magical volcanic crater lake of **Ipala** are close by.

From Guatemala City to El Salvador

Although several routes run between the capital and the El Salvadorean border, it's the highland route via Cuilapa that draws the most traffic. This not only provides the fastest connection between the two countries, but also offers the most spectacular scenery, weaving through a series of lush valleys. The highway leaves Guatemala City through the southern suburbs of Zona 10, and climbs steeply out of the city, passing the hillside villas of the wealthy. It then reaches a high plateau from where you get a good view of the eastern side of the smoking peak of Volcán de Pacaya. There are few towns out this way and you'll soon reach **CUILAPA**, some 70km from the capital. Cuilapa's claim to fame is that it is supposedly the very "centre of the Americas" – this doesn't, however, make it an especially interesting place to stop. There are a couple of hotels if you get stuck, including the very pleasant *Turicentro Los Esclavos* (Ⓣ7886 5139, Ⓕ7886 5158; ❺) on the highway, 4km beyond Cuilapa, where there's a small pool, a good café-restaurant and spotless rooms with TV and fridge. Right next to the hotel is a sixteenth-century stone bridge, one of the oldest in Central America, though it's now dwarfed by an adjacent modern steel replacement. South of Cuilapa, a branch road heads through stunning scenery, between the peaks of Volcán Tecuamburro and Volcán Cruz Quemada to the town of **Chiquimulilla** (buses every hour; see p.256).

Eleven kilometres beyond Cuilapa the highway splits at the **El Molino junction**. The southern fork, highway CA-8, is the most direct route to the border, heading straight for the crossing at **VALLE NUEVO**, less than 50km away. This road is straight, fast and scenic, but the border crossing is little more than a customs post and there's nowhere to stay when you get there, or on the way.

The northern fork, CA-1, is the continuation of the **Carretera Interamericana**. This road is much slower, as it passes through most of the main towns and is served only by second-class buses, but it's also considerably more interesting. If you're heading directly for El Salvador, the southern branch is the one to stick with, and if you wait at the junction a pullman for San Salvador will turn up sooner or later.

The Carretera Interamericana: Jutiapa

Heading west from El Molino, the Carretera Interamericana turns towards the mountains, running through an isolated valley planted with sugarcane, then climbing onto a high plateau. Here the landscape is more characteristic of the eastern highlands, with its open valleys and low ridges overshadowed by huge eroded volcanoes.

Bypassing the small town of Quesada, the road arrives at **JUTIAPA**. The centre of trade and transport for the entire eastern region, this is a busy and not particularly attractive place, with a steady stream of buses to and from the border and the capital, and to all other parts of the east, from Jalapa to Esquipulas. If you need **to stay**, there are plenty of places to choose from including the clean *Posada de Peregrino*, at C 15 de Septiembre 0–30 (Ⓣ7855 1770, ❸). You can **change money** at Banco G&T Continental, C 15 de Septiembre and 10 Avenida, which has an ATM that accepts MasterCard and Visa.

Frequent **buses** pass through Jutiapa, heading for the border and for Guatemala City, with at least one an hour in both directions; they pull in at the bus terminal right in the middle of town. Jutiapa is also the starting point for a trip across the eastern highlands to Chiquimula or Esquipulas. The quickest route takes you directly to Esquipulas, through Ipala, and buses from Jutiapa head this way. But if you'd rather take your time and see the best of this part of the country then take a bus to Jalapa, spend the night there, and then press on to Chiquimula.

Asunción Mita and the border at San Cristóbal

Heading on from Jutiapa towards the border with El Salvador, the Carretera Interamericana runs through El Progreso, and then drops into a vast open valley, before arriving at the small town of **ASUNCIÓN MITA**. Despite its jaded appearance, in colonial times Asunción was an important staging post on the royal route to Panama. Nowadays, its only real significance is as the last town before the **border**, thirty minutes away, for which there is a constant stream of buses and minibuses. The actual crossing point is marked by the small town of **SAN CRISTÓBAL**, where you'll find a couple of basic pensiones (❶–❷) and an Inguat desk. The last **bus** for Guatemala City leaves the border at around 5.30pm, and the last minibus for Asunción Mita leaves at around 6.30pm.

Jalapa to Ipala

Any trip through the eastern highlands should include the road **between Jalapa and Ipala**, which takes you through some truly breathtaking scenery. This is not actually on the way to anywhere, and it's a fairly long and exhausting trip, but if you've had enough of the tourist overkill of the western highlands and don't mind a bumpy ride, then it makes a refreshing change.

From Jutiapa direct buses run to Jalapa, passing over the shoulder of the Volcán Tahual and through a huge bowl-shaped valley, thick with fields of sugarcane, tobacco and maize. The main towns along the way are **Monjas** and **Morazán**, two busy agricultural centres. **JALAPA** itself is a prosperous but isolated town, resting on a high plateau in the heart of the eastern highlands and surrounded by low peaks and cattle pasture. Set away from all the major roads, its busy bus terminal links all the area's smaller towns and villages. There are plenty of places **to stay**: *Hotel Casa del Viajero*, at 1 Av 0–70 (Ⓣ7922 4086; ❷–❸), is a friendly place with a good comedor and rooms with or without bath, while the *Posada Don Antonio*, Av Chipilapa A 0–64 (Ⓣ7922 5751), is more comfortable; all rooms have a shower room here. The town also has several **banks**, including the G&T Continental at 1 Av 1–66, with a 5B ATM that accepts Visa and MasterCard. The best place to eat in town is the *Restaurante Casa Real* on 1 Calle where they serve huge salads, soups and grilled meats; or try *Antojitos Acuarios* opposite for a cheaper feed.

A paved road continues from Jalapa to **Sanarate**, on the Carretera al Atlántico, the fastest route back to the capital. **Buses** run hourly from Jalapa to Guatemala City (3hr) from 3am until 5pm via Jutiapa, and until 5pm via Sanarate. Buses leave Jalapa for Chiquimula (5hr) via Ipala every ninety minutes from 5am to 2.30pm.

San Luis Jilotepéque and Ipala

Heading on from Jalapa towards Chiquimula and Esquipulas the road climbs into the hills for the most beautiful section of the entire trip to Ipala, leading up onto a high ridge with superb views, and then dropping down to the isolated villages of San Pedro Pinula and **SAN LUÍS JILOTEPÉQUE**, two outposts of Maya culture. The plaza of San Luís is particularly impressive, with two massive ceiba trees, a colonial church, and a couple of replica stelae from Copán – and on Sundays it's the scene of a vast Maya market. There are two basic pensiones.

Fourteen kilometres beyond San Luís, this back road joins the main road from Jutiapa at the large village of **IPALA**, an important crossroads. The village itself is a pretty forlorn place, with a few shops and a couple of **hotels**. The best place to stay is the clean *Hopsedaje Pinal* (❷), with some rooms with private bath; failing that, head for *Hotel Ipala Real* (Ⓣ7923 7107; ❷), where the rooms have cable TV and en-suite showers and toilets.

Ipala inhabits an open plain at the base of **Volcán de Ipala** (1650m), which looks more like a rounded hill, and is similar in many ways to the cone of Chicabal near Quezaltenango. The cone is filled by a beautiful little **crater lake** ringed by trees, and has a patch of virgin cloudforest on its north side. A unique species of the *mojarra* fish, which apparently has six prominent spines on its back, is supposed to inhabit the lake. Unfortunately, the peace and quiet up here is slightly spoilt by the hum from a diesel generator that pumps out water for the surrounding villages. You can amble around the lake in a little over an hour, and it makes a wonderful place to **camp**, though you'll have to bring all your own supplies.

The easiest route to the top is via a trail (built by EarthCorps volunteers) from the village of **El Chagüitón**, south of the village of Ipala heading towards the village of Agua Blanca. It's two hours to the top via a visitor centre where you pay a US$1.30 entrance fee. Buses and pick-ups run from Ipala towards the village of Agua Blanca hourly; get off at **El Sauce** at Km 26.5, from where it's an hour and a half to the summit via El Chagüitón.

The north: Zacapa, Chiquimula and Esquipulas

What is true of the entire eastern highlands is particularly true of the string of towns that runs along the northern side of the mountains. Here eastern machismo is at its most potent and hardly anyone lives outside the towns. The vast majority of the population are ladinos, and furiously proud of it, with a reputation for quick tempers, warm hearts and violent responses. The trio of **Zacapa**, **Chiquimula** and **Esquipulas** are the most accessible towns in the eastern highlands, with a good road and fast bus service from the capital. They also offer access to two particularly interesting sites: the Maya ruins at **Copán** (see p.389) over the border in Honduras, and the shrine of the **Black Christ** in Esquipulas.

The direct road branches off the Carretera al Atlántico at the Río Hondo junction, running through dry, dusty hills to Zacapa, and on through Chiquimula and Esquipulas to the three-way border with Honduras and El Salvador. Before Zacapa the road passes the small, remote town of **ESTANZUELA**, which, oddly enough, has its own museum of paleontology, **El Museo de Paleontología Bryan Patterson** (daily 8am–5pm; free), dedicated to an American scientist who worked in the area for many years. The exhibits, which include the fossil of a blue whale, manatee bones, a giant armadillo shell, and the entire skeleton of a mastodon said to be some fifty thousand years old, are equally unexpected. There are also some more recent pieces such as a small Maya tomb, transported here from a site 66km away, and in the basement some copies of Copán stelae and one or two originals. The museum has a certain amateur charm and is well worth a look if you have half an hour to spare. To get here take any bus between El Rancho and Zacapa – including all the buses heading between Guatemala City and Esquipulas – ask the driver to drop you at the village, and simply walk straight through it for ten minutes, along the main street.

Zacapa

Just 13km from the Río Hondo junction, **ZACAPA** is reached from the main road by twin bridges across the Río Grande. In the dry months this is one of the hottest towns in the country, with maximum temperatures of 35–40°C. Its atmosphere is dominated by two things: ladino culture and the surrounding desert, which is irrigated to produce tobacco. The town is also famous for its rum – Ron Centenario Zacapa, the finest in Central America – and quesadilla cheesecake. There's not much to do in Zacapa, although it's pleasant enough, with a large, busy market, and some hot springs a few kilometres to the south. The town itself stretches out between the old train station and the plaza, a relaxed, tree-lined spot that boasts some of the finest public toilets in Guatemala. The plaza is also where you'll find the Banco G&T Continental, which has an ATM for Visa and MasterCard. There are two **hotels** of note: the good-value, eccentric Chinese-run *Hotel Wong*, 6 C 12–53 (❷), where the rooms come with or without private bathrooms, and the vast, chintzy *Hotel Miramundo*, 17 Av 5–41, Zona 3 (ⓣ7941 2674, ⓕ7941 0157; ❹–❺), whose rooms have a/c and TV. Zacapa has something approaching an epidemic of Chinese **restaurants**, most of which offer only fair food at inflated prices (around US$5 a meal), though portions are huge: the *Po Wing*, on the plaza, is a reasonable option and has an ice-cream parlour attached.

The **bus** terminal in Zacapa is a kilometre or so from the centre; take a local bus if you don't want to walk. From the terminal, buses leave hourly for Guatemala City. Microbuses run between the junction at El Rancho and all of the towns out this way including Chiquimula and Esquipulas: in Zacapa pick them up on 13 Avenida between 6 and 7 calles, near the *Hotel Wong*; they don't run to any timetable but departures are about every 20–30 minutes.

The hot springs of Santa Marta

The one good reason for stopping off in Zacapa is to take a trip to the **Aguas Thermales Santa Marta**, four or five kilometres south of town. There are no buses out this way so you'll either have to walk (you might be able to hitch some of the way) or go by taxi (around US$3 one way). To get to the hot springs on foot, walk up the street to the right of the church in Zacapa's plaza, past the Banco G&T Continental. After four blocks you come to a small park where you want to take the first left, then the next right and then another left. This brings you onto a track that heads out of town across a small river – stick with this track as it continues through the fields and, after about 3km, it will start to drop into another small valley. Just as it does so take the left-hand fork, at the end of which you'll find the baths – if you get lost, just ask for *los baños*.

The bathing rooms are set off a small courtyard built in a vaguely colonial style. Inside each room there's a huge tiled tub, filled with naturally heated water and a couple of beds. The tubs cost US$6 to rent, for as many people as you want to fit in, and the very friendly owner Rolando also sells beers, soft drinks and snacks. It's a superbly relaxing experience, sending you to the brink of sleep – if not beyond.

Chiquimula

From Zacapa the main road continues towards the border, heading up over a low pass and into a great open valley. Set to one side of this is the town of **CHIQUIMULA**, an ugly, bustling ladino stronghold. This is the largest of the three northern towns, with a population of around 37,000, and its huge plaza, shaded by ceiba trees, is permanently congested by the coming and going of assorted traffic. There's little to see here other than a massive ruined colonial **church**, the Iglesia Vieja, on the eastern side of town. Damaged in the 1765 earthquake and left behind as the town has shifted over the years, it retains an impressive, if fractured, Baroque facade.

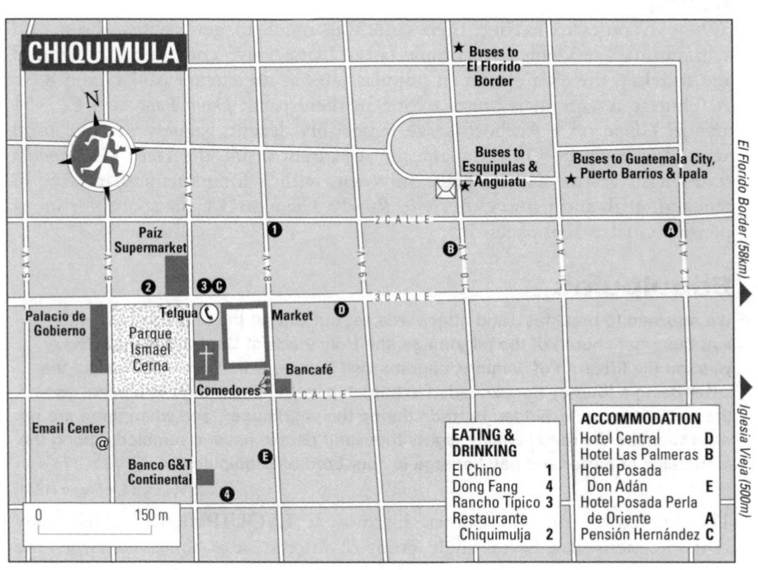

For **changing money** there's plenty of choice, including Bancafé, at 4 Calle and 8 Avenida, with a Visa ATM; and Banco G&T Continental, at 7 Av 4–75, for MasterCard cash advances. You can also cash dollars safely at Azujey, the largest of the sombrero shops in the daily **market**, which is always worth a browse in its own right for its kitsch selection of cowboy gear and leatherware. There's an **Internet** café, *Email Center*, at 6 Av 4–51 (daily 9am–9pm), and Telgua is on the corner of the plaza (daily 7am–midnight). The **bus terminal** is centred on 1A Calle, between 10 and 11 avenidas, midway between the plaza and the highway. Here you'll find hourly buses to Guatemala City (3hr 30min) and Puerto Barrios (4hr) until 6pm as well as microbuses to Esquipulas (every 30min; 1hr), Ipala (hourly; 1hr; some continuing on to Jalapa, 3hr) and Anguiatú (hourly; 1hr). A block to the north of the main terminal, buses leave for the border at El Florido (every 45min; 1hr 30min) until 4.30pm.

Accommodation

As Chiquimula is the starting point for routes to Copán in Honduras and Ipala, you might well end up **staying**. This is a very hot town, so shell out for a/c or make sure you have a good fan in your room.

Hotel Central 3 C 8–30 ⓣ7942 6352. A small hotel with five pleasant a/c rooms, all with private bath and cable TV. ❸

Hotel Las Palmeras 10 Av 2–00 ⓣ7942 4647. Basic rooms, some with a/c, bathroom and TV. ❷–❸

Hotel Posada Don Adán 8 Av 4–30 ⓣ7942 0549. Comfortable, if old-fashioned, and run by a hospitable elderly couple. Most of the eighteen large rooms have a/c and cable TV, plus there's parking here, too. ❹

Hotel Posada Perla de Oriente 2 C & 12 Av ⓣ7942 0014. Lush tropical gardens, a large swimming pool, and rooms, with or without a/c, that are spacious and clean, if not exactly stylish. ❹–❺

Pensión Hernández 3 C 7–41 ⓣ & ⓕ7942 0708, ⓔhotelh@guate.net. A well-run place with plenty of clean, simple rooms, all with fan and some with TV and private shower. It has safe parking, a small concrete pool for cooling off, and an owner who speaks good English. ❷–❸

Eating

When it comes to **eating**, there's nothing much to get excited about, and Chiquimula's residents have simple tastes. Inexpensive comedores are around the **market**: there's a cluster of popular ones at the corner of 4 C and 8 Av. A Chinese restaurant is pretty exotic in these parts: *Dong Fang* at 5 C 7–51 and *El Chino* on 8 Av both serve reasonably decent, vaguely oriental food at moderate prices. On the plaza, the restaurant inside the *Hotel Chiquimulja* styles itself as the flashest place in town, with a long menu that takes in chicken, steak and pasta. Otherwise *Rancho Típico* on 3 Calle scores for inexpensive Guatemalan *platos*.

Esquipulas

We returned to breakfast, and afterwards set out to visit the only object of interest, the great church of the pilgrimage, the Holy Place of Central America. Every year, on the fifteenth of January, pilgrims visit it, even from Peru and Mexico; the latter being a journey not exceeded in hardship by the pilgrimage to Mecca. As in the east, "it is not forbidden to trade during the pilgrimage", and when there are no wars to make the roads unsafe eighty thousand people have assembled among the mountains to barter and pay homage to "our Lord of Esquipulas".

John Lloyd Stephens (1841)

The final town on this eastern highway is **ESQUIPULAS**, which, now as in Stephens' day, has a single point of interest; it is almost certainly the

The Esquipulas pilgrimage

The history of the **Esquipulas pilgrimage** probably dates back to before the Conquest, when the valley was controlled by Chief Esquipulas. Even then the area was the site of an important religious shrine, perhaps connected with the nearby Maya site of Copán. When the Spanish arrived the chief was keen to avoid the usual bloodshed and chose to surrender without a fight; the grateful Spaniards named the city they founded at the site in his honour. The famed colonial sculptor Quirio Cataño was then commissioned to carve an image of Christ for the church constructed in the middle of the new town, and in order to make it more likely to appeal to the local people he chose to carve it from balsam, a dark wood. Another version has it that Cataño was hired by the Maya after one of their number had seen a vision of a dark Christ on this spot. In any event, the image was installed in the church in 1595 and soon accredited with miraculous powers. But after the bishop of Guatemala, Pardo de Figueroa, was cured of a chronic ailment on a trip to Esquipulas in 1737 things really took off. The bishop ordered the construction of a new church, which was completed in 1758, and had his body buried beneath the altar.

Although all this might seem fairly straightforward, it doesn't explain why this figure has become the most revered in a country full of miracle-working saints. One possible explanation is that it offers the Maya, who until recently dominated the pilgrimage, a chance to blend pre-Columbian and Catholic worship. It's known that the Maya pantheon included several Black deities such as Ek Ahau, the black lord, who was served by seven retainers, and Ek'Chuach, the tall black one, who protected travellers. When Aldous Huxley visited the shrine in 1934 his thoughts were along these lines: "So what draws the worshippers is probably less the saintliness of the historic Jesus than the magical sootiness of his image … numinosity is in inverse ratio to luminosity."

most important Catholic shrine in Central America, famous above all for its dark-hued statue of Christ. Arriving from Chiquimula the bus winds through the hills, beneath craggy outcrops and forested peaks, emerging suddenly at the lip of a huge bowl-shaped valley centring on a great open plateau. On one side of this, just below the road, is Esquipulas itself. The place is entirely dominated by the four perfectly white domes of the church, brilliantly floodlit at night. Beneath these, the rest of the town is a messy sprawl of cheap hotels, souvenir stalls and overpriced restaurants. The pilgrimage, which continues all year, has generated numerous sidelines, creating a booming resort where people from all over Central America come to worship, eat, drink and relax, in a bizarre combination of holy devotion and indulgence.

The principal day of **pilgrimage**, when the religious significance of the shrine is at its most potent, is January 15. Even the smallest villages will save enough money to send a representative or two on this occasion, their send-off and return invariably marked by religious services. These plus the thousands who can afford to come in their own right ensure that the numbers attending are still as high as in Stephens' day, filling the town to bursting and beyond. Buses chartered from all over Guatemala choke the streets, while the most devoted pilgrims arrive on foot (some dropping to their knees for the last few kilometres). There's a smaller pilgrimage annually on March 9, and faithful crowds visit year-round. The town has also played an important role in modern-day politics: it was here that the first **peace accord** initiatives to end the civil wars in El Salvador, Nicaragua and Guatemala were signed in 1987.

Inside the **church** today there's a constant scurry of hushed devotion amid clouds of smoke and incense. In the nave pilgrims approach the image on their

Fiestas

January
12–15 El Progreso (near Jutiapa), main day 15th
15 Esquipulas, the biggest pilgrimage in Central America
19–21 Cabañas (near Zacapa), main day 19th
20–26 Ipala, main day 23rd (includes bullfighting)

February
1–4 San Pedro Pinula, a fine traditional fiesta, main day 4th
5–10 Monjas, main day 7th
24–28 Río Hondo, main day 26th
Varies Both Pasaco (in the department of Jutiapa) and Huite (near Zacapa) have fiestas around carnival time

March
3–5 Jeréz (in the department of Jutiapa), main day 5th
9 Esquipulas, a smaller day of pilgrimage to the Black Christ
12–15 Moyuta (near Jutiapa) and Olapa (near Chiquimula)
15–21 Morales, main day 19th
Varies Jocotán

April
22–25 La Unión (near Zacapa), main day 25th

May
2–5 Jalapa, main day 3rd
5–9 Gualán (near Zacapa)

knees, while others light candles, mouth supplications or simply stand in silent crowds. The image itself is most closely approached by a separate side entrance, where you can join the queue to shuffle past beneath it and pause briefly in front before being shoved on by the crowds behind. Back outside you'll find yourself among swarms of souvenir and relic hawkers, and pilgrims who, duty done, are ready to head off to eat and drink away the rest of their stay. Many pilgrims also visit a set of nearby **caves**, Las Cuevas de las Minas (US$0.75), a ten-minute walk south of the basilica, said to have miraculous powers; and there are some **hot baths** – ideal for ritual ablution.

Practicalities

When it comes to staying in Esquipulas, you'll find yourself among hundreds of visitors whatever the time of year. **Hotels** probably outnumber private homes, and new ones are springing up all the time. Bargains, however, are in short supply, and the bulk of the budget places are grubby and bare, with tiny monk-like cells – not designed in a spirit of religiosity, but simply to up the number of guests. Prices are rarely in writing and are always negotiable, depending on the flow of pilgrims, so bargain hard. Avoid Saturdays when prices double.

Many of the least expensive places are clustered opposite the church on the other side of the main road, 11 Calle. The family-run *Hotel Villa Edelmira* (❷–❸), and *La Favorita*, on 10 Calle and 2 Avenida (❷), are two of the best simple budget hotels. For a touch more luxury, head for the *Hotel Los Ángeles*,

June
23–26 Usumatlán

July
16–22 Puerto Barrios, the (riotous) main day is the 19th
22–26 Jocotán (near Chiquimula)
23–27 Esquipulas, a fiesta in honour of Santiago Apóstol, main day 25th

August
11–18 Chiquimula, main day 15th (includes bullfighting)
12–15 Asunción Mita
25 San Luís Jilotepéque

September
22–25 Sansare (between Jalapa and Sanarate), main day 24th

November
7–14 Sanarate
10–16 Jutiapa, main day 13th
26 Lívingston, Garífuna day here is a huge celebration
26–30 Quesada (near Jutiapa).

December
4–9 Zacapa, main day 8th
13–16 San Luís Jilotepéque
22–27 Cuilapa
24–31 Lívingston, a Caribbean-style carnival

on 2 Avenida, the street just west of church (Ⓣ7943 1254; ❹), where the rooms have private bathrooms and TV; or the *Hotel Esquipulao*, next door (❹), a cheaper annexe to comfortable *Hotel Payaquí* (Ⓣ7943 2025, Ⓕ943 1371; ❺), where there's a pool and all rooms come with a TV and either fan or a/c.

There are also dozens of **restaurants** and **bars** to choose from. Breakfast is a bargain in Esquipulas, and you shouldn't have to pay more than US$1.50 for a good feed. There's a decent range of lunch specials later on, though dinner here can be expensive. The *Hacienda Steak House*, a block from the plaza at 2 Avenida and 10 Calle, is one of the smartest places in town, while many of the cheaper places are on 11 Calle and the surrounding streets – try the *Taquería Andale* at 2 Avenida and 10 Calle for inexpensive and tasty tacos. Among the **banks** in town, Banco Industrial has a branch with a Visa ATM at 9 Calle and 3 Avenida, and Banco G&T Continental, almost opposite, offers MasterCard cash advances; both will cash travellers' cheques.

Rutas Orientales runs a superb half-hourly **bus** service between Guatemala City and Esquipulas; its office is on the main street at 11 Calle and 1 Avenida. There are also regular microbuses to the borders with **El Salvador** (every 30min 6am–6pm; 1hr) and **Honduras** at Agua Caliente (every 30min 6am–5.30pm; 30min). If you want to get to the ruins of Copán, you'll need to catch a microbus to Chiquimula (every 30min) from 11 Calle and change there for the El Florido border post (see p.385).

On to the borders: El Salvador and Honduras

The **Honduran** border crossing at **Agua Caliente**, open 24 hours, is just 10km from Esquipulas, and served by a regular shuttle of minibuses and taxis from the main street that will shuttle you back and forth for a dollar a time (20min). There's a **Honduran consulate** (Mon–Fri 8am–1pm & 3–6pm) in the *Hotel Payaquí*, beside the church in Esquipulas, though most nationalities do not need a visa.

The border with **El Salvador** at Anguiatú (open 6am–7pm) is 33km from Esquipulas, down a branch road that splits from the main road just before you arrive at the town. Minibuses run from 11 Calle every half-hour (1hr) until 6pm. Most nationalities do not need a visa to enter El Salvador.

Travel details

Buses

Bus travel is convenient and pretty rapid in this region, and the main highways are all paved and in good condition. Details of services from Guatemala City can be found on pp.98–99.

Chiquimula to: El Florido (every 45min; 1hr 30min); Guatemala City (hourly; 3hr 30min); Ipala (hourly; 1hr).

Esquipulas to: Agua Caliente (every 30min; 30min); Anguiatú (every 30min; 1hr); Guatemala City (every 30min; 4hr 15min).

Morales to: Río Dulce (every 30min).

Puerto Barrios to: Chiquimula (hourly; 4hr); Corinto (every 30min; 1hr); Guatemala City (15 daily, including seven *especiales*; 5hr–5hr 30min), passing Quiriguá (1hr 30min).

Río Dulce to: El Estor (every 1hr 30min; 1hr 45min); Flores & Poptún (every 30min; 3hr); Guatemala City (every 30min; 5hr).

Boats

Lívingston to: Omoa, Honduras (charters only; 2hr 30min); Puerto Barrios, by ferry (2 daily; 1hr 30min) or *lancha* (about every 40min; 30min); Punta Gorda, Belize (2 weekly; 1hr); Río Dulce Town (regular services; about 2hr 30min).

Puerto Barrios to: Lívingston, by ferry (2 daily; 1hr 30min) or *lancha* (about every 40min; 30min); Punta Gorda, Belize (2 daily; 1hr 15min).

Río Dulce Town to: Lívingston (regular services until 4pm; about 1hr 30min).

5

Cobán and the Verapaces

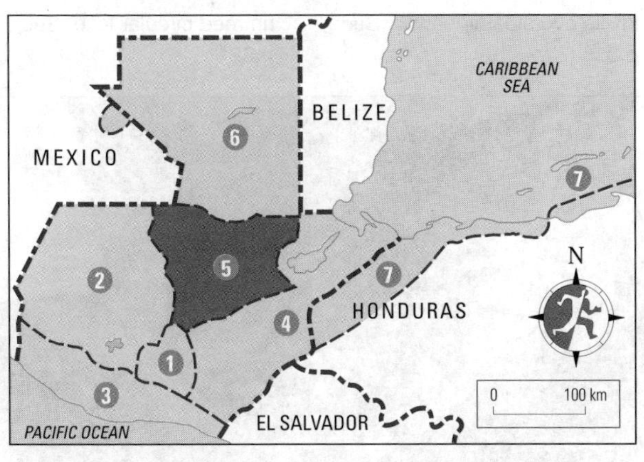

CHAPTER 5

Highlights

* **Fiestas** The towns of Baja Verapaz are famous for their festivals, enlivened by some unique traditional dances, like the Rabinal Achi and Palo Volador. **See p.302**

* **Quetzal** Catch a glimpse of Guatemala's national bird in the dense cloudforests of the Verapaces. **See p.306** & **p.314**

* **Semuc Champey** Cool off in the turquoise pools of this idyllic riverside hideaway. **See p.316**

* **Candelaria caves** An extraordinary limestone cave system, extending for more than 18km underground, with some immense chambers to explore. **See p.319**

* **Chisec** Explore the magical lakes of Lagunas de Sepalau and the sacred Maya cave of Bombil Pek near this peaceful little town. **See p.320**

* **Laguna Lachuá** An exceptionally beautiful, jungle-rimmed circular lake. **See p.321**

△ Coffee

5

Cobán and the Verapaces

While essentially a continuation of Guatemala's western highlands, the mountains of Alta (Upper) and Baja (Lower) Verapaz have always been set apart in a number of ways: certainly, the flat-bottomed Salamá valley and the mist-soaked hills around Cobán are physically unlike any of the country's other mountainous areas. **Baja Verapaz**, the more southerly of these two departments, is sparsely populated, a mixture of deep valleys and parched hills with patches of lush cloudforest coating the highest altitudes. Just two roads cross the department: one connects the fiesta towns of **Salamá**, **Rabinal** and **Cubulco**, the other runs from the Carretera al Atlántico up to Cobán.

Alta Verapaz, the wettest and greenest of Guatemala's highlands, occupies the land to the north. Local people say it rains for thirteen months a year here, alternating between straightforward downpours and the drizzle of the *chipi-chipi*, a misty rain that hangs interminably on the hills, although the mountains are now being deforested at such a rate that weather patterns may soon be disrupted. For the moment, however, the area's alpine terrain remains almost permanently moist and vivid with greenery. The pleasant town of **Cobán** is the departmental capital, and from here roads head north into Petén, west to El Quiché, and east to Lago de Izabal.

The **history** of the Verapaces is also quite distinct. Long before the Conquest, local Achi Maya had earned themselves a reputation as the most bloodthirsty of all the tribes, said to sacrifice every prisoner that they took. Their greatest enemies were the K'iche', with whom they were at war for a century. So ferocious were the Achi that not even the Spanish could contain them by force. Alvarado's army was unable to make any headway against them, and eventually he gave up trying to control the area, naming it *tierra de guerra*, the "land of war".

The Church, however, couldn't allow so many heathen souls to go to waste. Under the leadership of **Fray Bartolomé de Las Casas**, the so-called "Apostle of the Maya", the Church made a deal with the conquistadors: if Alvarado would agree to keep all armed men out of the area for five years, the priests would bring it under control. In 1537 Las Casas, accompanied by three other Dominican friars, set out into the highlands. Here they befriended the Achi chiefs, and learning the local dialects they translated devotional hymns and taught them to the bemused *indígenas*. By 1538 they had made considerable progress, converting large numbers of Maya and persuading them to move from their scattered hillside homes to the new Spanish-style villages. At the end of the five years the famous and invincible Achi were transformed into Spanish subjects, and the king of Spain renamed the province *Verapaz*, "True Peace".

Since the colonial era the Verapaces have remained isolated, and were for many years virtually independent: all their trade bypassed the capital by taking a direct route to the Caribbean along the Río Polochic and out through Lago de Izabal. The area really started to develop with the **coffee boom** at the turn of the century, when German immigrants flooded into the country to buy and run fincas, particularly in Alta Verapaz. By 1914 about half of all Guatemalan coffee was grown on German-owned lands, and Germany bought half of the exported produce.

Around Cobán the new immigrants intermarried with local families and established an island of European sophistication. A railway was built along the Polochic valley and Alta Verapaz became almost totally independent. This situation was brought to an end by World War II, when the US insisted that Guatemala do something about the enemy presence, and the government was forced to expel the landowners, many of whom were unashamed in their support for Hitler.

Although the Verapaces are now well connected to the capital, the area is still dependent on the production of coffee, and Cobán's economy is still heavily

Market days in the Verapaces

Monday
Senahú; Tucurú.

Tuesday
Chisec; El Chol; Cubulco; Lanquín; Purulhá; Rabinal; San Cristóbal Verapaz; San Jerónimo; Tres Cruces.

Saturday
Senahú.

Sunday
Chisec; Cubulco; Lanquín; Purulhá; Rabinal; Salamá; San Jerónimo; Santa Cruz; Tactic.

influenced by the huge coffee fincas and the wealthy families who own them. Taken as a whole, however, the Verapaces remain very much indigenous country: Baja Verapaz retains a small **Achi** Maya outpost around Rabinal, and in Alta Verapaz the Maya population, largely **Poqomchi'** and **Q'eqchi'** speakers, the two languages of the Poqomam group, is predominant. The production of coffee, and more recently **cardamom** for the Middle Eastern market, has cut deep into their land and their way of life, the fincas driving many people off prime territory to marginal plots. Traditional costume is worn less here than in the western highlands, and in its place many indigenous women have adopted a more universal Q'eqchi' costume, using the loose-hanging white *huipil* and locally made *cortes*. Maya men do not wear *traje* in the Verapaces.

The northern, flat section of Alta Verapaz includes a slice of Petén rainforest, and in recent years Q'eqchi' Maya have fanned out into this empty expanse, reaching the Río Salinas in the west, heading up into the Petén and making their way across the border into Belize. Here they carve out sections of the forest and attempt to farm, a process that threatens the future of the forest and offers little long-term security for the migrants.

Where to go

More and more travellers are discovering the attractions of the Verapaces, but far fewer people make it out this way compared with the western highlands or Petén. While it's true that Maya traditions are less evident here than in other parts of Guatemala, you'll find these highlands astonishingly beautiful, with their craggy limestone hills, moist, misty atmosphere and boundless fertility. The transport hub of the area is **Cobán**, a fairly attractive mid-sized mountain town with good accommodation and a couple of coffeehouses; it's a little subdued once the rain sets in, but still a decent base from which to explore the region. In Baja Verapaz, the towns of **Salamá**, **Rabinal** and **Cubulco** are rightly renowned for their fiestas, while **San Jerónimo** has some interesting historic sights.

In isolated patches of cloudforest in northern Baja Verapaz you can occasionally see the quetzal, Guatemala's national bird and one of Central America's rarest. The **quetzal sanctuary**, just off the Cobán highway, is an accessible and popular place to search, though you may have more luck inside the larger adjacent **Reserva Sierra de las Minas**. Northeast of Cobán, the exquisite natural bathing pools of **Semuc Champey** are surrounded by lush tropical forest and fast becoming a key travellers' hangout. Taking an alternative route, a couple of wonderful natural attractions can be found directly north of Cobán near the town of **Chisec**: the emerald **Lagunas de Sepalau** and the huge cavern of Bombil Pek, a focus for Maya worship. From Chisec it's a short hop to the vast system of **Candelaria caves** and the nearby ruins of **Cancuén**. Several seldom-travelled back roads offer adventurous escape routes from the region – east down the Polochic valley to **Lago de Izabal** (covered in Chapter Four) or to the western highlands, either via Uspantán or across remote frontier country to Barillas (covered at the end of Chapter Two).

Baja Verapaz

A dramatic mix of dry hills and fertile valleys, Baja Verapaz is crossed by a skeletal road network. The historic towns of **San Jerónimo**, **Salamá**, **Rabinal** and **Cubulco** are all regularly served by buses, and have interesting markets as well as being famed for their fiestas, where you'll see some unique traditional dances. The other big attractions are the **quetzal sanctuary**, on the western side of the Cobán highway, and the forested mountains, waterfalls and wildlife inside the **Reserva Sierra de las Minas** just to the east.

The main approach to both departments is from the Carretera al Atlántico, where the road to the Verapaz highlands branches off at the **El Rancho** junction. Lined with scrub bush and cacti, the road climbs steadily upwards, past the excellent, very popular roadside *Villa del Sol* restaurant (at Km 88), where a filling meal costs US$3. Soon the dusty browns and dry yellows of the Motagua valley give way to an explosion of green as dense pine forests and alpine meadows grip the mountains. The views from here are superb, though the hills can often be shrouded in a blanket of cloud. Some 48km beyond the junction is **La Cumbre de Santa Elena**, where the road for the main towns of Baja Verapaz turns off to the west, and immediately begins to drop towards the floor of the Salamá valley. Surrounded by steep, parched hillsides, with a level flood plain at its base, the valley appears entirely cut off from the outside world.

San Jerónimo

At the valley's eastern end lies the small town of **SAN JERÓNIMO**, 18km from the Cumbre junction. In the Conquest's early days, Dominican priests built a church and convent here and planted vineyards, eventually producing a wine lauded as the finest in Central America. In 1845, after the religious orders were abolished, an Englishman replaced the vines with sugarcane and began brewing an *aguardiente* that became equally famous. These days the area still produces cane, though the cultivation of flowers for export and fish farming have usurped alcohol production in importance.

Thanks to some active promotion by the municipal tourism authority, and a trio of sights, tranquil San Jerónimo attracts the odd curious visitor. Presiding over the central plaza, the village's seventeenth-century Baroque **church** contains a monumental gilded altar, brought here from France, which was crafted from sheets of eighteen-carat gold. Just down the hill from the church, in a wonderful rural position at the base of the foothills of the Sierra de las Minas, are the remains of the convent complex: the Hacienda de San Jerónimo. Its sugar-mill buildings now form the **Museo Regional del Trapiche** (Mon–Sat 8am–4pm, Sat & Sun 10am–4pm) with displays that explain the history of the hacienda and refining process, while the extensive grassy grounds here make an ideal place for a picnic. Also of interest is the colonial **aqueduct**, built in 1679, that once supplied the mill's waterwheels. Many of its 124 original stone arches are still standing on the southern outskirts of the village, about ten minutes' walk from the plaza – just ask the way to the *acueducto antiguo*.

The excellent *Hotel Hacienda Real el Trapiche* (ⓣ7940 2542; ❸), at the entrance to the town, has ten attractive rooms, all with good beds and reading lights. The hotel also offers great home-cooked food. On the plaza, *Comedor Los Arcos* serves tasty meals, though the pounding music can be a bit much. **Minibuses** connect Salamá and San Jerónimo between 6am and 7.30pm, running every half-hour.

Salamá

Eight kilometres west of San Jerónimo is **SALAMÁ**, capital of the department of Baja Verapaz. The town has a relaxed and prosperous air, and like many of the places out this way its population is largely ladino. There's not much to do outside **fiesta time** (Sept 17–21), other than browse in the Sunday market, although it's worth checking out the crumbling colonial **bridge**, now used only by pedestrians, on the edge of town, and the old **church**, the gilt of its huge altars darkened by age. If you decide to stay, the pick of the **hotels** is the modern *Hotel Real Legendario*, 8 Av 3–57 (ⓣ7940 0187; ❸), with a little café and very clean rooms, all with private bath, good beds and cable TV. *Hotel Tezulutlán*, just south of the plaza (ⓣ7940 1643; ❸), is a reasonable alternative, though the rooms, set round a leafy central courtyard, are not as clean. The less expensive *Pensión Juárez*, at the end of 5 Calle, past the police station (ⓣ7940 0055; ❷–❸), is a good budget hotel with plenty of rooms, some with bathroom. For **eating**, try one of the places around the plaza: *El Ganadero* is the best restaurant, while *Deli-Donus* and *Café Central* both score for coffee and snacks. Bancafé, opposite the church, has a 5B ATM for Visa and MasterCard holders, and will cash dollars and travellers' cheques.

To really explore the region you may want to consider getting in touch with Eco-Verapaz, 8 Av 7–12, Zona 1 (ⓣ7940 0146), who offer good mountain-biking, caving, hiking, horse-riding and cultural trips throughout the department. Prices are around US$40 a day for most activities. **Buses** from Guatemala City run hourly to Salamá (3hr 30min) between 6am and 5pm, from 11 Avenida and 17 Calle in Zona 1; many continue on to Rabinal (4hr 20min) and eight go all the way to Cubulco (5hr). From Salamá, buses depart for the capital between 3am and 6pm, while a steady stream of minibuses runs to San Jerónimo and to the La Cumbre junction, where there are connections with pullman buses running between Cobán and Guatemala City.

Rabinal

To the west of Salamá the road climbs out of the valley over a low pass and through a gap in the hills to **San Miguel Chicaj**, a large traditional village clustered around a colonial church. Beyond here the road climbs again, reaching a pass with magnificent views across the surrounding mountain ranges, which step away into El Quiché.

Less than an hour from Salamá, **RABINAL** is a dusty, isolated farming town where the one-storey adobe and cinderblock houses are dominated by a large colonial church. Here the proportion of indigenous inhabitants is considerably higher, making both the Sunday market and the fiesta well worth a visit. Founded in 1537 by Bartolomé de Las Casas, Rabinal was the first of the settlements he established in his peaceful conversion of the Achi nation; about 3km northwest, a steep ninety-minute hike away, are the ruins of one of their fortified cities, known locally as **Cerro Cayup**. Nowadays the place is known for its oranges, claimed to be the finest in the country – and they certainly taste like it.

Sights are slim in Rabinal itself, but the town's small **museum**, 4 Avenida and 2 Calle, Zona 3 (Mon–Sat 8.30–5pm), is worth a visit. Here you'll find exhibits on traditional medicinal practices, cultural history, local arts and crafts, and a room devoted to the impact of the civil war in the region – there were four massacres in 1982 alone in the Río Negro region north of the town. In the past few years, local people have exhumed several of the mass graves that pepper the hillsides around Rabinal and reburied some of the 4400 victims from the municipality, in an effort to give those killed during *la violencia* a more dignified resting place. Despite eight years of legal investigations, only three very junior members of the local PUC (paramilitary conscripts) have been jailed, and the army officers who directed the campaign remain free. Not surprisingly, when ex–military dictator Ríos Montt attempted to land his helicopter in Rabinal during the 2003 election campaign (on the very day the remains of massacre victims were being reburied) he was forced to retreat back to Guatemala City under a hail of rocks.

Rabinal's **fiesta**, which runs from January 19 to 24, is renowned for its dances, many of them pre-colonial in origin. The most famous of these, an extended dance drama known as the "Rabinal Achi" re-enacts a battle between the Achi and K'iche' tribes and is unique to the town, performed annually on January 23. Others include the *patzca*, a ceremony to call for good harvests, using masks that portray a swelling below the jaw, and wooden sticks engraved with serpents, birds and human heads. If you can't make it for the fiesta, the Sunday market is a good second-best; look out for some high-quality local artesanías, including carvings made from the *árbol del morro* (calabash tree) and traditional pottery.

The best of Rabinal's several fairly basic **hotels** is the *Posada San Pablo*, 3 Av 1–50 (Ⓣ7940 0211, ❶–❷), a decent budget affair with well-kept rooms, some with private bath. If it's full, try the *Hospedaje Caballeros*, 1 C 4–02 (❶). The most comfortable place is the three-storey, concrete *Gran Hotel Rabinal Achi*, also on 1 Calle, which has large rooms with private bath as well as a comedor. For an inexpensive **meal** count on *Cafetería Mishell del Rosario* on 1 Calle behind the church. The Banrural at 1 Calle and 3 Avenida cashes dollars only. Hourly **buses** connect the town with Salamá (50min). For Guatemala City, there are five daily via La Cumbre (4hr 20min), and three daily via El Chol and Granados (6hr).

Cubulco

Leaving Rabinal the road heads west, climbing yet another high ridge with fantastic views to the left, into the uninhabited mountain ranges. To the north, in one of the deep river valleys, lies the financially disastrous **Chixoy** hydro-electric plant (see p.308), responsible for producing around fifty percent of both Guatemala's electricity and its national debt.

A further 15km of rough road brings you into the next valley and to **CUBULCO**, an isolated town of Achi Maya and ladinos, surrounded on all sides by steep, forested mountains. Like Salamá and Rabinal, Cubulco is best visited for its fiesta, this being one of the few places where you can still see the **Palo Volador**, a pre-conquest ritual in which men throw themselves from a thirty-metre pole with a rope tied around their legs, spinning down towards the ground as the rope unravels, and hopefully landing on their feet. It's as dangerous as it looks, particularly when you bear in mind that most of the dancers are blind drunk; every few years an inebriated dancer falls from the top of the

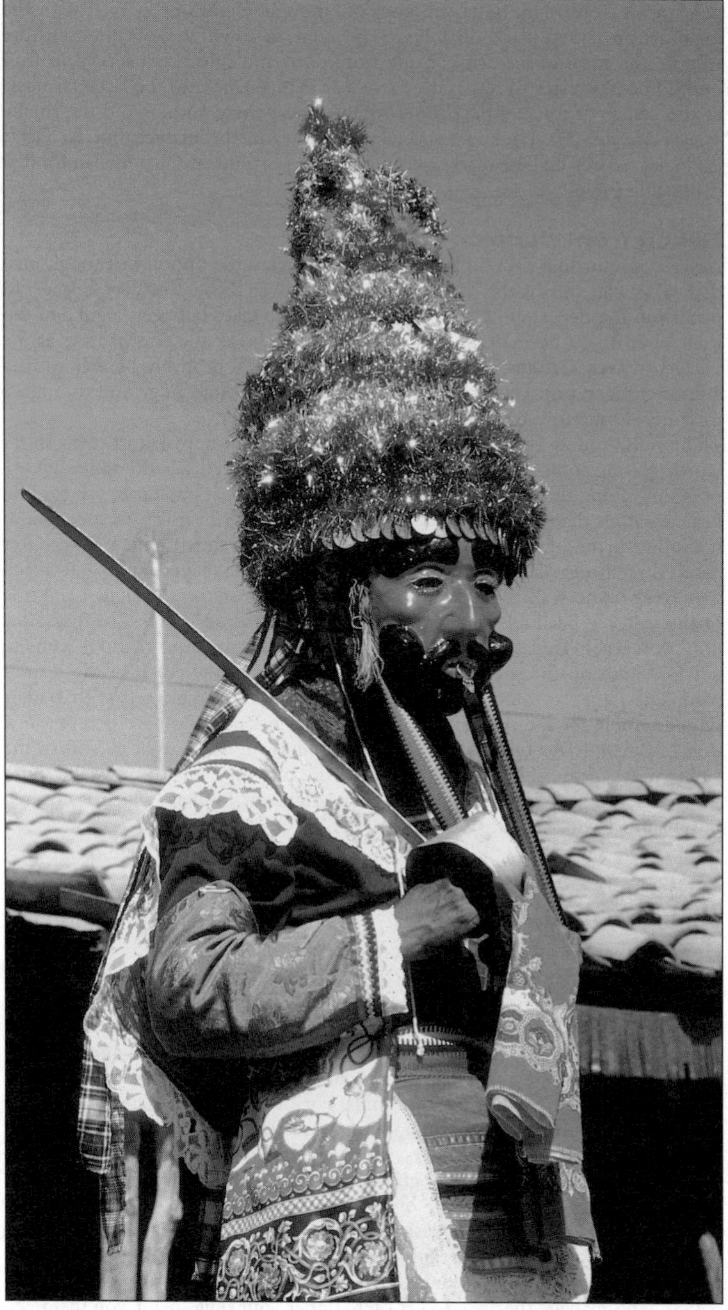

△ Rabinal fiesta dancer

pole to his death. The fiesta still goes on, though, as riotous as ever, with the main action taking place on July 25. If you're in town at fiesta time be sure to taste the local *chilate* drink, made from corn and spices and served in fruit husks. The best place to stay is the *Hospedaje Pías* (❶), next to the large farmacia in the centre of town, where some rooms have private bath. Avoid the smelly *Posada Morales* (❶). There are several comedores in the market, but *La Fonda del Viajero* scores highest marks, serving up big portions of Guatemalan food at reasonable prices.

Hiking from Cubulco to Joyabaj

Instead of returning back to Rabinal by road, there's the option of a tough hike that takes you out of the valley on foot, also over the Sierra de Chuacús, to Joyabaj in the department of El Quiché. The hike takes between eight and ten hours, but if you have a tent it's probably best to break the trip halfway at the village of **Tres Cruces** (if you don't have one, you'll probably be able to find a floor to sleep on). The views, as you tramp over a huge ridge and through a mixture of pine forest and farmland, are spectacular.

The hills around Cubulco are covered in a complex network of paths so it's worth getting someone to point you in the right direction, and asking plenty of people along the way – for the first half of the walk it's better to ask for Tres Cruces rather than Joyabaj. Broadly speaking, the path bears up to the right as it climbs the hillside to the south of Cubulco, crossing the mountain range after about three hours. On the other side is an open, bowl-shaped valley – to reach Tres Cruces you walk along the top of the ridge that marks the right-hand side of the valley – heading south from the pass. Don't drop down into the valley until you reach Tres Cruces. The village itself is the smallest of rural hamlets, perched high on the spine of the ridge, and far from the reach of the nearest road. On Thursday mornings the town's tiny plaza is crammed with traders who assemble for the market, but otherwise there's nothing here except a few *tiendas*. Beyond Tres Cruces you drop down into the valley that cuts in to the right (west) of the ridge, and then follow the dirt road out of the valley, onto the larger Joyabaj to Pachalum road – turn right for Joyabaj (which is covered in Chapter Two).

Reserva Sierra de las Minas and Biotopo del Quetzal

Heading for Cobán, and deeper into the highlands, the main road sweeps straight past the turning for Salamá and on around endless tight curves below forested hillsides. The steep slopes on the eastern side of the road form the foothills of the **Sierra de las Minas**, a mighty mountain range that soars to more than 3000m along a slender stretch of land between the Motagua and Polochic valleys. The peaks are often called the "dark mountains" because of the dense blanket of mist that hangs over the hills. Forming one of Guatemala's largest expanses of **cloudforest**, the almost unpopulated region harbours abundant wildlife including howler monkeys, white-tailed deer, coyotes and birds including the emerald toucan, hummingbirds and fairly plentiful numbers of quetzals (see box, p.306).

Much of the area has been designated the **Reserva Sierra de las Minas**, which is well off the tourist trail and not easy to **get to** independently. The most practical option is to arrange a trip with Defensores de la Naturaleza (see p.488), who manage the area. To get there under your own steam, you first need to get to the village of **San Rafael Chilascó**, which is 12km east of the Cobán highway, via the turn-off at Km 145. Monja Blanca buses between Guatemala City and Cobán pass by the turn-off every half-hour between 4am and 6pm, but you may have to wait a while at the junction for a pick-up to the village. Once in San Rafael, contact the village ecotourism committee, who work in conjunction with the Defensores de la Naturaleza and can organize accommodation (❶), meals with local families and guides. You'll need good-quality waterproofs and hiking boots. Trails lead to two spectacular **waterfalls**, El Saltó de Chilascó, which plunges 200m in two drops close to the entrance of the reserve, and the Laguneta falls, which drop an astounding 350m. There are many rare orchids and a liquidambar forest to admire along the way.

Back on the highway north to Cobán, just before the village of Purulhá, the **Biotopo del Quetzal** (daily 7am–4pm; US$2.50) is a much easier place to visit, though Guatemala's national bird is actually most common in the forests south of San Pedro Carchá (see p.314). The nature reserve is designed to protect the habitat of the endangered quetzal and covers a steep area of dense cloudforest, through which the Río Colorado cascades towards the valley floor, forming waterfalls and natural swimming pools. It is also known as the **Mario Dary Reserve**, in honour of one of the founders of Guatemala's environmental movement. A lecturer from San Carlos University, Mario Dary pioneered the establishment of nature reserves in Guatemala and spent years campaigning for a cloudforest sanctuary to protect the quetzal, causing great problems for the powerful timber companies in the process. He was murdered in 1988; an ecological foundation, Fundary, has been set up in his name to manage protected areas, including Punta de Manabique on the Caribbean coast.

Visiting the sanctuary

Two paths through the undergrowth from the road complete a circuit that takes you up into the woods above the reserve headquarters (where maps are available for US$0.75). Quetzals are occasionally seen here but they're extremely elusive. The best time of year to visit is just before and just after the nesting season (between March and June), and the best time of day is sunrise. In general, the birds tend to spend the nights up in the high forest and float across the road as dawn breaks, to spend the days in the forest below, and they can be easily identified by their jerky, undulating flight. A good place to look out for them is at one of their favoured feeding trees, the broad-leaved *aguacatillo*, which produces a small avocado-like fruit. Whether or not you see a quetzal, the forest itself, usually damp with *chipi-chipi*, a perpetual mist, is worth a visit: a profusion of lichens, ferns, mosses, bromeliads and orchids spread out beneath a towering canopy of cypress, oak, walnut and pepper trees.

Practicalities

Buses from Cobán and Guatemala City pass the entrance every half-hour, but make sure they know you want to be dropped at the *biotopo* as it's easy to miss – the entrance is at Km 161 on the Cobán highway.

There are several **places to stay, eat and drink** within a few kilometres of the quetzal sanctuary. Coming from Guatemala City, the first place you reach is the *Hotel Posada Montaña del Quetzal* at Km 156.5 (Ⓣ2331 0929, Ⓦwww.hposadaquetzal.com; ❺–❻), which has pleasant stone and timber bungalows with fireplaces and spacious rooms with private bathrooms; many have great forest views and there's a restaurant, bar, swimming pool, and orchid garden here. The next place is the bizarre-looking *Ram Tzul*, Km 158.5 (Ⓣ5908 4066; ❸–❺), where the main restaurant building is a towering glass-fronted construction. Behind this, however, the attractive accommodation looks over the Verapaz hills; the newest rooms are huge and very imaginative in design, with stained-glass windows and floors consisting of wood logs buried in cement. Just 100m past the entrance to the reserve, the simple *Hospedaje Ranchito del Quetzal* (☎2331 3579; ❷) offers basic accommodation either in very rustic palapa-roofed huts or in a concrete block, where some of the featureless rooms have private bath. You'll find a simple in-house comedor here too, and, compensating for the no-frills facilities, quetzals are sometimes seen in the patch of forest around the hotel. Heading on towards Cobán, the Swiss-style *Country Delight Inn* (☎5514 0955 or 5709 1149; ❹–❼), Km 166.5, offers attractive rooms with bath and a very comfortable, attractive chalet (that sleeps four) with a fireplace and full cooking facilities. The inn enjoys a lovely meadow setting just off the road, and there's ping pong and a small pool. Even if you're just passing by, it's well worth sampling some of the inn's really hearty, home-made cooking, which includes wonderfully flavoursome locally reared ham – try the *pan con pierna*.

Alta Verapaz

Beyond the quetzal sanctuary the main road crosses into the department of Alta Verapaz, and another 13km takes you beyond the forests and into a luxuriant alpine valley of cattle pastures hemmed in by steep, perpetually green hillsides. Most people speed through this region in an air-conditioned bus on their way to Cobán, but there are a few interesting attractions to detain you if you have the time to explore these evergreen hills and their towns' curiosities.

The resplendent quetzal

The **quetzal**, Guatemala's national symbol (after which the country's currency is named), has a distinguished past but an uncertain future. The bird's feathers have been sacred from the earliest of times, and in the strange cult of Quetzalcoatl, whose influence once spread throughout Mesoamerica, the bird was incorporated into the plumed serpent, a supremely powerful deity. To the Maya the quetzal was so sacred that killing one was a capital offence, and it is also thought to have been the *nahual*, or spiritual protector, of the Maya chiefs. When Tecún Umán faced Pedro de Alvarado in hand-to-hand combat, his headdress sprouted the long green feathers of the quetzal; and when the conquistadors founded a city adjacent to the battleground they named it Quetzaltenango, the place of the quetzals.

In modern Guatemala the quetzal's image saturates the country, and citizens honoured by the president are awarded the Order of the Quetzal. The bird is also considered a symbol of freedom, since caged quetzals die from the rigours of confinement. Despite all this, the sweeping tide of deforestation threatens the very existence of the bird, and the **Biotopo del Quetzal** is about the only concrete step that has been taken to save it.

The more resplendent of the birds, and the source of the famed feathers, is the male. The birds' heads are crowned with a plume of brilliant green, and their chests and lower bellies are a rich crimson; their unmistakeable, oversized golden-green tail feathers are only really evident in the mating season. The females, on the other hand, are an unremarkable brownish colour. The birds nest in holes drilled into dead trees, laying one or two eggs at the start of the rainy season, usually in April or May. Quetzals can easily be identified by the strangely jerky way they fly.

Tactic

The first place of any size is **TACTIC**, a small, mainly Poqomchi'-speaking town adjacent to the main road, which most buses bypass. Tactic has earned its share of fame as the site of an odd attraction, the **pozo vivo** or "living well", sited opposite the northern entrance road. However, it's certainly not worth going out of your way on the off-chance of a swirl in the mud, as the well remains completely dried up for most of the year. Far more interesting is the pagan **Chi-ixim** chapel, high above the town up a long flight of steps. This church has a dark-skinned Christ figure that attracts pilgrims from all over the country, but especially on January 15. Dozens of plaques of thanksgiving for miracles ascribed to the black saint of Chi-ixim, who also goes by the name Dios de Maíz ("Lord of Maiz"), adorn the walls here. The colonial **church** in the plaza is also worth noting; it boasts an elaborate facade decorated with mermaids and jaguars.

If you're hot from your hike to the chapel, you can cool off at the Balneario Cham-che, a crystal-clear spring-fed **pool** that's good for swimming. It's located on the other side of the main road, opposite the centre of town. For somewhere **to stay**, the *Hotel Villa Linda*, 4 C 6–25 (Ⓣ7953 9216; ❸), has clean rooms with private baths. Better still, head for the rustic *Chi'ixím Eco Hotel*, at Km 182.5 just off the highway (Ⓣ & Ⓕ7953 9198; ❹), which has eight comfortable bungalows with fireplaces and a spotless little dining room. For tasty ranch-style **food**, *Café La Granja*, a little further north at Km 187, has tempting Guatemalan favourites plus sandwiches and salads in a great log-cabin-style setting.

Santa Cruz Verapaz, San Cristóbal Verapaz and around

Further towards Cobán, the turn-off for Uspantán peels off to the left at the featureless town of **SANTA CRUZ VERAPAZ**. Right by the junction at Km 196.5, the huge *Park Hotel* (Ⓣ & Ⓕ7950 4539, Ⓔparkhotel@intel.net.gt; ❺) is a comfortable place to stay, with large, good-value doubles and suites, many overlooking a fairly miserable mini **zoo** (no charge) with cramped cages of squirrels, pizotes, owls and even some spider monkeys. It's a popular place with Guatemalans from the capital at weekends. Close by at Km 198.5, the *Ecocentro Holanda* (Ⓣ7952 1269, Ⓔholanda@intelnet.net.gt; ❹) has pleasant cabañas in landscaped grounds, a campsite (US$6.50 per tent) and a children's paddling pool.

Some 10km west of the junction, along the road to Uspantán, **SAN CRISTÓBAL VERAPAZ** is an attractive town surrounded by fields of sugarcane and coffee. It's set on the banks of **Lago de Cristóbal**, a favourite spot for swimming and fishing, although a shoe factory close to the shore has now badly polluted the water. Legend has it that the lake was formed in 1590 as a result of a dispute between a priest and local Maya over the celebration of pagan rites. According to one version the earth split and swallowed the *indígenas*, sealing their graves with the water, while another has it that the priest fled, hurling maledictions so heavy that they created a depression which then filled with water. The Poqomchi'-speaking Maya of San Cristóbal are among the last vestiges of one of the smallest and oldest highland tribes. You can find out more about their culture at an interesting little **museum**, located just off the plaza at C del Calvario 0–03. The Museo Katinamit (Mon–Sat 9am–1pm & 2–6pm, Sun 9am–noon; US$1) hosts exhibits on the maguey plant, the most important fibre of the region, which is woven into bags, hammocks and rope; Verapaz flora and fauna; and music. It also has an exhibition room with handicrafts for sale.

The museum building acts as a base for the Centro Comunitario Educativo Poqomchi' (CECEP; ⓣ7950 4039, ⓔcecep@internetdetelgua.com.gt), which can organize **ethnotourism** trips (US$10 for a half-day tour) of indigenous villages and sights around San Cristóbal, and also offers **Spanish language** classes for US$120 a week, including full board with a local family.

The town knows how to throw a good **fiesta** – it runs from July 21–26 (the main day is July 25) – and is an excellent, almost tourist-free place to head for **Semana Santa**, when a kilometre-long coloured sawdust carpet is created between the main church in the plaza and the Calvario chapel to the west. Try to avoid staying here if you can, though, as the only hotel, the *Pensión San Cristóbal*, 0 Avenida (❶), just up from the plaza, is very grim. Banco Industrial, almost next door at 0 and 1 calles, will give advances on Visa credit cards and cashes US dollars.

South of San Cristóbal is the billion-dollar disaster known as the **Chixoy dam** and hydroelectric plant, financed with money borrowed from the World Bank. The dam provides Guatemala with around half its electricity needs but the price of the project has been high. Unchecked deforestation in the area has increased sediment in the river thus reducing the efficiency of the power plant, and the cost of constructing the dam accounts for a sizable chunk of all Guatemala's considerable foreign-debt payments. Villagers displaced by the huge project are still fighting for compensation from the government more than twenty years after it was completed.

West from San Cristóbal the rough road continues to **Uspantán** (in the western highlands) from where buses run to Santa Cruz del Quiché, via Sacapulas, for connections to Nebaj and Huehuetenango. Two buses and four minibuses, plus pick-ups, make the Cobán–Uspantán trip daily, all passing through San Cristóbal. Local buses also run the Cobán–San Cristóbal route, leaving every thirty minutes from the Terminal Nuevo in Cobán.

Cobán

The heart of these rain-soaked hills and the capital of the department is **COBÁN**, Guatemala's principal centre for gourmet **coffee** production. Your initial impression of the town may not be that favourable – heavy traffic crawls past the central plaza and the main downtown shopping district is pretty nondescript – but away from here Cobán soon reveals its charm. It's not a large place (the population is 22,000) and suburbs fuse gently with outlying meadows and pine forests, giving the town the air of an overgrown mountain village.

If the rain sets in, Cobán's atmosphere can become a bit subdued, and in the evenings the air is often damp and cool. The sun does put in an appearance most days, though, and the town certainly makes a useful base for a day or two. Sights here include an excellent little Maya cultural museum, an orchid nursery, a coffee farm and a genteel café or two where you can sample a cup made from the world-renowned Verapaz bean. Outside the town, the spectacular mountains and rivers hold all kinds of exciting **ecotourism** possibilities, many of which can be done as day-trips.

Arrival and information

Transportes Escobar y Monja Blanca, one of Guatemala's best **bus** services, operates half-hourly departures between Guatemala City and its terminal in Cobán, at 2 C 3–77, Zona 4 (ⓣ7951 1793), a 4hr 30min journey. There's no main terminal for **local destinations**, with buses leaving from a variety of places – see the "Transport" box for details.

Inguat does not have a tourist office here, but luckily three hotels – namely *Hostal d'Acuña*, with helpful staff, a good folder of maps and bus times, and a useful notice board; *Posada Don Juan Matalbatz*; and *Hostal Doña Victoria* (see "Accommodation" for details) – more than fill the information gap. The **website** ⓦwww.cobanav.net is also well worth consulting. For expert guidance and advice about getting to very remote areas of the Verapaces, contact Proyecto Eco-Quetzal (see "Listings").

Like many other Guatemalan towns, Cobán is divided into a number of **zonas**, with the northeast corner of the plaza at 1 Calle and 1 Avenida the dividing point. Zona 1 is to the northwest, Zona 2 to the southwest, Zona 3 to the southeast and Zona 4 to the northeast.

Accommodation

Although you'll likely only pause here for a day or two, Cobán has plenty of **hotels**; most are good value, and some offer real colonial-style charm.

Hostal d'Acuña 4 C 3–17, Zona 2 ⓣ7951 0482, ⓔcasadeacuna@yahoo.com. Most visitors feel immediately at home at this superb place, which has excellent four-bed dorms (US$6.50 per person) and some small spotless rooms bordering the lush garden of a colonial house. Very fine food is served on the verandah, and tours are offered. Highly recommended. ❸

Hostal Doña Victoria 3 C 2–38, Zona 3 ⓣ7951 4213. Refurbished mansion decorated with antiques and artefacts, and oozing character. The stylishly presented bedrooms all have private bath (though avoid the noise-prone streetside rooms). On-site café/bar, restaurant and tour agency too. ❹

Hotel Alcázar Victoria 1 Av 5–34, Zona 1 ⓣ7952 1143. It's not that conveniently situated, being 750m north of the plaza, but this large modern hotel, where the decor is vaguely colonial in style, has 36 excellent rooms, all with good beds, TV and reading lights, set off a covered patio. ❹

Hotel Central 1 C 1–79, Zona 4 ⓣ7952 1442. Vaguely Germanic-influenced design and clean, though darkish, rooms with private bathrooms, set round a central garden. It costs a little extra for a TV. There's a comedor here too. ❸

Hotel La Paz 6 Av 2–19, Zona 1 ⓣ7952 1358. Safe, pleasant budget hotel run by a very vigilant *señora*. The rooms are fairly featureless, but kept clean and tidy – and most have private bath. Safe parking and café. ❷–❸

Hotel La Posada 1 C 4–12, Zona 2 ⓣ7952 1495, ⓔlaposada@c.net.gt. The finest hotel in town occupies an elegant colonial building with a beautiful, antique-furnished interior. The rooms, many with wooden Moorish-style screens (and some with four-poster beds), are set around two leafy courtyards and offer all the usual luxuries, though traffic noise can be a problem. There's also an excellent restaurant and café. ❻

Hotel Virgen del Rosario 2 Av 4–28, Zona 3 ⓣ7952 1914. Excellent-value, secure new place. The fourteen very comfortable, spotless rooms (with or without private bath) may have flowery bedspreads, but all have cable TV and most have reading lights; towels are provided too. There's a sitting area upstairs. ❷–❸

Pensión Monja Blanca 2 C 6–30, Zona 2 ⓣ7951 1900 or 7952 0531. Agreeably old-fashioned atmosphere and plenty of rooms, many with private bathroom. All choices are on the ground-level and set around two lovingly tended courtyard gardens. Don't miss the Victorian-style tearoom for breakfast. ❸–❹

Posada de Carlos V 1 Av 3–44, Zona 1 ⓣ7952 3502 About 500m north of the plaza, this mountain-chalet-style hotel has pine-trimmed rooms with cable TV and private bathroom. Check out the lobby photographs of old Cobán. ❹

Posada Don Juan Matalbatz 3 C 1–46, Zona 1 ⓣ7952 1599, ⓔdiscoverynat@intelnet.net.gt. Good new colonial-style place run by friendly people with very spacious superior rooms/suites set around a little garden, some with bathtubs and fridges, and a few basic but clean budget rooms upstairs. Pool table, garden courtyard and tour agency. ❷–❹

The Town

Cobán's imperial heyday, when it stood at the centre of its own isolated world, is long gone, and its glory faded. The **plaza**, however, remains an impressive triangle, from which the town drops away on all sides. It's dominated by the **cathedral**, which is worth peering into to see the remains of a massive ancient

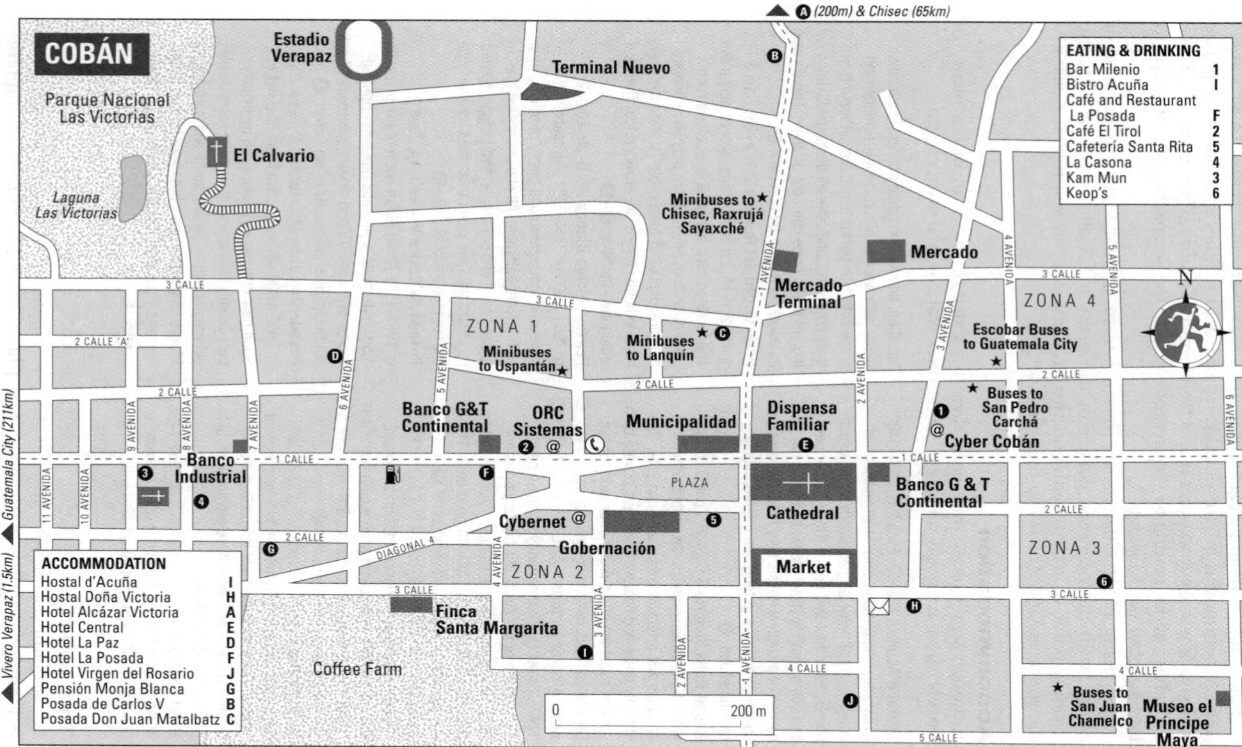
COBÁN
A (200m) & Chisec (65km)
Lanquín (60km)
Guatemala City (211km)
Vivero Verapaz (1.5km)
EATING & DRINKING
Bar Milenio 1
Bistro Acuña I
Café and Restaurant La Posada F
Café El Tirol 2
Cafetería Santa Rita 5
La Casona 4
Kam Mun 3
Keop's 6
ACCOMMODATION
Hostal d'Acuña I
Hostal Doña Victoria H
Hotel Alcázar Victoria A
Hotel Central E
Hotel La Paz D
Hotel La Posada F
Hotel Virgen del Rosario J
Pensión Monja Blanca G
Posada de Carlos V B
Posada Don Juan Matalbatz C
Parque Nacional Las Victorias
Laguna Las Victorias
El Calvario
Estadio Verapaz
Terminal Nuevo
Minibuses to Chisec, Raxrujá Sayaxché
Mercado
Mercado Terminal
Minibuses to Lanquín
Minibuses to Uspantán
Escobar Buses to Guatemala City
Buses to San Pedro Carchá
Cyber Cobán
Banco G&T Continental
ORC Sistemas
Municipalidad
Dispensa Familiar
Banco Industrial
PLAZA
Cathedral
Banco G & T Continental
Cybernet
Gobernación
Market
Finca Santa Margarita
Coffee Farm
Buses to San Juan Chamelco
Museo el Príncipe Maya
ZONA 1
ZONA 2
ZONA 3
ZONA 4
1 CALLE
2 CALLE
2 CALLE 'A'
3 CALLE
4 CALLE
5 CALLE
DIAGONAL 4
1 AVENIDA
2 AVENIDA
3 AVENIDA
4 AVENIDA
5 AVENIDA
6 AVENIDA
7 AVENIDA
8 AVENIDA
9 AVENIDA
10 AVENIDA
11 AVENIDA
N
0
200 m

cracked church bell. A block behind, the **market** bustles with trade during the day and is surrounded by food stalls at night. Hints of the days of German control can also be found here in the architecture, which incorporates the occasional suggestion of Bavarian grandeur.

Cobán's prosperity from coffee (and more recently cardamom and allspice) has built the colonial-style hotels and coffeehouses, nightclubs, and new **Plaza Magdalena** shopping and entertainment mall just west of the centre. Since the highway linked Cobán with the capital, the *finqueros*, wealthy owners of the coffee plantations, have mostly moved to Guatemala City, but a small residue still base themselves in Cobán. Meanwhile, the crowds that sleep in the market and plaza, assembling in the bus terminal to search for work, are migrant labourers heading for the plantations.

For a closer look at Cobán's principal crop, take the guided tour offered by the **Finca Santa Margarita**, a coffee plantation just south of the centre of town at 3 C 4–12, Zona 2 (Mon–Fri 8am–12.30pm & 1.30–5pm, Sat 8am–noon; US$2). The interesting tour (an English-speaking guide is available) covers the history of the finca, founded by the Dieseldorff family in 1888, examines all the stages of cultivation and production, and includes a walk through the grounds. You also get a chance to sample different low, middle and high-altitude Arabica coffee blends and, of course, purchase some beans.

Several blocks east of here you'll find an excellent assembly of Maya artefacts and carvings inside the small **Museo El Príncipe Maya**, 6 Av 4–26, Zona 3 (Mon–Sat 9am–6pm; US$2); all the priceless collection has been found in the departments of the Verapaces and Petén. The museum has some fine shell necklaces, polychrome bowls, jade earrings and a plethora of clay figurines, including warriors wearing animal masks. Don't miss the eccentric flints, early Classic urn or the main attraction – a stunning panel from a Cancuén altarpiece, embellished with 160 glyphs.

One of Cobán's most intriguing sights is the church of **El Calvario**, which is very popular with indigenous worshippers and a short stroll from the plaza. Head west out of town on 1 Avenida and turn right up 7 Avenida until you reach a steep cobbled path. You'll pass a number of tiny **shrines** on the way up – crosses blackened by candle smoke and decorated with scattered offerings. The faithful stoop to pray at these altars asking for divine help: to cure ills, bring love or wealth or cast misfortune on enemies. There's a commanding view over the town from the whitewashed church itself, which has a distinctly pagan identity, including both Christian and Maya crosses; inside the church hundreds of corn cobs (sacred in indigenous religion) hang from the roof. Next door the **Parque Nacional Las Victorias** (daily 8am–4.30pm; US$0.75) is Cobán's green lung, and a great place to stroll through the pines along attractive pathways; there's a children's playground here too.

In the southwest outskirts of town is another place worth visiting: the **Vivero Verapaz** (Mon–Sat 9am–noon & 2–5pm, Sun 9am–noon; US$0.75), a former coffee finca now dedicated to the growing of orchids, which flourish in these sodden mountains. The export of these blooms is illegal in Guatemala but the farm produces some seven hundred indigenous varieties, as well as a handful of hybrids that they've put together themselves, all of which are sold within Guatemala. The plants are nurtured in a wonderfully shaded environment, and a farm worker will show you around and point out the most spectacular buds, which are at their best between November and January. The farm is about 3km from the plaza: follow Diagonal 4 and then, at the bottom of the hill, turn left, go across the bridge and follow the road. A taxi here from the plaza will cost about US$3.

Eating and drinking

Eating in Cobán comes down to a choice between European-style restaurants and very basic, cheap comedores. Look out for the local speciality: *kak' ik*, a terrific turkey soup. You'll find the cheapest food at the **market**, but as it's closed by dusk, head to the street stalls set up around the plaza. Central Cobán is pretty quiet at night, though there are some half-decent **bars**: *La Casona*, at 8 Av and 2 C, has live music and gets lively on Thursdays and weekends; *Bar Milenio*, at 3 Av and 1 C, has live bands, too, plus pool tables. Best of the **clubs**, *Keop's*, 5 Av and 3 C, plays merengue and Latin dance. The **Plaza Magdalena** mall, 2km west of the plaza, boasts a multiplex cinema with three screens and plenty of fast-food restaurants.

Bistro Acuña 4 C 3–17, Zona 2. This very civilized and enjoyable place has a superb location in a period home with dining rooms set off a garden; tables are candlelit at night. The menu is not cheap (a sandwich is US$5), but there are great pizzas, salads and pasta, and the breads and cakes are even better. Breakfast options include pancakes with fresh blueberries.

Café and Restaurant La Posada 1 C 4–12, Zona 2, inside *Hotel La Posada*. The smartest restaurant in town, with a stylish formal dining room, serving traditional Guatemalan specialities and international cuisine. There's a long menu and always a daily special, and if the weather permits, you can eat on a verandah facing the hotel's garden. The more relaxed and inexpensive café (open daily 2.30–9pm) serves breakfasts, bagels and muffins.

Café El Tirol 1 C, north side of the plaza. Long-running place serving 52 different coffee possibilities, eight set breakfasts, hot chocolate, waffles and sandwiches. However, the service here can be woefully lethargic. Closed Mon.

Cafetería Santa Rita 2 C, on the plaza, close to the cathedral. Offering an alternative to the other European-style cafés, this almost archetypal comedor has filling *comida típica*, including huge breakfasts, and friendly service.

Kam Mun 1 C and 9 Av, Zona 2. Large, hygienic Chinese restaurant, with big portions and a solid line-up of economical choices.

Listings

Banks and exchange Banco Industrial, at 1 C and 7 Av in Zona 1, has a Visa ATM. Banco G&T Continental has two branches: 1 C and 4 Av in Zona 1, and 1 C and 2 Av in Zona 3 with MasterCard ATMs. All change travellers' cheques and dollars.

Car rental Tabarini, 7 Av 2–27, Zona 2 (Ⓣ7952 1504, Ⓕ7951 3282).

Email and Internet Cobán is well wired with email facilities. ORC Sistemas, in the same building as the *Café Tirol*, is very central, but Cyber Cobán, at 3 Av 1–11 in Zona 4, has the best rates and speeds.

Laundry La Providencia, at the west end of the plaza on Diagonal 4 (Mon–Sat 8am–noon & 2–5pm).

Post office 3 C and 2 Av, Zona 3 (Mon–Fri 8am–4.30pm).

Spanish schools Cobán's easy-going atmosphere and relative lack of English-speakers make it a good place to pick up Spanish. Schools include Active Spanish School, 3 C 6–12, Zona 1 (Ⓣ & Ⓕ7952 1432, Ⓔnirspanishschool@hotmail.com); and School of Arts and Language, Finca Tzalampec, 16 Av 2–50, Zona 1 (Ⓣ7953 9062, Ⓔalfonsotujab@yahoo.com.mx). Rates start at US$100 a week for 20 hours of tuition and full board with a family.

Telephones Telgua has its main office in the plaza (daily 7am–midnight).

Tours Proyecto Eco-Quetzal, at 2 C 14–36, Zona 1 (Ⓣ & Ⓕ7952 1047, Ⓦwww.ecoquetzal.org), is a highly recommended adventure and cultural tourism specialist that enables visitors to get off the beaten track and stay with indigenous villagers in remote areas of the Verapaces. These well-priced ecotourism initiatives are concentrated in two different areas. A two-night stay in the Chicacnab cloudforest (see p.314), where quetzals are abundant, costs US$45 per person; while a two-night stay in a village on the banks of the Río Ik'bolay (near Laguna Lachuá), where the birdlife includes toucans, parrots and guan, costs US$38. Otherwise, tours to Semuc Champey (around US$32), Laguna Lachuá (around US$45) and other destinations in the Verapaces are offered by agencies in the following hotels: *Hostal d'Acuña* (Ⓣ7951 0482), *Posada Don Juan Matalbatz* (Ⓣ7952 1599) and *Hostal Doña Victoria* (Aventuras Turísticas Ⓣ7951 4213).

Cobán Transport

Cobán does not have a central bus terminal and transportation coordination is chaotic to say the least. Buses, microbuses and pick-ups operate from a number of different bus stops scattered around town. Most chicken buses operate from the so-called Terminal Nuevo (also known as Terminal 2). Bewilderingly, buses to a couple of destinations leave from different places, depending on the time of day. Check departure points and schedules in advance in the *municipalidad*, the *Hostal d'Acuña* or *Posada Don Juan Matalbatz*, or on-line at ⓦwww.cobanav.net.

Note that you can "hop-on hop-off" the two **shuttle bus services** operated by *Hostal d'Acuña*. From Cobán to Tikal, you have the option of jumping off at places including Chisec, Candelaria, Sayaxché and Flores on the way north; or you could get off at the Biotopo del Quetzal en route to Antigua. These shuttles may be convenient, but they are much more expensive than public transport at US$8 to Candelaria or US$28 to either Antigua or Tikal.

To	Bus stop	Frequency	Journey time	Transport mode
Antigua	hotel pick-up	one daily at 6am	5hr 15min	*Hostal d'Acuña* shuttle bus
Chisec	1 Av, Zona 1	every 30min	1hr 30min	microbus
El Estor	Terminal Nuevo	6 daily	7hr	chicken bus
Flores	hotel pick-up	one daily at 6am	4hr 15min	*Hostal d'Acuña* shuttle bus
Fray Bartolomé de Las Casas (via Pajal)	Terminal Nuevo	5 daily	5hr	chicken bus
Guatemala City	2 C & 4 Av, Zona 4	every 30min	4hr 30min	pullman a/c bus
Lanquín	5am & 6am*	7 daily	2hr 30min	microbus
Playa Grande	Mercado Terminal	irregular	4hr	pick-up
Raxrujá	1 Av, Zona 1	hourly	2hr	microbus
San Juan Chamelco	4 C & 4 Av, Zona 3	every 20min	20min	chicken bus
San Pedro Carchá	2 C & 4 Av, Zona 4	every 20min	20min	chicken bus
Sayaxché	1 Av, Zona 1	2 daily (at 6am & noon)	3hr 30min	microbus
Senahú	Terminal Nuevo	4 daily	6hr	chicken bus
Tactic	Terminal Nuevo	every 30min	50min	chicken bus
Tikal	hotel pick-up	one daily at 6am	5hr 30min	*Hostal d'Acuña* shuttle bus
Uspantán	2 C & 3 Av, Zona 1	4 daily	4hr 30min	microbus**

* from Dispensa Familiar, later buses from 3 C near 1 Av, Zona 1

** also buses daily at 10am and noon from 1 C & 7 Av, Zona 2

San Pedro Carchá and around

Six kilometres away to the east, the much smaller town of **SAN PEDRO CARCHÁ** has silver rather than coffee money firing the economy and a greater percentage of Maya people. These days the two towns are merging into a single urban sprawl.

In San Pedro Carchá itself the small, newly renovated **regional museum** (Mon–Fri 9am–noon & 2–5pm; US$0.75), beside the church, is worth a quick visit if you're in town. It houses a collection of Maya artefacts, dolls dressed in local costume, and a collection of stuffed birds and animals, including the inevitable moulting quetzal. A couple of kilometres from Carchá's centre is the **Balneario Las Islas**, a stretch of cool water that's a popular place to swim. To get here walk along the main street beside the church and take the third turning on the right. Follow this street for about a kilometre, then take the right-hand fork at the end. **Buses** back to Cobán leave from the plaza every 15min.

Sierra de Caquipec

Southwest of Carchá, the dense cloudforests of the **Sierra de Caquipec** probably contain the greatest concentration of **quetzals** (see box, p.306) in Central America. German biologists have established that there are several hundred in this thinly populated region, which stretches south towards Tucurú, part of which has been declared a habitat sanctuary for Guatemala's national bird. It's now possible to visit the Caquipec mountains as part of an excellent low-impact **ecotourism** initiative run by Proyecto Eco-Quetzal (see p.312), staying in the Q'eqchi' Maya village of **Chicacnab**, from where local guides take you into the oak and pine forests where quetzals are abundant. Wild boar, kinkajous and the odd jaguar also live in the forest. The trips cost US$45 per person for a three-day, two-night excursion, which includes (very basic) accommodation, meals and a guide (but not public transport from San Pedro Carchá). It's a steep and often very slippy three-hour climb from the village to the forest for quetzal-spotting – you'll need stout walking boots, waterproofs and warm clothes (Chicacnab is at 2400m). The guides can also lead you to caves, a lagoon and a viewpoint from where the three towns of Cobán, Carchá and Chamelco can be seen, if the hills aren't wrapped in cloud that is.

San Juan Chamelco

Seven kilometres southeast of Cobán, connected by a stream of local buses, **SAN JUAN CHAMELCO** is the most important Q'eqchi' settlement in the area. Some of your fellow bus passengers are likely to be women dressed in traditional costume, wearing beautiful cascades of old coins for earrings, and speaking Q'eqchi' rather than Spanish. Chamelco's focal point is a large colonial **church**, whose facade is rather unexpectedly decorated with twin Maya versions of the Habsburg double eagle – undoubtedly a result of the historic German presence in the region. Inside, you will find the usual hushed devotional tones and flickering candles around the altars. The most significant treasure, the church bell, is hidden in the belfry; it was a gift to the Maya leader Juan Matalbatz from no less than the Holy Roman Emperor Charles V.

The large market around the church sells anything from local farm produce to blue jeans, but very little in the way of crafts. The best time to visit the village is for its annual **fiesta**, which runs from June 21 to 24 (the main day is the 24th). A special feature of the festival is the procession, during which participants dress up in a variety of outfits from pre-conquest Maya costumes to representations of local wildlife, in celebration of the local Q'eqchi' culture and environment.

Not far from Chamelco is a great **place to stay**, *Don Jerónimo's* (Ⓣ5301 3191, Ⓦwww.dearbrutus.com/donjeronimo; US$25 per person for full board), a vegetarian guest-house-cum-retreat in sublime rolling countryside, run by a friendly American who has been living off the land for a good twenty years. Guest bungalows are rustic but comfortable, and have private bathrooms. There's river tubing and good swimming close by, as well as ping-pong and an impressive library to browse on rainy days. It's a pleasant five-kilometre walk from Chamelco down a signposted road 150m west of the plaza; alternatively, you can catch a pick-up from 0 Calle and 0 Avenida heading for the village of Chamíl.

Just 500m from *Don Jerónimo's* are the **Grutas de Rey Marcos** (daily 9am–5pm; US$3 including guide service, hard hat and boot rental), a series of **caves** discovered in May 1998. The cave system is more than a kilometre long, though the tour only takes you a little way into the complex – you have to wade across an underground river at one stage to see some of the best stalactites and stalagmites, including one that's a dead ringer for the Leaning Tower of Pisa.

East to Lanquín, Semuc Champey and beyond

Northeast of Cobán and San Pedro Carchá, a rough dirt road (though some widening and paving work is ongoing) heads off into the hills, connecting a string of coffee fincas. For the first few kilometres, the hills are closed in around the road, but as it drops down into the richer land to the north the valleys open out. Their precipitous sides are patched with cornfields and the level central land is saved for the all-important coffee bushes. As the bus lurches along, clinging to the sides of the ridges, there are fantastic views of the valleys below.

After 43km the road reaches the **Pajal** junction (43km and 2hr by bus from Cobán), where a branch road cuts down deep into the valley to **LANQUÍN** (a further 12km and 30min away). This sleepy, modest Q'eqchi' village, where Spanish is very much a second language, shelters beneath towering green hills, whose lower slopes are planted with coffee and cardamom bushes. Virtually every visitor is here to enjoy the pools of Semuc Champey, and you'll probably be greeted by a worker from one of the hostels trying to get you to stay at their place.

Practicalities

There are several **accommodation** options in and around the village of Lanquín. The two most popular places are located in countryside outside the village. Nearest to Lanquín, the near-legendary backpackers' stronghold of *El Retiro* (❷–❹) is a ten-minute walk away along the road to Cahabón. This outstanding, English-Q'eqchi'-owned lodge is right by the Lanquín river, and has camping, fine palm-leaf-thatched cabañas (some with private bathroom) with mosquito screens, excellent four-bed dorms (US$4 per person) and plenty of hammocks. There's great food, and dinner (US$4.75) is a communal veggie affair, giving you a great opportunity to meet other travellers. A campfire is lit most nights, when acoustic guitars and bongos are brought out. You also can rent tubes here to float down the Lanquín river. The second rural place is just a fifteen-minute walk from Semuc Champey itself. *Las Marías* (❶–❷) is a very peaceful rustic-style hospedaje, built entirely from wood. The hospitable Q'eqchi' Maya owners offer comfortable dorms and double rooms, and serve tasty, inexpensive breakfast, lunch and dinner. Speak to them, too, about excellent tours to an extensive cave complex nearby for which you have to wade, swim and clamber your way through using candles.

Of the several basic **pensiones** in Lanquín village, the good, cheap hospedaje-cum-store-cum-comedor, *Divina Providencia* (❶), is the best, offering good grub, steaming hot showers and cold beers. The clapboard-built rooms are adequate enough, though you'll probably get to know all about your neighbours' nocturnal pursuits. More comfortable but hardly a luxury choice, the slightly dreary *Hotel El Recreo* (Ⓣ7952 2160, Ⓕ7952 2160; ❹), on the entrance road, has a choice of rooms in wooden buildings, a restaurant and a pool, though few guests.

There's **no bank** in Lanquín, so make sure you bring enough cash with you for your stay. The nearest banks are in Cobán and San Pedro Carchá (though the hotels should be able to cash some US dollars for you). **Transport schedules** around this remote region are subject to frequent change; for the latest information check at the *El Retiro* or *Las Marías*. Six daily public microbuses, plus two private shuttles, run to Cobán. If you're heading north, first get to the Pajal junction and then catch one of the five daily buses bound for Fray Bartolomé de Las Casas (from where regular minibuses run to Raxrujá, and a daily bus runs northeast to Poptún). Heading east, there are five daily buses to Cahabón, from where pick-ups and one daily bus head down to El Estor.

The Lanquín caves

Just a couple of kilometres from the village, the **Lanquín caves** are a maze of dripping, bat-infested chambers, stretching for at least 3km underground (daily 8am–4.30pm; US$2.75). To find them, simply walk along the road heading back to Cobán and turn right along a signposted dirt road which turns off towards the river, five minutes after you pass the *Recreo* hotel. A walkway, complete with ladders and chains, has been cut through the first few hundred metres and electric lights have been installed, which makes access substantially easier, though it remains dauntingly slippery. It's also well worth dropping by at dusk, when thousands of bats emerge from the mouth of the cave and flutter off into the night. The cave is also occasionally used for Maya religious rituals (particularly at fiesta time, and on December 5) when the whole village gathers for candelit ceremonies here.

Semuc Champey

The region's prime attraction is a great deal more spectacular than the caves however – the extraordinary pools of **Semuc Champey** (US$2.50, parking US$0.75), a shallow staircase of turquoise waters suspended on a natural limestone bridge. These idyllic pools, 8km south of Lanquín, sit at the base of a towering jungle-clad gorge, and make a sublime spot for a blissful day's wallowing and swimming, though watch out for the odd sharp edge. Just a few years ago very few visitors made it to this remote part of Guatemala, but the secret is now definitely out, and the pools are very much a key stop on the backpacking trail between Tikal and the western highlands. That said, you can usually find a peaceful spot without too much difficulty.

If you walk a few hundred metres upstream via a slippery path over rocks and roots, you come to the river source that feeds Semuc: the fast-flowing **Río Cahabón**, the bulk of which plunges into a cavern, cutting under the pools in an aquatic frenzy before emerging again downstream. For a photo-perfect view of the whole scene you can hike (and climb a little in sections) for twenty minutes up a slippery, vertiginous trail to a *mirador* high above the pools.

Don't leave your belongings unattended as the odd theft has been reported. Microbuses and some pick-ups (about every hour until 1pm; 20 min) run from Lanquín's plaza to Semuc Champey, or you can book a return tour from Cobán for around US$32 per person; see p.312 for tour operators.

Cahabón

Beyond Lanquín the road continues to **CAHABÓN** – which has two basic pensiones, the best being *Hospedaje Carolina* (❶) – an additional 24km to the east, and from there a very rough dirt track spirals around switchbacks to Panzós, cutting high over the mountains through spectacular scenery. Ask in the Cahabón municipality for the designated tourism officer who can help out with local excursions. One daily **bus** (at 1pm) makes the four-hour trip to El Estor, while pick-ups ply the route more frequently. There are five daily buses between Lanquín and Cahabón; the last buses leave both towns at 3pm. Another extremely rough trail connects Cahabón with Senahú, which is sometimes negotiable in a 4WD; check with the tourist officer about current conditions.

Down the Polochic valley to Panzós

If you're planning to head out towards the Caribbean from Cobán, or simply interested in taking a short trip along back roads, then the **Polochic valley** is an ideal place to spend the day being bounced around inside a bus. Travelling the length of the valley you witness an immense transformation as you drop down through the coffee-coated mountains and emerge into lush, tropical lowlands. To reach the head of the valley you have to travel south from Cobán along the main road to Guatemala City; shortly after Tactic at the San Julián junction, you leave the luxury of tarmac and head off into the valley. The scenery is pure Alta Verapaz: V-shaped valleys where coffee commands the best land and fields of maize cling to the upper slopes wherever they can. The towns are untidy-looking places where the Q'eqchi' and Poqomchi' Maya are largely ladinized and seldom wear the brilliant red *huipiles* that used to be traditional here.

The first place at the upper end of the valley is **Tamahú**, 15km below which the town of **Tucurú** marks the point where the valley starts to open out and the river loses its frantic energy. High above Tucurú, in the Caquipec mountains to the north, is a large protected area of pristine cloudforest which contains one of the highest concentrations of **quetzals** anywhere in the world, not to mention an array of other birds and beasts, including some very vocal howler monkeys. The reserve is extremely difficult to reach and you really need a four-wheel drive to get you up there – contact Proyecto Eco-Quetzal in Cobán (see p.312) who run excellent tours into these mountains and can arrange accommodation with local families in the region.

Beyond Tucurú the road plunges abruptly, with cattle pastures starting to take the place of the coffee bushes, and both the villages and the people have a more tropical look about them. After 28km you reach **LA TINTA**, a scruffy town with an excellent, very clean hospedaje, *Hotel Los Ángeles* (❶–❷) right on the highway, where some rooms have private bath. Continuing east, it's just 13km to **TELEMÁN**, the largest of the squalid trading centres in this lower section of the valley; here, the agreeable family-run *Hotel de los Ralda* on the highway (ⓣ7875 0074; ❷–❸) offers rooms with hot water and fans, while the *Ampakito Comedor* serves the town's best food.

A side trip to Senahú

From Telemán a side road branches off to the north and climbs high into the lush hills, past row upon row of neatly ranked coffee bushes. As it winds upwards a superb view opens out across the level valley floor below, exposing the river's swirling meanders and a series of oxbows and cut-offs.

Set back behind the first ridge of hills, the small coffee centre of **SENAHÚ** sits in a steep-sided bowl high above the Polochic valley. The village itself is a fairly unremarkable farming settlement, but is worth a visit, not least as an ideal starting point for a wander in the Alta Verapaz hills – with superb hikes to the nearby **Cuevas de Seamay**, used by Maya shamen for ceremonies, and to Semuc Champey and Lanquín. Of several simple pensiones, the best are the simple *Edilson* (❶) and, on the central plaza, the pleasant, twelve-room *Hotel El Recreo Senahú* (ⓣ7952 2160; ❸), where guides can be arranged. Four **buses** (plus some minibuses) connect Senahú and Cobán daily. Alternatively, microbuses and pick-ups shuttle between the highway at Telemán and Senahú.

Two kilometres to the east of Senahú a gravel road, occasionally served by buses, runs to the *Finca El Volcán*, beyond which you can continue towards Semuc Champey, passing the *Finca Arenal* en route. The walk takes two to three days, and with the uncertainty of local weather conditions you can expect to be regularly soaked, but the dauntingly hilly countryside and the superb fertility of the vegetation make it all worthwhile. The best way to find the route is to hire a guide in Senahú, though you do pass several substantial fincas where you can ask for directions. Another hike takes you to Cahabón through some equally stunning lush mountain terrain – ask at the *Edilson* or the *Hotel El Recreo Senahú* for directions. Sometimes you can make this trip in a four-wheel drive.

Panzós

Heading on down the Polochic valley you reach **PANZÓS**, the largest of the valley towns. Its name means "place of the green waters", a reference to the swamps that surround the river, infested with alligators and birdlife. It was here in Panzós that the old Verapaz railway from the Caribbean coast ended, and goods were transferred to boats for the journey across Lago de Izabal. In 1978, Panzós made international headlines when a group of campesinos attending a meeting to settle land disputes were gunned down by the army and local police, in one of the earliest and most brutal massacres of General Lucas García's regime. The day before the atrocity, bulldozers had prepared mass graves at two sites outside the town before the demonstrators even arrived. About a hundred men, women and children were killed, and the event is generally regarded as a landmark in the history of political violence in Guatemala, after which the situation deteriorated rapidly. García's interest in the dispute, however, may have been more personal than political, as he owned 78,000 acres of land in the area around Panzós.

Routes towards Petén

In the northern section of the Alta Verapaz, the lush hills drop away steeply onto the limestone plain that marks the frontier with the department of Petén. One good paved highway runs from Cobán, passing through Chisec, and then on up to Sayaxché in Petén. A second, much slower dirt road heads from San Pedro Carchá, via the Pajal junction up to Raxrujá, where it links up with the road from Chisec. Otherwise the road network here is rough and ready, though new tracks are running further and further into previously untouched forests, up to the Mexican border, and new settlements are being established all the time. Many of these immigrants are *repatriados*, Guatemalan exiles from highland villages who fled for their lives during the dark days of the civil war, only to return in the 1990s. Understandably, many maps of the area are riddled with errors.

North to Fray Bartolomé de Las Casas

From the **Pajal** junction it's a slow, very beautiful journey through typical alpine Verapaz scenery, a verdant landscape of impossibly green mountains, tiny adobe-built hamlets, pasture and pine forests. After more than two hours of twists and turns you'll reach the village of **Sebol**, a beautiful spot on the Río de la Pasión where waterfalls cascade into the river and a side road heads off for **FRAY BARTOLOMÉ DE LAS CASAS**, 5km to the east. This featureless town has been left off many maps, though it boasts several **hospedajes** – the best are the basic *Hotel Bartolo* (❶), which has a comedor, and the fairly clean *Hotel Diamelas* (❷) – and a Banrural bank just off the plaza. Buses leave Las Casas for Cobán hourly until 4pm, most via Chisec (2hr 30min) and five daily via the Pajal junction (5hr). Northeast to Poptún there's one daily bus at 3am (5hr) plus pick-ups.

Raxrujá and the Candelaria caves

Some 18km west of Fray, **RAXRUJÁ** is little more than a few streets and some ramshackle buildings straggling round a bridge over the Río Escondido, a tributary of the Pasión, but it does function as a gateway to the extensive ruins of Cancuén and the Candelaria caves, and offers the only **accommodation** for miles around. First choice is the *Hotel Cancuén* (ⓣ7983 0720), on the edge of town along the road to Candelaria, with basic simple rooms (❷) and spotless, excellent-value modern tiled rooms with TV and a/c (❸). For **food**, *Restaurant Tu Casa*, located next door, is a good choice with daily specials and friendly staff, or closer to the centre try the comedores *Vidalia* or *Doña Reina*. The Banrural will cash travellers' cheques. Microbuses leave hourly for Chisec (45min), continuing on to Cobán (2hr) until 4pm, and there are also infrequent buses (and additional pick-ups) along the slower road via Pajal (3hr) to Cobán (5hr 15min). Heading north, buses and microbuses leave about every ninety minutes for Sayaxché (2hr 30min) along a very fast, paved road, where you change to another microbus for Santa Elena/Flores.

The limestone mountains to the west of Raxrujá are full of caves. The most impressive are undoubtedly the **Candelaria caves**, 10km west, whose series of caverns stretches for around 18km and includes some truly monumental chambers such as the 200-metre-long, 60-metre-wide "Tzul Tacca". Skylight shafts flood through its roof ceiling, which create a spectacular light show on the rocks and cavern water below. The main caverns are located on private property jealously guarded by Daniel Dreux, who has set up the **Complejo Cultural de Candelaria** conservation area (and is trying to get the caves awarded national-park status). Entrance to the complex, including a two-hour tour and a guide to the first cave system, costs US$3 per person, while a two-day tour by *lancha* covering 33km (only possible March–July) can also be arranged. Alternatively, contact one of the Cobán travel agents (see p.312). The complex has some wonderfully atmospheric **accommodation** (ⓣ5710 8753, ⓔcuevascandelaria@aol.com; US$40–50 per person, including all meals) in very stylish cabins decorated with furniture, art and fabrics, though not all have private bath. The fab French cuisine here belies the jungle surrounds, but note there are a lot of rather picky hotel rules: no outside food is permitted, and all shoes have to be left at the entrance gate. You can also **camp** (US$2.50 per person) right opposite the entrance at the *Rancho Ríos Escondidos* (no sign).

It's also possible to visit some large caverns that are linked to the Candelaria system from the tiny settlement of **Comunidad Candelaria**, on the road to Chisec at Km 309.5. Ask at the tienda here (owned by Santiago Xuchup) for a guide (US$0.75). It's a short walk to the two main caves, Entrada de Sol – measuring some 70m in length and 30m in width – and the smaller Murciélago, where you might see some bats, and perhaps hear the roar of the howler monkeys that live nearby.

Cancuén

North of Raxrujá is the large Maya site of **Cancuén** (daily 8am–5pm; US$5), where a huge Classic-period palace has been unearthed. In 2000, newspapers across the world trumpeted the rediscovery of this ancient Maya city, lost for

1300 years, by an American–Guatemalan team of archeologists on the banks of the river Pasión. Although the reality was very different – Cancuén had been discovered in 1907 and was even plotted on tourist-board maps of the country – the sheer size of the ruins had certainly been underestimated, while new investigations revealed the site to be enigmatic in other ways. Uniquely, Cancuén seems to have lacked the usual religious and defensive structures characteristic of Maya cities and appears to have existed as an essentially secular, trading city. For most of the twentieth century, the absence of soaring temple-pyramids led archeologists to assume that Cancuén was a very minor site, and it was ignored for decades. However, the vast amounts of jade, pyrite, obsidian and fine ceramics found recently indicate that this was actually one of the greatest trading centres of the Maya world, with a paved plaza (which may have been a marketplace) covering two square kilometres. Cancuén is thought to have flourished because of its strategic position between the great cities of the lowlands, like Tikal and Calakmul, and the mineral-rich highlands of southern Guatemala. The vast, almost ostentatious **palace** complex (Structure L7-9) with 170 rooms and 11 courtyards, its sides adorned with dozens of life-sized stucco figures, is Cancuén's most arresting feature. Recent investigations at Cancuén have uncovered three stunning ball-court markers, a jade workshop and two glyph-covered altar panels. There's a camping area here (no fee) and a visitor centre is planned; call ⓣ5902 3074 for up-to-date information or consult ⓦwww.cancuen.org.

To **get to** Cancuén, pick-ups (approximately hourly) leave Raxruhá for the *aldea* of **La Unión**, 12km to the north where boatmen will take you by *lancha* (reservations ⓣ5902 3074) for the thirty-minute ride along the Río de la Pasión to the site. It's also possible to travel via the village of La Isla, but connections here are not as good.

Chisec and around

Some 26km west of Raxrujá and 60km north of Cobán, **CHISEC** is a quiet, agreeable little town spread out along the highway. Though presently a fairly featureless place, Chisec has grown quickly in the last years as land-hungry migrants have moved into the region. It's one of the very few places in Guatemala not to have a church on its (huge) central plaza – many of its population are former guerrillas and *repatriados* opposed to religious influence. Both **places to stay** are about 800m north of the plaza, the best being *Hotel La Estancia* (ⓣ7979 7748; ❸), with two floors of fairly plain but clean rooms, all with a/c and bathroom, a good comedor and a small swimming pool. On the other side of the road the *Hotel Nopales* (❷) is a slightly cheaper budget place with bare clean rooms. The best **food** in the centre of town is at *Cafetería La Huella* where you'll find *comida típica*, burgers, coffee and cakes, or at *Cafetería el Manantial* next to the *municipalidad*, where they serve great breakfasts. The very clean *Restaurant Bombil Pek* at the southern end of the village is also excellent, if a bit more pricey. Banrural on the plaza issues Visa cash advances and will cash travellers' cheques, and you can surf the **Internet** at Centro Electrónico just behind the bank. **Microbuses** run from Cobán to Chisec every half-hour (1hr 30 min), and to Raxrujá via Candelaria (hourly; 1hr).

Chisec makes the perfect base for visiting two remarkable natural attractions, the nearest being the "painted cave" of **Bombil Pek** some 2km north of town. There's a community-run guide office (daily 8am–3.30pm) beside the highway nearby where you pay your entrance fee (US$3) and collect a flashlight; they also have **tubes** (US$2.50; best July–Oct) for river exploration for rent here. A guide then leads you along a delightful forty-minute hike through the *milpa* fields and forest, and down a steep slippery wooden staircase into the sink hole and its vast 50m-high main cavern. Many ceramics have been found here, and the cave is still used for Maya religious ceremonies. Your guide will then try to persuade you to squeeze through a tiny hole at the rear to a second, much smaller cave where the faded painted images of two monkeys, possibly representing the hero twins of the Popol Vuh (see box, p.148), adorn the walls. From Chisec, microbuses heading north along the highway pass the guides' office hourly.

The three exquisite jade lakes of **Lagunas Sepalau**, Chisec's other outstanding attraction, are 9km from town along the road that heads west from the *municipalidad*. Pick-ups run all day from the plaza and there's a bus at 11am. You'll be dropped off at the Q'eqchi' village of **Sepalau Cataltzul** where you pay a US$3 entrance fee. A local guide will accompany you to the lakes, 1km further away with a *lancha* for paddling across the lake (and lifejackets). The first lake you come to, **Laguna Paraíso**, ringed by untouched dense jungle, is beautiful and peaceful, and makes the perfect spot for a swim. The second lake, **Atsam'ja**, is much smaller, but the third and largest lake, **Q'ekija**, a further kilometre down the track, is the most remarkable of all – a gorgeous blue-green colour, its near-vertical limestone sides backed by towering jungle. You'll almost certainly hear howler monkeys and see kingfishers, and perhaps toucans here; and there are jaguars in the region, too.

Playa Grande and Laguna Lachuá

Northwest from Chisec, it's 62km on a rough dirt road to the town of **PLAYA GRANDE** (also referred to as **CANTABÁL** or **IXCÁN**), a short distance west of the Río Negro. There's little traffic this way, mostly pick-ups. Most traffic from Cobán heads to Playa Grande via a turn-off on the main highway at the village of Bulbatz. Playa Grande itself is an authentic frontier settlement with scruffy tin-roofed, breezeblock-built houses and a few rough bars. It is, however, the main administrative centre for the Ixcán region and has a few **hotels**, the best options being the basic but clean *Hospedaje Torre Visión* (❷) and *Pensión Reyna* (❶). Banrural will change travellers' cheques.

The main point of interest in this area is the **Parque Nacional Laguna Lachuá** (US$5.50), a near-circular lake 4km off the main road east of Playa Grande – a sweltering walk. One of the least-visited national parks in Central America, this is a beautiful, tranquil spot, with azure blue waters completely surrounded by dense tropical forest. Though it smells slightly sulphurous, the water is good for swimming, with curious horseshoe-shaped limestone formations by the edge that make perfect individual bathing pools. You'll see otters and an abundance of birdlife, but watch out for mosquitoes.

Despite the Laguna Lachuá being officially protected as national park, thirty percent of the reserve's mahogany trees were illegally cleared by 150 highly organized **loggers** – who were accompanied by armed guards for protection – in 1999. Park officials who attempted to stop the plunder were forced to suspend patrols after the intruders threatened to lynch them. Though arrests were made, mobs connected with the timber companies quickly freed the loggers from Playa Grande police station where they were being held. They then kidnapped an official of the Nature Conservation Union, holding him until authorities agreed to release a jailed timber merchant. Similar incidents have occurred throughout northern Guatemala, where loggers enjoy virtual impunity from arrest, environmentalists live in fear of their lives, and a nature reserve often amounts to little more than lines on a map.

There's a large thatched *rancho* (shelter) with bunk beds (US$7) by the shore, or you can sling a hammock (available for rent), or camp (US$2.50). Fireplaces and wood are provided, though you'll need to bring food and drinking water. Rustic canoes can be rented here for a dollar an hour. On public holidays the park can quickly fill to its 84-person limit; call ahead on ⓣ5704 1508 to reserve your place.

Fiestas

The Verapaces are famous for their fiestas, and in Baja Verapaz especially you'll see an unusual range of traditional dances. In addition, Cobán hosts the **National Fiesta of Folklore**, at the start of August, which is attended by indigenous groups from throughout the country.

January

15 Tactic, large pilgrimage to the town's Chi-ixim chapel

19–24 Rabinal, most important dates are the 23rd (for the Rabinal Achi dance) and the main day, the 24th

22–25 Tamahú, main day 25th

Holy Week

San Cristóbal Verapaz, big religious processions

May

1–4 Santa Cruz Verapaz, includes the dances of Los Chuntos, Vendos and Mamah-Num

4–9 Tucurú, main day 8th

June

9–13 Senahú, main day 13th

10–13 Purulhá, main day 13th

21–24 San Juan Chamelco, main day 24th (includes spectacular costumed processions)

24–29 San Pedro Carchá, main day 29th

25–30 Chisec, main day 29th

July

20–25 Cubulco, includes the Palo Volador on the final day

21–26 San Cristóbal Verapaz, main day 25th

August

July 31–Aug 6 Cobán, followed by the National Fiesta of Folklore

11–16 Tactic, main day 15th

22–28 Lanquín, main day 28th

23–28 Chajal

23–30 Panzós

September

4–8 Cahabón, main day 6th

17–21 Salamá, main day 17th

25–29 San Miguel Chicaj, main day 29th

27–30 San Jerónimo, main day 30th

December

First week Cobán, orchid exhibition held in town's convent (next to the cathedral)

6–8 Santa Cruz El Chol, main day 8th

Getting to Lachuá is obviously easiest if you take a tour (see Cobán "Listings"), but it's by no means impossible under your own steam. Once you've made it to Playa Grande there's an irregular flow of traffic (pick-ups and the odd bus) heading from Playa Grande to the entrance road for the lake. Pick-ups leave Cobán for Playa Grande (4hr), mainly in the early morning. Coming south from Sayaxché, the most direct route means a change at the Cruce del Pato junction (though you may wait here a while), and there's generally more traffic from Raxruhá. From Chisec there's no schedule to Playa Grande, but a couple of pick-ups do run to Playa Grande most days.

Into the Ixcán

The Río Negro marks the boundary between the departments of Alta Verapaz and Quiché. The land to the west, known as the **Ixcán**, is comprised of tropical forest and swampland which became the scene of bloody fighting in the civil war. The region is the main focus for *repatriado* settlement in Guatemala, with new villages being established by refugees who have returned from exile in Mexico.

The journey further west across the Ixcán and into northern Huehuetenango is an arduous one along the worst roads in the country, even partly following a river bed in the dry season. Nevertheless, two daily buses and several pick-ups make the journey from Playa Grande to Barillas, through swampy lowland, parcels of remaining tropical forest, cattle pastureland and over the huge new Puente La Campaña de la Paz bridge that crosses the mighty Río Ixcán. The journey takes at least five hours, depending on the state of the road but it's a spectacular route as you watch the growing bulk of the Cuchumatanes rising ever higher on the horizon.

Travel details

Buses and microbuses

Baja Verapaz

Heading for Baja Verapaz from Cobán or Guatemala City you can also take any bus between the two and get off at **La Cumbre** (de Santa Elena) from where microbuses run to Salamá.

Rabinal to: Guatemala City (8 daily; 4hr 20min or 6hr via El Chal); Salamá (7 daily; 50min).

Salamá to: Cubulco (5 daily; 1hr 30min); Guatemala City (10 daily; 3hr 30min); Rabinal (7 daily; 50min).

Alta Verapaz

For all Cobán transport schedules see box, p.313.

Cahabón to: El Estor (1 daily; 4hr).

Chisec to: Cobán (every 30min; 1hr 30min); Raxrujá (hourly; 45min).

Fray Bartolomé de Las Casas to: Cobán, via Chisec (hourly; 2hr 30min), via Pajal (5 daily; 5hr); Poptún (1 daily; 5hr).

Lanquín to: Cobán (6 daily; 2hr 30min).

Panzós to: Cobán (6 daily; 6hr).

Raxrujá to: Cobán (hourly; 2hr); Sayaxché (every 1hr 30min; 2hr).

Petén

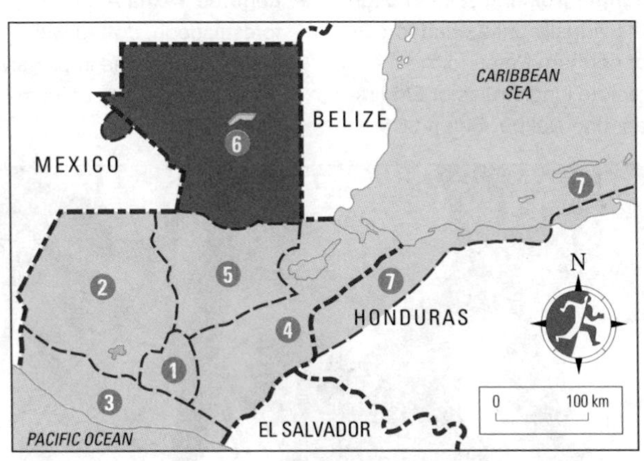
CARIBBEAN SEA
BELIZE
MEXICO
HONDURAS
EL SALVADOR
PACIFIC OCEAN
N
0 100 km
1
2
3
4
5
6
7
7

CHAPTER 6

Highlights

* **Finca Ixobel** Kick back and enjoy the wonderful home-cooking at this rural retreat, set in the pine-clad foothills of the Maya Mountains. **See p.332**

* **Tikal** Explore the spectacular ruins of an ancient Maya metropolis, set in a protected rainforest reserve that's teeming with wildlife. **See p.345**

* **Jungle trekking** Hike through the virtually untouched forests of northern Petén to the remote jungle ruins of El Mirador and Nakbé. **See p.361**

* **Lago de Petexbatún** Encircled by a series of small Maya sites, this beautiful remote lake is one of the best-kept secrets in Petén. **See p.367**

* **Yaxchilán** This imposing ruined city, its temples topped with mighty roof combs, is situated superbly on the banks of the Río Usumacinta. **See p.372**

* **Lago de Yaxhá** A sublime forest lagoon, dotted with ruins including the impressive, partly restored site of Yaxhá. **See p.375**

△ Spider monkey

Petén

The vast northern department of Petén occupies about a third of Guatemala but contains just over three percent of its population. This huge expanse of tropical rainforest, swamps and savannah forms part of an untamed wilderness that stretches into the Lacandón forest and Calakmul reserve of southern Mexico and across the Maya Mountains to Belize. Totally unlike any other part of the country, large expanses of the Petén remain virtually untouched, with ancient ceiba and mahogany trees that tower 50m above the forest floor. The area is extraordinarily rich in wildlife: some 285 species of bird have been sighted at Tikal alone, including a wide range of hummingbirds, toucans, blue and white herons, hawks, buzzards, wild turkeys and the motmot (a bird of paradise). Beneath the forest canopy lurk many other species that are harder to locate. Among the mammals are the lumbering tapir, ocelots, deer, coatis, jaguars and monkeys, plus crocodiles and thousands of species of plants, snakes, insects and butterflies.

In the past few decades, however, this privileged isolation has become increasingly under threat. Waves of **settlers** have cleared enormous tracts of jungle, while oil exploration and commercial logging have brought with them mountains of money and machinery, cutting new roads deep into the forest. The population of Petén, in 1950 just 15,000, is today estimated at close to 500,000, a number which puts enormous pressure on the remaining forest. Yet despite forty percent of Petén being officially protected as the **Reserva de la Biósfera Maya** (Maya Biosphere Reserve), regulations are loosely enforced and widely ignored. Today, though there are numerous Petén-based ecological groups committed to preserving the remaining forests, activists are subject to routine threats and protective laws are widely ignored.

Population boom and environmental failure have occurred before in the Petén, and most experts concur that these factors precipitated the collapse of the Classic Maya cities here eleven centuries ago. Petén was both the birthplace and heartland of the **Maya civilization**, which flourished for almost two thousand years between 1000 BC and the tenth century AD, by which time Maya culture had reached unparalleled architectural, scientific and artistic achievement. Great cities rose out of the forest, surrounded by huge areas of raised and irrigated fields and connected by a vast network of causeways to smaller settlements. But incredibly high population densities and a prolonged drought towards the end of the Classic period (250–909AD) brought about a swift collapse, leaving the forest to reclaim the temples and palaces.

Today the ruins of several hundred ancient Maya sites pepper the region, although many of them still remain completely buried in jungle, and others are known only to locals and looters. In the past few years, satellite imagery has

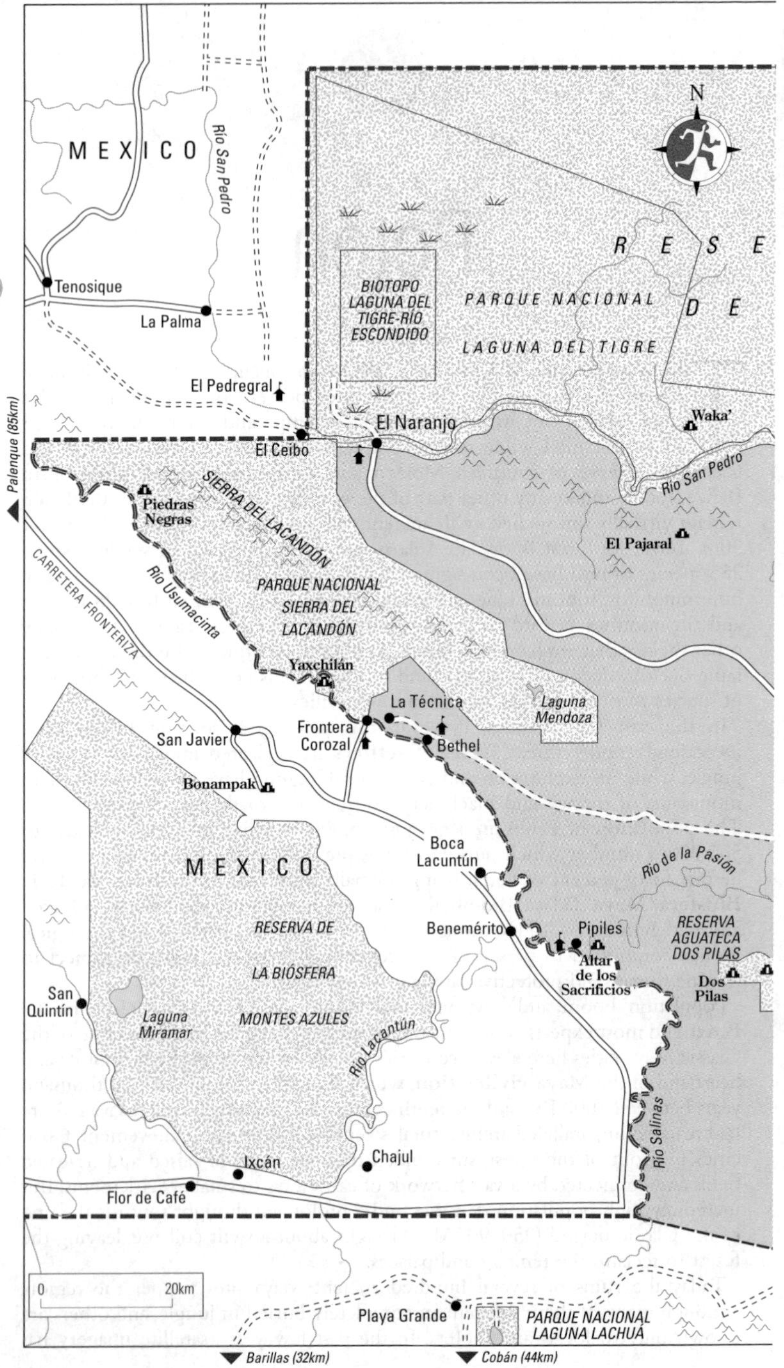
MEXICO
Río San Pedro
N
RESE
DE
BIOTOPO LAGUNA DEL TIGRE-RÍO ESCONDIDO
PARQUE NACIONAL
LAGUNA DEL TIGRE
Tenosique
La Palma
El Pedregral
El Naranjo
Waka'
El Ceibo
Río San Pedro
Palenque (85km)
Piedras Negras
SIERRA DEL LACANDÓN
El Pajaral
CARRETERA FRONTERIZA
Río Usumacinta
PARQUE NACIONAL SIERRA DEL LACANDÓN
Yaxchilán
La Técnica
Laguna Mendoza
San Javier
Frontera Corozal
Bethel
Bonampak
Boca Lacuntún
Río de la Pasión
MEXICO
RESERVA DE
LA BIÓSFERA
MONTES AZULES
Benemérito
Pipiles
RESERVA AGUATECA DOS PILAS
Altar de los Sacrificios
Dos Pilas
San Quintín
Laguna Miramar
Río Lacantún
Río Salinas
Ixcán
Chajul
Flor de Café
0
20km
Playa Grande
PARQUE NACIONAL LAGUNA LACHUA
Barillas (32km)
Cobán (44km)

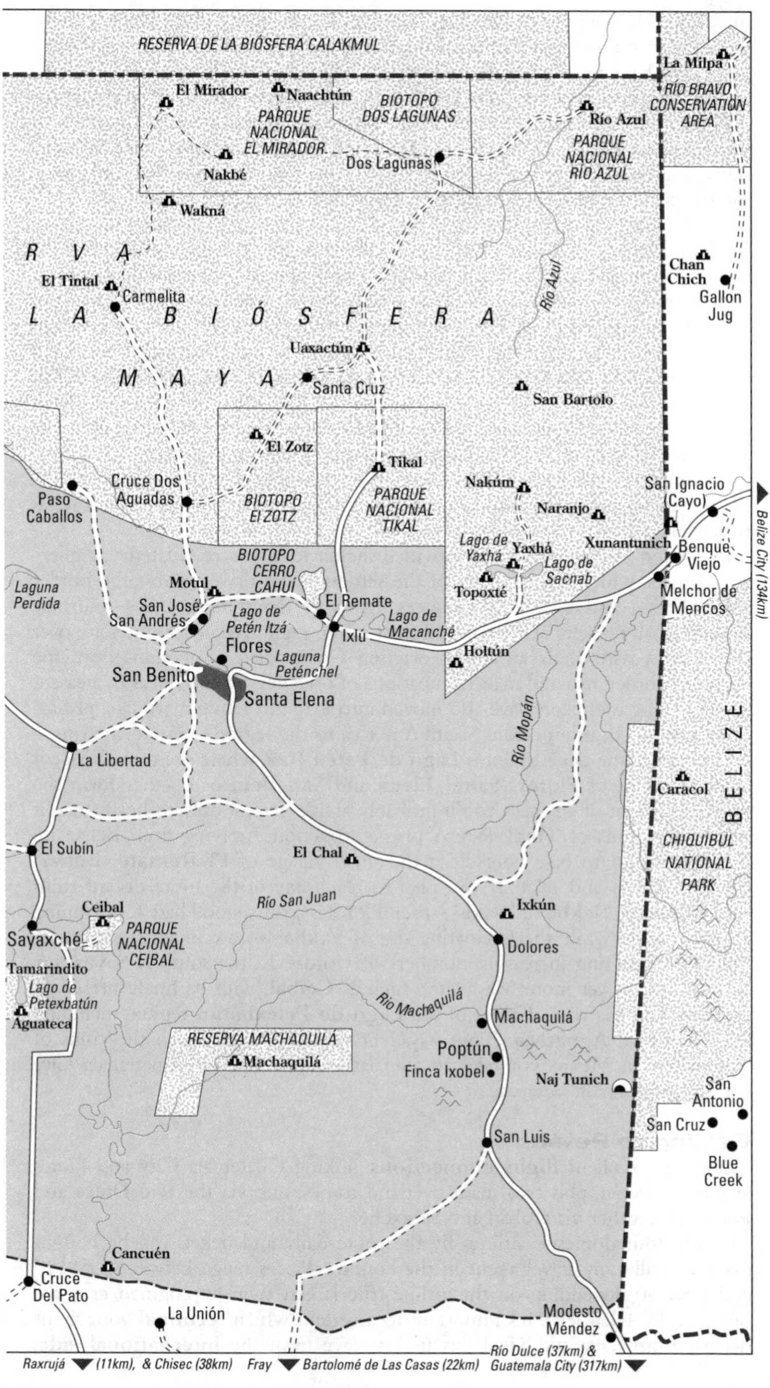

RESERVA DE LA BIÓSFERA CALAKMUL
La Milpa
RÍO BRAVO CONSERVATION AREA
El Mirador
Naachtún
PARQUE NACIONAL EL MIRADOR
BIOTOPO DOS LAGUNAS
Río Azul
PARQUE NACIONAL RÍO AZUL
Nakbé
Dos Lagunas
Wakná
R V A
L A B I Ó S F E R A
M A Y A
El Tintal
Carmelita
Río Azul
Chan Chich
Gallon Jug
Uaxactún
Santa Cruz
San Bartolo
El Zotz
Tikal
Nakúm
Naranjo
San Ignacio (Cayo)
Belize City (134km)
Paso Caballos
Cruce Dos Aguadas
BIOTOPO El ZOTZ
PARQUE NACIONAL TIKAL
Lago de Yaxhá
Yaxhá
Xunantunich
Benque Viejo
Lago de Sacnab
BIOTOPO CERRO CAHUÍ
Motul
Topoxté
Melchor de Mencos
Laguna Perdida
San José
San Andrés
Lago de Petén Itzá
El Remate
Ixlú
Lago de Macanché
Flores
Laguna Peténchel
Holtún
San Benito
Santa Elena
Río Mopán
BELIZE
La Libertad
Caracol
El Subín
El Chal
CHIQUIBUL NATIONAL PARK
Río San Juan
Ixkún
Ceibal
Sayaxché
PARQUE NACIONAL CEIBAL
Dolores
Tamarindito
Lago de Petexbatún
Aguateca
Río Machaquilá
Machaquilá
RESERVA MACHAQUILÁ
Machaquilá
Poptún
Finca Ixobel
Naj Tunich
San Antonio
San Cruz
San Luis
Blue Creek
Cancuén
Cruce Del Pato
La Unión
Modesto Méndez
Raxrujá (11km), & Chisec (38km)
Fray Bartolomé de Las Casas (22km)
Río Dulce (37km) & Guatemala City (317km)

uncovered the remains of two large cities, El Pajaral and Xulnal, while archeological excavations at other near-forgotten sites, including Cancuén, Wakná and Cival, have revealed them to be much larger than originally thought. Tikal and El Mirador are among the largest and most spectacular of all **Maya ruins** – Tikal alone has some 3000 buildings – but they represent only a fraction of what was once here. At the close of the tenth century the cities were mysteriously abandoned, after which some people moved north to the Yucatán, where the Maya civilization continued to flourish until the twelfth century.

By the time the Spanish arrived the area had been partially recolonized by the Itza, a group of Toltec Maya (originally from the Yucatán) who inhabited the land around Lago de Petén Itzá. The forest proved so impenetrable that it wasn't brought under Spanish control until 1697, more than 150 years after they had conquered the rest of the country. Although the Itza resisted persistent attempts to Christianize them, their lakeside capital was eventually conquered and destroyed by Martín de Ursúa and his army, thus bringing about the defeat of the last independent Maya tribe. The Spanish had little enthusiasm for Petén though, and under their rule it remained a backwater, with nothing to offer but a steady trickle of *chicle* – the basic ingredient of chewing gum, which is bled from sapodilla trees. Independence saw no great change, and it wasn't until 1970 that Petén became genuinely accessible by car. Even today, the network of roads is skeletal, and many routes are impassable in the wet season.

The Petén forests historically provided shelter for some of Guatemala's guerrilla armies, which led to many of the settlers being driven across the border into Mexico and becoming refugees. Most of the refugees have returned, though small pockets of tension still exist in the region. Many disputes are over land rights, with Belizean troops evicting Guatemalan campesinos from the disputed border area and mass occupations of privately owned fincas by peasant groups. Drug traffickers have also moved into Petén to set up marijuana plantations and fly cocaine in from South America to the region's remote airstrips.

The hub of the department is **Lago de Petén Itzá**, where the three adjacent lakeside towns of **Flores**, **Santa Elena** and **San Benito** together form the only settlement of any size. You'll probably arrive here, if only to head straight out to the ruins of **Tikal**, Petén's prime attraction. Arriving from Belize it's probably better to base yourself at the small village of **El Remate**, halfway between Flores and Tikal. If you plan to reach any of the more distant ruins – **El Mirador**, **Nakbé** or **Waka'** – then Flores is again a good base for planning an expedition, while the fascinating site of **Yaxhá** is now much more accessible and attracting increasing numbers of visitors. To the south is **Sayaxché**, surrounded by yet more Maya sites, such as **Ceibal**, with its finely preserved carvings, and the ruined cities of the **Lago de Petexbatún** region, including the impressive **Aguateca**. From Sayaxché you can easily reach the ruins of **Yaxchilán** in Mexico, or take an alternative route back to Guatemala City – via Cobán in Alta Verapaz.

Getting to Petén

There are excellent **flight connections** linking Guatemala City and Flores airport in Petén, plus two main overland routes: one via the Río Dulce and Poptún, the other via Cobán and Sayaxché.

By **air**, four domestic airlines fly the route daily, and tickets can be bought from virtually any travel agent in the country. Prices range between US$110 and US$150 depending on the airline (the largest twin-jet-engined craft are operated by Tikal Jets). It's important to ascertain which **terminal** your flight departs from: Taca and Tikal Jets flights leave from the **international side**,

The Reserva de la Biósfera Maya

The idea behind biosphere reserves, conceived in 1974 by UNESCO, was an ambitious attempt to combine the protection of natural areas and the conservation of their genetic diversity with scientific research and sustainable development. The **Reserva de la Biósfera Maya**, created in 1990, covers 16,000 square kilometres of northern Petén: in theory it is the largest tropical forest reserve in Central America.

On the premise that conservation and development can be compatible, land use in the reserve has three designations: **core areas** include the national parks, major archeological sites and the *biotopos*, areas of scientific investigation. The primary role of core areas is to preserve biodiversity; human settlements are prohibited though tourism is permitted. Surrounding the core areas are **multiple-use areas** where inhabitants, aided and encouraged by the government and NGOs, are able to engage in sustainable use of the forest resources and small-scale agriculture. The **buffer zone,** a fifteen-kilometre-wide belt along the southern edge of the reserve, is intended to prevent further human intrusion but contains many existing villages.

Fine in theory, particularly when you consider that much of the northern reserve skirts the Reserva de la Biósfera Calakmul in Mexico and that protected land in Belize forms much of the reserve's eastern boundary. In practice, however, the destruction of Petén's **rainforest** proceeds virtually unchecked. Less than fifty percent of the original cover remains and illicit logging, often conducted from Mexico with the complicity of Guatemalan officials, is reducing it further. Oil exploration is the other industry that has driven the destruction of the forest in the west of the reserve, as petroleum companies have pushed roads deep into the Parque Nacional Laguna del Tigre. Incredibly, successive Guatemalan governments have aided and abetted the oil companies, issuing concessions for exploration – though this practise was later ruled illegal by the Attorney General in 2000. As soon as a road exists, land-hungry migrants – mainly from Guatemala's agriculturally impoverished southeastern and Alta Verapaz departments – follow, carving out slash-and-burn *milpas*. Large areas of forest are torched by these migrants every year, particularly in the west of the reserve, but the families typically have to move on after a few years when the Petén's thin soil is depleted, leaving their plots to cattle ranchers. In 2003 the smoke from these fires was so thick it disrupted air traffic throughout Guatemala and Mexico and even affected southern Texas where children were sent home from school.

Although much has been lost in the west and south of the reserve, environmental groups and NGOs are fighting to conserve what remains. Foreign funding, from aid programmes and conservation organizations, provides much of the finance for protection, and many settlers realize that their future depends on sustainable use of forest resources. Tourism is an accepted part of the plan and, though few visitors see little outside Tikal and Flores, trips to the more remote *biotopos* and national parks are perfectly feasible. The next critical area is going to be the **Mirador Basin** (Ⓦwww.miradorbasin.com), which archeologists, including UCLA's Richard Hansen, hope to see turned into a national park, with ecotourism initiatives helping to secure the future of the forest and its dozens of ruins.

while all other airlines depart from their offices inside the airport perimeter (entrance on Avenida Hincapie). Most flights leave between 6am and 7.30am in the morning, enabling day-tripping visitors to spend several hours at Tikal before catching a flight back between 3.30pm and 5pm (though there are departures at other times of day). Flights are heavily in demand in the peak tourist season, and overbooking is common at all times of year.

Travelling by bus, several companies (see box, p.99) run direct services from Guatemala City, all operating from a run-down part of Zona 1 between 15 and 17 calles and 8 and 10 avenidas. The journey time is eight to ten hours. Between the various companies there are more than thirty buses a day, the quickest of which pass the Río Dulce bridge (for **Lívingston**) after about five hours and Poptún after about six and a half hours. The best buses are the luxurious a/c pullmans run by Línea Dorada (luxury at 10am, US$26; regular at 10pm and 10.30pm, US$15–18) and ADN (luxury services at 10am and 9pm; US$27), while Fuente del Norte run fairly decent-quality regular buses (hourly; US$10) and five daily "Maya de Oro" near-luxury buses (US$18). If you don't want to do this 554-kilometre trip in one go, it's easy enough to do it in stages – the best places to break the journey are at **Río Dulce** and **Poptún**.

An alternative route takes you from Guatemala City to **Cobán** from where most travellers head to **Lanquín** (for Semuc Champey) and then north via Raxrujá and **Sayaxché**. Or you could take the quicker road from Cobán to **Chisec**, then on to Sayaxché and Flores. This route is virtually all paved and is served by direct minibuses and a daily shuttle bus.

You can also enter Petén **from Belize** through the border at Melchor de Mencos or **from Mexico** via Frontera Corozal, or the much less travelled river route along the Río San Pedro via La Palma.

Poptún and around

Heading north from Río Dulce Town, the smooth paved highway to Flores cuts through a degraded landscape of small *milpa* farms and cattle ranches that was jungle a decade or two ago. Some 95km from Río Dulce, at an altitude of 500m, the first settlement of any interest is the small town of **POPTÚN**. For many travellers this dusty settlement is the embodiment of rustic bliss and organic food – thanks to the proximity of the *Finca Ixobel* (see below). There's no particular reason to stay in the town itself, but you may well stop by to use a cybercafé (try *Servicio de Internet* next to the Fuente del Norte bus office on Calle 15 de Septiembre) or hit one of the two banks (both on 5 Calle; Bancafé has a Visa ATM, Banrural a MasterCard ATM). If you do get stuck, you could **stay** at the friendly *Hotel Posada de los Castellanos* (ⓣ7927 7222; ❷), where basic rooms have hot water and a bathroom. The owner of this *posada*, Don Placido Castellanos, is an excellent source of information about the Petén and also has a much more comfortable place, *Villa de los Castellanos* (ⓣ7927 7541, ⓕ7927 7307; ❹) 6km north of town. The large comfortable cabañas (all with bathroom) at the latter spot offer a great riverside base for plotting trips to the forests, rivers and caves of central Petén; speak to Don Placido about excursions to the remote Reserva Machaquilá and its ruins.

The best food in Poptún is at *La Fonda Ixobel*, which has good bread and cakes. Minibuses shuttle between Poptún and Flores every thirty minutes until 6.30pm, while buses (around 30 daily) head south to Río Dulce and on to Guatemala City all day and night. There's also one daily bus to Fray Bartolomé de Las Casas (5hr) at 7am.

Finca Ixobel

About 4km south of Poptún, surrounded by aromatic pine forests in the cool foothills of the Maya Mountains, the *Finca Ixobel* (ⓣ5410 4037, ⓦwww.fincaixobel.com) is a rural retreat and farm that's also a legendary travellers' meeting point. It was originally run by Americans Mike and Carole DeVine, but on June 8, 1990, Mike was murdered by the army, an act which prompted the US government to suspend military aid to Guatemala. Five soldiers were convicted of the murder in September 1992, although a drawn-out investigation cast little light on their motives. Others involved have managed to evade capture, while the soldiers' commanding officer, Captain Hugo Contreras, escaped from jail shortly after his arrest. Carole fought the case for years and remains at the finca.

Finca Ixobel is a supremely beautiful and relaxing place, where you can swim in the pond, walk in the forest, dodge the resident "attack" parrots and stuff yourself with delicious homegrown (mostly organic) food. You run a tab for accommodation, food (dinner costs US$3–6) and drink, paying when you leave – which can be a rude awakening. Many travellers are quickly seduced by the tranquil nature of the finca and end up staying much longer than planned, some working as cooks or helpers in exchange for board and lodging. There are **hikes** into the jungle, horse-riding trips, tubing, 4WD jungle jaunts, and short excursions to nearby caves. Accommodation is either in attractive bungalows with two beds and a private bathroom (❹–❻), **rooms** (❸, with bathroom ❹) or **dorms** (US$3.75 per bed), and there's also camping, hammock space and tree houses (all US$3 per person). To get to the finca, ask the bus driver to drop you at the gate, from where it's a fifteen-minute walk through the pine trees; after dark, it's safest to head for the *La Fonda Ixobel* restaurant in Poptún and have them call a taxi for you (US$2.25).

Naj Tunich caves

The limestone hills surrounding Poptún are riddled with **caves** and coated in lush tropical forest. One of the largest caves contains an underground river and waterfall that you can swim through (if you don't mind leaping into a chilly pool in total darkness); walking trips to this cave system are organized by *Finca Ixobel*. The most impressive, however, is the remote **Naj Tunich** or "Stone House", 23km down a rough track from Poptún, close to the Belizean border. At the time of writing, the cave system, which is more than 1.2km long, was not open to the public because of the threat from looters, but speak to the owner of the *Villa de los Castellanos* (see p.332) who can sometimes organize special tours. If you're lucky enough to get inside, you'll find cave walls decorated with extensive hieroglyphic texts (400 glyphs in total) and **Maya murals**, which, in addition to depictions of religious ceremonies and ball games, include several graphic and well-preserved drawings of erotic scenes, a feature found nowhere else in Maya art. Caves were sacred to the ancient Maya, who believed them to be entrances to Xibalbá, the dreaded underworld, and Naj Tunich was one of the most revered sites of the central Maya region. Many of the glyphic inscriptions were painted by royal scribes from distant cities, including Calakmul in today's Mexico, and the cave was something of a place of pilgrimage for kings eager to secure favourable passage to the afterlife. If you can't make it to the caves, seek out the excellent feature on Naj Tunich in the August 1981 edition of *National Geographic*.

Dolores and El Chal

Most of the non-luxury buses to Flores call in at the village of **Dolores**, set back from the road about 20km north of Poptún. Founded in 1708 as an outpost for missionaries working out of Cobán, these days it's a growing town and the area around it has been settled by returning refugees and migrants from the eastern highlands. An hour's walk to the north are the unrestored Maya ruins of **Ixkún** (8am–5pm; US$1.80), a mid-sized site made up of eight plazas. Fifteen kilometres north of Dolores a road branches northeast at the village of Sabaneta, making a short cut to the **Belize border**. Some buses from

Guatemala to Melchor use this route, though it's liable to flooding and often in bad condition.

A further 30km brings you to the ruins of **El Chal** (daily 8am–5pm; no charge), signed on the west side of the village of the same name, and less than 500m from the road. Call in at the small hut by the entrance to the ruins for a free tour with the guard. The ruins include several plazas and a ball court, and the palace complex, built on a ridge, gives a view of the surrounding countryside. Some bush has been cleared, but the buildings are largely unrestored – the most remarkable features are a couple of stelae and nearby altars with clearly visible glyphs and carved features.

Flores

Although it's the capital of Petén, **FLORES** is a delightfully easy-going, sedate place with an old-fashioned atmosphere, quite unlike most of the region's towns, where commerce and bustle dominate. A cluster of cobbled streets and aging houses built around a twin-domed church, it sits beautifully on a small island in Lago de Petén Itzá, connected to the mainland by a short (man-made) causeway. The modern emphasis lies across the water in the twin towns of **SANTA ELENA** and **SAN BENITO**, both of which are ugly, chaotic and sprawling places, dusty in the dry season and mud-bound during the rains. Santa Elena, opposite Flores at the other end of the causeway, is strung out between the airport and the market, and takes in several hotels, banks, and bus and microbus transport terminals. San Benito, further west, has even less going for it, with a profusion of rough cantinas frequented by struggling settlers and a villain or two. The three once distinct towns are now often lumped together under the single name of Flores.

The **lake** is a natural choice for settlement, and its shores were heavily populated in Maya times. The city of **Tayasal**, capital of the Itza, lay on the island that was to become modern Flores. Cortés passed through here in 1525, on his way south to Honduras, and left behind a sick horse which he promised to send for. In 1618 two Franciscan friars arrived to find the people worshipping a large white idol in the shape of a horse called "Tzimin Chac", the thunder horse. Unable to persuade the Maya to renounce their religion they smashed the idol and left the city. Subsequent visitors were less well received: in 1622 a military expedition of twenty men was invited into the city by Canek, chief of the Itza, where they were set upon and sacrificed to the idols. The town was eventually destroyed by Martín de Ursúa and an army of 235 in 1697. The following year the island was fortified in order to be used as an outpost of the Spanish Empire on the Camino Real (Royal Road) to Campeche. For the entire colonial period (and indeed up to the 1960s) Flores languished in virtual isolation, having more contact with neighbouring Belize than the capital.

Today, despite the steady flow of tourists passing through for Tikal, the town retains an enjoyably genteel air, with residents greeting one another courteously as they meet in the streets. Though it has little to detain you in itself – a leisurely thirty-minute stroll around the cobbled streets and lanes is enough to become entirely familiar with the place – Flores does offer enjoyable surroundings and an excellent selection of hotels, restaurants, cybercafés and tour operators.

Arrival

Arriving by bus from Guatemala City you'll be dropped on 4 Calle in Santa Elena, just a few blocks from the causeway to Flores, though Línea Dorada buses will continue on to Flores. The **airport** is 3km east of the causeway, a US$2 taxi-ride from town. **Local buses** (*urbanos*) cover the route for US$0.15, but this entails a time-consuming change halfway to get on another bus across the causeway. (Getting **back** to the airport, local buses leave from the Flores end of the causeway about every ten minutes or so.)

Information

The knowledgeable staff at the **Inguat** desk in the arrivals hall at the airport (daily 7am–noon & 3–6pm; ⓣ7926 0533) can give you reasonable maps and

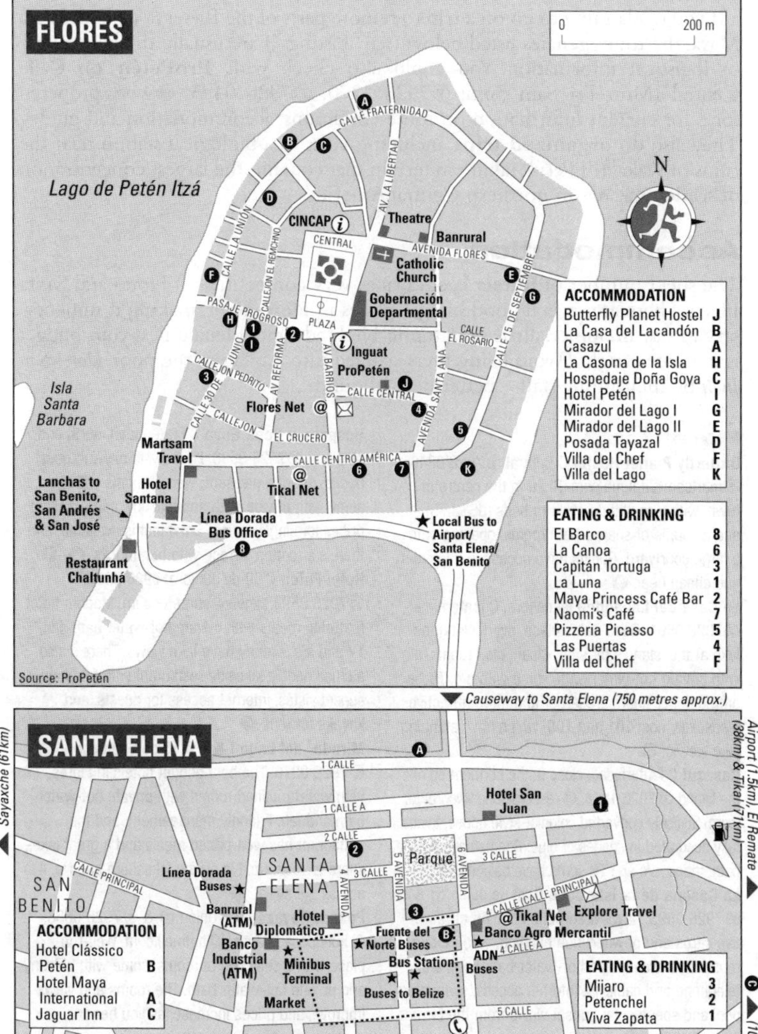

good information in English. There's another Inguat office on the central plaza in Flores (Mon–Fri 8am–4pm; ⓣ7926 0669), whose staff are helpful but will probably direct you across the plaza to **CINCAP** (Centro de Información sobre la Naturaleza, Cultura y Artesanías de Petén) in the **Castillo de Arismendi** building (Mon–Fri 9am–noon & 2–8pm; ⓣ7926 0718), to examine their more detailed maps, books and leaflets about northern Petén. Here at the Castillo, you can see exhibits on historical and contemporary Petén and buy medicinal herbs, collected as part of the effort to promote forest sustainability. This is also the base of the ecologist and ecotourism organization Alianza Verde (ⓦwww.alianzaverde.org), who manage CINCAP and publish *Destination Petén*, a useful free monthly listings and **information magazine**, available at most hotels and travel agencies.

If you're planning to go on a trip to remote parts of the Reserva de la Biósfera Maya, the tour agencies listed below (see "Listings") are usually the best source of logistical information. You could also check with **ProPetén** on Calle Central (Mon–Fri 8am–5pm; ⓣ7926 1370, ⓕ7926 0495, ⓦwww.propeten.org) for current information on route conditions, accommodation and guides. They also do **organized trips**, including visits to a biological station near the ruins of Waka' (El Perú), taking in terrain that contains the largest concentration of scarlet macaws in northern Central America.

Accommodation

The sheer number of **hotels** keeps prices very competitive in Flores and Santa Elena. There are several good budget places in Flores itself, making it unnecessary to stay in noisier, dirtier and traffic-blighted Santa Elena unless your budget is extremely tight. Avoid being press-ganged into staying at the poor *Hotel San Juan* by their pushy staff – better deals abound.

Flores

Butterfly Planet Hostel C Central ⓣ7926 0346, ⓔmartsam@itelgua.com. Right in the centre of town, with a multitude of dorm beds (US$3.75) and a couple of shared-bath rooms, opening onto a large courtyard. Guests have access to a kitchen and cheap beer. ❷

La Casa del Lacandón lakeshore, C Fraternidad ⓣ7926 3591. Good-value place, overlooking the lake at the island's far side. Clean, tiled rooms, all with private hot-water bath, some with a/c. Those on the upper floors are larger and more attractive (especially nos. 101 and 105, which have stunning lake views). ❷

Casazul C Fraternidad, close to the northern tip of the island ⓣ7926 1138, ⓔreservaciones@corpetur.com. Stylishly converted colonial-style house, tastefully decorated in shades of blue. Rooms have private bath, fridge, a/c and TV, some have balcony. ❺

La Casona de la Isla Calle C 30 de Junio ⓣ & ⓕ7926 0593, ⓦwww.corpetur.com. An attractive citrus and powder-blue building, with modern rooms with clean, tiled hot-water bathroom, a/c, telephone and cable TV. Internet access, swimming pool and spectacular sunset views from the terrace restaurant/bar. ❺

Hospedaje Doña Goya C Fraternidad, north end of island ⓣ7926 3538. Friendly, family-run guest house, offering pleasant, well-lit rooms with fans, some with private bath and balcony, and excellent prices for single rooms. Breakfast is available, and there's a rooftop terrace with hammocks. ❷–❸

Hotel Petén C 30 de Junio ⓣ7926 0692, ⓕ7926 0593, ⓦwww.corpetur.com. Modern hotel featuring rooms with private hot-water bath, fan, TV and a/c – many have lake views. There's also a small pool, a lakeside restaurant with fabulous sunset vistas, Internet access for guests, and kayaks for rent. ❻

Mirador del Lago I & II C 15 de Septiembre ⓣ7926 3276. The best budget hotels in Flores, with well-furnished rooms with private hot-water bath and fan. Friendly management, and the restaurant has well-priced meals and a great lakeshore terrace. No. I is on the lakeshore and No. II is across the street. ❷

Posada Tayazal C la Unión ⓣ & ⓕ7926 0568, ⓔhotelposadatayazal@hotmail.com. Well-run place with a selection of rooms, some with balcony and private hot-water bath. The rooms and views improve, and prices increase, as you head upstairs. ❷–❸

Villa del Chef C la Unión ⓣ7926 0926, ⓔenrico_ferrulli@yahoo.com. The best-value and most comfortable shared-bath budget rooms in Flores, with a small balcony and sitting area, above the recommended restaurant of the same name. ❷

Villa del Lago southeast corner of island ⓣ & ⓕ7926 0629, ⓔhotelvilladelago@itelgua.com. Modern, three-storey building with pretty, very comfortable rooms, all with private hot-water bath, some with a/c and great views. There's an upper-floor terrace which is a fine place to take breakfast and enjoy the sweeping vistas of the lake. ❹–❺

Santa Elena

Hotel Clássico Petén 4 C & 6 Av ⓣ7926 0672. Attractive new hotel with twenty very clean, fair-sized rooms, all with bathroom and either fan or a/c, set off well-kept communal areas. Parking. ❹

Hotel Maya International lakeshore ⓣ2334 1818, ⓦwww.villasdeguatemala.com. Right over the lakeshore opposite Flores. Large four-star hotel with good-sized rooms boasting private bath, cable TV, phone, safe and a balcony. There's a lakefront restaurant and a pool. Free transport to and from airport. ❽

Jaguar Inn Calzada Rodríguez Macal 8–79 ⓣ & ⓕ7926 0002, ⓦwww.jaguartikal.com. Large comfortable singles and doubles all with private baths and TV, plus a choice of a/c or fan, set off a slim plant-filled courtyard. Located a little out of town near the airport, but has a restaurant, safe parking and friendly management. ❸–❹

Eating, drinking and entertainment

Flores generally offers cosmopolitan, tourist-geared dining, and plenty of **restaurants** enjoy delightful lakeside views. However, prices are a little higher than elsewhere in Guatemala. Santa Elena has a very limited selection of comedores, so even if you're staying here you may want to cross the causeway for a little more atmosphere. Be warned: many restaurants serve wild game, often listed on menus as *comida silvestre*, and virtually all this has been taken illegally from reserves – avoid in particular ordering items such as *tepescuintle* (paca, a large relation of the guinea pig), *venado* (deer) and *coche de monte* (peccary, or wild pig).

For a Petén-style **night out** head to *Viva Zapata* at 2 Calle and 8 Avenida in Santa Elena, which is a popular dancehall, live music venue, theatre, bar and restaurant all rolled into one. In Flores, *Las Puertas* (see below) has live music some nights, while the *Maya Princess* shows videos. *La Luna* and *El Barco* are good places for a drink.

Flores

El Barco On a flat-decked boat to the left as you cross the causeway. Seafood, steak and chicken in reasonable portions at good prices, with some Guatemalan specialities and veggie dishes. Happy hour is 6–8.30pm.

La Canoa C Centro América. Popular, good-value place serving pasta, great soups, and some vegetarian and Guatemalan food, as well as excellent breakfasts.

Capitán Tortuga C 30 de Junio. Large place with a menu that takes in steaks, pizza and Mexican food at around US$4–7 a main. The ribs here are excellent.

La Luna C 30 de Junio. Set in a wonderfully atmospheric old building, with artwork on the walls, this is the most stylish restaurant in town, though it's not that pricey at around US$5–8 a main dish. Cuisine includes fish, falafel and pasta – and it doesn't serve wild game.

Maya Princess Café Bar Av Reforma. An interesting, inexpensive international menu – Thai-style chicken, salad with basil leaves – plus daily specials. Sociable vibe and free movies shown at 4pm and 9pm daily.

Naomi's Café C Centro América. Excellent café serving fresh bread and cakes and a range of local and international food and drinks, including pizza, pasta, cappuccinos and smoothies. Opens at 5am for breakfast, and has an evening happy hour plus book exchange, book and map sales, and Internet access.

Pizzeria Picasso C 15 de Septiembre ⓣ7926 0637. Great pizza served under cooling breezes from the ceiling fans; they also deliver.

Las Puertas signposted from Av Santa Ana. Paint-splattered walls and live music as well as very good pasta and healthy breakfasts. Worth it for the atmosphere. Doubles as a bar: try the margaritas.

Villa del Chef C La Unión. A quiet, stylish and romantic little restaurant with tables and wicker chairs on a lakeshore terrace (candlelit in the evenings) serving healthy cuisine at very good prices, including vegetarian choices like *pinchos*, and great desserts. Book exchange at the bar, too.

Santa Elena

Mijaro two locations: south of the causeway, and on C Principal. The best Guatemalan restaurants in Santa Elena, with good *típica*-style food and plenty of meat dishes at local prices, and a daily special. You can usually leave luggage here while you look for a room.

Restaurant Petenchel 2 C and 4 Av, a block past the park. Simple, good food: the nicest place to eat around the main street. They'll also look after your luggage here too.

Listings

Banks Banco Agro Mercantil, 6 Av and 4 C in Santa Elena (Mon–Sat 8.30am–8pm), has an ATM next door for MasterCard users. Banco Industrial, on 4 C, has a Visa ATM. In Flores, Banrural, just east of the plaza, changes travellers' cheques.

Bike and motorbike rental Backabush Bike Tours, Av Barrios (ⓣ5695 7481), has good mountain bikes for US$1.50 per hour, and also offers excellent tours. For motorbikes (US$15 for 2 hrs), see Martsam Travel, on C Centro América in Flores.

Car rental Budget, Hertz, Tabarini (with the widest choice; ⓣ7926 0253) and Koka operate from the airport. Rates (including insurance) start around US$37 a day for a small car, about US$65 for a 4WD.

Communications *Tikal Net*, on C Centro América in Flores and C Principal in Santa Elena, a cybercafé where you can also make cheap international phone calls.

Doctor The staff at the Centro Médico Maya, 4 Av near 3 C in Santa Elena (ⓣ7926 0180), are helpful and professional, though no English is spoken.

Language schools San Andrés and San José (two attractive villages on the north shore of the lake) both have good Spanish schools. Official rates are about US$150–175 a week for 20 hours of one-on-one lessons, food and lodging with a local family – a bit more expensive than some places in Guatemala, but very few people here speak English so you can progress quite quickly. In San Andrés, the Eco-Escuela (ⓣ5498 4539, ⓦwww.ecoescuelaespanol.org) is the largest, longest-established school in Petén, while the Escuela Nueva Juventud (ⓣ5711 0040, ⓦwww.volunteerpeten.com) is in a medicinal plant reserve and also offers environmental volunteer opportunities. In San José, there's the Escuela Bio-Itzá (ⓣ7926 1363, ⓔbioitza@guate.net), and also the newer Mundo Maya Ecological Spanish School (ⓣ7928 8321, ⓦwww.mundomayaguatemala.com). In Flores itself, the Ixchel Spanish Academy (ⓣ7926 3225, ⓔspanishacademy@martsam.com) is a new school with a good reputation.

Laundry Lavandería Amelia, behind CINCAP in Flores, or Petenchel on C Centro América.

Post offices In Flores, on Av Barrios; in Santa Elena, on C Principal, two blocks east of the Banco Agro Mercantil.

Travel agents and tour operators Every hotel seems to be offering tours, but most can simply sell you minibus trips to Tikal or bus and plane tickets. The best travel agent in Flores is Martsam Travel, C Centro América (ⓣ & ⓕ7926 3225, ⓦwww.martsam.com), where the owners speak good English. They run a daily trip to Yaxhá for US$20pp (minimum 2) and also offer overnight jungle trips to El Zotz, Waka' (El Perú) and many other sites. Explore, 4 C, Santa Elena (ⓣ7926 2375, ⓦwww.exploreguate.com), are experts in trips to Ceibal (US$35), on the Río de la Pasión, and Aguateca and Dos Pilas (overnight US$140, including Ceibal) on Lago de Petexbatún. Tikal Connection (formerly Eco Maya), C Centro América (ⓣ7926 4981, ⓦwww.tikalcnx.com), specialize in remote hikes to sites such as Río Azul, El Mirador and Nakbé.

Voluntary work The language schools listed above have programmes for volunteers, including helping women's groups, teaching children and doing environmental work. ARCAS (Asociación de Rescate y Conservación de Vida Silvestre), the Wildlife Rescue and Conservation Association (ⓣ7926 2022, ⓦwww.rds.org.gt/arcas), set in the forest on the lakeshore, runs an inspiring rescue and rehabilitation programme for animals and birds. To volunteer you need to donate $100 a week (the minimum stay required), which covers food, lodging and transportation.

Around Flores

If you have an afternoon, or a few days to spare, the lake and surrounding hills offer a few interesting diversions. The most obvious excursion is a **trip on the**

Moving on from Flores

If you're heading to **Tikal**, virtually all hotels and travel agencies can book you a shuttle bus (US$5 return), which will pick you up at your accommodation from 5am onwards.

All the **bus companies** have offices or depots on (or just off) 4 Calle in Santa Elena, while Línea Dorada/Mundo Maya have an additional office in Flores on the south side of the island. Heading for **Guatemala City**, Fuente del Norte (☎7926 0666) have hourly buses (8–9hr 30min; US$10–18), five of which are more comfortable "Maya de Oro" services. Línea Dorada (☎7926 1788, Ⓦwww.tikalmayanworld.com) offer luxury bus services (all with a/c and reclining seats, some with meals and movies included) that leave daily at 10am, 8pm and 10pm (8hr; US$16–30). ADN (☎7926 3827) also have luxury buses (8hr; US$30), which are of a similar standard and leave twice daily, at 10am and 9pm.

For travel **around Péten**, there are both chicken buses and microbuses, all leaving from the market area just south of Calle Principal. Services to destinations in the department include: five daily buses to Bethel (4hr), with three continuing on to La Técnica (4hr 30min); one daily bus (at 1pm; 3hr) to Carmelita; hourly microbuses and four daily buses to El Naranjo (4hr); half-hourly microbuses to Poptún (1hr 30min); hourly microbuses to San Andrés (30min) and San José (40min); and half-hourly microbuses and four daily buses to Sayaxché (1hr 30min).

For **Cobán** (4hr 15min), via Sayaxché, the Candelaria caves and Chisec, there's a daily shuttle-bus service at 1pm (book at one of the tour operators on p.312); you can do it cheaper by taking a regular microbus to Sayaxché and catching a southbound connection there. For **Río Dulce** (3hr) take a Guatemala City–bound bus.

Travelling **to Belize**, there are regular microbuses from the marketplace for the border at Melchor de Menchos (2hr), plus hourly chicken buses and the odd pullman bus (including a daily Fuente del Norte service at 4.30pm). Mundo Maya operate a/c express services leaving daily at 5am and 7.30am for Belize City Marine terminal (4hr; US$17) that continue on to the **Mexican border** at Chetumal (another 4hr; US$24 in all) for connections north to Cancún. San Juan Travel, not a recommended travel agency, operate a similar, less reliable service. For details on getting to Mexico via Frontera Corozal or Río San Pedro, see p.370 and p.374 respectively.

Tickets for **flights** to Guatemala City (50min–1hr; US$65–90 one way) on any of the four airlines that make the trip can be bought at the airport or at any travel agent. Other destinations from Petén include Belize City (five daily; 35min), with Tropic Air, Maya Island Air, Island Air and Tikal Jets; Cancún (Taca, 3 weekly; 1hr 20min); and the US city of Houston (Continental, 2 weekly on Wednesday and Saturday; 3hr 20min). You can also **charter flights** from Flores airport to Dos Lagunas, El Naranjo, Sayaxché, Playa Grande, Puerto Barrios, Río Dulce, Copán (Honduras) and Palenque (Mexico).

lake. Boatmen can take you on a circuit that includes a *mirador* and the small Classic-era ruins of Tayasal on the peninsula opposite, and the **Petencito zoo** (daily 8am–5pm; US$2.50), which features a pretty well-looked-after collection of sluggish local wildlife, pausing for a swim along the way. (Note, though, that the concrete waterslide by the zoo can be dangerous and has caused at least one death.) Alternatively, you could visit **ARCAS**, a kilometre to the west, which is a rescue and rehabilitation centre for animals formerly kept as pets or confiscated from wildlife traffickers. There's no public access to the rescue area itself, but there is an environmental education centre, botanical trail and bird observation spot here. Aim to pay around US$12–15 for a boat trip that takes in two of the above attractions. You'll find the boatmen behind the *Hotel Santana*, in the southwestern corner of Flores, and at the start of the causeway in Santa Elena just past the *Maya International* hotel.

Of the numerous **caves** in the hills behind Santa Elena, the most accessible is **Ak'tun Kan** (daily 8am–5pm; US$1.25) – simply follow the Flores causeway through Santa Elena, continue down 6 Avenida until it forks in front of a small hill, and then take the first right. Otherwise known as *La Cueva de la Serpiente*, the cave is the legendary home of a huge snake. The guard may explain some of the bizarre names given to the various shapes inside, some of which resemble animals and even a marimba.

Skyway Ixpanpajul

At the **Skyway Ixpanpajul**, 10km from Santa Elena, just off the road to Guatemala City (daily; adults US$25, children US$15; Ⓦwww.ixpanpajul.com), an amazing system of suspension bridges and good stone paths connects 3km of forested hilltops in a nine-square-kilometre private reserve. In the middle of the bridges, you enjoy a monkey's-eye view of the canopy and on top of the highest hill there's an enormous *mirador* with views of virtually the whole of the Petén Itzá basin. It's best to go in the early morning, after mid-afternoon or even at night, when the wildlife (particularly snakes, and kingcacuas) really comes to life; allow a few hours so you can take your time and see the trees and orchids. There's a good self-guided trail leaflet (in Spanish only) and you can get there by bike (45min) or any Poptún-bound *microbus* will drop you at the entrance. Martsam Travel in Flores offer a trip with return transport, a short horse ride and entrance ticket for US$30 per person.

You can also **camp** here for US$5 per person, and there are showers and toilets.

San Andrés and San José

Though accessible by bus and boat, the traditional villages of **San Andrés** and **San José**, across the lake from Flores, have until recently received few visitors. The pace of life is even slower here than in Flores, and the people are courteous and friendly. The streets, sloping steeply up from the shore, are lined with one-storey buildings, some of *palmetto* sticks and thatch, some coated with plaster, and others hewn in brightly painted concrete. Pigs and chickens wander freely.

In the past, the mainstay of the economy was the arduous and poorly paid collection of **chicle**, the sap of the sapodilla tree, for use in the manufacture

of chewing gum. This involves setting up camps in the forest, and working for months at a time in the rainy season when the sap is flowing. Today, natural *chicle* has largely been superseded by artificial substitutes, but there is still a demand for the original product, especially in Japan. Other forest products are also collected, including *xate* (pronounced "shatey"), palm leaves used in floral arrangements and exported to North America and Europe; and *pimienta de jamaica*, or allspice. Harvesters (*pimenteros*) use spurs to climb the trees and collect the spice, then dry it over a fire. Since the creation of the Reserva de la Biósfera Maya (see p.331), however, efforts have been made to provide villagers with alternative sources of income and four **Spanish schools** have been established in recent years.

Getting to the villages is simple by microbus, which leave about every half-hour from Santa Elena for the thirty-minute trip; there are no longer regular *lancha* services, though a few leave from the jetties near the *Hotel Santana* in Flores (about 45min; US$1.50 per person) and from San Benito, a suburb of Santa Elena.

San Andrés

Most outsiders in **SAN ANDRÉS** are students at the two **language schools**: the Eco-Escuela (the first to be set up in Petén) and the newer Escuela Nueva Juventud. Since virtually nobody in the village speaks English, a course here is an excellent opportunity to immerse yourself in Spanish, without the distractions of Antigua, though it may be daunting for absolute beginners. For more information see "Listings" at the end of the Flores account.

For somewhere to **stay** you'll find the basic but acceptable *Hotel Corina* (❷), on top of the hill as you enter the village, while 3km to the west is the attractive *Hotel Nitún* (Ⓣ2201 0759, Ⓦwww.nitun.com; ❻, including transport from Flores), set above the lakeshore with full-board **accommodation** in four stylish thatched stone cabañas, all with polished hardwood floors and private bathrooms, a restaurant serving superb food and a fantastic upper-deck bar-lounge with lake views. The guest house is run by Lorena Castillo and Bernie Mittelstaedt, a friendly, knowledgeable couple (both speak perfect English), who also operate Monkey Eco Tours and can organize well-equipped expeditions to remote archeological sites throughout northern Petén. There are several simple **comedores** in San José, including the *Restaurant La Troya*, which is 250m up from the lakeshore.

San José and around

Just 2km east along the shore from San Andrés, above a lovely bay, **SAN JOSÉ** is even more relaxed than its neighbour. Take a look at the Catholic **church**, where three sacred skulls are kept in a cabinet: they're paraded through the streets as part of a pagan ceremony on the Day of the Dead each year (see box, p.342). The village is undergoing something of a cultural revival: Itza, the pre-conquest Maya tongue is being taught in the school, and you'll see signs in that language dotted all around. The Asociación Bio-Itzá, a community partnership, has established an excellent **Spanish school**, the Bio-Itzá (one of two schools in the village: see p.338 for more information), just above the main dock and parque. Students get the chance to help out with the association's projects, which include a **women's cooperative** which has more than fifty members and runs a botanical garden, where visitors can learn about the use of traditional medicinal plants and their relation to the lunar cycle. The garden is located a kilometre inland from the centre in a district known as Nuevo San José. The association's other main project is the management of a **forest reserve**, north of the village, which abuts the Biotopo El Zotz, in the buffer zone of the Reserva Maya Biósfera. The area is rich in wildlife

San José's sacred skulls

San José is famous for its two **fiestas**. The first, to mark the patron saint's day, is held between March 10 and 19 and includes parades and fireworks plus an unusual, comical-looking costumed dance during which a girl (*la chatona*) and a horse skip through the village streets. The second fiesta is distinctly more pagan, with a unique mass, celebrated in the church on All Saints' Day (or Halloween) and a festival which continues on into November 1 – The Day of the Dead. For the evening service, one of three venerated human **skulls** (thought to be the remains of early founders of the village, though some claim they were Spanish missionaries) is removed from its glass case inside the church and positioned on the altar for the ceremony. Afterwards, the skull is carried through the village by black-clad skullbearers, accompanied by children dressed in traditional Itza *traje* and hundreds of devotees, many carrying candles and lanterns. The procession weaves through the streets, stopping at around thirty homes where prayers are said, chants made and the families ask for blessings. In each home, a corn-based drink called *ixpasá* is consumed and special fiesta food is eaten, part of a ceremony that can take over a day to complete. The exact origin of the event is unclear, but it clearly incorporates a degree of ancestor reverence (or even worship). After all the houses have been visited, the skull is returned to its case in the church, where it remains, and can be seen with the other two skulls, for the rest of the year.

and contains a thatched visitor shelter and some unexcavated, minor Maya ruins. There are no hospedajes in San José, but *El Bungalo*, right by the lakeshore, serves good *comida típica* dishes at fair prices.

Some 4km northwest of San José, down a signed track, are the recently restored ruins of the Classic-period settlement of **Motul** (free). The site, which was historically allied to Tikal, is fairly spread out and little visited (though there should be a caretaker about), with four plazas. In Plaza B a large stela in front of a looted temple depicts dancing Maya lords. Plaza C is the biggest, with several mounds and courtyards, while Plaza D has the tallest pyramid. It's a tranquil spot, ideal for bird-watching, and probably best visited by bicycle from either of the villages. If you'd rather just chill out for a while by the lake, there are secluded spots east of the village, including a rocky beach with good swimming.

Continuing east from San José along the dirt road that parallels the northern side of the lake towards El Remate, you pass the isolated villages of San Pedro and Jobompiché. Just west of the latter, *La Lancha* (ⓣ7928 8331, ⓦwww.lalancha.com; ⑨, depending on room and season), a wonderful rustic-chic hotel, has ten very stylish rooms, some with marble floors and tribal carvings, others with Guatemalan fabrics and painted wardrobes, that are perched on cliffs above Lago de Petén Itzá. The hotel, owned by film director Francis Ford Coppola, enjoys a peaceful location (apart from the local troop of howler monkeys) and has a lovely pool and gourmet food; breakfast is included and mountain bikes are free for guests to use.

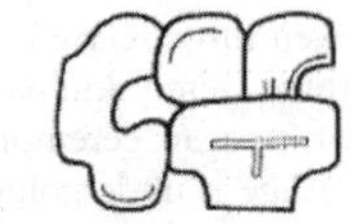

▲ Motul de San José emblem glyph

Two daily buses, plus irregular pick-ups, connect Jobompiché with Santa Elena, passing through El Remate (9km to the east) on the way.

El Remate and around

On the eastern shore of Lago de Petén Itzá, 37km from Santa Elena on the road to Tikal, **EL REMATE** offers a tranquil alternative to staying in Flores.

Just 2km north of the Ixlú junction, it's a small, friendly village, fast growing in popularity as a convenient base for visiting Tikal as well as several other nearby places, such as the **Biotopo Cerro Cahuí,** the ruins of **Ixlú** and the jungle-rich area around the **Laguna Macanché**. There are several high-quality artisan workshops on the lakeshore (close to the edge of the village, heading south to Ixlú) that sell beautifully carved **wooden handicrafts**; stop by Artesanía Ecológical to see expert carver Rolando Soto at work.

Getting to El Remate is easy: every minibus to Tikal passes through the village, while *colectivo* minibuses and public buses from the market in Santa Elena pass through about every forty minutes or so. Coming from the Belize border, get off at Ixlú – from here you can walk or hitch the 2km to El Remate. Leaving the village, local buses pass through El Remate at 5.30am, 7.30am and 8am for Santa Elena, and a swarm of minibuses from Tikal ply the same route from midday onwards. There's also a daily **shuttle bus** to Cobán (via Chisec), leaving at 12.30pm (4hr 45min); it costs US$24 to travel all the way to Cobán, or you could jump off at points including Sayaxché, Candelaria or Chisec on the way. Tickets for this shuttle bus can be bought at *La Casa de Don David*.

Accommodation and eating

El Remate has a good range of **accommodation**, particularly at the budget end of the market. Most of the places listed below have a distinctive charm, and they're fairly well spaced, with no sense of overcrowding. Note that most hotels use cellular phones, and network coverage can be unreliable. A few simple comedores around the village offer inexpensive Guatemalan **food**, and most of the hotels also provide meals. For something a bit more sophisticated, check out the mainly Italian *Restaurant las Orquideas* (just beyond *Casa Mobego*, about 800m west of *La Casa de Don David*), which serves fine pizza, pasta, *bruchette* and breakfasts. Places are listed in the order you approach them from the Ixlú junction.

Camping Sal Itzá 100m down a signed track opposite the lakeshore right at the beginning of the village ⓣ5701 8300. Simple but comfortable stick-and-thatch cabins with mosquito nets and camping on a steep hillside with lake views. Run by a very friendly family, headed by Juan and Catalina, who'll cook tasty local food on request. ❷

Las Sirenas on the right ⓣ7928 8477. Clean, comfortable rooms, some with private bath, in a wooden building with views of the lake. There's a café below and owner Beto Nuñez speaks English and offers guided tours. Telephone and laundry service. ❷

El Mirador del Duende high above the lake, reached by a stairway cut into the cliff ⓣ5301 5576 or 5806 2231, ⓔmicuchitril@hotmail.com. An incredible collection of igloo-like whitewashed stucco cabañas decorated with Maya glyphs, plus space for hammocks and tents. Great chill-out terrace overlooking the lake and cheap vegetarian food. ❷

La Mansión del Pájaro Serpiente just below *El Mirador del Duende* ⓣ & ⓕ7926 8498, ⓔpajaroserpiente@intelnett.com. American-Guatemalan–owned place that offers the best accommodation in the village, with wonderful thatched, two-storey stone cabañas in a tropical garden and smaller rooms, all with superb lake views. The honeymoon suite has its own plunge pool. Good food is also available at US$6 per meal, and there's a small swimming pool. ❺–❼

La Casa de Juan (John's Place) on the right, 300m beyond *La Mansión* ⓣ2224 2555. Simple place with four dark, very basic but nevertheless popular budget rooms. It's owned by an amiable family and has a good inexpensive restaurant and a plant-filled deck above. ❶

La Casa de Don David 300m beyond *La Mansión*, right on the junction ⓣ7928 8469 or 5306 2190, ⓦwww.lacasadedondavid.com. Very well run, spacious and secure accommodation in bungalows and rooms, some with a/c, and with either private cold- or hot-water baths, set in grassy grounds that reach down to the lakeshore. The American/Guatemalan owners really keep the place spotless, and offer great information and filling meals in the attractive restaurant, change money, arrange trips, and sell bus and shuttle bus tickets. ❺–❻, including a meal.

Casa Roja 500m down the road to Cerro Cahuí, on the right ⓣ5909 6999. Also known as *Casa Mobego*, this is a good budget deal right by the lake. Simple, well-constructed stick-and-thatch cabañas, plus camping and an inexpensive vegetarian restaurant. Kayaks for rent. ❷

Casa de Doña Tonita 800m down the road to Cerro Cahuí on the right ⓣ5701 7114. Four basic clapboard rooms, built high above the lake, with great views. The owner also runs a pleasant thatched-roofed restaurant next door with vegetarian food and snacks. ❷

Mon Ami 300m past *Dona Tonita's* ⓣ7928 8413. Attractive rooms and bungalows, with stylish, homely touches, run by an inimitable Frenchman who has lived in Petén for over a decade. Also superb in-house restaurant with many Gallic dishes. ❸–❹

Villa Jardín Maya 200m past *Mon Ami*, on the right above lake road ⓔhoteljardinmaya@hotmail.com. Two near-identical casas, each with four beds, private shower and mosquito nets, run by a very hospitable Guatemalan couple, Héctor and Virginia Monroy. ❷

El Gringo Perdido on the north shore, 3km from *Don David's* ⓣ & ⓕ2334 2305, ⓔgringo_perdido@hotmail.com. Long-established place in a really tranquil lakeside setting offering simple rooms with bath, good-value open-fronted cabañas and camping (US$3 per person), plus a restaurant (dinner is US$7–10). Guided canoe tours available. ❸–❺

Hotel Camino Real Tikal beyond Cerro Cahuí, 5km from the Tikal highway ⓣ7926 0207, ⓦwww.caminorealtikal.com.gt. Large luxury hotel in extensive lakeside grounds with excellent views over the water and a private beach. Rooms are a bit unimaginative and corporate, and there are attendant luxury trappings like electric buggies and a souvenir shop. Windsurfing and sailing, free use of kayaks and a guided tour of the Biotopo Cerro Cahuí is included. ❾, US$132 for a double, though discounted packages are also available.

Ixlú and the Biotopo Cerro Cahuí

Two kilometres south of El Remate, at the Belize and Melchor road junction (formerly known simply as El Cruce), is the tiny village of **Ixlú**, where you'll find a thatched information hut with toilets. Inside, a large map of the area shows the little restored **ruins of Ixlú**, 200m down a signed track from the road, on the shore of **Lago de Salpetén**. The *Zac Petén* restaurant, on the Melchor side of the junction, is the best place to eat; they'll also let you store your bags. A very basic **campsite** has been built on the lakeshore where you can rent canoes.

On the north shore of the lake, 3km west of the centre of El Remate, the **Biotopo Cerro Cahuí** (daily 7am–5pm; US$3.50) is a wildlife conservation area comprising lakeshore, ponds and some of the best examples of undisturbed tropical forest in Petén. The smallest and most accessible of Petén's *biotopos*, it contains a rich diversity of plants and animals, and is especially recommended for bird-watchers. There are hiking trails, a couple of small ruins and two thatched *miradores* on the hill above the lake; pick up maps and information at the gate where you sign in.

Laguna Macanché and around

From the Ixlú junction it's 7km east to the village of **MACANCHÉ**, on the shore of **Laguna Macanché**, where a signed track leads north for 1.8km to another wonderfully tranquil place to stay, the *Santuario Ecológico El Retiro* (ⓣ5704 1300, ⓦwww.retiro-guatemala.com; ❸–❺). Set in forested grounds on the north shore of the lake are private **bungalows** with hot shower and shady porch for US$40 double, as well as spacious, already set-up **tents** (US$7 per person); you can also **camp** for US$3.50 per person. There's a good restaurant and a dock for swimming – and the crocodiles are not usually seen at this end of the lake. In the base area is a **serpentarium** where more than twenty species of snakes native to Guatemala (including the deadly fer-de-lance) and a venomous beaded lizard – *escorpión* in Spanish – are housed in glass tanks in a very secure building. Owner Miguel Meillon keeps the reptiles under licence from the Guatemalan government and a tour, which can include watching the snakes catch and devour rats, costs US$5; other tours are described below. Volunteer workers are usually welcome too; contact Miguel for more information.

On top of the hill behind the base area lie the stone remains of ancient **Maya residential complexes** – but far more intriguing are the numbers of *chultunes* found here. A *chultun* is a gourd-shaped hole carved out of the rock, with a very narrow entrance on top capped by a circular stone. Their exact use is still unknown, though suggested functions include storage chambers, a refuge or a place to conduct ceremonial or religious rites. The best example found so far is just behind the bungalows; this has a main chamber with several side chambers accessed by a spiral ramp: anyone brave enough can sleep here.

El Retiro forms part of an extensive private nature reserve and **crocodile sanctuary** which extends along the lake and into two other lakes beyond. Alejandro, the caretaker and guide at *El Retiro*, can take you on a 45-minute hike through the forest or a ten-minute boat ride to reach the gorgeous **Laguneta El Burro**, just beyond the north shore of Laguna Macanché, and surrounded by thick rainforest dotted with Maya ruins; use of a canoe to paddle around the *laguneta* (small lagoon) is included in the tour. Other trails (each about 45min) lead to another large lake, **Laguna Tintal**, and then on to a *cenote*, a limestone sinkhole 100m across and almost 100m deep. A day tour including lunch, a visit to the serpentarium and all three lagoons costs US$20; a night tour including dinner and a hike and boat trip to spot the crocodiles is US$40.

Tikal

Towering above the rain forest, **Tikal** is possibly the most magnificent of all Maya sites. The ruins, 68km from Flores down a smooth paved road, are dominated by five enormous temples: steep-sided limestone pyramids that rise to more than 60m above the forest floor. Around them are literally thousands of other structures, many semi-strangled by giant roots and still hidden beneath mounds of earth.

The site itself is surrounded by the **Parque Nacional Tikal**, a protected area of some 576 square kilometres which is on the edge of the much larger Reserva de la Biósfera Maya. The trees around the ruins are home to hundreds of species, including howler and spider monkeys, toucans and parakeets. The sheer scale of the place is overwhelming, and its atmosphere spellbinding. Whether you can spare as little as an hour or as long as a week, it's always worth the trip.

Getting there

The best way to reach the ruins is in one of the **tourist minibuses** (US$5 return) that meet flights at Flores airport and pick up passengers from every hotel in Flores and Santa Elena, starting from 5am. It's wise to arrive early at Tikal when the air is fresh and heat less intense, but note that it's rare to witness an impressive **sunrise** over the ruins as the appearance of the sun is generally delayed by mist rising from the humid forest. At any rate, you can't get past the ticket inspection gate until 6am, by which time the sun is beginning to appear.

If you're travelling **from Belize**, change buses at **Ixlú**, the three-way junction at the eastern end of Lago de Petén Itzá, from where there are plenty of passing minibuses (US$2.50 one way) all day long.

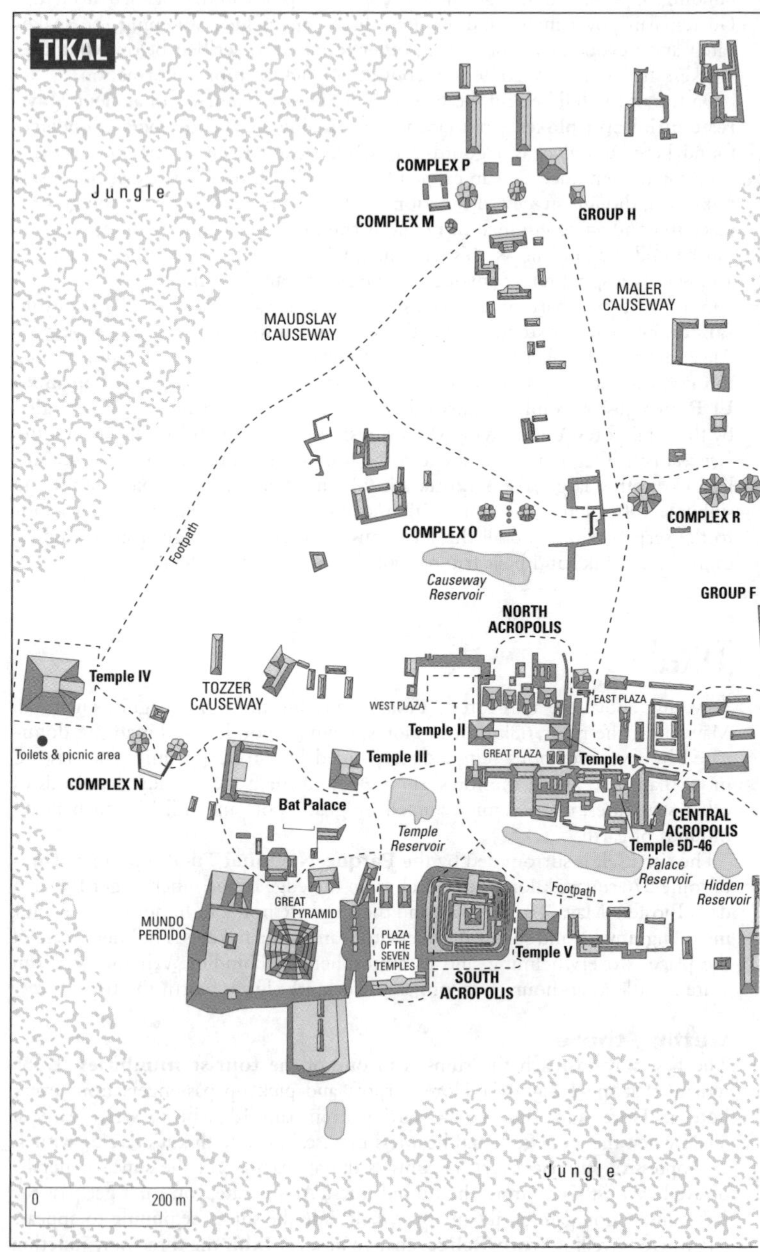
TIKAL
Jungle
COMPLEX P
COMPLEX M
GROUP H
MALER CAUSEWAY
MAUDSLAY CAUSEWAY
Footpath
COMPLEX O
COMPLEX R
Causeway Reservoir
GROUP F
NORTH ACROPOLIS
Temple IV
TOZZER CAUSEWAY
WEST PLAZA
EAST PLAZA
Temple II
GREAT PLAZA
Temple I
Toilets & picnic area
Temple III
COMPLEX N
Bat Palace
CENTRAL ACROPOLIS
Temple 5D-46
Temple Reservoir
Palace Reservoir
Hidden Reservoir
Footpath
GREAT PYRAMID
MUNDO PERDIDO
PLAZA OF THE SEVEN TEMPLES
Temple V
SOUTH ACROPOLIS
Jungle
0
200 m

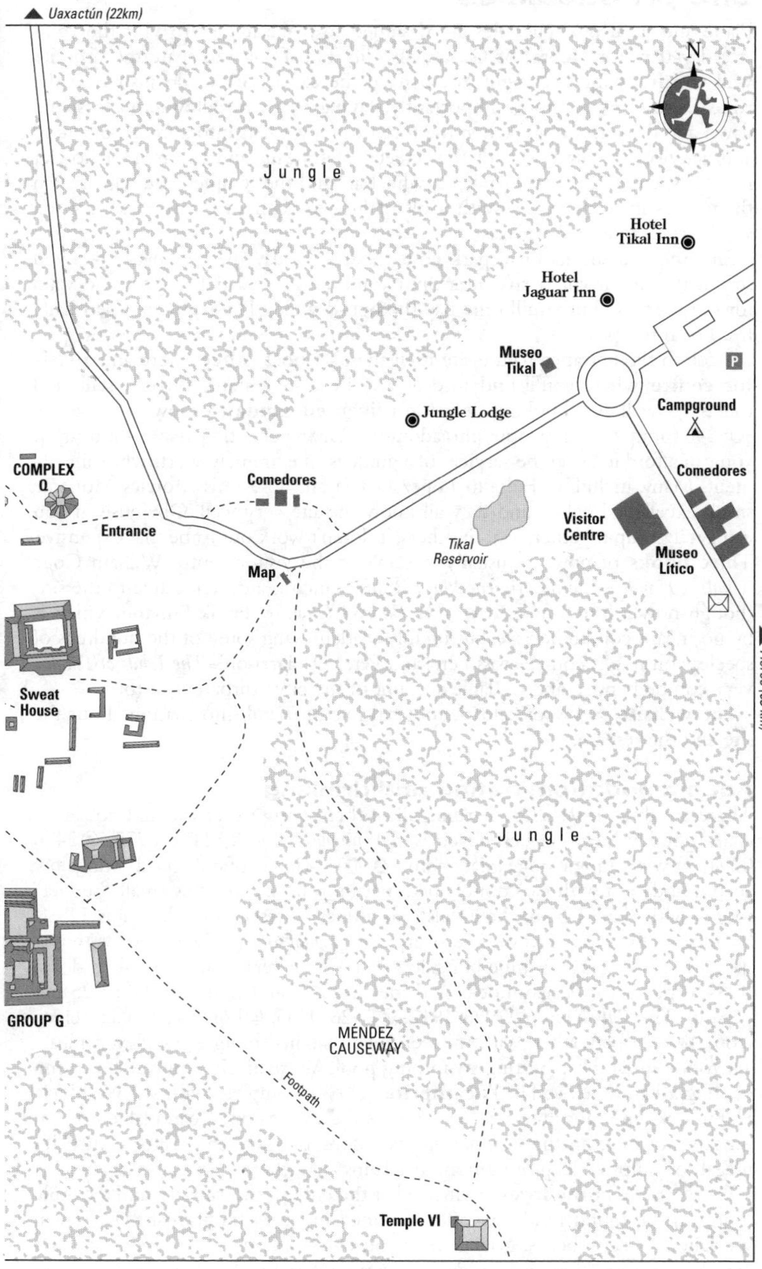

Uaxactún (22km)
N
Jungle
Hotel Tikal Inn
Hotel Jaguar Inn
Museo Tikal
P
Jungle Lodge
Campground
COMPLEX Q
Comedores
Comedores
Entrance
Visitor Centre
Tikal Reservoir
Museo Lítico
Map
Flores (63 km)
Sweat House
Jungle
GROUP G
MÉNDEZ CAUSEWAY
Footpath
Temple VI

Site practicalities

Plane and local bus schedules are designed to make it easy to visit the ruins as a day-trip from Flores or Guatemala City, but if you can spare the time it's well worth staying overnight. You'll need the extra time to do justice to the ruins themselves, but more importantly staying overnight allows you to spend dawn and dusk at the site, when the forest canopy bursts into a frenzy of sound and activity. The air fills with the screech of toucans and the roar of howler monkeys, while flocks of parakeets wheel around the temples, and bats launch themselves into the night. With a bit of luck you might even see a grey fox sneak across one of the plazas.

Entrance to the national park costs US$6.75 a day (payable every day you stay at the site; if you arrive after 3pm you'll be given a ticket that's also valid for the next day but you'll only pay the one-day fee). The ruins are open daily from 6am to 6pm.

Close to the entrance to the site itself there's a **post office**, shops and a **visitor centre**, where you'll find an overpriced café-restaurant, souvenir stalls and toilets, as well as a booking desk for a **licensed guide** to show you the site (US$40 for up to four people, plus additional US$5 per extra person; 4hr tour). If you can afford it, using the services of a guide is an extremely worthwhile investment. Many, including Eulogio López García and José Luis Morales Monzón, speak excellent English, and they all know the site very well. Obviously, if you can get a group together, or join others, it doesn't work out to be that expensive. Three **books** of note are usually available at the visitor centre: William Coe's *Tikal: A Handbook to the Ancient Maya Ruins*, which is a decent guide to the site, though now a little out of date; *The Birds of Tikal*, by Frank Smythe, which is by no means comprehensive, but useful for identifying some of the hundreds of species you might come across here; and Peter D. Harrison's *The Lords of Tikal*, a very comprehensive and readable account of the city's turbulent history.

The **website** Ⓦwww.tikalpark.com has lots of useful information about the site and the reserve.

Accommodation, eating and drinking

There are three **hotels** at the ruins, all of them fairly expensive and not especially good value. The best place is the *Jungle Lodge* (Ⓣ2476 8775, Ⓕ2476 0294, Ⓦwww.junglelodge.guate.com; ❺–❼), which offers good bungalow accommodation with two double beds per bungalow, and a few small "budget" rooms with shared bath; there's also an attractive restaurant (dinner is US$8, breakfast US$4) and a pool. The overpriced *Jaguar Inn* (Ⓣ7926 0002, Ⓦwww.jaguartikal.com; ❻) has nine bungalows with little verandahs, a five-bed dorm (US$10 per person), hammocks with nets (US$5) and camping (US$3.25 per person). The *Tikal Inn* (Ⓣ7926 1917, Ⓕ7926 0065, Ⓔhoteltikalinn@intelgua.com; ❻) is a better bet, with thirteen nice thatched bungalows, eleven pleasant rooms and a heat-busting swimming pool. Alternatively, you can also camp or sling a hammock at Tikal's **campsite** (US$4), complete with shower block. Hammocks and mosquito nets (essential in the wet season) are available for rent on the spot or from the *Comedor Imperio Maya*, opposite the visitor centre. It's illegal to camp or sleep out among the ruins.

Three simple **comedores** are located at the entrance to the site, and a couple more can be found inside; all offer a limited menu of traditional Guatemalan specialities – eggs, beans, grilled meat and chicken. For a more extensive and expensive menu, head for the decent restaurant at the *Jungle Lodge*. Cold soft drinks are sold around the ruins by vendors.

The site museums

At the entrance, between the *Jungle Lodge* and *Jaguar Inn* hotels, the one-room **Museo Tikal** (Mon–Fri 9am–5pm, Sat & Sun 9am–4pm; US$1.30) houses some of the artefacts found in the ruins, including ceramics, obsidian eccentric flints, the jade jewellery found in Tumba 116 and the magnificent **Stela 31**, which was inaugurated in 445 AD. This limestone monument shows Tikal ruler Siyah Chan K'awil (Stormy Sky) wearing a jaguar-head belt and a jade necklace, flanked by two warriors bearing non-Maya Teotihuacán-style spear throwers and darts as well as shields decorated with the "goggle-eyed" image of the rain god Tlaloc. The stela was cut to mark the completion of the first *katun* under Stormy Sky's rule, but the lengthy glyphic inscriptions on the rear confirm clear alliance with the Mexican metropolis of Teotihuacán.

The museum also has a spectacular reconstruction of the great ruler **Hasaw Chan K'awil's tomb**. One of the richest ever found in the Maya world, the tomb contained 180 worked jade items in the form of bracelets, anklets, necklaces and earplugs, and delicately incised bones, including a famous carving depicting deities paddling a canoe to the underworld. A larger bone, also found at the tomb, shows a poignant image of a bound captive, no doubt awaiting a sacrificial death. The accompanying text explains that this unfortunate individual is from the neighbouring city of Calakmul – the other "superpower" state to the north – a city that Hasaw Chan K'awil defeated in a seminal victory in 695 AD, reversing more than a century of subjugation. There are plans to renovate this museum soon.

The **Museo Lítico** (same hours as Museo Tikal; free), inside the visitor centre, holds nineteen more stelae, though they are very poorly labelled and there is no supplementary information in English.

The rise and fall of Tikal

The following account is a summary of the latest findings based on the interpretations of inscriptions from Tikal itself and texts gathered from numerous other sites throughout Petén, Mexico and Belize. According to this latest evidence, the first occupants of Tikal arrived around 900 BC, probably attracted by its position above surrounding seasonal swamps and by the availability of flint for making tools and weapons. For the next four hundred years, though the village grew and prospered slowly, there's nothing to suggest that it was anything more than a tiny settlement of thatched huts. By 500 BC, however, the first steps of a modest astronomical stone temple had been constructed (which were later used as foundations for the great pyramid in the Mundo Perdido), though burials at this time were still relatively simple and ceramics found had been crudely executed. Tikal remained a minor settlement during the latter years of the Middle Preclassic (1000–400 BC), while 50km to the north, towering temples were being built at **Nakbé**, the first city to emerge from the Petén forest.

It's in the Late Preclassic era, after 250 BC, that the first significant ceremonial structures began to be constructed. The Mundo Perdido structure was enlarged to form a pyramid, and small temples were built in the **North Acropolis**, though the absence of royal burials and the relatively modest size of these buildings mean that Tikal was a peripheral settlement at this stage. Dominating the entire northern region of Petén, the formidable city-state of **El Mirador** (see p.362) was the first Maya "superpower", though its Preclassic hegemony was later to be challenged by a distant, and even more powerful player – **Teotihuacán** in central Mexico.

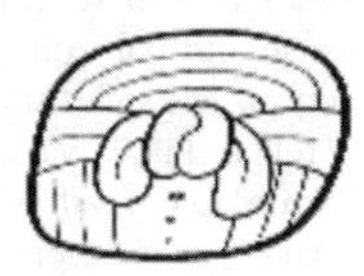

▲ Tikal emblem glyph

By the time of Christ, the **Great Plaza** had begun to take shape and Tikal was already established as an important site with a large permanent population. For the next two centuries, art and architecture became increasingly ornate and sophisticated as the great pyramid was enlarged to over 30m in height, its sides adorned by huge stucco masks. The styles that were to dominate throughout the Classic period were perfected in these early years, and by 200 AD all the major architectural traits had evolved. It's during this period that **Yax Ehb' Xok** (First Step Shark) established the first ruling dynasty of the city, somewhere between 100 and 200 AD. Though there were earlier kings, the royal lineage established by Yax Ehb' Xok was recognized by all 33 (known) subsequent kings of Tikal, until the record fades in 869 AD.

The closing years of the Late Preclassic era (400 BC–250 AD) were marked by the eruption of the Ilopango volcano in El Salvador, which smothered a huge area of the highlands, including much of Guatemala and Honduras, in a thick layer of volcanic ash. Trade routes were disrupted and alliance patterns altered. The ensuing years saw the decline and abandonment of El Mirador, creating a power vacuum and opening the way for the expansion of several smaller sites. To the south of El Mirador, Tikal and Uaxactún emerged as substantial centres of trade, science and religion. Less than a day's walk apart and growing rapidly, the cities engaged in heated competition.

Matters finally came to a head on January 31, 378 AD, when, during the last year of the reign of Chak Tok Ich'aak (Jaguar Paw I), Tikal's warriors overran Uaxactún. The secret of Tikal's success appears to have been its alliance with Teotihuacán, and the introduction of new warfare technology from central Mexico. Inscriptions attest that it was the arrival of a somewhat mysterious warrior, **Siyak K'ak'** (Fire-Born), "from the west" that helped seal the victory. This general is thought to have been dispatched by the Teotihuacán king, Spearthrower Owl, armed with the latest technology: an *atlatl* (a wooden sling capable of firing arrows). Recent re-valuation of texts suggests that it's probable that the warrior Siyak K'ak' ordered the execution of Jaguar Paw I. It's clear that this was nothing less than a Mexican-directed takeover, for the next king installed at Tikal, Yax Nuun Ayin I (First Crocodile but also known as Curl Nose), was the son of Spearthrower Owl. First Crocodile married into the Tikal dynasty, and started a new royal lineage, though efforts were made to pay careful reverence to the deposed ruler Jaguar Paw I, and his palace (Structure 5D-46) remained a revered royal residence for the next four centuries.

Tikal in the Classic period (400–909 AD)

The victory over Uaxactún enabled Tikal to dominate the central Petén for much of the next five hundred years. During this time it became one of the most elaborate and magnificent of all Maya city-states, monopolizing the crucial lowland trade routes, its influence reaching as far as Copán in Honduras and Yaxchilán on the Usumacinta. The elite immediately launched an extensive rebuilding programme, including a radical remodelling of the North Acropolis and the renovation of most of the city's finest temples. It's clear that Tikal's alliance with Teotihuacán remained an important part of its continuing power: stelae and paintings from the period show that subsequent Tikal rulers adopted central Mexican styles of clothing, pottery and warfare.

Yet as Tikal was expanding and growing in size during the fifth century, a formidable rival Maya "superpower" – **Calakmul**, or the Kingdom of the Snake – was emerging in the jungles to the north. Through an aggressive series of regional alliances, Calakmul steadily encircled Tikal with enemy cities, filling the power vacuum in the Maya heartland that had developed as the influence

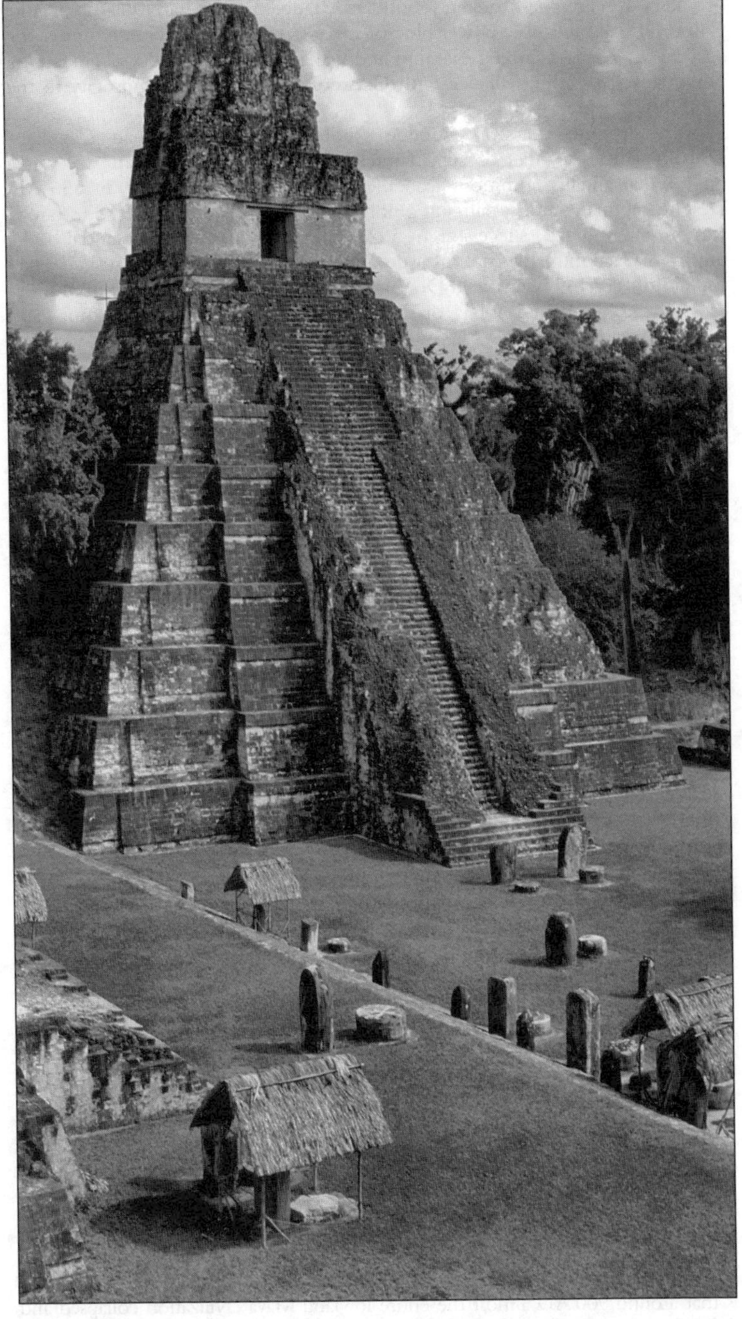

△ Temple I, Tikal

of Tikal's overstretched backer, Teotihuacán, faded. By the Early Classic period, Calakmul had built up a power bloc of vassal states, many previously under the auspices of Tikal, including Naranjo and Waka' (see p.374), and was courting a potentially devastating alliance with **Caracol**, a powerful emerging city to the southeast, in modern Belize.

In an apparent attempt to subdue a potential rival, Wak Chan K'awil, or **Double Bird**, the ruler of Tikal, launched an attack (known as an "axe war") on Caracol and its ambitious leader, Yahaw Te ("**Lord Water**"), in 556 AD. Despite capturing and sacrificing a noble from Caracol, Double Bird's strategy was only temporarily successful. In 562 AD, Lord Water (with substantial backing from Calakmul) hit back in a devastating "star war", which crushed Tikal and almost certainly sacrificed Double Bird. The victors stamped their authority over the humiliated nobles of Tikal, smashing stelae, desecrating tombs and destroying written records. The subsequent 130-year period, for which virtually no inscribed monuments have been uncovered at Tikal, has long been referred to as Tikal's "**hiatus**", but very recent findings at Temple V – which was probably built during this period – have forced Mayanists to re-evaluate the concept of an extended hiatus. It is clear, however, that despite the defeat in 562 AD, Tikal was never broken.

Towards the end of the seventh century, Calakmul's position of dominance had begun to weaken, and Tikal gradually started to recover its lost power under the formidable leadership of Hasaw Chan K'awil, or **Heavenly Standard Bearer** (682–723 AD). During his reign the main ceremonial areas, the East Plaza and the North Acropolis, were completely remodelled, reclaimed from the desecration suffered at the hands of Calakmul and Caracol. By 695 AD, Tikal was powerful enough to launch an attack against Calakmul, capturing and executing its king, Yich'aak K'ak' (known as **Fiery Claw** or **Jaguar Paw**) and severely weakening the alliance against Tikal. The following year, Hasaw Chan K'awil repeated his astonishing coup by capturing **Split Earth**, the new king of Calakmul, and Tikal regained its position as the dominant city in the Maya world.

Hasaw Chan K'awil's leadership gave birth to a revitalized and powerful ruling dynasty: in the hundred years following his death five of Tikal's main temples were built, and his son, Yik'in Chan K'awil, or **Divine Sunset Lord** (who ascended the throne in 734 AD), had his father's body entombed in the magnificent **Temple I**. He also constructed Temple VI, remodelled the Central Acropolis and principal city causeways, and defeated Waka' and Naranjo in 743 AD and 744 AD, breaking the ring of hostile cities that encircled Tikal. Around this time, at the height of the Classic period, Tikal's population had grown to somewhere around 100,000 (some Mayanists argue for much more) spread across a central area covering about thirty square kilometres. Its authority also extended to include a series of vassal states, among them Naranjo, Waka', Uaxactún and many more minor settlements – a domain of perhaps 500,000 subjects. During this time we know the city was called **Mutul** – "Knot of Hair" – the name taken from Tikal's emblem glyph, which depicts the rear view of a head, with what appears to be a knotted headband around it.

By the beginning of the ninth century, severe signs of crisis emerged across the entire Maya region – probably sparked by a period of climate change, including a catastrophic drought. Population levels at Tikal plummeted, as people fled the area, and Tikal's last recorded monument is inscribed on Stela 24, completed in 869 AD. What brought about Tikal's final **downfall** remains a mystery, but what is certain is that around 900 AD almost the entire lowland Maya civilization collapsed and that Tikal was effectively abandoned by the end of the tenth century. Afterwards, the site was used from time to time by other groups, who worshipped here and repositioned many of the stelae, but it was never occupied again.

Rediscovery

After its mysterious decline little is known of Tikal until 1695 when Father Avendaño, lost in the maze of swamps, stumbled upon a "variety of old buildings". The colonial powers were distinctly unimpressed by Petén and for the next 150 years the ruins were left to the jungle. In 1848 they were rediscovered by a government expedition led by Modesto Méndez. Later in the nineteenth century, a Swiss scientist visited the site and removed the beautifully carved wooden lintels from the tops of Temples I and IV – they are in a museum in Basel – and in 1881 the English archeologist Maudslay took the first photographs of the ruins, showing the main temples cloaked in tropical vegetation.

Until 1951 the site could only be reached – with considerable difficulty – on horseback, and although there was a steady trickle of visitors the ruins remained mostly uncleared. Then the Guatemalan army built an airstrip, paving the way for an invasion of archeologists and tourists. The gargantuan project to excavate and restore the site started in 1956, and involved teams from the University of Pennsylvania in the US and Guatemala's Institute of Anthropology. Much of the major work was completed by 1984, but thousands of minor buildings remain buried by roots, shoots and rubble. There's little doubt that an incredible amount is waiting to be found – as recently as 1996 a workman unearthed a stela (Stela 40, dating from 468 AD) while mowing the grass on the Great Plaza. In 2003 inscriptions discovered at Temple V have provided convincing evidence that Tikal may not have suffered a Classic-era hiatus at all.

The ruins

The sheer scale of the ruins at Tikal can at first seem daunting. The **central area**, with its five main temples, forms by far the most impressive section; if you start to explore beyond this, you can ramble seemingly forever in the maze of smaller, **unrestored structures** and complexes. Compared with the scale and magnificence of the main area, they're not that impressive, but armed with a good **map** (the best is in Coe's guide to the ruins, available in the visitor centre), it can be exciting to search for some of the rarely visited outlying sections. Don't even think about exploring the more distant structures without a map; every year at least one tourist gets lost in the jungle.

From the entrance to the Great Plaza

Walking into the ruins, a path bears to the right from the site **map** towards the prosaically named **Complex Q** and **Complex R**, two of the seven sets of twin pyramids. Commissioned by Yax Ain II, also known as **Chitam**, one of Tikal's last known rulers, they were built to mark the passing of a *katun* (twenty 360-day years). Twinned pyramids are an architectural feature found only in the Tikal region, with several at the city itself, and a few others found at sites nearby (including Nakúm, Yaxhá and Ixlú). At Complex Q (inaugurated in 771 AD), the first set you come to, only one of the pyramids has been restored, with the stelae and altars re-erected in front of it. The stelae at the base of the pyramid are blank, as a result of erosion, but there's a copy of a superbly carved example, **Stela 22** (the original of which can be seen in the Museo Lítico inside the visitor centre). The carvings on Stela 22 record the ascension to the throne of Chitam II, portrayed in full regalia, complete with an enormous sweeping headdress and the staff of authority.

Following the path as it bears around to the left after the twin temples of **Complex R** (built in 790 AD) you approach the back of Temple I through the **East Plaza**. On the left side, behind a small ball court, is a broad platform supporting a series of small buildings known as the **marketplace**, and in the southeast corner of the plaza stands an imposing temple, beneath which were found the remains of several severed heads, the victims of human sacrifice. Behind the marketplace, the **Sweat House** probably functioned as a kind of sauna (similar to those used by highland Maya today). Priests and rulers would have taken a sweat bath in order to cleanse themselves before conducting religious rituals.

From here, a few short steps bring you to the **Great Plaza**, the heart of the ancient city. Surrounded by four massive structures, this was the focus of ceremonial and religious activity at Tikal for around a thousand years, and was still in use long after the rest of the city had been abandoned. The earliest part is the North Acropolis; the two great temple-pyramids (which disrupted the city's original north–south axis) weren't built until the eighth century. The plaza covers an area of one and a half acres, and beneath today's grass lie four layers of paving, the oldest of which dates from about 150 BC and the most recent from 700 AD. Climbing Temple I has been prohibited for several years, but there are terrific views from Temple II (which is usually possible to climb, though access is periodically closed after heavy rain as the steps become very slippy).

Temple I, towering 44m above the plaza, is the hallmark of Tikal – it's also known as the Jaguar Temple because of the jaguar carved in its door lintel, though this is now in a museum in Basel. The temple was built as a burial monument to contain the magnificent **tomb of Hasaw Chan K'awil**, one of Tikal's greatest rulers, who ascended the throne in 682 AD (see p.352) and defeated the archenemy state of Calakmul. It was constructed shortly after his death in 721 AD, under the direction of his son and successor, Yik'in Chan K'awil, though it's now thought likely that Hasaw Chan K'awil planned his tomb and burial temple himself. Within the tomb at the temple's core, his remains were found facing north, surrounded by an assortment of jade, pearls, seashells and stingray spines, which were a traditional symbol of human sacrifice. There were also some magnificent bone ornaments, perhaps spoils of victory over Calakmul, depicting a journey to the underworld made in a canoe rowed by mythical animal figures. A reconstruction of the tomb (Tumba 116) is on show in the Museo Tikal.

Architecturally, Temple I was radically different from anything that had been constructed in the Maya region up to that point – an unequivocal statement of confidence no doubt designed to reassert Tikal's position as a dominant power. Comprising a series of nine ascending platforms, the style emphasises the vertical dimensions of the temple and draws the eye to the roof comb. To create this soaring effect, hundreds of tons of flint and rubble were poured on top of the completed tomb and the temple was built around this, with a staircase of thick plastered blocks running up the front. The staircase was a skeleton structure, over which the final surface would have been constructed. The whole thing is topped by a three-room building and a hollow roof comb that was originally painted in cream, red and possibly green. On the front of the comb it's just possible to make out a seated figure and a stylized serpent.

Standing opposite, like a squatter version of Temple I, is **Temple II**, also known as the Temple of the Masks for the two grotesque masks, now heavily eroded, that flank the central stairway. The temples were arranged to form a twin pyramid alignment, and their construction marked a seminal change to the ceremonial core of the city. Not only was the sheer size of these new temples a powerful statement, but their position purposely deflected attention away from the adjacent North Acropolis, rising above the monuments where Tikal's elite had been buried for at least five hundred years. It's not exactly certain when Temple II was completed, though it dates from the beginning of the eighth century, and almost certainly predates Temple I by a few years. As yet no tomb has been found beneath this temple, but it's thought to have been built to honour Hasaw Chan K'awil's wife, Lady Twelve Macaw. The structure now stands 38m high, although with its roof comb intact it would have equalled Temple I. If access is permitted, it's an easy climb up the staircase to the top, from where the echo is fantastically clear and crisp; and the view, almost level with the forest canopy, is incredible, with the great plaza spread out below.

The North Acropolis

Occupying the whole north side of the plaza, the **North Acropolis** is one of the most complex structures in the entire Maya world. In traditional Maya style it was built and rebuilt on top of itself, and beneath the twelve temples that can be seen today are the remains of about a hundred other structures. As early as 100 BC the Maya had constructed elaborate platforms supporting temples and tombs here; in about 250 AD the entire thing was torn down and rebuilt as a platform and four vaulted temples, each of which was rebuilt twice during Early Classic times. Archeologists have removed some of the surface to reveal these earlier structures, including two four-metre-high Preclassic stone **masks**, which can be glimpsed under thatched protective roofs, one of which depicts a hook-nosed god with earplugs wearing a crown-like headdress. Originally these great masks, which adorn many Maya Preclassic temple staircases, would have been finished with a stucco coating of limestone and painted in scarlet and green. In 1959 a trench was dug deep beneath the platform of the North Acropolis, unearthing a burial chamber in which the body of a ruler lay surrounded by nine retainers killed for the occasion, along with turtles, a crocodile and a mass of pottery.

Two lines of **stelae** with circular altars at their bases, all of which were originally painted a brilliant red, stand in front of the North Acropolis. These were once thought to show images of the gods, but it's now known that the carvings are of members of Tikal's ruling elite. These rulers were certainly obsessive in their recording of the city's dynastic sequence, linking it with great historical moments and reaching as far back into the past as possible. Many of the stelae bear the marks of ritual defacement, perpetrated by invaders from Caracol and Calakmul during the Classic era, acts carried out by conquerors as rites of humiliation. Several of the stelae now in the main plaza were set up in their current positions long after the decline of the city by people who still worshipped here.

The Central Acropolis

On the other side of the plaza, the **Central Acropolis** is a maze of 45 tiny interconnecting rooms and stairways built around six smallish courtyards. The buildings here are usually referred to as palaces rather than temples, although their precise use remains a mystery. Possibilities include law courts, temporary retreats, administrative centres and residences for Tikal's elite. What we do know is that the buildings were constantly altered and adapted, with rooms, walls and doorways added and repositioned regularly. One of the very few buildings whose function has been identified is **Structure 5D-46**, which sits towards the eastern end of the complex. This mundanely named, partly ruined rectangular building with short frontal and rear stone staircases dates from around

360 AD, when it was built as the residential home of Chak Tok Ich'aak I (Great Jaguar Paw). One of the most famous of Tikal's early kings, he was revered in the city's historical records until the inscriptions fade out in the ninth century. It's thought Structure 5D-46 was a royal residence for at least 400 years, and its importance deemed so hallowed that no ruler carried out any significant structural alterations after the fourth century AD. Take a look, too, at the large two-storey building in Court 2 known as **Maler's Palace**, named after the archeologist Teobert Maler who made it his home during expeditions in 1895 and 1904. Behind the acropolis is the palace reservoir, one of at least twelve clay-lined pools that were fed by a series of channels with rainwater from all over the city.

From the West Plaza to Temple IV

Behind Temple II is the **West Plaza**, dominated by a large Late Classic palace on the north side, and scattered with various altars and stelae, which, like those in the Great Plaza, owe their present position to Postclassic people, who rearranged many of the smaller monuments. From here the **Tozzer Causeway** – one of the raised routes that connected the main parts of the city – leads west to the unrestored **Temple III** (60m), covered in jungle vegetation and inaccessible to visitors. A fragment of Stela 24, found at the base of the temple, dates it at June 24, 810 AD, which marked the end of a *katun*. It was customary to construct twin temples to mark this auspicious event, but by this time it's clear that the Classic Maya were in severe difficulties across the region and just raising the manpower necessary to build Temple III would have been quite an achievement. Many Mayanists believe Temple III is a burial monument to Dark Sun, the last of Tikal's great rulers, and that it is he depicted as a portly figure wearing a magnificent jaguar costume on the badly eroded lintels that crown the temple's summit. Around the back of the building is a huge palace complex, of which only the broad-staircased **Bat Palace** has been restored. Further down the causeway, on the left-hand side, is **Complex N**, another set of Late Classic twin pyramids. In the northern enclosure of the complex, the superbly carved **Stela 16** shows a flamboyantly dressed Hasaw Chan K'awil, who was buried beneath Temple I, depicted with a huge plumed headdress. **Altar 5** at its base bears a sculpted scene of Hasaw presiding over a sacrificial skull and bones with a lord from Maasal, formerly a vassal state of Calakmul, a clear indicator that Tikal had successfully expanded into the orbit of its bitter rival by 711 AD when the altar was completed. The accompanying text mentions the death of Hasaw's wife, Lady Twelve Macaw. Both Altar 5 and Stela 16 are aligned with Temples I and II, the monuments dedicated to Hasaw and his wife in the great plaza.

At the end of the Tozzer Causeway, **Temple IV** is the tallest of all the Tikal structures at a massive 64.6m (212ft). Built in 741 AD by Yik'in Chan K'awil (Hasaw's son), it is thought by many archeologists to be his burial monument, though no tomb has yet been found here. It's most famous for the stunning carved **wooden lintels**, embellished with images of the victorious king and a riot of glyphs, that were built into the top of the temple. Nowadays you'll have to travel to Switzerland to see them – though you can see an excellent replica of Lintel 3 in Guatemala City's archeological museum.

Twin ladders, one for the ascent, the other for the descent, attached to the sides of the temple delineate the route up, past the tangle of roots and trees that grip the sides of the unrestored temple. Slow and exhausting as the climb is, the finest views of the whole site await. All around you the forest canopy stretches out to the horizon, over the ruins of Naranjo towards the Maya Mountains of

Belize, interrupted only by the great roof combs of the other temples. Given the vistas, it's not surprising that the sunrise tribe gather here in great numbers, and though the humidity and mist usually shroud the visuals somewhat, the dawn jungle chorus rarely fails to disappoint.

From Temple IV the **Maudslay Causeway** leads to **Group H**, which includes two more twin-pyramid structures, and from here the **Maler Causeway** takes you back down to the East Plaza, past yet another set.

The Mundo Perdido and the Plaza of the Seven Temples

The other main buildings in the centre of Tikal are to the southeast of Temple IV. The first of these, occupying the **Mundo Perdido**, or Lost World, form another magical and very distinct section of the site with its own atmosphere and architecture. Little is known about the ruins in this part of the city, but archeologists hope that further research will help to explain the early history of Tikal. The main feature is the **Great Pyramid**, a 32-metre-high structure whose surface hides four earlier versions, the first an astronomical temple from 500 BC. The top of the pyramid offers awesome views towards Temple IV and the Great Plaza and makes an excellent base to watch the visual dramatics at sunrise or sunset – though note that the temple is roped off after heavy rain, when the steps can be slippery. Just east of here, the **Plaza of the Seven Temples** forms part of a complex dating back to before Christ. There's an unusual triple ball court on the north side of this plaza and its eastern flank is formed by the unexcavated South Acropolis.

Temple V, Temple VI and beyond

A short trail from the southern part of the Plaza of the Seven Temples leads to the rear of the 58-metre-high **Temple V**, whose commanding, flared facade has now been fully restored after a seven-year restoration project. The latest evidence suggests that this monument, the construction of which took fifty years, was started around 600 AD by the ruler Animal Skull (which would make it the original of Tikal's six great temples) though very little about Temple III is currently known. A vertiginous wooden staircase (closed when it's been raining heavily) attached to the side of the temple accesses a very slender upper level, just beneath the roof comb, from where you get a stomach-churning perspective of the temples of the Great Plaza and an ocean of jungle beyond.

Finally, there's **Temple VI**, also known as the Temple of the Inscriptions, reached along the Méndez Causeway from the Central Acropolis. The temple (only rediscovered in 1957), about 1km from the plaza, is another of Yik'in Chan K'awil's constructions, completed in 766 AD. It's a medium-sized temple, famous for its twelve-metre roof comb, on the back of which is a huge hieroglyphic text, only just visible these days. More than 180 glyphs chart the history of the city from a founding date in 1139 BC (which is more than two hundred years before the first archeological evidence of settlement), though this date was almost certainly guesswork by the Classic Maya. Temple VI is another candidate as the burial place of Yik'in Chan K'awil, Tikal's most prodigious monument builder, along with Temple IV.

Outside the main area are countless smaller **unrestored structures**. Compared with the scale and magnificence of what you've seen already they're not that impressive, but armed with a good map (the best is in Coe's guide to the ruins), it can be exciting to explore some of the rarely visited outlying sections. Tikal is certain to exhaust you before you exhaust it.

Uaxactún and around

▲ Uaxactún emblem glyph

Twenty-three kilometres north of Tikal, the abode and clapboard houses that comprise the friendly village of **UAXACTÚN** are spread out on both sides of an airstrip, as are the ruins of the same name. With a couple of places to stay, a few comedores and a daily bus to Flores, the village is an ideal jumping-off point for the remote northern ruins of **El Zotz** and **Río Azul**. Substantially smaller than Tikal, the site (known as Sia'an K'aan in Maya times) rose to prominence in the Late Preclassic era when it grew to become a major player. It's known that both Uaxactún and Tikal were overshadowed by the presence of the El Mirador to the north until the first century AD, but once the influence of the Maya world's first superpower started to decline, rivalry between Tikal and Uaxactún took off as both cities began to expand, embarking on grand building programmes. The two finally clashed on January 16, 378 AD, when Tikal's warriors conquered Uaxactún. It's very likely that the key to this victory was the introduction of new warfare technology from Mexico – spearthrowing slings – by Teotihuacán warrior Siyak K'ak, who had just overturned the ruling Tikal dynasty. Tikal's victory at Uaxactún, within days of the arrival of the Mexicans, was to prove a seminal event, announcing the new leader's aggressive intent to the rest of the Petén's cities and condemning Uaxactún to six hundred years of subordinate status. Quite simply, Uaxactún never recovered.

Uaxactún **ruins** (no fee) may be a little disappointing after the grandeur of Tikal, but you'll probably have the site to yourself, giving you the chance to soak up the atmosphere as you explore the several substantial structures here. Village children will offer to guide you around; their charm is irresistible – as are the dolls made from corn husks decorated with beads and dried flowers you'll be implored to buy – though their archeological knowledge is limited. A tip of a quetzal or two is fine.

The most interesting buildings are in **Group E**, east of the airstrip, where three low, reconstructed temples – Temples E-1, E-II and E-III – built side by side, are arranged to function as an observatory. Viewed from the top of a fourth temple, the sun rises behind the north temple (E-I) on the longest day of the year and behind the southern one (E-III) on the shortest day. It's an architectural pattern that was first discovered here but has since been found at a number of other sites. This point of observation is above the famous **E-VII sub**, a buried Preclassic temple that was once thought to date back to 2000 BC, though a much later date is now accepted. The pyramid has simple staircases on all sides, the steps flanked by pairs of elaborate **stucco masks** of jaguar and serpent heads. It's clear that this was a sacred monument, a platform for bloodletting and sacrifice, for the jaguar signifies the Jaguar God of the underworld, one of the most powerful deities; the serpent is the fabled "vision serpent".

On the other side of the airstrip are **Groups A** and **B**, a series of larger temples and residential compounds, some of them reconstructed, spread out across the high ground. In amongst the structures are some impressive stelae, each sheltered by a small thatched roof, but most lying poignantly broken and supine.

Practicalities

A **bus** from Flores passes through Tikal en route for Uaxactún at around 3pm; alternatively, you could take a tour from Flores (see p.328). **Staying overnight** you have two options. The welcoming *Campamento Ecológico El Chiclero* (Ⓣ & Ⓕ7926 1095; ❸) offers clean rooms with decent mattresses and nets or a place to camp or sling up a hammock (US$3); bathrooms are shared but kept clean. Owner Antonio Baldizón also organizes 4WD trips to Río Azul and excursions to Naachtún, and his wife Neria prepares excellent food (large-portioned meals are served here for US$5 a time). Otherwise *Aldana's* (❷) run by Bárbara Aldana is friendly but very basic, with wooden rooms and camping (US$2 per person). For a cheap **meal**, head to *Comedor Uaxactún* on the north side of the airstrip.

Doña Neria at *El Chiclero* is also in charge of the **Museo Juan Antonio Valdes** (free) in the grounds of the hotel. Guarded only by chicken wire and a padlock, the museum has an astonishing collection of intact vases, plates and other ceramics crammed onto the wooden shelves. Many of the vessels are decorated with glyphs and animal figures, and some have a hole drilled in the centre to ceremonially "kill" the power they contain. Other items include a beautiful necklace and flint axe-heads, polished to a glass-like gleam.

El Zotz and Río Azul

Lost in a sea of jungle around Tikal are several other substantial **ruins** – unrestored and for the most part uncleared but with their own unique atmosphere. The bulk of the temples lies beneath mounds of earth, their sides coated in vegetation, and only the tallest roof combs are still visible. A dirt road heads north to Río Azul (a controversial plan is being considered to make this a highway into Mexico), and a track heads west to El Zotz. So if you're in search of adventure and want to see a virtually untouched Maya ruin, these sites are perfect.

El Zotz

Twenty-five kilometres west of Uaxactún, along a rough jeep track that's sometimes passable in the dry season (by 4WD), **El Zotz** is a large Maya site set in its own *biotopo* next to the Tikal national park. To **get there** speak to the owners of *El Chiclero* in Uaxactún or the tour operators in Flores (see p.328), who can arrange pack horses, equipment and a guide; a three-day trip costs about US$149. Setting out from Uaxactún, it's about a four-hour hike to **Santa Cruz**, where settlers, including Pablo Pérez, make a living from selling honey and crocodile skins. Pablo will direct you to the *aguada* for water (you'll need a filter) and will let you camp if you decide to split the journey. At the site itself, you'll be welcomed by the guards who look after the *biotopo* headquarters. You can camp here and, with permission, use the kitchen and drinking water. Remember to bring some food to share with the guards.

Totally unrestored, El Zotz has been systematically looted, although there are guards on duty all year now and there's also a CECON biological station close to the ruins. The three main temples are smothered in soil and vegetation, but using the workers' scaffold you can climb to the top of the tallest structure, the **devil's pyramid**, which is spectacular in itself. The roof combs of the Tikal temples, 23km west of here, can be glimpsed on clear days. Zotz means "bat" in Maya and each evening at dusk you'll see tens, perhaps hundreds, of thousands of **bats** of several species emerge from a cave near the campsite. It's especially impressive in the moonlight, the beating wings sounding like a river flowing over rapids – one of the most remarkable natural sights in Petén. Keep an eye out, too, for bat falcons, swooping with talons outstretched in search of their prey.

Walking on, it takes about four and a half hours to get to **Cruce Dos Aguadas**, a crossroads village populated by Q'eqchi' Maya on the bus route from Santa Elena to Carmelita. There are a couple of basic tiendas and comedores here, the best of which is *Comedor Patojas*, where they'll let you sling a hammock or camp. Northwards it's 41km to Carmelita for El Mirador and about the same distance west to Pasos Caballos for Waka' (a trip that's not possible in the rainy season). It's actually a little quicker to get to El Zotz independently if you do this trip in reverse, by getting a bus or pick-up from San Andrés to Cruce Dos Aguadas and walking or hitching from there. Some *xatero* trucks go right past the site and the guards usually know when one will pass by for the return journey. While this route is shorter, entailing less walking, there's also less forest cover than on the route from Uaxactún, and less chance of seeing wildlife.

Río Azul

The remote site of **Río Azul**, almost on the tripartite border where Guatemala, Belize and Mexico meet, was only rediscovered in 1962. The city and its suburbs are thought to have had a population of at least five thousand, scattered over 750 acres. Although totally unrestored, the core of the site resembles Tikal in many ways, though it is smaller. The tallest temple (A-III) stands some 47m above the forest floor, poking its head out above the treetops and giving magnificent views across the jungle.

▲ Río Azul emblem glyph

Investigations suggest that the site dates back to the Middle Preclassic period, though the population soared in the Early Classic era between 410 AD and 530 AD. This period of rapid expansion coincides with the emergence of the new Teotihuacán–Tikal alliance, and it's clear that the city became a crucial trading centre between the Caribbean coast (where cacao, the Maya currency, was abundant), Tikal and routes to central Mexico. Río Azul became a strategic outpost of the expanding Tikal empire, defining its northernmost boundaries, and an important defensive ally against the threatening presence of Calakmul, the other regional superpower, 60km to the northwest. It's likely that Tikal's ruler Stormy Sky installed one of his sons here as king. But by the sixth century Río Azul's position on the fringes of Tikal's domain had become alarmingly precarious, and Calakmul's Tuun K'ab' Hix (Stone Hand Jaguar) overran the city in 530 AD. After this defeat, Río Azul was forcibly allied to Calakmul and there followed a long hiatus when no monuments were constructed. Mirroring Tikal's fortunes, the city again saw a surge in population in Late Classic times, as Tikal reclaimed its former sphere of influence. It was again sacked in 830 AD, this time by marauding Puuc Maya from the Yucatán, and ended the Classic period as it had begun – a much squabbled over outpost city.

Several incredible **tombs** have been unearthed here, lined with white plaster and painted with vivid red glyphs. Tomb 1 is thought to have contained the remains of Stormy Sky's son, while nearby tombs 19 and 23 contained bodies of warriors dressed in clothing typical of the ancient city of Teotihuacán in central Mexico, further supporting the theory that Tikal derived much of its power from an alliance with this mighty city. Many of these finds, including a richly decorated jar with a curved handle which turns to open the vessel, are displayed in the archeology museum in Guatemala City (see p.92).

Extensive **looting** occurred after the site's discovery, however, robbing even greater burial treasures – a gang of up to eighty men plundering the tombs once the archeological teams had retreated to Flores in the rainy season. During the late 1960s and early 1970s, when the looting business reached its height, Río Azul supplied the international market with unique treasures, including some incredible green jade masks and pendants. The gangs stripped the tombs bare, hacking away many of their elaborately decorated walls and removing some of the finest murals in the Maya world. Despite its chamber being looted in 1981, Tomb 1's walls escaped the worst of the damage and remain mercifully intact. Working with simple tools, several of the robbers are thought to have died when tombs caved in on them, and in due course the bodies, buried alongside their Maya ancestors, will probably be unearthed by archeologists. More recently, several new tombs have been discovered, probably those of noblemen rather than royalty, though, and their murals don't compare with those that have been removed.

Today there are two resident guards, who'll accompany you throughout your visit. The tallest temples are now becoming unsafe to climb, so always heed the advice of the guards. For more information on the site, see *Río Azul: An Ancient Maya City*, by Richard Adams (University of Oklahoma).

Getting there

The **road** that connects Tikal and Uaxactún continues for an additional 95km north to Río Azul. This route is only passable in the dry season, and can be covered by 4WDs in as little as five hours, depending on the conditions. **Walking** or on **horseback** it's four days each way – three at a push. Trips can be arranged through *El Chiclero* in Uaxactún or through ProPetén or a number of travel agents in Flores.

Just beyond the halfway point you come to the **Biotopo Dos Lagunas**, an excellent point to take a break. The guards here have a *campamento* on the shore of one of the lagunas, and they'll be happy to let you cook a meal here or even stay the night – there are basic shelters and showers but you'll need a mosquito net. As always, bring some gifts of food or coffee for the guards – and the crocodiles in the lake will lunge at pieces of bread.

Once you arrive at Río Azul you'll be welcome to stay at the guard's **camp** at **Río Ixcán**, on the far side of the river; in the dry season a truck can drive through the river, otherwise you cross in an old dugout canoe. The ruins themselves are six kilometres from the campsite, along a wide, motorable road shaded by the forest, so take all the food and water you'll need for several hours at the site.

For much of the year the river is reduced to a series of pools, and the road continues a further 12km to **Tres Banderas**, where the borders of Guatemala, Mexico and Belize meet. Eventually, it may be possible to get your exit stamp in Uaxactún and continue to Mexico using this route. It's not currently possible to exit Guatemala this way, however, and many environmental groups oppose the upgrading of the road, fearing it will bring an invasion of land-hungry settlers who will clear the forest.

El Mirador and around

The remains of the first great cities of the Maya are still engulfed by the most extensive forests in the Maya region, tight against the Mexican border in the extreme north of the country. The importance of this remote region is only just beginning to be understood, and it's only very recently that archeologists have begun extensive excavations here, but exciting discoveries have already led to a major rethink about the origins of Maya civilization. The main focus of investigation has been the giant site of **El Mirador**, the first Maya "superpower", which is famous for its colossal triadic temple complexes. Neighbouring **Nakbé**, the first city to emerge in the Middle Preclassic (around

800 BC), and **Wakná** (which was only discovered in 1998) also now have teams of archeologists and workers anxiously trying to piece together the formative history of the Maya.

The conditions are very difficult – marshy mosquito-plagued terrain that becomes so saturated that excavations can only be attempted for five months of the year. However, undoubtedly the greatest challenge facing the archeologists and Guatemalan authorities is to save the ruins from the constant threat of well-organized gangs of tomb looters and timber merchants eager to plunder the forest hardwoods. Because of this insecurity, environmentalists and Mayanists are lobbying hard to get the entire Mirador region – 2169 square kilometres of jungle stretching from the Mexican border as far south as Carmelita and the ruins of El Zotz – declared the **Mirador Basin National Park**. The Guatemalan government is lobbying to have the basin declared a UNESCO World Heritage Site, and it did grant the area "Special Protected Area Status" in 2004. However, despite these encouraging official moves, effectual protective and financial measures have been less forthcoming. The University of California have had to hire 27 armed guards to patrol El Mirador alone; otherwise, according to Richard Hansen, who is leading the excavations here, "we'd lose the whole city". Meanwhile, the Foundation for Anthropological Research and Environmental Studies (FARES) have paid for forty rangers to protect the basin's jungle – ten percent of which had already been burnt by 2005.

Hansen sees strictly managed ecotourism, including the construction of jungle lodges, as the way to preserve the forests and 26 known Maya ruins of the Mirador Basin. Only 1200 visitors make it to Mirador each year, and it's hoped that this number will rise to about 10,000 by 2010. The jungle tracks to the main sites will no doubt improve by then, but for now the ruins are all very difficult to **get to** and require a minimum of a five-day (return) hike through dense jungle with pack horses and supplies. Trips can be organized through several tour operators in Flores (see p.328) or from the village of Carmelita (see p.364).

El Mirador

El Mirador is perhaps the most exotic and mysterious Maya site of all. Encircled by the Petén and Campeche jungles, this massive city matches Tikal's scale, and may even surpass it, although little is known about its history. Rediscovered in 1926, it dates from a period much earlier than Tikal, and came to dominate the Maya region. Occupying a commanding position on an outcrop of karstic (limestone) hills, at an altitude of 250m, the city was built on Middle Preclassic foundations, and could well have been originally settled by migrants from Nakbé. Mirador flourished between 200 BC and 150 AD, when it was unquestionably the largest city in Central America, home to tens of thousands of Maya. Though substantial archeological investigations have only just really begun, it's already clear that the site represents the peak of Preclassic Maya culture, which was far more sophisticated than was once believed.

The core of the site covers some sixteen square kilometres, stretching between two massive pyramidic groups that face each other across the forest on an east–west axis. The site's western side is marked by the massive **Tigre Complex**, made up of a huge single pyramid flanked by two smaller temples, a triadic design that's characteristic of El Mirador's architecture (and a design that's replicated at all of the area's Preclassic sites). The base of this complex measures 125m by 135m alone, which is enough to cover around three football fields, while the summit of the 2000-year-old pyramid touches 70m, making it the tallest structure anywhere in the Maya world (and matching the height of Teotihuacán's Pyramid of the Sun as the tallest pre-Columbian structure in the Americas). Giant stucco **jaguar masks** have been uncovered on lower flanking temples of the main pyramid, their teeth and claws painted red. In front of the Tigre Complex is El Mirador's sacred hub: a long, narrow plaza, the **Central Acropolis**, and a row of smaller buildings. Burial chambers unearthed in this central section had been painted with ferric oxide to prevent corrosion and contained the bodies of priests and noblemen, surrounded by the obsidian lancets and stingray spines used to pierce the penis, ears and tongue in ritual bloodletting ceremonies (see "Contexts", pp.460–461). The spilling of blood was seen by the Maya as a method of summoning and sustaining the gods, and was clearly common at all the great ceremonial centres.

South of the Tigre Complex, the **Monos Complex** is another triadic structure and plaza, named after the local howler monkeys that roar long into the night and after heavy rainfall. To the north, the **León Pyramid** and the **Casabel Complex** mark the boundary of the site. Heading away to the east, on the other side of the main plaza and the Central Acropolis, the Puleston Causeway runs some 800m to the smaller East Group, the largest of which (about 2km from the Tigre Complex) is the **Danta Complex**. Also a triadic structure, it rises in three stages to a height just below that of the Tigre pyramid, but gives even better views since it was built on higher land. It too has imposing masks built into the side of its temples, including some striking jaguar and vulture heads.

The area **around El Mirador** is riddled with other Maya sites – you'll pass through about a dozen small ruins on your way here. As you look out across the forest from the top of either of the main temples you can see others rising above the horizon on all sides – including the largest (as opposed to the tallest) Maya pyramid of all: Structure 2 at Calakmul in Mexico. Raised **causeways**, ancient trading routes called *sakbé* – some up to 50m wide and 4m in height – connect many of these smaller sites to El Mirador.

Nakbé, El Tintal and Wakná

About 10km to the southeast of El Mirador down one of the main *sakbé*, **Nakbé** was the first substantial city to emerge in the Maya region (though it's quite possible that earlier sites have yet to be rediscovered). There's now definitive evidence that people had settled here to farm by 1000 BC, possibly a few centuries earlier, and that the settlement grew to become a city of many thousands by 400 BC. These dates have necessitated a complete revision of the once-accepted timescale of the origin of the Maya civilization in the lowlands, and it's hoped that ongoing research here will reveal much more about the earliest development of Maya calendrics, religion and writing.

Today the site, which has only been partially cleared, is virtually unvisited by anyone except archeologists, *xateros* (palm-leaf gatherers) and *chicleros* (rubber tappers). Initial excavation work by Richard Hansen and his UCLA team has revealed that the city had a ceremonial core of **temples**, separated into two groups via a kilometre-long limestone causeway – much like El Mirador. At the eastern end, the temples rise from a platform to peak at 35m, while the western temple reaches 45m (around the same height as Temple I at Tikal, though it was constructed more than 1200 years previously, around 500 BC). The archeologists have also found evidence of skilful stucco work – a huge **mask** (measuring 5m by 8m) was found on the side of one of the temples, though it has since been covered in earth for protection. There are probably hundreds of outlying structures, including residential complexes grouped around plazas, though very limited excavation has yet been undertaken and doubtless many more exciting discoveries will follow.

El Tintal, another Preclassic site, 21km south of El Mirador, was also connected by a causeway to its giant neighbour, and the ruins, though severely looted, make an ideal campsite on the route to Mirador basin. The unrestored temples here are from a slightly later era, but also arranged in a triadic formation with a central staircase flanked by elaborate stucco masks – some of the earliest examples of Maya sculptural art. Climb to the top of the largest pyramid and there are spectacular views, including El Mirador in the distance.

There are dozens of other sites in the Mirador Basin that have barely been touched, including many very early Preclassic settlements. The large site of **Wakná**, or "house of six", was only rediscovered in 1998, after careful analysisof satellite photographs detected temple-like mounds in the jungle. It was still up to a ground crew to verify that these anomalies were indeed a Maya ruin, however. Dr Hansen, accompanied by *chicleros*, led a team to the region and confirmed that the mounds were indeed the remains of a city, later established to be Preclassic in origin. Unfortunately, they weren't the first people to discover the site – a trench cut into one of the temples confirmed that looters had already been active here, and had raided a tomb. Tour operators, including Martsam Travel (see Flores "Listings"), include Wakná on their seven-day trek itinerary to El Mirador.

Meanwhile, recent investigations at extremely remote **Naachtún**, about 25km east of El Mirador and just a kilometre south of the Mexican border, have revealed it to be a very substantial site that flourished in the Late Classic period. More than forty stelae have been unearthed here, and the architecture at the site (perilously located between the two giants of Tikal and Calakmul) reflects styles found in both cities: around its main plaza the temples show strong Tikal influence, while its royal palaces draw on Calakmul design traditions.

Getting to the Mirador basin

Getting to El Mirador is a substantial undertaking, involving a rough 77km bus or pick-up journey from Santa Elena to the *chicle*- and *xate*-gathering centre of **Carmelita**, followed by two days of hard jungle hiking – you'll need a horse to carry your food and equipment. The journey, impossibly muddy in the rainy season, is best attempted from mid-January to August (February to April is the driest period). The trip offers an exceptional chance to see virtually untouched forest, and perhaps some of the creatures that inhabit it. It's cheapest to get there independently by gathering some people together first (maybe in Flores) and then heading for Carmelita and getting in touch with the Tursimo Cooperativa (if you speak Spanish contact them first on the community phone ⓣ5800 0293 or 7861 0366). They will organize guides, packhorses, food, water and camping gear for you; a group of four people pay about US$180 each this way. Consult the highly informative website ⓦwww.mostlymaya.com for more information about organizing the hike, what to take and what to expect. Otherwise, if you'd rather set up a trip in Flores, Tikal Connection and Martsam Travel (see Flores "Listings") both offer five-day **tours** (around US$270 per person for a group of four) from Flores, including guides, packhorses and digs in Carmelita. If you'd rather organize a trip well in advance, contact Maya Expeditions (see Guatemala City "Listings"), who run excellent tours to the main sites (including Wakná) in the Mirador Basin region, led by prominent archeologists. Bring some supplies for the guards, who spend forty days at a time in the forest, subsisting on beans and tortillas.

One daily **bus** (at 1pm) plus pick-ups make the three-hour journey from Santa Elena to Carmelita via San Andrés and Cruce Dos Aguadas. *Campamento*

Nakbé (❷), 1.5km before Carmelita, offers basic but clean **accommodation**, with large thatched shelters with mosquito nets and hammocks. If you have your own tent, you can camp (US$2 per person). For a good feed, visit *Comedor Pepe Toño*, in the centre of the village, run by Brenda Zapata, who is a mine of information about the area and can introduce you to the local guides.

Sayaxché and around

Southwest of Flores on a lazy bend in the Río de la Pasión, **SAYAXCHÉ** is a fairly rough-and-ready frontier settlement that's an ideal base for exploring the forests of southern Petén and its huge collection of archeological remains. Situated at the junction of road and river, the town is an important point of storage for grain and cattle and the source of supplies for a vast surrounding area that is being steadily cleared and colonized. The complex network of rivers and swamps that cuts through the jungle here has been an important trade route since Maya times. Several ruins can be found in the area: upstream is **Ceibal**, a compact but beautiful site in a wonderful jungle setting, while to the south is **Lago de Petexbatún**, a stunning lakeside setting for the Maya sites of **Aguateca** and Punta de Chimino, and the trailhead for the substantial ruins of **Dos Pilas** and smaller Tamarindito. A visit to this region offers great opportunities to explore the Petén forest and watch the wildlife, including howler and spider monkeys, crocodiles, iguanas and superb birdlife.

Sayaxché practicalities

Getting to Sayaxché from Flores is very straightforward, with half-hourly minibuses and four daily buses plying the fairly good 62-kilometre road from Santa Elena, of which only the first 18km is not paved. A ferry (US$0.20 per person) takes you over the Río de la Pasión, directly opposite Sayaxché. **Hotels** in Sayaxché are on the basic side. *Guayacán* (ⓣ7926 6111; ❸), right beside the river, has clean, functional rooms with tiled floors and private bath, some with a/c; lovely sunset views from the terrace; and filling food. *Posada Segura* (ⓣ7928 6162; ❷–❸), 250m to the right of the dock, is cheaper but just as comfortable, with secure, clean rooms with TV and fans, some with private bath; it offers good rates for single travellers and has a cheap **comedor** on site. Other spots to grab a bite to eat include the surprisingly stylish *El Botanero*, on the second left street after the dock, which has fish and shrimp, great cocktails and music that's quite diverse (given the location), with jazz, merengue and African rhythms on the stereo. The *Restaurant Yaxkin* (closes 8pm) has huge portions of very Guatemalan-style *comida típica*.

You'll find plenty of **boatmen** eager to take you up- or downriver, though prices are quoted in dollars – you'll have to be patient and bargain hard to get a fair deal. Try Viajes Don Pedro (ⓣ & ⓕ7928 6109), which offer **tours** of the area from their office on the riverfront. The very helpful Julián Mariona, who owns *Posada El Caribe* (see p.367), can also arrange **trips** to the nearby ruins and fishing expeditions (both around US$45 a day). You can change travellers' cheques at the **bank**, Banora, a block up from the *Guayacán*.

Moving on from Sayaxché, there are two daily microbuses to Cobán (3hr 30min) via Chisec at 10am and 3.30pm (note, however, that microbus transport timetables are not exactly set in stone), as well as services to Raxrujá (2hr) via the Cruce del Pato junction about every hour and a half until around 4pm. From Raxrujá you'll find regular buses south to Cobán, via the Pajal junction (for Lanquín and Semuc Champey) and via Chisec. A daily **shuttle bus** service (run by *Hostal d'Acuña* in Cobán) also passes through Sayaxché at 9am for Flores (1hr), El Remate (1hr 45min) and Tikal (2hr 30min). On its return this shuttle bus passes through Sayaxché at around 2.15pm, Chisec about 4pm and gets to Cobán by about 5.15pm.

Ceibal (Seibal)

The compact site of **Ceibal** (sometimes spelt "Seibal"), which you can reach by land or river, is the most accessible Maya ruin near Sayaxché. By boat it's easy enough to make it there and back in an afternoon. Not much commercial river traffic heads upstream, however, so you'll probably have to **rent a boat** – ask around at the waterfront and be prepared to haggle: boats take up to six people and charge around US$45–50 for a round-trip journey, including two hours at the ruins. The hour-long boat journey is followed by a short walk through towering rainforest. **By road** Ceibal is just 17km from Sayaxché. Any transport heading south out of town towards Cruce del Pato passes the entrance road to the site, from where it's an eight-kilometre walk through the jungle to the ruins. Organizing a *privado* pick-up taxi from Sayaxché, including an hour at the ruins, should cost about US$18 – speak to the staff at the *Guayacán*. About halfway along the entrance road, you'll pass a sign denoting the start of the protected area of the Ceibal cultural monument, though this status hasn't prevented some campesinos clearing a chunk of forest. If you haven't hired a boat and decide to try and return by river, be prepared to wait a long time for a ride. It is possible to stay at the ruins, if you have a tent or hammock (with mosquito net) – bring food to share with the guards and you'll always be welcome.

▲ Ceibal emblem glyph

Surrounded by forest and shaded by huge ceiba trees, **the ruins** of Ceibal are partially cleared and restored, and beautifully landscaped into a mixture of open plazas and untamed jungle. During the Classic period Ceibal was a relatively minor site, but it grew rapidly between 830 and 910 AD, possibly after falling under the control of Putun colonists from what is now Mexico. In this period it grew to become one of the largest southern lowland sites, with an estimated population of around 10,000. Outside influence is clearly visible in some of the carving here: speech scrolls, straight noses, waist-length hair and serpent motifs are all decidedly non-Maya. The architecture also differs from other Classic Maya sites, including the round platforms that are usually associated with the Quetzalcoatl cult.

Ceibal has four main clusters of buildings, all connected by flagstone causeways (*calzadas*) that cut through the forest, and two ball courts. Although most of the largest temples (Structure 10 rises to 28m) lie buried under mounds, Ceibal does have some outstanding **carving**, superbly preserved due to the use of hard stone. Of the 57 **stelae** – some of which weigh more than four tonnes – found here, the most impressive are in the large Plaza Central (where the surrounding temples are unrestored and still jungle-clad) and in the neighbouring Plaza Sur. The latter plaza's low central temple, **Structure A-3**, has four fine stelae set around its cardinal points and another (Stela 21) in the room at the top of the temple – all were commissioned in 849 AD to commemorate the Maya year 10.1.0.0.0. Fragments of stucco found on Structure A-3 suggest that its doorways and roof were originally decorated with ornate **friezes**, carved with both low relief and free-standing fully rounded figures, and painted in brilliant shades of red, blue, green, pink, black and yellow. East of the plaza along Calzada I, the crudely carved but unusual monkey-faced Stela 2 is particularly striking, beyond which, straight ahead down the path, lies Stela 14, another impressive sculpture.

If you turn right here along Calzada II and walk for a few minutes, you'll reach the only other restored part, the highly unusual **Structure 79**, a massive circular stone platform superbly set in a clearing in the forest. The exact purpose of this platform, whose foundations date from the Late Preclassic period, is unclear, but it was certainly used for religious ceremonies (a niche where copal resin was burned has been found) and possibly also functioned as an observation deck for astronomy. In front of Structure 79's stairway, a huge, roughly carved **altar**, measuring more than 2m in diameter and bearing the face of a jaguar, is supported by two crouching humanoid figures.

Lago de Petexbatún

A similar distance to the south of Sayaxché, **Lago de Petexbatún** is a spectacular expanse of water ringed by dense forest and containing plentiful supplies of snook, bass, alligator and freshwater turtle. The shores of the lake abound with birdlife and howler monkeys, and there are a number of Maya ruins – the most impressive of which is Aguateca, subject to recent excavations and partial restoration. Their sheer number suggests that the lake was an important trading centre for the Maya.

As it's not that feasible to get around the lake independently, it's probably best explored as part of a **tour**. Most tour operators in Flores can organize excursions to Aguateca (these usually include Ceibal as well), though the ideal way to explore this beautiful region is to arrange a boat and guide locally (ask at *Posada El Caribe* or *Chiminos*; see below) to take you on a two- or three-day trip around the lake. There are plenty of options – touring the lake on foot, by boat or on horseback, exploring the jungle, fishing or bathing in the natural warm springs on the lakeshore.

You'll find three **hotels** in the lake area. It's a 45-minute speedboat trip from Sayaxché to the northern tip of Lago de Petexbatún, where you'll find the very friendly *Posada El Caribe* (Ⓣ7928 6114, Ⓕ7928 6168; ❻, full board). Run by the Mariona family, it has clean and comfortable screened cabins and good food. Don Julián, the owner, has lived in this part of the Petén all his life and is highly recommended for lake and ruin tours to Aguateca and Dos Pilas; he can arrange horses, 4WD and boat transport, though he speaks very limited English. About three kilometres south of here on the western shore of the lake, the seldom-occupied, European-owned *Petexbatún Lodge* (Ⓣ7926 0501 or 2331 7561) enjoys a great plot above the *lago* and has bunk-bed dorms (US$10 per person) and eight mediocre, moderately attractive bungalows (❻), each with two double beds and bathroom. Just south of here, the spectacular *Chiminos Island Lodge* (Ⓣ2335 3506, Ⓕ2335 2647, Ⓦwww.chiminosisland.com; US$88 per person including all meals) is an absolutely stunning place to stay, with six huge, commodious thatch-roofed bungalows, all with very stylish bathrooms and furnishings and wonderful private viewing decks above the lake. Bungalow "2 Norte" is the most attractive, with bungalow "1 Norte" second choice, though all are sublime. There are some minor ruins in the patch of jungle around the hotel, which is also home to howler monkeys. The hotel also has docks for sunbathing and swimming, cooking that's of a very high standard and an attentive and helpful staff.

Aguateca and Punta de Chiminos

Aguateca, perched on a high outcrop at the southern tip of the lake, is the furthest away from Sayaxché but the most easily reached Petexbatún site, as a boat can get you to within twenty minutes' walk of the ruins. This intriguing site (no fee), split in two by a natural chasm, was only rediscovered in 1957 and is currently undergoing extensive restoration work. The atmosphere is magical, surrounded by dense tropical forest and with superb views of the lake from two *miradores*. Throughout the Late Classic period, Aguateca was closely aligned with (or controlled by) nearby Dos Pilas, the dominant city in the southern Petén, and reached its peak in the eighth century, when the latter was developing an aggressive policy of expansion. Indeed, Aguateca may have been a twin capital of an ambitious Petexbatún state. Military successes, including a conclusive victory over Ceibal in 735 AD, were celebrated at both sites with remarkably similar stelae – Aguateca's Stela 3 shows Dos Pilas ruler Master Sun Jaguar in full battle regalia, including a Teotihuacán-style face mask. After 761 AD, however, Dos Pilas began to lose control of its empire and the members of the elite moved their headquarters to Aguateca, attracted by its strong defensive position. But despite the construction of 5km of walls around the citadel and its agricultural land, their enemies soon caught up with them, and sometime after 790 AD Aguateca itself was overrun.

The resident guards will provide you with stout walking sticks – essential as the slippery paths here can be treacherous – before escorting you around the site's steep trails. The tour, which takes a little more than an hour, takes in part of the site's palisade defences, temples and palaces (including the residence of Aguateca's last ruler, Tante K'inich) and a barracks (where restoration is ongoing). The carving at Aguateca is superbly executed and includes images of hummingbirds, pineapples and pelicans. The plazas are dotted with stelae, including one on the Plaza Principal depicting Tante K'inich lording it over a ruler from Ceibal, who is shown cowering at his feet, and another that has been shattered by looters who hoped to sell the fragments. Aguateca is also the site of the Maya world's only known **bridge**, which crosses a narrow gash in the hillside, but it's not that impressive in itself. The *Posada El Caribe* and *Chiminos* hotels (see p.367) run trips to all the sites in the area or you can book a tour in Flores (see p.338), where prices start at around US$120 for a two-day tour. A new visitor centre and café is under construction close to the entrance, where Aguateca's guards are based. The guards always welcome company, and if you want to **stay** they'll find some space for you to sling a hammock or pitch a tent. If you do stay, you'll need to bring a mosquito net and food.

About four kilometres to the north, jutting out from the west shore of the lake, is a club-shaped peninsula known as **Punta de Chiminos**. This site was the final refuge of the last of the Petexbatún Maya in the Late Classic era, as the region descended into warfare and chaos at the beginning of the ninth century. Here they constructed some formidable defences across the narrow stem of the peninsula, including three rock-hewn trenches and nine-metre ramparts, which created a man-made citadel. The point is now the spectacular location for the lovely *Chiminos Island Lodge* (see p.367), though there's very little to see there today.

Dos Pilas and around

Some 12km west of the northern tip of Lago de Petexbatún, still buried in the jungle, is another virtually unreconstructed site, **Dos Pilas**, which has one of the most fascinating and best documented histories of any Maya city. **Dos Pilas** was established around 640 AD by a renegade group from Tikal, who fled the great city during the dark ages that followed its defeat by Calakmul. The leader of this breakaway tribe, a lord named B'alaj Chan K'awil (Lightening Sky), was clearly a brazen individual. It's thought that, even though he claimed membership of the Tikal royal line, he swore a treacherous allegiance with Calakmul in 648 AD in an attempt to launch a rival dynasty at Tikal. Dos Pilas clashed with Tikal several times in the years afterwards, as Tikal sought to humble the upstart Dos Pilas ruler. Though B'alaj Chan K'awil ultimately failed in his bid to claim the Tikal lineage, he did repel Tikal in 679 AD, a victory which he celebrated by commissioning several new stelae and launching a substantial reconstruction of the plaza.

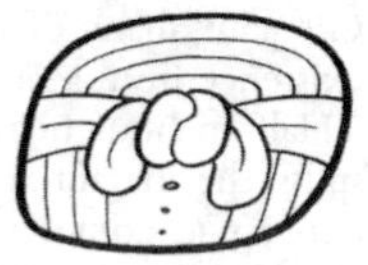
▲ Dos Pilas emblem glyph

Dos Pilas continued to throw its weight around for another century, provoking a series of battles with neighbouring cities, defeating Ceibal in 735 AD, and capturing lords from Yaxchilán and Motul. Monuments including three hieroglyphic stairways were built, though by the latter half of the eighth century the region was becoming so unstable (probably due to attacks by Putun Maya from Mexico) that the rulers fled Dos Pilas in 761 AD. Farmers continued to occupy the site for a few more years, tearing down the temple structures to build elaborate defensive walls in a vain attempt to keep out the invaders, but by the early ninth century Dos Pilas was abandoned completely. If you want to find out more about the history of Dos Pilas, check out the masterful account of the city's place in Classic Maya politics in Simon Martin's and Nikolai Grube's *Chronicle of the Maya Kings and Queens* (Thames and Hudson; see "Books", p.496).

Sadly, the remains of the city are less than spectacular, as many temples were partly dismantled during the chaos of the late eighth century. Nevertheless, there's some superb carving to admire, including several wonderful stelae and four small **hieroglyphic stairways**, now protected by thatched shelters grouped around the grassy plaza. On the south side of the plaza are the ruins of a palace, while on the east side a rich tomb was discovered under Temple L-51, probably belonging to the ruler Itzamnaaj K'awiil. Encircling the remains of this ceremonial core, it's still possible to make out the remains of the fortifications, a double defensive wall and stockade that the final occupiers erected.

Getting to Dos Pilas is by no means straightforward, or cheap. It's best to try and organize transport in Sayaxché or Flores, where several tour operators offer trips to the Ceibal and the Petexbatún region. Either way you'll have to travel from Sayaxché, and then via a 45-minute speedboat trip to the *Posada El Caribe* (see p.367) followed by a further 12km on foot or horseback to the ruins. The hike takes you past the small site of **Arroyo de Piedra**, where you'll find a plaza and two fairly well-preserved stelae, and the ruins of **Tamarindito** where another hieroglyphic stairway has been found. Two guards live at the site of Dos Pilas and it's certainly possible to **stay** here – as always, you should bring a tent or hammock and mosquito net, and enough food to share with the guards. Otherwise you can make a day-trip of it and return to Sayaxché in the evening.

South to the Ixcán

The quick, smooth paved road south from Sayaxché skirts round the edge of the **Ceibal natural reserve**, at first slicing through a stretch of jungle, then through a flat scrubland of lone tree stumps, cattle pasture and thatched cabañas where indigenous families and their swollen-bellied children live. These

Q'eqchi', many of whom are returning refugees, struggle to eke out a meagre existence from a near-exhausted land.

Half an hour before **Cruce del Pato**, where the road splits, the magnificent bulk of the Cuchumatanes mountain range comes into view, with the looming, forested ridges rising abruptly from the plain. Microbuses running between Raxrujá and Sayaxché pass this lonely junction about every ninety minutes in both directions until around 5pm, plus the odd chicken bus. A few trucks also run past Cruce del Pato heading to Playa Grande, but you're usually better off heading to Raxrujá and getting a connection there.

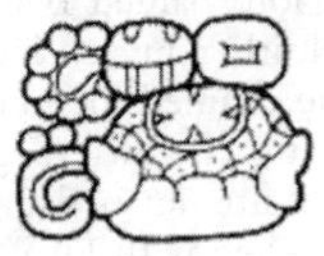

▲ Cancuén emblem glyph

Twelve kilometres east of Cruce del Pato is the large Maya site of **Cancuén** (see p.319), where a huge Classic-period palace has been unearthed. The city had close relations with both Dos Pilas and Calakmul in the Classic period, and flourished quite late after Dos Pilas had collapsed in 761 AD. Cancuén is best accessed from the town of Raxrujá in the Verapaces.

Routes to Mexico

Heading west to Mexico from Petén is fairly straightforward and highly scenic in places, passing remote ruins and patches of dense rainforest. Though the Mexican state of Chiapas has been relatively calm for several years, tensions do remain between government and Zapatista-aligned campesinos, and you can expect army security checks every hour or so as you get around. That said, travel is perfectly safe in the region, and the armed forces courteous and polite.

The most popular route by far involves crossing the Río Usumacinta into Chiapas at **Frontera Corozal**, from either **Bethel**, or a little upstream at **La Técnica** on the Guatemalan bank of the river. This trip enables you to pass the first-class ruins of **Yaxchilán** and Bonampak on the way. It's also possible to travel by boat **from Sayaxché** to Benemérito, on the Mexican bank of the Río Usumacinta, or, alternatively, head northwest **from Flores** to El Naranjo by bus, then along the Río San Pedro to La Palma in Mexico, though there are no regular boat schedules on either of these routes. **Border formalities** are relatively straightforward all round.

From Bethel to Frontera Corozal

The cheapest and most straightforward route to Mexico is via **BETHEL**, on the Río Usumacinta, where there's a Guatemalan **migración** post. Three daily minibuses (the last at 1.30pm; 3hr) and five daily buses (the last at 1pm; 4hr) leave Flores for Bethel passing the El Subín junction north of Sayaxché along a (mostly) paved road. At Bethel it's relatively easy to find a *lancha* heading downstream (around US$6; 30min) to Frontera Corozal. Alternatively, it's usually possible to get off the bus, obtain your exit stamp in Bethel and continue on the same bus for a further 12km to the tiny settlement of **La Técnica**, where you can cross the Usumacinta (US$0.50) to Corozal on the opposite bank. La Técnica lacks accommodation or other facilities. Some agencies in Flores (see p.338) offer cross-border tickets direct to Palenque using this route (about US$30 per person), though there are occasionally reports of Mexican drivers not accepting Guatemala-issued tickets and demanding additional payments, especially on services booked via the unreliable San Juan Travel in Santa Elena.

Bethel itself is a pleasant village with wide grassy streets, plenty of trees to provide shade and a couple of comedores. The tall, tree-covered mounds that comprise the **Bethel ruins**, unknown to archeologists until 1995, are 1.5km from the village. Though not that extensive, they occupy an imposing stretch of the Usumacinta, and the settlement must have played a key role in controlling trade along the river. A twenty-minute trail leads from the ruins up to a *mirador*, where you'll find the remains of a pyramid, probably a ceremonial centre, that's some 75m above the plaza floor.

Bethel has an excellent, community-run **place to stay**, the *Posada Maya* (☎7861 1799 or 7861 1800), that's set in a grassy plaza above the river and surrounded by forest. It offers comfortable wood-and-thatch cabins (❸), as well as camping and hammock space (❷) on concrete platforms under tall palapa roofs, as well as good food. Speak to Benjamín Rosales here about boat transport to Yaxchilán (a *lancha* costs around US$100 return) and hikes to a spectacular *cenote*, a limestone sink hole, close to the village or even into the Parque Nacional Sierra del Lacandón, perhaps the most remote and best-preserved rainforest in Guatemala.

From Sayaxché to Benemérito

It's also possible to get to Mexico via a much slower route **from Sayaxché**, heading downriver along the Río de la Pasión, though very few travellers take this trip as there are no fixed boat departures. That said, trading boats leave Sayaxché about every other day, most taking around eight hours (and some much longer) through an area of forest and swamp to make it to immigration at **Pipiles**, where the Pasión and Salinas rivers meet to form the Usumacinta. Get your exit (or entry) stamp here. If you've made it this far, you could stop to visit the small Maya site of **Altar de los Sacrificios**, a couple of kilometres south of Pipiles. Commanding an important river junction, this is one of the oldest sites in Petén, but these days there's not much to see beyond a solitary stela. The beach below, which is exposed in the dry season, is often scattered with tiny fragments of Maya pottery, uncovered as the river eats into the base of the site, carving into ancient burials.

Downstream along the Usumacinta from Pipiles it's about 15km to **BENEMÉRITO** in Mexico, a sprawling frontier town, with rough accommodation (and inhabitants – this is a drug-smuggling stronghold). Fortunately, transport connections are good here, enabling a quick getaway to Palenque (12 daily minibuses and 7 daily buses, the last at 4pm; 4hr) or south towards Comitán (4 daily, the last at 12.45pm; 7hr). Note that Mexican **immigration** in Benemérito is 2km north of town, where the road crosses the Río Lacantún (bus drivers will wait for you while you get your tourist card), or you can sort out your entry stamp in Palenque, Frontera Corozal or Comitán.

Frontera Corozal to Yaxchilán

Boats to the Maya ruins of Yaxchilán are best organized in the tiny village of **Frontera Corozal** (though it's also possible, but much more costly, to get there from Bethel or Benemérito) on the Mexican bank of the Usumacinta. Corozal is 18km east of the main Palenque–Comitán highway, *colectivo* taxis (US$2 per person), minibuses and the odd bus shuttle between the two. The town has two good **places to stay**: the riverside *Escudo Jaguar* (☎55 3290 0993; ❸–❺), which has very clean, attractive rooms and cabins plus a decent but expensive restaurant; and *Nueva Alianza* (☎55 5339 0995; ❷), a new budget place that offers decent rooms with nets in a large partitioned wooden structure (you can eat quite cheaply here too). If you have a minute, don't miss the village's excellent community **museum**, which has two superb stelae from the Maya site of Dos Caobas.

Most folk head straight to the dock to board a *lancha* for Yaxchilán, however. It's usually easy to hook up with other people or a tour group to share the costs of hiring the boat, a good idea as it's quite steep at US$60 return for four people or US$92 for up to eight. It's a lovely 45-minute run downstream to the ruins, and an hour to return. The banks of the Usumacinta are still covered in thick jungle, particularly on the Guatemalan side where it forms the eastern border of the virtually untouched Parque Nacional Sierra de Lacandón.

Yaxchilán

The Yaxchilán ruins (daily 8am–5pm; US$3) are undeniably the most spectacular on the Usumacinta, superbly positioned on the Mexican bank, spread out over several steep hills within a great loop in the river. This is an important location, and carvings at Yaxchilán, like those at the neighbouring sites of Bonampak and Piedras Negras, tell of repeated conflict with the surrounding Maya centres. By 514 AD, when its emblem glyph was used for the first time, Yaxchilán was already a place of some size, but its era of greatness was launched by the ruler Itzamnaaj B'alam II (Shield Jaguar II), who came to power in 681 and extended the city's sphere of influence through a campaign of conquest. At this stage it was sufficiently powerful to form a military alliance that included not only the Usumacinta centres but also Tikal and Palenque. Itzamnaaj B'alam II was succeeded by Pájaro Jaguar IV (Bird Jaguar IV), who continued the ambitious construction projects and military expansion. Less is known about the later years in Yaxchilán, although building continued well into the Late Classic period, so the site was probably occupied until at least 900 AD.

What you see today is a collection of plazas, temples and ball courts strung out along the raised banks of the river, while the low hills in the centre of the site are topped with impressive palaces. The structures are all fairly low, but each of the main temples supports the crumbling remains of a massive honeycombed roof, decorated with stucco carvings. The quality of this carving is quite exceptional, particularly the **door lintels**, 58 of which once spanned the doorways of the main temples here. There's much to still admire at the site, but many of the best pieces have been removed to museums around the world: one set of particularly fine lintels, depicting the bloodletting rituals of Itzamnaaj B'alam II and his wife Lady Xoc, is displayed in the British Museum in London. When the layers of vegetation are peeled back, the original stonework appears unaffected by the past thousand years, with flecks of red paint still clinging to the surface.

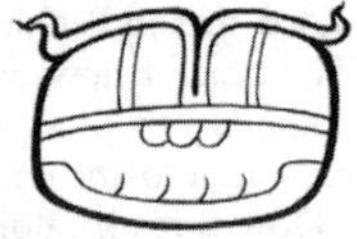
▲ Yaxchilán emblem glyph

The most impressive structure is **Temple 33**, topped by a towering honeycombed crest, which is reached by a grand staircase from the plaza. Look under its doorways and there are some wonderfully carved lintels, one of which depicts the infant prince Itzamnaaj B'alam III performing a "bird staff" dance with his father, the ruler Pájaro Jaguar IV. Yaxchilán's architecture focuses heavily on the river, and the remains of a built-up bank suggest that it might have been the site of a bridge or toll gate. At low water you can see a pyramid, about 8m square at the base, 6m high, with a carved altar on top. Built on the riverbed and completely submerged at high water, it is believed by archeologists to be a bridge abutment.

Until fairly recently, the site was still used by Lacandón Maya, who came here to burn incense, worship, and leave offerings to their gods. The whole place still has a bewitching atmosphere, with the energy of the forest, overwhelming in its fertility, threatening to consume the ruins. The forest here is relatively undisturbed and buzzes with life: toucans (and occasionally red macaws) as well as howler and spider monkeys loiter in the trees, while bats are now the main inhabitants of the palaces and temples.

Piedras Negras

Forty kilometres downstream from Yaxchilán, the Maya ruins of **Piedras Negras** loom high over the Guatemalan bank of the river. It's one of the most extensive sites in Guatemala, but it's also one of the least accessible and least visited. The city was called Yokib' ("the entrance") in Maya times; the Spanish name of Piedras Negras refers to the black stones lining the riverbank here. Founded around 300 AD, an unrelenting rivalry developed between the city and Yaxchilán for dominance over Usumacinta trade routes, contested by bloody battles and strategic pacts with Calakmul and Tikal. Like its adversary, Piedras Negras is best known for the extraordinary quality of its **carvings**, considered by many to be the very finest to emerge from the Maya world. Several of the best of these are on display in the Museo Nacional de Arqueología in Guatemala City, including a royal throne, some exquisitely carved stelae and panels. The most important of these panels, discovered in June 2000, has an unusually long hieroglyphic text which has allowed Mayanists to compile an excellent record of the city's Late Classic history under the ruler Itzamk'anahk K'in Ajaw (626–686 AD). However, there's still plenty to experience on site.

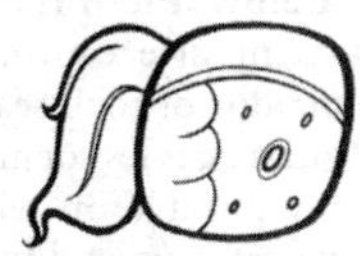
▲ Piedras Negras emblem glyph

Upon arrival, the most immediately impressive monument is a large rock jutting over the river bank with a carving of a seated male figure presenting a bundle to a female figure. This was once surrounded by glyphs, now badly eroded and best seen at night with a torch held at a low angle. Continuing up the hill, across plazas and over the ruins of buildings you get some idea of the city's size. Several buildings are comparatively well preserved, particularly the **sweat baths**, used for ritual purification; the most imposing of all is the **acropolis**, a huge palace complex of rooms, passages and courtyards towering 100m above the riverbank. A **megalithic stairway** at one time led down to the river, doubtless a humbling sight to visitors (and captives) before the forest invaded the city. Another intriguing sight is a huge double-headed turtle glyph carved on a rock overhanging a small valley. This is a reference to the end of a *katun*; inside the main glyph is a giant representation of the day sign Ahau (also signifies Lord), recalling the myth of the birth of the maize god. During research carried out at Piedras Negras in the 1930s, artist and epigrapher Tatiana Proskouriakoff noticed that dates carved on monuments corresponded approximately to a human life span, indicating that the glyphs might refer to events in one person's lifetime, possibly the rulers of the city. Refuted for decades by the archeological establishment, the theory was later proved correct. The site has been excavated since 1997 by a joint American and Guatemalan team led by archeologists Stephen Houston and Héctor Escobedo.

Traditionally, the presence of FAR guerrillas in the region protected the ruins from systematic looting – neither looters nor the army dared enter. Now that guerrillas are just a memory and access from the Mexican bank is becoming easier, it remains to be seen how long Piedras Negras can maintain its relatively untouched state, particularly as *narcotraficantes* (cocaine smugglers) have been highly active in this region.

Getting to Piedras Negras is by no means straightforward. The perfect way to arrive is by boat along the Usumacinta, following the ancient Maya trade route, though this involves booking an expensive tour (Maya Expeditions are highly recommended, see Guatemala City "Listings"; or speak to the owners of the *Posada Maya* in Bethel). The least expensive and most accessible route is from Mexico: Willy Fonseca, owner of the *Restaurante Vallescondido* (Ⓣ01 91634 80721) at Km 61 on the Palenque–Comitán road, runs very well organized day-trips by 4WD and boat for US$500, which works out at US$100 per person if there are five of you (the maximum number).

Below Piedras Negras the current quickens and the river drops through two massive canyons. The first of these, **Cañon de San José**, is a narrow corridor of rock sealed in by cliffs 300m high; the second, the **Cañon de las Iguanas**, is less dramatic. Travel on this part of the river is treacherous and really only possible on whitewater rafts: smaller craft have to be carried around the two canyons, and under no circumstances is it possible to travel upriver.

El Naranjo and the San Pedro river route

Now that there are no longer scheduled boat departures along the Río San Pedro, this route into Mexico is very seldom used by travellers. However, it is still possible to travel from Flores to Mexico via the San Pedro, through a remote, deforested area, though it could work out to be quite expensive. A (mostly) paved road runs from Santa Elena to **EL NARANJO**, a rough place consisting of little more than an army base. There's a **migración** here, stores (offering poor exchange rates), comedores and basic hotels. The only decent place **to stay** is the friendly, family-run *Posada San Pedro* across the river (❷). A boat does leave most days for La Palma in Mexico at 1pm, but be prepared to have to wait around for an extra day or so, and expect to pay US$20 for the four-hour ride; boats pass Mexican **migración** after an hour. La Palma has good bus connections to Tenosique (last bus 5pm).

Waka' (El Perú) and the Ruta Guacamaya

To the east of El Naranjo, in the upper reaches of the Río San Pedro, is Waka' (also called El Perú), a seldom-visited and almost unreconstructed archeological site buried in some of the wildest rainforest in Petén. Waka' ("stood up place") gets its name from its position on a 130-metre-high escarpment towering above a tributary of the Río San Pedro. The city grew to become an important middle-ranking Petén settlement in the Late Classic period, controlling important overland and water routes. Despite being the nearest place of any size west of Tikal, it sided with the other great "superpower" – distant Calakmul – in the power politics of the time. Around 650 AD, Yuknoom the Great of Calakmul attended the accession of Waka' ruler K'inich B'alam ("Great Sun Jaguar") here – the same leader later married a Calakmul princess. Waka' continued to remain under the Calakmul overlordship in the early eighth century, but would later pay for this affiliation when a resurgent Tikal overran the city in 743 AD, after which no monuments were carved here for 47 years.

Most of the site's temple mounds are still coated in vegetation, but Waka' is perhaps most famous for its many well-preserved **stelae**, and the recent discovery of a fascinating **royal tomb** of a female ruler dating from around 620 AD. This queen was clearly a formidable and highly revered figure as she was buried in a battle helmet with stingray spines (for ritual bloodletting) placed near her pelvis – burial customs usually only bestowed on male rulers. Mayanist David Freidel (see "Books" in Contexts) is excavating the site, so an archeologist may be available to show you around. The guards here welcome visitors, particularly if you bring along a little spare food. Though it's possible to get to Waka' by boat from El Naranjo, virtually everyone visits the site as part of an adventure tour, best arranged in Flores (see p.338). These tours, often dubbed **La Ruta Guacamaya** or "Scarlet Macaw Trail", are exciting two- or three-night trips by 4WD pick-up and boat along rivers and through primary forest, camping at the ruins; prices run between US$195 and US$280 per person via Martsam Travel in Flores or *La Casa de Don David* in El Remate. Close to the site, at the confluence of the San Pedro and Sacluc, there's a biological station at which rangers monitor forests that contain the largest concentrations of scarlet macaws in northern Central America. You've also an excellent chance of observing spider and howler monkeys, crocodiles, river turtles and the Petén turkey, and may even see a tapir on the banks of the Sacluc river. The best time to see scarlet macaws is between February and June when they nest in hollows of larger trees, but there are a plethora of other exotic birds in the Waka' region at all times of year.

Yaxhá to the Belize border

East of the Ixlú junction, a paved but potholed road runs 65km to the Belize border, passing a turn-off for gorgeous Laguna Macanché (see p.344). Thirty kilometres from Ixlú there's a sign on the right for **Holtún**, a site with tall, unrestored temples adorned with masks, a twenty-minute walk from the road. On the roadside, look out for the sign put up by Borman Peréz, who sells good-value wood and ceramic art from his house. He can guide you to the site and offers a couple of budget **rooms** (❷) and space for camping; he also rents bikes and horses to visit Yaxhá.

Continuing east along the road to Belize, it's about a kilometre to the junction for **Lago de Yaxhá**, a beautiful, shallow limestone depression, similar to, but smaller than, Lago de Petén Itzá. The lake is encircled by the dense jungle of the Monumento Natural Yaxhá–Nakúm–Naranjo, which harbours jaguar and margay cats, two species of crocodile, three species of turtle and dozens of other reptiles as well as prolific birdlife. It's one of the very few places in Guatemala where tapir are known to be breeding. The lake is also home to two Maya sites, the very extensive and impressive ruins of **Yaxhá** and smaller **Topoxté**, and offers access to a third, **Nakúm**, to the north. Several Flores-based tour operators offer half-day trips to the Yaxhá area, though Nakúm is less frequently included on tour itineraries.

In June 2005, CBS television commenced filming the **Survivor** TV series at Yaxhá, which is sure to put the site on the map (and close access to the ruins for months). Permission to permit filming the show inside the natural monument was granted despite opposition from Guatemala's protected-areas agency, CONAP, and the Ministry of Culture.

Yaxhá

Yaxhá (daily 8am–5pm), covering several square kilometres of a limestone ridge overlooking the lake, is a highly compelling and rewarding Maya site to visit. If you're not on a guided trip, one of the guards will show you around for a small tip. Its name means "green-blue water", a reference to the wonderful turquoise hue of the lake just below. Of all Guatemala's ruins, only Tikal and El

▲ Yaxhá emblem glyph

Mirador can trump the sheer scale and impact of this site, which is given added atmosphere because of the lack of crowds and the thriving wildlife (particularly howler monkeys and toucans). As yet, very little is known about the history of Yaxhá, partly due to a relative lack of inscriptions, and also because substantial archeological excavations have only recently begun, but it is predominantly a Classic-period site. The size of the city (only Tikal and El Mirador are larger in Guatemala) indicates that Yaxhá was undoubtedly an important force in the central Maya region during this era, its influence perhaps only contained by the proximity of the "superstate" Tikal, with which it shares several archeological similarities and close ties. For much of the Classic period, Yaxhá seemed locked in rivalry with the city of Naranjo, about 20km to the northeast, dominating its smaller neighbour for much of this time but suffering a heavy defeat in 799 AD when ruler Itzammnaaj K'awill of Naranjo defeated K'iinch Lakamtuun of Yaxhá.

Restoration work is ongoing at Yaxhá, but most of the buildings have yet to be cleared and many are still choked in dense forest. The ruins are spread out over nine plazas, with around five hundred structures having been mapped so far, including three ball courts. From the entrance head north towards Plaza F, and climb the staircase up the large **pyramid** here to get an overview of the ruins, its temple tops and Lago de Yaxhá far below. Continuing north from here up Calzada Blom, it's about 750m to the imposing **Grupo Maler** complex (named after the great early twentieth-century Austrian explorer Teobert Maler), where restoration is nearly complete. Here, a pair of temples face each other across a grassy plaza in an arrangement that follows the twin-temple alignment tradition established at Tikal. Several weathered stelae stand in front of the ruins of the palace structure here as well as the broken remains of a huge circular altar, possibly destroyed by invaders from Naranjo. Heading south back along Calzada Blom you come to the **Acropolis Norte**, where restoration is also nearing completion, its central plaza surrounded by temples on three sides. The rectangular structure with unusual curved edges on the northern side of this plaza reaches around 22m in height.

South from the Acropolis Norte you follow a grassy avenue-like trail, its sides overshadowed by soaring unrestored temples to Plaza D, then east up Vía 1 to Plaza B, an open area bordered by low walls. Steps lead up from here to Plaza A, from where you can scramble up a bank on its south side towards Yaxhá's tallest and most impressive pyramid, the fully restored **Structure 216**. This imposing, classically Maya temple rises in tiers to a height of more than 30m and has a broad central staircase. There are spectacular vistas over the forest and lake from its summit – particularly at sunset.

Practicalities

The main Flores–Belize road passes 11km to the south of Lago de Yaxhá and neighbouring Lago de Sacnab; the turn-off is clearly signposted. If you're not on a tour, then it's possible to hitch from the main road as there is some traffic to and from the village of La Máquina, 2km before the lakes. Just before you reach the lakes you pass a **control post** where you may be asked to sign in. From here it's 3km to the site: head along the road between the lakes then turn left (signposted) for Yaxhá.

If you want to **stay** near Yaxhá, the wonderful, solar-powered *Campamento El Sombrero* (Ⓣ7926 5229, Ⓕ7926 5198, Ⓦwww.ecosombrero.com; ❹–❺), 200m from the road on the south side of the lake, has fine rooms in thatched wooden jungle lodges and space for **camping**; the Italian owner can arrange boat trips on the *lagos* and horseback riding, and she'll pick you up from the bus stop

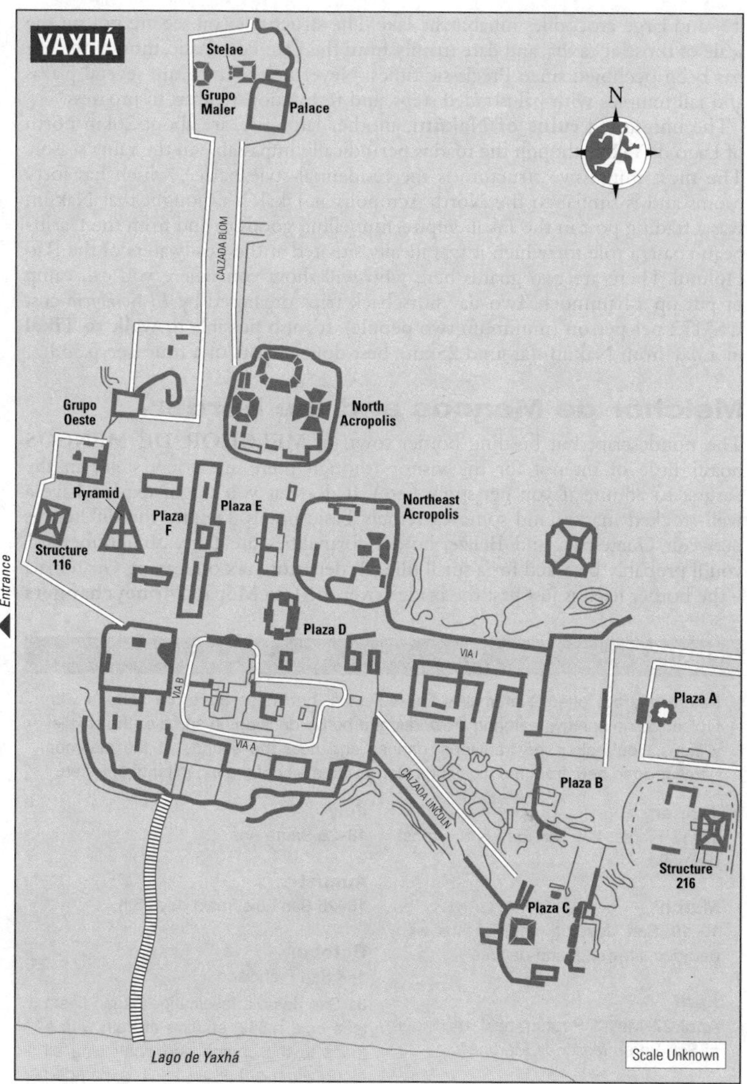

if you've called in advance. There's another *campamento* on the far side of the lake, below Yaxhá, where you can pitch a tent or sling a hammock beneath a thatched shelter for free.

Topoxté and Nakúm

Topoxté, a much smaller site on an island close to the west shore of Lago de Yaxhá, is best reached by boat from *El Sombrero* (see below). There's a four-kilometre trail to a spot opposite the island but you still have to get over to it – and large crocodiles inhabit the lake. The structures you see are not on the scale of those at Yaxhá, and date mainly from the Late Postclassic, though the site has been occupied since Preclassic times. Nevertheless, there are several plazas and tall temples with balustraded steps, and restoration work is in progress.

The unrestored **ruins of Nakúm**, another large site, are about 20km north of Lago de Yaxhá, though the road is periodically impassable in the rainy season. The most impressive structure is the residential-style palace, which has forty rooms and is similar to the North Acropolis at Tikal. It's thought that Nakúm was a trading post in the Tikal empire, funnelling goods to and from the Caribbean coast, a role for which it was ideally situated at the headwaters of the Río Holmul. There are two guards here who will show you where you can camp or put up a hammock. Two-day horseback trips organised by *El Sombrero* cost US$172 per person (minimum two people). It's also possible to **walk to Tikal** in a day from Nakúm (around 25km), best done as part of a tour (see p.338).

Melchor de Mencos and the border

The nondescript but bustling border town of **MELCHOR DE MENCOS** boasts little of interest for the visitor (though there are a few stelae in the parque to admire if you get stuck here). It does, as you might expect, have a well-stocked market and some extremely basic hotels. Despite the differences between Guatemala and Belize, border formalities are fairly straightforward; you'll probably be asked for a small (illegal) departure tax on leaving Guatemala – the border itself is just past the bridge over the Río Mopán. **Moneychangers**

Fiestas

Petén may not offer Guatemala's finest fiestas, but those there are abound with typical ladino energy, featuring fireworks and heavy drinking. In some of the smaller villages, you'll also see traditional dances and hear the sounds of the marimba – transported here from the highlands along with many of the inhabitants of Petén.

January
12–15 Flores, the final day is the most dramatic

March
10–19 San José, a small fiesta with parades, fireworks and dances

April
April 27–May 1 Poptún, held in honour of San Pedro Martír de Merona

May
1–9 San Benito, sure to be wild and very drunken
15–22 Melchor de Mencos, main day 22nd
23–31 Dolores, main day 28th

June
16 Sayaxché, held in honour of San Antonio de Padua

July
18–26 Santa Ana

August
16–25 San Luís, main day 25th

October
1–4 San Francisco
31 San José, a fascinating pagan fiesta (see box, p.342) starting at 8pm with a mass in the church and continuing all night when a human skull is paraded through the town's streets

November
21–30 San Andrés, main day 30th

December
9–12 La Libertad

will pester you on either side of the border – most give a fair rate, and you may choose to use their services as the **bank** just beyond the immigration building does not give cash advances or change dollars. Next to immigration, by the riverbank, is the recommended *Río Mopán Lodge* (Ⓣ7926 5196, Ⓦwww.tikaltravel.com; ❸). Swiss owner Marco Gross knows Petén and its archeology extremely well and organizes amazing trips to remote Maya sites; you can also safely change money here.

For details of microbuses and buses between Santa Elena and Melchor see p.339. It's worth noting that Línea Dorada/Mundo Maya also operate a twice-daily express **shuttle service** from Santa Elena to Belize City (4hr; US$17) which continues on to the Mexican border at Chetumal (another 4hr; US$24 in all), for connections north to Cancún. From the border **to Tikal** taxi drivers charge around US$10 per person for a shared ride (they leave when they have four people), or you can do it independently by catching a bus or minibus to Ixlú and getting another from there.

On the Belize side of the border, buses leave **for Belize City** every half-hour or so (3hr), usually right from the frontier. If there's no bus waiting, you may have to take a shared taxi to Benque Viejo or to San Ignacio (US$2 per person; 20min) and catch a connection there.

Travel details

For more detailed information about travel from Flores and Santa Elena, see the box on p.339.

Buses

Flores to: Belize City (3 daily; 4hr); Bethel (5 daily; 4hr); Carmelita (1 daily; 3hr); Cobán (1 daily; 4hr 15min); El Naranjo (hourly; 5hr); Guatemala City (about 30 daily; 8–10hr); La Técnica (3 daily; 4hr 30min); Melchor de Mencos (hourly; 2hr); Poptún (every 30min; 1hr 30min); San Andrés (hourly; 30min); San José (hourly; 40min); Sayaxché (every 30min; 1hr 30min); Tikal (frequent shuttles; 1hr).
Poptún to: Fray Bartolomé de Las Casas (1 daily; 5hr).
Sayaxché to: Cobán (2 daily; 3hr 30min); Flores (every 30min; 1hr 30min); Raxrujá (every 1hr 30min; 2hr).

Boats

Bethel to: Frontera Corozal (5min), leave when full.
El Naranjo to: La Palma in Mexico (4hr). No fixed schedule but a boat leaves most days at 1pm.
Flores to: San Andrés and San José (40min and 50min), irregular boats from Flores and San Benito in daylight hours only.
La Técnica to: Frontera Corozal (30min), leave when full.
Sayaxché to: Benemérito, Mexico. A trading boat leaves about every other day (8–24hr); private speedboats take 3–4hr.

Flights

Flores to: Belize City (5 daily; 35min); Cancún (3 weekly; 1hr 20min); Guatemala City (8–10 daily; 50min–1hr); Houston (2 weekly; 3hr 20min).

7

Into Honduras: Copán and the Bay Islands

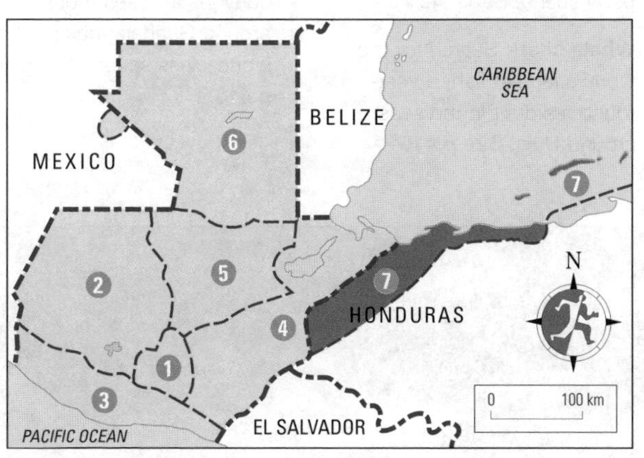

CHAPTER 7

Highlights

* **Copán Ruinas** A hospitable, easy-going charm makes this many travellers' favourite Honduran town. **See p.385**
* **Copán** Examine the exquisite carvings and temples at the archeological site dubbed the "Athens of the Maya World". **See p.389**
* **Utila** A travellers' mecca, this island is famed for its budget-priced scuba schools, its rum punch and its reggae-powered party scene. **See p.404**
* **Whale shark** Search for the world's largest fish, a year-round resident in the seas around Utila. **See p.410**
* **Roatán's West End** The region's finest beach-reef resort, with a selection of great seafood restaurants and cool bars. **See p.412**
* **West Bay** A perfect Caribbean beach: pale powdery sands, palm trees and pellucid water – though watch out for the sand flies. **See p.413**
* **Guanaja's coral reefs** The plunging reef walls, coral canyons and sea mounts around Guanaja make for world-class scuba diving. **See p.416**

△ Roatán beach

7

Into Honduras: Copán and the Bay Islands

Across the border in **Honduras**, about five hours by road from Guatemala City, are the ruins of **Copán**, one of the most magnificent of all Maya sites. While the compact scale of the site is not initially as impressive as Tikal or Mexico's Chichén Itzá, it boasts an astonishing number of decorative carvings, stelae and altars, including the longest Maya text in existence: a hieroglyphic stairway of some two thousand glyphs carved onto a flight of sixty stone steps. Throw in a wonderful site museum, perhaps the best in the Maya world, and the delightful and friendly village of Copán Ruinas, where most people stay, and it's not surprising that Copán now ranks as the second most-visited destination in the country. Within easy striking distance of Copán, the **Bay Islands** (Islas de la Bahía) of Utila, Roatán and Guanaja have a completely different, but equally alluring appeal: palm-fringed white-sand beaches, balmy Caribbean waters and near-pristine coral reefs perfect for snorkelling and scuba diving. Culturally distinct from the rest of Honduras, the islanders are the descendants of Cayman Islanders, buccaneers and shipwrecked African slaves, and most still speak a melodic, archaic-sounding English. There's little local affection for mainland Central American culture, with radios and satellite dishes tuned to North American broadcasts and reggae music dominating the dancehalls. For the visitor, **Utila** and **Roatán** offer a tremendous opportunity to visit affordable, friendly and accessible islands with none of the tourist overkill, high prices or hassle that can taint other Caribbean destinations. **Guanaja**, on the other hand, is not as set up for independent travellers, and mainly caters to scuba divers on pre-booked package trips. Its once-densely forested interior is also still recovering after being badly mauled by Hurricane Mitch in 1998.

Getting to Honduras is pretty straightforward from Guatemala. If you're heading to Copán, there are excellent transport links from Antigua and Guatemala City by direct daily shuttle and luxury buses (see p.98 and p.122), or you can also travel via Chiquimula (see p.290), a longer but cheaper route. From Copán you can (just) get to the Bay Islands the same day by travelling on an early bus via San Pedro Sula to La Ceiba and taking a flight or boat from there. The other main crossing between Guatemala and Honduras is close to the coastline from Puerto Barrios to Puerto Cortés (see p.399). It's a slow journey, but ongoing highway improvements in Honduras should mean that this route will be much faster soon.

Note that the **country code** for Honduras is 504 and there are no area codes.

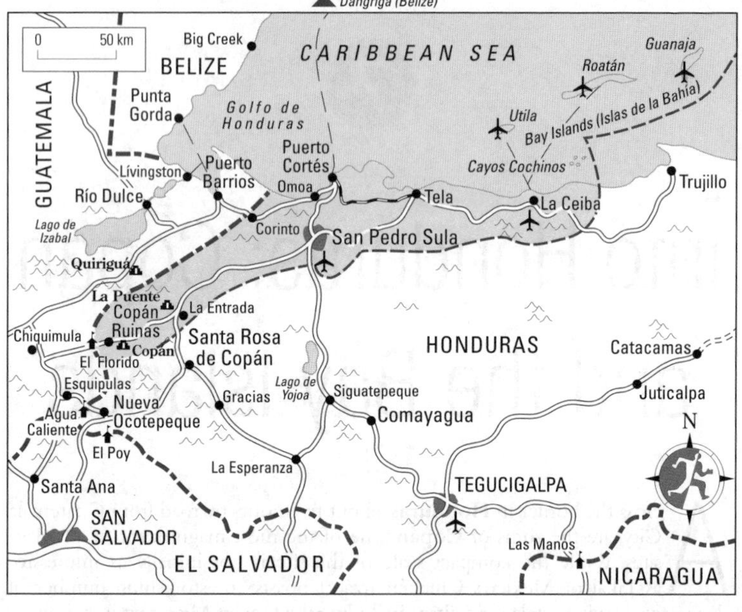

Copán and around

Delightfully located in a sweeping highland valley, the city-state of **Copán** was the southernmost centre of the Maya civilization. It's easy to understand what attracted the Maya to the site, which lies on the fertile banks of the Río Copán at a pleasingly temperate altitude of 600m. Today the countryside around Copán is equally appealing and fecund, with green rolling hills of pastureland, and tobacco and coffee farms interspersed with patches of pine forest. Though the archeological site is the main attraction, there's plenty more to explore in the surrounding area, with hot springs, an excellent bird park and the minor site of **Las Sepulturas** just a few kilometres away. A short walk west of the ruins, easy-going **Copán Ruinas** is not much more than an overgrown village, but it makes a great base, with attractive hotels, good cafés and restaurants, and fast onward transport connections with Guatemala and the rest of Honduras.

Getting to Copán

Speedy, direct **shuttle buses** (US$15 one way) leave Antigua daily at 4am, pausing to pick up passengers in Guatemala City an hour later on demand, and getting to Copán by around 10am; they return to Guatemala at 3pm from Copán. These shuttle buses are operated by Monarcas Travel, Alameda Santa Lucia Norte 7, Antigua (ⓣ7832 1939, ⓦwww.mayabus.com). A daily 5am luxury a/c pullman bus (US$35 one way) also covers the Guatemala City–Copán route, operated by Hedman Alas, based at 2 Av 8–73, Zona 10 (ⓣ2362 5072) in Guatemala City.

Alternatively, you could save a little cash by travelling via the Guatemalan town of **Chiquimula**, which is regularly served by Rutas Orientales buses from Guatemala City and local buses from Puerto Barrios. From Chiquimula buses leave every 45 minutes (1hr 15min) for the border at **El Florido** (open 6am–6pm), 57km to the west along an excellent paved road. Border formalities are straightforward, though they can be slow – and you'll almost certainly be asked for an unofficial US$1–2 "exit tax" to leave the country. Virtually all Western nationalities do not need to pay to enter Honduras as they are granted a free 30-day visa at the border (for more on this, see "Red tape and visas" in the Basics section of this book), though border officials, like their Guatemalan counterparts, may request a dollar or two. The Banrural **bank** (Mon–Sat 7am–6pm), at the border just inside Guatemala, changes travellers' cheques and cashes dollars, or you can deal with the ever-present moneychangers at the border post who handle dollars, lempiras and quetzals at pretty fair rates.

From El Florido, pick-ups and minibuses leave when full (about every 30min; US$1.75) to the town of Copán Ruinas, taking around twenty minutes; the last one leaves at 6pm. **Heading back** into Guatemala, the last bus leaves El Florido for Chiquimula at 4.30pm, though it's sensible to cross as early in the day as possible to ensure onward connections in Guatemala. If you plan to **drive** inside Honduras, note that you need permission from your Guatemalan rental car company. If time is really tight (and money is not), you can **charter a flight** from Guatemala City to Copán with Jungle Flying, Hangar L-22, Av Hincapié & 18 Calle, Zona 13, Guatemala City (Ⓣ2360 4917 & 2339 0502), for around US$240 return, based on four paying passengers.

Copán Ruinas: the town

One kilometre northwest of the archeological site of Copán lies the small town of **COPÁN RUINAS**, a charming place of steep cobbled streets and red-tiled roofs, set among the lush scenery of Honduras's western highlands. Despite a fast-increasing number of visitors, income from whom now forms the mainstay of the town's economy, it has managed to remain a largely unspoilt and genuinely friendly place. Many travellers are seduced by Copán's delightfully relaxed atmosphere, clean air and rural setting, and end up spending longer here than planned, studying Spanish, eating and drinking well, or exploring the region's other minor sites, hot springs and beautiful countryside.

Arrival and information

Almost everything of interest is within a few blocks of Copán's Parque Central. **Pick-ups** and minibuses to and from the border at El Florido leave from a block west of the parque. Monarcas shuttles operate from La Casa de Todo, a block east of the parque, while Hedman Alas buses use a new purpose-built terminal 500m south of the parque. Other Honduran bus companies leave from stops near the football pitch just east of the town centre; for schedules see "Moving On" box on p.390. Tuk-tuks (also called "mototaxis") are plentiful in Copán, and will whisk you around the village or to the ruins for around US$0.50 per person a journey.

For local information, check out the **tourist office** (daily 8am–7pm; Ⓣ651 4394, Ⓔinfo@copanhonduras.org), just off the Parque Central, or the two excellent local **websites**, Ⓦwww.copanruinas.com and Ⓦwww.copanhonduras.org. The **post office** is just off the parque behind the museum; **Hondutel** is just south of the plaza.

Accommodation

Many of the town's older **hotels** have undergone refits to attract the ever-expanding organized-tour market, while a swathe of new mid-range places

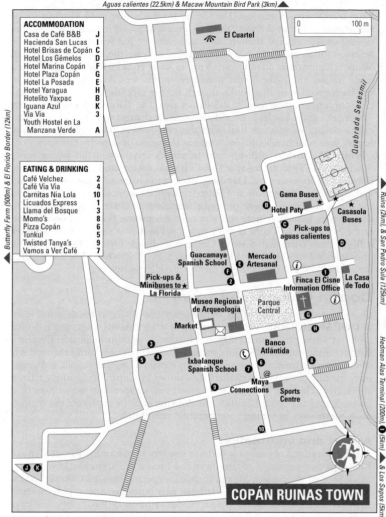

Aguas calientes (22.5km) & Macaw Mountain Bird Park (3km)

Butterfly Farm (500m) & El Florido Border (12km)

Ruins (2km), & San Pedro Sula (125km)

Hedman Alas Terminal (200m), 1 (5km) & Los Sapos (5km)

ACCOMMODATION

Casa de Café B&B	J
Hacienda San Lucas	I
Hotel Brisas de Copán	C
Hotel Los Gémelos	D
Hotel Marina Copán	F
Hotel Plaza Copán	G
Hotel La Posada	E
Hotel Yaragua	H
Hotelito Yaxpac	B
Iguana Azul	K
Via Via	3
Youth Hostel en La Manzana Verde	A

EATING & DRINKING

Café Velchez	2
Café Via Via	4
Carnitas Nia Lola	10
Licuados Express	1
Llama del Bosque	3
Momo's	8
Pizza Copán	6
Tunkul	5
Twisted Tanya's	9
Vamos a Ver Café	7

El Cuartel
0 100 m
Quebrada Sesesmil
Gama Buses
Hotel Paty
Casasola Buses
Pick-ups to aguas calientes
Guacamaya Spanish School
Mercado Artesanal
Pick-ups & Minibuses to La Florida
Finca El Cisne Information Office
La Casa de Todo
Museo Regional de Arqueología
Parque Central
Market
Banco Atlántida
Ixbalanque Spanish School
Maya Connections
Sports Centre
N

COPÁN RUINAS TOWN

helps keep prices competitive. Budget options tend to fill up quickly so book ahead, if arriving late in the day. If you'd prefer a well-equipped house to rent, speak to the owners of the *Casa de Café*.

Casa de Café B&B at the southwest edge of town, overlooking the Río Copán valley ⓣ651 4620, ⓦwww.casadecafecopan.com. A charming place owned by an American–Honduran couple, with ten comfortable and airy rooms, all with wood panelling, desks and nice individual touches, plus private bathrooms with steaming hot water. There's also a fabulous garden where you could lie in a hammock and enjoy the views all day. A huge ranch-style breakfast is included, and there's free coffee, a library with many guidebooks and Maya-related titles, videos and TV. 6

Hacienda San Lucas 5km south of parque ⓣ651 4106, ⓦwww.haciendasanlucas.com. Wonderful converted farmhouse accommodation set in the hills south of town, with startling views over the valley. There's an attached restaurant with excellent home-cooked food, plus horse-riding and the small Los Sapos archeological site in the grounds. A hearty breakfast is included and atmospheric evening meals are served by candlelight. Free transport is provided from their welcome centre two blocks north of the parque. ❽

Hotel Brisas de Copán one block north of parque ⓣ651 4118. Clean, good-sized accommodation all with bath, hot water and TV, and some with terraces. Parking. ❹

Hotel Los Gémelos a block east of parque ⓣ651 4077. Friendly backpackers' stronghold with basic but clean rooms with fans (all shared bath) set off a central garden. It's one of the best budget options in town, with reliable hot water, so it fills rapidly. ❷

Hotel Marina Copán just northwest of parque ⓣ651 4070, ⓦwww.hotelmarinacopan.com. The most luxurious accommodation in town. The stylish rooms, all with a/c and TV, are beautifully presented, plus there's a small pool, sauna, gym and bar on site. ❽

Hotel Plaza Copán east side of parque ⓣ651 4508, ⓦwww.hotelplazacopan.com. Twenty-one slightly pricey rooms, some overlooking the square and all with a/c and cable TV. The hotel also features a pleasant courtyard with a fountain and a small kidney-shaped pool, and a restaurant which serves all meals. ❻

Hotel La Posada northwest of parque ⓣ651 4059, ⓔlaposada@hotelmarinacopan.com. Under the same ownership as the *Hotel Plaza Copán*, rooms here are more basic but still good value considering the price. Verdant gardens and small but cosy rooms with TV and bathroom make this one of the better mid-range options. ❹

Hotel Yaragua half a block east of parque ⓣ651 4050, ⓦwww.yaragua.com. Pleasant hotel with 24 smallish but comfortable, good-value rooms, set around a verdant little courtyard, with good-quality double beds and cable TV. The in-house restaurant is open from 6am and has a typical Honduran-style menu. ❹

Hotelito Yaxpac a block north of parque ⓣ651 4025. Run by a friendly family, the *Yaxpac* features four simple and clean rooms, all with private bath and two with little balconies. The sole drawback is the 8am checkout time. ❷

Iguana Azul next to the *Casa de Café B&B* (and under the same ownership) ⓣ651 4620, ⓦwww.iguanaazulcopan.com. Very popular budget choice, with three private doubles and two pleasant dormitories, all with shared bath and decent mattresses. Amenities include private lockers for valuables, a pretty little garden, communal area and laundry facilities, plus great travel information. Dorm US$4; doubles ❷

Via Via two blocks west of parque ⓣ651 4652, ⓦwww.viaviacafe.com. Simple but spotless rooms with en-suite bathrooms and dorms (US$4 per bed) at the rear of a popular travellers' café. It can be noisy here at night, but it's great value. The hospitable Belgian owners speak excellent English and will help you organize trips, and the hotel's notice board also has information on local attractions and events. ❷

Youth Hostel en La Manzana Verde a block and a half north of parque ⓣ651 4652, ⓦwww.enlamanzanaverde.com. Under the same ownership as *Via Via*, this pleasant new youth hostel has basic but well-planned six- and four-bed dorm rooms (US$4), a double room, private guest lockers, kitchen and laundry facilities, a lounge with TV, and an information-rich notice board. They can also organize tours here. ❷

The Town

Half a day is enough to take in virtually all the town's attractions. The **Parque Central** – lined with banks, municipal structures and an attractive, whitewashed Baroque-style church – was designed and built by visiting archeologists Tatiana Proskouriakoff and Gustav Stromsvik. Unfortunately, the simple elegance of the original layout, which followed classical Spanish lines, has been somewhat spoilt by grandiose remodelling initiatives, including a series of sweeping pillars and arches, which have been unleashed by a local mayor in the past few years. It does remain a popular place to kill time, however, its benches filled with cowboy-booted farmhands and camera-touting visitors. A number of new **souvenir shops** on or close to the parque sell ceramics, wood and leather crafts from the region and elsewhere in the country; all of the shops are broadly similar in terms of price and range. Inside the **Mercado Artesanal**, on the north side of the plaza, you'll find more local handicrafts, including dolls made from dried maize leaves.

On the west side of the parque, and somewhat eclipsed by the sculpture museum at the site itself, is the **Museo Regional de Arqueología** (Mon–Sat 8am–4pm; US$2). Inside are some impressive Maya carvings collected from the Copán region, including the glyph-covered Altars T and U; Stela B, depicting the ruler Waxaklajuun Ub'aah K'awiil (Eighteen Rabbit); and some remarkable and intricately detailed flints – ornamental oddities with seven interlocking heads carved from obsidian. There are also two remarkable **tombs**. The first contains the remains of a female shaman, complete with jade jewellery and the skulls of a puma, deer and two human sacrificial victims. The other (10J-45), discovered in 1999 during road-building work, was created for an Early Classic period ruler of Copán during the sixth century and comprises a vaulted burial chamber where the as yet unidentified ruler was buried with numerous ceramics and two large, carved jade, pectoral pieces.

Just behind the museum (turn right beyond the post office), the tiny municipal **market** is worth a browse and has a fair selection of fresh fruit. For a fine view over the town and surrounding countryside, walk north from the Parque Central for about five blocks to the crumbling **El Cuartel**, the old military barracks up the hill.

Copán's outskirts

About 3km north of the plaza, the **Macaw Mountain Bird Park and Nature Reserve** (daily 9am–5pm; $10; Ⓦwww.macawmountain.com), with abundant parrots, parakeets, toucans, six species of macaw, grey hawks, and a great horned owl, is worth the hefty entrance fee. Most of the birds have been previously kept as pets and donated to the centre, and breeding programmes have been started for very rare species such as the great green macaw and the yellow-lored amazon. The reserve has enough of interest for a good half-day excursion, with walk-through aviaries and nature trails that wind through a lovely old-growth forest of cedar, mahogany fig and zapote trees, interspersed with elevated viewing decks. You'll also find a coffee-roasting house and café serving gourmet coffee from the Copán region, an information centre explaining the relationship between the Maya and birds, and a wonderful natural pool for swimming.

On the other side of town, a twenty-minute walk from the plaza along the road to Guatemala, stands the **Enchanted Wings Butterfly House and Nature Centre** (daily 8am–5pm; $5.50), owned by an American enthusiast and his Honduran wife. Butterflies to look out for include the speckled brown "giant owl" and the scarlet-and-yellow "helicopter", two of the hardier species. Butterflies hatch in the morning hours, so it's best to time your visit accordingly. There's also a display of more than two hundred orchids, around a third of Honduras's native species, with the periods of February to April and July to August being the best time to see them flowering.

Eating and drinking

Copán has a wide range of places to **eat** and **drink**, many of them catering specifically to the tourist market. Standards are usually very high, with generous portions and good service, although virtually all restaurants stop serving at 10pm. The most popular places for a drink are *Tunkul*, *Carnitas Nia Lola* and *Twisted Tanya's*. As for **nightlife**, some of the town's bars and cafés provide live music, especially at weekends, while the local sports centre hosts weekend discos twice a month. The Camino Maya centre (known locally as *la piscina)*, on the road east out of town, has the highly popular *Tavos* bar, a swimming pool, a restaurant and pool tables, plus discos on Friday and Saturday nights (until 2am; US$2.75).

Café Velchez northwest corner of parque. Upmarket European-style café, serving good but fairly pricey coffees (including espresso), juices and licuados, alcoholic drinks (wine by the glass), cakes and light meals.

Café Via Via two blocks west of parque. Belgian-owned establishment with a street-side terrace and leafy garden offering an array of sandwiches and good breakfasts, including pancakes and omelettes. There's also a very reasonably priced fixed menu with vegetarian options.

Carnitas Nia Lola two blocks south of parque. This highly atmospheric and enjoyable restaurant-bar serves large portions of delicious grilled and barbecued meats, plus vegetarian dishes, at reasonable prices. It's equally frequented as a drinking venue, with an early-evening happy hour and a good mix of locals and visitors.

Licuados Express one block east of parque. Open by 6.30am, this little juice bar serves delicious licuados, juices and breakfasts to the town's early birds. Try the gourmet licuados – mocaccino or chocobanana are best – or tuck into home-made cookies and bagels.

Llama del Bosque two blocks west of parque. Slightly old-fashioned restaurant with a reasonably priced menu that includes local breakfasts, meat and chicken dishes, *baleadas* and snacks.

Momo's one block south of parque. Fast becoming legendary for huge, bargain-priced meat dishes, this atmospheric log restaurant has an open-air barbecue where the food is cooked in front of you.

Pizza Copán opposite Hondutel. Popular with locals and tourists alike who come to indulge in decent pizza and pasta. No alcohol served but take-away available. Be sure to check out the original stone sculptures.

Tunkul Bar and Restaurant two blocks west of parque. Buzzing garden restaurant-bar with good food, including burritos, vegetarian dishes and a very popular garlic chicken, plus lively music and a happy hour (8–9pm).

Twisted Tanya's A block south and a block west of parque. The nearest thing Copán has to gourmet dining, this stylish and enjoyable English-owned bar-restaurant has an ambitious menu that includes seafood pasta with crab, mussels and conch, filet mignon and Indian-style curries. There's a great dessert list, wine from Spain and South America, and very fine tropical cocktails (happy hour 4–6pm). Around US$10 for two courses.

Vamos a Ver Café one block south of parque. Busy garden café that's popular with travellers thanks to affordable and delicious home-made soups, sandwiches and snacks.

Listings

Banks Banco Atlántida and BAC, both on the parque, have Visa ATMs and will change travellers' cheques, cash dollars and quetzals (at poor rates).

Book exchange Exchanges available at La Casa de Todo, near the *Hotel Los Gémelos*, and at *Carnitas Nia Lola*.

Internet There are several Internet places in town, including Maya Connections, just south of the plaza, and La Casa de Todo (daily 8am–8pm). Rates are around US$1.25 an hour.

Language schools Copán is an excellent place to study, with two Spanish schools to choose between, though it's a more expensive learning centre than Guatemala – four hours of classes plus full family-based accommodation and meals costs US$180–200 a week. Guacamaya (Ⓣ651 4360, Ⓦwww.guacamaya.com), north of the plaza, is the older of the two schools and more expensive, though Ixbalanque (Ⓣ651 4432, Ⓦwww.ixbalanque.com), west of the plaza, is also worth considering.

Laundry La Casa de Todo (see above) charges around US$0.90 for a normal load.

Tour operators Yaragua Tours (Ⓣ651 4147, Ⓦwww.yaragua.com), half a block east of the plaza, is a good local company that offers trips to the hot springs (US$15 per person), El Rubí waterfall (US$20), a spectacular local cave, the Cueva el Boquerón (US$35), horse-riding (US$20 for 3hr) and river tubing (US$15). Robert Gallardo at the butterfly farm (see p.388) runs top-class bird-watching tours from around US$40 for a half-day. Monarcas (Ⓣ651 4361, Ⓦwww.mayabus.com), one block north of the plaza, can also arrange trips in the Copán area and throughout Guatemala.

Copán ruins

COPÁN RUINS lie 1.5km east of town, a pleasant fifteen-minute walk along a raised footpath that runs parallel to the highway. Entrance to the site (daily 8am–4pm; US$10 including the Las Sepulturas ruins, though access to the archeological tunnels costs an extra US$12) is through the **visitor centre** on

Moving on from Copán

To reach other destinations **within Honduras**, including the Bay Islands, you'll have to travel on to the large industrial city of San Pedro Sula, from where there are regular flights to the Bay Islands, or press on to the coastal city of La Ceiba, which has daily boat connections to Roatán and Utila and several daily flights to all three islands. Direct Hedman Alas a/c luxury buses (Ⓣ651 4106, Ⓦwww.hedmanalas.com) to San Pedro Sula leave Copán from a private terminal 500m south of the plaza daily at 5.30am and 10.30am. There's an extra service on Fri, Sat, Sun and Mon at 2.30pm (US$8; 3hr). Casasola offer a less expensive bus service (US$4.50) to San Pedro Sula at 7am daily, leaving from a stop opposite the football pitch, while a Gama bus (same time and price) leaves from a spot nearby, next to *Hotel Paty*.

For Guatemala, direct Monarcas shuttle buses to Antigua (US$15; 6hr) leave from their office a block and a half north of Copán's plaza daily at 2pm; they travel via Guatemala City, if there are passengers. Hedman Alas run a luxury a/c bus service to Guatemala City (US$35; 5hr) daily at 1.30pm; the company can arrange an onward shuttle connection to Antigua for US$6 per person.

If you want to explore Guatemala's eastern highlands or Caribbean region, it's cheapest to take a pick-up or minibus (US$1.50) to the border at El Florido, then a local bus (every 45min, the last at 4.30pm; US$1.25) to Chiquimula from where there are regular buses to destinations including Puerto Barrios.

the left-hand side of the car park, where a small exhibition explains Copán's place in the Maya world. Inside the visitor centre there's a ticket office and a desk where you can hire a registered site **guide** (US$20 for 2hr) – an excellent investment if you really want to get the most out of Copán. On the other side of the car park is a **cafeteria**, serving drinks and reasonable meals, and a small souvenir shop.

Opposite the visitor centre is the terrific **Museum of Mayan Sculpture** (daily 8am–3.45pm; US$5), arguably the finest in the entire Maya region, with a tremendous collection of stelae, altars, panels and well-labelled explanations in English. You enter through a dramatic entrance doorway, resembling the jaws of a serpent, and pass through a tunnel (signifying the passage into *xibalba*, or the underworld). Dominating the museum is a full-scale, flamboyantly painted replica of the magnificent **Rosalila Temple**, built by Moon Jaguar in 571 and discovered intact under Temple 16. A vast crimson- and jade-coloured mask of the Sun God, depicted with wings outstretched, forms the main facade of the temple. Other ground-floor exhibits concentrate on aspects of Maya beliefs and cosmology, while the upper floor houses many of the finest original sculptures from the Copán valley, comprehensively displaying the skill of the Maya craftsmen.

From the museum it's a 200m walk east to the **warden's gate**, the entrance to the site proper, where your ticket will be checked and where there are usually several squabbling red macaws to greet your arrival – these are tame and sleep in cages by the gate at night.

A brief history of Copán

Archeologists now believe that settlers began moving into the Río Copán valley from around 1400 BC, taking advantage of the area's rich agricultural potential, although construction of the city is not thought to have begun until around 100 AD.

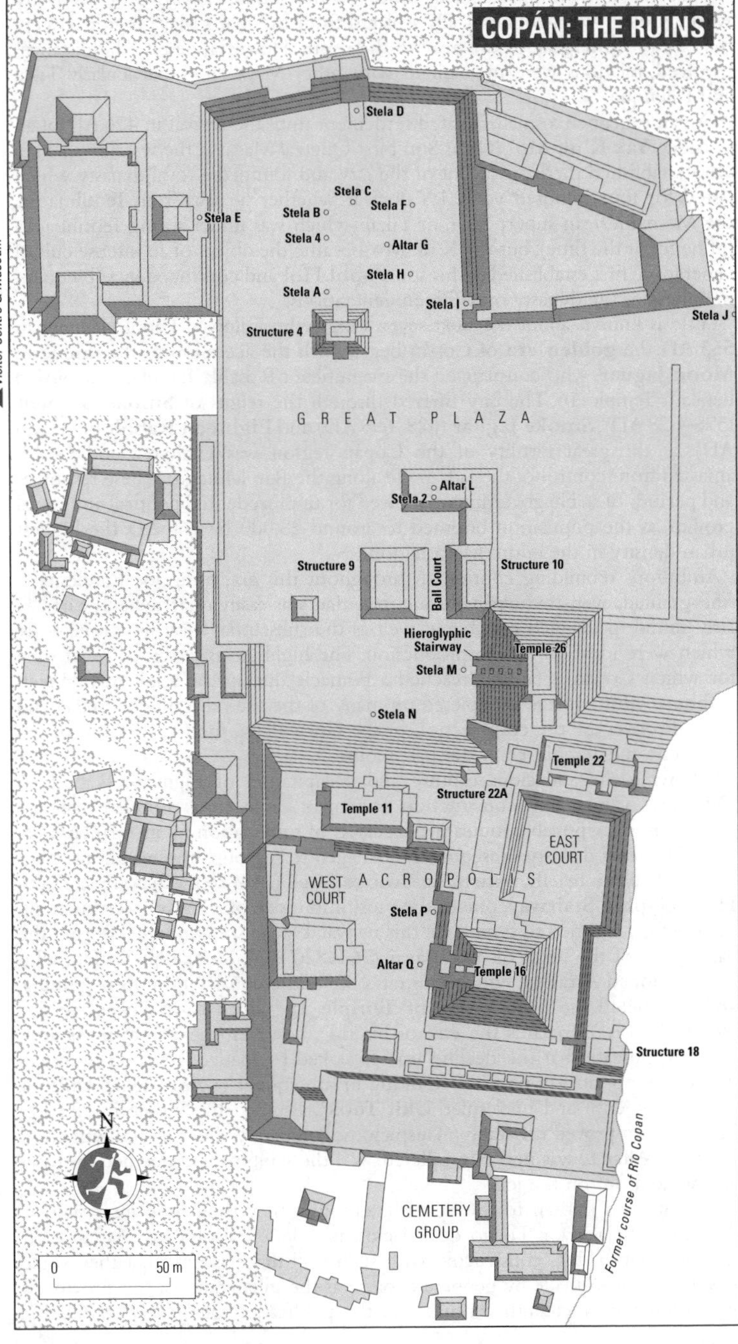

7 INTO HONDURAS: COPÁN AND THE BAY ISLANDS | Copán and around

Once the most important **city-state** on the southern fringes of the Maya world, Copán was geographically isolated from the main Maya region, except the city of **Quiriguá**, 64km away to the north. However, despite the distances involved, relations were maintained with other Maya cities, particularly Tikal and Palenque.

Copán remained a small, isolated settlement until the arrival in 426 AD of an outsider, **Yax K'uk Mo'** (Great Sun First Quetzal Macaw), the warrior-shaman who established the basic layout of the city and founded a royal dynasty which lasted for four hundred years. It's unclear whether he was from Teotihuacán, the Mesoamerican superpower, or Tikal (which was under strong Teotihuacán influence at the time), but Yax K'uk Mo' became the object of an intense cult of veneration, first established by his son **Popol Hol** and continued by subsequent members of the dynasty over fifteen generations.

Little is known about the next seven kings who followed Popol Hol, but in 553 AD the **golden era** of Copán began with the accession to the throne of **Moon Jaguar**, who constructed the magnificent Rosalila Temple, now buried beneath Temple 16. The city thrived through the reigns of **Smoke Serpent** (578–628 AD), **Smoke Jaguar** (628–695 AD) and **Eighteen Rabbit** (695–738 AD), as the great fertility of the Copán region was exploited and wealth amassed from control of the jade trade along the Río Motagua. These resources and periods of stable government allowed for unprecedented political and social growth, as the population boomed to around 28,000 by 760 AD, the highest urban density in the entire Maya region.

Ambitious rebuilding continued throughout this era, using local andesite, a fine-grained, even-textured volcanic rock that was easily quarried and particularly suited to detailed carving, as well as the substantial local limestone beds, which were ideal for stucco production. The highly artistic carved-relief style for which Copán is famous reached a pinnacle during the reign of Eighteen Rabbit – whose image is depicted on many of the site's magnificent stelae and who also oversaw the construction of the Great Plaza, the final version of the ball court and Temple 22 in the East Court.

Following the audacious capture and decapitation of Eighteen Rabbit by Quiriguá's Cauac Sky, construction at Copán came to a complete halt for seventeen years, possibly indicating a period of subjugation by its former vassal state. The royal dynasty subsequently managed to regroup, however, flourishing gloriously, albeit briefly, once more. **Smoke Shell** (749–763 AD) completed the **Hieroglyphic Stairway**, one of the most impressive of all Maya constructions, in an effort designed to symbolize this revival. Optimism continued during the early years of the reign of **Yax Pasaj** (763–820 AD), Smoke Shell's son, who commissioned **Altar Q**, which illustrates the entire dynasty from its beginning, and completed the final version of **Temple 16**, which towers over the site, around 776 AD. Towards the end of his rule, however, the rot set in: skeletal remains indicate that the decline was provoked by inadequate food resources created by population pressure, resulting in subsequent environmental collapse. The seventeenth and final ruler, **Ukit Took'**, assumed the throne in 822 AD, but his reign proved miserably inauspicious. Poignantly, the only monument to his reign, Altar L, was never completed, as if the sculptor had downed his tools and walked out on the job.

The site was known to the Spanish, although they took little interest in it. A court official, Don Diego de Palacios, in a letter written in March 1576, mentions city ruins "constructed with such skill that it seems that they could never have been made by people as coarse as the inhabitants of this province". Not until the nineteenth century and the publication of *Incidents of Travel in*

Central America, Chiapas and Yucatán by **John Lloyd Stephens** and **Frederick Catherwood** did Copán become known to the wider world. Stephens, the then acting US ambassador, succeeded in buying the ruins in 1839 and, accompanied by Catherwood, a British architect and artist, spent several weeks clearing the site and mapping the buildings. Stephens' plans to float Copán's monuments down the Río Copán and on to the US were never realized, but the instant success of the book and the interest it sparked in Mesoamerican culture ensured that Copán became a magnet for explorers.

British archeologist **Alfred Maudsley** began a full-scale mapping, excavation and reconstruction of the site in 1891 under the sponsorship of the Peabody Museum at Harvard University. A second major investigation was begun in 1935 by the Washington Carnegie Institute, during which the Río Copán was diverted to prevent it carving into the site. A breakthrough in the understanding not only of Copán but of the whole Maya world came in 1959–60, when archeologists Heinrich Berlin and Tatiana Proskouriakoff first began to decipher Maya **glyphs**, leading to the realization that they record the history of the cities and their dynasties.

Since 1977, the Instituto Hondureño de Antropología e Historia has been running a series of projects with the help of archeologists from around the world. Copán is now perhaps the best understood of all Maya cities, and a series of **tunnelling projects** beneath the Acropolis has unearthed remarkable discoveries including, in 1989, the Rosalila Temple, which is now open to the public. In 1993 the Papagayo Temple, built by Popol Hol and dedicated to his father Yax K'uk Mo', was uncovered, and in 1998 further burrowing revealed the tomb of the founder himself.

The Great Plaza

Straight ahead through the avenue of trees lies the **Great Plaza**, a large rectangular arena strewn with the magnificently carved and exceptionally well-preserved stelae that are Copán's outstanding features. Initially, however, the visual impact of this grassy expanse may seem a little underwhelming: the first structure you see is **Stucture 4**, a modestly sized pyramid-temple, while the stepped buildings bordering the northern end of the plaza are low and unremarkable. This part of the Great Plaza was once a public place, the stepped sides bordered by a densely populated residential area. The grandest buildings are confined to the monumental temples that border the southern section of the plaza, rising to form the Acropolis, the domain of the ruling and religious elite.

▲ Copán emblem glyph

Dotted all around are Copán's famed **stelae** and altars, made from local andesite. Most of the stelae represent **Eighteen Rabbit**, Copán's "King of the Arts" (stelae A, B, C, D, F, H and 4). **Stela A**, dating from 731 AD, has incredibly deep carving, although the faces are now eroded; its sides include a total of 52 glyphs, translating into a famous inscription that includes the emblem glyphs of the four great cities of Copán, Palenque, Tikal and Calakmul – a text designed to show that Eighteen Rabbit saw his city as a pivotal power in the Maya world. **Stela B** depicts a slightly oriental-looking Eighteen Rabbit, wearing a turban-like headdress intertwined with twin macaws, while his hands support a bar motif, a symbol designed to show the ruler holding up the sky. **Stela C** (730 AD) is one of the earliest stones to have faces on both sides and, like many of the central stelae, has an altar at its base, carved in the shape of a turtle. Two rulers are represented here: facing the turtle (a symbol of longevity) is Eighteen

△ Stela at Copán

Rabbit's father, Smoke Jaguar, who lived well into his eighties, while on the other side is Eighteen Rabbit himself. **Stela H**, perhaps the most impressively executed of all the sculptures, shows Eighteen Rabbit wearing the latticed skirt of the Maize God, his wrists weighed down with jewellery, while his face is crowned with a stunning headdress.

The Ball Court and Hieroglyphic Stairway

South of Structure 4, towards the Acropolis, is the I-shaped **Ball Court**, one of the largest and most elaborate of the Classic period, and one of the few Maya courts still to have a paved floor. It was completed in 738 AD, just four months before Eighteen Rabbit's demise at the hands of Quiriguá; two previous versions lie beneath it. Like its predecessors, the court was dedicated to the great macaw deity, and both sloping sides of the court are lined with three sculpted macaw heads. The rooms that line the sides of the court, overlooking the playing area, were probably used by priests and members of the elite as they watched the game.

Pressed up against the Ball Court and protected by a vast canvas cover is the famed **Hieroglyphic Stairway**, perhaps Copán's most astonishing monument. The stairway, which takes up the entire western face of the Temple 26 pyramid, is made up of some 72 stone steps; every block is carved to form part of the glyphic sequence – around 2200 glyph blocks in all. It forms the longest-known Maya hieroglyphic text, but, unfortunately, attempted reconstruction by early archeologists left the sequence so jumbled that a complete interpretation is still some way off. What is known is that the stairway was initiated to record the dynastic history of the city: some of the lower steps were first put in place by Eighteen Rabbit in 710 AD, while Smoke Shell rearranged and completed most of the sequences in 755 AD as part of his efforts to reassert the city's dignity and strength. At the base of the stairway, the badly weathered **Stela M** depicts Smoke Shell and records a solar eclipse in 756 AD.

Adjacent to the Hierogylphic Stairway, and towering over the extreme southern end of the plaza, are the vertiginous steps of **Temple 11** (also known as the Temple of the Inscriptions). The temple was constructed by Smoke Shell, who is thought to be buried beneath it, though no tomb has yet been found. At its base is another classic piece of Copán carving, **Stela N** (761 AD), representing Smoke Shell, with portraits on the two main faces of the stela and glyphs down the sides. The depth of the relief has protected the nooks and crannies, some of which still bear traces of paint – originally the carvings and buildings would have been painted in a whole range of bright colours, but for some reason only the red has survived.

The Acropolis

From the southwestern corner of the plaza, a trail runs past some original drainage ducts beyond which stone steps climb steeply up the side of Temple 11 to a soaring cluster of temples, dubbed the **Acropolis**. This lofty inner sanctum was the preserve of royalty, nobles and priests; it was the political and ceremonial core where religious rituals were enacted, sacrifices performed and rulers entombed. The whole structure grew in size over four hundred years, the temples growing higher and higher as new structures were built over the remains of earlier buildings. A warren of excavated tunnels, some open to the public, bores through the vast bulk of the Acropolis to the Rosalila Temple and several tombs. From the summit of Temple 11, beside a giant ceiba tree (a tree held sacred by the Maya), there's a panoramic view of the site below, over the Ball Court and Great Plaza to the green hills beyond.

A few metres east of Temple 11 are the **Mat House** (Structure 22A), a governmental building distinguished by its interlocking weave-like patterns, and **Temple 22**, which boasts some superbly intricate stonework around the door frames. Constructed by Eighteen Rabbit, Temple 22 functioned as a "sacred mountain" where the elite performed religious blood-letting ceremonies. Above the door is the body of a double-headed snake, its heads resting on two figures, which are in turn supported by skulls. The decoration here is unique in the southern Maya region – only Yucatán sites such as Kabáh and Chicanna have carvings of comparable quality.

The East Court

Below Temple 22 are the stepped sides of the **East Court**, a graceful plaza which also bears elaborate carvings, including life-sized jaguar heads with hollow eyes which would have once held pieces of jade or polished obsidian. In the middle of the western staircase, flanked by the jaguars, is a rectangular Venus mask, carved in superb deep relief. Rising over the court and dominating the Acropolis is the tallest structure in Copán, **Temple 16**, a thirty-metre pyramid completed by the city's sixteenth ruler, Yax Pasaj, in 776 AD. To construct the temple Yax Pasaj had to build on top of the **Rosalila Temple**, though it was built with extraordinary – and atypical – care so as not to destroy the earlier temple; generally, it was Maya custom to ritually deface or destroy obsolete temples or stelae. The temple served as a centre for worship during the reign of Smoke Serpent, or Butz' Chan (578–628 AD), Copán's eleventh ruler, a period that marked the apogee of the city's political, social and artistic growth – so the discovery of the Rosalila has been one of the most exciting finds of recent years. You can now view the brilliant original facade of the buried temple by entering through a short **tunnel** – an unforgettable, if costly (US$12), experience, as it may be sealed again in future years. The admission price does at least include access to two further tunnels, which extend below the East Plaza past some early cosmological stucco carvings – including a huge macaw mask – more buried temple facades and crypts including the Galindo tomb.

At the southern end of the East Court, **Structure 18** is a small square building with four carved panels in which Yax Pasaj was buried in 821 AD. The diminutive scale of the structure reveals how quickly decline set in, with the militaristic nature of the panels symptomatic of the troubled times. The tomb was empty when excavated by archeologists and is thought to have been looted on a number of occasions. From Structure 18 there's a terrific view of the valley, over the Río Copán, which eroded the eastern buildings of the Acropolis over the centuries until its path was diverted by early archeologists. South of Structure 18, the **Cemetery Group** was once thought to have been a burial site, though it's now known to have been a residential complex and home to the ruling elite. To date, however, little work has been done on this part of the ruins.

The West Court

The second plaza of the Acropolis, the **West Court**, is confined by the south side of Temple 11, which has eight small doorways, and Temple 16. **Altar Q**, at the base of Temple 16, is the court's most famous feature and an astonishing example of ancestral symbolism. Carved in 776 AD, it celebrates Yax Pasaj's accession to the throne on July 2, 763. The top of the altar is carved with six hieroglyphic blocks, while the sides are decorated with sixteen cross-legged figures, all seated on cushions, who represent previous rulers of Copán. All are pointing towards a portrait of Yax Pasaj which shows him receiving a ceremonial staff from the city's first ruler Yax K'uk Mo', thereby endorsing Yax Pasaj's right to rule. Behind the altar is a small crypt, discovered to contain the remains of a macaw and fifteen big cats, sacrificed in honour of his ancestors when the altar was inaugurated.

Las Sepulturas

Two kilometres east of the ruins along a pleasant, newly laid stone pathway is the much smaller site of **Las Sepulturas** (daily 8am–4pm; entrance with the same ticket as for Copán), the focus of much archeological interest in recent years because of the information it provides on daily domestic life in Maya times. Eighteen of the forty-odd residential compounds at the site have been excavated, comprising one hundred buildings that would have been inhabited by the elite. Smaller compounds on the edge of the site are thought to have housed young princes, as well as concubines and servants. It was customary to bury the nobility close to their residences, and more than 250 tombs have been excavated around the compounds – given the number of women found in the tombs it seems likely that the local Maya practised polygamy. One of the most interesting finds – the tomb of a priest or shaman, dating from around 450 AD – is on display in the museum in Copán Ruinas.

Around Copán

Los Sapos (US$1.50), dating from the same era as Copán, is set in the hills to the south of town, about an hour or so away by foot; cross the river after the Hedman Alas bus terminal, bear left and follow the signs. The site, whose name derives from a rock carved in the shape of a toad, is thought to have been a place where Maya women came to bear children, though unfortunately time and weather have eroded much of the carving. To get there, follow the main road south out of town, turn left onto a dirt track just past the river bridge and follow this as it begins to climb gently into the hills, past the *Hacienda San Lucas* (see p.386) on whose grounds the ruins reside. The views across the tobacco fields of the river valley are beautiful, and there are plenty of spots for swimming along the way.

Pick-ups leave Copán regularly throughout the day for the peaceful town of **Santa Rita**, 9km to the northeast. At the river bridge, just before entering the town, a path leads up to **El Rubí**, a pretty double-waterfall on the Río Copán, about 2km away. Attacks on tourists were often reported up until a few years ago, when, under local advice, people stopped visiting independently. The implementation of a new tourist police in the Copán area may improve the security situation in the future, but you should always seek local information before setting out. In any case, an organized trip is probably a better option; Yaragua Tours in Copán charge US$20 per person.

Around 22km north of Copán are some (very) **hot springs** (US$1.25), set in lush highland scenery dotted with coffee fincas and patches of pine forest. Once there you can either wallow around in man-made pools or head to the source via a short trail where cool river water and near boiling-hot spring waters combine. One way to get to the *aguas calientes* is to hitch a ride on a passing pick-up, which are reasonably frequent from outside *Hotel Paty* in Copán and also pass the bird park; expect to pay around US$1 for the ride, which takes about 50 minutes. (If you're planning to hitch back to Copán, don't leave the springs any later than 3.30pm.) Alternatively, speak to one of Copán's tour operators.

A kilometre or so further north is the *agroturismo* centre at **Finca El Cisne** (Ⓣ651 4695, Ⓔfincaelcisne@copanruinas.com), a working finca involved in the production of cardamom, coffee and cattle. Tours involving you in the daily running of the centre as well as providing information on farming and agricultural practices in the region are well-organized and can be arranged through the Finca El Cisne office opposite La Casa de Todo in Copán Ruinas town. Day tours start from around US$35 including all meals, or you can stay over in comfortable rooms for around US$70 per night, which includes nocturnal visits to the hot springs (when they are closed to the public).

From Copán to the coast

Excellent road transport links connect Copán to the large and unappealing city of **San Pedro Sula**, where you'll have to change buses for the slightly more attractive coastal town of **La Ceiba**. If you leave Copán early enough, it's possible to make it to the Bay of Islands in a day, catching a flight in San Pedro or a ferry or flight from La Ceiba.

San Pedro Sula

Though it's Honduras's second city and the country's driving economic force, **SAN PEDRO SULA** is uninspiring as well as uncomfortably hot and humid for most of the year. This is a place for business rather than sightseeing, so if you can, press on to La Ceiba or catch a flight from here to the Bay Islands. The city lacks a central **bus terminal**, although one is planned for the near future. If you're looking to get out quickly, however, **taxis** are plentiful and pretty cheap: expect to pay around US$2.50 per journey in the central area, or around US$9 to the airport, 12km southeast of town.

If you do stay, San Pedro has a wide range of accommodation, restaurants and shops. Be prepared to pay more for a **hotel**, though, as the cheapest options are very rough. If you've arrived on a Casasola or Gama bus from Copán, the slightly ramshackle-looking but clean *Hotel Palmira*, at 6 C, 6–7 Av SO (Ⓣ557 6522; ❷–❹), couldn't be more convenient since it's right next to their shared terminal. All of the *Palmira*'s rooms come with private bathroom, and some also have a/c. Alternatively, the *Gran Hotel San Pedro*, a block east of the main parque at 3 C, 1–2 Av SO (Ⓣ553 1513, Ⓦwww.hotelsanpedrosa.com; ❸–❺), is a perennial favourite with travellers and has a good choice of rooms. The best mid-range hotel in town is the *Hotel Ejecutivo*, at 10 Av, 2 C SO (Ⓣ552 4289, Ⓦwww.hotel-ejecutivo.com; ❺–❻), which has large and comfortable rooms with a/c and TV.

Moving on from San Pedro Sula, three companies operate frequent buses for **La Ceiba** (3hr–3hr 30min), the gateway city to the Bay Islands. Two of the companies run luxury buses: Hedman Alas, at 3 Calle & 8 Avenida NO (Ⓣ553 1361, Ⓦwww.hedmanalas.com), with four daily departures; and Viana, at Av Circunvalación, 200m from *Wendy's* (Ⓣ556 9261), with two daily departures. Meanwhile, Catisa-Tupsa, located six blocks east of the Casasola bus terminal at 2 Av 5–6 C SO (Ⓣ552 1042), runs twelve standard daily buses that stop at towns en route. If you'd rather get to the Bay Islands as quickly as possible, **flights** in Honduras are quite reasonably priced. Three airlines – Taca/Isleña (Ⓣ668 3333, Ⓦwww.flyislena.com), Sosa (Ⓣ668 3223) and Atlantic Air (Ⓣ668 1309, Ⓦwww.atlanticairlines.com.ni) – connect San Pedro with Utila (3 daily; US$84), Roatán (7 daily; US$86) and Guanaja (2 daily; US$90); all flights are via La Ceiba.

La Ceiba

Some 190km east along the coast from San Pedro Sula, steamy **LA CEIBA** is one of the more approachable Honduran cities. Though it lacks sights and its beaches are not the cleanest, the city has a cosmopolitan mix of inhabitants, including a large Garífuna community (see p.274), and a bustling, self-assured atmosphere by day. However, it's the night that's really celebrated in La Ceiba – the city is unquestionably the **party capital** of the country, with a vibrant dancehall scene and a legendary May carnival.

All Catisa-Tupsa buses arrive at the **bus terminal**, 2km west of the Parque Central, while Viana buses pull in 200 west of here on the same road. Hedman Alas buses use a private terminal a five-minute walk south of the Megaplaza mall, which is about 1.5km south from the parque. Local buses and shared taxis run very frequently to the centre from all terminals. La Ceiba's **airport** is 9km south of town; a taxi to the centre costs US$4.50. Of Ceiba's **hotels** the best budget bet is the excellent *Banana Republic Guesthouse*, Av Morazón (Ⓣ440 1282; ❸), a five-minute walk from the vast Megaplaza mall and ten minutes north of the Hedman Alas terminal. It has private rooms and dorms (US$5–7 per bed), helpful staff, laundry, Internet connections and a garden with hammocks. Of the downtown hotels, *Hotel San Carlos*, Av San Isidro, 5–6 C (Ⓣ443 0330; ❷–❸), is a basic but safe place with a selection of simple accommodation, all with fans. The landmark *Gran Hotel Paris*, on the Parque Central (Ⓣ443 2391, Ⓦwww.granhotelparis.com; ❻), has an excellent location and large, comfortable rooms (all with a/c, phone and TV), plus a pool, bar and restaurant. For a beachfront location head to *Posada del Puerto*, just off 1 Calle (Ⓣ440 0030; ❹–❺), which has very spacious, tastefully presented rooms. If you want to sample La Ceiba's club scene, the action is concentrated in the string of bars and dance venues along the seafront.

Moving on from La Ceiba, ferries run twice daily to Utila, at 9.30am and 4.30pm (US$15 one way; 1hr), and Roatán, at 10am and 4pm (US$17 one way; 2hr). Ferries leave from the Muralla de Cabotaje municipal dock, about 5km to the east of the city; there's no bus service, so you'll need to take a taxi (US$5 from the centre; US$9 from the airport). **Flying** to the islands is also uncomplicated, with about a dozen flights daily to Roatán (30min; US$34), four daily to Utila (20min; US$32) and five daily to Guanaja (40min; US$36). Availability is rarely a problem, and you can usually buy your tickets on the spot at the airport, though it's best to book ahead in the peak holiday seasons (Christmas–Easter and August). The domestic airlines Taca/Isleña (Ⓣ443 0179) and Sosa (Ⓣ443 2519) have offices on the Parque Central in La Ceiba, while Atlantic Airlines (Ⓣ440 2343) has an office on Avenida La República; all have desks at the airport, too.

Overland from Guatemala to Tela

Although the beach and village of **Omoa** has a laid-back appeal and the faded resort of **Tela** some terrific nature reserves close by, few people linger long on Honduras's north coast, such is the appeal of the Bay Islands. Travelling overland this way you'll have to negotiate the sprawling, unattractive cities of Puerto Cortés and San Pedro Sula.

Minibuses leaving Puerto Barrios in Guatemala take an hour to reach the border crossing with Honduras, just past the huge Arizona bridge over the Río Motagua. Immigration is generally straightforward for travellers, with US$1–2 entry and exit charges being levied by the border officials. (However, drivers with foreign plates entering Honduras here have reported customs officials demanding that the necessary permit, and fee of around US$120, are processed in Puerto Cortés). Pick-ups leave when full for the ramshackle town of **Corinto**, a couple of kilometres or so away. There's absolutely no reason to hang around here, but if you get stuck head to the *Pulperia Arnold*, in the centre of town by the crossroads from the border, where the owner rents out some simple **rooms** (❷) and can provide good grub. Buses leave Corinto every 90 minutes for Puerto Cortés (the last at 3.30pm) along an excruciatingly slow and bumpy road, which is scheduled to be paved in its entirety by 2007.

Omoa

Fifty kilometres from Corinto there's a turn-off for the sleepy little fishing village of **Omoa**, 2km from the highway down a side road, which draws a steady trickle of travellers. Omoa is most famous for the monumental remains of a colonial **fort** (Mon–Fri 8am–4pm, Sat & Sun 9am–5pm; US$1.10) that stands in mute witness to the region's colourful history. Although the Spanish began construction of the fort in 1759, it was never fully completed because of a combination of bureaucratic inefficiency, problems with materials and a labour shortage; it also was temporarily occupied by British and Miskito military forces in October 1779. Omoa's narrow beach is lined with fishing boats and offers stunning views west across the curve of the bay to the Sierra de Omoa peaks in the distance. It can get busy with day-trippers at weekends, however. For a **room**, the highly popular *Roli's Place* (Ⓣ658 9082; ❷) is an excellent budget base with comfortable rooms as well as camping (US$2 per person), hammocks (US$2.50 per person) and dorms (US$3.50 per person); they also have kayaks and bikes, a kitchen and laundry facilities. Otherwise *Hotel Tatiana* (Ⓣ658 9182; ❹) is a decent-value option with en-suite rooms. The best places for meals are the *champas* along the seafront, which serve freshly caught seafood at very reasonable prices; *Jardín Romantico* is particularly recommended. Buses leave from the highway every thirty minutes for Puerto Cortés.

Puerto Cortés

Honduras's main port, **PUERTO CORTÉS**, 19km from Omoa, is a run-down town where the unstinting heat and dilapidated wooden buildings merely add to the rough-and-ready feel of the place. You'll hopefully pass through only to change buses en route to San Pedro Sula, but if you do stay, *Hotel Formosa*, a block west of the centre (Ⓣ665 0853; ❷–❸), is a good cheap option with en-suite rooms, some with TV and a/c. There is little choice in terms of places to eat. Buffet meals are available at *Reposteria Plata*, at 3 Avenida and 2 Calle, popular with locals and open on Sundays when everywhere else is closed. Three companies run **buses** between Puerto Cortés and San Pedro Sula, including the reliable Citul, who run the hour-long trip every thirty minutes between 6am and 6pm from their terminal a block north of the main plaza at 4 Avenida and 4 Calle. Travelling in the other direction, there are buses to Corinto every ninety minutes (8am–3.30pm; 3hr) and half-hourly connections to Omoa (1hr); buses leave from the Transportes Citral terminal on 4 Calle around the corner from the Citul terminal.

Tela

Though grand plans are periodically proposed to create a string of swanky resorts on the coastline around **TELA**, 96km from San Pedro Sula, for now the town retains a somewhat weathered, slightly run-down air. A certain faded appeal and Caribbean character may be evident in places, but Tela's trump card is undoubtedly the ravishing sandy shoreline that stretches for miles east and west of its centre, and the terrific protected reserve of Punta Sal close by. Established by the United Fruit Company in the late nineteenth century, Tela slipped into a lengthy period of provincial stupor until relatively recently when a pioneering, largely successful attempt to improve local security problems by introducing a **tourism police** has helped transform the town's previously seedy image – you'll see plenty of the beige-and-khaki-clad officers around, and most speak some English.

Buses running between San Pedro and La Ceiba drop you off on the highway 2km south of the centre; taxis make the trip into town for US$0.50 per person. Tela's **tourist information** centre (Mon–Fri 8am–6pm, Sat 8am–noon; Ⓦwww.telahonduras.com) is located in the municipal building off the southeast corner of the parque. Best choice for a budget **room** is the rambling *Hotel Tela*, two blocks west of the parque on 9 Calle (Ⓣ448 2150; ❸). It offers large, clean en-suite rooms, somewhat dated in style but with plenty of character. For somewhere more comfortable head to *Cesar's Mariscos*, on the beach at 3 Avenida (Ⓣ448 2083, Ⓦwww.hotelcesarmariscos.com; ❺), a pretty hotel above a good seafood restaurant with spacious rooms, each uniquely decorated and many with balconies with sea views and hammock. Five blocks west of the parque, the *Mango Café*, on 8 Calle, is a good place for a snack or *tapado* seafood. For **tours** to the stunning mangrove swamps, lagoons and beaches of **Punta Sal** and Punta Izopo contact Garífuna Tours, 9 Calle (Ⓣ448 2904, Ⓦwww.garifunatours.com), who run trips for US$18 per person, as well as the EcoPass tour, encompassing Punta Sal, Punta Izopo and Pico Bonito for US$58. **Moving on** from Tela, head to the main highway and wait for a bus there; they run to both La Ceiba and San Pedro Sula about every forty minutes.

The Bay Islands

Strung along the southern fringes of the world's second-largest barrier reef, the **Bay Islands** (Islas de la Bahía) are Honduras's major tourist attraction. With their clear, calm waters and abundant marine life, the islands are the ideal destination for inexpensive diving, sailing and fishing, while less active types can sling a hammock on one of the many palm-fringed, sandy beaches and snooze in the shade, watching the magnificent sunsets that paint the broad skies with colours as vibrant as the coral below.

Composed of three main islands and some 65 smaller cayes, this sweeping 125-kilometre island chain lies on the Bonacca Ridge, an underwater extension of the Sierra de Omoa mountain range that disappears into the sea near Puerto Cortés on the coast. **Utila**, the island closest to the mainland, attracts budget travellers from all over the world, while **Roatán** is the largest and most developed. **Guanaja**, to the east, is a more upmarket and exclusive resort destination. All three islands offer superb diving and snorkelling.

Even old hands get excited about **diving** the waters around the Bay Islands, where lizard fish and toadfish dart by, scarcely distinguishable from the coral; eagle rays glide through the water like huge birds flying through the air; parrot fish chomp steadily away at the coral; and barracuda and harmless nurse sharks circle the waters, checking you out from a distance. In addition, the world's largest fish, the **whale shark** (which can reach up to 16m in length), is a resident of the Cayman Trench, which plummets to profound depths just north of the islands. It's most frequently spotted close to Utilan waters between March and

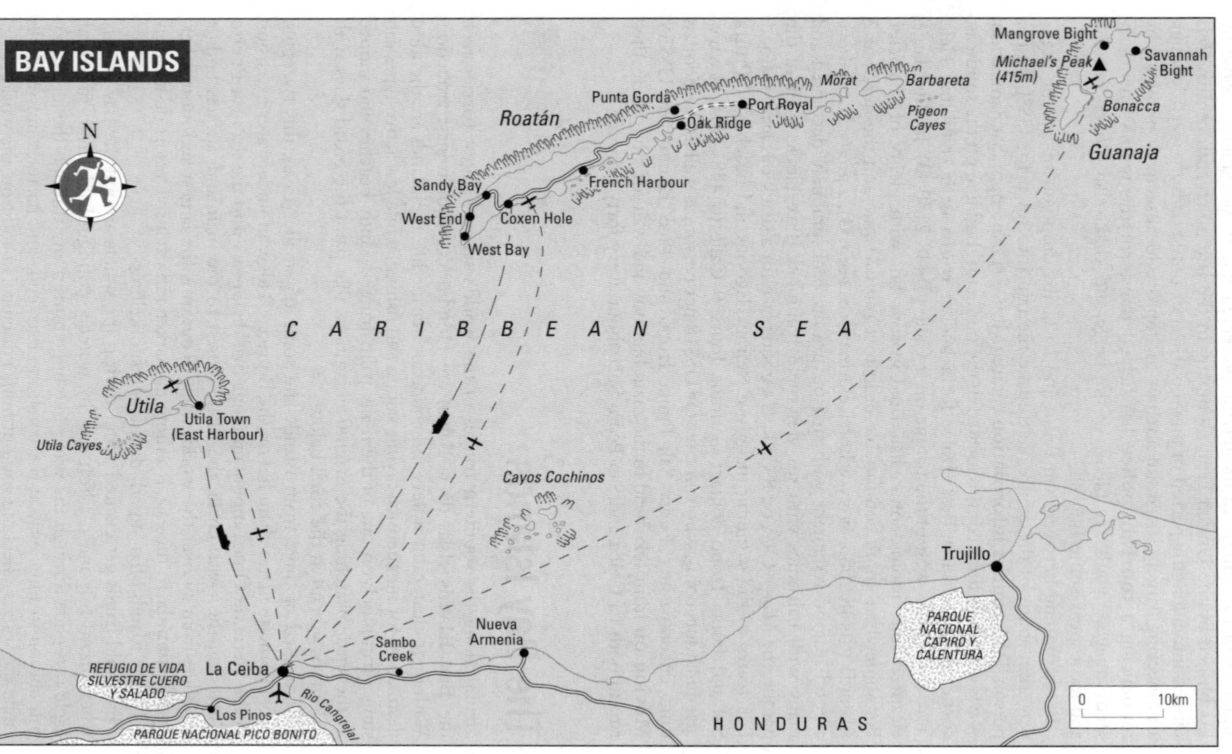
BAY ISLANDS
N
Roatán
Punta Gorda
Port Royal
Oak Ridge
Morat
Barbareta
Pigeon Cayes
Sandy Bay
French Harbour
West End
Coxen Hole
West Bay
Mangrove Bight
Michael's Peak (415m)
Savannah Bight
Bonacca
Guanaja
C A R I B B E A N S E A
Utila
Utila Town (East Harbour)
Utila Cayes
Cayos Cochinos
Trujillo
PARQUE NACIONAL CAPIRO Y CALENTURA
Nueva Armenia
Sambo Creek
La Ceiba
REFUGIO DE VIDA SILVESTRE CUERO Y SALADO
Río Cangrejal
Los Pinos
PARQUE NACIONAL PICO BONITO
HONDURAS
0 10km
Tela & San Pedro Sula

June and in October and November, when dive boats run trips to look for it, but can be encountered year round.

The best **time to visit** the islands is from March to September, when the water visibility is good and the weather is clear and sunny. The rains start in October, while late November and December are usually very wet, with squally showers continuing until late February. Daytime temperatures range between 25°C and 29°C year round, though the heat is rarely oppressive, thanks to almost constant east–southeast trade winds. Mosquitoes and sandflies are endemic on all the islands, and at their worst when the wind dies down; lavish coatings of baby oil help to keep the latter away.

Some history

The Bay Islands' history of conquest, pirate raids and constant immigration has resulted in a society that's unique in Honduras. The islands' original inhabitants are thought to have been the **Pech**, described by Columbus on his fourth voyage in 1502 as being a "robust people who adore idols and live mostly from a certain white grain from which they make fine bread and the most perfect beer". Post-conquest, the indigenous population declined rapidly as a result of enslavement and forced labour. The islands' strategic location as a provisioning point for the Europe-bound Spanish fleets ensured that they soon became the targets for **pirates**, initially Dutch and French, and subsequently English. The Spanish decision to evacuate the islands in 1650 left the way open for bands of pirates, including Henry Morgan, to move in and set up bases in Guanaja and Port Royal in Roatán. For nearly a century the islands were a stronghold from where buccaneers launched sporadic attacks on Spanish ships and against the mainland settlements.

British forces occupied the Bay Islands in 1742, and then contested control of Port Royal in Roatán (the main settlement at that time) with the Spanish for the next forty years. But in 1782 the Spanish left Roatán, and the island was deserted until the arrival of the **Garífuna** in 1797. Forcibly expelled from the British-controlled island of St Vincent following a rebellion, most of the 3000-strong group were persuaded by the Spanish to settle in Trujillo on the mainland, leaving a small settlement at Punta Gorda on the island's north coast. Further waves of settlers came after the abolition of slavery in 1830, when white **Cayman Islanders** and freed **slaves** arrived first on Utila, later moving on to Roatán and Guanaja. These new inhabitants fished and built up a very successful fruit industry – until a hurricane levelled the plantations in 1877.

Honduras acquired rights to the islands following independence in 1821, yet many – not least the islanders themselves – still considered the territory to be British. In 1852, Britain declared the islands a Crown Colony, breaking the terms of the 1850 Clayton–Bulwer Treaty, an agreement not to exercise dominion over any part of Central America. Forced to back down under US pressure, Britain finally conceded sovereignty to Honduras in the Wyke–Cruz Treaty of 1859.

Today, the islands retain their cultural separation from the mainland, although with both Spanish-speaking Hondurans and North American and European expats settling in growing numbers, the island's ethnic make-up continues to change. A unique form of **Creole English** is still spoken on the street, but due to the increasing number of mainlanders migrating here, Spanish – always the official language – is becoming almost as common. This government-encouraged migration has sparked tensions between English-speaking locals and the Latino newcomers, especially in Roatán, where many islanders feel they are being swamped by land-hungry outsiders with whom they have little in common. The huge growth in **tourism** since the early 1990s, a trend that shows no signs of abating, has also been controversial, with growing concerns about the environmental impact of the industry and the question of who, exactly, benefits most from the boom.

For full details of **getting to the islands** from the rest of Honduras, see p.399 and p.417. There are also several **international flights** to Roatán: Continental fly twice daily on Saturdays from Houston, at 9.30am and 12.50pm, while Taca and Aerohonduras both operate direct flights on Sundays from Miami.

Utila

Smallest of the three main Bay Islands, **UTILA** is a key destination for budget travellers, and one of the cheapest places in the world to **learn to dive** – and even if you don't want to don tanks, the superb waters around the island offer great swimming and snorkelling. Utila is still the cheapest of the Bay Islands, with a cost of living only slightly higher than that on the mainland, although prices are gradually rising. Though the island is now largely dependent on tourism, it stills retains a good deal of old-fashioned charm. The well-swept streets are lined with wonderful old wooden Caribbean-style houses, built on stilts, with shuttered windows and sunny verandahs, their gardens bursting with bougainvillea. Life is laid-back and people are generally friendly, though watch out for the odd dancehall brawl. As elsewhere, respect local customs in dress and don't walk around in your bathing suit. Note also that drinking from glass bottles on the street is prohibited.

Arrival and information

All **boats** dock in the centre of **Utila Town** (also known as East Harbour), a large, curved harbour that's the island's only settlement and home to the vast majority of its 2500-strong population. The island's principal road, about a forty-minute walk end to end, runs along the seafront from The Point in the east to Blue Bayou in the west. The airstrip is 4km north of Utila Town, at the end of the island's other main street, Cola de Mico Road, which heads inland from the dock.

Wherever you arrive, you'll be met by representatives from the **dive schools** laden with maps and information on special offers. Many schools offer free accommodation during their courses, but it's worth checking out the various options before signing up. For more objective information, the Utila branch of the Bay Islands' Conservation Association (BICA) has a **visitor and information office** on the main street, 100m east of the dock (Mon–Fri 9am–noon and 2–5pm; ⓣ425 3260, ⓦwww.bica-utila.org). Consult the excellent community **website** ⓦwww.aboututila.com for more information and news about the island, including a link to the *Utila East Wind* newsletter.

Accommodation

Utila has more than 25 affordable **guest houses and hotels**, and a profusion of rooms for rent; there's always somewhere available, even at Christmas and Easter. Most of the dive schools have links with a hostel, so that enrolling on a scuba course gets you a few free or discounted nights' accommodation. Everywhere is within walking distance of the dock, and the accommodation listed below is in the order that you come to it, walking west along the road from the airstrip. Be sure that your room has adequate security as there are regular burglaries of backpackers' rooms. There are no designated places to **camp** except on the cayes.

East of the dock

Rubi's Inn a two-minute walk from the dock ⓣ425 3240, ⓔrubisinn@yahoo.com. Very clean, with twelve airy rooms, each with two double beds and fridge, and some with a/c. Amenities include pleasant gardens with sea views, use of a communal kitchen and swimming opportunities in the sheltered bay. ❹

Cooper's Inn a five-minute walk from the dock ⓣ425 3184. One of the best budget places on the island, with sixteen orderly, basic rooms (all with fans) and friendly management, plus use of a shared kitchen, shared bathrooms and a restaurant. ❷

Sharkey's Reef Hotel behind *Sharkey's Reef Restaurant*, near the old airstrip ⓣ425 3212. Set in a peaceful garden, the five rooms and two apartments here all have a/c, private bathrooms and cable TV, and some have kitchens. There's also a terrace with great views over the lagoon. ❺–❻

Tropical Sunset opposite *Sharkey's* ⓣ425 3190. Comfortable, modern rooms and apartments, some with sea views. The cheaper rooms come with a fan, while the more expensive apartments boast a/c, TV and a balcony. There's also an on-site bar and restaurant. ❺–❻

Cola de Mico Road

Mango Inn a five-minute walk up the road from the dock ⓣ425 3335, ⓦwww.mango-inn.com. A beautiful, well-run place, timber-built in Caribbean style and set in shady gardens with a lovely pool. The range of rooms stretches from thatched, a/c bungalows and cabins to pleasant dorms with shared bath. Also on offer: a book exchange, laundry service, and the lively *Mango Café* (see "Eating"). Rates drop considerably if diving with the affiliated Utila Dive Centre; a number of packages are available. Dorms US$5, rooms ❹, bungalows and cabins ❺–❻

Tony's Place opposite *Mango Inn* ⓣ425 3376. The twelve simple but spotless rooms (with fan) here are amongst the best value on the island. The shared bathrooms are squeaky clean and the owner is friendly and informative. Hummingbird feeders attract birds, including the Canivet's Emerald, found only on the Bay Islands and a small area of adjacent Guatemala and Mexico. ❷

Jade Seahorse next to *Tony's Place* ⓣ425 3270, ⓦwww.jadeseahorse.com. Unquestionably the most eccentric place to stay on the island. Owned by an American artist and designed in his own unique fantasy-meets-Gaudí style, the highly quirky rooms are modern and well-equipped with a/c, two double beds, minibar and tiled bathroom. ❼

West of the dock

Deep Blue Resort just across the lagoon west of Blue Bayou ⓣ425 3211 ⓦwww.deepblueutila.com. Very well set up, professionally run, small-scale dive resort with ten spacious rooms, all with two double beds, a/c and fridges, and balconies with commanding ocean views. It's located next to a pleasant, private white-sand beach and, though there's no road or pedestrian access into town, the hotel provides boat transport links. ❾ from US$1000 including full board and all diving

Tropical Hotel opposite Hondutel ⓣ425 3568. This backpackers' stronghold offers small, functional rooms with fans and a communal kitchen. ❷

Seaside Inn opposite Ecomarine-Gunter's Dive Shop ⓣ425 3150, ⓔhotelseaside@yahoo.com. Recently refurbished, the inn has an ample number of plain but comfortable en-suite rooms, all with two double beds and some with a/c, plus two apartments available for monthly rent. Internet access available. ❸–❺

Margaritaville Beach Hotel a ten-minute walk west of the dock ⓣ425 3366, ⓔmargaritavillehotel@yahoo.com. *Margaritaville* offers large, airy rooms, all with two beds and private bath and some with a/c; a hammock-filled terrace; and a tranquil seafront location that's well away from the main dock and handy for the beach. ❸–❹

Diving

Most visitors come to Utila specifically for the **diving**, attracted by the low prices, clear warm water (temperatures fluctuate between 25–28°C), and abundant marine life. Even in winter, the water is generally calm, and common sightings include turtles, parrot fish, trumpet fish, spotted eagle rays and yellow stingrays, porcupine fish and tarpon. As it's the north coast of Utila that offers the best diving, make sure your dive school regularly goes to that side of the island. The reef walls are near-vertical on this side, where the best sites include Blackish Point, Duppy Waters and The Maze. On the east side of Utila the seamount of Black Hills offers prolific sealife, but on the south coast the sea bottom is much shallower and the reef in poorer condition. That said, the south coast's Black Coral Wall and Pretty Bush are usually enjoyable. Many of the schools with larger, more powerful boats head to the dive sites of the north coast via seamounts where currents converge and **whale sharks** (see box, p.410) are frequently seen. The good schools will be happy to spend time talking to you about the merits of the various sites.

Rather than signing up with the first dive-school representative who approaches you, it's worth spending a morning walking around checking out all the schools. **Price** is not really a consideration, with the dozen or more dive shops all setting a uniform rate (US$199) for Open Water, Advanced and Rescue Diver PADI courses. Divemaster (US$550) and various levels of Instructor courses are also on offer, as are fun dives at US$175 for a package of ten. **Safety** is a more pertinent issue: for peace of mind, you should make sure that you understand – and get along with – the instructors, many of whom speak a number of languages. Before signing up, also check that classes have no more than six people, that the equipment is well maintained and that all boats have working oxygen and a first-aid kit. Anyone with asthma or ear problems should not be allowed to dive. Diving **insurance** sold by BICA is a compulsory extra at US$3 per day and helps fund the island's decompression chamber and medical treatment in the event of an emergency.

Recommended schools include the Utila Dive Centre (Ⓣ425 3326, Ⓦwww.utiladivecentre.com), about 300m east of the dock; its sister school, Cross Creek (Ⓣ425 3334, Ⓦwww.crosscreekutila.com), about 200m east of the dock; Alton's (Ⓣ425 3108, Ⓦwww.altonsdiveshop.com), 350m east of the dock; Deep Blue Divers Ⓣ425 3211, Ⓦwww.deepblueutila.com) just west of the dock, and Ecomarine-Gunter's Dive Shop (Ⓣ425 3350, Ⓦwww.riconet.de/ecomarine), about 400m west of the dock. Many of the dive shops also rent out **snorkelling** equipment for around US$5 a day, free for divers.

It's important to bear in mind that the coral reef dies when it is touched. BICA has installed buoys at each of the sites to prevent boats anchoring on the reef, and all the reputable schools will use these.

Around Utila

The best swimming near town is at the attractive, recently cleaned-up little bay known locally as **Chepe's Beach**, a fifteen-minute walk west of the centre, where the sands are gently shelving. The beach has a small snack bar and hammocks slung in the shade of coconut trees, and locals gather here at weekends to barbecue and play Latin, country and western, and reggae music. Five minutes further on, the **Blue Bayou** bay has excellent snorkelling (US$1.50 charge to use the area), particularly just before sundown when barracuda, turtles and eagle rays are often seen. There's also a rickety wooden pier here where you can sunbathe in peace away from the sandflies.

East of town, **Airport Beach**, at the end of the old dirt airstrip past the Point, also offers good snorkelling just offshore (though access is more difficult), as does the little reef beyond the lighthouse. The path from the end of the airstrip up the east coast of the island leads to a couple of small coves – the second is good for swimming and sunbathing. Five minutes beyond the coves, you'll come to the **Ironshores**, a mile-long stretch of low volcanic cliffs with lava tunnels cutting down to the water.

A kilometre inland from Utila Town, down a well-signposted route from Cola de Mico road is the **Iguana Research Station** (Mon, Wed & Fri 2–5pm; US$2), where an environmental charity is trying to breed the rare Utila iguana, known locally as the "swamper". Found nowhere else in the world, the swamper is under threat from poachers (locals have traditionally eaten them) and habitat loss. You can see the swamper up close in the centre's enclosures, along with the two other kinds of iguana found in Utila; there's also information here about the island's environment.

Another pleasant diversion is the five-kilometre walk or cycle along Cola de Mico Road up to the northern tip of the island to **Pumpkin Hill and beach**, passing the site of the new airport. The 82-metre hill, the eroded crest of an extinct volcano, gives good views over the island and across to the mainland and the dark bulk of the Pico Bonito mountains. Down on the beach, lava rocks cascade into the sea, forming underwater caves – there's good snorkelling here when the water is calm, though it's not safe to free dive down into the caves.

The Cayes

Utila Cayes – eleven tiny outcrops strung along the southwestern edge of the island – were designated a wildlife refuge in 1992. **Pigeon Caye** (also known as Suc Suc Caye) and **Jewel Caye**, connected by a narrow causeway, are both inhabited by descendants of the original settlers from the Cayman Islands, and the pace of life here is even slower than that on Utila. Small launches regularly shuttle between Suc Suc and Utila (US$1.50), or can be hired with a skipper for a day's snorkelling, if you have your own equipment. *Vicky's Rooms* on Suc Suc (❷) offers basic accommodation, and a couple of reasonable restaurants and a good fish market complete the scene.

Water Caye, a blissful stretch of white sand, coconut palms, pellucid water and a small coral reef, is even more idyllic, given its absence of sandflies. You can **camp** here, but you'll need to bring all your own food, fuel and water; a caretaker turns up every day to collect the US$1 fee for use of the island, and hammocks can be rented for an extra US$1. Water Caye is also the venue for occasional **full-moon parties** as well as a spectacular annual two-day rave held in July or August each year, with international house and techno DJs, organized by Sunjam (see Ⓦwww.sunjamutila.com for information). **Transport** to the caye is organized during such events; at other times, dive boats will often drop you off on their way to the north coast for a small fee, or you can ask the owner of the *Bundu Café* (see "Eating") in Utila Town.

Eating

Fish, crab and lobster are obviously staples on the islands, along with the usual rice and beans. With the tourists, however, have also come European and American foods – pasta, pizza, burgers, pancakes and granola. Since most things have to be brought in by boat, **prices** are higher than on the mainland: main courses start at about US$4, and beers cost at least US$1. For eating on the cheap, head for the evening stalls on the road by the dock, which do a thriving trade in *baleadas*. Note that many restaurants stop serving at around 10pm.

Bundu Café on the main street, east of the dock. A very popular travellers' hangout serving European-style breakfasts and lunches along with *lassi*-style milkshakes. Curry night on Thursdays and occasional live music.

Camila's Bakery a five-minute walk east of the dock. The finest pastries, cakes and bread in town, run by a long-time Danish resident.

Captain Jack's a five-minute walk west of the dock. Dutch-Utilan–owned café-restaurant serving excellent-value lunches, including burritos and sandwiches, freshly squeezed orange juice, and delicious dinners such as fish cakes and grilled kingfish steaks. Don't be put off by the run-down building.

Cross Creek at the Point. Near-legendary Caribbean cooking from one of Utila's best chefs, served in a quiet spot beside the lagoon and majoring in flavoursome pan-fried fish and seafood. Menu changes daily, and portions are enormous and cheap – around US$4 per main dish.

Island Café a two-minute walk west of the dock. A well-run, locally owned restaurant with excellent fish and seafood at moderate prices and friendly service.

Mango Café *Mango Inn.* A popular place with an interesting selection of tasty, well-presented

European food to go along with espresso drinks and a lively bar. The daily special, usually seafood, is great value, and the pizzas (baked in a wood-fired oven) are definitely the best on the island. Closed Mon.

Mermaid's a two-minute walk east of the dock. Fast-food buffet with pizza, Chinese food and pasta at reasonable rates, served under a breezy canvas roof.

Munchie's a one-minute walk west of the dock. The best breakfasts on the island, with a range of cooked food and fresh fruit, smoothies and licuados. Check out the Iguana Garden at the rear, a steep wall inhabited by a group of spiny-tailed iguanas.

La Piccola a one-minute walk west of the dock. The island's only specialist Italian restaurant boasts a wide selection of pasta, salads and daily specials, including a free starter (try the grilled aubergine and pesto). Bread is home-made, and many of the dishes are more imaginative than the standard fare sold elsewhere. Also has a good wine list. Closed Mon and Tues.

RJs at The Point beside the bridge. Popular with dive crews and students, with a gregarious atmosphere and excellent meat and fish barbecues. Get there early if you want a table, as it fills up quickly. Open Wed, Fri and Sun only.

Nightlife

Despite its tiny population, Utila is a fearsomely hedonistic party island, except on Saturday night as most islanders are Seventh-Day Adventists. The hottest place in town for travellers is the *Coco Loco Bar*, just west of the dock, which has tables on a pier above the sea and draws a lively bunch of party heads with its extended happy hour and regular house, techno and reggae parties. *Tranquilo*, just next door, is equally popular though the music policy can be banal, while the *Bundu Café*, east of the dock, can get lively and occasionally has live music. On Cola de Mico road, you simply have to see the amazingly eccentric *Treetonic* bar inside the *Jade Seahorse* hotel, while almost opposite here the *Mango Café* is another popular spot for a quiet drink. The dancehall *Bar in the Bush*, about 200m further north up the same road, boasts a booty-shakin' sound system that revs right up on Wednesdays and Fridays.

Listings

Airlines Tickets for Sosa and Atlantic, covering domestic routes in Honduras, can be purchased (cash only) in the captain's office by the dock.

Banks BGA and Atlántida bank, both just east of the dock, change money and offer cash advances on Visa cards. BGA also has an ATM. Henderson's store, just west of the dock, will change cash and travellers' cheques outside bank hours.

Bicycles can be rented for around US$5 a day from Delco, just west of the dock.

Book exchange The *Bundu Café*, on the main street, east of the dock, has a book exchange.

Doctor The Community Medical Clinic is two minutes west of the dock (Mon–Fri 9am–noon).

Immigration office at the port building (Mon–Fri 9am–noon & 2–4.30pm).

Internet access Two minutes west of the dock, Utila Phone Company (daily 8am–8pm) offers Internet access for US$4 an hour, plus discounted international calls.

Post office in the large building at the main dock (Mon–Fri 9am–noon & 2–4.30pm, Sat 9–11.30am).

Spanish School Central American Spanish school, east of the dock (ⓦwww.ca-spanish.com), charges US$150 per week for 20 hours of tuition including full board.

Telephones see "Internet" above. Avoid the Hondutel office, next to the *migración*, where the rates are extortionate.

Travel agents Morgan's Travel at the dock can help you with ferry and flight tickets.

Roatán

Some 50km from La Ceiba, **ROATÁN** is the largest of the Bay Islands, a curving ridged hump almost 50km long and 5km across at its widest point. It still draws backpackers, but the island is increasingly chasing higher-spending tourists. Many of the dozen or so luxury resorts are geared towards divers on all-in packages, though there are some fine guest houses and smaller hotels too.

The rich reefs do offer superb **diving**, but Roatán's hills also offers some great hiking and horse-riding, while stretches of idyllic sands provide the chance to do nothing except laze on a beach. **Coxen Hole** is the island's commercial centre, while **West End** is the most lively resort.

Arrival, information and getting around

Regular **flights** from La Ceiba (and the US) land at the airport, on the road to French Harbour, 3km from Coxen Hole. A taxi to West End from here costs US$10, or you could walk to the road and wait for one of the public minibuses that head to Coxen Hole every 20 minutes or so (US$0.75) and change there. There's an information desk, a hotel reservation desk, car rental agencies and a bank at the airport. **Ferries** to the island dock in the centre of Coxen Hole.

A paved road runs west–east along the island, connecting the major communities. **Minibuses** leave regularly from Main Street in Coxen Hole, heading west to Sandy Bay and West End (every 20min until late afternoon) and east to Brick Bay, French Harbour, Oak Ridge and Punta Gorda (every 30min or so until late afternoon); fares are US$0.70 to $1. If you really want to explore, you'll need to rent a **car** or **motorbike**: several agencies at the airport can sort you out, including Sandy Bay Rent-a-Car (Ⓣ445 1871, Ⓦwww.roatanet.com/rentacar), who also have offices at Sandy Bay and West End and rent out Jeeps (US$40–45 per day) and motorbikes (US$25 per day).

For **information** about the island and its events, consult the excellent monthy magazine *Bay Islands Voice* or its **website**, Ⓦwww.bayislandsvoice.com; alternatively, try Ⓦwww.roatanisland.net.

Coxen Hole

COXEN HOLE (also known as Roatán Town) is dusty and run-down,

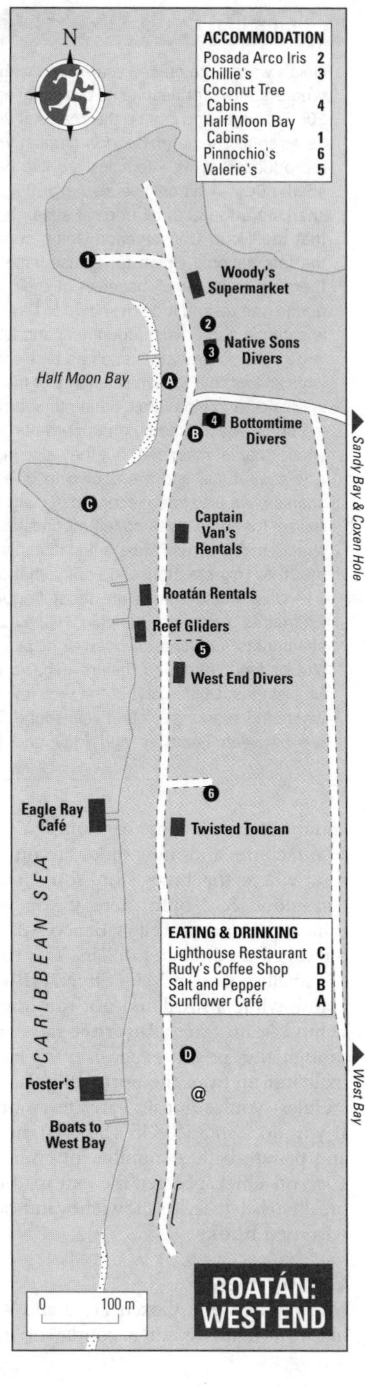

Whale sharks

Utila's waters are graced year-round with the presence of the world's biggest fish, the **whale shark**. Yet despite its proximity to land and its size – it grows to an estimated 20m in length and can tip the scales at 20 tonnes – little is known about this creature. Its scientific name (*rhincodon typhus*) wasn't even determined until 1984, and their reproductive cycle – females are live bearers of around 300 fully developed 50cm shark pups – was only verified in 1995. Largely solitary, pelagic (oceanic) fish, whale sharks are found in all tropical seas, though so little is known about their numbers that the World Conservation Union consider their status to be "indeterminate" and the International Union for Conservation of Nature and Natural Resources classify them as "vulnerable" because of their size and late maturity. Whale sharks have a gentle nature, and are not known to have any natural enemies except man (their meat is eaten in some Asian countries) and killer whales, though juveniles are targeted by large oceanic predators such as blue sharks and marlin.

It's known that the whale sharks of the western Caribbean travel between Cozumel in Mexico and Honduras, timing their arrival at feeding spots to coincide with incoming tides, which create rich upcurrents. Plankton and microscopic crustaceans form whale sharks' main diet, but they also ingest some sardine-sized fish and, occasionally, small tuna, and are known to dive as deep as 1000m in search of food. The sharks have also been recorded circling around coral reefs (including Gladden Spit in Belize) for hours awaiting full-moon snapper-egg spawns. It's highly likely that whale sharks move across substantial distances in the western hemisphere, as it's known that they migrate thousands of kilometres across the Indian and Pacific oceans.

In Utila whale sharks are most frequently spotted in open waters two or three kilometres north of Pumpkin Hill, where currents converge around underwater seamounts, creating an upswell of plankton, krill and baitfish on which the whale sharks feed. Although they're occasionally encountered in the seas off the other Bay Islands, Utila is one of the very few places in the world (alongside the Maldives) where the sharks are found year-round. The **best times of year** to see whale sharks are between February and May and between September and early November.

and most visitors come here only to change money or shop. All the town's practical facilities and most shops are on a hundred-metre stretch of **Main Street**, near where the buses stop. You'll find the headquarters of BICA (Mon–Fri 9am–noon & 2–5pm) here, if you want to learn more about Roatán's reefs, flora and fauna, as well as Banco Atlántida, which has a Visa ATM and changes travellers' cheques and dollars. The **migración** and **post office** are both near the small square on Main Street. HB Warren is the largest **supermarket** on the island, while a small and not too impressive general market can be found just behind Main Street. **Internet** rates are lower here than the rest of the island, though they're still expensive; try Hondusoft, on the second floor of a small mall, just up from the port (daily 9am–6pm; US$5 per hour).

Unless you've got an early ferry or flight, it's unlikely you'll want **to stay**. If you do, *Sarita* (☎445 1541; ❸), next to the dock, has basic rooms with TV and private bath. A number of comedores dish out cheap eats, while *Qué Tal Café*, on Thicket Street, the exit road towards Sandy Bay, serves European-style breakfasts, deli-style sandwiches and cappuccinos. Next door, Librería Casi Todo sells used **books**.

Sandy Bay

Midway between Coxen Hole and West End, **SANDY BAY** is an unassuming community with a couple of interesting attractions. The **Institute for**

When the sea is too rough, dive boats don't set out to look for them, and afternoon searches are very rare at any time of year because of choppy water.

When conditions are favourable, dive boats seek out whale sharks in a favourable region between Utila Town and the dive sites of the north coast of the island, with the captain first scanning the horizon for seabirds, particularly diving terns (which also feed on baitfish). Next, all eyes look out for "**boils**" created by the frenzied feeding of bonito (black-fin tuna), which also prey on krill and baitfish. Whale sharks glide around just below the surface, hoovering up mouthfuls of plankton-rich seawater. Often the shark surfaces to feed in a vertical position – an unforgettable sight as the great fish steadies itself upright (a little like a performing seal), exposing its white underbelly, vast mouth agape and sucking in seawater, which it filters through a gill-raker and then expels via five pairs of huge gill slits. The captain then gives a signal and everyone aboard jumps into the ocean for a glimpse of the shark – though they rarely hang around for more than a minute or two under these circumstances. Whale sharks are not considered dangerous to humans, but snorkellers are not permitted to attempt to touch the behemoths.

The sharks themselves are quite astonishing to behold. They have a broad, flat head, the upperside of their body usually steely grey-blue and covered in white spots and square checkerboard-style markings. By photographing the intricate patterns of lines and spots directly behind the sharks' gill slits, individuals can be recognized. A database of Utila sightings is being compiled as part of a study of the island's sharks; see Ⓦwww.utilawhalesharkresearch.com for more information.

The initial findings show that the whale sharks average between six and nine metres – though local fishermen talk about an 18-metre barnacle-encrusted specimen they've nicknamed Old Tom. The sheer concentration of numbers in Utilan waters suggest that the seas north of the island could perhaps be a breeding ground. Fortunately, with Utila now gaining a reputation as a whale shark hotbed, dive operators have agreed upon "whale shark **encounter guidelines**" designed to ensure that boats do not encroach too closely on the feeding sharks, with a maximum of eight snorkellers permitted in the water with the shark at one time.

Marine Sciences (Mon–Tues; Thurs–Sun 9am–5pm; US$3), based at *Antony's Key Resort* (see below), has exhibitions on the marine life and geology of the islands and a museum with useful information on local history and archeology. The institute also puts on bottle-nosed **dolphin shows** (weekdays 10am & 4.30pm, Sat & Sun 10am, 1pm & 4pm; US$5), and offers the chance to dive or snorkel with the dolphins (US$100 and US$75 respectively; must be booked in advance on Ⓣ445 1327). Across the road from the institute, several short nature trails weave through the jungle at the **Carambola Botanical Gardens** (daily 8am–5pm; US$3), a riot of flowers, lush ferns and tropical trees. A twenty-minute walk from the gardens up Monte Carambola, the **Iguana Wall** is a section of cliff that's a breeding ground for iguanas and parrots. From the top of the mountain you can see across to Utila on clear days.

The Sandy Bay area has several places **to stay**, all of which are clearly signposted, including the pleasant *Tri R Resort* (Ⓣ445 1623; ❺), with large a/c rooms with private bath and a good restaurant; and several dive resorts, the best of which is PADI five-star *Anthony's Key Resort* (Ⓣ445 1003, Ⓕ445 1140, Ⓦwww.anthonyskey.com; weekly packages from US$600). *Anthony's* is one of the smartest places on the island, with cabins set among the trees and on a small caye. Popular places **to eat** include *Rick's American Café* (closed Wed) set on the hillside above the road and serving giant US-style burgers and ribs.

West End

With its calm waters and incredible white beaches, **WEST END**, 14km from Coxen Hole, makes the most of its ideal setting, gearing itself mainly towards independent travellers on all budgets, with a good selection of attractive accommodation. Set in the southwest corner of the island, round a shallow bay, the village has retained a laid-back charm, and the gathering pace of tourist development has done little to dent the locals' friendliness.

The paved road from Coxen Hole finishes at the northern end of the village, not far from **Half Moon Bay**, a beautifully sheltered sandy beach ringed with hotels. Turning to the south at the end of the paved road from Coxen Hole, a sandy track runs alongside the water's edge through the heart of West End, passing a merry bunch of guest houses, bars and restaurants set between patches of coconut palms. You can rent **cars** from Roatán Rentals, at the north of West End, or Sandy Bay Rent-a-Car close by; Captain Van's rent out overpriced bicycles (US$9), mopeds (US$29) and motorbikes (US$39). Though widely available, **Internet access** is overpriced and the connections slow; Beach House (Mon–Fri 10am–10pm), opposite the entrance road from Coxen Hole, is the cheapest at US$10, while the fastest connection is at *King's Café* further down the road, though they close at 6pm and charge US$12 per hour.

Accommodation

Most of the **accommodation** in West End and Half Moon Bay is charmingly individualistic, and heavy discounts are available during low season (April–July & Sept to mid-Dec), particularly for longer stays.

Chillie's Half Moon Bay ⓣ445 5365, ⓔnatives@hondutel.hn. Nicely set-up backpackers' choice, with dorm beds (US$7.50) and private rooms, a kitchen and camping (US$6) available. Also home to Native Sons Divers. ❸

Half Moon Bay Cabins Half Moon Bay ⓣ445 1075. Luxurious and refined option with fourteen secluded cabins scattered around wooded grounds close to the water's edge; all have fan or a/c. There's also an expensive restaurant with silver-service and cocktail bar on site. Kayaks and snorkel gear are free for guests. ❻–❼

Mariposa Lodge on a side street half-way down the main beach road ⓔmariposalodge@yahoo.com (no phone). A good-value, quiet lodge with two apartments – complete with sundecks, kitchen and cable TV – plus small three-bed dorms (US$8.50). Extras include an on-site massage service ($35 for a full-body massage). ❹

Pinocchio's ⓣ445 1481, ⓔpinocchio69@bigfoot.com. A small, personable hotel, occupying a wooden building set on a small hill above the village. Rooms are clean and airy, if a little basic, though all have bath. The owners are a good source of information, plus a recommended restaurant is downstairs (see "Eating and drinking"). ❺

Posada Arco Iris Half Moon Bay ⓣ445 1264, ⓦwww.roatanposada.com. Set in attractive gardens just off the beach, with excellent, imaginatively furnished and spacious rooms, studios and apartments, all with fridge and hammocks, and some with a/c. ❺–❼

Valerie's about 100m along West End, then up a signposted dirt track ⓦwww.roatanonline.com/valeries (no phone). Venerable love-it-or-hate-it bohemian hostel set up with a profusion of quirky accommodation, including two trailer-style rooms, two apartments, a small house, a flat with hot tub and a large dorm (US$5 per person); guests can also use the kitchen. ❷–❸

Eating and drinking

There's a more than adequate range of **places to eat** in West End, with fish, seafood and pasta featuring heavily on many menus, though prices are well above mainland Honduran rates. **Drinking** can also drain your pocket fast, so it's best to seek out the half-price happy hours at many of the restaurants and bars – they start at around 4.30pm, and many of them last until 10pm. The *Twisted Toucan*, halfway along the seafront, is the liveliest place in town most nights, except Fridays, when everyone heads to *Foster's* for the weekly reggae jump-up.

Argentinian Grill Half Moon Bay. Argentinean-run restaurant with authentic *churrascos*, grilled meat and seafood at reasonable (by Roatán standards) prices. Portions are huge and service efficient, making this spot the best value for money in the West End.
Bertie's Criolle Cuisine at village entrance. Small menu of Creole specials, mainly grilled fish along with the odd meat dish. Prices are far from cheap, but the sea views from the terrace make it worth the extra expense.
Lighthouse Restaurant close to the seafront, between West End and Half Moon Bay. Big portions of reasonably priced Caribbean food served in friendly, diner-like surrounds.
Pinocchio's in the hotel of the same name. One of the finest restaurants in West End, with an eclectic range of creative, but fairly pricey, European meat and fish dishes. Open after 6pm and closed Wed.
Rudy's Coffee Stop The spot for legendary breakfasts, including banana pancakes, omelettes, fresh coffee and juices. Opens early at 6.30am, so it's ideal for an early breakfast and a quick getaway. Closed Sun.

West Bay

Two kilometres southwest of West End, towards the extreme western tip of Roatán, is the stunning white-sand beach of **WEST BAY**, fringed by coconut palms and washed by crystal-clear waters. The beach's tranquillity has been mildly disrupted by a rash of cabaña and hotel construction, but provided you avoid the sandflies by sunbathing on the jetties, it's still a sublime place to relax and enjoy the Caribbean. There's decent **snorkelling** at the southern end of the beach too, though the once pristine reef has suffered in recent years from increasing river run-off and the close attentions of unsupervised day-trippers.

From West End, it's a pleasant 45-minute stroll south along the beach and over a few rock outcrops; alternatively, take one of the small **launches** that leave *Foster's* regularly – the last one returns around 7pm (9pm in high season). A dirt road also runs here: from West End, head up the road to Coxen Hole and take the first turning on the right. If you want **to stay**, the Swiss-owned *Bananarama* (ⓣ992 9679, ⓦwww.bananaramadive.com; ❼) has overpriced but

West End watersports

Diving courses for all levels are available in West End. Prices are officially standardized, with a four-day PADI open-water course costing around US$220. It's worth asking around, however, as some schools include basic accommodation, and sporadic price wars have been known to break out. Fun dives are set at US$25 a dive, though substantial discounts are often on offer, with ten-dive packages set at around US$200. Recommended West End–based **schools** include West End Divers (ⓔreefglides@yahoo.com) and Bottom-Time Divers (ⓦwww.coconuttree.com). Native Sons (ⓔnatives@hondutel.hn), located at *Chillie's* hotel on Half Moon Bay, is another good school. Nearby West Bay also has a few dive schools (see below).

The reef lying just offshore provides superb **snorkelling,** with the best spots being at the mouth of Half Moon Bay and at the Blue Channel, which can be accessed from the beach 100m south of *Foster's* bar. You can also rent **sea kayaks** from the *Sea Breeze Inn*, close to the entrance road; expect to pay around US$12 for a half-day or US$20 for a full day. Underwater Paradise, based in the *Half Moon Bay Resort*, runs popular, hour-long glass-bottomed **boat tours** for US$18 per person, as well as a tourist submarine which, at US$200 per person, isn't cheap but makes for an unforgettable experience. Yush Tours at Half Moon Bay (ⓣ966 9643, ⓔkemrflowers@hotmail.com) offer snorkelling packages to reefs and shipwrecks from US$30 per boat (maximum 6 people) as well as fishing trips and dolphin tours.

comfortable wood cabins with mosquito nets and suites, while for something really luxurious, head for the Canadian-owned *Island Pearl Resort* (Ⓣ991 1858, Ⓦwww.roatanpearl.com; ❾, from US$150), which boasts stunning two-storey houses equipped with kitchens and hot tubs, plus a gourmet restaurant set in a spacious beachside plot. Both hotels have good in-house **dive schools**.

Northern Roatán

Leaving Coxen Hole, the paved road runs northeast past the small secluded cove of Brick Bay to **FRENCH HARBOUR**, a busy fishing port and the island's second largest town. Less run-down than Coxen Hole, it's a lively place to stay for a couple of days. In the centre the *Harbour View Hotel* (Ⓣ455 5390; ❹) has clean a/c rooms with bath and hot water, while the fabulously decadent *Fantasy Island Beach Resort* (Ⓣ455 5222; ❾, from US$850 weekly including full board and dive package) nearby has a huge plot, luxury rooms, pool, a marina and opportunities for numerous watersports. The best place **to eat** is *Gio's*, by the Credomatic building on the waterfront, where you can dine on excellent but pricey seafood – the speciality is king crab – on an outdoor deck with a view of the harbour. Should you have time, stop by the town's private **Iguana Reserve** (daily 9am–5pm; US$1), home to more than 2800 specimens of four species; all the proceeds of the entry fee go towards the care of the reptiles. To get there follow the signs to the *Fantasy Island* resort until you see signs leading to the centre.

From French Harbour the road cuts inland along a central ridge to give superb views of both the north and south coasts of the island. After about 14km it reaches **OAK RIDGE**, an attractive fishing port with wooden houses strung along its harbour. There are some nice unspoiled beaches to the east of town, accessible by launches from the main dock. The best place to stay is the clean and pleasant *Hotel San José* (Ⓣ435 2328; ❸–❹), on a small caye a short distance across the water from the dock. Launches run from the main dock to the caye on demand (US$0.50).

About 5km from Oak Ridge on the northern coast of the island is the village of **PUNTA GORDA**, the oldest Garífuna community in Honduras. The best time to visit is for the anniversary of the founding of the settlement (April 6–12), when Garífuna from all over the country attend the celebrations. At other times it's a quiet and slightly dilapidated little port with no historical buildings. The very basic *Los Cincos Hermanos* (❷) offers fairly clean rooms and has an attached comedor.

From the end of the paved road at Punta Gorda you can continue driving along the dirt track which runs east along the island, passing the turn-off for the secluded **Paya Beach** after around 1.5km, where there's a dive hotel, the pleasant little *Paya Beach Resort* (Ⓣ924 2220, Ⓦwww.payabay.com; ❾, US$975 for a week package including full board, diving and meals). A further 5km or so along is **Camp Bay Beach**, an idyllic, undeveloped stretch of white sand and coconut palms, though development is imminent. The road ends at the village of **PORT ROYAL**, on the southern edge of the island, where the faint remains of a fort built by the English can be seen on a caye offshore. The village lies in the **Port Royal Park and Wildlife Reserve**, the largest refuge on the island, set up in 1978 in an attempt to protect endangered species such as the yellow-napped Amazon parrot, as well as the watershed for eastern Roatán.

The eastern tip of Roatán is made up of mangrove swamps, with the small island of **Morat** just offshore. Beyond is **Barbareta Caye**, which has retained much of its virgin forest cover. The island's only accommodation, the *Barbareta Beach Resort*, can be rented in its entirety (in the US Ⓣ888/500 DIVE, Ⓦwww.bay-islands-scuba-diving.com; packages from US$1400 per person for a week), with diving, windsurfing, hiking, mountain-biking and fishing tours thrown in. The reef around Barbareta and the nearby Pigeon Cayes offers excellent snorkelling; launches can be hired to reach these islands from Oak Ridge for around US$45 for a return trip.

Guanaja

The easternmost Bay Island, **GUANAJA**, was the most beautiful, densely forested and undeveloped of them all until Hurricane Mitch laid siege to it for more than two days during October 1998, lashing the land with winds of up to 300kph. Although buildings have been patched up and reforestation projects have been implemented, the landscape will take decades to recover. The island is some 25km long and up to four kilometres wide, and is divided into two unequal parts by a narrow canal – the only way to get between the two sections of the island is by water taxi, which adds both to the atmosphere and to the cost of living. The island is very thinly populated – most of Guanaja's 12,000 inhabitants live in **Bonacca** (also know as Guanaja Town), a crowded settlement that sits on a small caye a few hundred metres offshore. It's here that you'll find the island's shops, as well as the bulk of the reasonably priced accommodation. The only other settlements of any substance are **Savannah Bight** (on the east coast) and **Mangrove Bight** (on the north coast).

Arrival and information

Guanaja **airstrip** is on the larger section of the island, next to the canal. There are no roads, aside from a couple of dirt tracks (though a controversial plan to start building some has been proposed), and the main form of transport is in small launches. **Boats** from the main dock in Bonacca meet all flights and rides can be hitched on private boats to Mangrove Bight for a nominal fee. There are no scheduled boat services to Guanaja from the mainland, but regular cargo ships sail to the island from La Ceiba and other ports in Honduras.

Virtually all the houses in Bonacca are built on stilts – vestiges of early settlement by the Cayman islanders – the buildings clinging to wooden causeways over the canals, many of which have now been filled in. The main causeway, running for about 500m east–west along the caye, with a maze of small passages branching off it, is where you'll find all the shops, banks and businesses. You can **change dollars** and travellers' cheques and get cash advances at Bancahsa, to the right of the dock (Mon–Fri 8–11.30am & 1.30–4pm, Sat 8–11.30am).

Accommodation

Most hotels in Guanaja are all-inclusive luxury **dive resorts** offering weekly packages. You'll also find a small number of mid-range **hotels** in Bonacca – though none are particularly good value for money.

Bonacca

Hotel Miller halfway along the main causeway ⓣ453 4327. In a slightly run-down building, though the rooms are in reasonable condition; most have hot water and, for a little extra, a/c and cable TV. ❹

Hotel Nights Inn at the extreme western end of the causeway ⓣ453 4465. Family-run place with clean, comfortable and fairly spacious rooms, all with cable TV and a/c. ❺

The rest of the island

Bayman Bay Club on the north side of the island ⓣ991 0913, ⓦwww.baymanbayclub.com. Large cabins set in plenty of space on a wooded hillside above a small beach. ❼

End of the World north side of the island ⓣ991 1257, ⓦwww.guanaja.com. Simply furnished but attractive cabins, each with two beds, above a slim sandy beach. Dive (all-inclusive packages start at US$750) and fishing trips can be organized. ❾

Island House Resort on the north side of the island ⓣ 453 4299. Pleasant accommodation in a large house run by a friendly local dive instructor, close to several expanses of beautiful beach and a quick swim from the reef wall. Rooms with full board ❻, with full board and diving ❽

Posada del Sol on the south side of the island ⓣ & ⓕ 453 4186, ⓔ posadadelsol@aol.com. Attractive Spanish-style villas scattered around sixty acres of grounds, with amenities including a pool, tennis courts, sea kayaks and snorkelling equipment. All-inclusive dive packages from US$775 per person.

Around the island

Though Guanaja's Caribbean pine forests were flattened by Mitch, there's still some decent **hiking** across the island. A wonderful trail leads from Mangrove Bight up to **Michael's Peak** (415m), the highest point of the entire Bay Islands, and down to Sandy Bay on the south coast, affording stunning views of Guanaja, Bonacca and the surrounding reef. Fit walkers can do the trail in a day, or you can camp at the summit, provided you bring your own provisions.

Some of the island's finest white-sand **beaches** lie around the rocky headland of **Michael's Rock**, near the *Island House Resort* on the north coast, with good snorkelling close to the shore. **Diving** is excellent all around the main island, but particularly off the small cayes to the east, and at **Black Rocks**, off the northern tip of the main island, where there's an underwater coral canyon. The **Mestizo Dive Site** was opened in 2002 to mark the 500th anniversary of Columbus's visit, with sunken statues of the explorer and national hero Lempira on a reef surrounded by genuine Spanish colonial artefacts, including a cannon.

To get to these sites you'll have to contact one of the hotel-based dive schools: the *Island House Resort* usually has the best rates at around US$70 for two dives including equipment. **Fishing** and **snorkelling** can be arranged with local boatmen, who charge US$10–15 for an hour and a half on the reef. In many areas, however, the reef is close enough to swim to if you have your own snorkel gear.

Eating and drinking

There are several **restaurants** in Bonacca, though none is particularly cheap, as most of the supplies have to be shipped in from the mainland; note, too, that many of them close on Sundays. In the centre of Bonacca itself, try *Pirate's Den* for fresh seafood with daily lunch specials and Friday barbecues. For Mexican food head to *Mexi-Treats*, located opposite the Banco Atlántida on the caye. *Best Stop*, next to the basketball court, is good for snacks, cakes and sticky buns, as well as a variety of fast food including hot wings, burgers and yummy sticky buns. The funkiest **bar** in town is *Nit's Bar*, just east of the main dock, where the clapboard walls shake to classic reggae sounds; while the main dancehall is *Pirate's Landing* at Savannah Bight, home to live DJs every night save Tuesdays.

Cayos Cochinos

Lying 17km offshore from the mainland, the **CAYOS COCHINOS** (Hog Islands) comprise two thickly wooded main islands – **Cochino Grande** and **Cochino Pequeño** – and thirteen cayes, all of them privately owned. The small amount of effort it takes to get there is well worth it for a few days' utter tranquillity. Fringed by a reef, the whole area has been designated a marine reserve, with anchoring on the reef and commercial fishing both strictly prohibited. The US Smithsonian Institution, which manages the reserve, has a research station on Cochino Pequeño. On land, the island's hills are studded with hardwood forests, palms and cactus, while Cochino Grande has a number of trails across its interior, and a small peak rising to 145m.

Organized accommodation on the islands is limited to the *Plantation Beach Resort* on Cochino Grande (ⓣ442 0974, ⓦwww.plantationbeachresort.info), which has a stunning location and twelve fine cabins and does weekly dive packages for around US$850, including all meals and three dives a day. They collect guests by launch from the Muralla de Cabotaje dock in La Ceiba on Saturdays. It can be more rewarding, however, to stay in the traditional Garífuna fishing village of **CHACHAUATE** on Lower Monitor Caye, south of Cochino Grande. The villagers have allocated a hut for visitors to sling their hammocks in for a minimal charge, and will cook meals for you. Basic groceries are available in the village, though you should bring water and your main food supplies with you from the mainland.

Unless you're staying at the *Plantation Beach*, the only way to the Cayos is to charter a boat from the Muralla de Cabotaje dock at La Ceiba (US$60–80 return for up to six people, but be sure to bargain hard).

Travel details

Buses

Copán Ruinas Town to: El Florido (every 30min; 20min); Guatemala City (1 daily; 5hr); San Pedro Sula (7–8 daily; 3hr).
Corinto to: Puerto Cortés (every 1hr 30min, last at 3.30pm; 3hr).
El Florido border to: Chiquimula (every 45min; 1hr 15min); Copán Ruinas Town (every 30min; 20min).
La Ceiba to: San Pedro Sula (18 daily; 3hr); Tela (every 40min; 1hr 30min).
Puerto Cortés to: Corinto (every 1hr 30min; 3hr); San Pedro Sula (every 30min; 1hr).
San Pedro Sula to: La Ceiba (18 daily; 3hr); Puerto Cortés (every 30min; 1hr); Tela (every 40min; 1hr 30min).
Tela to: La Ceiba (every 40min; 1hr 30min); San Pedro Sula (every 40min; 1hr 30min).

Shuttle buses

Antigua to: Copán (1 daily at 4am; 6hr).
Copan to Antigua (1 daily at 2.30pm; 6hr).

Boats

La Ceiba to: Roatán (2 daily; 2hr); Utila (2 daily; 1hr).

Flights

Houston to: Roatán (2 weekly; 3hr 30min).
La Ceiba to: Guanaja (5 daily; 40min); Roatán (12 daily; 30min); Utila (4 daily; 20min).
Miami to: Roatán (2 weekly; 2hr 15min).

Contexts

Contexts

History

Little is known about the area that is now called Guatemala in the days before the advent of Maya civilization, and even the early origins of the Maya remain fairly mysterious. Today, the Maya region is one of the world's hottest archeological areas, and recent excavations have fostered a greater understanding of the region's history but also cast doubts on many previously accepted theories. Although the historical picture, including the names of rulers, is becoming much clearer, many issues are still subject to furious academic polemic.

Prehistory

Opinions differ as to when the first people arrived in the Americas, but the most widely accepted theory is that **Stone Age hunter-gatherers** crossed the Bering land bridge from Siberia to Alaska in several waves beginning 25,000 years ago. Travelling along an ice-free corridor (and possibly in small boats along the coastline) they migrated south into Central America. The first recognizable culture, known as **Clovis**, had emerged by 11,000 BC, and worked stone tools, including spearpoints, blades and scrapers, dating from 9000 BC have been found in the Guatemalan highlands.

In **Mesoamerica**, an area defined as stretching from north central Mexico through Central America to Panama, the first settled pattern of development took place around 8000 BC, as a warming climate forced the hunter-gatherers to adapt to a different way of life. The glaciers were in retreat and the big game, which the hunters depended upon, became scarce due to the warmer, drier climate (and possibly over-hunting). This period, in which the hunters turned to more intensive use of plant foods, is known as the Archaic period and lasted until about 2000 BC. During this time the food vital to the subsequent development of agriculture, such as corn, beans, peppers, squash and probably maize, were domesticated, and research on ancient pollen samples indicates that the Petén region was an area of savannahs and broad-leaved woodlands. Current theory suggests that tropical forest did not appear until the Classic period, by which time the Maya could more easily control its profuse growth.

The early Maya

After 2000 BC we move into the **Preclassic** (or **Formative**) era, a name used by archeologists to describe the earliest developments in the history of the **Maya**, marking the first phase on a long road of evolution and increasing sophistication which culminates with the Classic period. During the **Early Preclassic** (2000–1000 BC), the Maya settled in villages throughout the region, as the foragers became farmers and began making pottery. By 1100 BC, the **Olmec**, often called Mesoamerica's "mother culture", were constructing pyramid-like ceremonial platforms and carving colossal stone heads at San Lorenzo, just to the northwest of the Maya region. Their artistic, polytheistic religious (and almost certainly political) influence spread throughout Maya lands, and Olmec-style carvings have been found at numerous sites along Guatemala's Pacific coast, in El Salvador and at Copán, in Honduras. The Olmec also developed an early writing system and a calendar known as the "Long Count", which was later adopted by the Maya.

The population increased substantially across the Maya region during the **Middle Preclassic** period (1000–400 BC). In northern Petén, **Nakbé** had, by 750 BC, grown to become perhaps the first Maya city, complete with imposing temples and stucco sculptures – evidence that the Maya had progressed far beyond a simple peasant society. At the same time, other settlements – including Tikal and El Mirador – were building their first ceremonial structures, though they still remained little more than village-sized agricultural centres until the Late Preclassic era. It is thought that a common language was spoken throughout the Maya lands, and that a universal belief system, practised from a very early date, may have provided the stimulus and social cohesion to build bigger towns and religious temples. Materials including obsidian and jade from the Guatemalan highlands and granite and salt from Belize were widely traded. Pottery, including red and orange jars and dishes of the *Mamon* style, has been found at a number of settlements, indicating increasing pan-Maya communication. At the same time, food surpluses and rising prosperity levels gradually enabled some inhabitants to eschew farming duties and become seers, priests and astronomers.

Greater advances in architecture were achieved in the **Late Preclassic** (400 BC–250 AD) as other cities prospered in Petén. At the start of this era, Nakbé was the dominant city – its ceremonial core rebuilt to include a soaring cluster of temples and its plazas studded with carved stelae. But the focus quickly shifted to **El Mirador**, 12km to the north, which expanded to become a massive city, spread over twenty square kilometres, with a population of around 100,000. Almost nothing is known about the power politics of these times, but the sheer size of El Mirador indicates that the city must have acquired "superstate" status

Maya Archeological Periods

The names given to **Maya archeological periods** are confusing, not least because when the time periods were established in the mid-twentieth century very little was known about the formative years of Maya civilization. Recent findings have pushed back the dates when the earliest breakthroughs were made and it's only in the past fifteen years that remote cities like El Mirador and Nakbé have begun to be substantially excavated, revealing that the Preclassic period was far more advanced than previously thought.

The archeological periods vary according to the source. This guide follows those used in the *Chronicle of the Maya Kings and Queens* by Simon Martin and Nikolai Grube (see "Books", p.496).

PRE-2000 BC	ARCHAIC
2000 BC–1000 BC	Early Preclassic
1000 BC–400 BC	Middle Preclassic
400 BC–250 AD	Late Preclassic
250 AD–600 AD	Early Classic
600 AD–800 AD	Late Classic
800 AD–909 AD	Terminal Classic
909 AD–1200 AD	Early Postclassic
1200 AD–SPANISH CONQUEST	Late Postclassic

by around 100 BC. Positioned at the heart of a vast trading network, one of its gargantuan temple complexes was constructed to a height of 70m – the highest building ever to have been built by a pre-Columbian culture in the Americas.

El Mirador's only serious rival during the Late Classic era was located several hundred kilometres to the south, on the site of the modern capital of Guatemala City. **Kaminaljuyú** had established a formidable commercial empire based on the supply of obsidian and jade, and held sway over a string of settlements along the Pacific coast, including Takalik Abaj. It's clear that the southern Maya area was much more influenced by Olmec advances at this time, and that Meso-american writing and calendar systems first developed in this region before being introduced to Petén.

From 1 AD pyramids and temple platforms were emerging at Tikal, Uaxactún, Calakmul and many other sites in Petén, in what amounted to an explosion of Maya culture. The famous Maya corbelled arch was developed in this period, and architectural styles became more ambitious. (The corbelled arch was not a true arch, with a keystone, but consisted of two sides, each with stones overlapping until they eventually met, and thus could only span a relatively narrow gap.) A stratified **Maya society** was also becoming established, the nascent states led by rulers and shamanic priests who presided over religious ceremonies dictated by astronomical and calendrical events. There were specialist craftsmen, architects, scribes and artists capable of creating the exquisite murals of San Bartolo (which were only rediscovered in 2002). Intensive agriculture was also practised using irrigation from vast reservoirs via extensive canal networks.

But towards the end of the Late Preclassic period, during the second and third centuries AD, environmental disasters, and possibly protracted warfare, plagued the region. El Mirador, the greatest city in the Maya world, had collapsed by 150 AD, after a long dry climatic period which would have severely cut agricultural production. In the southern region, the eruption of the **Ilopango volcano** in central El Salvador smothered a vast area in ash, probably provoking mass migration from cities as far away as Kaminaljuyú, which was virtually abandoned around 250 AD. Temple building and stelae carving ceased. Pacific trade routes between the southern Maya region and Mexico were disrupted, and much of the trade was rerouted to the north, bringing prosperity (but also Central Mexican influence) to the cities of Petén.

The Classic Maya

The development that separates the Late Preclassic from the **Classic period** (250–909 AD) is the introduction of the Long Count calendar and a recognizably Maya form of writing. This occurred by the end of the third century AD and marks the beginning of the greatest phase of Maya achievement.

During the Classic period all the cities we now know as ruined or restored sites were built, almost always over earlier structures. Elaborately carved **stelae**, bearing dates and emblem glyphs, were erected at regular intervals. These tell of actual rulers and of historical events in their lives – battles, marriages, dynastic succession and so on. As these dates have come to be deciphered they have provided confirmation (or otherwise) of archeological evidence and offered a major insight into the nature of Maya dynastic rule.

Developments in the Maya area during the Early Classic period were still heavily influenced by a giant power to the north – **Teotihuacán**, which dominated Central Mexico and boasted a population of around 250,000. Its **armed merchants**, called *pochteca*, spread the authority of Teotihuacán as far as Petén, the Yucatán and Copán. It's unlikely that Teotihuacán launched an outright military invasion of Maya territory, but the city's influence was strong enough to precipitate fundamental changes in the region. In 378 AD, an armed merchant called Siyak K'ak ushered in a takeover of Tikal, establishing a new dynasty, while at Copán, Yax K'uk Mo' (who was almost certainly from Teotihuacán) founded that city's royal lineage in 426 AD. These Mexicans also brought alternative religious beliefs, and new styles of ceramics, art and architecture – Kaminaljuyú was rebuilt in Teotihuacán style, and Tikal and Copán temples and stelae from the era depict Central Mexican gods.

Yet while Tikal was positioning itself within the Teotihuacán sphere of influence and dominating the Petén region, an increasingly precocious rival Maya state was emerging to the north in Campeche: **Calakmul**, "the kingdom of the snake". From the fifth century, these two states grew to eclipse all other cities in the Maya world, establishing dominion over huge swathes of the region. Each controlling sophisticated trade networks, they jostled for supremacy, a struggle which eventually erupted into open warfare once Teotihuacán influence faded in the sixth century. Calakmul formed an alliance with **Caracol** (today located in Belize) and defeated Tikal in 562 AD – detailed carvings depict elaborately costumed lords trampling on bound captives. This victory caused a hiatus in Tikal's empire building during which there was little new construction at the city or in the smaller centres under its patronage.

The prosperity and grandeur of the **Late Classic** period (600–800 AD) reached across the Maya lands: from Bonampak and Palenque in the west, to Labná, Sayil, Calakmul and Uxmal in the north, Altun Ha in the east, and Copán and Quiriguá in the south, as well as hundreds of smaller centres. Bound together by a coherent religion and culture, Maya architecture, astronomy and art reached degrees of sophistication unequalled by any other pre-Columbian society. Trade prospered and populations grew – by 750 AD it's estimated that the region's people numbered around ten million. Many Maya states were larger than contemporary western European cities, then in their "Dark Ages". Masterpieces of painted pottery and carved jade (their most precious material) were created, often to be used as funerary offerings. Shell, bone and, occasionally, marble were also exquisitely carved; temples were painted in brilliant colours, inside and out. Most of the pigments faded long ago, but vestiges remain, enabling experts to reconstruct vivid images of the appearance of the ancient cities.

In the power politics of the era, Tikal avenged its bitter defeat by overrunning Calakmul in 695 AD and reasserting its influence over its former vassal states of Río Azul and Waka' (El Perú). In a furious epoch of monument building, five of the great temples that define the ceremonial heart of the city were finished between 670 and 810 AD. Elsewhere across Maya lands, cities including Piedras Negras, Yaxhá, Yaxchilán and Dos Pilas flourished as never before, giving rise to more and more imposing temples and palaces, and unparalleled artistic achievements.

The Maya in decline

The glory days were not to last very long, however. By 750 AD political and social changes were beginning to be felt; alliances and trade links broke down, wars increased and stelae recording periods of time were carved less frequently. After 800 AD we move into a period known as the **Terminal Classic** during which the great cities gradually became depopulated, and new construction virtually ceased in the central area after about 830 AD. Bonampak was abandoned before its famous murals could be completed, while many of the great sites along the Usumacinta river (now part of the border between Guatemala and Mexico) were occupied by militaristic outsiders.

The reason for the decline of the Maya is not (and may never be) known, though it was probably a result of several factors. It's known that Maya lands were already under severe pressure from deforestation by the late ninth century, when the region was struck by a terrible **drought**. An incredibly high population density put great strains on food production, possibly exhausting the fertility of the soil, and epidemics may have combined to cause the abandonment of city life. Some Mayanists speculate that there may have been a peasant revolt caused by mass hunger and the demands of an unproductive elite. Whatever the causes, strife and disorder appear to have spread throughout Mesoamerica by the end of the Classic period. In the Maya heartland, virtually all the key cities were abandoned, and those few that remained were reduced to a fairly primitive state. Some survived on the periphery, however, particularly in northern Belize, with Lamanai and other cities remaining inhabited throughout the **Postclassic** period (909 AD to the Spanish conquest). The settlements in the Yucatán peninsula also struggled on, and though the region escaped the worst of the depopulation, it was conquered by the militaristic **Toltecs** from central Mexico in 987 AD, creating a hybrid of Classic Maya culture.

With the decline of Maya civilization in the Petén lowlands undoubtedly came an influx of population into Belize, Yucatán and the Guatemalan highlands to the south. These areas, formerly marginal regions of relatively little development, now contained the last vestiges of Maya culture, and it's at this time that the Guatemala highland area began to take on some of the tribal characteristics still in evidence today. By the end of the Classic period there were small settlements throughout the highlands, usually built on open valley floors and supporting large populations sustained by terraced farming and irrigation. Little was to change in this basic village structure for several hundred years.

Pre-conquest: the highland tribes

Towards the end of the thirteenth century, however, the great cities of the Yucatán, such as Chichén Itzá and Uxmal, which had been under the control of **Toltec–Maya** from the gulf coast of Mexico, were also abandoned. At around the same time, Toltec–Maya invaded the central Guatemalan highlands (although whether they came from the Yucatán or from the Gulf of Mexico remains uncertain). Some argue that they travelled due south into the highlands along the Usumacinta and Chixoy river valleys, while others claim that they came from further west and entered the area via the Pacific coast, which has always been a popular route for invading armies. Their numbers were probably small but their impact was profound, and following their arrival life in the highlands was radically altered.

What once had been a relatively settled, peaceful and religious society became, under the influence of the Toltecs, fundamentally secular, aggressive and militaristic. The Toltec invaders were ruthlessly well organized and in no time at all they established themselves as a ruling elite, founding a series of competing empires.

The greatest of these were the **K'iche'**, who dominated the central area and established their capital, **K'umarkaaj** (later known as Utatlán), to the west of the modern town of Santa Cruz del Quiché. Next in line were the **Kaqchikel**, who were originally based around the modern town of Chichicastenango, but moved their capital to **Iximché** to the south. On the southern shores of Lago de Atitlán, the **Tz'utujil** had their capital on the lower slopes of the San Pedro volcano. To the west the **Mam** occupied the area around the modern town of Huehuetenango, with their capital at **Zaculeu**, while the northern slopes of the Cuchumatanes were home to a collection of smaller groups such as the **Chuj**, the **Q'anjob'al**, and further to the east the **Awakateko** and the **Ixil**. The eastern highlands, around the modern city of Cobán, were home to the notoriously fierce **Achi** nation, with the **Q'eqchi'** to their north, while around the modern site of Guatemala City the land was controlled by the **Poqomam**, with their capital at **Mixco Viejo**. Finally, along the Pacific coast, the **Pipil**, a tribe that had also migrated from the north, occupied the lowlands.

The sheer numbers of these tribes give an impression of the extent to which the area was fragmented, and it's these same divisions, now surviving on the basis of language alone, that still shape the highlands today (see map, p.463).

The Toltec rulers probably controlled only the dominant tribes – the K'iche', Mam and Kaqchikel – while their lesser neighbours were still made up entirely of people indigenous to the area. Arriving in the latter part of the thirteenth century, the Toltecs must have terrorized the local K'iche'–Kaqchikel highlanders and gradually established themselves in a new, rigidly hierarchical society. They brought with them many northern traditions – elements of a Nahua-based language, new gods and an array of military skills – and fused these with local ideas. Many of the rulers' names are similar to those used in the Toltec heartland to the north, and they claimed to trace their ancestry to Quetzalcoatl, a mythical ruling dynasty from the Toltec city of Tula. Shortly after the Spanish conquest, the K'iche' wrote an account of their history, the *Popol Vuh*, in which they lay claim to a Toltec pedigree, as do the Kaqchikel in their account, *The Annals of the Kaqchikel*.

The Toltec invaders were not content with overpowering just a tribe or two, so under the direction of their new rulers the K'iche' began to expand their empire – between 1400 and 1475 they brought the Kaqchikel, the Mam and several other tribes under their control. At the height of their power, around a million highlanders bowed to the word of the K'iche' king. But in 1475 the man who had masterminded their expansion, the great K'iche' ruler **Quicab**, died, and the empire lost much of its authority. The Kaqchikel were the first to break from the fold, anticipating the death of Quicab and moving south to a new and fortified capital, Iximché, in around 1470. Shortly afterwards the other tribes managed to escape the grip of K'iche' control and assert their independence. For the next fifty years or so the tribes were in a state of almost perpetual conflict, fighting for access to the inadequate supplies of farmland. The archeological remains from this era give evidence of this instability; gone are the valley-floor centres of pre-Toltec times, and in their place are fortified hilltop sites, surrounded by ravines and man-made ditches.

When the Spanish arrived, the highlands were in crisis. The population had grown so fast that it had outstripped the food supply, forcing the tribes to fight for any available land in order to increase their agricultural capacity. With a growing sense of urgency both the K'iche' and the Kaqchikel had begun to encroach on the lowlands of the Pacific coast. The situation could hardly have been more favourable to the Spanish, who fostered this intertribal friction, playing one group off against another.

The Spanish conquest

While the tribes of highland Guatemala were fighting it out amongst themselves, their northern neighbours, in what is now Mexico, were confronting a formidable new enemy. In 1521, the Spanish conquistadors had captured the Aztec capital at Tenochtitlán and were starting to cast their net further afield. Amidst the horrors of the Conquest there was one man, **Pedro de Alvarado**, whose evilness stood out above the rest. He could hardly have been better suited to the job – ambitious, cunning, intelligent, ingenious, dashingly handsome and ruthlessly cruel.

In 1523, conquistador leader Hernán Cortés dispatched Alvarado to Guatemala, entreating him to use the minimum of force "and to preach matters concerning our Holy Faith". His army included 120 horsemen, 173 horses, 300 soldiers and 200 Mexican warriors, largely Tlaxcalans who had allied themselves with Cortés in the conquest of Mexico. Marching south they entered Guatemala along the Pacific coast, where they met with the first wave of resistance, a small army of K'iche' warriors. These were no match for the Spaniards, who cut through their ranks with ease. From here Alvarado turned north, taking his troops up into the highlands and through a narrow mountain pass to the Quetzaltenango valley, where they came upon the deserted city of **Xelajú**, a K'iche' outpost.

Warned of the impending arrival of the Spanish, the K'iche' had struggled to build an alliance with the other tribes, but old rivalries proved too strong and the **K'iche'** army stood alone. Three days later, on a nearby plain, they met the Spaniards in open warfare. Alvarado claimed the invaders were confronted by some 30,000 K'iche' warriors (though this figure is almost certainly an exaggeration) led by their leader **Tecún Umán** in a headdress of quetzal feathers. Despite the huge disparity in numbers, slingshot and foot soldiers were no match for cavalry and gunpowder, and the Spaniards were once again able to wade through the Maya ranks. Legend has it that the battle was brought to a close when Alvarado met Tecún Umán in hand-to-hand conflict – and cut him down. After this defeat, the K'iche' invited the Spaniards to their capital, where they planned to trap and destroy them. But when Alvarado saw their city he grew suspicious and took several K'iche' lords as prisoners. When hostilities erupted once again, he killed the captives and had the city burnt to the ground.

Having dealt with the K'iche', Alvarado turned his attention to the other tribal groups. The **Kaqchikel**, recognizing the military superiority of the Spanish, decided to form some kind of alliance with them. As a result, the Spaniards established their first headquarters, in 1523, alongside the Kaqchikel capital of **Iximché**. From here they ranged far and wide, overpowering the countless smaller tribes. Travelling east, Alvarado's army met the **Tz'utujil** on the shores of Lago de Atitlán. Here the first battle took place at a site near the modern village of Panajachel, and the second beneath the Tz'utujil capital, at the base of the San Pedro volcano, where the Spaniards were helped by a force of Kaqchikel warriors who arrived on the scene in some 300 canoes. Moving on, the Spanish headed south to the Pacific coast, where they overcame the **Pipil** before making their way back to Iximché.

In 1524, Alvarado sent his brother Gonzalo on an expedition against the **Mam**, who were conquered after a month-long siege during which they holed up in their fortified capital, **Zaculeu**. The next year, Alvarado himself set out to take on the **Poqomam** at their capital, **Mixco Viejo**, where he came up against an army of some 3000 warriors. Once again they proved no match for the well-disciplined Spanish ranks.

Despite this string of relatively easy victories, it wasn't until well into the 1530s that Alvarado managed to assert control over the more remote parts of the highlands. Moving into the Cuchumatanes his forces were beaten back by the **Uspanteko** and met fierce opposition in the **Ixil** region. And while Alvarado's soldiers were struggling to contain resistance in these isolated mountainous areas, problems also arose at the very heart of the campaign. In 1526, the Kaqchikel revolted against the Spanish, abandoning their capital and moving into the mountains, from where they waged a guerrilla war against their former partners. The Spanish were forced to abandon their base at Iximché, and moved instead to a site near the modern town of Antigua.

Here, on St Cecilia's Day, November 22, 1527, they established their first permanent capital, the city of **Santiago de los Caballeros**. For ten years indigenous labourers toiled in the construction of the new city, neatly sited at the base of the Agua volcano, building a cathedral, a town hall, and a palace for Alvarado. The land within the city was given out to those who had fought alongside him, and plots on the edge of town were allocated to his remaining Maya allies.

Meanwhile, one particularly thorny problem for the Spanish was presented by the **Achi** and **Q'eqchi'** Maya, who occupied what are now the Verapaz highlands. Despite all his efforts, Alvarado was unable to conquer either of these tribes, who fought fiercely against the invading armies. In the end he gave up on trying to control the area, naming it Tierra de Guerra. The situation was eventually resolved by the Church. In 1537, **Fray Bartolomé de las Casas**, the "protector of the Indians", travelled into the region in a bid to persuade the locals to accept both Christianity and Spanish authority. Within three years the priests had succeeded where Alvarado's armies had failed, and the last of the highland tribes was brought under colonial control in 1540. Thus did the area earn its name of Verapaz, "true peace".

Alvarado himself grew tired of the Conquest, disappointed by the lack of plunder, and his reputation for brutality began to spread. He was forced to return to Spain to face charges of treason, but returned a free man with a young wife at his side. Life in the New World soon sent his bride to an early grave, however, and Alvarado set out once again, in search of the great mineral wealth that had eluded him in Guatemala. First he travelled south to Peru, where it's said that Francisco Pizarro, conqueror of the Inca nation, paid him to leave South America. He then returned to Spain once again, where he married **Beatriz de la Cueva**, his first wife's sister, and the two of them made their way back to Guatemala, where he dropped off his new bride before setting sail for the Spice Islands. Along the way he stopped in Mexico, to put down an uprising, and was crushed to death beneath a rolling horse.

From 1524 until his death in 1541, Alvarado had ruled Guatemala as a personal fiefdom, desperately seeking adventure and wealth, and enslaving and abusing the local population in order to finance his urge to explore. By the time of his death all the Maya tribes had been overcome (except for tiny numbers of Itza), although local uprisings had already started to take place.

Colonial rule

The early years of colonial rule were marked by a turmoil of uprisings and political wrangling, and while the death of Alvarado might have been expected to bring a degree of calm, it was in fact followed by fresh disaster. When Alvarado's wife Beatriz de la Cueva heard of his death, she plunged the capital into a period of prolonged mourning. She had the entire palace painted black, inside and out, and ordered the city authorities to appoint her as the new governor. Meanwhile, the area was swept by a series of storms, and on the night of September 10, 1541, it was shaken by a massive earthquake. The sides of the Agua volcano shuddered, undermining the walls of the cone and releasing its contents. A great wall of mud and water swept down the side of the peak, burying the city of Santiago and most of its inhabitants.

The surviving colonial authorities moved up the valley to a new site, where a second **Santiago de los Caballeros** was founded in the following year. This new city served as the administrative headquarters of the **Audiencia de Guatemala**, which was made up of six provinces: Costa Rica, Nicaragua, San Salvador, Honduras, Guatemala and Chiapas (now part of Mexico). With Alvarado out of the way, the authorities began to build a new society, recreating the splendours of the homeland. Santiago was never endowed with the same wealth or freedom as Mexico City and Lima, but it was nevertheless the centre of political and religious power for two hundred years, accumulating a superb array of arts and architecture. By the mid-eighteenth century its population approached 80,000. Here colonial society was at its most developed, rigidly structured along racial lines with pure-blood Spaniards at the top, indigenous slaves at the bottom, and a host of carefully defined racial strata in between. The city was regularly shaken by scandal, intrigue and earthquakes, and it was eventually destroyed in 1773 by the last of these, after which the capital was moved to its modern site: Guatemala City.

Perhaps the greatest power in colonial Central America was the **Church**. The first religious order to reach Guatemala was the Franciscans, who arrived with Alvarado himself, and by 1532 the Mercedarians and Dominicans had followed suit, with the Jesuits arriving shortly after. **Francisco Marroquín**, the country's first bishop, rewarded these early arrivals with huge concessions, including land and indigenous people, which later enabled them to earn fortunes from sugar, wheat and indigo, income boosted by the fact that they were exempt from tax. In later years a whole range of other orders arrived in Santiago, and religious rivalry became an important shaping force in the colony. Through its wealth and power, the Church fostered the splendour of the colonial capital while ruthlessly exploiting the native people and their land. In Santiago alone there were some eighty churches, and alongside these were schools, convents, hospitals, hermitages, craft centres and colleges. The religious orders became the main benefactors of the arts, amassing a wealth of tapestry, jewels, sculpture and painting, and staging concerts, fiestas and endless religious processions. Religious persecution was at its worst between 1572 and 1580, when the office of the **Inquisition** sought out those who had failed to receive the faith and dealt with them harshly.

By the eighteenth century the power of the Church had started to get out of control, and the Spanish kings began to impose taxes on the religious orders and to limit their power and freedom. The conflict between church and state came to a head in 1767, when Carlos III banished the Jesuits from the Spanish colonies.

The Spanish must have been disappointed with their conquest of Central America as it offered none of the instant plunder that had been found in Mexico and Peru. They found small amounts of silver around the modern town of Huehuetenango and a few grains of gold in the rivers of Honduras, but nothing that could compare with the vast resources of Potosí (a huge silver mine in Bolivia) or highland Mexico. In Central America the **colonial economy** was based on agriculture. The coastal area produced cacao, tobacco, cotton and, most valuable of all, indigo; the highlands were grazed with sheep and goats; and cattle, specially imported from Spain, were raised on coastal ranches. In the lowlands of Petén and the jungles of the lower Motagua valley, the mosquitoes and forests remained unchallenged, although here and there certain aspects of the forest were developed: chicle, the raw material of chewing gum, was bled from the sapodilla trees, as was sarsaparilla, used to treat syphilis.

At the heart of the colonial economy was the system of *repartamientos*, whereby the ruling classes were granted the right to extract labour from the indigenous population. It was this that established the system whereby the Maya population was transported to work in the plantations, a pattern – though no longer legally enforced – that remains a tremendous burden today.

Meanwhile, in the capital it was graft and corruption that controlled the movement of money, with titles and appointments sold to the highest bidder. All of the colony's wealth was funnelled through the city, and it was only here that the monetary economy really developed.

The impact of the Conquest was perhaps the greatest in the highlands, where the **Maya population** had their lives totally restructured. The first stage in this process was the *reducción*, whereby scattered native communities were combined into new Spanish-style towns and villages. Between 1543 and 1600 some seven hundred new settlements were created, each based around a Catholic church. Ostensibly, the purpose of this was to enable the Church to work on its newfound converts, but it also had the effect of pooling the available labour and making its exploitation that much easier. The highland villages were still bound up in an ancient system of subsistence farming, although this tradition was now disturbed by demands for tribute.

Maya **social structures** were also profoundly altered by post-conquest changes. The great central authorities that had previously dominated were now eradicated, replaced by local structures based in the new villages. *Caciques* (local chiefs) and *alcaldes* (mayors) now held the bulk of local power, which was bestowed on them by the Church. In the distant corners of the highlands, however, priests were few and far between, only visiting the villages from time to time. Those that they left in charge developed not only their own power structures but also their own religion, mixing the new with the old. By the start of the nineteenth century, the Maya population had largely recovered from the initial impact of the Conquest, and in many places these local structures became increasingly important. In each village *cofradías* (brotherhood groups) were entrusted with the care of saints, while *principales* (village elders) held the bulk of traditional authority, a situation that still persists today. Throughout the highlands, village uprisings became increasingly commonplace as the new indigenous culture became stronger and stronger.

Even more serious for the indigenous population than any social changes were the **diseases** that arrived with the conquistadors. Waves of plague, typhoid and fever swept through a population without any natural resistance to them. In the worst-hit areas the native population was cut by some ninety percent, and in many parts of the country their numbers were halved.

Two centuries of colonial rule totally reshaped the structure of Guatemalan society, giving it new cities, a new religion, a transformed economy and a racist hierarchy. Nevertheless, the impact of colonial rule was perhaps less marked than in many other parts of Latin America. Only two sizable cities had emerged and the outlying areas had received little attention from the colonial authorities. And although the indigenous population had been ruthlessly exploited and suffered enormous losses at the hands of foreign weapons and imported diseases, its culture was never eradicated. It simply absorbed the symbols and ideas of the new Spanish ideology, creating a dynamic synthesis that is neither Maya nor Catholic.

Independence

The apartheid-style nature of colonial rule had given birth to deep dissatisfaction amongst many groups in Central America. Spain's policy was to keep wealth and power in the hands of those born in Spain (*chapetones*), a policy that left growing numbers of Creoles (including those of Spanish blood born in Guatemala) and mestizos (of mixed blood) resentful and hungry for power and change. (For the majority of the indigenous people, both power and wealth were way beyond their reach.) As the Spanish departed, Guatemalan politics were dominated by a struggle between **conservatives**, who sided with the Church and the Crown, and **liberals**, who advocated a secular and more egalitarian state. One result of the split was that independence was not a clean break, but was declared several times.

The spark, as throughout Spanish America, was Napoleon's invasion of Spain and the abdication of King Fernando VII. In the chaos that followed, a liberal constitution was imposed on Spain in 1812 and a mood of reform swept through the colonies. At the time, Central America was under the control of **Brigadier Don Gabino Gainza**, the last of the Captains General. His one concern was to maintain the status quo, in which he was strongly backed by the wealthy landowners and the Church hierarchy. Bowing to demands for independence, but still hoping to preserve the power structure, Gainza signed a formal **Act of Independence** on September 15, 1821, enshrining the authority of the Church and seeking to preserve the old order under new leadership. Augustín de Iturbide, the short-lived emperor of newly independent Mexico, promptly sent troops to annex Guatemala to the Mexican empire, a union which was to last less than a year.

Through a second Declaration of Independence, in 1823, Guatemala joined the Central American states in a loose **federation**, adopting a constitution modelled on that of the United States, abolishing slavery and advocating liberal reforms. These moves were bitterly opposed by the Church and conservatives throughout Central America, and provoked several inter-federation (and internal) conflicts. But in 1830 the political left of Salvador, Honduras and Guatemala united under the leadership of **Francisco Morazán**, a Honduran general, under whom **Mariano Gálvez** became the chief of state in Guatemala: religious orders were abolished, the death penalty done away with, and trial by jury, a general school system, civil marriage and the progressive Lívingston law code were all instituted.

This liberal era lasted until 1838 when the ailing Central American Federation was dissolved and the reforming Guatemalan administration overthrown by a revolt from the mountains. Throughout the turmoil of independence and brief years of the federation, life in the highlands remained harsh, with the indigenous population still bearing the burdens imposed on them by two centuries of colonial rule. Seething with discontent, the Maya were united behind an illiterate but charismatic leader, the 23-year-old **Rafael Carrera**, under whose command they marched on Guatemala City. Independence was declared in 1839, with Carrera installed first as a *caudillo* (strongman), and later as president.

Carrera respected no authority other than that of the Church, and his immediate reforms swept aside the changes instituted by the liberal government. The religious orders were restored to their former position and traditional Spanish titles were reinstated. The conservatives had little in common with Carrera, but they could see that he offered to uphold their position with the weight of popular support, and hence they sided with him. Under Carrera, Guatemala fought a succession of conflicts against liberals in other parts of Central America, and eventually established itself as an independent republic in 1847. Carrera's greatest internal challenge came from the state of **Los Altos**, which included much of the western highlands and proclaimed itself an independent republic in defiance of him. It was a short-lived threat, however, and the would-be state was soon brought back into the republic.

When Carrera died, at the age of fifty in 1865, Guatemala was an impoverished nation (the export of indigo and cochinel had plummeted after the invention of artificial dyes), while its transport network was backward at best. Little was to change under his successor, **Vicente Cerna**, another conservative, who ruled until 1871, but during this period liberal opposition was again gathering momentum, and 1867 saw the first **liberal uprising**, led by **Serpio Cruz**. His bid for power was unsuccessful, but it inspired two young liberals, Justo Rufino Barrios and Francisco Cruz, to follow suit. In the next few years, they mounted several other unsuccessful revolts, and in 1870 Serpio Cruz was captured and hanged.

Rufino Barrios and the coffee boom

The year 1871 marked a major turning point in Guatemalan politics. In that year Rufino Barrios and Miguel García Granados set out from Mexico with an army of just 45 men, entering Guatemala via the small border town of Cuilco. The **liberal revolution** thus set in motion was an astounding success, the army growing by the day as it approached the capital, which was finally taken on June 30, 1871. Granados took the helm of the new liberal administration but held the presidency for just a few years, surrounding himself with aging comrades and offering only very limited reforms.

Meanwhile, out in the district of Los Altos, **Rufino Barrios**, now a local military commander, was infuriated by the lack of action. In 1872 he marched his troops to the capital and installed them in the San José barracks, demanding immediate elections. These were granted and he won with ease. Barrios was a charismatic leader with tyrannical tendencies (monuments throughout the country testify to his sense of his own importance) who regarded himself as a great reformer. His most immediate acts were classic liberal gestures: the restructuring of the education system and an attack on the Church. The University of San Carlos was secularized and modernized, while clerics were forbidden to wear the cloth and public religious processions were banned. The Church was outraged and excommunicated Barrios, which prompted him to expel the archbishop in retaliation. Barrios' liberal perspective was undoubtedly instilled with a deep arrogance, and he would tolerate no political opposition, developing an effective network of secret police and ensuring that the army became an essential part of his political power base.

Barrios also set about reforming agriculture, and he presided over a boom period, largely as a result of the cultivation of **coffee**. It was this more than anything else that distinguished the era and was to fundamentally reshape the country. When the liberals came to power coffee already accounted for half the value of the country's exports, and by 1884 the volume of output had increased five times. To foster this expansion Barrios founded a Ministry of Development, which extended the railway network (begun in 1880), established a national bank, and developed the ports of Champerico, San José and Iztapa. Between 1870 and 1900 the volume of foreign trade increased twenty times.

All this had an enormous impact on Guatemalan **society**. Many of the new plantations were owned and run by German immigrants, and the majority of the coffee eventually found its way to Europe. The newcomers soon formed a powerful elite and, although most of the Germans were later forced out of Guatemala (during World War II), their influence can still be felt, directly in the Verapaz highlands, and more subtly in the continuing presence of an extremely powerful political clique. The new liberal perspective maintained that foreign ideas were superior to indigenous ones, and while European immigrants were welcomed with open arms, the Maya population was still regarded as hopelessly inferior.

Indigenous society was also deeply affected by the needs of the coffee boom, as Barrios instituted a system of **forced labour**. By 1876 up to one quarter of the male Maya population could be dispatched to work on the coffee fincas, often under appalling conditions, while in the highlands landowners continued to employ a system of debt peonage.

As a result of the coffee boom, many Maya lost not only their freedom but also their land. From 1873 onwards the government began confiscating land that was either unused or communally owned and selling it to the highest bidder. Huge amounts of the country were seized, and land that had been communally owned for centuries was gobbled up by the new wave of agribusiness. In many areas the villagers rose up in defiance, with significant **revolts** throughout the western highlands continuing into the twentieth century. In Momostenango some five hundred armed men faced the authorities, only to find their village overrun by troops and their homes burnt to the ground. In Cantel troops shot all of the village officials, who were campaigning against plans to build a textile factory on their land. These land seizures forced the Maya to become dependent on seasonal labour.

Jorge Ubico and the banana empire

Rufino Barrios, who was eventually killed in 1885 while fighting to re-establish a unified Central America, was succeeded by a string of short-lived but like-minded presidents. The next to hold power for any time was **Manuel Estrada Cabrera**, a stern authoritarian who restricted union organization and supported the interests of big business. He ruled from 1898 until he was overthrown in 1920, by which time he was on the verge of insanity.

Meanwhile, a new and exceptionally powerful player was becoming involved in the country's affairs – the **United Fruit Company**, which would assert its influence over much of Central America until the 1960s. The company, which got its start in Costa Rica, moved into Guatemala in 1901, when it bought a small tract of land on which to grow bananas. Three years later, it was awarded a contract to complete the railway from Guatemala City to Puerto Barrios, and in 1912 ownership of the Pacific railway network also fell to the company, giving it a virtual transport monopoly. Large-scale banana cultivation really took off, and by 1934 United Fruit controlled a massive amount of land, exporting around 3.5 million bunches of bananas annually and reaping vast profits. In 1941 some 25,000 Guatemalans were employed in the banana industry.

The power of the United Fruit Company was by no means restricted to agriculture, and its influence was so pervasive that the company earned itself the nickname *El Pulpo*, "the octopus". Control of the transport network brought with it control of the coffee trade: by 1930, 28 percent of the country's coffee output was handled by the company's Caribbean port, Puerto Barrios. During the 1930s it cost as much to ship coffee from Guatemala to New Orleans as it did from Río de Janeiro to New Orleans.

Against this background the power of the Guatemalan government was severely limited, with the influence of the United States increasing alongside that of the United Fruit Company. In 1919, Guatemala faced a financial crisis and Cabrera was ousted by a coup the following year, replaced by the moderate **Carlos Herrera**, whose reforms threatened to terminate United Fruit Company contracts. As a result, Herrera lasted little more than a year, ousted by **General José María Orellano** in December 1921. Orellano had no qualms about repressive measures – his minister of war, Jorge Ubico, killed some 290 opponents in 1926, the year in which Orellano died of a heart attack. Orellano's death prompted a bitter power struggle between Ubico, a fierce radical, and **Lazaro Chacón**, who won the day and was elected as the new liberal president. In the next few years, indigenous farmers began to express their anger at the United Fruit Company monopoly, while the company demanded the renewal of long-standing contracts, squeezing Chacón from both sides. His rule came to an end in 1930, when he suffered a stroke.

The way was now clear for **Jorge Ubico**, a charismatic leader who was well connected with the ruling and land-owning elite. Ubico had risen fast through the ranks of local government as *jefe político* in Alta Verapaz and Retalhuleu, earning a reputation for efficiency and honesty. As president, however, he inherited financial disaster. Guatemala had been badly hit by the Depression, accumulating debts of some US$5 million: in response Ubico fought hard to expand the export market for Guatemalan produce, managing to sign trade agreements that exempted local coffee and bananas from import duties in the United States. But increased trade with the great American power was only possible at the expense of traditional links with Europe.

Within Guatemala, Ubico steadfastly supported the United Fruit Company and the interests of US business. This relationship was of such importance that by 1940 ninety percent of all Guatemalan exports were being sold to the United States. Trade and diplomacy drew Guatemala ever closer to the US, a relationship exemplified when Ubico, against his will, was forced to bow to US pressure to expel German landowners in the run-up to World War II.

Internally, Ubico embarked on a radical programme of reform, including a sweeping drive against corruption and a massive road-building effort, which bought him great popularity in the provinces. Despite his liberal pretensions, however, Ubico sided firmly with big business when the chips were down, always offering his assistance to the United Fruit Company and the landowning elite. The system of debt peonage was replaced by the **vagrancy law**, under which all landless peasants were forced to work 150 days a year – in fincas or on public-works schemes like road building – and additional draconian legal measures ensured that landowners in effect were given total authority over their workforce. Not surprisingly, sporadic local protests and revolts against landowners continued in the late 1930s and early 1940s.

Internal security was another obsession that was to dominate Ubico's years in office, as he became increasingly paranoid. He maintained that he was a reincarnation of Napoleon and was fascinated by all aspects of the military: he operated a network of spies and informers whom he regularly used to unleash waves of repression, particularly in the run-up to elections. In 1934, when he discovered an assassination plan, three hundred people were killed in just two days. To prevent any further opposition he registered all printing presses in the country and made discipline the cornerstone of state education.

But while Ubico tightened his grip on every aspect of government, the rumblings of opposition grew louder. In 1944 discontent erupted in student violence, and Ubico was finally forced to resign after fourteen years of tyrannical rule. Power was transferred to **Juan Frederico Ponce Vaides**, who attempted to continue in the same style, but by the end of the year he also faced open revolt. The pair of them were driven into exile.

Ten years of "spiritual socialism"

The overthrow of Jorge Ubico released a wave of opposition, with students, professionals and young military officers all demanding democracy and freedom. It was a mood that was to transform Guatemalan politics, one so extreme a contrast to previous transitions in power that the handover was dubbed **the 1944 revolution**.

A joint military and civilian junta took control in the interim period before elections, and in March 1945 a new constitution was instituted, extending suffrage to include all adults and prohibiting the president from standing for a second term. In the elections **Juan José Arévalo**, a teacher, won the presidency with 85 percent of the vote. His political doctrine was dubbed **"spiritual socialism"**, and he immediately set about implementing much-needed structural reforms. Under a new budget, a third of the government's income was allocated to social welfare, to be spent on the construction of schools and hospitals, a programme of immunization, and a far-reaching literacy campaign. The vagrancy laws were abolished, a national development agency was founded, and in 1947 a labour code was adopted, granting workers the right to strike and union representation.

Some former coffee farms were turned into cooperatives, while new laws protected tenant farmers from eviction. Other policies were intended to promote industrial and agricultural development, for example technical assistance and credit were made available to peasant farmers.

In Arévalo's final years the pace of reform slackened somewhat as he concentrated on consolidating the gains made in early years and on evading various attempts to overthrow him. Despite his popularity, Arévalo was still wary of the traditional elite: Church leaders, old-school army officers and wealthy landowners all resented the new wave of legislation, and repeated coup attempts were made.

Elections were scheduled for 1950, and during the run-up the two main candidates were both colonels: **Francisco Arana** and **Jácobo Arbenz**, both members of the junta that had taken over at the end of the Ubico era. In 1949, Arana, who was favoured by the right, was assassinated. Suspicion fell on Arbenz, who was backed by the peasant organizations and unions, but there was no hard proof. Arana was replaced by **Brigadier Ydígoras Fuentes**, an army officer from the Ubico years.

Arbenz won the election with ease, taking 65 percent of the vote, and declared that he would transform the country into an independent capitalist nation and raise the standard of living. But the process of overthrowing feudal society and ending economic dependency was to lead to a direct confrontation between

Che Guevara in Guatemala

Ernesto "Che" Guevara arrived in Guatemala on New Year's Eve 1953, broke and with no place to stay. He had graduated as a doctor in his native Argentina five months previously, and immediately left to explore Latin America – hitching rides, sleeping rough and cadging meals along the way.

The future *comandante* spent eight months in Guatemala City, living in Zona 1, the historic heart of the capital, in a number of cheap hospedajes. Most of his days were spent in a fruitless search for work as a doctor, surviving on the generosity of the people he met and scratching a meagre income from a series of casual jobs: teaching a few Spanish classes, doing some translation work, and peddling encyclopedias and images of the Black Christ of Esquipulas in the capital's streets.

But Guevara had not just come to Guatemala to look for work. In the early 1950s, Guatemala City was a mecca for political idealists, communists and budding revolutionaries from Latin America, all attracted to the country by reformist president Arbenz and his party's doctrine of "spiritual socialism". In a letter to his aunt, Guevara wrote of his travels through the region, and avowed his intentions to challenge American hegemony:

Along the way, I had the opportunity to pass through the dominions of the United Fruit ... I have sworn before a picture of the old and mourned comrade Stalin that I won't rest until I see these capitalist octopuses annihilated. In Guatemala I will perfect myself and achieve what I need to be an authentic revolutionary.

One of the first people he met in Guatemala was Hildea Gadea, a well-connected young Peruvian who later became his first wife. Gadea, an exiled member of Peru's ARPA rebels, introduced Che to a number of other young political activists, including Rolando Morán, who was to become the leader of the Guatemalan EGP guerrillas (see p.156). Guevara formed his political consciousness in Guatemala City, his beliefs shaped by hours spent reading Marx, Trotsky and Mao, an instinctive hatred of US imperialism, and marathon theological debates. Of the city's myriad Latino leftist groups, the Cubans most impressed Che, for they alone had actually launched an armed uprising against a dictatorship (the failed Moncada assault after Batista had cancelled the 1952 Cuban elections). Guevara met Ñico López, the Cuban who would later introduce him to Fidel and Raúl Castro, and with whom he would later regroup in Mexico, set sail for Cuba in 1956 and initiate the revolution.

Guevara remained in Guatemala City throughout the attacks on the capital in June 1954. The young radical wrote to his family denouncing the indecisiveness of the Arbenz government and its inability to organize local militias to defend the country. He swore allegiance to the Soviet Union, and joined the Communist Party while holed up in the Argentine embassy, awaiting deportation after Arbenz had been deposed.

Many of the young Guatemala-based comrades later reassembled in Mexico City where they digested the downfall of Arbenz. Perhaps the biggest lesson Guevara learned was that rather than attempt to negotiate with Washington, it was essential to combat American interference with armed resistance. He was convinced that Guatemala had been betrayed "*inside and out*", and argued that future revolutionaries must be prepared to establish their internal authority by force and eliminate enemies using repression and firing squads if necessary – "*victory will be conquered with blood and fire, there can be no pardon for the traitors*".

the new government and the American corporations that still dominated the economy.

Aware of the size of the task that faced him, Arbenz enlisted the support of the masses, encouraging the participation of peasants in the programme of agrarian reform and inciting the militancy of students and unions. He also attempted to break the great monopolies, building a state-run hydroelectric plant to rival the American-owned generating company and a highway to compete with the railway to the Caribbean, as well as planning a new port alongside Puerto Barrios, which was still owned by the United Fruit Company. At the same time, Arbenz began a series of suits against foreign corporations, seeking unpaid taxes. Internally, these measures aroused a mood of national pride, but they were strongly resented by the US companies whose empires were under attack.

The situation became even more serious with the **law of agrarian reform** passed in July 1952, which stated that idle and state-owned land would be distributed to the landless. Some of this land was to be rented out for a lifetime lease, but the bulk of it was handed over outright to the new owners, who were to pay a small percentage of its market value. The former owners of the land were to be compensated with government bonds, but the value of the land was calculated on the basis of the tax they had been paying, usually a fraction of its true value.

The new laws outraged landowners, despite the fact that they were given the right to appeal. Between 1953 and 1954 around 8840 square kilometres were redistributed to the benefit of some 100,000 peasant families – the first time since the arrival of the Spanish that the government had responded to the needs of the indigenous population. The landowner most seriously affected by the reforms was the United Fruit Company, which only farmed around fifteen percent of its land holdings, and lost about half of its property.

As the pace of reform gathered, Arbenz began to take an increasingly radical stance. In 1951, the Communist Party was granted legal status, and in the next election four party members were elected to the legislature, which was staunchly anti-American.

In the United States the press repeatedly accused the new Guatemalan government of being a communist beachhead in Central America, and the US government attempted to intervene on behalf of the United Fruit Company. Tellingly, Allen Dulles, the new director of the CIA, also happened to be a member of the fruit company's board.

In 1953, President Dwight Eisenhower approved plans to overthrow the government. The CIA set up a small military invasion of Guatemala to depose Arbenz and install an alternative administration more suited to their tastes. A ragtag army of exiles and mercenaries was put together in Honduras, and on June 18, 1954, Guatemala City was bombed with leaflets demanding the resignation of Arbenz. Aware that the army would never support him, Arbenz had bought a boatload of Czechoslovakian arms, hoping to arm the people, but the guns were intercepted by the CIA before they reached Puerto Barrios. On the night of June 18, Guatemala was strafed with machine-gun fire while the invading army, described by Arbenz as "a heterogeneous Fruit Company expeditionary force", was getting closer to the city by the hour.

On June 27, Arbenz declared that he was relinquishing the presidency to **Colonel Carlos Enrique Díaz**, the army chief of staff. And on July 3 John Peurifoy, the US ambassador to Guatemala, flew the new government to Guatemala aboard a US Air Force plane. Guatemala's attempt to escape the clutches of outside intervention and bring about social change had been brought to an abrupt end.

Counter-revolution and military rule

Following the overthrow of Arbenz, the army rose to fill the power vacuum; it would dominate politics for the next thirty years, propelling the country into a spiral of violence and economic decline. Since the time of Jorge Ubico the army had become increasingly professional and political, and now it began to receive increasing amounts of US aid, expanding its influence to include a wide range of public works and infrastructure projects.

In 1954 the US ambassador persuaded a provisional government to accept **Castillo Armas** as the new president, and Armas wasted no time sweeping away the progressive legislation of the previous ten years. The constitution of 1945 was replaced by a more restrictive version; illiterates were disenfranchised; left-wing parties were outlawed; and large numbers of unionists and reformers were simply executed. The regime lifted the restrictions that had been placed on foreign investment and returned all the land that had been confiscated to its previous owners, a measure which badly affected the indigenous population. Meanwhile, Armas surrounded himself with the traditional Guatemalan elite and drew heavily on US assistance in order to develop the economy.

A referendum was rigged to provide a supportive response to Armas' rule, but his government had only limited backing from the armed forces, and coup rumblings persisted until finally he was shot by his own bodyguard in 1957.

The assassination was followed by several months of political turmoil, out of which **Ydígoras Fuentes** (a former candidate) emerged as the next president. His disastrous five-year rule was marked by corruption, incompetence, outrageous patronage and economic decline caused by a fall in coffee prices; the formation of the Central American Common Market during his tenure did help to boost light industry, however. A coup failed in 1960, and two years later a large section of Congress withdrew its support from the government.

Ydígoras was eventually overthrown when Arévalo threatened to return to Guatemala and contest the 1963 elections, which he might well have won. The possibility of another socialist government sent shock waves through the establishment in both Guatemala and the United States, and President John F. Kennedy gave the go-ahead for another coup. In 1963 the army once more took control, under the leadership of **Peralta Azurdia**.

Peralta was president for just three years, during which he fiddled with the constitution and took his time in restoring the electoral process. Meanwhile, the authoritarian nature of his government came up against the first wave of armed resistance. Two failed coupsters from 1960, Turcios Lima and Marco Yon Sosa, both army officers, took to the eastern highlands and waged a **guerrilla war** against the state. Trained in counterinsurgency by the US, and both in their early twenties, they began to attack local army posts. A second organization, FAR, emerged later that year, and the Guatemalan Labour Party (PGT) formed a shaky alliance with the guerrillas, attempting to represent their grievances in the political arena and advocating a return to Arévalo's rule.

Peralta finally lost control in the 1966 elections, which were won by **Julio Cesar Montenegro** of the centre-left Partido Revolucionario. Before taking office, however, Montenegro was forced to sign a pact with the military, obliging him to give them a totally free hand in all affairs of national security. Then, after Montenegro's offer of amnesty to the guerrillas was rejected, a ruthless counterinsurgency campaign swung into action. Specially trained units, backed by US advisers, undermined peasant support for the guerrillas by terrorizing the local population. The guerrillas were soon forced to spend much of their time on the move, and further damage was done to the movement by the death of Turcios Lima in a car crash. By the end of the decade, the guerrilla movement had been virtually eradicated in the eastern highlands, and its activities, greatly reduced, shifted to Guatemala City, where the US ambassador was assassinated by FAR rebels in 1968.

Meanwhile, Montenegro declared his government to be "the third government of the revolution", aligning it with the socialist administrations of Arévalo and Arbenz. But despite the support of reformers, students, professionals and a large section of the middle classes, his hands were tied by the influence of the army. Political violence became commonplace as **death squads**, backed by the military and right-wing Movimiento de Liberación Nacional (MLN), operated with impunity, killing anyone they deemed subversive to the state.

Economic decline and political violence

Extreme political violence, economic crises and electoral fraud dominated Guatemala's history between 1970 and the early 1990s. At the heart of the crisis was the injustice and inequality of Guatemalan society: although the country remained fairly prosperous, the benefits of its success never reached the poor, who were denied access to land, education or healthcare, with many of their number forced instead to work in the coastal plantations that fuelled the capital's affluence.

The 1970 elections confirmed the power of the military and the far right (represented by the MLN and PID), and **Colonel Arana Osorio**, who had directed the counterinsurgency campaign in the east, was elected president. The turnout was under fifty percent, of which Arana polled just under half, giving him the votes of around four percent of the population (bearing in mind that only a small percentage was enfranchised).

Once in power he set about eradicating armed opposition, declaring that "if it is necessary to turn the country into a cemetery in order to pacify it, I will not hesitate to do so". The reign of terror, conducted by both the armed forces and the "death squads", reached unprecedented levels. Once again the violence claimed the lives of students, academics, opposition politicians, union leaders and agrarian reformers. According to one estimate, 15,000 political killings occurred during the first three years of Arana's rule.

Presidential elections followed in 1974, contended by a broad coalition of centre-left parties under General Efraín Ríos Montt. The campaign was marked by manipulation and fraud, and the declaration of the right's candidate, **Kjell Laugerud**, as the winner caused uproar. Eventually, things simmered down when Ríos Montt was persuaded to accept defeat and packed off to a diplomatic post in Spain. Laugerud offered limited reforms, allowing greater tolerance towards unions and the cooperative movement, and the government launched a plan for the colonization of Petén and the Northern Transversal Strip in an attempt to provide more land. The army, though, continued to consolidate its authority, spreading its influence across a wider range of business and commercial interests and challenging Laugerud's moderation.

All of this was interrupted by a massive **earthquake** on February 4, 1976. The quake left around 23,000 dead, 77,000 injured and a million homeless. The poor, their homes built from makeshift materials on unstable ground, suffered the most, and subsistence farmers were caught out just as they were about to plant their corn.

In the wake of the earthquake, during the process of reconstruction, fresh centres of regional control emerged on both sides of the political spectrum. The electoral process seemed to offer no respite from the injustice that was at the heart of Guatemalan society, and many of the victims felt the time had come to take action. A revived trade-union organization championed the cause of the majority, while a new guerrilla organization, the Guerrilla Army of the Poor (EGP), emerged in the Ixil area, and army operations became increasingly ferocious. In 1977, US President Jimmy Carter suspended all military aid to Guatemala because of the country's appalling human-rights record.

In the following year, Guatemala's elections were once again dominated by the army, which engineered a victory for **Brigadier General Fernando Lucas García**, who had served as defence minister in the Laugerud administration. Lucas García promised to bring the situation under control, and things took a significant turn for the worse as the new administration unleashed a fresh wave of violence. All opposition considered subversive was met with severe repression. Conditions throughout the country were deteriorating rapidly, and the economy was badly affected by a fall in commodity prices, while several guerrilla armies were developing strongholds in the highlands.

As chaos threatened, the army resorted to extreme measures, and within a month there was a major massacre in **Panzós** that left more than a hundred dead. In Guatemala City the situation became so dangerous that political parties were driven underground. Two leading members of the Social Democrats, who were expected to win the next election, lost their lives in 1979. Once they were out of the way, the government turned on the Christian Democrats, killing more than a hundred of their members and forcing the party's leader, Vinicio Cerezo, into hiding.

Throughout the Lucas García administration the **army** became increasingly powerful and the death toll rose steadily. In rural areas the war against the guerrillas was reaching new heights as army casualties rose to 250 a month, and the demand for conscripts grew rapidly. The four main guerrilla groups had an estimated 6000 combatants and some 250,000 unarmed collaborators. Under the Lucas García administration the horrors of **repression** were at their most intense, both in the highlands and in the cities. The victims again included students, journalists, academics, politicians, priests, lawyers, teachers, unionists, and above all peasant farmers, massacred in their hundreds. Accurate figures are impossible to calculate but it's estimated that around 35,000 Guatemalans were killed during the four years of the Lucas García regime.

But while high-ranking officers became more and more involved in big business and political wrangling, the officers in the field began to feel deserted. Here there was growing discontent as a result of repeated military failures, inefficiency and a shortage of supplies, despite increased military aid and weaponry from Israel.

Ríos Montt

The 1982 elections were also manipulated by the far right, who ensured a victory for **Aníbal Guevara**. However, on March 23 a group of young military officers led a successful coup, which installed **General Efraín Ríos Montt** (who had been denied the post in 1974) as the head of a three-member junta. The coup leaders argued that they had been left with no option as the ruling elite had overridden the electoral process three times in the last eight years, and the takeover was supported by the majority of the opposition parties.

Ríos Montt was an evangelical Christian, a member of the Iglesia del Verbo, and throughout his rule Sunday-night television was dominated by marathon presidential sermons. He immediately declared his determination to defeat the guerrillas, restore law and order, and eradicate corruption. Government officials were issued with identity cards inscribed with the words "I do not steal. I do not lie." A state of siege was declared.

Initially, repression dropped in the cities, corrupt police and army officers were forced to resign, and trade and tourism began to return. However, in the highlands the war intensified, as Ríos Montt declared that he would defeat the guerrillas by Christmas. An **amnesty** was offered, which only a few rebels accepted, and the army descended on the highlands and set about destroying the guerrillas' infrastructure by undermining their support base. Villagers were forcibly organized into **civil defence patrols** (PACs), armed with ancient rifles, and ordered to patrol the countryside. Those who refused were denounced as "subversives" and carted off to re-education camps or army-base torture chambers. Thus the people of the villages were forced to take sides, caught between the attraction of guerrilla propaganda and the extreme brutality of the armed forces.

Ríos Montt's iron-fist policy was as successful as it was murderous, unleashing a further wave of violence, as soldiers swept through the mountains committing massacre after massacre, wiping villages off the map that were deemed to have collaborated with the enemy and leaving nothing but scorched earth. The guerrillas, their network of support virtually eradicated, were driven into remote corners, and occasionally responded with desperate measures, including the ambush and slaughter of PAC members and villagers. The massacre carried out at the village of Txacal Tze in the Ixil region on June 13, 1982, by EGP guerrillas left an estimated 125 dead.

Meanwhile, the "state of siege" became a "state of alarm", under which special tribunals were given the power to try and execute suspects. By the middle of 1983, Ríos Montt faced growing pressure from all sides. Leaders of the Catholic Church were outraged by the murders of dozens of priests and catechists and an influx of evangelical preachers, while politicians, business people, farmers and professionals were angered by the lack of progress towards democratic rule, and landowners were frightened by rumours of land reform.

In August 1983, Ríos Montt was overthrown by yet another military coup, this one backed by a US government keen to see Guatemala set on the road to democracy. **General Mejía Víctores** became president, and although the death squads and disappearances remained a fixture, elections were held for an 88-member Constituent Assembly, which was given the task of drawing up a new constitution in preparation for presidential elections. Under Víctores rural repression also continued, though the process of reconstruction accelerated as internal refugees were rehoused in "model villages", where they were under the control of the army. Scarcely any money was available for rebuilding the devastated communities, and it was often widows and orphans who were left to construct their own homes. In the Ixil Triangle alone the war had displaced 60,000 people (72 percent of the population), and nine model villages were built to replace 49 that had been destroyed. Nationwide more than 600 villages had been destroyed and around 180,000 had lost their lives.

In 1985 presidential elections were held, the first free vote in Guatemala for thirty years.

Cerezo and the return to democratic rule

The elections were won by **Vinicio Cerezo**, a Christian Democrat not associated with the traditional ruling elite who had already been the target of several assassination attempts. His election victory was the result of a sweeping wave of popular support, and in the run-up to the election he offered a programme of reform that he claimed would rid the country of repression.

Once in office, however, Cerezo knew that his room for manoeuvre was severely limited, and he declared that the army still held 75 percent of the power. From the outset he could promise little: "I'm a politician not a magician. Why promise what I cannot deliver? All I commit myself to doing is opening up the political space, giving democracy a chance."

Throughout his six-year rule Cerezo offered a **non-confrontational approach**, seeking above all else to avoid upsetting the powerful alliance of business interests, landowners and generals. To protect himself, he courted the support of a group of sympathetic officers, and with their aid survived several coup attempts. But the administration remained trapped in the middle; the right accused Cerezo of communist leanings, while the left claimed that he was evading his commitment to reform.

Political killings dropped off a great deal under civilian rule, although they by no means stopped. Murder remained a daily event in Guatemala in the late 1980s as the civil war raged on in remote parts of the highlands and death squads continued to operate in the capital. No one accused Cerezo of involvement in the killings but it was clear that they were often carried out by rogue elements in the security forces determined to direct and control the political situation.

In many ways the Cerezo administration was a disappointment to the Guatemalan people. Although the early years of civilian rule did create a breathing space, it was clear that the army was still actively controlling political opposition. The generals sanctioned Cerezo's government in order to present a democratic face to the world, while the army continued to control the countryside and the economy continued to serve the oligarchy.

The country's leading **human-rights organization**, the Mutual Support Group (GAM), hoped that civilian rule would present them with a chance to investigate the fate of the "disappeared" and bring the perpetrators of violence to trial. Cerezo, however, chose to forget the past, and ongoing abuses went largely uninvestigated and unpunished. GAM's leaders, meanwhile, became victims of the death squads.

Nevertheless, the promise of civilian rule created a general thaw in the political climate, fostering the growth of numerous pressure groups and fresh demands for reform, making protests and strikes a regular feature of Guatemalan life. Real change, however, never materialized. Despite the fact that at least 65 percent of the population still lived below the official poverty line, little was done to meet their needs in terms of education, health, employment or tax reform. The thirst for **land reform** reared its head once again, and under the leadership of Padre Andrés Girón some 35,000 peasants demanded action. Acknowledging that his greatest achievement had been to survive, Cerezo organized the country's first civilian transfer of power in decades, in 1990.

The Serrano and de León administrations

The **1990 elections** were dogged by controversy. Former dictator Ríos Montt was banned from standing as a candidate, but **Jorge Serrano**, a former minister in his government, won. However, with a third of the population not registered to vote and an abstention rate of 56 percent, Serrano had the support of less than a quarter of the people. An engineer and evangelical with a centre-right economic position, Serrano once again proved both uninterested and incapable of effecting any real reform or bringing an end to the civil war. The level of human-rights abuse remained high, death-squad activity continued, the economy remained weak and the army was still a powerful force, using intimidation and murder to stamp out opposition. Economic activity was still controlled by a tiny elite: less than two percent of landowners owned more than 65 percent of the land, and some 85 percent of the population lived in poverty.

Nevertheless, Guatemala's dispossessed and poor continued to clamour for change. Maya peasants became increasingly organized and influential, denouncing the continued bombardment of villages and rejecting the presence of the army and the system of civil patrols. Matters were brought into sharp focus in 1992 when **Rigoberta Menchú** was awarded the Nobel Peace Prize for her campaigning work on behalf of Guatemala's indigenous population. In spite of the efforts of the Serrano administration, the country's civil war still rumbled on and three main guerrilla armies, united as the **URNG**, continued to confront the state army.

Small groups of refugees began to return from exile in Mexico and start civil communities, though an estimated 45,000 still remained. The territorial dispute with **Belize** was officially resolved when the two countries established full diplomatic relations in 1991; but the decision to recognize Belize as an independent country provoked hostility with ultra-nationalists and the Guatemalan military.

By early 1993, Serrano's reputation had plummeted following a series of **scandals** involving corruption and his business ventures, some of which had suspected links with Colombian drug cartels. In May 1993, Serrano responded to the wave of popular protest with a self-coup, declaring he would rule by decree because the country was endangered by civil disorder and corruption. He also argued that the drug mafia planned to take over Guatemala; few were convinced and the US responded by suspending its annual US$67 million of aid. Two days later, protests from the left and right and widespread international condemnation spurred generals to oust Serrano, while further demonstrations blocked a subsequent army-backed appointee. The whole sorry affair revealed much about Guatemala: that the army allowed civilians to run the government so that they could get on with the more serious business of running the country. Guatemala still retained its hopelessly unbalanced structure, but the army was now susceptible to the pressure of popular and international protest.

Congress appointed **Ramiro de León Carpio**, the country's human-rights ombudsman, as the new president. One of his first moves was a reshuffle of the senior military command, although he rejected calls for revenge, declaring that stability was the main goal. Although great early optimism greeted de León's appointment, public frustration quickly grew as the new government failed to address fundamental issues, such as crime, land ownership, tax and constitutional reform. Some progress was made in peace negotiations with the URNG guerrilla leadership, however, and the Indigenous Rights Act, passed in 1995, allowed greater constitutional freedom for Guatemala's *indígenas* and legal provision for state education in Maya languages.

Arzú and the peace accords

In January 1996, polls to elect a new president were tarnished by low turnout as 63 percent of registered voters stayed at home. Only a strong showing in Guatemala City ensured the success of **Álvaro Arzú**, a former mayor of the capital, who represented the country's so-called modernizing right. His party, the PAN or National Advancement Party, had strong oligarchic roots, and was committed to private-sector-led growth and the free market, though Arzú's early adoption of a relatively progressive stance, appointing new defence, foreign and economic ministers and shaking up the armed forces' power structure, surprised many. Arzú's presidency is now generally regarded as a relatively stable period in modern Guatemalan history, and on a personal level he departed office with a reputation untainted by corruption.

Arzú moved quickly to bring an end to the 36-year civil war, meeting the URNG guerrilla leaders and working towards a final settlement. The **Peace Accords**, signed on December 29, 1996, concluded almost a decade of talks and terminated a conflict that had claimed 200,000 lives. The core purpose of the accords was to investigate previous human-rights violations through a Truth Commission overseen by MINUGUA (the UN mission to Guatemala), to recognize the identity of indigenous people and to eliminate discrimination and promote socioeconomic development for all Guatemalans. However, progress on these issues was slow during the Arzú years, and a constitutional amendment to allow greater Maya rights was rejected by the electorate.

There were token cuts in military numbers, but the army's influence and position remained unchallenged throughout his term. Though blamed for more than eighty percent of the atrocities of the civil war, army officers implicated in orchestrating massacres successfully avoided prosecution – Arzú simply dared not touch them. Then in April 1998, two days after publishing a long-awaited human-rights investigation into wartime slaughters (see p.475), **Bishop Juan Geradi** was bludgeoned to death in his own garage. The murder stunned the nation; though most Guatemalans had long been accustomed to horrific levels of political violence, most thought the days of disappearances and death squads were over, and as one newspaper put it, "This wasn't supposed to happen. Not any more."

The acute fragility of the nascent Guatemalan democracy was revealed – most observers immediately recognized Geradi's assassination as an act sanctioned by a vengeful military intent on preserving its dominant power base. Despite international and domestic outrage – hundreds of thousands attended a silent protest in the capital days after the killing – the Arzú government proved incapable of reigning in the real perpetrators of the murder. The investigation descended to near-farcical levels at times (a priest's dog was implicated at one stage) as terrified judges, prosecutors and key witnesses fled abroad following death threats. As Arzú departed the presidential palace in December 1999, Geradi's murderers remained at large and the investigation unsolved.

Despite this horrific killing, the level of political violence fell in the Arzú years, though there was an alarming upsurge in the **crime rate**. Petty theft, muggings, robberies, kidnappings, drug- and gang-related incidents and murders soared. A new police force, the PNC, quickly gained a reputation as bad as its predecessor for endemic corruption and ineffectualness. Not surprisingly, law and order became the key issue of the 1999 election campaign.

President Portillo

Former lawyer and professor **Alfonso Portillo** won Guatemala's 1999 presidential elections, the first peacetime vote in nearly forty years, with a mandate to implement the Peace Accords and tackle the criminal gangs. In the grossest of ironies, Portillo confessed to killing two men in Mexico in 1982, declaring, "A man who defends his life will defend the lives of his people." He claimed he had acted in self-defence. But perhaps the most decisive factor in his victory was the support of his political mentor, former general and founder of the right-wing FRG party, Ríos Montt. Montt, Guatemala's most controversial politician, had been ruled ineligible to stand for the presidency because of his role in an earlier coup, but he was widely perceived to be really in control, pulling all the strings behind the scenes.

Initially, there was a positive groundswell of optimism as the new president unveiled a diverse cabinet which included academics, indigenous activists and even human-rights advocates. Nevertheless, many of the key institutions were placed under the control of right-wing FRG politicians and pro-business groups.

Portillo immediately set about attempting to solve the **Geradi case** – another key campaign pledge – as three senior military personnel were charged with murder within weeks of his inauguration. Credibly, the military suspects (an intelligence chief and two members of the elite presidential guard) and a priest (who was found guilty of acting as an accomplice) were eventually brought to trial, and found guilty of plotting Geradi's murder in June 2001. Despite intense pressure on the prosecution, and a bomb exploding outside the home of one judge on the first day of the trial, justice prevailed.

The Geradi case aside, Portillo lurched from crisis to crisis, and after four years of catastrophic presidency he departed office leaving Guatemala virtually bankrupt. The stench of **corruption** pervaded his entire term as a series of scandals were unearthed and public coffers were emptied, including an allegation that hundreds of millions of dollars were transferred from the social security fund into Panamanian bank accounts. According to the UN mission to Guatemala, only 36 percent of the government's commitments to ratify the Peace Accords had been met by 2001, and little or no progress had been made on indigenous issues, improving health and education, or increasing income from tax collection.

Crime levels soared during his term. Human-rights workers, journalists and environmentalists who dared to challenge powerful political interests were threatened and killed, while gangs terrorized the city suburbs. Hardly a week seemed to pass without an armed bank robbery or a public lynching of a suspected thief. Seventy of the country's most notorious criminals – murderers, rapists, kidnappers and gang leaders – blasted their way out of jail in 2001 and Portillo even dispatched his own family to Canada after threats from a kidnapping gang.

Meanwhile, the **economy** continued to falter, as traditional exports (principally coffee, sugar and bananas) slumped, and low commodity prices affected profitability. On the other hand, the cocaine trade boomed, as Guatemala became a key transit country in the route between Colombia and North America. Behind this boom were shadowy organized crime cartels – locally known as *poderes ocultos* "hidden powers", – thought to be headed up by retired generals and including a network of corrupt officials, with links to the very highest echelons of Guatemalan politics. The Organization of American States condemned "the existence of clandestine structures linked to the state … who operate with the participation or tolerance of state agents", while the US decertified Guatemala as a partner country in their so-called "war against drugs" in 2002.

With Guatemala seemingly teetering on the brink, Ríos Montt declared he would stand as the FRG candidate for the 2003 elections, busing in thousands of supporters who rioted in the capital in July 2003 demanding a constitutional change that would allow him to contest the vote. The constitutional court yielded to this demand, but mercifully the subsequent campaign was not tainted with widespread violence. Montt fell at the first hurdle in November, polling less than 20 percent of the vote, and dropped out of the race. Most Guatemalans heaved a collective sigh of relief as the enigma of the Montt legend, which had cast a shadow over Guatemala for more than twenty years, at last seemed extinguished.

Guatemala today

Óscar Berger, inaugurated as president in January 2004, got off to an encouraging start. A former mayor of Guatemala City from the right-wing GANA coalition, he declared that the country was nearly broke and that his goal would be to govern in an austere, cost-conscious manner that would bring long-term prosperity. Berger's background as a member of Guatemala's oligarchy was reflected in his choice of cabinet, as key financial and industrial members of the elite were placed in senior positions, but he also made several progressive appointments. The most notable of these were persuading Nobel laureate and Maya rights campaigner Rigoberta Menchú to act as a goodwill ambassador with a brief to implement the Peace Accords; placing Frank LaRue, founder of human-rights group CALDH, as a commissioner to deal with the issue on a governmental basis; and positioning Rosalina Tuyuc, a respected indigenous leader, as head of a programme to support victims of the civil war. Berger reasoned that national reconciliation would be aided by bringing in leaders of grass-roots developmental and social pressure groups, with the added long-term benefit of encouraging stability and foreign investment.

He attempted to deal with Guatemala's appalling internal **security problems** by supporting the establishment of CICIACS, a UN-backed commission to strengthen the judiciary in the fight against organized crime – though this move was later rejected as unconstitutional by Congress. Very significantly, Berger signalled a commitment to curb the power of the **armed forces** by implementing sweeping cuts to military spending, reducing it to 0.66 percent of the national budget, slashing army numbers from 27,000 to 15,500, and closing thirteen military bases. But despite these positive actions, Berger also ordered the army back onto the streets in an effort to improve security, a move that went against the recommendations of the Peace Accords, which had called for the demilitarization of society. Four thousand troops and policemen were assigned to *zonas rojos*, poor barrios of Guatemala City, in an effort to combat the intimidation, extortion and violence wreaked on the capital by its notorious gangs; the army were also assigned to patrol state highways in an effort to maintain law and order and counter banditry.

Criminal investigations into allegations of fraud and corruption were launched against ex-president Portillo, who fled to Mexico the day his parliamentary immunity from prosecution ended. Portillo's vice-president, his finance minister and forty other senior officials in his administration were issued with arrest warrants on corruption charges. Meanwhile, Ríos Montt, accused of inciting the riots in Guatemala City in June 2003 that led to the death of a journalist, was placed under (comfortable) house arrest.

Unsurprisingly, given his links to big business and the country's oligarchy, Berger was an enthusiastic supporter of **CAFTA** (the US–Central American Free Trade Agreement), which was ratified by the Guatemalan Congress in March 2005. This accord proved highly contentious, leading to demonstrations in Guatemala City and in other departments, with a protestor dying in Huehuetenango. Opponents reasoned that heavily subsidized US agricultural exports would mean ruin for small-scale Central American farmers and pointed out that eighty percent of Central American goods entered the US without being subject to tariffs anyway.

The other key issue in the countryside, the seemingly intractable issue of **agrarian reform**, proved even more combustible. Landless campesinos had been seizing and occupying fincas across the country since the late 1990s, during which time Portillo pursued a relatively softly-softly approach, with one eviction every six months. Berger, by contrast, immediately adopted a much tougher stance with the squatters, cranking up the eviction rate to eight per month, a course of action which provoked demonstrations in twenty of the country's 22 departments in July 2004, as protestors encircled government buildings and blocked roads. Eleven protestors died at Finca Nuevo Linda near Retalhuleu as 2000 police violently ejected 3000 squatters. Campesino and human-rights leaders charged Berger with pandering to his privileged support base, the landowning elite, though he continued the evictions and the volatile issue of agrarian reform looks set to rumble on for many years yet.

These protests served to confirm the desperately poor living standards affecting most Guatemalans – 56 percent live below the poverty line according to the World Bank – and especially the Maya who face the additional burden of institutionalized discrimination. Income retribution remains woefully skewed, with taxation accounting for less than teb percent of GDP, the lowest in the Western Hemisphere. Guatemala also has little industry of its own, except for a booming foreign-owned *maquiladora* textile-factory sector where garments are assembled for export to the US and Korea. Most of these factories operate in special tax-exempt zones, free from any import or export duties or union influence, where workers earn a typical daily wage of around US$4–5.

As far as developing nations go, Guatemala has returned pretty modest economic figures, averaging 2–3 percent GDP growth per year since the mid-1990s, a little behind most of Latin America, and trailing India, China and most of Southeast Asia. The country's poor education system (30 percent of adults are illiterate) and weak infrastructure are serious handicaps, while social instability and crime levels also impact upon international competitiveness and inward investment. Businesses operating in Guatemala are forced to pay vastly increased security costs compared with other parts of the world. This lawlessness also hampers the potential of the nation's **tourism industry**. Though tourist arrivals have accelerated and now approach one million visitors per year, most experts consider these numbers to be well short of what could be achieved given Guatemala's unique cultural and natural diversity, low cost of living, and location just a couple of hours' flight from the southern US.

The country's promise is undeniable, but given the limited progress achieved since the return to civilian rule twenty years ago, it will take a period of sustained stability, judicial reform, and a real commitment to tackle Guatemala's pressing social issues before significant economic progress and prosperity can be realized.

Chronology of the Maya

c.20,000–10,000 BC ▸ Paleo-Indian culture (also called Lithic or Early Hunter periods). Waves of hunter-gatherers from Asia cross the Bering land bridge (and possibly also use a maritime route) to the American continent.

c.10,000 BC ▸ Clovis culture. Worked-stone projectile points – first identified at Clovis, New Mexico – used to hunt large herbivores, including mammoths, found at many sites in North and Central America.

c.6000–2000 BC ▸ Archaic (Proto-Maya) period. General warming of the climate following the retreat of northern ice sheets. The Pacific littoral region in Guatemala is the most intensely inhabited area of the Maya world, though there are well-established villages and trade routes throughout the region. Villagers farm maize and beans, catch fish and make pottery. Clay figures discovered from this period may be the first religious artefacts. A Proto-Maya language is thought to have been spoken.

August 13, 3114 BC ▸ The mythical starting date of the Maya Calendar (13.0.0.0.0. 4 Ahau 8 Kumk'u) marks the beginning of the current "Great Cycle", the creation of the present world; the cycle is due to end on December 21, 2012.

2000 BC–250 AD ▸ Preclassic (or Formative) period. The **Olmec** culture, the first emergent civilization of Mesoamerica, brings an early calendar and new gods. Trade in jade, salt and cacao increases between villages in Guatemala, and the first Maya great cities, Nakbé and El Mirador, emerge towards the end of the period.

1700 BC ▸ Olmec civilization emerges on Gulf coast of Mexico, just outside the Maya region.

1400 BC ▸ First settlement in Copán valley.

c.1000 BC ▸ Earliest confirmed settlement at Nakbé and Cival.

1000–400 BC ▸ Middle Preclassic period. Relatively sophisticated building construction at Nakbé in northern Petén. Many of the earliest foundations of the central region's sites established. Olmec, then Iztapa cultures, dominate the Pacific coast.

750 BC ▸ Nakbé is flourishing. Possibly the very first Maya "city", it is dominated by eighteen-metre-high temples. Maya culture eclipses Olmec influence in Petén.

500 BC ▸ First evidence of ceremonial buildings at **Tikal**.

400 BC–250 AD ▸ Late Preclassic. Early development of the foundations of Maya civilization: calendar, writing, architectural design and sophisticated artistic style. Monumental temple cities emerge. Causeways (*sacbes*) are built and trade links flourish.

300 BC ▸ Nakbé temples rebuilt to 45-metre height, and colossal stucco masks constructed. Early building work at **El Mirador** and Stela 2 carved at Cival.

200 BC ▸ Miraflores culture thrives on Pacific coast and Guatemalan highlands, centred at **Kaminaljuyú**; elaborate stelae carved. First ceremonial structures built at **Tikal**, **Uaxactún** and possibly **Calakmul** (in Mexico).

150 BC ▸ The first great Maya city-state, **El Mirador**, emerges;

seventy-metre-high temples are built, their soaring stone staircases framed by giant masks.

36 BC ▸ First known Long Count date, corresponding to December 7, 36 BC, inscribed on Stela 2 at **Chiapa de Corzo**, Chiapas.

c.1 AD ▸ Major pyramids, platforms and giant stucco masks constructed at Uaxactún, Tikal and Cerros, but the region is dominated by El Mirador with a population that peaks at around 100,000. Emergence of **Teotihuacán** in Mexico.

36 AD ▸ Stela 1 carved at **El Baúl** on Pacific coast using Long Count date.

c.150 AD ▸ **El Mirador** and other cities abandoned, possibly due to disease or environmental collapse; Yax Ehb' Xok establishes the first ruling dynasty at Tikal. **Calakmul** emerges as a major power. San Bartolo murals painted.

199 AD ▸ Earliest recorded use of Long Count date in central region.

250 AD ▸ **Kaminaljuyú** all but abandoned.

250–600 AD ▸ **Early Classic period.** Maya region and much of Mexico influenced, or even dominated by, the great metropolis of Teotihuacán, north of modern-day Mexico City, until around 450 AD. Calakmul later emerges as the regional superpower, challenging and defeating Tikal. Dated inscriptions emerge in the lowlands. Elaborate carved stelae erected throughout central region after 435 AD. Extensive trade network along Caribbean coast between Yucatán and Honduras.

292 AD ▸ Stela 29 carved at **Tikal**, with Long Count calendar date.

c.359 AD ▸ Yoaat B'alam I (Progenitor Jaguar) becomes first king of **Yaxchilán**.

378 AD ▸ Siyak K'ak' (Lord Fire-Born), probably from **Teotihuacán**, ejects (and almost certainly kills) **Tikal**'s ruler Chak Tok Ich'aak (Great Jaguar Paw I) and defeats **Uaxactún**.

400 AD ▸ Guatemalan highlands under strong Teotihuacán influence; **Kaminaljuyú** rebuilt in its style.

426 AD ▸ Yax K'uk Mo' (Great Sun First Quetzal Macaw), probably from Teotihuacán, founds dynasty at **Copán**.

435 AD ▸ Completion of Baktun 8 (9.0.0.0.0). Population of **Copán** rises and building work accelerates.

c.514 AD ▸ Warriors from **Piedras Negras** return home with prisoners from Yaxchilán, including the king, Knot-eye Jaguar I.

556 AD ▸ Wak Chan K'awil (Double Bird) of **Tikal** (537–562 AD) enacts an "axe war" against **Caracol**.

562 AD ▸ Yajaw Te' K'inich II (Lord Water) of **Caracol** retaliates in concert with Sky Witness of **Calakmul** and overruns Tikal. Calakmul becomes regional superpower.

534–593 AD ▸ **Middle Classic hiatus**: dearth of stelae carving and building throughout region previously under Tikal control.

c.600 AD ▸ Population density in core Maya region reaches an estimated 965 people per square kilometre.

600–800 AD ▸ **Late Classic period.** Golden age of the Maya, as civilization reaches intellectual and artistic peak and numerous powerful city-states emerge in central region, though the mighty superpowers of **Calakmul** and a re-emergent **Tikal** dominate. Monumental construction of temples, plazas, pyramids and palaces. Puuc, Río Bec and Chenes cities all flourish in northern area;

spectacular construction throughout the Maya world.

611 AD ▸ Scroll Serpent of **Calakmul** attacks Palenque and destroys the city centre.

615 AD ▸ K'inich Hanaab Pakal (Great Sun Shield) begins 68-year reign at **Palenque**.

628 AD ▸ Smoke Imix's (Ruler 12) 67-year reign begins at **Copán**.

645 AD ▸ B'alaj Chan K'awil (Lightening Sky) founds city of **Dos Pilas**.

c 650 AD ▸ Latest evidence suggests Tikal's **Temple V** completed around this date.

657 AD ▸ Yuknoom the Great of **Calakmul** attacks Tikal, whose ruler Nuun Ujol Chaak (Shield Skull) takes refuge in Palenque.

659 AD ▸ Nuun Ujol Chaak of **Tikal** wins battle against Yaxchilán, probably launched from his exile.

672 AD ▸ Nuun Ujol Chaak of **Tikal** returns from exile and launches a "star war" against **Dos Pilas**. B'alaj Chan K'awil takes refuge (probably in Calakmul). In 677 AD he returns to Dos Pilas, and in 679 AD successfully repels Tikal.

682 AD ▸ Hasaw Chan K'awil (Heavenly Standard Bearer) begins 52-year reign at **Tikal** and achieves its resurgence in a series of successful military campaigns against Calakmul and vast construction projects. Lightening Sky of **Dos Pilas** sends his daughter Lady Six Sky to **Naranjo** to re-establish the royal house there. Itzamnaaj B'alam II (Shield Jaguar) begins reign at **Yaxchilán**.

693 AD ▸ K'ak Tilaw Chan Chaak (Smoking Squirrel), new ruler of **Naranjo**, retaliates against **Caracol** by repeatedly attacking its allies, Ucanal (693 AD and 698 AD), Yaxhá (710 AD) and Sacnab (711 AD).

695 AD ▸ Smoke Imix of Copán dies; succeeded by Waxaklajuun Ub'aah K'awil (Eighteen Rabbit). Hasaw Chan K'awil of **Tikal** captures Yich'aak K'ak (Fiery Claw) of **Calakmul**, breaking its power in the central Petén.

c.700 AD ▸ **Yaxchilán** dominates the Usumacinta region. Population of Caracol estimated at more than 100,000.

734 AD ▸ Hasaw Chan K'awil of **Tikal** dies; succeeded by his son, Yik'in Chan K'awil (Divine Sunset Lord). He organizes Tikal's attacks on **Waka'** (743 AD) and **Naranjo** (in 744 AD). These are the last recorded "star war events" in Petén.

735 AD ▸ Ruler 3 of **Dos Pilas** captures Yich'aak B'alam (Jaguar Claw) of **Ceibal**, and reduces Ceibal to subjugation for the next sixty years.

738 AD ▸ **Copán**'s Waxaklajuun Ub'aah K'awil killed by Cauac Sky of **Quiriguá**, a subordinate city. No monuments are built at Copán for seventeen years.

c.750 AD ▸ Population peaks in central region, total Maya numbers estimated to be around ten million.

790 AD ▸ **Bonampak** murals painted, but site abandoned shortly afterwards. **Dos Pilas** overrun. End of the *katun* celebrated across the Maya world with carved stelae.

800–909 AD ▸ **Terminal Classic period.** Overpopulation and intense agricultural cultivation in region, and an epochal drought, leads to environmental collapse. **Ceibal** flourishes briefly in isolation. Most main cities almost abandoned by 900 AD except in the northern area (Mexico) and in Belize, where trade continues along the rivers and coast.

808 AD ▸ Skull Mahk'ina III of **Yaxchilán** captures Ruler 7 of

Piedras Negras' ending Classic Maya culture in the upper Usumacinta region.

810 AD ▸ Dark Sun builds Temple III, the last of **Tikal**'s temple pyramids. Last dated inscription at **Quiriguá**.

830 AD ▸ Completion of Baktun 9.

849 AD ▸ **Ceibal** erects five stelae to commemorate the *katun* (10.1.0.0.0).

c.860 AD ▸ Population of central region down to a third of previous level.

869 AD ▸ Last recorded date at **Tikal**.

c.900 AD ▸ **Uxmal** and **Chichén Itzá** abandoned.

909 AD ▸ Erection of the last stela in Maya region at **Toniná** (to commemorate the *katun* ending 10.4.0.0.0.0).

909–c.1530 AD ▸ **Postclassic period.**

909–1200 AD ▸ **Early Postclassic period.** Maya collapse sees cities abandoned throughout the region.

The **Toltec** from Central Mexico invade Yucatán, bringing a new religious cult and architectural styles such as the *Chacmool*. Itza influence replaces Toltec.

1200 AD ▸ **Chichén Itzá** reoccupied by Toltec; new construction begins. Itza driven from Campeche coast.

c.1250 AD ▸ Toltec enter Guatemala. **Utatlán** founded.

c.1450 AD ▸ Itza establish **Tayasal** (also called Noh Petén) on Lago de Petén Itzá.

1450 AD ▸ K'iche' state dominates warring highlands.

1470 AD ▸ Kaqchikel throw off K'iche' control and found their capital at **Iximché**.

1500 AD ▸ Continual conflict in Guatemalan highlands between the main tribal groups.

1519 AD ▸ **Cortés** lands in Cozumel.

1521 AD ▸ Aztec capital of **Tenochtitlán** falls to Spanish under Cortés.

Chronology of Guatemala

1523 ▸ Alvarado arrives in Guatemala. Establishes capital at Tecpán next to Iximché in 1524.

1523–40 ▸ **Spanish conquest** of Guatemala proceeds: first Spanish capital founded 1527.

1541 ▸ Alvarado dies; new capital founded at **Antigua**.

17th c. ▸ **Colonial rule** is gradually established throughout the country. Antigua is the capital of the whole of Central America, and the power of the Church grows.

1697 ▸ Conquest of the Itza at Tayasal on Lago de Petén Itzá: the last of the independent Maya.

1773 ▸ Earthquake destroys Antigua.

1776 ▸ Guatemala City becomes capital.

18th c. ▸ Colonial Guatemala remains a backwater, with no great riches for the Spanish.

1821 ▸ Mexico and Central America gain **independence** from Spain; Guatemala annexed by Mexico, then joins Central American Federation.

1847 ▸ Guatemala becomes a republic, independent of Central America, under **Rafael Carrera**.

1850 ▸ Guatemala and Britain continue to squabble over Belize.

1862 ▸ Belize becomes part of the British Empire.

1867 ▸ First **liberal uprising** under Serpio Cruz.

1871 ▸ Liberal revolution; **Rufino Barrios** becomes president. Start of coffee boom.

1906 ▸ Railway to Pacific coast completed.

1930 ▸ **Jorge Ubico** president – banana boom and height of **United Fruit Company** power.

1944–54 ▸ "Spiritual Socialism" presidencies of **Arévalo** and **Arbenz**; ended by CIA-backed military coup.

1954 ▸ **Castillo Armas** president: the start of **military rule** and a series of military-backed dictators.

1960s ▸ First **guerrilla** actions, rapidly followed by repressive clamp-downs and rise of **death squads** under **Colonel Carlos Arana**.

1968 ▸ US ambassador John Gordon Mein killed by FAR guerrillas in Guatemala City; Guatemalan writer Miguel Ángel Asturias wins Nobel Prize for Literature.

1970 ▸ **Colonel Arana Osorio** president.

1974 ▸ Electoral fraud wins presidency for **Kjell Laugerud**.

1976 ▸ **Earthquake** leaves 23,000 dead, a million homeless.

1978 ▸ **Lucas García** president; thousands die through repression. US bans arms sales to Guatemala. Intense fighting in the highlands between army and guerrillas.

1982 ▸ **Ríos Montt** seizes presidency. Army begins scorched earth campaign in the highlands. Belize becomes independent.

1986 ▸ **Vinicio Cerezo** elected: return to civilian rule though power of military remains great.

1990 ▸ **Jorge Serrano** elected with less than 25 percent of vote.

1991 ▸ Guatemala recognizes Belizean independence. Peace talks between guerrillas and government.

1992 ▸ **Rigoberta Menchú** wins Nobel Peace Prize.

1993 ▸ Serrano ousted by generals – **Ramiro de León Carpio** appointed.

1996 ▸ **Álvaro Arzú** and the PAN elected. **Peace Accords** signed.

1998 ▸ **Hurricane Mitch** devastates much of Central America and kills hundreds in Guatemala; Bishop Juan Geradi assassinated.

2000 ▸ FRG's **Alfonso Portillo** sworn in as president, backed by Ríos Montt.

2001 ▸ Growing instability and disillusion with Portillo: crime wave and riots against VAT tax increases.

2003 ▸ Lawlessness continues. US decertifies Guatemala as "war on drugs" partner as cocaine smuggling gangs' influence proliferates. Ríos Montt and FRG defeated in elections.

2004 ▸ **Óscar Berger** inaugurated as president. Armed forces numbers are slashed. Portillo flees to Mexico.

2005 ▸ CAFTA trade agreement approved by Guatemalan Congress. Land evictions continue in countryside.

The Maya achievement

For some three thousand years before the arrival of the Spanish, Maya civilization dominated Mesoamerica, leaving behind some of the most impressive architecture in the entire continent. The scale and grandeur of some Maya cities, such as El Mirador, built around 100 BC, rivalled their European contemporaries, and the artistry and splendour of Maya civilization at the height of the Classic era arguably eclipsed that in the Old World. Maya culture was complex and sophisticated, fostering the highest standards of engineering, astronomy, stone carving and mathematics, as well as an intricate writing system.

To appreciate all this you have to see for yourself the remains of the great centres. Despite centuries of neglect, abuse and encroaching jungle, they are still astounding – the biggest temple-pyramids tower up to 70m above the forest floor, well above the jungle canopy. Stone monuments, however, leave much of the story untold, and there is still a great deal that we have to learn about Maya civilization. What follows is the briefest of introductions to the subject, hopefully just enough to whet your appetite for the immense volumes that have been written on it; some of these are listed in "Books", on pp.489–498.

The Maya society

By the Early Classic period, the Maya cities had become organized into a hierarchy of power, with cities such as Tikal and Calakmul dominating vast areas and controlling the smaller sites through a complex structure of **alliances**. The cities jostled for power and influence, occasionally erupting into open warfare, which was also partly fuelled by the need for sacrificial victims. The distance between the larger sites averaged around 30km, and between these were myriad smaller settlements consisting of religious centres and residential groups. The structure of the alliances can be traced through the use of **emblem glyphs**. Only the glyphs of the main centres are used in isolation, while the names of smaller sites are used in conjunction with those of their larger patrons. Of all the myriad Classic cities, the dominant ones were clearly Tikal and Calakmul, with Palenque, Copán, Caracol, Piedras Negras, Yaxhá and Yaxchilán accepting secondary status until the early eighth century when the hierarchy began to dismantle. Cancuén, Dos Pilas, Naranjo, and Quiriguá were other key cities, each lording it over, and probably extracting tribute from, many more minor settlements. Trade, marriages and warfare between the large centres were commonplace as the cities were bound up in an endless round of competition and conflict.

By the Late Classic period, population densities across a broad swathe of territory in the central area were as high as 965 people per square kilometre – an extraordinarily high figure, equivalent to densities in rural China or Java today – and as many as ten million people lived in the wider Maya region. It's thought there were strict divisions between the classes, with perhaps eighty percent being preoccupied with intensive cultivation to feed these vast numbers. The peasant farmers, who were at the bottom of the social scale, also provided the labour necessary to construct the monumental temples that decorate the centre of every city (the Maya did not have the wheel) as well

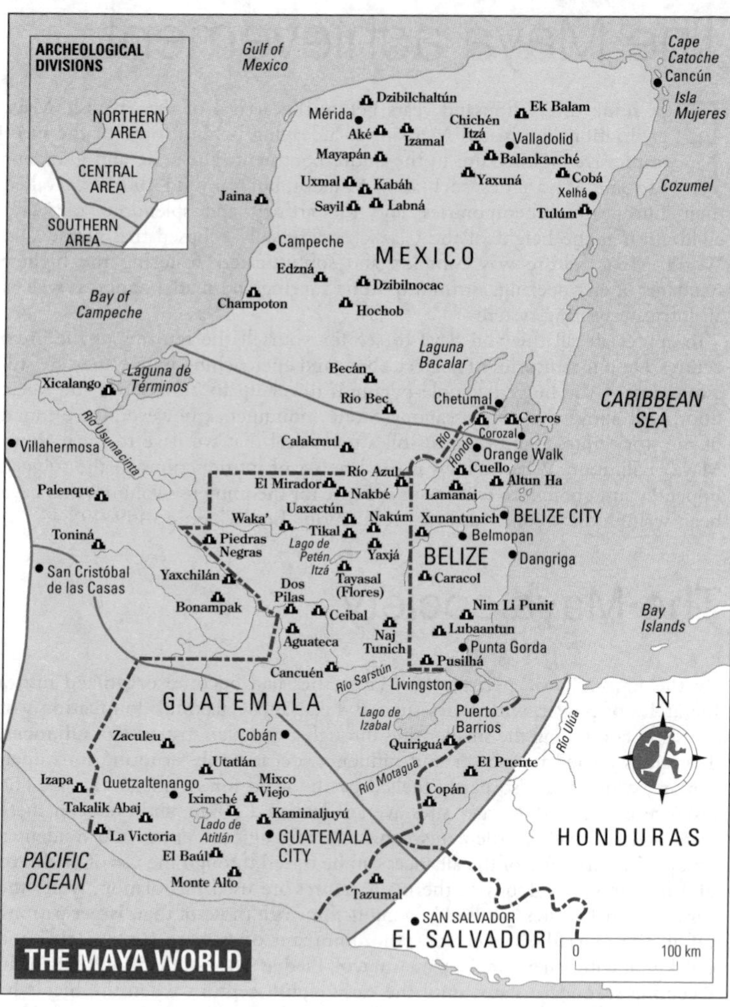

as perform regular "military service" duties. Even in the suburbs where the peasants lived, there are complexes of religious structures with simple, small-scale temples where ceremonies took place.

Although the remains of the great Maya sites are a testament to the scale and sophistication of Maya civilization, they offer little insight into daily life in Maya times. To reconstruct the lives of the ordinary Maya, archeologists have turned to the smaller residential groups that surround the main sites, littered with the remains of household utensils, pottery, bones and farming tools. These groups are made up of simple structures made of poles and wattle-and-daub, each of which was home to a single family. The groups as a whole probably housed an extended family, who would have farmed and hunted together and may well have specialized in some trade or craft. The people living in these groups were commoners, their lives largely dependent on agriculture. Maize, beans, cacao, squash, chillies and fruit trees were cultivated in raised and irrigated fields, while wild fruits were harvested from the surrounding forest. It's not certain whether the land was privately or communally owned.

Until the 1960s, Mayanists had long shared the view that the ordinary Maya were ruled by a scholarly astronomer–priest elite, who were preoccupied with religious devotion and the study of calendrics and the stars. They were thought to be men of reason, with no time for the barbarity of war and conquest, and were often likened to the ancient Greeks. However, this early utopian vision could not have been further from the truth: the decipherment of Maya glyphs has shown that the Maya rulers were primarily concerned with the glories of battle and conquest and the preservation of their royal bloodlines; human sacrifice and bloodletting rituals were also a pivotal part of elite Maya society. The rulers considered themselves to be god–humans and thought that the line of royal accession could only be achieved by sacred validation in the form of human **bloodletting** (see box, p.460).

There were two **elite classes**: *ahau* and *cahal*, who between them probably made up two or three percent of the population. The *ahau* title was reserved exclusively for the ruler and extremely close blood relatives – the top echelon of Maya society; membership could only be inherited. One step down was the *cahal* class, most of whom would have shared bloodlines with the *ahau*. The *cahal* were mainly governors of subsidiary settlements that were under the control of the dominant city-state, and their status was always subordinate to the *ahau*. Although *cahal* lords commissioned their own stelae, the inscriptions always declared loyalty to the regional ruler.

The rulers lived close to the ceremonial centre of the Maya city, in imposing palaces, though the rooms were limited in size because the Maya never mastered the use of the arch. Palaces doubled as administrative centres and were used for official receptions for visiting dignitaries, with strategically positioned thrones where the ruler would preside over religious ceremonies.

The "**middle class**" of Maya society consisted of a professional class (*ah na:ab*) of architects, senior scribes (*ah tz'ib*), sculptors, bureaucrats and master artisans, some of whom were also titled, and probably young princes and important court performers. Priests and shamans can also be included in this middle class though, surprisingly, no title for the priesthood has yet been recognized. It's possible that not giving the priests a title may have been a method used by a fearful ruler to limit their influence. Through their knowledge of calendrics and supernatural prophecies, the priests were relied upon to divine the appropriate time to plant and harvest crops.

There's no doubt that **women** played an influential role in Maya society, and in the Late Classic period there were even some women rulers – Lady Ahpo Katun at Piedras Negras, Lady Ahpo-Hel at Palenque and a Lady Six Sky at Naranjo. Women also presided at court and were given prestigious titles – Lady Cahal of Bonampak, for example. More frequently, however, as in Europe, dynasties were allied and enhanced by the marriage of royal women between cities. One of the best-documented strategic marriages occurred after the great southern city of Copán had suffered the humiliation of having its leader captured and sacrificed by upstart local rival Quiriguá in 738 AD – a royal marriage was arranged with a noblewoman from Palenque more than 500km away.

Maya **agriculture** was continually adapting to the needs of the developing society, and the early practice of slash-and-burn was soon replaced by more intensive and sophisticated methods to meet the needs of a growing population. Some of the land was terraced, drained or irrigated in order to improve its fertility and ensure that fields didn't have to lie fallow for long periods, and the capture of water became crucial to the success of a site.

The large lowland cities, which are today hemmed in by forest, were once surrounded by open fields, canals and residential compounds, although slash-and-burn agriculture probably continued in marginal and outlying areas. Agriculture became a necessary absorption, with the ordinary Maya trading at least some of their food in markets, although all households still had a kitchen garden where they grew herbs and fruit.

Maize has always been the basis of the Maya **diet**, in ancient times as much as it is today. Once harvested it was made into *saka*, a cornmeal gruel that was eaten with chilli as the first meal of the day. During the day labourers ate a mixture of corn dough and water, and we know that tamales were also a popular speciality. The main meal, eaten in the evenings, would have been similarly maize-based, although it may well have included meat and vegetables. As a supplement to this simple diet, deer, peccary, wild turkey, duck, pigeon and quail were all hunted with bows and arrows or blowguns. The Maya also made use of dogs, both for hunting and the dinner table. Fish were also eaten, and the remains of fishhooks and nets have been found at some sites, while there is evidence that those living on the coast traded dried fish and salt far inland. The forest provided firewood as well as food, and cotton was cultivated to be dyed with natural colours and then spun into cloth.

The Maya calendar

One of the cornerstones of Maya thinking was an obsession with **time**. For both practical and mystical reasons the Maya developed a highly sophisticated understanding of arithmetic, calendrics and astronomy, all of which they believed gave them the power to understand and predict events. All great occasions were interpreted on the basis of the Maya calendar, and it was this precise understanding of time that gave the ruling elite its authority. The majority of the carvings, on temples and stelae, record the exact date at which rulers were born, ascended to power, and died.

The basis of all Maya **calculation** was the vigesimal counting system, which used multiples of twenty. All figures were written using a combination of three symbols – a shell to denote zero, a dot for one and a bar for five – which you can still see on many stelae. When calculating calendrical systems, the Maya used a slightly different notation known as the head-variant system, in which each number from one to twenty was represented by a deity, whose head was used to represent the number.

When it comes to the Maya **calendar** things start to get a little more complicated, as the Maya used a number of different counting systems, depending on the reason the date was being calculated. The basic unit of the Maya calendar was the day, or *kin*, followed by the *uinal*, a group of twenty days roughly equivalent to our month; but at the next level things start to get even more complex as the Maya marked the passing of time in three distinct ways. The **260-day almanac** (16 *uinals*) was used to calculate the timing of ceremonial events. Each day was associated with a particular deity that had strong influence over those born on that particular day. This calendar wasn't divided into months but had 260 distinct day-names – a system still in use among some Kaqchikel and Mam Maya who name their children according to its structure and celebrate fiestas according to its dictates. A second calendar, the so-called "**vague year**" or *haab*, was made up of eighteen *uinals* and five *kins*, a total of 365 days, making it a close approximation of the solar year. These two calendars weren't used in isolation but operated in parallel so that once every 52 years the new day of the solar year coincided with the same day in the 260-day almanac, a meeting that was regarded as very powerful and marked the start of a new era.

Finally, the Maya had another system for marking the passing of history, which is used on dedicatory monuments. The system, known as the **long count**, is based on the great cycle of thirteen *baktuns* (a period of 5128 years). The current period dates from August 13, 3114 BC, and is destined to come to an end on December 10, 2012. The dates in this system simply record the number of days that have elapsed since the start of the current great cycle, a task that calls for ten different numbers – recording the equivalent of years, decades, centuries, and so on. In later years, the Maya sculptors obviously tired of this exhaustive process and opted instead for the short count, an abbreviated version.

Astronomy

Alongside their fascination with time, the Maya were obsessed with the sky and devoted much time and energy to unravelling its patterns. Several large sites such as Copán, Uaxactún and Chichén Itzá have **observatories** carefully aligned with solar and lunar sequences.

The Maya showed a great understanding of **astronomy**, and with their 365-day "vague year" they were just a quarter of a day out in their calculations of the solar year. At Copán, towards the end of the seventh century AD, Maya astronomers had calculated the lunar cycle at 29.53020 days, not too far off our current estimate of 29.53059. In the Dresden Codex (a copy of which can be found in Guatemala City's Popol Vuh museum), their calculations extend to the 405 lunations over a period of 11,960 days, as part of a pattern that set out to predict eclipses. At the same time, they had calculated with astonishing accuracy the movements of Venus, Mars, and perhaps Mercury. Venus was of particular importance to the Maya as they linked its presence with success in war; several stelae record the appearance of Venus prompting the decision to strike at an enemy – an attack known as a "**star war**".

Maya time: the units

1 *kin* = 24 hours
20 *kins* = 1 *uinal*, or 20 days
18 *uinals* = 1 *tun*, or 360 days
20 *tuns* = 1 *katun*, or 7200 days
20 *katuns* = 1 *baktun*, or 144,000 days
20 *baktuns* = 1 *pictun*, or 2,880,000 days
20 *pictuns* = 1 *calabtun*, or 57,600,000 days
20 *calabtuns* = 1 *kinchiltun*, or 1,152,000,000 days
20 *kinchiltuns* = 1 *alautun*, or 23,040,000,000 days

Religion

Maya cosmology is far from straightforward as at every stage an idea is balanced by its opposite and each part of the universe is made up of many layers. To the ancient Maya (and many indigenous people today) this is the third version of the earth, the previous two having been destroyed by deluges. The current version is a flat surface, with four corners, each associated with a certain colour: white for north, red for east, yellow for south and black for west, with green at the centre. Above the earth, the sky is supported by four trees, each a different colour and species – these are also sometimes depicted as gods, known as *Bacabs*. At its centre, the sky is supported by a ceiba tree. Above the sky is a heaven of thirteen layers, each of which has its own god, with the very top layer overseen by an owl. Other attested models of the world include that of a turtle (the land) floating on the sea. However, it's the underworld, *Xibalbá*, the "Place of Fright",

Ritual bloodletting and the Maya

Ritual bloodletting was a fundamental part of Maya religious life, practised by all strata of society. It took many forms, from cursory self-inflicted blood offerings to elaborate ceremonies involving the mass sacrifice of captive kings and enemy warriors. The Maya modelled their lives according to a vision of the cosmos, and within this arena, human actions could affect the future, auspiciously or otherwise. Pivotal to this vision was the concept that blood-spilling helped repay man's debt to the gods, who had endowed the gift of life.

The K'iche' Maya creation story, the **Popol Vuh**, tells of the creation, destruction and recreation of previous imperfect worlds before their own was made. Earlier races had been conceived and then destroyed for failing to praise their creators. The Maya people were made by mixing ground maize, the region's food staple, with the sacrificial blood of the gods. Consumed by the omnipresent fear that the world could again be destroyed, the Maya sought to appease the gods and ensure continued prosperity through bloodletting.

First practised by the **Olmec**, Mesoamerica's "mother culture", more than 3000 years ago, bloodletting continued until the arrival of the conquistadors. Among the early Maya, ritual blood offerings were primarily concerned with renewal and agricultural fertility, closely linked to creation mythology. Later, in the Classic period, with increasing social complexity and proven agricultural reliability, bloodletting may have become more related to the shifting concerns of the day, including warfare and political alliances. The practice later grew to apocalyptic degrees of carnage among the **Aztecs**, horrifying the Spanish, whose chronicler Diego Duran describes the sacrifice of 80,000 victims at the rededication of the Templo Mayor in their capital.

As well as direct representations of the sacrificial act, the Maya developed a symbolic iconography of bloodletting, so that the smallest motif, such as three knotted bands or smoke scrolls, could express blood sacrifice. Maya bloodletting iconography had its roots in Olmec art, including the elaborate vision quest serpent, depicted in the eighth-century Yaxchilán lintels, which grew from the corpus of Olmec serpentine motifs. Through their wealth and control of resources, the Maya nobility recorded their actions by using non-perishable artistic mediums – the fact that depictions of bloodletting were chosen for preservation on **stone**, a costly and laborious medium, confirms its religious, social and political significance.

A common bloodletting ritual may have consisted of cutting earlobes, cheeks, thighs or other fleshy parts of the body and collecting the blood to burn, or sprinkling it directly on a shrine or idol. Undertaken for numerous reasons – to bless a journey, which was of greatest importance to the ancient Maya (and many traditionalists today), as it is in this direction that they pass after death, on their way to the place of rest. The nine layers of hell are guarded by the "Lords of the Night", and deep caves are thought to connect with the underworld.

The ancient Maya also recognized an incredible array of gods, though today this concept of a pantheon is much less common. Every divinity had four manifestations based upon colour and direction, and many also had counterparts in the underworld and consorts of the opposite sex. In addition, the Maya also had an extensive array of patron deities, each associated with a particular trade or particular class, while every activity from suicide to sex had its deity.

Religious ritual

The combined complexity of the Maya pantheon and calendar gave every day a particular significance, and the ancient Maya were bound up in a demanding **cycle of religious ritual**. The main purpose of ritual was the procurement

the planting of crops, or the passing of a family member – these rites may have been performed individually or by an entire community, accompanied by prayers, the sacrifice of animals and the burning of copal incense.

Elite bloodletting rituals often took place at important or auspicious occasions: during accession ceremonies, at the birth of an heir, to mark the passing of a calendar round, in times of war, drought or disease, and to ensure regeneration and prosperity. Bloodletting also served as a rite of passage, or the individual quest for a prophetic vision and communication with the gods, providing access to the spiritual world.

There seem to have been two main **auto-sacrificial rituals** practised by the Maya elite. These were not undertaken lightly and carried severe physical and psychological repercussions. As part of a larger ceremony, the actual act of letting blood may have been preceded by days of preparation, meditation, fasting, sexual abstinence and bodily purification with sweat baths. A male rite was to draw blood by pricking the penis with either a stingray spine, obsidian lancet or flint knife. The second rite – piercing the tongue – was probably performed by both sexes, although it's most famously illustrated by Lady Xoc in the **Yaxchilán lintels** (now housed in the British Museum). The blood offering was then soaked into bark paper and collected in ceremonial bowls to be burnt as a presentation and petition to the Gods.

The Maya also practiced bloodletting in the form of **captive sacrifice**, a highly ceremonial affair in which prolonged death and torture were features – gruesomely depicted in the Bonampak murals. Prisoners then either faced death by decapitation, or by having their heart removed. Hearts were then burnt as an offering to the gods, while decapitated heads might be displayed on a skull-rack.

Maya **warfare** often reflected the need for ritual bloodletting, as warriors frequently sought to capture alive rulers of rival cities, who would then be imprisoned and sacrificed at a later date. The soaring temples of the city centre served as ceremonial theatres for elaborate religious rituals, allowing victories to be proclaimed to the entire community. Sacrificial victims would have been especially important to mark the accession of a new ruler, the bloodletting adding legitimacy to the king and affirming his power.

Blood offerings were integral to ancient Amerindian life, a tradition passed from the Olmec to the Maya and then on to the Aztec. Bloodletting developed from culture to culture through material and ideological exchange but always retained its central elements – links to the supernatural, mythical origins, and a vital connection with the continued prosperity of mankind and mother earth.

Simone Clifford-Jaeger

of success by appealing to the right god at the right time and in the right way. As every event, from planting to childbirth, was associated with a particular divinity, all of the main events in daily life demanded some kind of religious ritual. For the most important of these, the Maya staged elaborate ceremonies.

Although each ceremony had its own format, a certain pattern bound them all. The correct day was carefully chosen by priestly divination, and for several days beforehand the participants fasted and remained abstinent. The main ceremony was dominated by the expulsion of all evil spirits, the burning of incense before the idols, a sacrifice (either animal or human), and **bloodletting** (see box, pp.460–461).

In divination rituals, used to foretell the pattern of future events or account for the cause of past events, the elite used various **drugs** to achieve altered states of consciousness. Perhaps the most obvious of these was alcohol, either made from fermented maize or a combination of honey and the bark of the balnche tree. Wild tobacco, which is considerably stronger than the modern domesticated version, was also smoked. The Maya also used a range of hallucinogenic mushrooms, all of which were appropriately named, but none more so than the *xibalbaj obox*, "underworld mushroom", and the *k'aizalah obox*, "lost judgement mushroom".

Indigenous Guatemala

A vital indigenous culture is perhaps Guatemala's most unique feature. Although the Maya people may appear quiet and humble, their costumes, fiestas and markets are a riot of colour, creativity and celebration. Most Maya people remain extremely attached to local traditions and values, and regard themselves as *indígenas* first and Guatemalans second.

The indigenous Maya, the vast majority of whom live in the western highlands, make up just over half of Guatemala's population, although it's extremely hard to define exactly who is Maya. For the sake of the national census, people who consider themselves indigenous are classed as such, regardless of their parentage. And when it comes to defining the Maya as a group, culture is more important than pedigree, as the Maya define themselves through

their relationships with their land, gods, villages and families. Holding aloof from the melting pot of modern Guatemalan society, Maya people adhere instead to their traditional *costumbres*, codes of practice that govern every aspect of life.

As a result, the only way to define Maya culture is by describing its main traits, acknowledging that all indigenous Guatemalans will accept some of these attributes, and accepting that many are neither *indígena* nor ladino, but combine elements of both.

Indigenous culture

When the Spanish set about destroying the Maya tribes of Guatemala they altered every aspect of life for the indigenous people, uprooting their social structures and reshaping their communities. Before the Conquest the bulk of the population had lived scattered in the hills, paying tribute to a tribal elite, and surviving through subsistence farming and hunting. Under Spanish rule they were moved into new **villages** known as *reducciones*, where their homes were clustered around a church and a marketplace. Horizons shrank rapidly as allegiances became localized and the village hierarchies that still dominate the highlands today replaced existing tribal structures.

For almost five hundred years the Maya population has suffered repeated abuse, as the predominantly white elite have exploited indigenous land and labour, regarding the Maya as an expendable commodity. But within their own communities indigenous Guatemalans were left pretty much to themselves and developed an astoundingly introspective culture that is continually adapting to new threats, reshaping itself for the future. **Village life** has been insulated from the outside world and in some areas few people speak fluent Spanish, the remainder speaking one of the 28 indigenous languages and dialects (see map, p.463). Today's indigenous culture is a complex synthesis which includes elements of Maya, Spanish and modern American cultures.

The majority of the indigenous population still live by **subsistence agriculture**, their homes either spread across the hills or gathered in small villages. Farmers tend their milpas, growing beans, chillies, maize and squash – the staple diet for thousands of years. To the Maya, land is sacred and the need to own and farm it is central to their culture, despite the fact that few can survive by farming alone. Some cash crops are also grown – including broccoli, snow peas and coffee – much of it for export.

Many Maya migrate to the coast for several months a year, where they often work in appalling conditions on plantations to supplement their income. However, huge numbers are now choosing to head north to the US to work illegally instead, their overseas **remittances** now forming a crucial part of the local economy in virtually every mountain village. In the central highland region, where transport and communications are better, the prosperity of many villages is boosted by a local **craft**: in Momostenango they produce wool and blankets, around Lago de Atitlán the villagers make reed mats, and in Cotzal and San Pablo La Laguna they make rope. Meanwhile, other villages specialize

Throughout this guide we have used the terms "Maya" or "*indígenas*" to refer to those Guatemalans of Maya origin. You may also hear them called *Indio* (or Indian), though in Guatemala this term has racially pejorative connotations.

in market gardening, pottery, flowers or textiles. **Tourism** dollars also make a financial impact in some regions, particularly around Lago de Atitlán, but also in the Ixil, Todos Santos and Quetzaltenango areas, too.

Family life tends to bow to tradition, with large families very much a part of the indigenous culture. Marriage customs vary from place to place but in general the groom is expected to pay the bride's parents, and the couple may

Evangelism in Guatemala

One of the greatest surprises awaiting first-time travellers in Guatemala is the number of evangelical churches in the country, with fundamentalist, Pentecostal or neo-Pentecostal services taking place in most towns and villages. Although early Protestant missions came to Guatemala as far back as 1882, the impact of US-based churches remained marginal and largely unnoticed until the 1950s, when **state repression** and the subsequent **guerrilla war** began to weaken the power of the Catholic Church. Up until this time, more than 95 percent of the population was officially Catholic, though the rural Maya had their own hybrid forms of worship that mixed Catholic ceremony with pagan rite.

While the hierarchy of the Catholic Church remained fervently anti-Communist and closely aligned with the economic, political and military elite, during the early 1960s many rural Catholic priests became heavily influenced by liberation theology, supporting peasant leagues and development projects, and some even joined the guerrillas. Subsequently, the ruling class of generals, politicians and big landowners began to consider the Catholic Church as being riddled with Communist sympathizers, and targeted perceived troublemakers accordingly. By the early 1980s, so many priests had been murdered by the state-sponsored death squads that the Catholic Church pulled out of the entire department of El Quiché in protest. In contrast, many evangelical missionaries preached the importance of an army victory over the guerrillas and, with their pro-business, anti-Communist rhetoric, attracted many converts anxious to avoid suspicion and survive. In addition, the early evangelicals had made it a priority to learn the native Maya languages, and had the Bible translated into K'iche', Mam, Kaqchikel and other tongues.

However, it was the devastating **1976 earthquake** that really sparked the march of US evangelism in Guatemala. Church-backed disaster-relief programmes brought in millions of dollars of medicine, food and toys to those prepared to convert, and shattered villages were rebuilt with new schools and health centres. In the eyes of the impoverished rural villagers, Protestantism became linked with prosperity, and lively evangelical church services, where dancing, music and singing were the norm, quickly gained huge popularity.

The movement received another boost in 1982, when **General Ríos Montt** seized power in a military coup to become Guatemala's first evangelical leader. The population was treated to Montt's maniacal, marathon Sunday sermons, and a new flood of mission teams entered the country from the southern United States. For many Guatemalans, Ríos Montt represented the best and worst of evangelism: he was frenzied and fanatical, yet also fostered a reputation for strictness and probity (despite the terrible human-rights violations under his brief tenure). Ríos Montt was ousted after just seventeen months in power, though he was to dominate Guatemalan politics through the 1990s as leader of the FRG party, and ran for president himself in 2003, only to be soundly defeated.

Guatemala is today the least Catholic country in Latin America, with around sixty percent of the population looking to the Vatican for guidance and about forty percent supporting the evangelicals. However, as some denominations have been promising miracles, such as bumper harvests, which have failed to materialize, it remains to be seen whether the latter can retain this level of worship.

well live with their in-laws. Authority within the village is usually given to men, although in the Ixil area women are involved in all decision making. Customs are slowly changing, but generally men spend most of the day tending the milpas and vegetable plots, while woman are based in the family home, looking after the children, cooking and weaving. However, Maya women are by no means confined to the house and frequently travel to distant markets to sell excess fruit, vegetables and textiles and to buy, or barter for, thread and supplies. In some places particularly noted for their weavings, such as Nebaj or Chajul, whole families decamp to Antigua or Panajachel for three or four days to sell their crafts to tourists.

Indigenous religion

Every aspect of Maya life – from the birth of a child to the planting of corn – is loaded with religious significance, based on a complicated **fusion of the Maya pantheon and Catholic religion**. Christ and the saints have taken their place alongside *Dios Mundo*, the God of the World, and *Hurakan*, the Heart of Heaven. The two religions have merged to form a hybrid, in which the outward forms of Catholicism are used to worship the ancient pantheon, a compromise that was probably fostered by Spanish priests. The symbol of the cross, for example, was well known to the Maya, as used to signify the four winds of heaven, the four directions, and everlasting life. Today many of the deities have both Maya and Hispanic names, and are usually associated with a particular saint. All the deities remain subordinate to a mighty and remote supreme being, and Christ takes a place in the upper echelons of the hierarchy.

For the Maya, **God** is everywhere, bound up in the seasons, the mountains, the crops, the soil, the air and the sky. Prayer and offerings mark every important event, with disasters often attributed to divine intervention. Even more numerous than the gods, **spirits** are found in every imaginable object, binding together the universe. Each individual is born with a *nahaul*, or spiritual counterpart, in the animal world, and his or her destiny is bound up with that particular animal. The spirits of dead ancestors are also ever-present and have to be looked after by each successive generation.

Traditionally, a community's religious hierarchy organizes its worship. All office-holders are male, and throughout their lives they progress through the system, moving from post to post. The various posts are grouped into *cofradías*, ritual brotherhoods, each of which is responsible for a particular saint. Throughout the year the saint is kept in the home of an elder member, and on the appointed date, in the midst of a fiesta, it's paraded through the streets, to spend the next year somewhere else. The elder responsible for the saint will have to pay for much of the fiesta, including costumes, alcohol and assorted offerings, but it's a responsibility, or cargo, that's considered a great honour. In the traditional village hierarchy, it's these duties that give the elders, known as *principales*, a prominent role in village life and it's through these duties that they exercise their authority, such as the organization of the annual **fiesta**. (In some villages, such as Chichicastenango and Sololá, a *municipalidad indígena*, or indigenous council, operates alongside the *cofradías*, and is similarly hierarchical. As men work their way up through the system they may well alternate between the civil and religious hierarchies.) The *cofradías* don't necessarily confine themselves to the traditional list of saints, and have been known to foster "evil" saints, such as

San Simón or **Maximón**, a drinking, smoking ladino figure, sometimes referred to as Judas or Pedro de Alvarado.

On a more superstitious level, native priests (*costumbristas*, or *aj'itz* in K'iche' and Kaqchikel areas) communicate with the gods and spirits to cater to people's personal religious needs. This is usually done on behalf of an individual client who's in search of a blessing, and often takes place at shrines and caves in the mountains, with offerings of *copal*, a type of incense, and alcohol. The *costumbristas* also make extensive use of old Maya sites, and small burnt patches of grass litter many of the ruins in the highlands. Indigenous priests are also credited with the ability to cast spells, predict the future and communicate with the dead. For specific medical problems, the Maya appeal to *zahorines* who practise traditional medicine with a combination of invocation and herbs, and are closely associated with indigenous religious traditions.

Until the 1950s, when Catholic **missionaries** became active in the highlands, many indigenous Guatemalans had no idea that there was a gulf between their own religion and orthodox Catholicism. At first, the missionaries drew most of their support from the younger generation, many of whom were frustrated by the rigidity of the village hierarchy. Gradually, this eroded the authority of the traditional religious system, undermining the *cofradías*, disapproving of traditional fiestas, and scorning the work of the native priests. As a part of this, the reforming movement Catholic Action, which combines the drive for orthodoxy with an involvement in social issues, has also had a profound impact.

After the 1976 earthquake, waves of Protestant missionaries, known as *evangélicos* arrived in Guatemala, and their presence has also accelerated the decline of traditional religion (see box, p.465). In the 1980s their numbers were greatly boosted by the influence of Ríos Montt, at a time when the Catholic Church was suffering severe repression. These days there are at least three hundred different sects, backed by a huge injection of money from the US, and offering all sorts of incentives to fresh converts. But indigenous religion is no stranger to oppression, and despite the efforts of outsiders the *costumbristas* and *cofradías* are still in business, and fiestas remain drunken and vaguely pagan. Indeed, since the end of the civil war there has been an upsurge in interest in Maya religious practice.

Markets and fiestas

At the heart of the indigenous economy is the **weekly market**, which remains central to life in the highlands and provides one of the best opportunities to see Maya life at close quarters. The majority of the indigenous population still lives by subsistence farming but spares a day or two a week to gather together in the nearest village and trade surplus produce. The market is as much a social occasion as an economic one and people come to talk, eat, drink, gossip and have a good time. In some places the action starts the night before with marimba music and heavy drinking.

On market day itself the village is filled by a steady flow of people, arriving by pick-up or bus, on foot, or by donkey. In no time at all trading gets under way, and the plaza is soon buzzing with activity and humming with conversation, although raised voices are a rarity, with deals struck after protracted, but always polite, negotiations. Markets certainly don't operate in the way that you might expect and rival traders will happily set up alongside one another, seemingly more concerned about the day's conversation than the volume of trade.

The scale and atmosphere of markets varies from place to place. The country's largest is in **San Francisco el Alto**, on Fridays, and draws traders from throughout the country. Other renowned ones are the vegetable market of **Almolonga** and **Sololá**'s huge Tuesday and Friday affairs, but almost every village has its day. **Chichicastenango**'s vast Thursday and Sunday markets are probably Guatemala's most famous, and remain important gatherings for highlanders, though the tourist-orientated souvenir stalls are mushrooming here. But perhaps the most enjoyable of Guatemala's markets are well away from the Carretera Interamericana, in tiny, isolated hamlets. Up high in the folds of the mountains, in places like lonely Chajul or isolated Santa Eulalia, the pleasure is simply soaking up the scene, as traders and villagers barter and banter in hushed clicks and near-whispers, in the unhurried commercial ritual that so defines Maya highland life.

Once a year every village, however small, indulges in an orgy of celebration in honour of its patron saint – you'll find a list of them at the end of each chapter. These **fiestas** are a great swirl of dance, music, religion, endless firecrackers, eating and outrageous drinking, and express the vitality of indigenous culture. They usually centre on religious processions, in which the image of the local patron saint is paraded through the streets, accompanied by the elders of the *cofradía*, who dress in full regalia. (All members of a *cofradía* usually have special ceremonial costumes, superbly woven and beautifully decorated.) The larger fiestas also involve funfairs and week-long markets. Traditional music is played with marimbas, drums and flutes; professional bands also may be hired, blasting out popular tunes through crackling PA systems.

Dance, too, is very much a part of fiestas, and incorporates routines and ideas that date from ancient Maya times. Dance costumes are incredibly elaborate, covered in mirrors and sequins, and have to be rented for the occasion. Despite the cost, which is high by highland standards, the dancers see their role both as an obligation – to tradition and the community – and an honour. Most of the dances form an extension of dramatic tradition through which local history was retold in dance dramas. The *Dance of the Conquistadors* is one of the most popular, modelled on the *Dance of the Moors* and introduced by the Spanish as a re-enactment of the Conquest, although in some cases it's been instilled with a significance that can never have been intended by the invaders. The dancers often see no connection with the Conquest, but dance instead to release the spirits of the dead, a function perhaps closer to Maya religion than Catholicism. The *Palo Volador*, a dramatic spectacle in which men swing perilously to the ground from a twenty-metre pole, certainly dates from the pre-Columbian era (these days you'll only see it in Cubulco, Chichicastenango and Joyabaj), as does the *Dance of the Deer*, while the *Dance of the Bullfight* and the *Dance of the Volcano* relate incidents from the Conquest itself. Most of the dances do have steps to them, but the dancers are usually blind drunk and sway around as best they can in time to the music, sometimes tumbling over each other or even passing out – so don't expect to see anything too dainty.

Maya costume

To outsiders the most obvious and impressive feature of indigenous culture are the **hand-woven textiles** that are worn by the majority of the women and some of the men. This, like so much else in the Maya world, is not simply a relic of the past but a living skill, responding to new ideas and impulses and recreated by each generation.

Weaving is one of the oldest of Maya crafts, and was practised for centuries before the arrival of the Spanish. We know that it was a highly valued talent, and the Maya goddess Ix Chel, "she of the rainbow", who presided over childbirth, divination and healing, is often depicted at her loom. In pre-Columbian times the majority of the population probably wore long white cotton tunics, similar to those worn by the Lacandón Maya today. In the highlands it's a style that has been largely superseded, although in some villages, such as Soloma and San Mateo Ixtatán, the basic format is still the same, now embellished with magnificent embroidery. We also know, from Maya tombs and sculptures, that the nobility wore elaborate headdresses and heavily decorated cloth, using blues and reds created with vegetable dyes. Here it seems that tunics and robes were also the fashion of the day.

After the Conquest, the indigenous nobility was virtually eradicated and the focus of Maya society was shifted from large regional centres to small village communities. The Spanish introduced silk and wool, as well as a whole range of new dyes. Not much is known about the development of Maya costume in colonial times, and it's impossible to say when or why each village developed a distinctive style of dress. Some argue that the styles were introduced by the Spanish as a means of control, rather like the branding of sheep, while others claim that they developed naturally from the introspective nature of village culture. The truth is probably to be found somewhere between the two: we know that Spanish symbols were introduced into traditional costume designs, but that at times the Spanish had little influence over life in the villages.

Women's clothing

Today, women in around 150 villages still wear **traditional costume**, each with its own patterns, designs and colours. The basic element of a Maya woman's costume is the *huipil*, a loose-fitting blouse, normally woven by the women themselves on a **back-strap loom**. All *huipiles* are intricately decorated, either as a part of the woven pattern or with complex embroidery, and these designs are specific to each village. To protect the embroidery some women wear their *huipiles* inside out, saving the full splendour for market days. Longer ceremonial *huipiles*, reserved for fiestas, are usually more extravagant, often hanging low in the most traditional style.

Under the *huipil* a skirt, or *corte*, is worn, and these are becoming increasingly standardized. Usually woven on a foot loom, it is a simple piece of cloth, up to five metres long, joined to form a tube into which the women step. Most common are the *jaspeado cortes* woven on looms in Salcajá, San Francisco Totonicapán and Cobán by commercial weavers, and tie-dyed in universally worn patterns. In some cases there are distinct styles, but these tend to be used in a general region rather than in specific villages: the brilliant reds of the Ixil or the yellows of San Pedro and San Marcos. To add individuality to their skirts the women decorate them with thin strips of coloured embroidery, known as *randa*. And to hold them up they use elaborate **sashes**, woven in superb colours and intricate patterns, and often including decorative tassels.

Perhaps the most outlandish part of women's costume is the **headdress**, which varies widely and seems to have no connection with modern styles. The *halos* of Santiago Atitlán – twelve-metre strips of cloth – are the most famous of the headdresses, while the turbans of Nebaj and Aguacatán are some of the

△ Male *traje*, Todos Santos Cuchumatán

finest. In addition to the cloth that they wear, the women also weave *tzutes*, used to carry babies or food, and shawls that ward off the highland chill.

Fashions are constantly changing, particularly in the past decade as weavers travel further from their villages than ever before, gaining influences and ideas from other regions and using new hues and patterns in their own designs. Until recently, the women of Chajul dressed almost completely in scarlet, though nowadays other colours are just as common; while in Santa Catarina Palopó the traditional red fabric went out of favour some years ago, and has been almost universally replaced by blues and mauves.

The advent of literacy, a recent development in most areas, means that modern *huipiles* might include the name of the weaver's school, village, or even a pop star. Synthetic thread, including garish silvers and golds, has also been absorbed into many of the patterns. As village society starts to open up, some designs, once specific to a single village, are coming to be used throughout the country.

Nevertheless, the basic style of the clothing worn by women has changed little over the centuries. The most significant development is simply that the *huipil*, which once hung loose, is now tucked into the skirt. Sleeves are now much more commonplace and some women also gather their skirts, their costume emphasizing the shape of the body.

Men's clothing

Highland men have always had greater contact with the outside world than women, and as a result their clothing has been more susceptible to change. From the outset male attire was influenced to a greater extent by the arrival of the Spanish, and today **men's traditional costume** is worn in only a few villages. The more traditional styles are generally reflected in ceremonial costume, while everyday clothes are heavily influenced by non-traditional "Western" styles. If you're around for a fiesta, you'll probably see some fantastic costumes worn by men who wear jeans every other day of the year.

On the whole even "traditional costumes" now have more in common with your typical shirt and trousers than the ancient loose-hanging tunic. Nevertheless, men's costumes do include superb weaving and spectacular designs. Their jackets are particularly unusual, ranging from the superb reds of Nebaj, modelled on those worn by Spanish officers, to the ornate tuxedo style of Sololá. (Those worn in Sololá seem to undergo regular changes, and the greys of late have now been superseded by a very ornate white version.) In the Cuchumatanes the men wear *capixays*, small ponchos made from wool, and in San Juan Atitán these bear a slight similarity to monks' habits. Other particularly unusual features are *rodilleras* (or *delanteras*), short woollen skirts, worn in Nahualá and San Antonio Palopó, the superbly embroidered knee-length shorts of Santiago Atitlán and Santa Catarina Palopó, and the astounding cowboy-style shirts of Todos Santos and Sololá.

Although fewer men wear traditional costume, the styles that remain are astonishingly diverse, their scarcity making them appear all the more outlandish. The *tzute*, a piece of cloth worn either on the head or folded on the shoulder, is of particular significance, often marking out an important member of the *cofradía*. In some villages the mayor, dressed in jeans and a T-shirt, will still wear a woven *tzute* on his shoulder as a symbol of office.

Designs

The **designs** used in the traditional costume of both men and women are as diverse as the costumes themselves, an amazing collection of sophisticated patterns, using superb combinations of colour and shape. They include a range of animals, plants and people, as well as abstract designs, words and names. Many of them probably date from long before the Conquest: we know that the double-headed eagle, or *k'ot*, was emblematic in San Juan Cotzal, and the sun, moon and snake were commonly used in classic Maya design, while the peacock, horse and chicken can only have been introduced after the arrival of the Spanish. The **quetzal** is perhaps the most universal feature and is certain to date from pre-conquest times, when the bird was seen as the spiritual protector of K'iche' kings. The significance of the designs is as imprecise as their origins, although according to Lily de Jongh Osborne, an expert on Maya culture, designs once expressed the weaver's position within the social hierarchy, and could also indicate marital status. One particularly interesting design is the bat on the back of the jackets of Sololá, which dates back to the bat dynasty, among the last Kaqchikel rulers. In days gone by each level of the village hierarchy wore a different style of jacket, although today fashion is the prime consideration, and each generation is simply more outrageous than the last.

The Maya today

The Maya were the main victims of the decades-long civil war, which not only killed 160,000 highlanders and left a million homeless, but also attacked the very foundation of indigenous culture in Guatemala. The military viewed the Maya as inherently subversive, and communities were set against each other as men were conscripted into PAC paramilitary patrols and pressured to betray anyone showing signs of dissidence against the state.

But under civilian rule, a **Maya cultural revival** has steadily matured, as Guatemala's indigenous people have pursued the freedom of organization, protest and participation denied them for centuries. Hundreds of schools have been founded to educate Maya children in their own tongues, increasing numbers of indigenous writers and journalists have emerged, more and more Maya books and magazines are being published, and *indígena* radio stations have been set up. The shifting mood has even influenced youth culture, with Maya shamanic courses becoming popular and ladino university students asserting their mixed-race identity and proclaiming a Maya heritage. Yet despite these changes Guatemala remains a seismically divided country. Racism is endemic and most Maya, still subject to institutionalized discrimination, live in poverty (77 percent, according to the government's own figures).

Human rights in Guatemala

Since the arrival of the Spanish, Guatemalan history has been characterized by political repression and economic exploitation, involving the denial of the most basic human rights. A horrific catalogue of events stretches across the past five hundred years, but reached levels as barbaric as any previously seen in the late 1970s and the early 1980s when the civil war was at its peak. The chief victims have always been the indigenous Maya, generally regarded as backward, ignorant and dispensable. Some progress has been made in recent years to improve the human-rights situation, but campaigners who speak out routinely face intimidation, violence and death if they dare to upset the country's shadowy hidden powers.

A brief history

When conquistador **Pedro de Alvarado** arrived in the region in 1523, he introduced the notion of race-based exploitation that has dominated Guatemala to the present day. Once the initial conquest was over the majority of survivors were systematically herded into villages, deprived of their land, and forced to work in the new plantations. Revolts against colonial and ladino rule were common throughout the eighteenth and nineteenth centuries, but these tended to flare up in specific towns rather than amount to nationwide rebellions. All were met with severe repression. The demands of the coffee industry put fresh strains on the indigenous population, as their land and labour were once again exploited for the benefit of foreign investors and the ruling elite.

The most significant human-rights developments came during the governments of **Arévalo** and **Arbenz** (1945–55), which for the first time sought to address the needs of the indigenous population. Local organizations such as unions and cooperatives were free to operate, suffrage was extended to include all adults, health and schooling were expanded, and land was redistributed to the dispossessed. For the first time in the country's history the issues of inequality and injustice were seriously addressed. However, in 1954 the government was overthrown by a CIA-backed coup, which cleared the stage for military rule and ushered in the modern era of repression.

After 1954 the army dominated the government, operating in alliance with the landowning elite and foreign business interests to consolidate their power. Large-scale repression of leftists followed in the mid-1960s, which was countered by a **guerrilla** movement in the eastern highlands. The army was unable to strike directly at its enemy and opted instead to eradicate their support in the community: between 1966 and 1977 some 10,000 noncombatants were killed. **Death squads** became a permanent feature of Guatemalan politics during military rule – assassinating unionists, left-wing politicians and students.

By 1975 the guerrilla movement was once again on the rise, as were peasant organizations like the Committee for Campesino Unity (CUC), cooperatives and unions, many inspired by the move towards **liberation theology**, under which the Catholic Church began to campaign on social issues. By 1979 three **guerrilla movements** were well established, operating across the country from Petén to the Pacific coast. **General Lucas García** unleashed an era of unprecedented mass repression against politicians, labour leaders, priests and leftists in the cities, while in the countryside the war against the guerrillas also reached a new intensity, as selective killings were replaced by outright massacres. Once again the army found itself pitched against an elusive enemy and resorted to indiscriminate killings in a bid to undermine peasant support for the guerrillas. It's estimated that perhaps 35,000 died during the first four years of the Lucas administration, the vast majority killed either by the security forces or by death squads.

Under the next military leader, **General Efrían Ríos Montt**, the state's tactics changed as the government offered the guerrillas amnesty and ordered PAC paramilitary groups to patrol the countryside. The level of violence increased as the army began to make big gains in the fight against the rebels. Amnesty International charge Montt with operating a genocidal campaign in the department of Quiché, where the slaughter was worst.

Ríos Montt was replaced by **Mejía Víctores** in August 1983, and there followed a drop in the level of rural repression, and the process of reconstruction began. Guerrilla forces fell to around 1500, and although military campaigns continued, "model villages" were now being built to replace those that had been destroyed. Important grassroots **human-rights organizations** began to spring up in this period, including the Mutual Support Group (GAM), comprising families of the disappeared, and the National Commission of Guatemalan Widows (CONAVIGUA), a very significant and largely indigenous group. Though the members of these groups faced routine intimidation and frequent death threats, they marked the emergence of a new period of Maya political activism.

Towards the end of 1985 the country faced its first free elections in thirty years.

Civilian rule and the Peace Accords

A marked decrease in the quantity of human-rights violations followed the election of civilian president **Vinicio Cerezo** in 1986, although things quickly started to deteriorate once again and abductions, killings and intimidation remained widespread. No one accused Cerezo of involvement in the murders; however, members of the security forces apparently carried them out, and so it was a measure of his inability to control them. Violence dropped in rural areas, and with the guerrilla forces on the back foot the army had little need to use the same brutality it had employed in the past. But Cerezo's non-confrontational approach not only ensured a reprieve for the guilty but also allowed for the continued abuse of human rights and the unchallenged hegemony of the army.

Although the early 1990s saw limited progress in improving the human-rights situation, the government was forced to tackle several high-profile cases, including the murder of street children and the assassinations of US citizen Michael Devine and anthropologist Myrna Mack Chang, and for the first time members of the armed forces were convicted of human-rights violations. A number of defiant local groups continued to denounce these abuses, particularly GAM, many of whose members and leaders were kidnapped and murdered. The government's Human Rights Commission received more than one thousand complaints of human-rights violations and acted on none of them.

Meanwhile, out **in the highlands**, the people of Santiago Atitlán expelled the army from their village, after troops shot and killed thirteen people (see p.176), and a number of other villages called for army bases to be closed. The confidence of the Maya population was further boosted in 1992, when the Nobel Peace Prize was awarded to **Rigoberta Menchú**, briefly focusing world attention on the plight of Guatemala's indigenous population. The Indigenous Rights Accords of 1995 sought to tackle outstanding issues relating to the Maya, including education and the promotion of indigenous languages, but only limited progress has been made on these issues to date.

One of the most crucial strands of the **Peace Accords of December 1996** was the establishment of a Truth Commission, overseen by MINUGUA (the UN mission to Guatemala), to investigate human-rights abuses committed during the civil war. Though the commission lacked legal teeth, military forces (including the army, civil patrols, police and death squads) were held culpable for 93 percent of the killings. A parallel investigation, REMHI, established by the Catholic Church, also concluded that the military and civil patrols were accountable for 91 percent of the killings, while the guerrillas and unknown assailants were responsible for the remainder.

Two days after the report was presented, **Bishop Juan Geradi**, who was in charge of the REMHI project, was found beaten to death at his home in Guatemala City. The assassination of one of Guatemala's most prominent human-rights campaigners outraged the nation, bringing thousands onto the streets in protest. For three years the murder investigation dragged on, and a succession of prosecutors and witnesses received death threats. Finally, in June 2001, three elite military chiefs and a priest were found guilty in the case. The Geradi case confirmed in the starkest terms the weakness of the nation's justice system and the extreme obstacles to obtaining prosecutions in Guatemala. A climate of fear persists and those who dare to challenge the interests of the elite, hidden powers and criminal gangs face intimidation and violence.

The situation today

Amnesty International's 2005 report on Guatemala praised President Berger's appointment of several important human-rights activists to posts in his government as well as his decision to curb military spending and army personnel. But the report also stressed that little had been done to tackle the country's deep-rooted human-rights issues, and highlighted new concerns that urgently needed attention. Above all, the report cited the level of violence in society, and the culture of impunity that shielded the perpetrators of these attacks.

The most perturbing of these issues is the inexorable rise in the number of women murdered in Guatemala, many dying the most gruesome of deaths for apparently motiveless reasons, a sadistic phenomenon known as **femicide**. Murders have risen from the 163 women killed in 2002 to 527 in 2004, with many of the victims' bodies showing evidence of torture, mutilation and rape in the moments before death. It's widely believed in Guatemala that these deaths are related to gang violence and territorial disputes, but a UN investigation found that – in contrast to generally held public perceptions – the majority of the victims had no gang affiliations, and were butchered as part of street-gang initiation rituals. A new police unit was set up to investigate these killings in 2004, though when an Organization of American States team visited seven months later, they found the unit woefully under-resourced. According to the Guatemalan Human Rights Ombudsman's Office ninety percent of femicide cases have not been investigated, and groups including Amnesty believe the number of victims is under-reported. Not surprisingly, human-rights workers have been appalled that the government has allocated thousands of police officers to deal with agrarian disputes (see below), but only feeble resources to the femicide issue.

Another pressing human-rights issue is the plight of the several thousand **street children**, most of whom live in the capital and are frequently subject to violent attack by vigilantes, security guards and policemen. Large numbers of children, many orphans, descended on the capital in the years after the civil war, many scratching a living on the city's streets through petty crime and begging. Using meticulous documentation and dogged perseverance, charities including Casa Alianza have pursued the perpetrators through the courts and scored a number of successes, including the payment of US$500,000 in June 2001 to the families of five children who had been tortured and murdered by two policemen.

Campaigning against violent crime or corruption, or challenging the authority of Guatemala's organized crime networks, is dangerous work. Those most at risk include journalists, like radio presenter Jorge Alegría, who was gunned down in Puerto Barrios in September 2001; trade-union leaders, like Carlos Mejía of the UTESP, who received death threats in October 2002; and environmental workers, such as Diego Xon Salazar, an indigenous human-rights activist kidnapped and killed in 2003. Activists' families are often targeted, too, like 2year-old Yira Argueta López, daughter of a REMHI project leader investigating civil war deaths who was strangled to death in Chimaltenango in January 2005. The judiciary is certainly not exempt from these attacks – Attorney General Carlos de León had six bullets pumped into his car in December 2002 when he was investigating organized crime and drug trafficking, and twelve judges reported receiving threats in the first three months of 2005. Few in Guatemala doubt that these attacks are carried out by *poderes ocultos*, or "hidden powers", mafia-like crime structures fearless of retribution.

"Clandestine and **illegal armed groups** still operate with impunity in Guatemala," Amnesty says. "These groups have been linked to organized crime and are thought to have infiltrated the police, army and some state institutions." According to GAM, the human-rights group, "these structures are made up of those who violated human rights in the recent past and today seek the manner to enrich themselves and prevent the investigation of their crimes." A plan to create a commission to investigate clandestine groups (CICIACS) was widely welcomed, though Congress ruled it unconstitutional in August 2004.

Land reform, the other critical issue cited in the Amnesty report, has never been tackled in Guatemala. Though the hard statistics are difficult to pin down, it's generally accepted that seventy percent of the country's agricultural land is owned by just three percent of the population. The squatting of fincas by landless campesinos has proliferated in recent years, and today Guatemala has dozens of potentially incendiary disputes. Since his inauguration, President Berger has ramped up the eviction rate in such cases, with two thirds of these expulsions turning violent in 2004. The worst incident occurred at Finca Nuevo Linda, where roughly two thousand police took on some three thousand peasant squatters, resulting in eleven deaths and hundreds of injured. As disputes with (often absent) landowners have escalated, Berger has reacted unequivocally by applying the full might of the law against these landless peasants in actions that placate his natural constituency, the landowning elite or, as MINUGUA put it,

Human rights in Guatemala

For more information on human rights in Guatemala contact either the Guatemalan Human Rights Commission – USA (®www.ghrc-usa.org), Amnesty International (®www.amnesty.org) or Human Rights Watch (®www.hrw.org). These organizations all publish regular bulletins and reports on the current situation in the country.

"with an undue deference by the government to the demands of landowners". The biggest criticism is that there have been no real attempts to find alternative land or a practical solution to help the campesinos involved.

The state's efforts to deal with the perpetrators of **civil war crimes** – and safeguard the security of the victims' families who are pressing for investigation – has been woeful, contrary to the demands of the Peace Accords. Indeed, MINUGUA says "Witnesses and others involved in the few legal proceedings initiated in order to seek justice for gross violations of human rights have suffered intimidation and attacks."

Despite these threats, Guatemalan human-rights groups are attempting to prosecute ex-military leaders through the international and national courts. The Rigoberta Menchú Foundation has filed suits abroad against former generals Lucas García and Ríos Montt, using the Pinochet and Milosevic cases as references. Other organizations have successfully obtained compensation from the Guatemalan government through the inter-American justice system for the families of victims of violence. In Guatemala, all prosecutions are fraught with difficulty, but the CALDH (Centre for Legal Action on Human Rights) has aided indigenous massacre survivors to file suits against the military high command from the Lucas García administration for killings in their villages. It has been essential to organize international accompaniment for the communities who have presented the legal actions, in order to prevent reprisals against them.

Amnesty sees the progress and outcome of these actions as a vital test of Guatemalan democracy. This is the first time that victims of massive human-rights violations have brought charges against the intellectual authors of these crimes, and a positive outcome could lead to genuine reconciliation in the country and break the impunity of the army forces. It would also show that Guatemala is subscribing to international standards of human rights and demonstrate that the nation's legal system can be used to obtain justice and seek redress for offences.

Rigoberta Menchú and the Nobel Peace Prize

Five hundred years after Columbus reached the Americas the Nobel committee awarded their peace prize to Rigoberta Menchú Tum, a 33-year-old K'iche' Maya woman who had campaigned tirelessly for peace in Guatemala and for the advancement of indigenous people across the world. In their official statement, the Nobel institute described Menchú as "a vivid symbol of peace and reconciliation across ethnic, cultural and social dividing lines".

Within Guatemala, however, the honour provoked controversy. Few doubted that Menchú had firm connections and deep sympathies with Guatemala's guerrillas, although after she was awarded the prize she distanced herself from the armed struggle. Nevertheless, many people argued that her support for armed uprising made her an inappropriate winner of a peace prize. A couple of days before the announcement, army spokesman Captain Julio Yon Rivera said she had "defamed the fatherland", although once the prize was awarded he claimed to have been expressing a personal opinion that was not the official view of the Guatemalan army. Others feared that the prize would be interpreted as a vindication of the guerrillas and only serve to perpetuate the civil war.

The first volume of Menchú's autobiography, *I, Rigoberta Menchú*, shows her to be essentially a pacifist and suggests that her unspoken support for the guerrillas was very much a last resort. "For us, killing is something monstrous. And that's why we feel so angered by all the repression… Even though the tortures and kidnappings had done our people a lot of harm, we shouldn't lose faith in change. This is when I began working in a peasant organization and went on to another stage of my life. There are other things, other ways."

Menchú's story is undeniably tragic, and her account offers a harrowing look into the darkest years of Guatemalan history and the plight of the nation's indigenous people. However, the accuracy of sizable parts of her life story, as recounted in her autobiography, were later challenged in *Rigoberta Menchú and the Story of All Poor Guatemalans,* an iconoclastic biography published in 1998 by David Stoll. Stoll concluded that substantial sections of the Menchú legend had been fabricated or greatly exaggerated, and that she had "drastically revised the pre-war experience of her village to suit the needs of the revolutionary organization she had joined".

In *I, Rigoberta Menchú*, Menchú describes how the barbaric cruelty of the Guatemalan civil war affected her family, who were political activists, and how they were branded guerrilla sympathizers by the military. Menchú recounts the fight to protect the family farm from greedy ladinos, her family's days working in the plantations of the Pacific coast, and her lack of formal schooling. The deaths of her brother, mother and father at the hands of the armed forces are agonizingly retold. Expanding to cover the wider picture in Guatemala, Menchú condemns the massive disparities between the country's ladino and Maya, and rich and poor. The biography has gone on to sell more than 500,000 copies, while Menchú has been invited to speak at events and conferences all over the world. Campaigning for the rights of the Guatemalan Maya and other oppressed minorities from exile in Mexico, she frequently travelled to the United Nations in Geneva and New York to press her case. This period of the Nobel laureate's life is narrated in

Crossing Borders, the second volume of her autobiography, and an altogether less traumatic and controversial read.

Rigoberta Menchú returned to Guatemala in 1994 as an iconic but refractory figure; in the global arena, however, her reputation was unblemished until the publication of David Stoll's biography. Stoll's book provided compelling evidence that Menchú's family's land dispute was an internecine family feud rather than a racially charged indigenous–ladino altercation; that she never had toiled in the fields of Pacific-coast plantations and had been educated at two private convent schools. He alleged a guerrilla past and questioned the accuracy of her account about the deaths of two of her brothers.

After the biography's publication an international furore ensued, with allegations from *The New York Times* that she had received "a Nobel prize for lying". Menchú evaded responding directly to Stoll's charges, though admitted that she had received some formal education at a convent school in Chiantla. She later sought to distance herself somewhat from *I, Rigoberta Menchú*, and inferred the input of her editor and translator – Arturo Taracena, a guerrilla attaché – had distorted her testimony. Geir Lundestad, director of the Nobel institute, has expressed support for Menchú, declaring that the decision to give Menchú the award was because of her work on behalf of indigenous people, and not because of her family history.

As the dust settled, a roster of academics lined up to support Menchú's reputation, questioning Stoll's motives and defending the value of her *testimonio* – which, they reasoned, was recounting the civil war experiences of indigenous Guatemalans as a whole – and followed a tradition of Maya testimonial writing that dated back to the time of the Conquest. No one disputed that her mother, father and brothers died at the hands of the military (with another 200,000 Guatemalans) whose extreme brutality has been documented in exhaustive reports compiled by the UN and Catholic Church. Her success bringing global attention to the terrible suffering inflicted on (and continuing repression of) Guatemala's Maya is incontestable, and her work on behalf of the world's indigenous peoples has been unrelenting and highly effective. The two sides of the debate are set out in *The Rigoberta Menchú Controversy* published in 2001, a collection of articles edited by Arturo Arias.

Today, Menchú is adored by most Guatemalan Maya and the political left, many of whom see her as a future presidential candidate, mistrusted by most of the Guatemalan oligarchy, and tends to be despised by the military and those on the right. This hasn't stopped her acting as a goodwill ambassador for the Peace Accords under the Berger government, and through her foundation, campaigning for human rights in Guatemala, and beyond. Menchú has been closely involved with indigenous issues and a drive to increase indigenous electoral participation and filed genocide charges in the international courts against the former military rulers Lucas García and Ríos Montt. Declaring "that there's no peace without justice" she has fought to end the impunity of the armed forces for their civil war atrocities.

For more information on the Rigoberta Menchú Foundation, consult the website ⓦwww.frmt.org (in Spanish).

Landscape and wildlife

Guatemala embraces an astonishingly diverse collection of environments, ranging from the permanently moist rainforests and mangroves of the Caribbean coast to the exposed *altiplano* highlands, where the ground can be hard with frost. Its wildlife is correspondingly varied; undisturbed forests provide a home to both temperate species from the north and tropical ones from the south, as well as a number of indigenous species found nowhere else in the world.

The Pacific coast

Guatemala's **Pacific coastline** is marked by a thin strip of black volcanic sand, pounded by the surf. There are no natural harbours and boats have to take their chances in the breakers or launch from one of the piers (though Puerto Quetzal takes large, ocean-going ships). The sea itself provides a rich natural harvest of shrimp, tuna, snapper and mackerel, most of which go for export. The coastal waters are also ideal for sport fishing. A couple of kilometres offshore, dorado, which grow to around forty pounds, are plentiful, while farther out marlin, sailfish, wahoo and skipjack ply the waters.

The **beach** itself rises from the water to form a large sandbank, dotted with palm trees, behind which the land drops off into low-lying mangrove swamps and canals. In the east, from San José to the border, the **Chiquimulilla Canal** runs behind the beach for around 100km. For most of the way it's no more than a narrow strip of water, but here and there it fans out into swamps, creating a maze of waterways that are an ideal breeding ground for young fish, waterfowl and a range of small mammals. The sandy shoreline is an ideal nesting site for three species of **sea turtle**, including the giant leatherback (see box, p.254), which periodically emerge from the water, drag themselves up the beach and deposit a clutch of eggs before hauling their weight back into the water. At Monterrico, east of San José, a nature reserve protects a small section of the coastline for the benefit of the turtles, and with luck you might see one here. The **Reserva Monterrico-Hawaii** is in fact the best place to see wildlife on the Pacific coast as it includes a superb mangrove swamp, which you can easily explore by boat.

The **mangroves** are mixed in with water lilies, bulrushes and tropical hardwoods, amongst which you'll see **herons**, **kingfishers** and an array of **ducks** including **muscovies** and **white whistling ducks**. In the area around Monterrico, flocks of **wood stork** are common, and you might also see the **white ibis** or the occasional **great jabiru**, a massive stork that nests in the area. With real perseverance and a bit of luck you might also catch a glimpse of a **racoon**, **anteater** or **opossum**. You'll also be able to see **alligators** and **iguanas**, if not in the wild then at the reserve headquarters where they are kept in a breeding programme. Other birds that you might see almost anywhere along the coast include **plovers**, **coots** and **terns**, and a number of winter migrants including **white** and **brown pelicans**.

Between the shore and the foothills of the highlands, the **coastal plain** is an intensely fertile and heavily farmed area, where the volcanic and alluvial soils are ideal for sugarcane, cotton, palm oil, banana and rubber plantations and cattle ranches. In recent years soya and sorghum, which require less labour, have been added to this list. Guatemala's coastal **agribusiness** is high cost and high yield: the soils are treated chemically and the crops regularly sprayed with a cocktail of pesticides, herbicides and fertilizers. There's little land that remains untouched by the hand of commercial agriculture so it's hard to imagine what this must once have looked like, but it was almost certainly very similar to Petén, a mixture of savannah and rainforest supporting a rich array of wildlife. These days it's only the swamps, steep hillsides and towering hedges that give any hint of its former glory, although beautiful flocks of white **snowy** and **cattle egrets** feed alongside the beef cattle.

Finally, one particularly interesting lowland species is the **oropendola**, a large oriole which builds a long woven nest hanging from trees and telephone wires. They tend to nest in colonies and a single tree might support fifty nests. You'll probably notice the nests more than the birds, which thrive throughout Guatemala and neighbouring countries.

The Boca Costa

Approaching the highlands, the coastal plain starts to slope up towards a string of volcanic cones, and this section of well-drained hillside is known as the **Boca Costa**. The volcanic soils, high rainfall and good drainage combine to make it ideal for growing **coffee**, and it's here that some of Guatemala's best beans are produced, with rows of olive-green bushes ranked beneath shady trees.

Where the land is unsuitable for coffee, lush tropical forest still grows, clinging to the hills. As you head up into the highlands, through deeply cleft valleys, you pass through some of this superb forest, dripping with moss-covered vines, bromeliads and orchids. Close to the most active volcanoes, in areas where farming has not disturbed the environment, are some incredibly rich ecosystems. Around Volcán Santiaguito near Quetzaltenango, more than 120 species of bird have been sighted here, including some real rarities such as **solitary eagles**, **quetzals** and **highland guans**. The **azure-rumped tanager**, **maroon-chested ground dove** and **Pacific parakeet** are endemic to this region. The Guatemala Birding Resource Center (@www.xelapages.com/gbrc), a specialist tour operator, runs excellent trips to the Boca Costa region.

The highlands

The highlands proper begin with a chain of **volcanoes**. There are 37 peaks in all, the main backbone ranged in a direct line that runs parallel with the Pacific coastline from the southwestern border with Mexico into El Salvador. (In the eastern highlands, away from the main chain, there's another sprinkling of older, less spectacular weathered cones.) The highest of the main peaks is **Tajumulco** (4220m), near the Mexican border, while three highly active cones – **Fuego**, **Pacaya** and **Santiaguito** – all belch sulphurous fumes, volcanic ash and the occasional fountain of molten rock. Beneath the surface their subterranean fires heat the bedrock, and in several places hot spring water emerges, offering the luxury of a warm, mineral-rich bath (for the best of these see Fuentes Georginas, p.198, and the *Las Cumbres* hotel, p.198).

On the southern side of the central highlands, volcanic peaks surround two large lakes, Lago de Amatitlán and Lago de Atitlán, both of which are set in superb countryside. South of Guatemala City, **Lago de Amatitlán** has suffered years of environmental mismanagement, and its waters are heavily contaminated and blackened by pollution. The lake remains a popular picnic spot for the capital's not-so-rich. Farther west, **Lago de Atitlán** is still spectacularly beautiful, with crystal blue water, but increasing tourist development and a population explosion threaten to damage its delicate ecological balance. Atitlán's ecosystem was upset as far back as 1958, when **black bass** were introduced in a bid to create sport fishing. The bass is a greedy, rapacious fish and in no time at all its presence had reshaped the food chain. Smaller fish became increasingly rare, as did crabs, frogs, insects and small mammals. The **Atitlán grebe**, a small, flightless water bird unique to the lake, was worst hit. Young grebes were gobbled up by the hungry bass, and by 1965 just eighty of them survived. By 1984, falling water levels caused by the 1976 earthquake, combined with tourist development of the lakeshore, cut their numbers by a further thirty. Today the bird is extinct.

On the northern side of the volcanic ridge are the **central valleys** of the highlands, a complex mixture of sweeping bowls, steep-sided valleys, open plateaux and jagged peaks. This central area is home to the vast majority of Guatemala's population, and all the available land is intensely farmed, with hillsides carved into workable terraces and portioned up into a patchwork of small fields. Here the land is farmed by campesinos using techniques that predate the arrival of the Spanish. The *milpa* is the mainstay of Maya farming practices: a field is cleared, usually by slash and burn, and planted with maize as the main crop, with beans, chillies and squash grown as well. Traditionally, the land is rotated between *milpa* and pasture, and also left fallow for a while, but in some areas it's now under constant pressure, the fertility of the soil is virtually exhausted and only with the assistance of fertilizer can it still produce a worthwhile crop. The pressure on land is immense and each generation is forced to farm more marginal territory, planting on steep hillsides where exposed soil is soon washed into the valley below.

Some areas remain off limits to farmers, however, and substantial tracts of the highlands are still **forested**. In the cool valleys of the central highlands, pine trees dominate, intermixed with oak, cedar and fir. To the south, on the volcanic slopes and in the warmth of deep-cut valleys, lush subtropical forest thrives in a world kept permanently moist – similar in many ways to the forest of Verapaz, where constant rain fosters the growth of cloudforest.

Heading on to the north, the land rises to form several **mountain ranges**. The largest of these are the Cuchumatanes, a massive chain of granite peaks that reach a height of 3837m above the town of Huehuetenango. Further to the east there are several smaller ranges such as the Sierra de Chuacús, the Sierra de las Minas and the Sierra de Chamá. The high peaks support stunted trees and open grassland, used for grazing sheep and cattle, but are too cold for maize and most other crops.

Bird life is plentiful throughout the highlands; you'll see a variety of **hummingbirds**, flocks of screeching **parakeets**, **swifts**, **egrets** and the ever-present **vultures**. Slightly less commonplace are the **quails** and **wood partridges**, **white-tailed pigeons**, and several species of doves including the **little Inca** and the **white-winged dove**. Last but by no means least is the **quetzal**, which has been revered since Maya times. The male quetzal has fantastic green tail-feathers which snake behind it through the air as it flies: these have always been prized by hunters and even today the bird is very rare indeed. Near Cobán is the **Biotopo del Quetzal**, a protected area of cloudforest in the department of Baja Verapaz where quetzals breed, but you'll have a better chance of spotting Guatemala's national bird in the more remote mountains of the **Sierra de Caquipec** to the northeast.

The highlands also support a number of small **mammals**, including foxes and small cats, although your chances of seeing these are very slim.

The rainforests of Petén

Northeast of the highlands the land drops away into the **rainforests** of Petén, a large chunk of which remains undisturbed, although recent oil finds and a huge influx of cattle ranchers, timber merchants and migrant settlers have cut a swathe through virgin jungle in the past thirty years. The forest of Petén extends across the Mexican border, where it merges with the Lacandón and Campeche rainforests, and into Belize, where it skirts around the lower slopes of the Maya Mountains, reaching to the Caribbean coast.

Today around forty percent of Petén is still covered by **primary forest**, with a canopy that towers between 30 and 50m above the forest floor, made up of hundreds of species of trees, including ceiba, mahogany, aguacate, ebony and sapodilla. The combination of a year-round growing season, plenty of moisture and millions of years of evolution have produced an environment that supports literally thousands of species of plants and trees. While temperate forests tend to be dominated by a single species – fir, oak or beech, say – it's diversity that characterizes the tropical forest. Each species is specifically adapted to fit into a particular ecological niche, where it receives a precise amount of light and moisture.

This biological storehouse has yielded some astonishing **discoveries**. Steroid hormones, such as cortisone, and diosgenin, the active ingredient in birth-control pills, were developed from wild yams found in these forests; and the highly potent anesthetic tetrodoxin is derived from a species of Central American frog.

Despite its size and diversity the forest is surprisingly **fragile**. It forms a closed system in which nutrients are continuously recycled and decaying plant matter fuels new growth. The forest floor is a spongy mass of roots, fungi, mosses, bacteria and microorganisms, in which nutrients are stored, broken down with the assistance of insects and chemical decay, and gradually released to the waiting roots and fresh seedlings. The thick canopy prevents much light reaching the forest floor, ensuring that the soil remains damp but warm, a hotbed of chemical activity. The death of a large tree prompts a flurry of growth as new light reaches the forest floor, and in no time at all a young tree rises to fill the gap. But once the trees are removed the soil is highly vulnerable, deprived of its main source of fertility. Exposed to the harsh tropical sun and direct rainfall, an area of cleared forest soon becomes prone to flooding and drought. Recently cleared land will contain enough nutrients for four or five years of good growth, but soon afterwards its usefulness declines rapidly and within twenty years it will be almost completely barren. If the trees are stripped from a large area, soil erosion will silt the rivers and parched soils will disrupt local rainfall patterns.

Settlement needn't mean the end of the rainforest. In the past this area supported a huge population of Maya, who probably numbered as many as ten million during the Late Classic era. (Some archeologists, however, argue that during Maya occupation Petén was a mixture of savannah and grassland, and

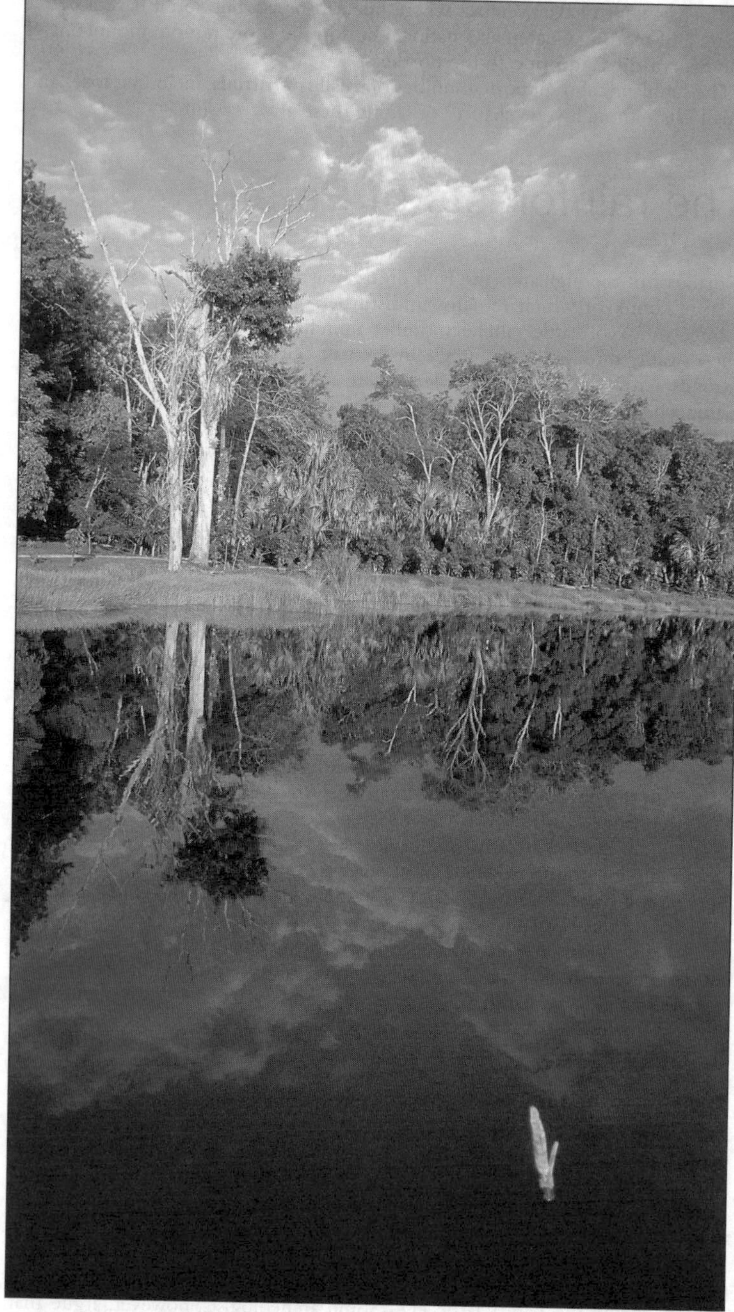

△ Petén rainforest

that relatively recent climatic changes have enabled it to evolve into rainforest.) Only one small group of Maya, the Lacandones, still farm the forest using traditional methods. They allow the existing trees to point them in the right direction, avoiding areas that support mahogany, as they tend to be too wet, and searching out ceiba and ramon trees, which thrive in rich, well-drained soils. In April a patch of forest is burnt down and then, to prevent soil erosion, planted with fast-growing trees such as banana and papaya, and with root crops to fix the soil. A few weeks later they plant their main crops: maize and a selection of others, from garlic to sweet potatoes. Every inch of the soil is covered in growth, a method that mimics the forest and thereby protects the soil. The same land is cultivated for three or four years and then allowed to return to its wild state – although they continue to harvest from the fruit-bearing plants – and in due course return to the same area. The whole process is in perfect harmony with the forest, extracting only what it can afford to lose and ensuring that it remains fertile. Sadly, the traditional farming methods of the Lacandones are now very rarely practiced. New settlers burn the forest and plant grass for cattle pasture, and vast areas of former jungle now have very little biodiversity or fertility.

In its undisturbed state the rainforest is still superbly beautiful and is home to an incredible range of wildlife. Amongst the birds, the spectacular scarlet, blue and emerald green **ocellated turkey**, found only in Petén, is perhaps the most famous. But the forest is also home to three species of **toucan**, **motmots** (a type of bird of paradise), several species of **parrot** including **Aztec** and **green parakeets**, and the endangered **scarlet macaw**, which is said to live to at least fifty. As in the highlands, **hummingbirds**, **buzzards** and **hawks** are all common. A surprising number of these can be seen fairly easily in the **Parque Nacional Tikal**, particularly if you hang around until sunset.

Although **mammals** are widespread, they are almost always elusive, and your best chance of seeing them is at the bigger reserves and archeological sites, where they may have lost some of their fear of humans. At many forest sites you'll almost certainly see **monkeys**, including the acrobatically agile **spider** and the highly social **howlers**, which emit a chilling, deep-throated roar. The largest land animal in Guatemala is the **tapir** (dante), weighing up to 300kg, and usually found near water. Tapirs are endangered and you're not likely to see one without a guide. Two species of **peccary** (wild pig), the collared and the white-lipped, wander the forest floors in large groups, seeking out roots and palm nuts. The smaller herbivores include the **paca** (also known as the tepescuintle and agouti), a rodent about the size of a piglet, which is hunted everywhere for food. You'll often see **coati** (locally known as *pizotes*), inquisitive and intelligent members of the raccoon family, foraging in the leaf litter around archeological sites with their long snouts, often in family groups of several dozen. Coatis and small **grey foxes** are frequently seen at Tikal, and in many places you can see **opossums** and **armadillos**.

Five species of wild **cat** are found in the region, though most are now rare outside the protected areas. **Jaguars** (called *tigres* in Guatemala) formerly ranged over the whole of the country, but today the densest population is found in the northern Petén, though they are very rarely seen. **Pumas** live in remote forest areas; less rare but still uncommon are the much smaller **ocelot** and the **margay**, which is about the size of a large domestic cat. The **jaguarundi** is the smallest and commonest of the wild cats, and as it hunts during the day you might spot one on a trail.

Take a trip along almost any river in Petén and you've a good chance of seeing **green iguanas**, **mud turtles** or **Central American river turtles** sunning themselves on logs. **Egrets** and **kingfishers** fish from overhanging branches, while large rivers such as Río de la Pasión and lakes, including Lago de Petexbatún, are also rich, packed with **snook**, **tarpon** and **mullet**.

Crocodiles are becoming increasingly common in Petén, after previously being hunted almost to extinction, and are now frequently spotted at Lago de Yaxhá and Laguna Perdida. They are not dangerous to humans unless they are very large – at least 3m long – but heed the warnings of locals if they advise against swimming in particular lagoons.

Although there are at least fifty species of **snake** in the region, only a few are venomous and you're unlikely to see any snakes at all. The **boa constrictor** is one of the most common and also is the largest, growing up to 4m, though it poses no threat to humans. Others you might see are **coral snakes** (which are venomous) and **false coral snakes** (which are not); in theory they're easily distinguished by noting the arrangement of adjacent colours in the stripes, but it's best to admire all snakes from a distance unless you're an expert.

At night in the forest, you'll hear the characteristic chorus of frog mating calls, and you'll also frequently find the **red-eyed tree frog** – a beautiful pale green creature about the size of the top joint of your thumb – in your shower in any rustic cabin. Less appealing perhaps are the giant **marine toads**, the largest toad in the Americas, weighing in at up to 1kg and growing to more than 20cm. Like most frogs and toads, the marine toad has toxic glands, and its toxin has hallucinogenic properties – an effect put to use in ceremonies by the ancient Maya, who licked the toad's glands and interpreted the resultant visions.

The Caribbean coast and the Bay Islands

Much of Guatemala's small **Caribbean coastline** is protected as part of the Biotopo Punta del Manabique, a rich wetland habitat, while just inland there are several additional ecologically diverse reserves around the Río Dulce and Lago de Izabal. This region offers some of the country's finest bird-watching territory, with more than three hundred species spotted inside the Reserva Bocas del Polochic alone. Though there are tiny coral outcrops in Guatemalan waters, there's much more to see around the exceptional reefs of the **Bay Islands**, where the three main islands all have excellent scuba-diving schools.

Immediately inland from the Guatemalan coast, the **littoral forest** is characterized by salt-tolerant plants, often with tough, waxy leaves which help conserve water. Species include red and white **gumbo limbo**, **black poisonwood**, **zericote**, **palmetto** and, of course, the **coconut**, which typifies Caribbean beaches, though it's not actually a native. The littoral forest supports a very high density of fauna, especially **migrating birds**, owing to the succession of fruits and seeds yet, due to its location, it's also facing increased development pressure.

Much of the shoreline around Punta del Manabique and Lívingston is still largely covered with **mangroves**, which play an important economic role, not merely as nurseries for commercial fish species but also for their stabilization of the shoreline and their ability to absorb the force of gales and hurricanes. The dominant species of the coastal fringe is the **red mangrove**, although in due course it undermines its own environment by consolidating the sea bed until it becomes more suitable for the less salt-tolerant black and white mangroves. The basis of the shoreline food chain is the nutrient-rich mud, held in place by the mangroves, whose roots are home to **oysters** and **sponges**. In the shallows, "meadows" of **seagrass beds** provide nurseries for many fish and invertebrates, and pasture for conch and turtles. The extensive root system of seagrasses also protects beaches from erosion by holding the fragments of sand and coral together.

The coastal zone is home to sparse numbers of the **West Indian manatee**, which can reach 4m in length and weigh up to 450kg. These placid and shy creatures move between freshwater lagoons and the open sea. They were once hunted for their meat but are now protected, and the Biotopo Chocón Machacas has been established in the Golfete region of the Río Dulce as a manatee sanctuary. Despite this measure, the manatee remains very rare in Guatemala, and you've a much better chance of spotting one in Belize, where their habitat is much less depleted.

In the **Bay Islands**, the **coral reefs** are some of the best preserved in the Caribbean, forming an astoundingly beautiful world where fish and coral come in every imaginable colour. The corals look like a brilliant underwater forest, but in fact each coral is composed of colonies of individual **polyps**, feeding off plankton wafting past in the current. There are basically two types of coral: the hard, calcareous, reef-building corals, such as **lettuce coral**, **brain coral** and **elkhorn coral** (known scientifically as the **hydrocorals**; 74 species), and the soft corals such as **sea fans** and **feather plumes** (the **ococorals**; 36 species). On the reefs you'll find the **chalice sponge**, which is a garish pink, the appropriately named **fire coral**, the delicate **feather-star crinoid** and the **apartment sponge**, a tall thin tube with lots of small holes in it.

Incredibly, the extensive reefs surrounding the Bay Islands survived the ten-metre waves of **Hurricane Mitch** in 1998 almost intact. Even in Guanaja, which took a direct hit (Mitch pounded the island for more than two days), the coral remains in generally excellent condition, though fish numbers have declined a little because of overfishing around the reefs, despite the island's marine reserve status. The Bay Islands' reef environment is characterized by between 500m and a kilometre or so of shallow **fringing reef**, interspersed with sandy patches, which extends from the shoreline – this area is no deeper than 12m. This fringing reef then reaches a **reef crest**, where the waves break, from where the coral plummets almost vertically off the northern coasts of Roatán, Utila and Guanaja. These steep drop-offs form dramatic **reef walls**, spectacular topographic features for which the Bay Islands are particularly renowned. The reef walls form the edge of the **continental shelf**, which plunges down to a depth of 3000m within a few kilometres north of the islands, forming a vast underwater canyon called the Cayman Trench.

It's the Bay Islands' position between these shallow and deep-water habitats that makes for such exciting scuba-diving. When cruising the reef walls on the northern coasts of the islands, it's possible to observe the abundant coral life while keeping an eye on the big blue, and perhaps spot **pelagic sealife** like tarpon or manta rays swept close to the shore. The southern coasts of all the islands are a little different: here the reef has a shallower profile with coral outcrops interspersed with channels and small cayes, and pelagic species are less common.

The seas around the Bay Islands are rich with all the main marine species found in the Caribbean. You're pretty much guaranteed to see a wide variety of reef life including **angel-** and **parrotfish**, **tiger groupers**, **trumpet fish** and small striped **sergeant-majors**, while **seahorses** and **hawksbill turtles** are also frequently spotted. **Yellow stingrays** and **spotted eagle rays** are usually a little more elusive, while **reef sharks** (the harmless nurse shark is the most common species) are only occasionally encountered. Keep an eye out for

Conservation organizations

Alianza Verde (Green Alliance, Ⓦwww.greendeal.org). Based in CINCAP, Flores (see p.336), and supported by Conservation International, this is a consortium of ecotourism operators and conservation organizations, working closely with Guatemala's National Protected Areas Commission (CONAP) and ProPetén (see p.336), focusing primarily on sustainable development in the Maya Biosphere Reserve. It is developing "Green Deal", a code of practice and certification for ecotourism businesses.

Arcas (Ⓦwww.arcasguatemala.com). Conservation group that provides a refuge for wild animals in Petén (see p.339) and also runs a sea-turtle project in the Monterrico–Hawaii area (see p.254).

Bay Islands Conservation Association (BICA, Ⓦwww.bica-utila.org). A well-organized environmental group (see p.404), involved with establishing and managing marine parks in the Bay Islands, Honduras. BICA volunteers are needed to monitor coral-reef health and sea-turtle numbers.

Centre for Conservation Studies (CECON). A department of Guatemala's University of San Carlos, with head offices at the Botanical Gardens of Guatemala City (see p.89). CECON manages and conducts scientific research in all seven of the nation's biotopos. These are often the best-protected areas within reserves, such as Cerro Cahuí in Petén, Monterrico on the Pacific coast and the Biotopo del Quetzal in Baja Verapaz.

Defensores de la Naturaleza (Ⓦwww.defensores.org.gt). Ecological group that combines conservation with sustainable tourism in the Sierra de las Minas and the Bocas de Polochic reserves (see p.304 and p.283). It also manages the vast Sierra de Lacandón national park in Petén and the small Parque Nacional Naciones Unidas.

Fundary (Ⓦwww.guate.net/fundarymanabique). Working with communities in Punta de Manabique (see p.270) to establish sustainable tourism in this biotopo on Guatemala's Caribbean coast. Spanish-speaking volunteers, preferably with a background in biology or ecotourism, are sometimes needed to patrol marine-turtle nesting beaches or undertake manatee and dolphin observation.

ProPetén (Ⓦwww.propeten.org). Petén's largest NGO works on numerous conservation and resource-management projects in the Maya Biosphere Reserve including Las Guacamayas, a biological station near Waka' (El Perú) ruins. Volunteers are needed.

Proyecto Eco-Quetzal (Ⓦwww.ecoquetzal.org). Long-established NGO (see p.312), with a successful record in protecting the forests around Cobán by offering economic alternatives to indigenous people, including excellent ecotourism projects in two remote areas where visitors stay with Q'eqchi' Maya villagers.

conger and **moray eels**, **spiny lobster** and the giant **king crab** hiding in holes and crevices in the reef wall, while solitary **great barracuda** can often be seen hunting on the reef crest at dawn and dusk.

The world's largest fish, the plankton-feeding **whale shark**, is resident to the waters around Utila. The fish, which can grow to 20m, also visits the coasts around Roatán and Guanaja in October and November to gorge on snapper and grouper eggs (see box, pp.410–411). Dolphins are sometimes seen just offshore as well – mostly the **Atlantic bottle-nosed dolphin**, though farther out large schools of smaller **spotted dolphin** sometimes follow ocean-going ships.

Books

Guatemala has never inspired a great deal of writing until the past few decades, when the civil war and political turmoil has spawned plenty of nonfiction. In recent years, there has also been a boom in titles about contemporary and ancient Maya culture. Most travel and historical accounts deal with Central America as a whole, devoting only a small slice to Guatemala.

For contemporary Latin American books, the US-based International Relations Center (ⓦwww.irc-online.org) produces an interesting range of publications, and some Guatemala-specific titles. Yax Te' Books (ⓦwww.csuohio.edu/yaxte), the publishing arm of Cleveland State University's K'inal Winik Cultural Center, produce a fascinating collection of titles, concentrating on indigenous Maya culture, literature and language. The London-based Latin America Bureau (ⓦwww.lab.org.uk) publishes books about Central America and the region's society, current affairs and politics. In London, The Guatemalan Maya Centre (see p.35) has a library of more than two thousand books about Guatemala, including many very rare volumes, while the Canning House Library (see p.35) has the UK's largest publicly accessible collection of books and periodicals on Latin America.

Books that we especially recommend are marked with a symbol (★). Where possible, we have given both the US and UK publishers, with the US publisher first (US; UK); o/p means a book is out of print.

Travel

Stephen Connoly Benz *Guatemalan Journey* (University of Texas Press, US). A contemporary perspective on the complexities of Guatemalan society and the impact of US culture and evangelism, with informative accounts of life in the capital and the textile-factory businesses.

Fabío Bourbon *The Lost Cities of the Mayas: The Life, Art and Discoveries of Frederick Catherwood* (Abbeville Press, UK). Fabulous colour reproductions of Catherwood's amazing paintings of lost Maya cities, the originals dating from the nineteenth century when he travelled around the region with John Lloyd Stephens (see p.490).

Peter Canby *Heart of the Sky – Travels Among the Maya* (HarperCollins). The author treads a familiar path through the Maya World, encountering an interesting collection of expats, Mayanists, priests, Guatemala City's idle rich and a female shaman. If not as erudite as Ronald Wright's masterful account (see p.490), it's still an accessible and informative read.

Anthony Daniels *Sweet Waist of America* (Trafalgar Square; Arrow; both o/p). A delight to read. Daniels takes a refreshingly even-handed approach to Guatemala and comes up with a fascinating cocktail of people and politics, discarding the stereotypes that litter most books on Central America. The book also includes interesting interviews with prominent characters from Guatemala's recent history.

Thomas Gage *Travels in the New World* (University of Oklahoma Press, US; UK o/p). Unusual account of a Dominican friar's travels through Mexico and Central America between 1635 and 1637, including some intriguing insights into colonial life as well as some great attacks on the greed and pomposity of the Catholic Church abroad.

★ **Aldous Huxley** *Beyond the Mexique Bay* (Academy Chicago; Flamingo. Huxley's travels in 1934 took him from Belize through Guatemala to Mexico, swept on by his fascination for history and religion, and sprouting bizarre theories on the basis of everything he saw. There are some terrific descriptions of Maya sites and indigenous culture, with superb one-liners summing up people and places.

Patrick Marnham *So Far from God* (Viking Penguin, o/p; Bloomsbury). A saddened and vaguely right-wing account of Marnham's travels through the Americas from the US to Panama (missing out Belize). Dotted with amusing anecdotes and interesting observations, the book was researched in 1984, and its description of Guatemala is dominated by the reign of terror. The Paraxtut massacre, mentioned by Marnham, has since been unmasked as a fabrication.

Jonathan Evan Maslow *Bird of Life, Bird of Death* (Dell; Penguin; both o/p). Maslow sets out in search of the quetzal, using the bird's uncertain future as a metaphor for contemporary Guatemala in a work that merges travel and political comment.

Peter Moore *The Full Montezuma* (Bantam). Puerile backpacking yarn about an Australian's misadventures with the "girl next door" around Mexico and Central America. About as lucid as a muddy puddle.

Nigel Pride *A Butterfly Sings to Pacaya* (Constable, UK, o/p). An enjoyable tale of a family's Jeep journey from the US border to the Maya region, illustrated by drawings of landscapes, people and animals. The trip was in the 1970s but the pleasures and privations they experience rarely appear dated, and the description of the climb of the Pacaya volcano is one of the highlights of the book.

Christopher Shaw *Sacred Monkey River: A Canoe Trip with the Gods* (W.W. Norton). Engaging account of the author's canoe journey along the Usumacinta River that divides Mexico and Guatemala. Nicely crafted prose is enlivened with convincing analysis of ancient Maya cosmology and culture, and the contemporary political and environmental issues affecting the region.

★ **John Lloyd Stephens** *Incidents of Travel in Central America, Chiapas, and Yucatán* (Dover; Prentice Hall). Stephens was a classic nineteenth-century explorer. Acting as US ambassador to Central America, he indulged his own enthusiasm for archeology; while the republics fought it out among themselves, he was wading through the jungle stumbling across ancient cities. His journals, told in a restrained Victorian style punctuated with sudden waves of enthusiasm, make great reading. Some editions include fantastic illustrations by Catherwood of the ruins overgrown with tropical rainforest.

★ **Ronald Wright** *Time Among the Maya* (Henry Holt; Abacus). A vivid and sympathetic account of travels from Belize through Guatemala, Chiapas and Yucatán, meeting the Maya of today and exploring their obsession with time. The book's twin points of interest are the ancient Maya and the recent violence. An encyclopedic bibliography offers ideas for exploration in depth, and the author's knowledge is evident in the superb historical insight he imparts through the book. Certainly one of the best travel books on the area.

Fiction, autobiography and poetry

★ **Miguel Ángel Asturias** *Hombres de Maíz* (University of Pittsburgh; Verso o/p). Guatemala's most famous author, Asturias is deeply indebted to Guatemalan history and culture in his work. "Men of Maize" is generally regarded as his masterpiece, classically Latin American in its magic realist style, and bound up in the complexity of indigenous culture. His other works include *El Señor Presidente*, a grotesque portrayal of social chaos and dictatorial rule, based on Asturias's own experience; *El Papa Verde*, which explores the murky world of the United Fruit Company; and *Weekend en Guatemala*, describing the downfall of the Arbenz government. Asturias won the Nobel Prize in literature before his death in 1974.

Paul Bowles *Up Above the World* (Ecco Press; Peter Owen). Bowles is at his chilling, understated best in this novel based on experiences of Guatemala in the late 1930s. **Jane Bowles** used the same visit for *A Guatemalan Idyll* and other tales republished in *Everything is Nice: Collected Stories of Jane Bowles* (Peter Owen, UK).

★ **Francisco Goldman** *The Long Night of White Chickens* (Grove-Atlantic; Faber & Faber). Drawing on the stylistic complexity of Latin American fiction, this novel tells the tale of a young Guatemalan orphan who flees to the US and works as a maid. When she finally returns home to her politically turbulent nation, she is murdered. It's an interesting and ambitious story, though its chaotic timeline gives the book a Byzantine intricacy that make it a dense and laborious read at times. Goldman's third novel, *A Divine Husband* (Atlantic), set in the nineteenth century, adopts a similar prose, following the adventures of a charismatic half-Maya girl and her many suitors in New York and Central America.

Gaspar Pedro Gonzáles *A Mayan Life* (Yax Te' Books, US). Absorbing story about the personal and cultural conflicts facing a Q'anjob'al Maya in the Cuchumatanes mountains as he seeks a higher education. Gonzáles claims this is the first novel ever written by a Maya author, though it is obviously highly autobiographical.

Norman Lewis *The Volcano Above Us* (Penguin, UK, o/p). Vaguely historical novel published in 1957 that pulls together all the main elements of Guatemala's history. The image that it summons is one of depressing drudgery and eternal conflict, set against a background of repression and racism. In the light of what's happened it has a certain prophetic quality, and remains gripping despite its miserable conclusions.

Víctor Perera *Rites: A Guatemalan Boyhood* (Mercury House; Eland). Autobiographical account of a childhood in Guatemala City's Jewish community. It may not cast much light on the country, but it's an interesting read, pulling together an unusual combination of cultures.

Kathy Reichs *Grave Secrets* (Simon & Schuster; Heinemann). In this compelling thriller forensic scientist Tempe Brennon flies to Guatemala to investigate the mass graves of civil war victims, but is then persuaded to look into the disappearances of four wealthy girls from the capital. Her efforts are thwarted by violence, judicial inadequacies and corruption.

History, politics and human rights

Tom Barry *Guatemala – A Country Guide* (International Relations Center, US). A concise account of the political, social and economic situation in Guatemala, with a mild left-wing stance. Published in 1990.

William V. Davidson *Historical Geography of the Bay Islands, Honduras* (South University Press, US). An interesting study of how waves of settlers, from pirates to Hondurans from the mainland, have shaped the culture of the islands. Useful for pieces of interesting background information.

Edward F. Fisher and R. McKenna Brown (eds) *Maya Cultural Activism in Guatemala* (University of Texas Press, US). Effectual summary of the indigenous movement in Guatemala, with strong chapters on clothing and identity, and the revival of interest in Maya language and hieroglyphic writing.

★ **Greg Grandin** *The Blood of Guatemala – A History of Race and Nation* (Duke University, US). Terrific study of Quetzaltenango's elite class of K'iche' Maya and their impact on the region and nation. Covers the period between the mid-eighteenth century and the fall of the Arbenz government in 1954.

★ **Jim Handy** *Gift of the Devil* (South End Press). Superb history of Guatemala: concise and readable with a sharp focus on the Maya population and the brief period of socialist government. Though now a little out of date (it was written in the mid-1980s), the book nevertheless manages to offer a convincing perspective on the modern Guatemalan state. By no means objective, Handy sets out to expose the development of oppression and point the finger at the oppressors.

George Lovell *A Beauty That Hurts: Life and Death in Guatemala* (Between the Lines, Canada). A good contemporary analysis enlivened by interviews with exiles and community leaders. The book scrutinizes political events through newspaper articles, and reviews the historical context that has shaped twenty-first-century Guatemala.

Víctor Montejo *Testimony: Death of a Guatemalan Village* (Curbstone Press, US). Yet another horrifying account of murder and destruction. In this case it's the personal testimony of a school teacher, describing the arrival of the army in a small highland village and the killing that follows.

★ **Trish O'Kane** *In Focus: Guatemala – A Guide to the People, Politics and Culture* (Latin American Bureau; Interlink). Very accessible introduction to Guatemala, offering a concise summary of the historical, political, economic and social situation, plus an enlightening look at modern Maya culture and activism.

★ **Víctor Perera** *Unfinished Conquest* (University of California Press, US). Superb, extremely readable account of the civil war tragedy, plus comprehensive attention to the deep inequalities that affect the late author's native country. The book's strength comes from the extensive interviews with both ordinary and influential Guatemalans and incisive analysis of recent history. A great introduction to the subject.

REMHI *Guatemala: Never Again* (Orbis; LAB; o/p). Abridged translation of the seminal report published by the Catholic Church of Guatemala into the civil war atrocities. The investigation contains an excellent historical background to the conflict, harrowing personal testimonies, incisive analysis of military and guerrilla strategies and a chapter devoted to preventing a recurrence.

Victoria Sanford *Buried Secrets: Truth and Human Rights in Guatemala* (Palgrave Macmillan). Recently published, this powerful, exhaustively researched investigative study of *la violencia* is based on more than four hundred interviews with massacre survivors, the military and guerrilla forces.

Jennifer Schirmer *The Guatemalan Military Project: A Violence Called Democracy* (University of Pennsylvania, US). Offers an insider's view of the ideology and mentality of the Guatemalan armed forces, based on numerous interviews with senior officers, six ex-defence ministers and three former heads of state.

Stephen Schlesinger and Stephen Kinzer *Bitter Fruit: The Untold Story of the American Coup in Guatemala* (Harvard University Press, US). This book traces the US connection in the 1954 coup, delving into the murky water of United Fruit Company politics and showing that the invading army received its orders from the White House.

Jean-Marie Simon *Eternal Spring – Eternal Tyranny* (Norton). Highly authoritative photojournalistic study of Guatemala's civil war period, with crisp text and evocative imagery.

Daniel Wilkinson *Silence on the Mountain: Stories of Betrayal and Forgetting in Guatemala* (Houghton Mifflin). Part historical narrative, part personal travelogue and part public testimony, Wilkinson's book gives a voice to those who suffered most during Guatemala's civil war.

Central American politics

Tom Barry *Central America Inside Out* (Grove-Atlantic; Avalon). Well-informed background reading on the entire region, though a little dated.

Peter Dale-Scott and Jonathan Marshall *Cocaine Politics: Drugs, Armies and the CIA in Central America* (University of California Press, US). Polemical but well-researched exposé of CIA involvement in cocaine trafficking and political oppression in Central America in the 1980s. Reveals the truth behind the Iran–Contra scandal and gives the lie to the rhetoric of the war on drugs.

James Dunkerley *Power in the Isthmus* (Norton; Verso Editions). Detailed account of Central American politics offering a good summary of the contemporary situation, albeit in a rather turgid academic style. His later book, *The Pacification of Central America* (Verso Editions), published in 1994, is a similarly well-compiled account with plenty of supporting statistics, covering the period up to the beginning of the peace process.

Walter Lafeber *Inevitable Revolutions: The United States in Central America* (W.W. Norton). A highly critical analysis of US involvement in Central America, from the 1823 Monroe Doctrine through the United Fruit Company years to the Reagan era.

Susan C. Stonch (ed) *Endangered Peoples of Latin America* (Greenwood, US). Assesses the problems facing the minorities of the region, including a chapter about the English-speaking Bay Islanders.

William Weinberg *War on the Land: Ecology and Politics in Central America* (Zed Books; Humanities Press). The author tells a story of intertwining conflicts and causes between conservation (and to a small extent ecotourism), land rights and politics in Central America.

Ralph Lee Woodward Jr *Central America: A Nation Divided* (Oxford University Press). Despite its daft title, a good general summary of the Central American situation that's written in an accessible style. The latest edition covers the aftermath of the peace treaties and the neoliberal economics of the late 1990s.

Indigenous culture

Linda Asturias de Barrios *Comalapa: Native Dress and Its Significance* (Ixchel Museum, Guatemala). Only available in Guatemala, this is a work of skilled academic research, investigating weaving skills and their place within modern Maya communities.

Robert Carmack *Quichean Civilization* (University of California Press, US). Thorough study of K'iche' history and highland society, drawing on archeological evidence and accounts of the Conquest.

Gareth W. Cook *Renewing the Maya World: Expressive Culture in a Highland Town* (University of Texas, US). Absorbing look at the annual fiesta traditions and dances that renew the cosmic order in the highland town of Momostenango, and their link to ancient Maya creation myths.

Krystyna Deuss *Indian Costumes from Guatemala* (K. Deuss, UK, o/p). A useful survey of the traditional costumes worn in Guatemala, and one of the best introductions to the subject. The author is also soon to publish a book devoted to Maya customs and culture in the Cuchumatanes mountains, based on two decades of research.

Ann Hecht *Textiles from Guatemala* (British Museum Press). Slim volume that documents the richness of Guatemala's textile weaving traditions.

Grant D. Jones *The Conquest of the Maya Kingdom* (Stanford University Press, US). A massive academic tome that's also a fascinating history of the Itza Maya and a gripping tale of how the Spanish entered and finally defeated the last independent Maya kingdom, at Tayasal, site of present-day Flores.

★ **Rigoberta Menchú** *I, Rigoberta Menchú – An Indian Woman in Guatemala* and *Crossing Borders* (Verso; Norton). Momentous story of one of Latin America's most remarkable women, Nobel Peace Prize–winner Rigoberta Menchú. The first volume is a horrific account of family life in the Maya highlands, recording how Menchú's family were targeted, terrorized and murdered by the military. The book also reveals much concerning K'iche' Maya cultural traditions and the enormous gulf between the ladino and indigenous societies in Guatemala. The second volume is more optimistic, documenting Menchú's life in exile in Mexico, her work at the United Nations fighting for indigenous people and her return to Guatemala. Although Menchú's courage and determination are undeniable, some, including author David Stoll (see p.495), have criticized the accuracy of parts of her story.

Hans Namuth *Los Todos Santeros* (Nishen, UK, o/p). Splendid book of black-and-white photographs taken in the village of Todos Santos Cuchumatán, to the north of Huehuetenango. The book was inspired by the work of anthropologist Maud Oakes (see below).

Maud Oakes *Beyond the Windy Place: The Two Crosses of Todos Santos* (Farrar, Straus & Young, o/p; Gollancz, o/p).

An anthropologist who spent many years in the Mam-speaking village of Todos Santos. Oakes' studies of life in the village were published in the 1940s and 1950s and still make fascinating reading.

★ **The Popol Vuh** (Touchstone; Scribner's). The great K'iche' creation epic, written shortly after the Conquest, is an amazing swirl of mythological characters and their wanderings through the K'iche' highlands, tracing the tribe's ancestry. There are several versions on offer though many of them are half-hearted, including only a few lines from the original. The best is translated by Dennis Tedlock.

★ **James D. Sexton** (ed) *Son of Tecún Umán* (University of Arizona Press; Waveland Press); *Campesino* (University of Arizona Press); and *Ignacio* (University of Pennsylvania Press). Three excellent autobiographical accounts written by a Tz'utujil Maya from Lago de Atitlán. The books give an impression of life inside a modern Maya village, bound up in poverty, local politics and a mixture of Catholicism and superstition, and manage to avoid the stereotyping that usually characterizes description of the indigenous population. Sexton's *Mayan Folktales: Folklore from Lake Atitlán, Guatemala* is another fascinating read, unveiling a world of wonderfully imaginative fables that underpin a society's strict moral codes and notions of justice and fate.

David Stoll *Rigoberta Menchú and the Story of All Poor Guatemalans* (Westview Press in US and UK). Iconoclastic biography that delivers a formidable broadside against considerable pieces of the Menchú legend, though some academics have criticized Stoll's literal interpretation of Maya testimonial traditions.

Philip Werne *The Maya of Guatemala* (Minority Rights Group, UK, o/p). A short study of repression and the Maya of Guatemala. The latest edition (published in 1994) is now a little out of date but still interesting.

Archeology

★ **Michael D. Coe** *The Maya* (Thames & Hudson). Now in its seventh edition, this clear and comprehensive introduction to Maya archeology is one of the best on offer. Coe has also written several more weighty, academic volumes. His *Breaking the Maya Code* (Penguin; Thames & Hudson), a very personal history of the decipherment of the glyphs, owes much to the fact that Coe was at many of the most important meetings leading to the breakthrough. The book demonstrates that the glyphs did reproduce Maya speech. *The Art of the Maya Scribe* (Thames & Hudson), written with Justin Kerr, developer of "rollout" photography – a technique enabling the viewer to see the whole surface of a cylindrical vessel – is a wonderfully illustrated history of Maya writing which also takes the reader on a journey through the Maya universe and mythology via the astonishingly skillful calligraphy of the Maya artists themselves.

★ **David Drew** *The Lost Chronicles of the Maya Kings* (University of California Press; Weidenfeld and Nicolson). Superbly readable and engaging, Drew draws on a wealth of material to deliver an excellent account of ancient Maya political history. The alliances and rivalries between the main cities are skillfully unravelled, and there's a particularly revealing analysis of Late Classic Maya power-politics. This is currently one of the most up-to-date references to consult.

William L. Fash *Scribes, Warriors and Kings* (Thames & Hudson). The definitive study of the ruins of Copán, including the complete historical background, superb maps, and lavish drawings and photographs.

Peter D. Harrison *The Lords of Tikal* (Thames & Hudson). Outstanding study of the Petén metropolis that includes the latest hieroglyphic readings and a tremendous amount of detail about the city's monuments and artefacts and the rulers who commissioned them, Temple V excepted.

★ **Simon Martin and Nikolai Grube** *Chronicle of the Maya Kings and Queens* (Thames & Hudson). Published to universal acclaim, this groundbreaking work is based on exhaustive new epigraphic studies, and the re-reading of previously translated glyphic texts. It also includes the historical records of several key Maya cities – including Tikal, Piedras Negras and Dos Pilas – complete with biographies of 152 kings and 4 queens, full dynastic sequences and all the key battles. As Michael D. Coe, author of *The Maya*, says: "There's nothing else like this book. It supersedes everything else ever written on Maya history."

Mary Miller and Simon Martin *Courtly Art of the Ancient Maya* (Thames & Hudson). Sumptuously illustrated with images of jade, stucco, stonework and pottery artistry, this book also explains the rituals and customs that defined daily life in the royal courts.

John Montgomery *Tikal: An Illustrated History of the Ancient Maya Capital* (Hippocrene, US). An instructive history of the site that's packed with information about the Maya, including a thorough chronology.

Linda Schele and David Freidel (et al) The authors, in the forefront of "new archeology", have been personally responsible for decoding many Maya glyphs. *A Forest of Kings: The Untold Story of the Ancient Maya* (Quill, US), in conjunction with *The Blood of Kings* by Linda Schele and Mary Miller (Thames & Hudson), shows that, far from being governed by peaceful astronomer-priests, the ancient Maya were ruled by hereditary kings, lived in populous, aggressive city-states, and engaged in a continual entanglement of alliances and war. *The Maya Cosmos* (Quill, US), by Schele, Freidel and Joy Parker, is perhaps more difficult to read, but it also examines Maya ritual and religion in a unique and far-reaching way. *The Code of Kings* (Scribner, US), written in collaboration with Peter Matthews and illustrated with Justin Kerr's famous "rollout" photography of Maya ceramics, examines the significance of the monuments at selected Maya sites. It's her last book – Linda Schele died in April 1998 – and a classic of epigraphic interpretation.

Peter Schmidt, Mercedes de la Garza and Enrique Nalda (eds) *Maya Civilization* (Thames & Hudson). Monumental collaborative effort, with sections written by many prominent Mayanists, lusciously presented with more than six hundred colour images of some breathtaking Maya art. The scholarly text is also impressive, with contributions on the importance of Calakmul to the Classic Maya history and detailed essays on the highlands of Guatemala, Maya cosmology and codices.

Robert Sharer *The Ancient Maya* (Stanford University Press; Cambridge University Press). The classic, comprehensive account of Maya civilization, now in its fifth edition, yet as authoritative as ever. Required reading for archeology students, it provides a fascinating reference for the non-expert, as does his *Daily Life in Maya Civilization* (Greenwood, US).

J. Eric S. Thompson *The Rise and Fall of the Maya Civilization* (University of Oklahoma Press, US). A major authority on the ancient Maya during his lifetime, Thompson produced many academic studies, of which this is one of the more accessible. Although recent researchers have overturned many of Thompson's theories, his work provided the inspiration for the postwar surge of interest in the Maya, and he remains a respected figure.

Wildlife and the environment

Les Betelsky *Belize and Northern Guatemala* (Academic Press). Other specialist wildlife guides may cover the subject in more detail but this is a reasonably comprehensive and well-organized single-volume guide to the mammals, birds, reptiles, amphibians and marine life of the region.

Louise H. Emmons *Neotropical Rainforest Mammals* (University of Chicago Press, US). Supported by François Feer's colour illustrations, this highly informative book is written by experts for non-scientists. Local and scientific names are given, along with plenty of interesting snippets.

Steve Howe and Sophie Webb *The Birds of Mexico and Northern Central America* (Oxford University Press). A tremendous work, this is the definitive book on the region's birds. Essential for all serious birders.

★ **Thor Janson** *In the Land of Green Lightning* (Pomegranate, US). Exquisite photographic collection, concentrating on the diverse wildlife and environment of the Maya region. Includes some astounding images of an exploding Volcán Pacaya.

C. Kaplan *Coral Reefs of the Caribbean and Florida* (Houghton Mifflin, US). Useful handbook on the abundant undersea wildlife of the Atlantic coasts of Guatemala and Honduras.

John C. Kricher *A Neotropical Companion* (Princeton University Press, US). Subtitled "An Introduction to the Animals, Plants and Ecosystems of the New World Tropics", this tome contains an amazing amount of valuable information for nature lovers. Researched mainly in Central America, so there's plenty that's directly relevant.

Frank B. Smythe *The Birds of Tikal* (Natural History Press, US). This near-comprehensive book is fairly widely available in Guatemala, and can be bought in Tikal.

Guides

Elizabeth Bell *Antigua Guatemala: The City and Its Heritage*. The best guide to Antigua, written by a long-term resident and prominent historian. It's available from several shops in Antigua, as is the author's *Lent and Easter Week in Antigua*.

William Coe *Tikal: A Handbook to the Ancient Maya Ruins* (University of Pennsylvania Press, US). A detailed account of the site, usually available at the ruins, though it does not include the latest findings. The map of the main area is essential for in-depth exploration.

Sharon Collins *Diving and Snorkeling Roatán and Honduras' Bay Islands* (Lonely Planet). Covers many of the main dive sites in Utila and Roatán, though the Guanaja content is sketchy.

Barbara Balchin de Koose *Antigua for You* (Watson, Guatemala). A very comprehensive account of Antigua's colonial architectural wonders, but doesn't offer much else.

★ **Joyce Kelly** *Archaeological Guide to Northern Central America* (University of Oklahoma Press). Detailed and practical guide to dozens of sites with excellent photographs and accurate maps. The "star ratings" may affront purists, but they do offer a valuable opinion on how worthwhile a particular visit might be. This volume covers 38 Maya sites and 25 museums in Guatemala, Belize, Honduras and El Salvador, and though now a little outdated, it still makes an indispensable companion.

Lily de Jongh Osborne *Four Keys to Guatemala* (Mayflower Publishing, UK, o/p). One of the best guides to Guatemala ever written, including a short piece on every aspect of the country's history and culture. Osborne also wrote a good book on indigenous arts and crafts in Guatemala. Sadly, both books are now out of print.

Cookbooks

Copeland Marks *False Tongues and Sunday Bread: A Guatemalan and Maya Cookbook* (Donald I. Fine, US). If you've traveled widely in Guatemala and suffered an endless onslaught of beans and tortillas, it may be a surprise to find that the country has an established culinary tradition. Marks' book includes many fine Guatemalan recipes like chicken with *mole* sauce as well as the staples like black beans.

Catalina B. Figueroa *Cocina Guatemalteca: Arte, Sabor y Colorido* (Editorial Piedra Santa). This recently published recipe book has a comprehensive range of national dishes and regional specialities, and is available in many bookshops in Antigua.

Language

Language

Language

Guatemala takes in a bewildering collection of languages, but fortunately for the traveller, Spanish will get you by in all but the most remote areas. Some middle-class Guatemalans speak English, but it's essential to learn at least a few Spanish phrases or you're in for a frustrating time.

The **Spanish** spoken in Guatemala has a strong Latin American flavour to it, and if you're used to the dainty intonation of Madrid then this may come as something of a surprise. If you're new to Spanish it's a lot easier to pick up than the Castilian version. Everywhere you'll find people willing to make an effort to understand you, eager to speak to passing gringos.

The rules of **pronunciation** are pretty straightforward and, once you get to know them, strictly observed. Unless there's an accent, words ending in d, l, r and z are **stressed** on the last syllable, all others on the second last. All **vowels** are pure and short.

A somewhere between the A sound of back and that of father.

E as in get.

I as in police.

O as in hot.

U as in rule.

C is soft before E and I, hard otherwise: *cerca* is pronounced serka.

G works the same way, a guttural H sound (like the ch in loch) before E or I, a hard G elsewhere – *gigante* becomes higante.

H is always silent.

J is the same sound as a guttural G: *jamón* is pronounced hamON.

LL sounds like an English Y: *tortilla* is pronounced torteeya.

N is as in English unless it has a tilde (accent) over it, when it becomes NY: *mañana* sounds like manyana.

QU is pronounced like an English K.

R is rolled, RR doubly so.

V sounds more like B, *vino* becoming beano.

X is slightly softer than in English – sometimes almost SH – *Xela* is pronounced shela.

Z is the same as a soft C, so *cerveza* becomes servesa.

Below is a list of a few essential words and phrases, though if you're travelling for any length of time a **dictionary** or **phrase book** is obviously a worthwhile investment. Any good Spanish phrase book or dictionary should see you through in Guatemala, but specific Latin American ones are the most useful. The *University of Chicago Dictionary of Latin-American Spanish* is a good all-rounder, while *Mexican Spanish: A Rough Guide Phrasebook* has a menu reader, rundown of colloquialisms and a number of cultural tips that are relevant to many Latin American countries, including Guatemala. If you're using a dictionary, remember that in Spanish CH, LL and Ñ count as separate letters and are listed after the Cs, Ls and Ns respectively. If you really want to get to grips with Guatemalan slang, swear words and expressions, look out for *¿Qué Onda Vos?* by Juan Carlos Martínez López and Mark Brazaitis, which includes a superb round-up of *guatemaltequismos*. It's available from several bookshops and the La Unión language school in Antigua (see p.65).

Maya languages

After years of state-backed *castellanización* programmes when Spanish was the only language of tuition and Maya schoolchildren were left virtual classroom spectators, a network of Maya schools has now been established, with hundreds alone in Q'eqchi' areas of Guatemala. A strong indigenous cultural movement has now developed in the country, intent on preserving the dozens of different Maya languages still spoken (for a comprehensive map, see p.463). Because the Maya birthrate is much higher than the ladino, there is now every chance that the main languages like K'iche', Kaqchikel and Mam will survive, though the fate of the more isolated tongues is far from secure.

If you're planning an extended stay in a remote indigenous region to do development work, it's extremely helpful to learn a little of the local language first. There are a number of language schools (see p.65) where you can **study a Maya language** and pick up the essentials. Cleveland State University's K'inal Winik Cultural Center (ⓦwww.csuohio.edu/kinalwinik) is devoted to Maya linguistics and culture and publishers of Yax Te' Books, who have several titles on indigenous Guatemalan languages and literature. The Yax Te' Foundation (ⓦwww.yaxte.org), devoted to promoting and supporting Maya culture and language, has some excellent study material and dictionaries.

Maya words do not easily translate into Spanish (or English) so you may see the same place spelt in different ways: *K'umarkaaj* can be spelt *K'umarcaah* or even *Gumarcaj*. Nearly all Maya words are pronounced stressing the final syllable, which is often accented: Atitlán is A-tit-LAN, Wakná is wak-NA.

C is always hard like a K, unlike Spanish.

J is a guttural H, as in Spanish.

U like a W at the beginning of a word and like an OO in the middle or at the end of a word – Uaxactún is pronounced wash-ak-TOON.

X sounds like SH – *Ixcún* is pronounced ish-KOON.

Spanish words and phrases

Basics

Sí, No	Yes, No	**Abierto/a, Cerrado/a**	Open, Closed
Por favor, Gracias	Please, Thank you	**Con, Sin**	With, Without
¿Dónde?, ¿Cuándo?	Where?, When?	**Buen(o)/a, Mal(o)/a**	Good, Bad
¿Qué?, ¿Cuánto?	What?, How much?	**Gran(de), Pequeño/a**	Big, Small
Aquí, Allí	Here, There	**Más, Menos**	More, Less
Este, Eso	This, That	**Hoy, Mañana**	Today, Tomorrow
Ahora, Más tarde	Now, Later	**Ayer**	Yesterday

Greetings and responses

Hola, Adiós	Hello, Goodbye	**Hasta luego**	See you later
Buenos días	Good morning	**Lo siento/discúlpeme**	Sorry
Buenas tardes/noches	Good afternoon/night	**Con permiso/perdón**	Excuse me

¿Cómo está (usted)?	How are you?	**Soy inglés(a)**	I am English
(No) Entiendo	I (don't) understand	**americano (a)**	American
¿Podría hablar más lento?	Could you speak more slowly?	**australiano(a)**	Australian
De nada	Not at all/You're welcome	**británico(a)**	British
¿Habla (usted) inglés?	Do you speak English?	**canadiense**	Canadian
No hablo español	I don't speak Spanish	**holandés(a)**	Dutch
¿Mande?	What (did you say)?	**irlandés(a)**	Irish
Me llamo…	My name is…	**neocelandés(a)**	New Zealander
¿Cómo se llama usted?	What's your name?	**escosés(a)**	Scottish
		sudafricano(a)	South African
		galés(a)	Welsh

Needs – hotels and transport

Quiero	I want
Quisiera	I'd like
¿Sabe…?	Do you know…?
No sé	I don't know
(¿)Hay(?)	There is (is there)?
Deme…(uno así)	Give me…(one like that)
¿Tiene…?	Do you have…?
…la hora	…the time
…un cuarto	…a room
…con dos camas/ cama matrimonial	…with two beds/ double bed
Es para una persona (dos personas)	It's for one person (two people)
…para una noche (una semana)	…for one night (one week)
¿Está bien, cuánto es?	It's fine, how much is it?
Es demasiado caro	It's too expensive
¿No tiene algo más barato?	Don't you have anything cheaper?
¿Se puede…?	Can one…?
¿…acampar aquí (cerca)?	…camp (near) here?
¿Hay un hotel aquí cerca?	Is there a hotel nearby?
¿Por dónde se va a…?	How do I get to…?
Izquierda, derecha, derecho	Left, right, straight on
¿Dónde está…?	Where is…?
…el terminal de camionetas	…the bus station
…el banco más cercano	…the nearest bank
…el correo/la oficina de correos	…the post office
…el baño/sanitario	…the toilet
¿De dónde sale la camioneta para…?	Where does the bus to…leave from?
Quisiera un boleto (de ida y vuelta) para…	I'd like a (return) ticket to…
¿A qué hora sale (llega en…)?	What time does it leave (arrive in…)?
¿Qué hay para comer?	What is there to eat?
¿Qué es eso?	What's that?
¿Cómo se llama este en español?	What's this called in Spanish?

Numbers and days

cero	0
un/uno/una	1
dos	2
tres	3
cuatro	4
cinco	5
seis	6
siete	7

ocho	8
nueve	9
diez	10
once	11
doce	12
trece	13
catorce	14
quince	15
dieciséis	16
veinte	20
veintiuno	21
veintidós	22
treinta	30
treinta y uno	31
cuarenta	40
cincuenta	50
sesenta	60
setenta	70
ochenta	80
noventa	90
cien	100
ciento uno	101
doscientos	200
doscientos uno	201
quinientos	500
mil	1000
dos mil	2000
un millión	1,000,000
primero/a	first
segundo/a	second
tercero/a	third
cuarto/a	fourth
quinto/a	fifth
sexto/a	sixth
séptimo/a	seventh
octavo/a	eighth
noveno/a	ninth
décimo/a	tenth

lunes	Monday
martes	Tuesday
miércoles	Wednesday
jueves	Thursday
viernes	Friday
sábado	Saturday
domingo	Sunday

Menu reader

Basics

Azúcar	Sugar
Carne	Meat
Ensalada	Salad
Huevos	Eggs
Mantequilla	Butter
Pan	Bread
Pescado	Fish
Pimienta	Pepper
Queso	Cheese
Sal	Salt
Salsa	Sauce
Verduras/Legumbres	Vegetables

Soups (*sopas*) and starters

Sopa	Soup
de arroz	with rice
de fideos	with noodles
de lentejas	Lentil
de verduras	Vegetable
Consome	Consomme
Caldo	Broth (usually with meat)
Ceviche	Raw fish salad, marinated in lime juice
Entremeses	Hors d'oeuvres

Meat (*carne*) and poultry (*aves*)

Alambre	Kebab	**Guisado**	Stew
Bistec	Steak	**Higado**	Liver
Cabrito	Kid goat	**Lengua**	Tongue
Carne (de res)	Beef	**Milanesa**	Breaded escalope
Carnitas	Stewed chunks of meat	**Pato**	Duck
Cerdo	Pork	**Pavo/Guajalote**	Turkey
Chorizo	Sausage	**Pechuga**	Breast
Chuleta	Chop	**Pierna**	Leg
Codorniz	Quail	**Pollo**	Chicken
Conejo	Rabbit	**Salchicha**	Hot dog or salami
Cordero	Lamb	**Ternera**	Veal
Costilla	Rib	**Venado**	Venison

Specialities

Chile relleno	Stuffed pepper	**Taco**	Rolled and stuffed tortilla
Chuchitos	Stuffed maize dumplings	**Tamale**	Boiled and stuffed maize pudding
Enchilada	Flat, crisp tortilla piled with salad or meat	**Tapado**	Fish stew with plantain and vegetables, served on Caribbean coas
Mosh	Porridge		
Pan de banana	Banana bread		
Pan de coco	Coconut bread		
Quesadilla	Toasted or fried tortillas with cheese		

Vegetables (legumbres, verduras)

Aguacate	Avocado	**Lechuga**	Lettuce
Ajo	Garlic	**Pacaya**	Bitter-tasting local vegetable
Casava/Yuca	Potato-like root vegetable	**Papas**	Potatoes
Cebolla	Onion	**Pepino**	Cucumber
Col	Cabbage	**Plátanos**	Plantain
Elote	Corn on the cob	**Tomate**	Tomato
Frijoles	Beans	**Zanahoria**	Carrot
Hongos	Mushrooms		

Fruit (frutas)

Banana	Banana	**Guayaba**	Guava
Ciruelas	Greengages	**Higos**	Figs
Coco	Coconut	**Jocote**	Small, plum-like fruit
Frambuesas	Raspberries	**Limon**	Lime
Fresas	Strawberries	**Mamey**	Pink, sweet, full of pips
Guanabana	Pear-like cactus fruit	**Mango**	Mango

Melocotón	Peach
Melón	Melon
Naranja	Orange
Papaya	Papaya
Piña	Pineapple
Pitahaya	Sweet, purple fruit
Sandía	Watermelon
Toronja	Grapefruit
Tuna	Cactus fruit
Uvas	Grapes
Zapote	Sweet, pink-fleshed fruit

Eggs (huevos)

a la Mexicana	Scrambled with mild tomato, onion and chilli sauce
con Jamón	with ham
con Tocino	with bacon
Fritos	Fried
Motuleños	Fried, served on a tortilla with ham, cheese and sauce
Rancheros	Cheese-fried and smothered in hot chilli sauce
Revueltos	Scrambled
Tibios	Lightly boiled

Common terms

a la Parilla	Grilled
al Horno	Baked
al Mojo de ajo	Fried in garlic and butter
Asado/a	Roast
Empanado/a	Breaded
Picante	Hot and spicy
Recado	A sauce for meat made from garlic, tomato and spices

Sweets (postres)

Crepas	Pancakes
Ensalada de Frutas	Fruit salad
Flan	Crème caramel
Helado	Ice cream
Pie de queso	Cheesecake
Plátanos al Horno	Baked plantains
Plátanos en Mole	Plantains in chocolate sauce

Glossary of frequently used terms

Aguardiente Raw alcohol made from sugarcane.

Aguas Bottled fizzy drinks such as Coca-Cola or Pepsi.

Alcalde Mayor.

Aldea Small settlement.

Altiplano The highlands of western Guatemala.

Atol Drink usually made from maize dough, cooked with water, salt, sugar and milk. Can also be made from rice.

Ayuntamiento Town hall.

Baleada Stuffed tortilla street snack (Honduras only).

Barranca Steep-sided ravine.

Barrio Residential district.

Biotopo Protected area of ecological interest, usually with limited tourist access.

Boca Costa Western volcanic slopes of the Guatemalan highlands, prime coffee-growing country.

Brujo Maya shaman.

CAFTA Central American Free Trade Agreement.

CALDH Centre for Legal Action on Human Rights. Pressure group campaigning for justice on behalf of the victims of the civil war violence.

Calvario Church, often with pagan religious traditions, always located on the western outskirts of a town; also known as the house of the ancestors.

Camioneta Second-class, or "chicken", bus. In other parts of Latin America the same word means a small truck or van.

Campesino Peasant farmer.

Cantina Local hard-drinking bar.

Casita Hut, small house.

Cayuco Canoe.

Chapín Nickname for a citizen of Guatemala.

Chicle Sapodilla tree sap from which chewing gum is made.

Chuj Maya steam sauna.

Classic Period during which ancient Maya civilization was at its height, usually given as 250–909 AD.

Codex Maya manuscript made from the bark of the fig tree and written in hieroglyphs. Most were destroyed by the Spanish, but a copy of the Dresden Codex can be found in the Popol Vuh museum in Guatemala City (see p.90).

Cofradía Religious brotherhood dedicated to the protection of a particular saint. These groups form the basis of religious and civil hierarchy in traditional highland society and combine Catholic and pagan practices.

Comedor Basic Guatemalan restaurant, usually with just one or two things on the menu, and always the cheapest place to eat.

Comida típica Literally "typical food", this indicates a menu of regular Guatemalan-style dishes, nothing fancy but always filling and inexpensive.

Conavigua National Coordination of Guatemalan Widows. Influential, mainly indigenous pressure group.

Copal Pine-resin incense burned at religious ceremonies.

Corriente Another name for a second-class bus.

Corte Traditional Guatemalan skirt.

Costumbres Guatemalan word for traditional customs of the highland Maya, usually of religious and cultural significance. The word often refers to traditions that owe more to paganism than to Catholicism; practitioners are called **costumbristas**.

Creole Guatemalan of mixed Afro-Caribbean descent.

Cuadra Street block.

CUC Committee of Peasant Unity.

Cusha Home-brewed liquor.

Don/Doña Sir/Madam. A term of respect mostly used to address a professional person or employer.

Efectivo Cash.

EGP (Ejército Guerrillero de los Pobres) (Guerrilla Army of the Poor). A Guatemalan guerrilla group that operated in the Ixil Triangle and Ixcán areas.

Evangélico Christian evangelist or fundamentalist, often missionaries. Name given to numerous Protestant sects seeking converts in Central America.

FAR (Fuerzas Armadas Rebeldes) (Rebel Armed Forces). Guatemalan guerrilla group that was mainly active in Petén.

Finca Plantation-style farm.

FRG (Frente Republicano Guatemalteco) (Guatemalan Republican Front). Right-wing political party of Ríos Montt and Alfonso Portillo.

GAM (Mutual Support Group). Pressure group campaigning for justice for the families of the "disappeared".

GANA Right-wing political coalition currently in power.

Garífuna Black Carib with a unique language and strong African heritage living in Livingston and villages along the Caribbean coast between Belize and Nicaragua. See p.274.

Gringo/gringa Any white-skinned foreigner, not necessarily a term of abuse.

Hospedaje Another name for a small basic hotel.

Huipil Woman's traditional blouse, usually woven or embroidered.

Indígena Indigenous person of Maya descent.

Indio Racially abusive term to describe someone of Maya descent. The word **indito** is equally offensive.

Inguat Guatemalan tourist board.

I.V.A. Guatemalan sales tax of twelve percent.

Ixil Highland tribe grouped around the three towns of the Ixil Triangle – Nebaj, Chajul and San Juan Cotzal.

Kaqchikel (Also spelt "Cakchiquel"). Indigenous highland tribe occupying an area between Guatemala City and Lake Atitlán.

K'iche' (Also spelt "Quiché"). Largest of the highland Maya tribes, centred on the town of Santa Cruz del Quiché.

Ladino A vague term – at its most specific defining someone of mixed Spanish and Maya blood, but more commonly used to describe a person of "Western" culture, or one who dresses in "Western" style, be they pure Maya or of mixed blood.

Legua The distance walked in an hour, used extensively in the highlands.

Leng Slang for **centavo**.

Mam Maya tribe occupying the west of the western highlands, the area around Huehuetenango.

Mariachi Mexican musical style popular in Guatemala.

Marimba Xylophone-like instrument used in traditional Guatemalan music.

Maya General term for the large tribal group who inhabited Guatemala, southern Mexico, Belize, western Honduras and a slice of El Salvador since the earliest times, and still do.

Mestizo Person of mixed native and Spanish blood, more commonly used in Mexico.

Metate Flat stone for grinding maize into flour.

Milpa Maize field, usually cleared by slash and burn.

Minugua United Nations mission, in Guatemala to oversee the peace process.

MLN (Movimiento de Liberación Nacional) (National Liberation Movement). Right-wing political party in Guatemala.

Natural Another term for an indigenous person.

PAC Village civil defence patrols, set up by Ríos Montt in the 1980s. They were responsible for many massacres, and still form a powerful pressure group today.

Palapa Thatched palm-leaf hut.

Parque Town's central plaza; or a park.

Pensión Simple hotel.

Pila Washhouse; sink for washing clothes.

Pipil Indigenous tribal group that occupied much of the Guatemalan Pacific coast at the time of the Conquest. Only their art survives, around the town of Santa Lucía Cotzumalguapa.

Pisto Slang for cash.

Pullman Fast and comfortable bus, usually an old Greyhound.

Punta rock The music of the Garífuna.

Q'eqchi' (Also spelt "Kekchi"). Maya tribal group based around Cobán, the Verapaz highlands, Lake Izabal and the Petén.

Remhi The Catholic Church's Truth Commission, set up to investigate the civil war atrocities.

Repatriados Guatemalan refugees from the civil war, who have now returned to their country.

Sierra Mountain range.

Tecún Umán Last king of the K'iche' tribe, defeated in battle by Alvarado.

Telgua National telecom company.

Tienda Shop.

Típica Clothes woven from multicoloured textiles, usually geared towards the Western customer.

Traje Traditional Maya costume.

Tzute Headcloth or scarf worn as a part of traditional Maya costume.

Tz'utujil Indigenous tribal group occupying the land to the south of Lake Atitlán.

URNG (Unidad Revolucionaria Nacional Guatemalteca) (Guatemalan National Revolutionary Unity). Umbrella organization of the four former guerrilla groups, now disbanded.

USAC (Universidad de San Carlos) University of San Carlos. Guatemala's national university, formerly a hotbed of political activism.

La Violencia Term often used to describe the bloodiest civil war years; literally "the violence".

Xate Decorative palm leaves harvested in Petén for export to the US, to be used in flower arrangements.

Xela Another name for the city of Quetzaltenango.

Maya architectural terms

Altar Elaborately carved altars, often of a cylindrical design, were grouped round the fringes of the main plaza. Used to record historical events, they could have also functioned as sacrificial stones. See also **zoomorphs**.

Ball court Narrow, stone-flagged rectangular court with banked sides where the Maya ball game was played. The courts symbolized a stage between the real and supernatural worlds and for the ball players it could be a game of life and death: losers were sometimes sacrificed.

Corbel arch "False arch" where each stone slightly overlaps the one below. A relatively primitive technique which severely limits the width of doorways and interiors.

Glyph Element in Maya writing, roughly the equivalent of a letter or phrase; used to record historical events. Some glyphs are phonetic, while others represent an entire description or concept as in Chinese characters. Dominant Classic and Postclassic sites had unique emblem glyphs; some like Copán and Tikal used several.

Lintel Top block of stone or wood above a doorway or window, often carved to record important events and dates. Those from Yaxchilán are especially well executed.

Palace Maya palaces occupied prominent locations near the ceremonial heart of the city, usually resting on low platforms, and almost certainly housed the royal elite. There are particularly striking palaces at Tikal and Cancuén.

Postclassic Period between the decline of Maya civilization and the arrival of the Spanish, 909–1530 AD.

Preclassic Archeological era preceding the blooming of Maya civilization, usually given as 2000 BC–250 AD.

Putún Style dominant at Ceibal in central Petén, exhibiting strong Mexican characteristics.

Roof comb Decorative top crest on stone temples, possibly intended to enhance verticality. Originally painted in arresting colours and often framed by giant stucco figures.

Sacbé Paved Maya road or raised causeway near the centre of Maya cities. Probably designed for ceremonial processions and to save rulers from sloshing through the lowland marshes. **Sacbés** were also trade routes and there are hundreds of kilometres still evident in northern Petén today.

Stela Freestanding, often exquisitely carved, stone monument. Decorating major Maya sites, stelae fulfilled a sacred and political role commemorating historical events. Among the largest and most impressive are the ones at Quiriguá and Copán.

Temple Monumental stone structure of pivotal religious significance built in the ceremonial heart of a city, usually with a pyramid-shaped base and topped with a narrow room or two used for secretive ceremonies and bloody sacrifices. Those at Tikal and El Mirador reach more than 60m.

Toltec Style of the central Mexican tribal group who invaded parts of the Maya region.

Zoomorph Spectacular stone altar intricately carved with animal images and glyphs; there are wonderful examples at Quiriguá.

Travel store

Rough Guides travel...

UK & Ireland
Britain
Devon & Cornwall
Dublin DIRECTIONS
Edinburgh DIRECTIONS
England
Ireland
Lake District
London
London DIRECTIONS
London Mini Guide
Scotland
Scottish Highlands & Islands
Wales

Europe
Algarve DIRECTIONS
Amsterdam
Amsterdam DIRECTIONS
Andalucía
Athens DIRECTIONS
Austria
Baltic States
Barcelona
Barcelona DIRECTIONS
Belgium & Luxembourg
Berlin
Brittany & Normandy
Bruges DIRECTIONS
Brussels
Budapest
Bulgaria
Copenhagen
Corfu
Corsica
Costa Brava DIRECTIONS
Crete
Croatia
Cyprus
Czech & Slovak Republics
Dodecanese & East Aegean
Dordogne & The Lot
Europe
Florence & Siena
Florence DIRECTIONS
France
French Hotels & Restos
Germany
Greece
Greek Islands
Hungary
Ibiza & Formentera DIRECTIONS
Iceland
Ionian Islands
Italy
Italian Lakes
Languedoc & Roussillon
Lisbon
Lisbon DIRECTIONS
The Loire
Madeira DIRECTIONS
Madrid DIRECTIONS
Mallorca & Menorca
Mallorca DIRECTIONS
Malta & Gozo DIRECTIONS
Menorca
Moscow
Netherlands
Norway
Paris
Paris DIRECTIONS
Paris Mini Guide
Poland
Portugal
Prague
Prague DIRECTIONS
Provence & the Côte d'Azur
Pyrenees
Romania
Rome
Rome DIRECTIONS
Sardinia
Scandinavia
Sicily
Slovenia
Spain
St Petersburg
Sweden
Switzerland
Tenerife & La Gomera DIRECTIONS
Turkey
Tuscany & Umbria
Venice & The Veneto
Venice DIRECTIONS
Vienna

Asia
Bali & Lombok
Bangkok
Beijing
Cambodia
China
Goa
Hong Kong & Macau
India
Indonesia
Japan
Laos
Malaysia, Singapore & Brunei
Nepal
The Philippines
Singapore
South India
Southeast Asia
Sri Lanka
Taiwan
Thailand
Thailand's Beaches & Islands
Tokyo
Vietnam

Australasia
Australia
Melbourne
New Zealand
Sydney

North America
Alaska
Boston
California
Canada
Chicago
Florida
Grand Canyon
Hawaii
Honolulu
Las Vegas DIRECTIONS
Los Angeles
Maui DIRECTIONS
Miami & South Florida
Montréal
New England
New Orleans DIRECTIONS
New York City
New York City DIRECTIONS
New York City Mini Guide
Orlando & Walt Disney World DIRECTIONS
Pacific Northwest
Rocky Mountains
San Francisco
San Francisco DIRECTIONS
Seattle
Southwest USA
Toronto
USA
Vancouver
Washington DC
Washington DC DIRECTIONS
Yosemite

Caribbean & Latin America
Antigua & Barbuda DIRECTIONS
Argentina
Bahamas
Barbados DIRECTIONS
Belize
Bolivia
Brazil
Cancùn & Cozumel DIRECTIONS
Caribbean
Central America
Chile
Costa Rica
Cuba
Dominican Republic
Dominican Republic DIRECTIONS
Ecuador
Guatemala
Jamaica

...music & reference

Mexico
Peru
St Lucia
South America
Trinidad & Tobago
Yúcatan

Africa & Middle East
Cape Town & the Garden Route
Egypt
The Gambia
Jordan
Kenya
Marrakesh DIRECTIONS
Morocco
South Africa, Lesotho & Swaziland
Syria
Tanzania
Tunisia
West Africa
Zanzibar

Travel Theme guides
First-Time Around the World
First-Time Asia
First-Time Europe
First-Time Latin America
Travel Online
Travel Health
Travel Survival
Walks in London & SE England
Women Travel

Maps
Algarve
Amsterdam
Andalucia & Costa del Sol
Argentina
Athens
Australia
Baja California
Barcelona
Berlin
Boston
Brittany
Brussels
California
Chicago
Corsica
Costa Rica & Panama
Crete
Croatia
Cuba
Cyprus
Czech Republic
Dominican Republic
Dubai & UAE
Dublin
Egypt
Florence & Siena
Florida
France
Frankfurt
Germany
Greece
Guatemala & Belize
Hong Kong
Iceland
Ireland
Kenya
Lisbon
London
Los Angeles
Madrid
Mallorca
Marrakesh
Mexico
Miami & Key West
Morocco
New England
New York City
New Zealand
Northern Spain
Paris
Peru
Portugal
Prague
Rome
San Francisco
Sicily
South Africa
South India
Sri Lanka
Tenerife
Thailand
Toronto
Trinidad & Tobago
Tuscany
Venice
Washington DC
Yucatán Peninsula

Dictionary Phrasebooks
Croatian
Czech
Dutch
Egyptian Arabic
European Languages (Czech, French, German, Greek, Italian, Portuguese, Spanish)
French
German
Greek
Hindi & Urdu
Hungarian
Indonesian
Italian
Japanese
Latin American Spanish
Mandarin Chinese
Mexican Spanish
Polish
Portuguese
Russian
Spanish
Swahili
Thai
Turkish
Vietnamese

Music Guides
The Beatles
Bob Dylan
Cult Pop
Classical Music
Elvis
Frank Sinatra
Heavy Metal
Hip-Hop
Jazz
Opera
Reggae
Rock
World Music (2 vols)

Reference Guides
Babies
Books for Teenagers
Children's Books, 0–5
Children's Books, 5–11
Comedy Movies
Conspiracy Theories
Cult Fiction
Cult Football
Cult Movies
Cult TV
The Da Vinci Code
Ethical Shopping
Gangster Movies
Horror Movies
iPods, iTunes & Music Online
The Internet
James Bond
Kids' Movies
Lord of the Rings
Macs & OS X
Muhammad Ali
Music Playlists
PCs and Windows
Poker
Pregnancy & Birth
Sci–Fi Movies
Shakespeare
Superheroes

Unexplained Phenomena
The Universe
Weather
Website Directory

Football
Arsenal 11s
Celtic 11s
Chelsea 11s
Liverpool 11s
Newcastle 11s
Rangers 11s
Tottenham 11s
Man United 11s

Visit us online

roughguides.com

Information on over 25,000 destinations around the world

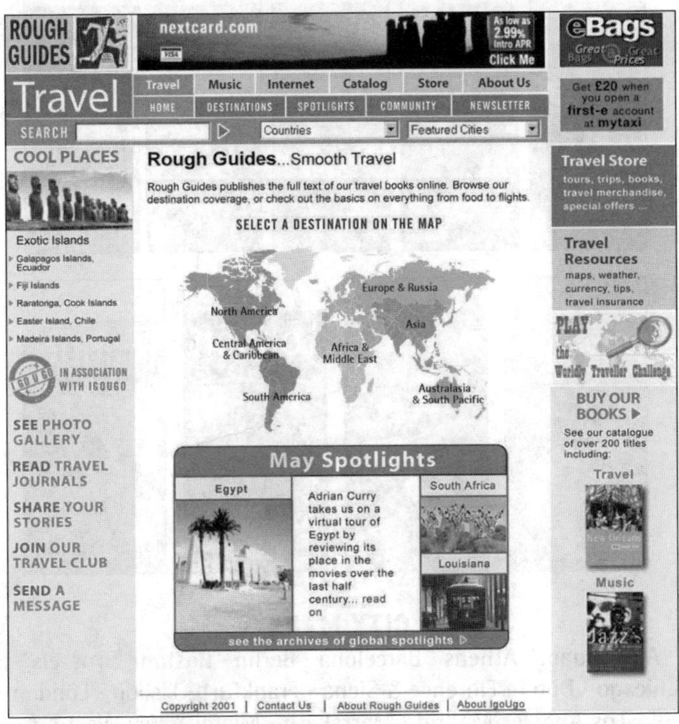

- **Read** Rough Guides' trusted travel info
- **Share** journals, photos and travel advice with other readers
- Get exclusive Rough Guide **discounts** and travel **deals**
- Earn membership points every time you contribute to the Rough Guide **community** and get **free** books, flights and trips
- Browse thousands of CD reviews and artists in our **music** area

roughnews

Stay in touch

Rough Guides FREE full-colour newsletter has news, travel issues, music reviews, readers' letters and the lastest dispatches from authors on the road.

If you would like to receive Rough News, please send us your name and address:

Rough Guides

80 Strand London
WC2R 0RL

4th Floor, 345
Hudson St, New York
NY10014, USA

newslettersubs@roughguides.co.uk

ROUGH GUIDES SOFTWARE

Share your adventures on the move

Rough Guides have launched **intouch**, a new all in one software package for planning your trip and staying in touch with people back home before, during and after your travels.

Create an itinerary and budget using on-screen information and maps, and take advantage of the diary to keep family and friends informed of your whereabouts.

The diary can be linked to your mobile phone so that you can send a text message, **intouch** will automatically send an email or cheap SMS to those listed on your account.

You can also post photos and diary entries online and then download them to make a journal on your return.

Rough Guides **intouch** is easy to install and you don't need to take anything with you - just hit the synchronize button and then use it from any internet café in the world.

Rough Guides **intouch** includes:
Planning tools
Free email address
Free personal website
Digital photo storage

And much more...

£5 OFF your purchase of Rough Guides **intouch** if you buy online at www.roughguidesintouch.com reference code: Rough Guide Books

Recommended retail price £24.99 available through leading retailers e.g. WH Smith, Waterstones and PC World

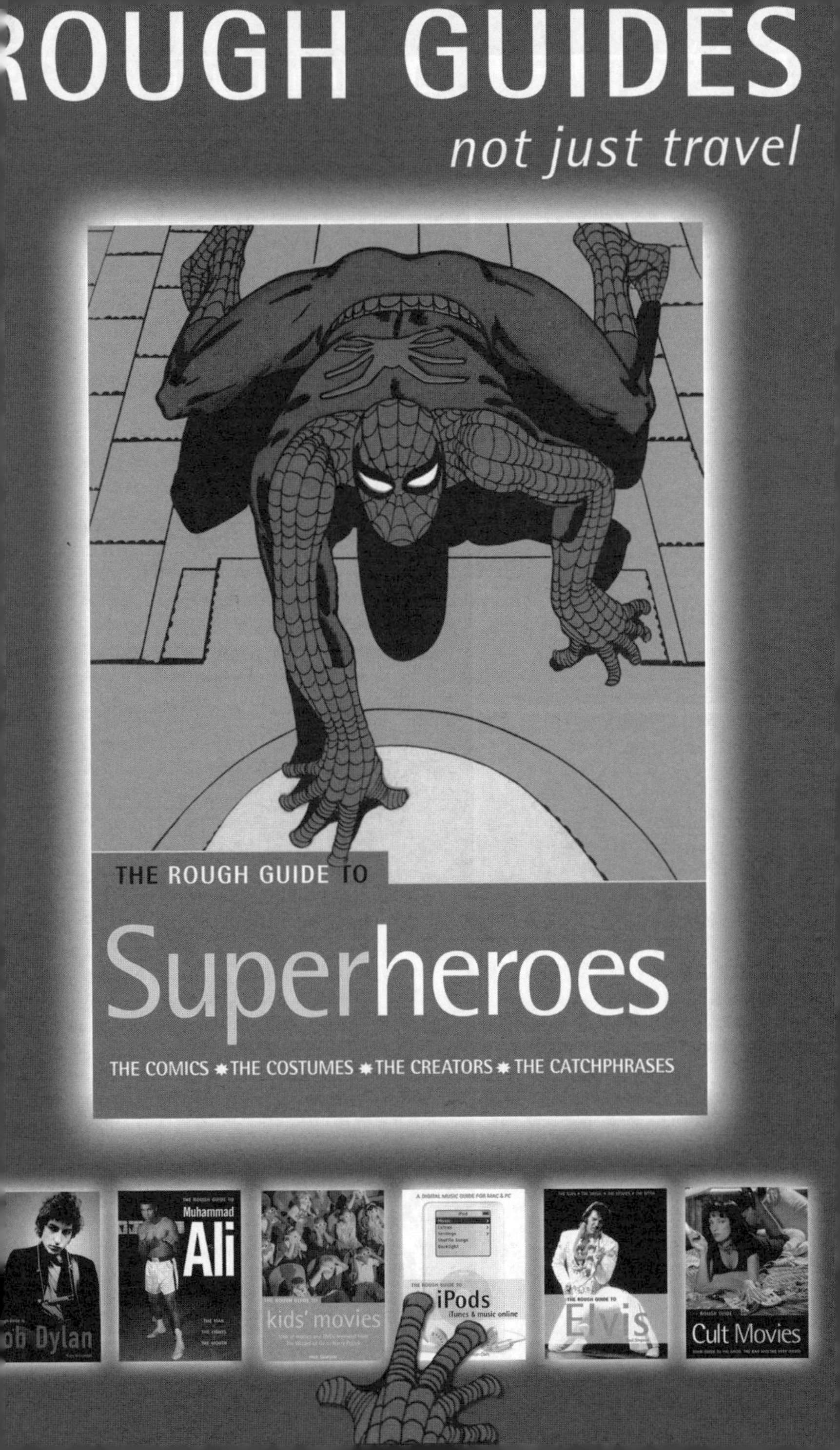
ROUGH GUIDES
not just travel
THE ROUGH GUIDE TO
Superheroes
THE COMICS ✸ THE COSTUMES ✸ THE CREATORS ✸ THE CATCHPHRASES
Muhammad
Ali
kids' movies
iPods
iTunes & music online
Elvis
Cult Movies

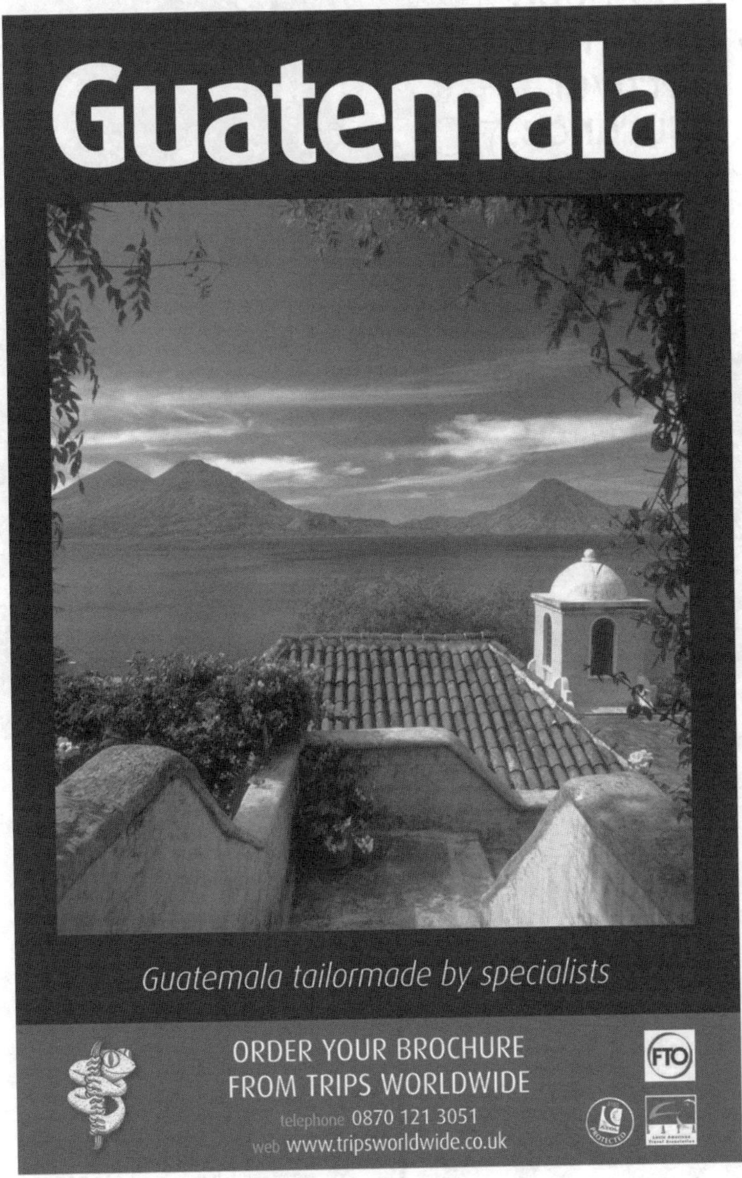
Guatemala
Guatemala tailormade by specialists
ORDER YOUR BROCHURE
FROM TRIPS WORLDWIDE
telephone 0870 121 3051
web www.tripsworldwide.co.uk
FTO

small print and

Index

A Rough Guide to Rough Guides

In the summer of 1981, Mark Ellingham, a recent graduate from Bristol University, was travelling round Greece and couldn't find a guidebook that really met his needs. On the one hand there were the student guides, insistent on saving every last cent, and on the other the heavyweight cultural tomes whose authors seemed to have spent more time in a research library than lounging away the afternoon at a taverna or on the beach.

In a bid to avoid getting a job, Mark and a small group of writers set about creating their own guidebook. It was a guide to Greece that aimed to combine a journalistic approach to description with a thoroughly practical approach to travellers' needs – a guide that would incorporate culture, history, and contemporary insights with a critical edge, together with up-to-date, value-for-money listings. Back in London, Mark and the team finished their Rough Guide, as they called it, and talked Routledge into publishing the book.

That first *Rough Guide to Greece*, published in 1982, was a student scheme that became a publishing phenomenon. The immediate success of the book – with numerous reprints and a Thomas Cook Prize shortlisting – spawned a series that rapidly covered dozens of destinations. Rough Guides had a ready market among low-budget backpackers, but soon also acquired a much broader and older readership that relished Rough Guides' wit and inquisitiveness as much as their enthusiastic, critical approach. Everyone wants value for money, but not at any price.

Rough Guides soon began supplementing the "rougher" information about hostels and low-budget listings with the kind of detail on restaurants and quality hotels that independent-minded visitors on any budget might expect, whether on business in New York or trekking in Thailand.

These days the guides – distributed worldwide by the Penguin Group – offer recommendations from shoestring to luxury and cover more than 200 destinations around the globe, including almost every country in the Americas and Europe, more than half of Africa, and most of Asia and Australasia. Our ever-growing team of authors and photographers is spread all over the world, particularly in Europe, the USA, and Australia.

In 1994, we published the *Rough Guide to World Music* and *Rough Guide to Classical Music*, and a year later the *Rough Guide to the Internet*. All three books have become benchmark titles in their fields – which encouraged us to expand into other areas of publishing, mainly around popular culture. Rough Guides now publish:

- Travel guides to more than 200 worldwide destinations
- Dictionary phrasebooks for 22 major languages
- History guides ranging from Ireland to Islam
- Maps printed on rip-proof and waterproof Polyart™ paper
- Music guides running the gamut from Opera to Elvis
- Restaurant guides to London, New York, and San Francisco
- Reference books on topics as diverse as the Weather and Shakespeare
- Sports guides from Formula 1 to Man Utd
- Pop culture books from *Lord of the Rings* to Cult TV
- World Music CDs in association with World Music Network

Visit **www.roughguides.com** to see our latest publications.

Rough Guide credits

Text editor: Jeff Cranmer
Layout: Jessica Subramanian
Cartography: Manish Chandra, Rajesh Chhibber, Maxine Repath
Picture editor: Jj Luck
Proofreader: Diane Margolis
Editorial: **London** Kate Berens, Claire Saunders, Geoff Howard, Ruth Blackmore, Polly Thomas, Richard Lim, Clifton Wilkinson, Alison Murchie, Sally Schafer, Karoline Densley, Andy Turner, Ella O'Donnell, Keith Drew, Edward Aves, Nikki Birrell, Helen Marsden, Joe Staines, Duncan Clark, Peter Buckley, Matthew Milton; **New York** Andrew Rosenberg, Richard Koss, Steven Horak, AnneLise Sorensen, Amy Hegarty, Hunter Slaton, April Isaacs
Design & Pictures: London Simon Bracken, Dan May, Diana Jarvis, Mark Thomas, Harriet Mills, Chloë Roberts; **Delhi** Madhulita Mohapatra, Umesh Aggarwal, Ajay Verma, Amit Verma, Ankur Guha
Production: Julia Bovis, Sophie Hewat, Katherine Owers
Cartography: **London** Ed Wright, Katie Lloyd-Jones; **Delhi** Jai Prakash Mishra, Ashutosh Bharti, Rajesh Mishra, Jasbir Sandhu, Karobi Gogoi, Animesh Pathak
Online: **New York** Jennifer Gold, Suzanne Welles, Kristin Mingrone; **Delhi** Manik Chauhan, Narender Kumar, Shekhar Jha, Rakesh Kumar, Lalit Sharma, Chhandita Chakravarty
Marketing & Publicity: London Richard Trillo, Niki Hanmer, David Wearn, Demelza Dallow, Louise Maher; **New York** Geoff Colquitt, Megan Kennedy, Katy Ball; **Delhi** Reem Khokhar
Custom publishing and foreign rights: Philippa Hopkins
Manager India: Punita Singh
Series editor: Mark Ellingham
Reference Director: Andrew Lockett
PA to Managing and Publishing Directors: Megan McIntyre
Publishing Director: Martin Dunford
Managing Director: Kevin Fitzgerald

Publishing information

This third edition published January 2006 by
Rough Guides Ltd,
80 Strand, London WC2R 0RL
345 Hudson St, 4th Floor,
New York, NY 10014, USA
14 Local Shopping Centre, Panchsheel Park,
New Delhi 110017, India.
Distributed by the Penguin Group
Penguin Books Ltd,
80 Strand, London WC2R 0RL
Penguin Putnam, Inc.,
375 Hudson St, NY 10014, USA
Penguin Group (Australia)
250 Camberwell Road, Camberwell,
Victoria 3124, Australia
Penguin Books Canada Ltd,
10 Alcorn Avenue, Toronto, ON,
M4V 1E4 Canada
Penguin Group (New Zealand),
Cnr Rosedale and Airborne Roads,
Albany, Auckland, New Zealand

Typeset in Bembo and Helvetica to an original design by Henry Iles.
Printed and bound in China

536pp includes index
A catalogue record for this book is available from the British Library.
ISBN 978-1-84353-499-0

3 5 7 9 8 6 4 2

Help us update

We've gone to a lot of effort to ensure that the third edition of **The Rough Guide to Guatemala** is accurate and up to date. However, things change – places get "discovered", opening hours are notoriously fickle, restaurants and rooms raise prices or lower standards. If you feel we've got it wrong or left something out, we'd like to know, and if you can remember the address, the price, the time, the phone number, so much the better.

We'll credit all contributions, and send a copy of the next edition (or any other Rough Guide if you prefer) for the best letters. Everyone who writes to us and isn't already a subscriber will receive a copy of our full-colour thrice-yearly newsletter. Please mark letters: "**Rough Guide Guatemala update**" and send to: Rough Guides, 80 Strand, London WC2R 0RL, or Rough Guides, 4th Floor, 345 Hudson St, New York, NY 10014. Or send an email to **mail@roughguides.com**.

Have your questions answered and tell others about your trip at **www.roughguides.atinfopop.com**.

Acknowledgements

Thanks to Philippa Myres in Antigua, Lorena Artola and *Dos Lunas* in la ciudad, José Manuel Briz, INGUAT (especially Migdalia de Barillas and Marlon Laz), Tom Lingenfelter in Xela, Pieter and Patrick of Adrenalina Tours, Don David in El Remate, Deedle and Dave and the staff of *La Iguana* at the lake, Martsam Travel in Flores, Howard Rosenzweig in Copán Ruinas, Mike Shawcross, UDC and the *Mango Inn*, Andrea Bellavita, Fernando for the gourmet coffee and cakes, Gail of *Posada La Merced*, Malia Dewse for her enthusiastic help with *cocina guatemalteca*, John of *Café No Sé*, Jamie Marshall and Maya in London, *Chiminos Island Lodge*, Geert Van Vaeck and James Stone. I'd particularly like to acknowledge the skill and dedication of my editor, Jeff Cranmer; Peter Eltringham for his all-round expertise in Petén and beyond; Mark Whatmore for getting the whole project off the ground in the first place; and my wife, Fiona, for holding the fort (and kids) back home.

Readers' letters

Thanks to all the readers who took the trouble to write in with their comments and suggestions (and apologies to anyone whose name we've misspelt or omitted):

Tina Maria Abich, Alec Beardsell, Bettina Berch, Flavia Bertini, Lara Bianciardi, Pieter Burkhardt for superb highlands information, Brooke Casey, Adrian Cashman and Sara Humphreys, Sile Nic Chormaic, Luis Ciani,Greg Clough,Celina Conroy, Guy Crotty, Ed Desautels, Helen Dimaras, Antonietta Fabrizio, Michael Foss, Bianca González, Susan Gutelman, Mike Haaijer, Susan Happ, Felicity Harrison, Nigel Hashim, Céline Heinbecker, Sven Hermans, Erica Hill, Caitlin Hollister, Karma Ingersoll-Thorp, Anton Jansen, Willem Joost Kemp, Will Koch, Ivanka Lakova and Arnaud Pasquali, Jonathan T. Lane for an excellent update, Christina Lather, Donia Lilly, Mathieu van Loon, Robert Lyman, Debby Lyttle, Shannon MacConnell, Campbell Macdonald and Sharon Friesen, Margo in North Carolina, Fernando Mejía and Pauline Déchamps, Clancy Mendoza, Marlo Mora, Janice Owen, Sharon Petrie, Fernando Pichiya, Jason Pielemeiser, Ryan Pohl, Josephine Reeves, Scott Reilly, Jaime Robeck, Deborah and Noah Rosenberg, Fran Rothstein, Erik Rozentuin, Elke Sagniewicz, Andrew Scherer and Giovanna Vidoli for the Maya update and more, Graham Sherrif for a superbly informative letter, Chris Shine, Donald M. Smith, Timothy J. Smith, Peggy Stauffen, Helen Stolman for the very full account, Albert Sun, Tom Sweeney, Patricia Swope, Yuki Takagaki, Isabelle and Didier Torchut, Ileana Valenzuela, Linda Veldmeijer, Richard Veul, Giovanna Vidoli and Andrew Scherer, Robert Wagner, and Heidi Zotter.

Photo credits

Cover
Main front picture: Lake Atitlán © Powerstock
Small front top picture: White orchid © Getty
Small front lower picture: Green chillies © Alamy
Back top picture: Antigua market © Alamy
Back lower picture: Doorway, Antigua © Alamy

Title page
Bus to Todos Santos de Cuchumatán © Pep Roig/Alamy

Full page
El Baul © David Hiser/Getty Images

Introduction
Toucan © Felix Stensson/Alamy
Holy week © Michel Friang/Alamy
Tikal El Peten - Maya ruins © J. Marshall/ Tribaleye Images/Alamy
Nebaj © J. Marshall/Tribaleye Images/Alamy
Dance of the Conquerors, San Sebastian Retalhuleu © J. Marshall/Tribaleye Images/ Alamy
Maya funeral urn © James Strachan/Robert Harding
Iguana, Punta de Manabique © D. Hoey/Trip
Maize © James Strachan/Robert Harding
Ceremonial masks © Axiom
Iglesia Church, Antigua © Terrance Klassen/ Alamy
Embroidered belts and hats © Robert Francis/ South American Pictures

Things not to miss
01 Parque Central at night, Antigua © Paul A. Souders/Corbis
02 Volcán de Pacaya © mediacolor's/Alamy
03 Temple of the Giant Jaguar at Tikal © Jan Butchofsky-Houser/Corbis
04 Quetzal © Kennan Ward/Corbis
05 Río Dulce © Westend61/Alamy
06 Whale shark and diver © Louie Psihoyos/ Corbis
07 Fuentes Georginas © Iain Stewart
08 Chichicastenango © Jamie Marshall
09 Chicken buses © Iain Stewart
10 Leatherback turtle © courtesy of Costa Rica Tourist Board
11 Coffee © T. Bognar/Trip
12 Quiriguá © Iain Stewart
13 Hiking from Todos Santos © Iain Stewart
14 Esquipulas © Iain Stewart
15 San Francisco el Alto market © Iain Stewart
16 Maximón © Reuters/Corbis
17 Diving shop, Lívingston © Iain Stewart
18 Maya mask © J. Monaco/Trip
19 Lagunas de Sepalau © Iain Stewart
20 Lívingston © Iain Stewart
21 Santo Tomás Church, Chichicastenango © Jamie Marshall
22 Todos Santos Cuchumatán © James Nelson/ Getty Images
23 Eastern highlands © Iain Stewart
24 Finca el Paraíso © Iain Stewart
25 Yaxhá © Iain Stewart
26 Lago de Atitlán © W. Jacobs/Trip
27 Ceiba tree © Macduff Everton/Corbis
28 Studying Spanish © Neil Julian/Alamy
29 Semuc Champey © Iain Stewart
30 Semana Santa © C. Rennie/Trip
31 Copán ruins © R. Powers/Trip
32 Ixil women © Jacques Jangoux/Alamy

Black and whites
p.74 Holy Week © Michel Friang /Alamy
p.116 Ruins, Antigua © Galen Rowell/Corbis
p.125 Volcán de Agua © Suzanne Murphy/Taxi/ Getty Images
p.132 Village church © Iain Stewart
p.155 Nebaj church, Ixil Triangle © J. Marshall/ Tribaleye/Alamy
p.199 Las Cumbres © Iain Stewart
p.234 Leatherback hatchling © Rebecca Whitfield/South American Pictures
p.247 Mangroves around Monterrico © Neil Julian/Alamy
p.260 Hotel Del Norte © Bruce Goodison
p.278 Río Dulce © Patrick Wass/Travel Ink
p.296 Coffee beans © xela/Alamy
p.303 Rabinal, fiesta dancers © Iain Stewart
p.326 Spider Monkey © Tony Morrison/South American Pictures
p.351 Maya ruins, Tikal © Robert Francis/South American Pictures
p.382 Roatán Island beach, Honduras © Nick Gregory/Alamy
p.394 Stela at Copán © Iain Stewart
p.470 Traditional men's jacket © Iain Stewart
p.484 Rainforest in Petén © Macduff Everton/ Corbis

Index

Map entries are in colour

D

E

F

G

H

I

J

K

L

M

N

O

P

Q

R

S

INDEX

T

U

INDEX

V

W

Y

Z

Map symbols

Maps are listed in the full index using coloured text

- International border
- Chapter division boundary
- Carretera Interamericana
- Other major highways
- Minor highways & roads (paved)
- Unpaved highways & roads
- Seasonal track
- Footpath
- Railway
- Ferry route
- Mountain range
- Waterfall
- Volcano
- Cave
- Ruin
- Castle
- Statue
- Immigration post
- Airport
- Bus stop
- Parking
- Gas station
- Campground
- Accommodation
- Information office
- Telephone
- Post office
- Internet access
- Building
- Church
- Cemetery
- Park
- Beach